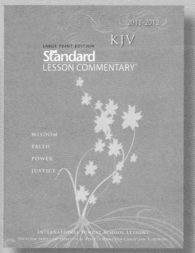

Standard® Lesson Quarterly Curriculum
Teacher Resources

For over 100 years, **Standard® Lesson Quarterly** has provided quality, biblically sound Sunday school lessons based on the ISSL / Uniform Series. Each quarter contains **13 weeks of lessons,** including verse-by-verse Bible exposition, discussion questions, and ready-to-use resources to enhance study. Teachers will appreciate the ease with which they are able to produce quality lessons.

Why you will love it—

- **Credible** – Based on International Sunday School Lessons/Uniform Series
- **Comprehensive** – Provides a comprehensive overview of the Bible in 6 years
- **Adaptable** – Can be used in different class sizes, large or small
- **Relevant** – Encourages students to apply what they are learning to daily life

KJV Adult Teacher's Convenience Kit
978-0-7847-4908-1

KJV Bible Teacher and Leader
978-0-7847-4909-8

The **KJV Adult Teacher's Convenience Kit** includes *KJV Bible Teacher & Leader* (teacher book) as well as:

- *Adult Bible Class* (student book)
- *Adult Resources*—Maps, charts, posters, and a CD with PowerPoint® presentations and reproducible student activity pages
- *Devotions®*—Daily devotions that correlate with the upcoming weekly lessons
- *SEEK®*—8-page take-home papers to give to students

SLQ is released quarterly starting in July, October, January, and April.

Powerpoint® is a trademark registered in the United States Patent and Trademark Office by Microsoft Corporation. Used by permission.

Available at your local Christian bookstore

Standard® Lesson Quarterly Curriculum
Student Resources

Students will appreciate how easy the lessons are to understand. Every lesson contains the printed Scripture text, condensed commentary on the text, and a student response page for involvement learning.

A **KJV Adult Bible Class**
978-0-7847-4911-1

B **KJV Adult Bible Class Large Print**—30% larger than the regular size!
978-0-7847-4912-8

C **Devotions®**—available in pocket size
978-0-7847-4867-1
large print
978-0-7847-4914-2

D **Adult Resources**—
contains maps, charts, posters, and a CD with PowerPoint® presentations and reproducible student activity pages
978-0-7847-4910-4

E **Seek®**—take-home papers, including articles, stories, questions, and daily Bible readings
978-0-7847-4913-5

Standard®
LESSON QUARTERLY

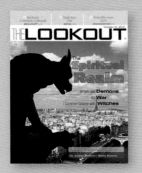

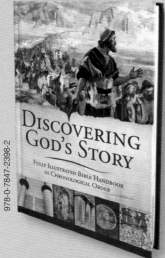

2011-2012

KJV

Standard
LESSON COMMENTARY®

KING JAMES
VERSION

Volume 59

Edited by
Ronald L. Nickelson

Jonathan Underwood,
Senior Editor

Standard®
PUBLISHING

Cincinnati, Ohio

IN THIS VOLUME

Cover design by Brigid Naglich
Lessons based on International Sunday School Lessons © 2007 by the Lesson Committee.

INDEX OF PRINTED TEXTS

The printed texts for 2011–2012 are arranged here in the order in which they appear in the Bible.

CD-ROM AVAILABLE

The *Standard Lesson Commentary*® is available in an electronic format in special editions of this volume. The compact disc (CD) contains the full text of the King James *Standard Lesson Commentary*® and *The NIV*® *Standard Lesson Commentary*® powered by Bible Explorer® from WORDsearch™ Bible Software, additional study helps, and a collection of presentation helps that can be projected or reproduced as handouts. Order 020510211. Some 200 additional books and resources are available by FREE download from http://www.wordsearchbible.com/freebooks.

If you have questions regarding the installation, registration, or activation of this CD, please contact WORDsearch Customer Service at (800) 888-9898 or (512) 832-2125.

If you have problems with the CD, please contact WORDsearch Technical Support by telephone at (512) 835-6900 or by e-mail at Support@WORDsearchBible.com.

Logos users! Purchase the *Standard Lesson eCommentary* as a direct download from www.logos.com.

CUMULATIVE INDEX

A cumulative index for Scripture passages used in the STANDARD LESSON COMMENTARY
for September 2010—August 2012 is provided below.

Abana *Ab*-uh-nuh or Uh-*ban*-uh.
Abraham *Ay*-bruh-ham.
Abram *Ay*-brum.
Absalom *Ab*-suh-lum.
Ahaz *Ay*-haz.
Ahaziah Ay-huh-*zye*-uh.
Ai *Ay*-eye.
Amariah *Am*-uh-**rye**-uh.
Amnon *Am*-nun.
Amorites *Am*-uh-rites.
Amos *Ay*-mus.
Annas *An*-nus.
Antioch *An*-tee-ock.
apostasy uh-*pahs*-tuh-see.
Aqaba *Ock*-uh-buh.
Aquinas Uh-*kwi*-nuss.
Aramaic *Air*-uh-**may**-ik.
Arimathaea *Air*-uh-muh-**thee**-uh
  (*th* as in *thin*).
Aristotle **A**-reh-*stot*-tuhl.
Asenath *As*-e-nath.
Ashtaroth *Ash*-tuh-rawth.
Ashtoreth *Ash*-toe-reth.
Asiatics A-zhee-*ah*-tiks.
Assyria Uh-*sear*-ee-uh.
Assyrian Uh-*sear*-e-un.
Assyrians Uh-*sear*-e-unz.
Astarte A-*star*-te (first *a* as in *had*).
Athaliah Ath-uh-*lye*-uh.
Athena Uh-*thee*-nuh.

Baal *Bay*-ul.
Baalim Bay-uh-*leem*.
Babel *Bay*-bul.
Babylon *Bab*-uh-lun.
Babylonian Bab-ih-*low*-nee-un.
Babylonians Bab-ih-*low*-nee-unz.
Barnabas *Bar*-nuh-bus.
Bathsheba Bath-*she*-buh.
Bede Beed.
Beersheba Beer-*she*-buh.
Belial *Bee*-li-ul.
Bethabara Beth-**ab**-uh-ruh.
Bethany *Beth*-uh-nee.
Beth-aven Beth-**ay**-ven.
Bethel *Beth*-ul.
Bethlehem *Beth*-lih-hem.

Bethsaida Beth-*say*-uh-duh.

Caedmon *Kad*-mun.
Caesar Augustus
  See-zer Aw-*gus*-tus.
Caesarea Maritima Sess-uh-*ree*-uh
  Mar-uh-*tee*-muh.
Caiaphas *Kay*-uh-fus or
  Kye-uh-fus.
Cana *Kay*-nuh.
Canaan *Kay*-nun.
Canaanites *Kay*-nun-ites.
Capernaum Kuh-*per*-nay-um.
Carchemish *Kar*-key-mish.
Coenaculum Ken-*ock*-you-loom.
Colossians Kuh-*losh*-unz.
Corinthians Ko-*rin*-thee-unz (*th* as
  in *thin*).
Cyrenius Sigh-*ree*-nee-us.

Damascus Duh-*mass*-kus.
Davidic Duh-*vid*-ick.
Derbe *Der*-be.
Deuteronomy Due-ter-*ahn*-uh-me.
Dothan *Doe*-thun (*th* as in *thin*).

Ebal *Ee*-bull.
Ebenezer *Eb*-en-**ee**-zer.
Ecclesiastes Ik-*leez*-ee-**as**-teez.
Egypt *Ee*-jipt.
Egyptians Ee-*jip*-shuns.
ekklesia *(Greek)* ek-lay-*see*-uh.
Eliezer El-ih-*ee*-zer.
Elijah Ee-*lye*-juh.
Elisha Ee-*lye*-shuh.
Elohim *(Hebrew)* El-o-*heem*.
Eos *Heh*-ohs.
ephah *ee*-fah.
Ephesians Ee-*fee*-zhunz.
Ephraim *Ee*-fray-im.
Esau *Ee*-saw.
Essenes *Eh*-seenz.
Euphrates You-*fray*-teez.
Ezekiel Ee-*zeek*-ee-ul or
  Ee-*zeek*-yul.
Eziongeber *Ee*-zih-on-**ge**-ber (g as
  in get).

Galatia Guh-*lay*-shuh.
Galatians Guh-*lay*-shunz.
Galilean Gal-uh-*lee*-un.
Galilee *Gal*-uh-lee.
Gehazi Geh-*hay*-zye (G as in *get*).
Gehenna Geh-*hen*-uh (G as in
  get).
Gentiles *Jen*-tiles.
Gerar *Gear*-rar (G as in *get*).
Gerizim *Gair*-ih-zeem or Guh-
  rye-zim.
Gilead *Gil*-ee-ud (G as in *get*).
Goshen *Go*-shen.

Habakkuk Huh-*back*-kuk.
Hagar *Hay*-gar.
Hai *Hay*-eye.
Haran *Hair*-un.
heathen *hee*-thun.
Hebrews *Hee*-brews.
heresy *hair*-uh-see.
heretics *hair*-uh-tiks.
Hermon *Her*-mun.
Herod Antipas
  Hair-ud *An*-tih-pus.
Herod Archelaus *Hair*-ud Are-
  kuh-*lay*-us.
Hezekiah Hez-ih-*kye*-uh.
Hinnom *Hin*-um.
Hohokam Huh-*hoe*-kum.
Hosea Ho-*zay*-uh.
Hyksos *Hik*-sus.

Iconium Eye-*ko*-nee-um.
Isaac *Eye*-zuk.
Isaiah Eye-*zay*-uh.
Ishmael *Ish*-may-el.
Ishmaelites *Ish*-may-el-ites.
Isis *Eye*-sus.
Israelites *Iz*-ray-el-ites.

Jehoiachin Jeh-*hoy*-uh-kin.
Jehoiada Jee-*hoy*-uh-duh.
Jehoram Jeh-*ho*-rum.
Jehoshaphat Jeh-*hosh*-uh-fat.
Jehovahjireh Jeh-*ho*-vuh-*jye*-ruh.
Jehu *Jay*-hew.

Jerusalem Juh-*roo*-suh-lem.
Jezebel *Jez*-uh-bel.
Jezreel *Jez*-ree-el or *Jez*-reel.
Joash *Jo*-ash.
Joram *Jo*-ram.
Josiah Jo-*sigh*-uh.
Judah *Joo*-duh.
Judaism *Joo*-duh-izz-um or
  Joo-day-izz-um.
Judaizers **Joo**-duh-*ize*-ers.
Judaizing **Joo**-duh-*ize*-ing.
Judas Maccabee *Joo*-dus *Mack*-
  uh-bee.
Judea Joo-*dee*-uh.
Justitia *Yus*-tih-tee-uh.

Keturah Keh-*too*-ruh.
Kirjathjearim *Kir*-jath-**jee**-uh-rim
  or jee-**a**-rim.
koheleth (*Hebrew*) ko-*hel*-eth.

Lamentations Lam-en-*tay*-shunz.
Lebanon *Leb*-uh-nun.
Lemuel *Lem*-you-el.
Levites *Lee*-vites.
Leviticus Leh-*vit*-ih-kus.
logos (*Greek*) *law*-goss.
Lystra *Liss*-truh.

Machir *May*-ker.
Magdala *Mag*-duh-luh.
Magdalene *Mag*-duh-leen or
  Mag-duh-*lee*-nee.
Magnificat Mag-*nif*-ih-cot.
Maher-shalal-hash-baz
  May-her-*shal*-al-**hash**-bas.
Manasseh Muh-*nass*-uh.
Marcion *Mahr*-shuhn.
medieval me-*dee*-vuhl.
Mediterranean
  Med-uh-tuh-**ray**-nee-un.
Megiddo Muh-*gid*-doe.
Mesopotamia
  Mes-uh-puh-**tay**-me-uh.
Messiah Meh-*sigh*-uh.
messianic mess-ee-*an*-ick.
Messias Mes-*sigh*-us.
Micaiah My-*kay*-uh.
Midian *Mid*-ee-un.
Midianites *Mid*-ee-un-ites.
Minerva Meh-*nur*-vuh.

Miriam *Meer*-ee-um.
Moreh *Moe*-reh.
Moriah Mo-*rye*-uh.
Mosaic Mo-*zay*-ik.
Moses *Mo*-zes or *Mo*-zez.

Naaman *Nay*-uh-mun.
Naboth *Nay*-bawth.
Naphtali *Naf*-tuh-lye.
Nathanael Nuh-*than*-yull (*th* as
  in *thin*).
Nazareth *Naz*-uh-reth.
Nebuchadnezzar
  Neb-yuh-kud-**nez**-er.
Nehemiah *Nee*-huh-**my**-uh.
Nicodemus *Nick*-uh-**dee**-mus.
Nineveh *Nin*-uh-vuh.

obeisance oh-*bee*-sunts.
Octavian Ok-*tay*-vee-an.
Oviedo Oh-vee-*a*-doh (*a* as in *day*).

pagan *pay*-gun.
patriarch *pay*-tree-ark.
patriarchal pay-tree-*are*-kul.
patriarchs *pay*-tree-arks.
Perea Peh-*ree*-uh.
Pharaoh *Fair*-o or *Fay*-roe.
Pharaohnecho *Fay*-ro-*nee*-ko
Pharisees *Fair*-ih-seez.
Pharpar *Far*-par.
Philippians Fih-*lip*-ee-unz.
Philistine Fuh-*liss*-teen or
  Fill-us-teen.
Pietism **Pie**-uh-*tih*-zim.
Pisidia Pih-*sid*-ee-uh.
Pontius Pilate *Pon*-shus or *Pon*-ti-
  us *Pie*-lut.
Potiphar *Pot*-ih-far.
Potipherah *Pot*-i-**fee**-ruh.
praetorium *pree*-tor-ee-um.
Psalter *Sal*-ter.

Qohelet (*Hebrew*) Koe-*hel*-it.
Quran Kuh-*ran*.

rabbi *rab*-eye.
rabbinical ruh-*bin*-ih-kul.
Raca *Ray*-kuh or Ray-*kah*.
Ramah *Ray*-muh.
Rehoboam Ree-huh-*boe*-um.

Reuben *Roo*-ben.

Samaria Suh-*mare*-ee-uh.
Samaritans Suh-*mare*-uh-tunz.
Sanhedrin *San*-huh-drun or
  San-*heed*-run.
Sarai *Seh*-rye.
sarcophagus sar-*coff*-uh-gus.
Sennacherib Sen-*nack*-er-ib.
Sepphoris *Sef*-uh-ris.
Septuagint Sep-*too*-ih-jent.
sepulchre *sep*-ul-kur.
Sheba *She*-buh.
Shechem *Shee*-kem or *Shek*-em.
Shenir *She*-nur.
Shulamite *Shoo*-lum-ite.
Shunammite *Shoo*-nam-ite.
Shunem *Shoo*-nem.
Sichem *Sigh*-kem.
Siloam Sigh-*lo*-um.
Sinai *Sigh*-nye or *Sigh*-nay-eye.
Sinope Suh-*no*-pea.
Sodom *Sod*-um.
Solomon *Sol*-o-mun.
Sudarium Sue-*deh*-ree-um.
Sychar *Sigh*-kar.
Syria *Sear*-ee-uh.

Terah *Tair*-uh.
Thessalonians *Thess*-uh-**lo**-nee-
  unz (*th* as in *thin*).
Tiberias Tie-*beer*-ee-us.
Tiglathpileser *Tig*-lath-pih-*lee*-zer.
Tithonus Tith-oh-*nus*.

Uriah Yu-*rye*-uh.

victuals *vih*-tulz.

Wadi el-Arish Wah-dee el-Uh-*rish*.

Yahweh (*Hebrew*) *Yah*-weh.
Yom Kippur Yom Kih-*purr*.

Zaphnathpaaneah **Zaf**-nath-*pay*-
  uh-nee-uh.
Zebadiah *Zeb*-uh-**dye**-uh.
Zebulun *Zeb*-you-lun.
Zedekiah Zed-uh-*kye*-uh.
Zeus Zoose.
Zoan Zo-an.

TEN YEARS ON

by Ronald L. Nickelson

As I write these words in September 2010, I have just completed 10 years as editor of the *Standard Lesson Commentary.* Reflecting on those 10 years brings to mind my all-time favorite illustration (so far). I repeat it here, from the lesson of November 19, 2006:

❧ Longings, Worthwhile and Otherwise ❧

Between 1830 and 1850, the total mileage of railroad track in the United States went from 23 to 9,000. At the same time, steamboats were providing a new form of transportation. In 1844 the first telegraph message was sent. It was about the year 1850 that former New York City mayor Philip Hone, age 69, bemoaned, "The world is going too fast!" He longed for the good ol' days when horse-drawn coaches sped along at the rate of six miles an hour (*Newsweek,* November 29, 2004).

The nineteenth-century Industrial Revolution was just the beginning. The rate of change has been accelerating ever since. Some of us lament the increasing complexity of technology. The classic example is the inability of some of us to program our VCRs. We might as well give up: DVDs are now the state of the art. Yet even they will likely be outmoded soon by another technology.

"Even nostalgia ain't what it used to be!" That comic's quip says a lot about our longing for a more peaceful past, or a healthier past, or an [add your own longing here] past. We catch some of that spirit in Psalm 137. But it contains more than a longing for days past, lost in the "daze" of imperfect memory. There is a recognition that some values of the past are worth keeping. When we think wistfully about the past, is it to long for something important—something that is "of God"—or is it for something trivial?   —C. R. B.

I confess that I empathize with Philip Hone! I recently finished converting my home movies from VCR tapes to DVD, knowing full well that the DVD format is giving way to the Blu-ray Disc format. I don't want any more change in this area.

Yet change happens, and it's happening fast. The church ignores this fact at her peril. Think about Facebook. This social media did not exist 10 years ago. Launched in 2004, Facebook boasted that it had 500 million users as of July 21, 2010. For good or for ill, many people now prefer to build their social networks through this format. This is a cultural change of epic proportions.

The enduring challenge for the church is to convince an ever-changing culture that it needs the never-changing Word of God. This challenge is always before us as we create the *Standard Lesson Commentary* product line each year. The discussion questions address the church as it exists in today's culture, not the culture of the 1960s. The same is true of the verbal illustrations. The learning activities encourage the teacher to use the latest technology to enhance the learning experience. For the most up-to-date, culturally relevant teaching aid, check out *In the World,* a free download at standardlesson.com.

Behind the scenes, our editorial team now uses Wikispaces and Facebook as collaborative tools to create this commentary. I did not in my wildest dreams envision being able to do this 10 years ago. Some churches use social media to help keep their members informed. All this makes me wonder what changes the next 10 years will bring.

I wonder, but I do not worry because God is still in control. And to keep myself from getting grumpy about change, I take Solomon's advice: "Say not thou, What is the cause that the former days were better than these? for thou dost not inquire wisely concerning this" (Ecclesiastes 7:10). Now if you will excuse me, I have some YouTube videos to watch.

TRADITION AND WISDOM

Special Features

Lessons

Unit 1: Teaching and Learning

Unit 2: Jesus Teaches Wisdom

QUARTERLY QUIZ

Use these questions as a pretest or as a review. The answers are on page iv of This Quarter in the Word.

Lesson 1

1. Proverbs promises that God will direct the paths of those who trust Him. T/F. *Proverbs 3:6*

2. Proverbs states that God won't correct those He loves. T/F. *Proverbs 3:12*

Lesson 2

1. Following wisdom means "when thou runnest, thou shalt not _____." *Proverbs 4:12*

2. Wisdom's words are what? (life and health; food and water; rod and staff?). *Proverbs 4:22*

Lesson 3

1. Purposes or plans are established with a multitude of counselors. T/F. *Proverbs 15:22*

2. The fear of the Lord is the instruction of what? (holiness, grace, wisdom?) *Proverbs 15:33*

Lesson 4

1. The men of King _____ copied the proverbs of Solomon. *Proverbs 25:1*

2. The guest of a king should take the place of highest honor. T/F. *Proverbs 25:6, 7.*

Lesson 5

1. The people perish when there is no what? (vision, law, sunlight?) *Proverbs 29:18.*

2. Who has less hope than even a fool? (a man hasty with words, a man who seeks revenge, a thief?) *Proverbs 29:20*

Lesson 6

1. Wisdom is better than _____ of war. *Ecclesiastes 9:18*

2. "A wise man's heart is at his _____ hand; but a fool's heart is at his _____." *Ecclesiastes 10:2*

Lesson 7

1. Ecclesiastes challenges the reader to "remember now thy Creator in the days of thy _____." *Ecclesiastes 12:1*

2. "The whole duty of man" is to _____ God and _____ His commandments. *Ecclesiastes 12:13*

Lesson 8

1. The spice paprika is listed in Song of Solomon 4. T/F. *Song of Solomon 4:13, 14*

2. What is under the spouse's tongue? (pick two: milk, wine, honey, air?) *Song of Solomon 4:11*

Lesson 9

1. The kingdom of Heaven belongs to those who are "poor in _____." *Matthew 5:3*

2. In the Beatitudes, Jesus pronounced blessing on the "pure in _____." *Matthew 5:8*

Lesson 10

1. Jesus said that He came to replace the law, which was obsolete. T/F. *Matthew 5:17*

2. Jesus says that those who enter the kingdom of Heaven must have righteousness greater than that of the _____ and _____. *Matthew 5:20*

Lesson 11

1. Jesus says to bless those who do what to you? (curse, bless, ignore?) *Matthew 5:44*

2. God sends the rain on the _____ and the _____. *Matthew 5:45*

Lesson 12

1. Jesus said to pray how? (with shoes removed, in secret, with many words?) *Matthew 6:5-7*

2. Jesus warned that God does not forgive the trespasses of what kind of person? (disobedient, unforgiving, unrighteous?) *Matthew 6:15*

Lesson 13

1. Jesus said that God provides for His people even more than He does for what? (birds, Gentiles, sinners?) *Matthew 6:26*

2. Jesus said, "Seek ye first the kingdom of God, and his _____." *Matthew 6:33*

QUARTER AT A GLANCE

by Douglas Redford

THE LESSONS for this quarter cover the theme of *wisdom* in two units. Each unit focuses on the teachings of an individual who exemplified wisdom: Solomon in the Old Testament and Jesus in the New Testament.

Solomon

King Solomon "exceeded all the kings of the earth for riches and for wisdom" (1 Kings 10:23). Yet Solomon is one of the Bible's most tragic figures, with the end of his reign characterized by sin and many adversaries (1 Kings 11:1-25). How could someone who began his reign with seemingly unlimited potential (1 Kings 3:5-14) end in such a pitiful state?

The biblical record tells us why: "For it came to pass, when Solomon was old, that his wives turned away his heart after other gods: and his heart was not perfect with the Lord his God, as was the heart of David his father" (1 Kings 11:4). The threefold emphasis on the heart makes this factor hard to overlook. Even the wisest man in history will find nothing but futility (or "vanity," to use Solomon's word in Ecclesiastes) if his heart is not right with God. Any gift of God (not just wisdom) is useless if the recipient is not in close fellowship with the giver.

And that was Solomon's downfall. This is ironic, given his emphasis in Proverbs on the importance of the heart: "Keep thy heart with all diligence; for out of it are the issues of life" (Proverbs 4:23, Lesson 2). Because Solomon could not keep his own heart true to God, he was unable to maintain the kingdom his father David had entrusted to him. Yet we can become wiser by studying both Solomon's wisdom and mistakes.

Jesus

Jesus, the one "greater than Solomon" (Matthew 12:42), strongly emphasized the heart in His Sermon on the Mount. There He addressed people who had been led to think of religion in terms of duties and obligations performed to the letter of the law and personified faithfully (or so it seemed) by the scribes and Pharisees. One can only imagine the audible gasp uttered by Jesus' audience when He told them, "Except your righteousness shall exceed the righteousness of the scribes and Pharisees, ye shall in no case enter into the kingdom of heaven" (Matthew 5:20, Lesson 10). But Jesus proceeded to draw their attention to the importance of the heart, in the areas of anger (vv. 21, 22) and lust (vv. 27, 28).

The heart behind our deeds is what matters (Lesson 12). The model for our deeds is God himself. His heart is not that of a rigid rule-maker, but that of a loving Father. He is more than willing to provide for the needs of His children who trust His care and seek His kingdom first (Matthew 6:25-34, Lesson 13).

You?

Today many foods are labeled as "heart healthy." Wouldn't it be helpful if books, television programs, etc., came with a similar spiritual warning: "This may be hazardous to the health of your heart and may hinder your spiritual prog-

Do we know God "by heart"?

ress"? Of course, they don't. It is up to each follower of Jesus to cultivate a holy discernment that guides us in embracing right choices.

We can study the writings and teachings of both Solomon and Jesus, and we can even know some of them by heart. But the bigger question is: do we know God "by heart"? Only the one "greater than Solomon" can provide us with a new heart and set us on a path of wisdom that prepares us for eternity.

GET THE SETTING

by Walter D. Zorn

THIS QUARTER'S LESSONS are taken from what is called *the wisdom literature* of the Old Testament as well as the "wisdom teaching" of Jesus as recorded in the Sermon on the Mount in Matthew's Gospel. Tradition and wisdom, as presented in the Bible, can be great practical help in living the Christian life. Although centuries have passed since the Old and New Testaments were written, their wise insights into human nature are timeless.

Pre-Christian Wisdom Literature

Three books in the Old Testament deserve the title *wisdom books:* Job, Proverbs, and Ecclesiastes. Some students also put the Psalms and Song of Solomon (Song of Songs) in this category, but it comes down to a matter of definition.

One of the major characteristics of Job, Proverbs, and Ecclesiastes is the absence of "covenant talk," such as the promises to the patriarchs, the exodus events and Moses, or God's eternal promise to David. Wisdom texts are also identified by the very practical ideas for daily living, where day-to-day decisions have "in the now"

consequences, most of which are learned by experience. That is the point of wisdom literature: to learn from the experience of others.

Stepping outside the inspired Old Testament while still remaining within the experience of the covenant people, we find more wisdom texts. Two of these are Wisdom of Solomon and Ecclesiasticus. But wisdom literature is not exclusive to God's people. Such literature can be found in all the great cultures of the Ancient Near East, such as those of Egypt, the Syro-Arabian Desert, and the Mesopotamian regions.

Wisdom texts may take the form of autobiographies, hymns, poetry, and personal letters. Such literature may exhibit a variety of linguistic features such as parallelisms, similes, and metaphors to communicate ideas that demand reflection. The metaphors used to describe old age in Ecclesiastes 12:1-7 are both humorous and insightful.

First-century Wisdom Teaching

Jesus, the one "greater than Solomon" (Matthew 12:42), had much wisdom to impart. This is especially evident in His famous Sermon on the Mount. His instructions in Matthew 5:13-20 can be compared with Old Testament proverbs.

But the wisdom teaching of Jesus didn't come in a vacuum. The Greek and Roman empires had risen after the close of the Old Testament era, and those empires promoted their own ideas about wisdom. Paul, who traveled extensively throughout the Greco-Roman world, was acutely aware of this. We find Paul's sharpest critique of pagan wisdom in 1 Corinthians 1:18–2:16; 3:18-23. Paul was determined that it was the wisdom of Jesus that had to prevail (Colossians 2:2, 3).

But were Jesus' teachings on wisdom absolutely contradictory with pagan teaching? One could write thousands of words on that topic! But in our limited space here, we think the pagan philosophers would agree with Jesus in at least one regard: wisdom is proven true by the outcome (Matthew 11:19). And so it still is.

THIS QUARTER IN THE WORD

Answers to the Quarterly Quiz on page 2

Lesson 1—1. true. 2. false. **Lesson 2**—1. stumble. 2. life and health. **Lesson 3**—1. true. 2. wisdom. **Lesson 4**—1. Hezekiah. 2. false. **Lesson 5**—1. vision. 2. a man hasty with words. **Lesson 6**—1. weapons. 2. right, left. **Lesson 7**—1. youth. 2. fear, keep. **Lesson 8**—1. false. 2. milk, honey. **Lesson 9**—1. spirit. 2. heart. **Lesson 10**—1. false. 2. scribes, Pharisees. **Lesson 11**—1. curse. 2. just, unjust. **Lesson 12**—1. in secret. 2. unforgiving. **Lesson 13**—1. birds. 2. righteousness.

LESSON CYCLE CHART

International Sunday School Lesson Cycle, September 2010—August 2016

Year	Fall Quarter (Sep, Oct, Nov)	Winter Quarter (Dec, Jan, Feb)	Spring Quarter (Mar, Apr, May)	Summer Quarter (Jun, Jul, Aug)
2010-2011	The Inescapable God (Exodus, Psalms)	Assuring Hope (Isaiah, Matthew, Mark)	We Worship God (Matthew, Mark, Philippians, 1 & 2 Timothy, Jude, Revelation)	God Instructs His People (Joshua, Judges, Ruth)
2011-2012	Tradition and Wisdom (Proverbs, Ecclesiastes, Song of Solomon, Matthew)	God Establishes a Faithful People (Genesis, Exodus, Luke, Galatians)	God's Creative Word (John)	God Calls for Justice (Pentateuch, History, Psalms, Prophets)
2012-2013	A Living Faith (Psalms, Acts, 1 Corinthians, Hebrews)	Jesus Is Lord (John, Ephesians, Philippians, Colossians)	Undying Hope (Daniel, Luke, Acts, 1 & 2 Thessalonians, 1 & 2 Peter)	God's People Worship (Isaiah, Ezra, Nehemiah)
2013-2014	First Things (Genesis, Exodus, Psalms)	Jesus and the Just Reign of God (Luke, James)	Jesus' Fulfillment of Scripture (Pentateuch, 2 Samuel, Psalms, Prophets, Gospels, Acts, Revelation)	The People of God Set Priorities (Haggai, Zechariah, 1 & 2 Corinthians)
2014-2015	Sustaining Hope (Psalms, Job, Isaiah, Jeremiah, Ezekiel, Habakkuk)	Acts of Worship (Psalms, Matthew, Luke, John, Ephesians, Hebrews, James)	The Spirit Comes (Mark, John, Acts, 1 Corinthians, 1, 2, & 3 John)	God's Prophets Demand Justice (Isaiah, Jeremiah, Ezekiel, Amos, Micah, Zechariah, Malachi)
2015-2016	The Christian Community Comes Alive (Acts)	Sacred Gifts and Holy Gatherings (Pentateuch, Song of Solomon, Hosea, Micah, Gospels)	The Gift of Faith (Mark, Luke)	Toward a New Creation (Genesis, Psalms, Zephaniah, Romans)

"God"	"Hope"	"Worship"	"Community"	"Tradition"	"Faith"	"Creation"	"Justice"

TEACHING THE BORED

Teacher Tips by Brent L. Amato

WE ARE CALLED by God to teach His people (2 Timothy 2:2, 24). Each student in your class is precious in His sight, each a gift from Him. Your students are the reason for and the object of your teaching ministry. No students, no need for a teacher!

"But you don't know some of my students!" Admit it: in a weaker moment, haven't you contemplated how much easier, exciting, and rewarding teaching would be if you could select your own students? Haven't you wished from time to time that certain students wouldn't show up?

But "problem students" come with the teaching turf. In our mind's eye, we can almost see each problem student marching into our classroom with a big sign hanging around his or her neck proclaiming one of four identities: *the bored, the barrier, the boss,* and *the bomber.* We may wish they wouldn't come, but they must be taught!

Before you get too discouraged in teaching problem students, keep in mind that Jesus had struggles as well with students in His day (compare Matthew 10:14; 15:16; Luke 9:51-55; John 6:60-66). Jesus sought to reach them, and we should seek to do so as well.

Four Types, One Imperative

Pray for these students. Pray for them by name. Intercessory prayer is commanded frequently in the New Testament (Colossians 4:3; 1 Thessalonians 5:25; Hebrews 13:18). What could happen if you started praying daily this week for them?

Your prayers on behalf of these students should be as specific as possible: that the Word of God you teach will accomplish what God desires in them (Isaiah 55:11) and pierce them to the depths of their soul and spirit (Hebrews 4:12).

God is in the business of redemption, and that includes students in Bible study classes. To accomplish the goal of redemption, He first must get the attention of His children! Intercessory prayer is vital for connecting these students with our awesome God, who is the antidote for all that cuts against your teaching.

One Focus, Three Strategies

For this installment of Teacher Tips, we'll focus on *the bored* and deal with the other three in later quarters. For whatever reason, you aren't connecting with *the bored.* It appears that they wish they were somewhere else. Although physically present, they are absent mentally, emotionally, and—most important—spiritually. It seems like your teaching is falling among the thorns or the stony soil in Jesus' Parable of the Sower (Matthew 13:1-23). Let's consider three ways to make progress with your bored students.

First, shift into a higher gear. Vary your teaching methods; this will keep you out of "teaching ruts" that can fuel boredom. Make frequent eye contact with your bored students. Give them special attention. Ask them questions. Ask them to do some research ("homework") in preparation for your next class. Show that you care for them and are not bored in teaching them.

Second, probe for passion. Take every opportunity to engage your bored students in conversation. Cultivate a relationship with them outside the classroom. In so doing, you may discover some of their passions, which you can build into your teaching as an antidote to their boredom.

Third, don't beat up either "the bored" or yourself. Accept the fact that there will be some students in your class who would rather be somewhere else on a given day. The fact that some students are bored doesn't necessarily mean that you are a bad teacher. Realizing these facts will reduce the pressure to be "the perfect teacher" and reduce your frustration toward "the imperfect student." Keep teaching in spite of them.

I can't wait for my next class! I hope my bored students show up. What about you?

PURSUING RIGHTEOUSNESS

DEVOTIONAL READING: Psalm 115:3-11
BACKGROUND SCRIPTURE: Proverbs 3

PROVERBS 3:1-12

1 My son, forget not my law; but let thine heart keep my commandments:

2 For length of days, and long life, and peace, shall they add to thee.

3 Let not mercy and truth forsake thee: bind them about thy neck; write them upon the table of thine heart:

4 So shalt thou find favour and good understanding in the sight of God and man.

5 Trust in the LORD with all thine heart; and lean not unto thine own understanding.

6 In all thy ways acknowledge him, and he shall direct thy paths.

7 Be not wise in thine own eyes: fear the LORD, and depart from evil.

8 It shall be health to thy navel, and marrow to thy bones.

9 Honour the LORD with thy substance, and with the firstfruits of all thine increase:

10 So shall thy barns be filled with plenty, and thy presses shall burst out with new wine.

11 My son, despise not the chastening of the LORD; neither be weary of his correction:

12 For whom the LORD loveth he correcteth; even as a father the son in whom he delighteth.

KEY VERSE

Trust in the LORD with all thine heart; and lean not unto thine own understanding. —**Proverbs 3:5**

TRADITION AND WISDOM

Unit 1: Teaching and Learning

LESSON AIMS

After participating in this lesson, each student will be able to:

1. Identify principles that lead to a blessed life.

2. Explain why "the fear of the Lord" is foundational to other proverbial principles.

3. Identify an area of life that can be aligned more closely with the Lord's will by application of a proverbial principle and make a plan to do so.

LESSON OUTLINE

Introduction
    A. Healthy Fear
    B. Lesson Background
I. Key to Successful Living (PROVERBS 3:1, 2)
    A. Principle (v. 1)
    B. Benefits (v. 2)
        The Secret to Long Life
II. Key to Good Reputation (PROVERBS 3:3, 4)
    A. Principle (v. 3)
    B. Benefits (v. 4)
III. Key to Right Path (PROVERBS 3:5, 6)
    A. Principle (vv. 5, 6a)
        "Know-it-alls"
    B. Benefits (v. 6b)
IV. Key to Healthy Life (PROVERBS 3:7, 8)
    A. Principle (v. 7)
    B. Benefits (v. 8)
V. Key to Blessings (PROVERBS 3:9, 10)
    A. Principle (v. 9)
    B. Benefits (v. 10)
VI. Key to Love (PROVERBS 3:11, 12)
    A. Principle (v. 11)
    B. Benefits (v. 12)
Conclusion
    A. Learning to Fear the Lord
    B. Prayer
    C. Thought to Remember

Introduction

A. Healthy Fear

Growing up I had a healthy fear of my dad. He was a fairly strict disciplinarian who did not hesitate to spank with his hands on my rear end when I did something that displeased him. My fear, however, did not always translate into obedience.

Once when I was about 10 years old, I spent a leisurely day during Christmas break shooting at birds with a new slingshot I had made. It was my responsibility to keep the wood box full for the stove in our house, our only source of heat. On a cold January day as the sun was going down, I realized I had let the box get empty, and there was no fire in the stove. I could see my dad coming home from work from the sawmill, and I knew I was in trouble. So I ran to the woodpile behind the house and started chopping wood as fast as I could.

It was too late. Dad had already been in the house and discovered the empty wood box and a cold house. It was very difficult to cut wood while my dad was spanking me!

Years later we talked and joked about that incident, for it was one of the last spankings I received from my dad. I told him what made it so memorable was that I had both back pockets full of rocks since I was shooting at birds throughout the day and I needed plenty of ammunition. Dad said: "I wondered why my hand hurt so badly after that!" Well, I didn't have to wonder why I hurt on the other side of that hand. I determined then that I would obey my dad from that point on. Such are the benefits of discipline that results in wisdom.

B. Lesson Background

Proverbs is a collection of wisdom sayings. The book as a whole is credited to "Solomon the son of David, king of Israel" (Proverbs 1:1). This is probably based on the fact that Solomon was the patron of wisdom during the period of the unified kingdom (see 1 Kings 4:29-34; 5:12). Those who described Solomon's reign did so on the basis of wisdom (see 1 Kings 3:16-28 for a wise decision and 10:6-9 for the Queen of Sheba's conclusion). The major role wisdom plays in the book of Proverbs is clearly stated in the opening verses of 1:2-7.

Pursuing Righteousness

The book divides itself into three major sections: (1) a long introduction to the collections of proverbs (Proverbs 1–9), (2) the collections of the proverbs themselves (10:1–31:9), and (3) an acrostic conclusion (31:10-31). The collections themselves form six subdivisions: (a) proverbs of Solomon (10:1–22:16), (b) words of the wise (22:17–24:22), (c) more words of the wise (24:23-34), (d) more proverbs of Solomon (25:1–29:27), (e) words of Agur (chapter 30), and (f) words of King Lemuel (31:1-9).

Most scholars see 10 fatherly appeals or lectures in Proverbs 1–9. These are 1:8-19; 2:1-22; 3:1-12; 3:21-35; 4:1-9; 4:10-19; 4:20-27; 5:1-23; 6:20-35; and 7:1-27. Our text for today is the third of these lectures. It includes 6 basic principles (the odd-numbered verses) and the benefits derived from them if obeyed (the even-numbered verses). I call them *principles* because they are not specific commands or detailed things to do. Rather, they have more to do with attitudes and a stance one takes in a lifestyle. The benefits are not necessarily immediate or magical, but they can be expected as coming from the God of wisdom himself.

I. Key to Successful Living
(PROVERBS 3:1, 2)
A. Principle (v. 1)

1. My son, forget not my law; but let thine heart keep my commandments.

The address to *my son* begins at Proverbs 1:8 and continues throughout the long prologue (see 1:8, 10, 15; 2:1; 3:1, 11, 21; 4:10, 20; 5:1, 20; 6:1, 3, 20; 7:1). Most education in ancient Israel is given from father to son, mother to daughter in what we call today a "home schooling" context.

The Hebrew text emphasizes the words *law* and *commandments* by placing them first in the two clauses after the opening *my son*. In other words, it's written something like "my law do not forget, and my commandments let your heart keep." The words *law* and *command(ment)s* are often associated in the Old Testament in such a way as to be synonymous (see Genesis 26:5; Exodus 24:12; 2 Kings 17:34, 37). Thus it is probably a mistake to draw a fine distinction between the terms.

THE BOOK OF PROVERBS

INTRODUCTION (1:1–9:18)	TEN FATHER-TO-SON APPEALS
	• Choose Your Friends Wisely [1:8-19]
	• Pursue Wisdom, part 1 [2:1-22]
	• PUT GOD FIRST (3:1-12) LESSON 1
	• Act with Discretion [3:21-35]
	• Pursue Wisdom, part 2 [4:1-9]
	• AVOID THE WAY OF THE WICKED (4:10-19) LESSON 2
	• Stay on the Right Path [4:20-27]
	• Avoid the Adulteress, part 1 [5:1-23]
	• Avoid the Adulteress, part 2 [6:20-35]
	• Avoid the Adulteress, part 3 [7:1-27]
THE PROVERBS (10:1–31:9)	SIX SUBDIVISIONS
	• PROVERBS OF SOLOMON (10:1–22:16) LESSON 3
	• Words of the Wise [22:17–24:22]
	• More Words of the Wise [24:23-34]
	• MORE PROVERBS OF SOLOMON (25:1–29:27) LESSONS 4, 5
	• Words of Agur [30:1-33]
	• Words of King Lemuel [31:1-9]
EPILOGUE (31:10-31)	ACROSTIC CONCLUSION

Visual for Lesson 1. *This chart will help your learners maintain a "big picture" perspective as you study the book of Proverbs.*

We may wonder if *my law* refers to the instruction of the father only, or to God's law. Many think that it refers to the father's own teaching and advice as given in Proverbs 1–9. This approach is plausible in light of Proverbs 6:20; 7:2. However, it seems best to view the *law* and *commandments* as being from God—laws that the father interprets and passes along to his son (see Proverbs 6:23). Such laws and commandments are firm in the father's mind, and the son must not forget them! This is more than just simple advice. The father desires complete obedience from the son.

The word *heart* in these texts usually refers to the core personality of the person being addressed. Thus the heart of the son includes his mind, emotions, and will. Keeping the commandments affects the inner being from which actions flow.

B. Benefits (v. 2)

2. For length of days, and long life, and peace, shall they add to thee.

A child has the best chance at experiencing a healthy and full life as he or she obeys the Word of God as taught and lived by dedicated parents. Whoever finds wisdom, finds life (see Proverbs 3:16; 8:35, where the words *her* and *me* refer to wisdom). The negative side is found in Proverbs 11:19: "he that pursueth evil pursueth it to his own death." Other texts that address *length of days* or *long life* include Exodus 20:12; Job 12:12; and Psalm 91:16.

❧ THE SECRET TO LONG LIFE ❧

The actress Dorothea Kent (1916–1990) once told of a 90-year-old who was asked how he had managed to live so long. With a twinkle in his eye he replied, "It's because most nights I went to bed and slept when I should have sat up and worried."

This gets to the truth of what our text says. Worry is our attempt to control things without input from God. But people who live by God's instructions in Scripture aren't nearly as likely as others to "sit up and worry" about what to do. Focusing on a godly lifestyle and behaviors promotes a longer and happier life.

Of course, there are no guarantees of how many days we shall have. Accidents, illness, and birth defects can cut our lives short. But godly living will produce a peace of soul that blesses us. Remember: the longest life there is is eternal life!

—C. R. B.

II. Key to Good Reputation
(PROVERBS 3:3, 4)
A. Principle (v. 3)

3. Let not mercy and truth forsake thee; bind them about thy neck; write them upon the table of thine heart.

The principle here is an admonition to bind *mercy and truth* about the neck as if a necklace. Further, these two are to be written on the heart as if the heart were a tablet (compare 2 Corinthians 3:3). But what do these images imply?

The words *mercy* and *truth* appear together often in the Old Testament, although the Hebrew words are not always translated *mercy* and *truth* as we see here. For example, Genesis 24:49 translates these words as "kindly and truly." The word *mercy*

can take various shades of meaning, depending on context. But *mercy* is connected so often with the word *covenant* that many students think of it as "covenant loyalty" (examples: Deuteronomy 7:9, 12; 1 Kings 8:23). The word *truth,* for its part, carries the idea of "reliability" (examples Psalm 71:22; Isaiah 61:8).

Both covenant loyalty and reliability are attributes of God; it is His character to exhibit covenant loyalty, and He does so with absolute reliability. As these two ideas are part of God's character, so they should be part of our character as well (compare Proverbs 16:6; 20:28).

To *bind them about thy neck; write them upon the table of thine heart* presents a lofty challenge indeed (compare Deuteronomy 6:8; Proverbs 6:21; 7:3; Jeremiah 31:33)! Although these phrases are figurative, they should be taken seriously. Rebellious and disobedient people are often described as being "stiffnecked" (examples: Exodus 32:9; Jeremiah 17:23; Acts 7:51) and having hardened hearts (examples: 2 Chronicles 36:13; Matthew 19:8). Thus it is appropriate to learn those characteristics that will keep the neck from stiffening and the heart from hardening—namely, mercy and truth. When we allow such godly characteristics to become a part of our core being, we find ourselves reaping the benefits.

B. Benefits (v. 4)

4. So shalt thou find favour and good understanding in the sight of God and man.

The Hebrew text literally begins with an imperative: ***Find** favour and good understanding.* But the translators of the *King James Version* rightly see this "finding" as a result of the challenge of verse 3; thus we have *so shalt thou find.* If a person's character includes the couplet of "mercy/covenant loyalty" and "truth/reliability," then the result will be *favour and good understanding in the sight of God and man.* The word *favor* implies "acceptance"; *good understanding* signifies "prudence" or "insight." Thus, the combination of these ideas means having a good reputation with both God and people.

God wants His own character developed in His people (compare Romans 8:29), and He is able to recognize when that is happening. A good name and reputation are cherished goals (see Proverbs 22:1; 1 Timothy 3:7). This takes time and commitment. The benefit of mercy and truth is a good relationship with both the divine and the human.

III. Key to Right Path
(Proverbs 3:5, 6)
A. Principle (vv. 5, 6a)

5a. Trust in the LORD with all thine heart.

The preposition *in* that we see here carries the idea of "direction toward." Thus to *trust in the Lord* is a very active concept. Similar expressions are found in 2 Kings 18:22, 30; Psalms 4:5; 31:6; 56:4; 86:2; Isaiah 36:7, 15. The kind of trust we are talking about demands a commitment of a person's whole being—mind, emotions, will, and body. The word *heart* is prominent throughout the first part of our text (compare Proverbs 3:1, 3).

What Do You Think?
How will you practice trust in the Lord in the various areas of life?
Talking Points for Your Discussion
- Mind
- Emotions
- Will
- Body

(handwritten: 9 1-405- 218-1754)

5b. And lean not unto thine own understanding.

We get into trouble when we begin to trust in our own resources and abilities (Isaiah 5:21). Life is filled with complexities, and we need the Lord's help with those. The next time you think you have

something "all figured out," stop and meditate on what God's viewpoint might be. The spiritually mature person allows the word and wisdom of Christ to direct his or her path (Colossians 3:16).

❧ "Know-it-alls" ❧

"Why don't you just stop and ask for directions?" That's the classic (and perhaps unfairly stereotyped) question of a wife to her stubborn husband while driving far from home. Global Positioning System units would seem to offer the ideal solution. But occasionally the programming is faulty, and the GPS unit sends you to a road that doesn't exist. Also, solar flares can result in lower signal strength. Of course, all this will have no effect on a "Mr. or Mrs. Know-it-all" who is behind the wheel of the family car!

We can think of the Bible as our Eternal Positioning System. God has "programmed" it to be perfectly reliable. Its signal strength never fades. But we must consult it. Each of us is tempted at times to be a "know-it-all." But those who pridefully trust in their own understanding will find themselves spiritually lost and, perhaps, not willing to admit that fact. —C. R. B.

6a. In all thy ways acknowledge him.

The simple message here is to know God. The prophet Hosea is especially concerned about this issue (see Hosea 2:20; 4:1, 6; 5:4; 6:3; 8:2; 13:4). To know God means that we have such an intimate relationship with Him that we practice the presence of God in all aspects of our lives (see Philippians 3:7-11). This principle will lead to a great benefit (next verse).

HOW TO SAY IT

Colossians	Kuh-*losh*-unz.
Ecclesiastes	Ik-*leez*-ee-*as*-teez.
Hosea	Ho-*zay*-uh.
Isaiah	Eye-*zay*-uh.
Lemuel	*Lem*-you-el.
Philippians	Fih-*lip*-ee-unz.
Septuagint	Sep-*too*-ih-jent.
Sheba	*She*-buh.
Solomon	*Sol*-o-mun.

B. Benefits (v. 6b)

6b. And he shall direct thy paths.

When we humbly seek to know God, then He will make our ways straight or smooth. Walking a straight and smooth path directed by God is the only way to go (compare Jeremiah 10:23).

Proverbs has much to say about the straight path, both positively and negatively (see Proverbs 1:15; 2:12-15, 19, 20; 3:17; 4:11, 26; 5:6, 21; 7:25; 8:20; 10:9; 11:5; 15:21b; 22:5). One of the most foolish things is to have full awareness of both the right and wrong paths and intentionally choose the wrong one (example: Jeremiah 44:15-18).

IV. Key to Healthy Life

(PROVERBS 3:7, 8)

A. Principle (v. 7)

7. Be not wise in thine own eyes: fear the LORD, and depart from evil.

Be not wise in thine own eyes is another way of saying, "Lean not unto thine own understanding" (Proverbs 3:5b, above). This thought is restated in several ways in Proverbs (see 12:15; 26:5, 12; 28:11, 26). One cannot fear God until arrogance and conceit are gone (compare Romans 12:16; James 3:13-16). The fear of God is the heartbeat of the Proverbs (see 1:7, 29; 2:5; 10:27; 14:27; 15:16, 33, among others). The "fear of God" concept is used as bookends for the introductory chapters of Proverbs 1–9 (see 1:7 and 9:10). Such fear will help us *depart from evil* (see 8:13; 16:6).

We note in passing that fear of the Lord is a major theme in the poetic parts of the Old Testament (examples: Job 28:28; Psalm 111:10; Ecclesiastes 12:13). Such fear will result in avoidance of evil (see Proverbs 14:15, 16). The Christian is not exempt from the need to fear God (Acts 9:31; 2 Corinthians 5:11; Hebrews 12:28, 29; 1 Peter 2:17).

B. Benefits (v. 8)

8. It shall be health to thy navel, and marrow to thy bones.

This Hebrew idiom offers us a certain difficulty in the original text. The word *navel* is accurately translated here, but the old Greek version known as the Septuagint has *body* instead of *navel*. Perhaps the translators of the Septuagint thought that *navel* does not create a parallel with *bones,* but that *flesh/body* does. Either way, the meaning is clear: the writer is talking about one's entire body. *Marrow* is describing the bones as being moist and lubricated, a sign of health (Job 21:24; Proverbs 15:30; Isaiah 58:11). Dry bones are a sign of ill health or even death (see Proverbs 17:22; Ezekiel 37:11).

Humility, the fear of God, and turning from evil will bring health spiritually, psychologically, and physically. There is a clear connection between one's spiritual well-being and one's physical and mental well-being. Each influences the others.

V. Key to Blessings

(PROVERBS 3:9, 10)

A. Principle (v. 9)

9. Honour the LORD with thy substance, and with the firstfruits of all thine increase.

This verse refers to the system of tithes and offerings under the Law of Moses (see Numbers 18:21-29; Deuteronomy 14:22-29). The tithe supported the priestly ministries. The tithing system encouraged worshipers to celebrate at the temple during required festivals (see Leviticus 23).

During the celebration of the Festival of Unleavened Bread, a brief ceremony called *firstfruits* is performed. This is an act of faith on the worshiper's part (see Leviticus 23:9-14): God is to receive the *first* and *best* of the harvest ahead of the farmer himself. The ancient Israelites need to be exhorted periodically to give in this manner (see Malachi 3:6-12). A generous heart is in imitation of the Lord (compare Psalm 111:5 with 112:5). The concept of *firstfruits* comes over into the New Testament in important ways (Romans 8:23; 11:16; 1 Corinthians 15:20, 23; James 1:18).

> *What Do You Think?*
> What specific ways will you honor God with your "firstfruits" in the week ahead?
> *Talking Points for Your Discussion*
> - Firstfruits of time
> - Firstfruits of money
> - Firstfruits of relationships

B. Benefits (v. 10)

10. So shall thy barns be filled with plenty, and thy presses shall burst out with new wine.

Malachi records God's challenge to the ancient Israelites to give the entire tithe so that He might bless them abundantly (see Malachi 3:10-12). This should not be thought of as a health-and-wealth gospel. However, in general God blesses those who are faithful, generous, and sacrificial in their giving (see Mark 10:29, 30). One should meditate on Jesus' parable of the greedy farmer in Luke 12:16-21.

VI. Key to Love
(PROVERBS 3:11, 12)
A. Principle (v. 11)

11. My son, despise not the chastening of the LORD; neither be weary of his correction.

This verse and the next are quoted in Hebrews 12:5, 6. *The chastening of the Lord* is mediated through the father to the son (compare Deuteronomy 8:5). Only a fool despises such discipline (see Proverbs 1:7; 15:5).

As a first principle, God's discipline and correction include suffering. Even so, we should be careful to understand that not all affliction results from wrongdoing. In Job's case, he was afflicted although he had done nothing wrong. But all wrongdoing will one day be punished.

B. Benefits (v. 12)

12. For whom the LORD loveth he correcteth; even as a father the son in whom he delighteth.

The benefit of discipline and correction by the Lord is the assurance that He loves us. Our human parents also disciplined us for our good. Think about it: what kind of parent never disciplines a child? One who just doesn't care! Even though my father disciplined me quite harshly at times, I was always assured of his love by being in his lap a short time later.

Not all affliction is discipline for wrongdoing, as mentioned above. But affliction develops our character that we can share in God's holiness (see Romans 5:3-5).

What Do You Think?
What was a time that you benefited from receiving the discipline and correction of the Lord?
Talking Points for Your Discussion
- In a time of distress (sin, discouragement, etc.)
- In a time of plenty

Conclusion
A. Learning to Fear the Lord

Let us review the six principles we have discovered, along with their benefits.

First, obey the instructions of your parents and God—that will give you the best shot at a long and successful life! *Second,* be committed in your innermost being to God's truth—you will win a good reputation with God and humanity! *Third,* trust only in the Lord and not in yourself—He will make your paths smooth! *Fourth,* have great reverence and awe for God while fleeing evil—you will live a very healthy life indeed! *Fifth,* put God first in your giving by giving your most and your best—you will discover more blessings than you can imagine! *Sixth,* accept the sufferings and difficulties in life—you will find behind them a loving Father who desires your best!

Learning to fear God gives meaning and purpose to our lives. Living a lifestyle that embraces the six principles above will produce the best kind of life: one that pleases God.

B. Prayer

Father, we bow before You with reverence and awe. Teach us to trust in You and not in ourselves. May we put You first. In Jesus' name, amen.

C. Thought to Remember

Obeying God's principles brings great benefits.

VISUALS FOR THESE LESSONS

The visual pictured in each lesson (example: page 11) is a small reproduction of a large, full-color poster included in the *Adult Resources* packet for the Fall Quarter. That packet also contains the very useful *Presentation Helps* on a CD for teacher use. Order No. 020019211 from your supplier.

INVOLVEMENT LEARNING

Some of the activities below are also found in the helpful student book, Adult Bible Class.
Don't forget to download the free reproducible page from www.standardlesson.com to enhance your lesson!

Into the Lesson

Inform your students that for the next eight weeks they will be studying from the books of Proverbs, Ecclesiastes, and Song of Solomon. Since these books deal with wisdom and are primarily the writings of Solomon, you want to find out how wise your students are by giving them a pop quiz. To that end, distribute the following True/False quiz:

1. Solomon was the author of all the sayings in the book of Proverbs. 2. Solomon was the son of David and Bathsheba. 3. Solomon's wisdom was a special gift from God. 4. These verses are from Proverbs: "To every thing there is a season, and a time to every purpose under the heaven." 5. Most scholars believe Ecclesiastes was written late in Solomon's life. 6. A primary theme of Proverbs is found in 1:7: "The fear of the Lord is the beginning of knowledge: but fools despise wisdom and instruction." 7. Song of Solomon is the Israelites' song of victory after defeating the Philistines. 8. Solomon was wise in faithfully following the Lord all the days of his life.

Answers: 2, 3, 5, and 6 are true; 1, 4, 7, and 8 are false. After discussing the answers, say, "Solomon has a lot to teach us because of all the wisdom that God gave him. As we read some of his proverbs today, see if any seem especially meaningful to you."

Alternative: Download the reproducible page and distribute copies of the Proverbs in Tension activity. Have learners complete the activity according to the instructions given. Ask for volunteers to share their best stories.

Into the Word

Prepare a handout chart with two columns and six rows. The column headings are *Principles* and *Promised Benefits*. Put the following six items under the *Principles* column: (A) Don't depend on your own smarts; trust God. (B) Hang love and truth around your neck and write them on your heart. (C) Accept God's discipline. (D) Listen to your dad and to God. (E) Give the best you've got to God. (F) Revere God and avoid evil. Put the following six items under the *Promised Benefits* column: (G) Your life will be long and worthwhile. (H) You will experience good health. (I) You'll receive God's abundant blessings. (J) God will help you stay on the right path. (K) You will know God loves you enough to correct you. (L) You will have favor with God and man.

Include these instructions at the top: "As we work though Proverbs 3:1-12, write the number of the verse that corresponds to the principles and benefits below. (Hint: the principles are odd-numbered verses; the benefits, even-numbered.) Draw lines to match the principles with the promised benefit."

Distribute a copy of the chart to each learner. They can fill out their charts in study groups or individually as you teach the lesson. *Answers:* verses 1 and 2, D/G; verses 3 and 4, B/L; verses 5 and 6, A/J; verses 7 and 8, F/H; verses 9 and 10, E/I; verses 11 and 12, C/K. Wrap up this segment by asking, "Which of these principles seems the most difficult to follow? Which of these benefits would you most like to enjoy?"

Into Life

Option 1: Download the reproducible page and distribute copies of the Fearful Mixture activity. Have learners complete the activity in small groups and compare their answers with 1 Corinthians 13:13. Discuss.

Option 2: Give a colored index card to each learner. Say, "Select a pair of proverbs that contain a command and a promise and write those verses on the card. Put the card in a conspicuous place at home where it will serve as a reminder." Close with prayer that asks for God's help in creating a desire to learn and obey His commands.

MAKING RIGHT CHOICES

DEVOTIONAL READING: Jeremiah 31:7-11
BACKGROUND SCRIPTURE: Proverbs 4:1-27

PROVERBS 4:10-15, 20-27

10 Hear, O my son, and receive my sayings; and the years of thy life shall be many.

11 I have taught thee in the way of wisdom; I have led thee in right paths.

12 When thou goest, thy steps shall not be straitened; and when thou runnest, thou shalt not stumble.

13 Take fast hold of instruction; let her not go: keep her; for she is thy life.

14 Enter not into the path of the wicked, and go not in the way of evil men.

15 Avoid it, pass not by it, turn from it, and pass away.

. . . .

20 My son, attend to my words; incline thine ear unto my sayings.

21 Let them not depart from thine eyes; keep them in the midst of thine heart.

22 For they are life unto those that find them, and health to all their flesh.

23 Keep thy heart with all diligence; for out of it are the issues of life.

24 Put away from thee a froward mouth, and perverse lips put far from thee.

25 Let thine eyes look right on, and let thine eyelids look straight before thee.

26 Ponder the path of thy feet, and let all thy ways be established.

27 Turn not to the right hand nor to the left: remove thy foot from evil.

KEY VERSE

Take fast hold of instruction; let her not go: keep her; for she is thy life. —**Proverbs 4:13**

TRADITION AND WISDOM

Unit 1: Teaching and Learning

LESSONS 1–8

LESSON AIMS

After participating in this lesson, each student will be able to:

1. Identify choices that the writer of Proverbs says one must make.

2. Compare and contrast Proverbs 4:14 with Psalm 1:1.

3. Select three verses from today's text to make into a prayer of supplication and do so.

LESSON OUTLINE

Introduction
  A. Making Right Choices
  B. Lesson Background
 I. Attentive Son (PROVERBS 4:10-15)
  A. Wisdom Walk (vv. 10-13)
  B. Wicked Walk (vv. 14, 15)
II. Healthy Person (PROVERBS 4:20-27)
  A. Ear (v. 20)
    Failing to Hear
  B. Eyes, Part 1 (v. 21a)
  C. Heart (vv. 21b-23)
  D. Mouth/Lips (v. 24)
  E. Eyes, Part 2 (v. 25)
    From Seeing to Perceiving
  F. Feet (vv. 26, 27)
Conclusion
  A. The Way of Wisdom
  B. Prayer
  C. Thought to Remember

Introduction

A. Making Right Choices

Sometimes it seems that the younger you are, the more critical the choices. I made three choices in my younger days that completely changed my life's direction and destiny. The first two were right choices, while the third may have been.

The first of the three choices was my decision to become a Christian. That was in 1957. It was the most important, wisest decision I ever made. But it easily could have gone the other way because I was reared in a non-Christian environment. That one decision kept my feet from "the path of the wicked." This does not mean I was perfect in that regard, but at least I was encouraged by many Christian friends to walk on right paths.

The second of the three choices was my 1967 decision to take a wife. I am so glad she said "Yes"! She has been my confidante, best friend, lover, counselor, helper, teacher, and organizer. She is much more, of course, but that one decision lifted my abilities in ministry and teaching because of her care, concern, support, and love through the years. She is the reason I have been able to continue a high-paced ministry of teaching and preaching. Our children are a blessing to us and have given us six grandchildren whom we adore. After God, I attribute most of our success to my wife. What a choice!

The third of the three choices was my 1988 decision to become the academic dean at a Bible college. I had attended the seminary of the institution, and thus I loved the school. My decision to become dean of the college may not have been the best choice for me, for I remained in administration only for 5 years. However, I was able to stay with the school and become part of the faculty. That was where my talents and giftedness were best put to use.

For more than 20 years I have been able to see the ultimate fruit of that third decision. I am able to continue a meaningful teaching ministry, with many students flowing through our lives year after year.

Making right, godly choices can bring happiness and fulfillment to life.

B. Lesson Background

Last week we noted that Proverbs 1–9 is organized as 10 lectures. Today's lesson includes part of what we may call "Lecture 6" (Proverbs 4:10-19) and all of "Lecture 7" (4:20-27). But before we launch into the commentary, let us observe some basic principles of interpretation required for the book of Proverbs.

First, it is important to recognize the structure of the book of Proverbs as a whole. Proverbs 1–9 is different from Proverbs 10–31, for the first nine chapters function as a long introduction to the collections of proverbs in Proverbs 10–31 (see last week's Lesson Background). Second, proverbs are usually parallel in structure. That is, the second line often adds to or contrasts with the idea of the first line.

Third, the nature of the imagery in a proverb is important to discern as we try to determine how things are compared or contrasted. Fourth, sometimes it is important to note the source of the proverb or wisdom saying: is it experience, observation, tradition, or something else? Fifth, we must recognize that proverbs are relative to the situation. This means we should evaluate circumstances for applying a proverb in any given life context (example: contrast Proverbs 26:4 with 26:5).

Sixth, a proverb addressed to those of a certain age group should be evaluated for relevance to other age groups. Seventh, we can enhance our understanding of the book of Proverbs by consulting sources that help us understand the background from which the proverbs emerged. Eighth, we should master what various proverbs say about a particular topic by grouping them together.

Ninth, we should be alert to biblical stories or characters who illustrate a proverb's application (or lack thereof). Tenth, we should evaluate how the New Testament addresses issues found in the book of Proverbs.

HOW TO SAY IT

Deuteronomy	Due-ter-*ahn*-uh-me.
Ezekiel	Ee-*zeek*-ee-ul or Ee-*zeek*-yul.
Leviticus	Leh-*vit*-ih-kus.
Potiphar	*Pot*-ih-far.

I. Attentive Son
(PROVERBS 4:10-15)
A. Wisdom Walk (vv. 10-13)

10a. Hear, O my son, and receive my sayings.

The command to hear is characteristic of Proverb's opening lectures. This imperative occurs seven times in Proverbs 1–9, compared with only five times in Proverbs 10–31. It reminds us of the Hebrew creed "Hear, O Israel: The Lord our God is one Lord" (Deuteronomy 6:4).

To *hear* signifies having an open mind that accepts a teaching and is willing to obey it; *receive my sayings* is the parallel phrase to this. This command comes after a discussion of the supreme importance of wisdom (Proverbs 4:1-9).

10b. And the years of thy life shall be many.

The son's obedience to the father's sayings will yield a significant result: long life. This theme of long life as a positive consequence is repeated from Proverbs 3:2 and will be repeated again in 9:11 in the book's opening lectures (compare 3:16 and 28:16). Walking in the right path not only holds out the promise of long life (compare Exodus 20:12; Ephesians 6:2, 3), it clearly includes quality of life as well (see Proverbs 4:13, 22, 23). The latter verses will be discussed below.

What Do You Think?
In what ways can walking in or not walking in the ways of God affect one's life expectancy?
Talking Points for Your Discussion
- Lifestyle (behavioral) choices
- Vocational choices
- Speech choices
- Choices of friends

---

11. I have taught thee in the way of wisdom; I have led thee in right paths.

The Scriptures often speak of walking *in* a way or path, both physically (Genesis 24:48; Exodus 23:20) and spiritually (Deuteronomy 5:33; 8:6). Spiritually, "the father" leads "the son" by teaching *the way of wisdom*. The father's teaching is authoritative. *Right paths* indicate the old, beaten paths that many a righteous person has walked. To depart from such paths has serious consequences (Jeremiah 18:15). The young person would be wise to walk along the same paths that the godly and elderly wise have traveled. All of us should "ask for the old paths" (Jeremiah 6:16). The word *right* signifies "morally straight." Thus *right* is "right"!

12. When thou goest, thy steps shall not be straitened; and when thou runnest, thou shalt not stumble.

The son has a choice to make. He can hear his father's instructions concerning the way of wisdom and choose to follow them, or he can choose to go his own way. In this verse, the walking *(goest)* and running are figures of speech for the daily grind and difficulties that come in life. When one walks, he or she may be slowed down *(straitened)* or hampered by some obstacle. Running affords more chances of stumbling, since it's harder to avoid obstacles while moving at a higher rate of speed. In either case, the person who makes wise decisions is in the best position to avoid difficulties. He or she will walk well and run smoothly in a spiritual sense.

> *What Do You Think?*
> What are some times in your life when you have failed to walk in the ways of God? What were the results, and how did you grow spiritually as a result?
>
> *Talking Points for Your Discussion*
> - Consider sins you have committed
> - Consider things you should have done but failed to do
> - Consider when you did "a good thing" but not "the best thing"

13. Take fast hold of instruction; let her not go: keep her; for she is thy life.

When we read this verse, our minds are forced to return to verse 10. There the son is commanded to hear and receive the sayings of the father, with the resulting promise of long life. These similarities between verses 10 and 13 lead us to think of them as bookends to what lies between. The son must grasp the father's instruction. So must we.

The Hebrew word translated *instruction* includes the ideas of discipline, chastening, and correction.

We see these ideas in, for example, Proverbs 15:10 and Jeremiah 2:30, although the translation is not *instruction* in those cases.

Although the word *instruction* is masculine in the Hebrew, it is treated as feminine on the basis that the word *wisdom* (v. 11) is feminine. Thus, instruction must be accepted just as we would accept wisdom. *Let her not go: keep her!* The figurative idea is that of a marriage. "Marriage" to Lady Wisdom demands faithfulness. Why? Because *she is thy life*.

While verse 10 makes reference to length of life, the verse before us includes the idea of quality of life (see also reference to the "tree of life" in Proverbs 3:18). Most people do not choose to be disciplined or corrected voluntarily. But such a choice, difficult as it may be, will result in both quantity and quality of life.

B. Wicked Walk (vv. 14, 15)

14. Enter not into the path of the wicked, and go not in the way of evil men.

Now we switch to the negative—what not to do. Just as there are well-worn paths that the righteous enter and walk upon (v. 11, above), so also there is *the path of the wicked* to be avoided. *The wicked* are criminals deserving punishment, regardless of who they are (see Proverbs 25:5). The warning against *evil men* (a synonym of *the wicked*) is pronounced throughout Proverbs 1–9 (examples: 2:14; 8:13).

Essentially, there are two paths in life: the way of wisdom and the way of the wicked (contrast Jeremiah 6:16 with 18:15). We must not walk the road of the wicked. We must not even get on that road! We are able to avoid that road only after we learn right from wrong (Leviticus 10:10; Ezekiel 22:26; 44:23; Hebrews 5:14).

> *What Do You Think?*
> In what ways are you most tempted to follow the ways of evil people? How do you resist?
>
> *Talking Points for Your Discussion*
> - "Everybody's doing it" (Exodus 23:2)
> - "To get along you have to go along" (Acts 4:19; 5:29)
> - "Just this once won't hurt" (1 Timothy 6:11)

15. Avoid it, pass not by it, turn from it, and pass away.

Wow—such forceful language! To the commands *avoid . . . pass not . . . turn from . . . pass away* we may contrast *take fast hold . . . let her not go . . . keep* of verse 13, above. There is no sense that one is allowed to swap roads back and forth at whim. That is not an option. There is to be no flirting with evil. There is to be no living one way during the day while living a different way at night. We should not even get close to the wicked way to take a peek—*pass not by it!*

An interesting feature of this verse is that the word translated *pass away* is also the word that is stated negatively as *pass not by it.* The play on words can be illustrated with a literal reading of the Hebrew: "Avoid it! You must *not cross over* on it. Turn from upon it and *cross over*!"

The existence of these two paths is the main subject in this first section of our text (Proverbs 4:10-15). There is the way of wisdom and the way of the wicked. The choices we make in terms of these two ways will determine perhaps our quantity of life (contrast Ecclesiastes 7:15), but certainly our quality of life. When we choose the right path, it is as if we are walking in the light (Proverbs 4:18, not in today's text) unto a perfect day. Those who choose the wicked way walk in darkness and do not know why they stumble (Proverbs 4:19).

II. Healthy Person
(PROVERBS 4:20-27)
A. Ear (v. 20)

20. My son, attend to my words; incline thine ear unto my sayings.

The image of the straight or right path will come back into view in verses 26, 27, below. In the meantime, the attention shifts to certain body parts that, if used properly, contribute to the son's ability to walk wisely and, in the end, to experience health. The opening words of "Lecture 7" (that is, Proverbs 4:20-27) are similar to those of "Lecture 6" (that is, Proverbs 4:10-19). The two phrases in verse 20 here are perfect examples of parallelism: *Attend to* equals to *incline thine ear,* while *my words* equate to *my sayings.*

Visual for Lesson 2. *Use this visual to start a discussion as you ask, "What are examples of 'wicked paths' in our area?"*

The body part that is responsible for capturing the father's words is the ear. The picture is like a person who cups an ear in order to better hear (contrast Acts 7:57). Before one can obey a word, one must first hear it (Romans 10:17). But hearing by itself is no guarantee of understanding (Acts 28:26a).

❧ *FAILING TO HEAR* ❧

On October 21, 2009, Northwest Airlines flight 188 from San Diego to Minneapolis overflew its destination by 150 miles. Repeated attempts to contact the plane by radio went unheard. It took authorities more than 90 minutes to reestablish radio contact. In fear of a terrorist hijacking, military jets were ready to scramble and intercept the plane.

After the flight landed safely, pilots told federal authorities they had been working on their personal laptop computers. Both pilots ended up losing their commercial flying licenses as a result of violating regulations. Their failure to stay in touch with air traffic controllers could have resulted in the loss of life of many people.

Some people thought the punishment was too drastic. But that may be a reflection of a cultural attitude that minimizes personal and individual accountability. Such an idea is far from what Scripture teaches. Failing to hear and heed wise counsel will cause us to lose our way. It may even shorten our life!

—C. R. B.

B. Eyes, Part 1 (v. 21a)

21a. Let them not depart from thine eyes.

The concern of the lecture is still the father's instructions (disciplines). Total concentration and focus on what the father has said is emphasized by the use of *thine eyes.* Even so, seeing is no guarantee of perceiving (Acts 28:26b).

C. Heart (vv. 21b-23)

21b. Keep them in the midst of thine heart.

While the eyes and ears are gateways into the life of a person, the heart, figuratively speaking, is the center of a person's being—intellect, emotions, will, and attitudes (Luke 12:34; John 14:1; etc.). The next two verses will elaborate on the importance of the heart in this regard.

22. For they are life unto those that find them, and health to all their flesh.

The word *for* introduces a reason for the exhortation to the son to keep the father's words. These words are life in so many ways (Proverbs 4:4, 10, 13). The second clause tells us that the entire body is healthy by ingesting the father's instructions. Keep in mind this is figurative and is not referring to the physical body exclusively, although sound spiritual disciplines increase the health of the body (see Proverbs 14:30; 1 Timothy 4:8).

> *What Do You Think?*
> In what ways have you found "life" and "health" as you have followed the ways of God? How can you be a witness in this regard?
> *Talking Points for Your Discussion*
> - In your family
> - In your workplace
> - In your church

23. Keep thy heart with all diligence; for out of it are the issues of life.

Ancient people find the basis for behavior in "the heart," and we moderns understand that (see Proverbs 2:2; 12:23; 15:13, 28). Jesus said that "out of the heart proceed evil thoughts, murders, adulteries, fornications, thefts, false witness, blasphemies" (Matthew 15:19). Thus out of the heart *are the issues of life.* Is it any wonder, then, that the author of Proverbs stresses *diligence* in guarding

the heart? The heart can easily go astray into various forms of evil (Jeremiah 17:9).

D. Mouth/Lips (v. 24)

24. Put away from thee a froward mouth, and perverse lips put far from thee.

Here we see parallelism again, this time in an X-shaped arrangement:

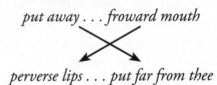

put away . . . froward mouth

perverse lips . . . put far from thee

The mouth speaks according to the heart (Luke 6:45; Romans 10:10). *Froward* means "crooked" or "twisted" (also Proverbs 6:12; 19:1). Such speech pours out mindless chatter and gossip, plays with half-truths to the detriment of others, and misuses the name of God in fitful spurts of anger. Not only must we put away these types of speaking, we must put them far away. It begins in the heart.

E. Eyes, Part 2 (v. 25)

25. Let thine eyes look right on, and let thine eyelids look straight before thee.

Again we see parallelism: *let thine eyes* equates to *let thine eyelids,* while *look right on* equates to *look straight before thee.* The second of these sets of parallels places us back with the road imagery of Proverbs 4:10-19. The verse before us assumes the road is straight, and therefore the eyes must focus in that direction, not diverting to either side (see 17:24). The close positioning between discussions of mouth and eye here in 4:24, 25 is found also in Proverbs 6:12, 13.

> *What Do You Think?*
> In what area do you need the most help in preventing what you see from leading you to sin? What will you do to get this help?
> *Talking Points for Your Discussion*
> - Areas leading to covetousness (Joshua 7:21)
> - Areas leading to lust (Matthew 5:28)
> - Areas leading to false conclusions about others (1 Samuel 16:7)
> - Areas leading to idolatry (Ezekiel 6:9; 20:7, 8, 24)

Making Right Choices

Tanya Vlach lost her left eye in a car accident in 2005. As a result, she received an artificial eye that she says is aesthetically satisfactory. However, she wants to use modern technology to put into that prosthetic a video camera, a working iris, memory, etc. The anticipated result would be a bionic eye that allows her to achieve an "augmented reality." At the time of this writing, however, the technology is not quite there.

The writer of Proverbs has no such high-tech concept in mind when he refers to the use of the eye. The writer's concept, ancient as it is, is actually more profound: his challenge doesn't deal with *seeing* in terms of the mere transmission of visual images, but with *perceiving* (compare Isaiah 6:9; Matthew 13:14).

We are urged to look straight ahead. That involves not only seeing the various paths, but also being able to perceive which is right and which is wrong. How can we get better at doing that?

—C. R. B.

F. Feet (vv. 26, 27)

26. Ponder the path of thy feet, and let all thy ways be established.

We are clearly back on "the road" with the discussion of feet. This verse tells us what to do while verse 27 (below) tells us what not to do. The Hebrew word translated *ponder* can be taken in more than one way. One is the idea of "weigh," which fits the translation of *ponder* that we see here: we are to evaluate (weigh, ponder) the path where we place our feet. We can be sure that the Lord is doing the same evaluation as He watches us (see Proverbs 5:21, which uses the same verb). The person who thinks through choices along life's journey will be established on a smooth and straight road.

27. Turn not to the right hand nor to the left: remove thy foot from evil.

What not to do is to turn to the right or to the left on this road. To do so is interpreted as *evil* (compare Deuteronomy 5:32; 17:11, 20; 28:14; Joshua 1:7; 23:6; 2 Kings 22:2). The word *turn* functions as a bookend with the same word that is translated "incline" in Proverbs 4:20, above. We

also see a bookend between *remove thy foot from evil* and "go not in the way of evil men" of verse 14, above. Thus we have come full circle. The way of wisdom avoids the way of evil. Thus, both "Lecture 6" and "Lecture 7" are bound by reference to the wise walk.

Conclusion
A. The Way of Wisdom

Making wise, godly choices is the right way. We have examples in the Bible. One such example is Joseph, who made a wise choice when he avoided the evil approaches of Potiphar's wife, even though it cost him his freedom at the time (Genesis 39).

On the other hand, people often make wrong choices. Such choices frequently are based on covetousness and selfishness in violation of God's Word. The Bible offers many examples. Achan sinfully kept plunder for himself (Joshua 7). King Saul violated God's command with regard to sacrifice (1 Samuel 13). King David committed adultery with Bathsheba (2 Samuel 11). A startling example in the New Testament is that of Ananias and Sapphira, who made an unwise decision to tell a lie about a property transaction (Acts 5). They forfeited their lives for that!

Two paths lie before us all: the wise way and the wicked way. There is no middle ground. We choose one or the other every time we make small and large choices in life. Make sure you don't fool yourself. Today is the tenth anniversary of the 9/11 terrorist attacks. The perpetrators fooled themselves into thinking they were doing God's will (1 Samuel 15:20). We have a great capacity for self-delusion, don't we?

B. Prayer

Father, we ask for Your wisdom. We also ask for the will to make the right choices in life. Fill our hearts with a desire to hear Your voice, see the way more clearly, speak truthfully, and have feet that stay on the way of wisdom. In the name of Jesus who is our wisdom, amen.

C. Thought To Remember

Watch where you put your eyes and feet.

INVOLVEMENT LEARNING

Some of the activities below are also found in the helpful student book, Adult Bible Class.
Don't forget to download the free reproducible page from www.standardlesson.com to enhance your lesson!

Into the Lesson

Write *Major Life Choices* on the board. Under it write the following in a scattered fashion: Education, Job/Profession, Renting vs. Buying Housing, Church Family, Where to Live.

Distribute index cards and ask learners to think about their own life choices in the areas indicated. Have them write one or two of these for which they made right choices and put their lives on the right path. Then ask them to pair off and share with partners what they have written and why it was the right choice.

Next, say, "A right choice early in life can have a long-lasting effect on making our lives happier, more fulfilling, and—most importantly—blessed. As we read today's text, we'll get some good advice on how to make more of those right choices."

Into the Word

Option 1: Create a chart titled *Which Way Will You Choose?* Below that title have three columns labeled "Questions," "The Way of Wisdom," and "The Way of the Wicked." In the rows under "Questions" (the far left) have the following list: A. "How do you respond to godly advice?" *(Proverbs 4:10, 13, 20)*; B. "What kind of paths do you walk on?" *(Proverbs 4:11, 26)*; C. "What happens when you walk or run?" *(Proverbs 4:12)*; D. "When you see the way the wicked are going, what do you do?" *(Proverbs 4:14, 15, 27)*; E. "How do you respond to advice about staying healthy?" *(Proverbs 4:21-23)*; F. "What kind of speech do you use?" *(Proverbs 4:24)*; G. "Where do you keep your focus?" *(Proverbs 4:25, 27)*

Ask learners to work on the chart in study groups. Assign groups to answer the questions for either "The Way of Wisdom" or "The Way of the Wicked." Tell the groups assigned the "Wicked Way" that they will have to use their imaginations sometimes to turn positive advice into negative advice.

When groups are finished, discuss the following questions: What did you learn about staying on the wise path? What is life like for those on the wicked path? What are some advantages for those who do things God's way? What are the disadvantages of following the wicked?

Option 2: Download the reproducible page and distribute copies of the How to Stay Healthy activity. Ask learners to form study groups and work together to read through the text and identify the various body parts that are mentioned. Going beyond identification, learners also should discuss the significance of those parts as they relate to today's lesson.

After about 10 minutes, call out each of the following parts and pause for volunteers to read what they have written: ears, eyes, heart, mouth/lips, feet, whole body. Then lead a discussion by asking the following questions: "In what ways can following God's Word help you to stay healthy? Give specifics." "How do these proverbs help you stay spiritually healthy?" "What can we do to keep God's instructions in our heart?"

Into Life

Option 1: Write the text of Proverbs 4:14 and Psalm 1:1 on the board. As a class, have learners answer these questions: In what way do these verses say similar things about whether or not to associate with wicked people? In what way are the verses different? What was a time when hanging out with the wrong person got you in trouble? How can the wrong kind of friends lead us into wrong choices in life?

Option 2: Download the reproducible page and distribute copies of the Prayer for Help activity. Encourage learners to use phrases from today's verses to write a prayer asking God to help them make better choices. Suggest that they use these prayers during their devotional times in the coming week.

TEACHING
VALUES

DEVOTIONAL READING: Proverbs 1:1-7
BACKGROUND SCRIPTURE: Proverbs 10:1–15:33

PROVERBS 15:21-33

21 Folly is joy to him that is destitute of wisdom: but a man of understanding walketh uprightly.

22 Without counsel purposes are disappointed: but in the multitude of counsellors they are established.

23 A man hath joy by the answer of his mouth: and a word spoken in due season, how good is it!

24 The way of life is above to the wise, that he may depart from hell beneath.

25 The LORD will destroy the house of the proud: but he will establish the border of the widow.

26 The thoughts of the wicked are an abomination to the LORD: but the words of the pure are pleasant words.

27 He that is greedy of gain troubleth his own house; but he that hateth gifts shall live.

28 The heart of the righteous studieth to answer: but the mouth of the wicked poureth out evil things.

29 The LORD is far from the wicked: but he heareth the prayer of the righteous.

30 The light of the eyes rejoiceth the heart: and a good report maketh the bones fat.

31 The ear that heareth the reproof of life abideth among the wise.

32 He that refuseth instruction despiseth his own soul: but he that heareth reproof getteth understanding.

33 The fear of the LORD is the instruction of wisdom; and before honour is humility.

KEY VERSE

He that refuseth instruction despiseth his own soul: but he that heareth reproof getteth understanding.
—**Proverbs 15:32**

TRADITION AND WISDOM

Unit 1: Teaching and Learning

LESSONS 1–8

LESSON AIMS

After participating in this lesson, each student will be able to:

1. Summarize the nature of the Lord's relationship to both the righteous and the wicked.

2. Relate three proverbs to modern situations.

3. Memorize the one proverb that speaks to his or her most pressing need.

LESSON OUTLINE

Introduction
  A. Person of Understanding
  B. Lesson Background
 I. Preamble (PROVERBS 15:21)
    Joy in Folly
 II. Good Counsel (PROVERBS 15:22-32)
    A. Seeker (v. 22)
    B. Encourager (v. 23)
    C. Wise (v. 24)
    D. Humble (v. 25)
    E. Pure (v. 26)
    F. Honest (v. 27)
      The Ripple Effects of Greed
    G. Righteous (vv. 28, 29)
    H. Cheerful (v. 30)
    I. Teachable (v. 31)
    J. Disciplined (v. 32)
 III. "The Fear of the Lord" (PROVERBS 15:33)
Conclusion
    A. The Importance of Wise Counsel
    B. Prayer
    C. Thought To Remember

Introduction

A. Person of Understanding

Sometimes college graduates think they know it all! Four years of hard work seemed like a great hurdle to me, especially when very few in my extended family ever went to college. To be content with a bachelor's degree in ministry, especially when churches were willing to hire preachers at that level, was tempting. After all, I knew everything!

Before I could get away from the graduation ceremonies of that day, however, a preacher friend of mine came to me with some good advice. He said, "Walt, you ought to go to seminary. There are some good people there you need to get to know." He had been our commencement speaker. I valued his counsel and decided to heed it.

I enrolled in graduate school. Three years later, I moved to the very church where my friend had preached. Following that ministry and two others, I entered the academic arena, eventually to become a faculty member at a Bible college.

Heeding my friend's counsel completely changed my life—for the better! People need good and effective counsel in order to live well. Proverbs is a divine source of counsel that can guide us toward a godly life. Just as higher education led me to ever higher academic abilities, so heeding the good counsel of Proverbs can lead us to ever greater spiritual maturity.

B. Lesson Background

Michael V. Fox notes that "Proverbs' guiding belief is that the human intellect—wisdom—founded on fear of God and tutored in traditional teachings, is the prime virtue of character, and as such is the necessary (and almost sufficient) means for creating a life of success—materially, physically, socially, and morally." That, in a nutshell, is what our lesson is about.

We observed in previous lessons that Proverbs 1–9 functions as a long introduction to the collections of proverbs in the rest of the book. The 10 "lectures" of Proverbs 1–9 swirl around the themes of the two paths (righteousness and wickedness) and the importance of holding fast to Lady Wisdom rather than Woman Folly.

Teaching Values

Proverbs 10–29 consists of short, pithy wisdom phrases, as we commonly understand the proverbs. Many scholars have tried to discover a structure to these collections, but no consensus has been reached. The various proverbs seem to be more randomly arranged than not. We do not have the original contexts of the individual proverbs. All this makes it very difficult to compose and outline this lesson! However, the wise person reading the collected proverbs can discern the meaning.

Some scholars have divided the first collection of Solomon's proverbs (that is, Proverbs 10:1–22:16) into two parts: 10:1–15:32 and 15:33–22:16. Others see a slightly different division, with the first part ending at 15:29. Either way, this means that our text for this lesson crosses this dividing line. The major characteristic of the first part of 10:1–15:32 is *antithetical parallelism;* this means that the second line of the proverb contrasts with the thought of the first line. The most prominent theme is between the righteous wise and the wicked fool.

English translations have difficulty in communicating the pithiness and subtleties of the Hebrew text. An attempt will be made in this commentary to give very literal renderings of the original Hebrew form in order to communicate the Hebrew flavor of words, phrases, and their order. If this is a distraction to you, simply ignore it. However, I think it would be a good idea to note at least a few literal renditions of the text to your class.

I. Preamble
(PROVERBS 15:21)

21. Folly is joy to him that is destitute of wisdom: but a man of understanding walketh uprightly.

Literal: "Folly, joy to one who lacks heart [sense], but a man of understanding goes straight ahead."

The Hebrew word for *heart* usually signifies the mind, although it certainly includes the will and emotions of a person—the person's inner core of being. Here the irony is that the person who lacks sense somehow finds *joy* in embracing folly (see Proverbs 12:23; 14:29). This is contrasted with *a*

man of understanding: one who walks uprightly on a straight path, meaning the righteous way.

How does one walk in this way and stay away from folly and avoid rejoicing in it? The answer is to heed the good counsel found in the next 10 proverbs. Each proverb describes the kind of person we all ought to become. Proverbs 15:21 thus makes an excellent introduction to the proverbs that follow.

❧ *JOY IN FOLLY* ❧

A few years ago, we witnessed the spectacle of several players in the National Football League being accused of wrongdoing. One player was arrested for giving alcohol to three underage females in a hotel room. Another player was found to have six illegal firearms in his home. A quarterback was convicted of running illegal dog fights. The list went on and on.

We wonder why star athletes who make millions of dollars a year would risk everything by engaging in foolishly criminal behavior. This kind of stupidity makes many of us gasp.

Yet "the rest of us" don't have a lot of room to talk. Everyone has the capability to demonstrate folly at times. This is why it's important to meditate on God's Word. Heeding the wisdom of Scripture will help us to walk uprightly in spite of temptations to do otherwise.   —C. R. B.

II. Good Counsel
(PROVERBS 15:22-32)
A. Seeker (v. 22)

22. Without counsel purposes are disappointed: but in the multitude of counsellors they are established.

Literal: "Ineffectual, plans with no counsel, but in many counselors it [a plan] will be established [succeed]."

Just as a child ought to listen to father or mother for good counsel, so also when one becomes an adult it is a good idea to listen to wise counsel from several sources. When a person relies solely on himself or herself, plans often go awry. The reason is that sometimes the person deceives himself or herself in the process. Think of how often you've talked yourself into something! This is less likely to happen if many wise counselors are consulted (see Proverbs 13:10; 19:20).

However, the availability of several counselors does not guarantee that their advice will be wise. King Rehoboam, Solomon's son (1 Kings 11:43), listened to the counsel of both the older men and the younger men (12:1-14). Instead of accepting the wise counsel of the former, he listened to the bad advice of the latter. The sad result was a divided kingdom (12:16). When one has a purpose or plan, it is a good idea to seek out wise people who will challenge our thinking and presuppositions.

> *What Do You Think?*
> What was a time when you failed to secure wise counsel before proceeding? What was the outcome, and how did you grow spiritually as a result?
> *Talking Points for Your Discussion*
> - With regard to finances
> - With regard to vocation
> - With regard to education
> - With regard to dating

B. Encourager (v. 23)

23. A man hath joy by the answer of his mouth: and a word spoken in due season, how good is it!

Literal: "Joy to the man with a response of his mouth and a word in its time [timely]—how good!"

On the subject of *joy,* we read in Proverbs 15:20 that "a wise son maketh a glad father"; now we are reminded that wise adults have joy over the good counsel of verse 22, above. And while the senseless and unwise consider their folly as a joy in 15:21, now we see that joy is experienced when one gives good counsel at the proper time *(in due season).*

The context of *the answer* refers to a good reply in a particular circumstance. We have all experienced the truth of the saying "timing is everything" (compare Proverbs 12:23). A dear friend of mine gave me advice just before I launched into a new move and new church work. He said, "If the

Lord is not in it, don't do it!" His words were not only right, they were also timely.

> *What Do You Think?*
> What was a time when someone said just the right thing that made a difference in the person you are today?
> *Talking Points for Your Discussion*
> - A word of encouragement
> - A word of counsel/advice
> - A word of rebuke
> - A word of comfort

C. Wise (v. 24)

24. The way of life is above to the wise, that he may depart from hell beneath.

Literal: "The path of life—upward for the prudent, in order to turn from Sheol downward."

The prudent or insightful (the wise) always seek to walk the way of life. This is the way upward (presumably where God is) in contrast with *hell beneath.* Once again we see the two-path outlook of the book of Proverbs (see Proverbs 1:15; 10:17). The contrast in this proverb, of course, is the upward and downward directions. By walking the path of life, the wise are on a course to be forever with the Lord. Thus they avoid the opposite, which is the downward spiral with all its ramifications.

Proverb 10:27 is a good commentary on this one: "The fear of the Lord prolongeth days: but the years of the wicked shall be shortened" (see also 13:14). The wise person will choose the upward way of life and not the one spiraling out of control to death.

D. Humble (v. 25)

25. The LORD will destroy the house of the proud: but he will establish the border of the widow.

Literal: "The house of proud men Yahweh will tear down and he shall [cause] to establish the border of the widow."

The Lord will destroy the oppressors by taking away their means of sustaining life, while He restores the life and property of the widow. Widows are the most vulnerable people in Israelite society. They are without a protector or power. As such, widows are often mentioned together with orphans (see Job 22:9; Psalm 94:6; Isaiah 10:2; Malachi 3:5). Boundary stones in ancient times mark a person's property line. Powerful people sometimes slowly shift such stones against the widow, who may have no recourse in the courts. Passages such as Proverbs 22:28; 23:10, 11 and Isaiah 5:8 give fair warning to such oppressors. God will step in to protect the weak.

E. Pure (v. 26)

26. The thoughts of the wicked are an abomination to the LORD: but the words of the pure are pleasant words.

Literal: "An abomination to Yahweh—thoughts of the wicked, but the pure—pleasant sayings."

One could possibly interpret the words *wicked* and *pure* as adjectives describing thoughts and words. It would then read, "An abomination to the Lord, evil plans, but pleasant words—pure."

However, the translation of the *King James Version* is quite acceptable. This means that the proverb is contrasting God's estimation of *the thoughts of the wicked* with the *pleasant words* of *the pure*. God knows the evil thoughts of the wicked before they even utter them. But God is pleased with the utterances of the pure for they are pleasant to His ears (compare Proverbs 16:24). Perhaps this echoes the "word spoken in due season" of Proverbs 15:23. The pure have a special relationship to God. As Jesus said, "Blessed are the pure in heart: for they shall see God" (Matthew 5:8). It is good to be of the pure.

F. Honest (v. 27)

27. He that is greedy of gain troubleth his own house; but he that hateth gifts shall live.

Literal: "Troubling his [own] house a greedy getter, but one who hates gifts [for bribery] shall live."

HOW TO SAY IT

obeisance	oh-*bee*-sunts.
Rehoboam	Ree-huh-*boe*-um.
Yahweh *(Hebrew)*	*Yah*-weh.

Sometimes the greedy getters gain their goods by violence. At other times such people resort to bribery, which is the sense of the word *gifts* here. Greed and bribery seem to go hand in hand (see Proverbs 17:23; 18:16).

Whether greed results in overt violence, covert bribery, or something else, the result is trouble for one's *own house,* especially when family members turn their greed against one another. We see greed tear families apart today when a large inheritance is involved. The result may be a family rift that never heals. Note how this proverb with the word *house* is related to verse 25, above. On the other hand, the nongreedy person is one who hates instruments of greed such as gifts (here used as bribery; compare 1 Samuel 12:3).

> *What Do You Think?*
> Which result of greediness do you think is the most damaging? How do you protect yourself from this danger?
> *Talking Points for Your Discussion*
> - Dissatisfaction (Ecclesiastes 5:10)
> - Foolishness (Jeremiah 17:11)
> - Rage and harm to others (Acts 16:19)
> - Spiritual wandering (1 Timothy 6:10)

❧ THE RIPPLE EFFECTS OF GREED ❧

Bernie Madoff became infamous a few years ago. For a time, he was apparently so successful that he was a "shaker and mover" of Wall Street, even becoming chairman of the NASDAQ stock exchange. But he had a darker side. In the economic meltdown of 2008, Madoff was discovered to have "made off" with approximately $65 *billion* of other people's money (including fictitious gains) in the most brazen Ponzi scheme ever.

The New York Times described Madoff as "a charlatan of epic proportions, a greedy manipulator so hungry to accumulate wealth that he did not care whom he hurt to get what he wanted." Madoff's wife, Ruth, also suffered from his disgrace, as if in confirmation of what Proverbs says about troubling one's own house. Although not charged with any crime, Ruth Madoff came to be described as "the loneliest woman in New York"

Choose the way of wisdom.

Visual for
Lessons 3 & 6

Point to this visual as you ask, "What are some early warning indicators that we are on the way of folly?"

as friends and businesses refused to have anything to do with her.

Perhaps there would be less greed in the world if folks would stop to think about how their actions affect their loved ones! —C. R. B.

G. Righteous (vv. 28, 29)

28, 29. The heart of the righteous studieth to answer: but the mouth of the wicked poureth out evil things. The LORD is far from the wicked: but he heareth the prayer of the righteous.

Literal: "The heart of the righteous meditates to answer but the mouth of the wicked (causes to) pour out evil (things). Far Yahweh from the wicked but the prayer of the righteous he hears."

Our English translation is very close to the Hebrew. These two verses say some special things about speech. First, there is the way the righteous speak in contrast with the wicked. The righteous use *the heart* (mind, will, emotions, spirit) before using *the mouth*. The righteous stop to think what effect their words will have before they are uttered (see again v. 23). By contrast, the wicked don't stop to think first; they simply blabber away (also 15:2). Evil speech is destructive (see Proverbs 11:11). We know that God is listening!

Second, God is far from the blabbering wicked because what they say is far from wholesome and certainly not prayerful! By contrast, the righteous continually pray, and God hears them (see Psalm 145:18; Proverbs 15:8). As we all know: "The effec-

tual fervent prayer of a righteous man availeth much" (James 5:16b).

H. Cheerful (v. 30)

30. The light of the eyes rejoiceth the heart: and a good report maketh the bones fat.

Literal: "The light of the eyes makes joyful the heart—a good report makes fat the bones."

I once had a student who lit up the room every time she walked in. She beamed optimism, and her cheery disposition was expressed primarily through her eyes. She made everyone around her feel better. That is the thrust of this proverb. In ancient times to be *fat* is to be healthy, an idea far from our thoughts today! Also, *the bones* represent the whole body. Therefore, receiving *a good report* makes a person feel good all over—healthy!

Our church recently hired a receptionist, and one of the primary hiring criteria was "Does the person smile immediately when someone walks through the doorway and approaches the desk?" First impressions are always important. A cheerful disposition ought to be the hallmark of God's people.

What Do You Think?
  If you had a "cheerful meter," what would it
    reveal about you right now? What can you do
    to get it to move up a notch?
Talking Points for Your Discussion
  ▪ Empty—at a complete stop spiritually
  ▪ Running on fumes—ready to give up
  ▪ Half full (or half empty)—could go either way
    depending on circumstances
  ▪ Full to overflowing—the joy of the Lord is your
    strength

I. Teachable (v. 31)

31. The ear that heareth the reproof of life abideth among the wise.

Literal: "An ear that hears the reproof of life—in the midst of the wise it lodges."

The listening ear is a treasured possession among God's people (see Proverbs 23:12; 25:12). Having an *ear that heareth* is a sign of being teachable. Only the wise can listen to a rebuke, change

▪   Teaching Values behavior as a result, and become a better person (Proverbs 9:8, 9).

I have a young student assistant who has taken several pieces of reproof or correction from me. He has accepted them, changed his behavior, and become a better person as a result. Recently he even recounted something I had said to him: "You build your character one brick at a time until you have built a sturdy house!" One of the best attitudes a Christian can have is to be teachable.

J. Disciplined (v. 32)

32. He that refuseth instruction despiseth his own soul: but he that heareth reproof getteth understanding.

Literal: "He who refuses [lets go of] discipline —one who despises his (own) soul [life], but he who hears reproof acquires heart."

This proverb takes us deeper into the realm of disciplined instruction that involves chastening and correction. The truly wise person is one who has learned to accept instruction in all areas of life (compare Proverbs 13:18; 15:5, 10). When one is willing to be instructed by heeding reproof and correction, that person gains understanding.

The instructed person is a person of substance, a person of understanding (see Proverbs 19:8). On the other hand, those who reject the discipline of instruction end up despising themselves (see Proverbs 5:11-14). Those who yield to the discipline of instruction are the happiest people on the earth!

III. "The Fear of the Lord"
(PROVERBS 15:33)

33. The fear of the LORD is the instruction of wisdom; and before honour is humility.

Literal: "The fear of Yahweh—discipline of wisdom and before honor—humility!"

This phrase *the fear of the Lord* is found many times in Proverbs. Indeed, the fear of the Lord is the foundation to all the proverbs. A healthy fear of God is the reverence necessary to create in our hearts a sense of humility and obeisance in His presence. *Humility* is parallel to *the fear of the Lord* in this text and is necessary as expressed elsewhere in the book (see Proverbs 11:2; 22:4).

What Do You Think?
What was a time you "learned the hard way" to fear the Lord? How did you grow spiritually as a result?
Talking Points for Your Discussion
- A time when you "knew better"
- A time when you "didn't know better"

Conclusion
A. The Importance of Wise Counsel

The fear of the Lord is the foundation to all wisdom. It motivates us to become people of understanding. This fact helps us to move forward in our maturing process as Christians. Much like what 2 Peter 1:5-7 teaches us in terms of adding to our Christian character, so now we may do the same with these 10 proverbs of good counsel. We restate them in modern terms this way:

1. Seeker: Listen to wise counsel; don't rely on your own understanding. *2. Encourager:* Good counsel at the right time can bring joy. *3. Wise:* Live the heavenly life, not the life that spirals down to death. *4. Humble:* Depend upon the Lord for support; the arrogant and prideful oppressor will be destroyed. *5. Pure:* Please God with pleasant words; He recoils at the plans of the wicked. *6. Honest:* Experience fullness of life by avoiding the greed that will trouble your family. *7. Righteous:* Be one who prays the prayers of the righteous, and God will listen. *8. Cheerful:* Bringing good news with a smile will gladden the heart of friends. *9. Teachable:* Accept correction to become wise. *10. Disciplined:* Learn to accept discipline to become a person of substance.

Choose one of these 10 to focus on. Seek to become that person for the next several months.

B. Prayer

Our Father, teach us what to say and when to say it. We pray for the wisdom that comes from above. In Jesus' name, amen.

C. Thought to Remember

Accepting good counsel develops character for life and eternity.

INVOLVEMENT LEARNING

Some of the activities below are also found in the helpful student book, Adult Bible Class.
Don't forget to download the free reproducible page from www.standardlesson.com to enhance your lesson!

Into the Lesson

Download the reproducible page and make copies of the Word Search: Righteous vs. Wicked activity. Distribute these to learners as they arrive. Encourage them to look at Proverbs 15:21-33 if they need help distinguishing between the qualities and God's response to them. When most are done say, "God gives either blessings or consequences depending on the values we choose to live by. Let's take a closer look of some of those."

Into the Word

Option 1: Prepare the following assignments and make enough copies so that each group of four to six will have one. Encourage learners to begin by reading Proverbs 15:21-33 aloud before completing their assignments.

Assignment A: Relating to God. What advice does the text give to those who want to receive blessings from God for a righteous life? What consequences will befall those who live a wicked life? Give specific examples from your own lives that illustrate both.

Assignment B: Relating to Family. What advice does the text give for having a happy family life? What are the consequences to the family when this advice isn't followed? Give specific examples from your own lives that illustrate both types.

Assignment C: Relating to Friends. What advice does the text give on how to be a good friend? What qualities of a bad friend are described, and how can they harm a relationship? Give examples from your own lives that illustrate both.

Allow time for each group to share with the class the answer to one of their questions.

Option 2: Divide the class into small groups. Prepare copies of the following "letter of recommendation" and distribute to the groups. Do not include the suggested answers, given in italics. Say, "Look in the text and find a verse that contains observations about the quality being discussed."

✁✁✁

"I recommend that you consider hiring Matthew Wright as your senior minister for the following reasons: (1) he lives by high standards of personal purity in thought and action *(v. 26)*; (2) he has a knack for listening to good advice *(v. 22)*; (3) he has a positive attitude that makes him a joy to be around *(v. 30)*; (4) he thinks carefully before he speaks *(v. 28)*; (5) he always seems to have the right answer at the right time *(v. 23)*; (6) he listens to constructive criticism *(v. 31)*; and (7) he is a man of prayer who praises God when his prayers are answered *(v. 29)*."

✁✁✁

Have each group share at least one of their answers. Verses other than the ones suggested may also be appropriate. To expand this discussion, you can create a "negative" letter of recommendation using Proverbs 15:21, 24, 25, 27, 32, and 33.

Into Life

Option 1. Relate the following situations to your class and ask them to counsel each person based on verses from today's text.

A. Shawn has an idea for a home-based business that he believes will allow him to support his family. He's not sure how to set it up and is wondering how long he should wait before quitting his job.

B. Mikayla is quick to give members of her family and her friends lots of advice on what they should do. But she has complained to you that she's frustrated because no one ever seems to appreciate or follow her "words of wisdom."

C. Bret has confided that he and his wife are having marital problems and are seeing a counselor. But he thinks it's a waste of time and has no intention of heeding the counselor.

Option 2. Download the reproducible page and distribute copies of the Taking Advice to Heart exercise as a take-home activity.

Teaching Values

ACTING WITH DISCERNMENT

DEVOTIONAL READING: 1 Kings 3:5-14
BACKGROUND SCRIPTURE: Proverbs 25:1-28

PROVERBS 25:1-10

1 These are also proverbs of Solomon, which the men of Hezekiah king of Judah copied out.

2 It is the glory of God to conceal a thing: but the honour of kings is to search out a matter.

3 The heaven for height, and the earth for depth, and the heart of kings is unsearchable.

4 Take away the dross from the silver, and there shall come forth a vessel for the finer.

5 Take away the wicked from before the king, and his throne shall be established in righteousness.

6 Put not forth thyself in the presence of the king, and stand not in the place of great men:

7 For better it is that it be said unto thee, Come up hither; than that thou shouldest be put lower in the presence of the prince whom thine eyes have seen.

8 Go not forth hastily to strive, lest thou know not what to do in the end thereof, when thy neighbour hath put thee to shame.

9 Debate thy cause with thy neighbour himself; and discover not a secret to another:

10 Lest he that heareth it put thee to shame, and thine infamy turn not away.

KEY VERSE

Debate thy cause with thy neighbour himself; and discover not a secret to another. —**Proverbs 25:9**

TRADITION AND WISDOM

Unit 1: Teaching and Learning
LESSONS 1–8

LESSON AIMS

After participating in this lesson, each student will be able to:

1. Restate some principles of behavior that affect relationships.

2. Compare and contrast Proverbs 25:6, 7 with Luke 14:7-11.

3. Write a paraphrase of one of the proverbs of today's text that most helps guard himself or herself from the influences of secular culture.

LESSON OUTLINE

Introduction

A. Neighborly Advice

One of the best pieces of advice I ever received was from a preacher friend who would later become a key person in directing my future service to God. I had graduated from Bible college and was doing summer evangelistic work (1965) with young people in various churches and Christian service camps throughout the southern states. My friend Bill and I were in Florida in a Christian service camp, and I was preaching the sermons for morning chapels and evening vespers.

The preacher friend, Jim, was the camp dean. After a couple of sermons Jim approached me very warmly but firmly and told me to tone down my criticism of other preachers, whether they were liberal or not. He pointed out that most of the young people in the camp knew only one preacher (in their home church), and that I need not condemn the whole lot just because I was arguing for truths of the gospel and against those who did not preach the truth. I was young and brash. Perhaps arrogant would be a better description. Jim tried to help me see the value of preaching more positively rather than negatively. He was right, of course, and it took me some time to adjust my thinking. I have never quit working on it.

Years later, I met Jim by happenstance on Highway 1 in Illinois while we were both driving through Danville. We stopped at a fast-food restaurant to eat and catch up on our past friendship. Jim had just been inaugurated as president at a Bible college. He offered me a faculty position at the college to teach. That was the beginning of my academic life, and without the neighborly mentoring of Jim it never would have happened.

The book of Proverbs provides, among other things, principles for developing good and equitable relationships. Our printed text presents five principles of behavior, positive things to do and negative things to avoid, in dealing with other people and even with God.

B. Lesson Background (Proverbs 25:1)

1. These are also proverbs of Solomon, which the men of Hezekiah king of Judah copied out.

Acting with Discernment

This first verse of today's printed text provides a little background information for the rest of our lesson. After moving beyond the preamble of Proverbs 1:1-7 and the extended discourses on wisdom of 1:8–9:18, we find two collections of Solomon's proverbs. These are found in 10:1–22:16 and 25:1–29:27; they are separated by a brief double collection of sayings of the wise in 22:17–24:22 and 24:23-34. Our text for today thus begins the second collection of proverbs by Solomon himself.

Solomon spoke 3,000 proverbs (1 Kings 4:32). However, the two collections noted above contain only a little over 500 proverbs. Thus the majority of Solomon's proverbs are lost to us, although there are a few in other places such as Ecclesiastes. Solomon reigned about 970–930 BC.

Hezekiah king of Judah reigned two centuries after Solomon, about 727–696 BC. Hezekiah was considered one of the "good" kings of Judah. This second collection of Solomon's proverbs may have been assembled in connection with Hezekiah's efforts to reestablish the worship of the true God after the apostasy of the evil King Ahaz. (For Hezekiah's reforms, see 2 Kings 18–20; 2 Chronicles 29–32; and Isaiah 36–39.)

It is clear that a lot of the proverbs from Proverbs 25, the source of today's text, emerge from the royal court. They are vivid in figures of speech, with many admonitions. Some scholars consider Proverbs 25:2-27 to be a small wisdom-book that was transcribed by *the men of Hezekiah* from a source that was a literary unit in and of itself. As with most proverbs, the application of these sayings may cover a variety of settings.

HOW TO SAY IT

Ahaz	*Ay*-haz.
apostasy	uh-*pahs*-tuh-see.
Athaliah	Ath-uh-*lye*-uh.
Ezekiel	Ee-*zeek*-ee-ul or Ee-*zeek*-yul.
Hezekiah	Hez-ih-*kye*-uh.
Isaiah	Eye-*zay*-uh.
Jehoiada	Jee-*hoy*-uh-duh.
Joash	*Jo*-ash.
Judah	*Joo*-duh.
Solomon	*Sol*-o-mun.

I. Searchable and Unsearchable
(PROVERBS 25:2, 3)
A. Reality (v. 2)

2. It is the glory of God to conceal a thing: but the honour of kings is to search out a matter.

The Hebrew text itself is very straightforward. Yet, in either the Hebrew or the English, the two phrases are somewhat puzzling in their relation to one another. What we see here is called *antithetic parallelism;* that means that the phrases contrast with one another while sharing similar elements.

The parallels are much tighter in Hebrew than they appear to be in English, since the Hebrew for *glory* and *honour* is the exact same word; the same is true for the words *thing* and *matter.* The contrast (antithesis) is that God conceals while kings must search.

There is a certain irony as this verse is connected with the one that follows. But first let us offer an interpretation. At its heart it is saying, "Let God be God and man be man." There are some things that human wisdom has difficulty understanding about God (see Job 28:20-27). Yet Solomon was the one who asked for wisdom, and God gave him wisdom beyond his peers (1 Kings 3:12). This thought helps us understand the next verse.

> *What Do You Think?*
> What are some things you have difficulty understanding about God? How does this affect your faith?
> *Talking Points for Your Discussion*
> - Regarding His abilities
> - Regarding His nature
> - Regard His merciful disposition

B. Irony (v. 3)

3. The heaven for height, and the earth for depth, and the heart of kings is unsearchable.

The last word of this verse is what binds verses 2 and 3 together. When searching out a matter, a king may look for answers as high as the heavens or in the depths of the earth, but ironically there is no searching out *the heart of kings.* Perhaps this is what people thought about King Solomon when he made his decision concerning the two prostitutes who claimed the same baby (see 1 Kings 3:16-27). Because of his wisdom in the matter, Solomon was held in awe by the people (3:28).

We do well to admit that any ability to govern wisely ultimately comes from God. Kings, who must search out a matter, who may even give astounding judgments, must recognize the source of their wisdom. Searching God's heart will result in wisdom, while searching only the human heart will not. Proper understanding of the distance between God and humans is the first step in discerning appropriate behaviors in many settings and situations.

❧ Searching High and Low ❧

I searched high and low for it. That old expression describes an intensive search for something. In a literal sense, the "highest" searches that humans have ever conducted involve investigations and missions to outer space, while the "lowest" searches are those that have been conducted thousands of feet below the surface of the ocean.

But even with all the knowledge we have gained of sea, land, and the cosmos, we must admit that there is much yet to learn. Creation holds mysteries that only God knows the answers to.

Yet, perhaps the greatest mystery of all is the human heart. Theologians and philosophers have explored its heights and depths for centuries with only partial success. We still find our senses shocked by the inhumanity of an Adolf Hitler. We still find ourselves amazed at the sacrificial attitude of a Mother Teresa. The human heart is capable of many things. To search our hearts in that regard is an important step in making right, godly choices.
—C. R. B.

II. Righteous vs. Wicked
(Proverbs 25:4, 5)
A. Analogy (v. 4)

4. Take away the dross from the silver, and there shall come forth a vessel for the finer.

The wise saying that is intended to be applied occurs in verse 5, below. But first comes the analogy. The Hebrew word translated *take away* is

used in both verses 4 and 5, thus binding the two verses together.

One does not think of commanding dross to come out of silver by itself. The silversmith *(the finer)* must do something to remove the dross—placing the metal in fire hot enough to cause the dross to rise to the top and be skimmed off. The result is a purified metal *(the silver)* fit for fashioning into whatever shape the silversmith wishes to make of it.

Such analogy becomes well known in ancient Israel. The prophets use it to speak of God's judgment on the city of Jerusalem and the people of God (see Isaiah 1:22, 25; Ezekiel 22:18-22).

> **What Do You Think?**
> What one area of your life do you most need to purify of dross in order to make you better fit for use by God?
> *Talking Points for Your Discussion*
> - A particular way of thinking
> - An area of habitual behavior
> - An area of priorities
> - An area of relationships

B. Application (v. 5)

5. Take away the wicked from before the king, and his throne shall be established in righteousness.

When a king is surrounded by wicked people who function as counselors or friends, destruction is not far away. Certainly the king's rule will not be characterized as righteous. Rehoboam comes to mind as one who listened only to foolish advisers (see 1 Kings 12:8-15 and discussion in last week's lesson); thus, Rehoboam's kingdom ended up being divided (12:16-24).

On the other hand, one can think of Joash who was proclaimed king at the age of 7 when Athaliah was killed (2 Kings 11). As long as Jehoiada the priest had influence over Joash, he was a "good" king. Righteousness reigned. When Jehoiada died, Joash turned away from God, and his reign deteriorated (see 2 Chronicles 24:17-27).

In essence, King David's prayer of Psalm 101 is the application of this proverb, for David said,

"I will not know a wicked person. . . . I will early destroy all the wicked of the land; that I may cut off all wicked doers from the city of the Lord" (Psalm 101:4b, 8). Wickedness seems to override the good far more often than the good overrides wickedness. Good companions encourage righteousness, but wicked companions will lead one to destruction (1 Corinthians 15:33).

III. Humiliation and Exaltation
(Proverbs 25:6-7b)
A. What Not to Do (v. 6)

6. Put not forth thyself in the presence of the king, and stand not in the place of great men.

While the first two proverbs are bound together by the use of key words, this proverb of command is bound to the "better" saying of the verse that follows it. Humility is one of the greatest of virtues. Yet to talk about it is somehow to lose it! An example of this is in Numbers 12:3: "(Now the man Moses was very meek, above all the men which were upon the face of the earth.)" It is clear that someone other than Moses wrote this. Otherwise, if Moses wrote it, then he ceases to be meek. That is why the verse is in parentheses.

It is always interesting to observe what happens during a change of national leadership today, especially when the move is from one political party to another: people crave to be close to the new leader. People love power. When one is not powerful, then standing next to a powerful person is the next best thing. This proverb says: "Don't do it!" Don't promote yourself excessively or push yourself forward. The next verse shows us a better way.

Visual for Lesson 4. *Point to this visual as you introduce the discussion question that is associated with Proverbs 25:4.*

B. Why Not to Do It (vv. 7a, b)

7a, b. For better it is that it be said unto thee, Come up hither; than that thou shouldest be put lower in the presence of the prince.

The wisdom of modesty is that it often is rewarded. The one who has talents and abilities above normal can be observed and promoted by others (examples: Genesis 41:41-43; Daniel 1:20; 2:48, 49; 5:29). The proverbs of Proverbs 25 are somehow connected with the royal court and the circumstances surrounding the king and his rule. However, the proverbs can be applied in many different ways by almost anyone.

Jesus may have used this saying in one of His teaching moments noted in Luke 14:7-11. Jesus' teaching of this principle is one we must accept, but it is also very difficult to put into practice. After the last supper, Jesus' disciples argued among themselves about who was going to be the greatest (Luke 22:24). A short time later, Jesus' crucifixion provided them the ultimate example of humility.

IV. Hasty Action
(Proverbs 25:7c-8)
A. Slow Down (vv. 7c-8b)

7c-8b. Whom thine eyes have seen. Go not forth hastily to strive, lest thou know not what to do in the end thereof.

What Do You Think?

What are some subtle ways you have tried to promote self? How do you keep from rationalizing in this regard?

Talking Points for Your Discussion
- A time when you "dropped a hint"
- A time when you "name dropped"
- A time when you attempted to make yourself look better by making someone else look worse

The chapter and verse divisions in our modern Bibles were not put there by the original authors of Scripture. Those divisions were added hundreds of years later. Having chapter and verse divisions is a great convenience, of course, but sometimes we wonder if a better decision could have been made. In the case before us, for example, most commentaries place the last phrase of verse 7, *whom thine eyes have seen,* with verse 8. The balance of the Hebrew text supports this.

The word *strive* suggests a courtroom scene, but it can also be any striving between two people where one is being confronted on the basis of a witness. As a result, the two phrases *whom thine eyes have seen* and *go not forth hastily to strive* mean something like "do not take a person to court too hastily on the basis of what you have witnessed." Sometimes your interpretation of what you see is wrong.

My grandfather found out the truth of this the hard way. On one occasion he was taking groceries into the house of a widow who was trying to raise several children. A woman living close by saw him enter the house and began a chain of gossip that damaged my grandfather's reputation. He was doing a good deed, but was accused falsely of impropriety. That one incident forever kept my grandparents from attending any church, for it was a church lady who had spread the gossip. Though this is no real reason to cease one's relationship to the church or to Christ, it was enough for my grandfather to abandon what little faith he had.

There also is a lesson here in not putting oneself in a situation that can be misinterpreted. Perhaps my grandfather could have avoided the false accusation by remaining outside the widow's house while he handed the groceries across the doorway.

What Do You Think?
  How do you initially tend to react when you witness something wrong and do not know the details of why something apparently is happening? How should you react?
Talking Points for Your Discussion
  - Reporting the issue to a church leader
  - Doing your own private investigation
  - Asking others for their opinion

B. Avoid Shame (v. 8c)

8c. When thy neighbour hath put thee to shame.

False or trumped-up charges can bring down the one who accuses. In my grandfather's case, he did not answer his critic. But imagine the shame that will be placed on the false accuser when this is unveiled on Judgment Day! We must hold our tongue in all kinds of situations (the teaching of many proverbs), including being slow to accuse by what we think our eyes are seeing.

V. Improper Procedures
(Proverbs 25:9, 10)
A. Indiscretion (v. 9)

9. Debate thy cause with thy neighbour himself; and discover not a secret to another.

Verses 9, 10 may go with verses 7c, 8 if all are concerned about a judicial (legal) contention. I prefer to see verses 9, 10 as addressing a private situation. Instead of going to court (v. 8), you should go to your offended neighbor first and in private (see Matthew 18:15-17; compare 5:22-26). This is wise protocol for dealing with a perceived problem with a neighbor. What is to be kept secret is the criticism itself, for to let it out in public could fit the category of backbiting or slander (Psalm 15:3; 2 Corinthians 12:20). Being discreet about confidential communication builds a good reputation. The opposite brings something else (next verse).

What Do You Think?
  What are some issues in the practice of discretion regarding communication with others? How do you prioritize these?
Talking Points for Your Discussion
  - Proverbs 12:23; Ecclesiastes 5:2; 1 Thessalonians 4:11
  - Legal issues of confidential communication
  - Making an unwise promise not to disclose information

B. Disrespect (v. 10)

10. Lest he that heareth it put thee to shame, and thine infamy turn not away.

Acting with Discernment

No one likes to be put to shame. But one of the quickest ways to be shamed is to betray a confidence. Respect for another's privacy is a great virtue. Otherwise, one quickly can develop a bad reputation, and it will be difficult to shake!

Character is developed one brick at a time. Each time there is contention with another and confidences are kept, there is trust and a strengthened relationship. We can't control all factors that come our way, but we can control ourselves. How we respond to life's ordeals reveals what kind of persons we really are. Good relationships with others promote a pleasant life and keep lines of communication open. So let it be.

❧ ARE YOU A TALKATIVE TESS? ❧

One day Talkative Tess observed that Silent Sam's truck had been parked in front of a bar for several hours. To Tess, this was all the "proof" she needed that Sam was a drunkard. So Tess began spreading the rumor that Sam was an alcoholic.

Sam, more a man of action than of words, said nothing. He simply retaliated by parking his truck in front of Tess's house several evenings in a row and leaving it there all night!

Proverbs speaks of the "infamy" that results from a loose tongue. This infamy includes, at least, the loss of credibility. Further infamy makes itself known in an unwillingness to talk to a person known to have a loose tongue. The cure, according to Proverbs, is simple: *Shut up!* —C. R. B.

Conclusion

A. Discernment as Wisdom

Discernment is a wisdom characteristic. People of discernment can see the true nature of situations and make good judgments about them. The discerning person can evaluate others' spirits (Proverbs 28:11) and accept the point of a rebuke (17:10). The introductory statements of Proverbs promote the discerning person (1:5, 6).

Acting with discernment is to put feet and hands to any given situation where there is need for good judgment. Let us recapitulate the five principles of conduct in our lesson and note the character needed for each.

First, let God be God and man be man. This takes discernment regarding the distance between God and humanity. Even kings must recognize where true wisdom comes from and that there are some concealed matters that belong only to God. The character needed is a heart that is submissive to the divine.

Second, remember that good companions encourage righteousness. On the other hand, wicked companions will bring corruption and then destruction. The character needed is self-discipline to rid oneself of evil influences, whether it be so-called friends or aspects of culture. Maintain righteousness through good companions.

Third, always take the humble position. By taking the best seat in the house (either literally or figuratively), one could be asked to move to the back in humiliation. Let praise of you come from others. Do not promote yourself. The character needed, of course, is genuine humility of heart and spirit.

Fourth, don't jump to conclusions. Judge not lest you be judged. Do not accuse another of wrong too quickly. Seeing is not always believing! False accusations can destroy others, but it can also bring shame upon you. The character needed is a nonjudgmental heart.

Fifth, keep confidences. When you must confront a neighbor directly, make the criticism without going public. This calls for an honest heart and a tight tongue. Respect the dignity of others even when they are blameworthy.

Learning to act with discernment with regard to these five principles will enhance one's relationships with neighbors, friends, and family. The result will be peace.

B. Prayer

Father, teach us how to get along with our neighbors, friends, and family. Give us a submissive heart toward You, a humble and nonjudgmental heart toward others, and the self-discipline needed to confront evil while keeping confidences. Forgive the foolish sins we commit against one another. In Jesus' name, amen.

C. Thought to Remember

Discernment is part of wisdom.

INVOLVEMENT LEARNING

Some of the activities below are also found in the helpful student book, Adult Bible Class.
Don't forget to download the free reproducible page from www.standardlesson.com to enhance your lesson!

Into the Lesson

Read the following brainteaser exactly as written: "I read this story in the newspaper. A man and his wife arrived at church late and were unable to sit together. So he sat in a seat directly in front of her. During the sermon, the husband fell asleep and began dreaming he was in the French Revolution and was being led up the steps to the guillotine. Just as the blade was about to drop in his dream, his wife noticed he had fallen asleep. So she picked up a hymnal and poked him in the back of the neck just as he dreamed the blade was falling. The shock killed him instantly. What's wrong with this story?"

Allow learners to ask questions and make guesses. You may need to read the story several times; be sure to read it exactly as written. When someone finally comes up with the answer *(the newspaper writer had no way of knowing what the man was dreaming, since the man died before he could tell anyone),* congratulate that person for discernment. Say, "As we'll see in today's text, having good discernment is very helpful when dealing with interpersonal relationships, whether it's someone in authority or with our friends."

Into the Word

Early in the week, contact one of your learners who has teaching ability. Ask this person to prepare a short lecture on King Hezekiah and his actions in collecting and copying some of Solomon's proverbs. Provide the person with the information contained in the commentary on verse 1 under Lesson Background.

If you are unable to find someone to do this, give the brief lecture yourself. Then say, "As we read today's text, we'll see that many of these proverbs give instructions on how to behave in the king's court. That may have been why the king was so interested in preserving them. In any case, let's see what they have to teach us today."

Put your learners into study groups of no more than five to complete the following assignments, one per group. If your class is large enough to have more than three groups, make duplicate assignments.

Assignment 1. Read Proverbs 15:1-5 and answer these questions: A. What is the difference between how God handles things and how a king or leader does? B. What is an example of something God might "conceal"? C. In what way is a king's heart "unsearchable"? D. How does the illustration about silver guide a leader in choosing people with whom to associate?

Assignment 2. Read Proverbs 15:6, 7a and Luke 14:7-11 and answer these questions: A. According to Proverbs, what is the right way to approach someone of importance? the wrong way? B. How does Jesus' parable expand on the basic truth of Proverbs? C. According to Jesus' parable, how does humility pay off in the long run?"

Assignment 3. Read Proverbs 15:7b-10 and answer these questions: A. What danger is involved in reporting and making accusations on the basis of what you've seen? B. What is an example of a time when you thought you knew what happened, but found out later there was more to the story? C. How can betraying someone's confidence destroy our own reputation, and how do we prevent that from happening?

Into Life

Download the reproducible page and distribute copies of the What Would You Say? activity as learners stay in their groups. Make assignments according to the number of groups and the time remaining.

Verses that may be used to generate the answers are as follows: Friendless Francine (vv. 9, 10), Ambitious Adam (vv. 6, 7a), Wondering Juan (vv. 4, 5), Curious Kate (vv. 7b, 8). Allow groups to share their answers with the class as a whole.

LIVING AN ORDERED LIFE

DEVOTIONAL READING: Deuteronomy 1:9-17
BACKGROUND SCRIPTURE: Proverbs 28:1–29:27

PROVERBS 29:16-27

16 When the wicked are multiplied, transgression increaseth: but the righteous shall see their fall.

17 Correct thy son, and he shall give thee rest; yea, he shall give delight unto thy soul.

18 Where there is no vision, the people perish: but he that keepeth the law, happy is he.

19 A servant will not be corrected by words: for though he understand he will not answer.

20 Seest thou a man that is hasty in his words? there is more hope of a fool than of him.

21 He that delicately bringeth up his servant from a child shall have him become his son at the length.

22 An angry man stirreth up strife, and a furious man aboundeth in transgression.

23 A man's pride shall bring him low: but honour shall uphold the humble in spirit.

24 Whoso is partner with a thief hateth his own soul: he heareth cursing, and bewrayeth it not.

25 The fear of man bringeth a snare: but whoso putteth his trust in the LORD shall be safe.

26 Many seek the ruler's favour; but every man's judgment cometh from the LORD.

27 An unjust man is an abomination to the just: and he that is upright in the way is abomination to the wicked.

KEY VERSE

The fear of man bringeth a snare: but whoso putteth his trust in the LORD shall be safe.. —**Proverbs 29:25**

Photo: Jupiterimages / Liquidlibrary / Thinkstock

TRADITION AND WISDOM

Unit 1: Teaching and Learning

LESSONS 1–8

LESSON AIMS

After participating in this lesson, each student will be able to:

1. Identify the connections between discipline, correction, and restraint.

2. Summarize the principles that promote an ordered life.

3. Identify one area in his or her life that needs to be reordered and explain how today's text will help bring that about.

LESSON OUTLINE

Introduction
  A. Living an Ordered Life
  B. Lesson Background
I. Introductory Proverb (PROVERBS 29:16)
II. Principles for an Ordered Life (PROVERBS 29:17-26)
  A. Having Peace (v. 17)
  B. Applying Scripture (v. 18)
    When God Is Forgotten
  C. Gaining Respect (v. 19)
    What Secular Culture Realizes
  D. Avoiding Haste (v. 20)
  E. Instructing Properly (v. 21)
  F. Understanding Anger (v. 22)
  G. Having Honor (v. 23)
  H. Staying Honest (v. 24)
  I. Trusting God (v. 25)
  J. Receiving Justice (v. 26)
III. Final Proverb (PROVERBS 29:27)
Conclusion
  A. The Ordered Life in Christ
  B. Prayer
  C. Thought to Remember

Introduction

A. Living an Ordered Life

Gordon MacDonald's well-known book *Ordering Your Private World* appeared in 1984. It received the Gold Medallion Book Award for evangelical Christian literature. It was written for all those who felt disorganized or even a failure. MacDonald wrote about principles that help a person order his or her inner life. With over a million and a half copies in print, the book struck a chord.

However, the Christian world was shocked when in 1987 Gordon MacDonald admitted to having been unfaithful in his marriage. There was a collective groan among Christian leaders, for such sins had occurred (and still occur) far too often. The good news is that Gordon MacDonald acknowledged his sin, submitted to pastoral discipline, and recommitted himself to his family. Returning to Christian ministry would wait, but it did happen. Restoration was complete. In other words, MacDonald (eventually) followed his own principles.

The book of Proverbs provides many principles that help a person lead an ordered public and private life. No one is perfect in applying these principles, but that does not excuse God's people from trying. Most of these principles can be found in the New Testament, and thus we discover how relevant they are for today's Christian. Living an ordered life should be a priority for all Christians. This lesson is developed to help us understand, identify, and apply some principles from Proverbs.

B. Lesson Background

The background for our lesson is the same as last week, thus that information need not be repeated here. The contrast between the righteous and the wicked seems to be a way of structuring Proverbs 28 and 29, within which today's lesson text occurs (see Proverbs 28:1, 12, 28; 29:16, 27). Thus, we can discern four sections in these two chapters (that is, Proverbs 28:1-11, 12-28; 29:1-15, and 16-27). Our lesson addresses the fourth of these sections.

In general, Proverbs 28:1–29:27 presents the wicked or greedy person as one who disrupts

Living an Ordered Life

harmony and security by ignoring God's law. Examples illustrate this in a variety of ways. In presenting these principles and illustrations, the proverbs are given in Hebrew poetic style, which is characterized by *parallelism*. Sometimes the parallel lines are set in opposition to one another (which is called *antithetic parallelism*); at other times the second line continues the thought of the first line (which is called *synthetic parallelism*).

In addressing the principles from Proverbs 29:17-26 for ordering one's life, I have turned many of the negative statements into positive principles by taking the opposing thought that is implied to the proverb at hand.

I. Introductory Proverb
(PROVERBS 29:16)

16. When the wicked are multiplied, transgression increaseth: but the righteous shall see their fall.

The Lesson Background notes that the contrast between the righteous and the wicked is found several times in Proverbs 28, 29. We may see the final two references—here in 29:16 and later in verse 27—as bookends for the principles that occur in between.

The proverb warns that when wicked people multiply so do their transgressions. Common experience tells us that this, sadly, is a natural progression. The more wicked people there are, the more sin there is as the wicked encourage one another in their misdeeds.

However, this is not the last word. The righteous will see the ruin or overthrow of the wicked. How can this be? In a "this world" sense, the wicked sow the seeds of their own destruction. We can think of turf wars in which members of gangs or drug cartels kill one another. In a "next world" sense, the wicked provoke divine retribution. The righteous win in the end because God is a just God. He will see to the fall of the wicked (Revelation 20:15). In the meantime, there is constant tension between the righteous and the wicked (more on this when we get to v. 27).

> **What Do You Think?**
> How should we react when the wicked fall? Why?
>
> *Talking Points for Your Discussion*
> - Rejoice in that they "got what was coming to them"?
> - Adopt an "I told you so" attitude?
> - Be thankful that it was not you?
> - Grieve over them and their sin?

II. Principles for an Ordered Life
(PROVERBS 29:17-26)
A. Having Peace (v. 17)

17. Correct thy son, and he shall give thee rest; yea, he shall give delight unto thy soul.

The correction in view deals with verbal rebuke or physical punishment, depending on what the situation calls for. Such correction and discipline of children also is found in Proverbs 22:15; 23:13, 14; 29:15.

A sad account of a parental failure to correct bad behavior is found in 2 Samuel 13. That chapter describes the rape of Tamar by her brother Amnon. Although the father, King David, "was very wroth" (v. 21), there is no record that he actually punished Amnon. Two years later, Tamar's brother Absalom (also David's son) exacted personal revenge by having Amnon murdered (13:23-29). Things spiraled further out of control when Absalom orchestrated a coup that ended in his own death (15:1–18:18). Parents who do not discipline their children properly will not have *rest*. *Delight* will not be a description of life for the parents who do not correct their children's behavior.

Overly harsh parental discipline can be as bad as no discipline (Ephesians 6:4). Discipline should never be done out of anger, hatred, or bitterness. Rather, love and concern for a child's welfare and maturity is to be the motivation for discipline. The parent who does this is modeling discipline after God (see Proverbs 3:11, 12). The well-ordered family life requires disciplined children.

HOW TO SAY IT

Amnon	*Am*-nun.
Absalom	*Ab*-suh-lum.
Habakkuk	Huh-*back*-kuk.

My wife and I were not perfect in our discipline of our two children, but we tried to be consistent and compassionate in our periods of correction. Today we enjoy the peace that comes with responsible adult children. They in turn are trying their best to discipline their own children.

B. Applying Scripture (v. 18)

18. Where there is no vision, the people perish: but he that keepeth the law, happy is he.

This proverb has often been used to promote the importance of having "a vision" in terms of a church building project, developing new programs, or increasing support for missions. But that is a misinterpretation. The problem lies in a misunderstanding of the word *vision*. This word does not mean "having a visionary leader or goal." Rather, the word *vision* refers to "prophetic vision"—that is, revelation from God (see 1 Samuel 3:1; Isaiah 1:1; Habakkuk 2:2, 3). When there is no word from God, the people will perish—that is, they will run wild. They do whatever they want to do without regard to God's will.

The second line is a contrast: *he that keepeth the law, happy is he.* Keeping the law means to obey God's Word, thereby restraining behavior that is destructive to life. It is not enough to know God's Word; one must apply the Scriptures to daily life and obey it (James 1:22, 23)! If anyone will obey consistently day in and day out, that person will live a well-ordered life.

Visual for Lesson 5. *As you discuss Proverbs 29:25, point to this visual and ask for examples of ways your learners can put trust in the Lord today.*

At one time it was common to speak of "Christian Europe." However, it can be argued that the decisive shift to secularization of society began with the French Revolution (1789–1799). This revolution was atheistic, seeking to free the state from religious influence—specifically that of the Roman Catholic Church. Instead, "Reason" was to be enthroned as god. Thus started a secularizing trend that saw the decline of Christianity in Europe.

Critics of Christianity argue that the church has a vivid history of violence and persecution, citing the Crusades and the Inquisition as examples. The critics have a point. But the two examples cited are but a shadow of the death and misery wrought by secular philosophies such as Marxism and Nazism.

Experience proves what Proverbs says: when God's Word—God's prophetic vision—is set aside, the wicked thrive. Our hope is in the power of the gospel to bring God's plans to fruition. He will allow himself to be forgotten for only so long.

—C. R. B.

C. Gaining Respect (v. 19)

19. A servant will not be corrected by words: for though he understand he will not answer.

Slaves and indentured servants in ancient cultures are subject to strict discipline, as are children. However, bodily harm is punishable by God's law (see Exodus 21:20, 21, 26, 27). This proverb seems to address the case where servants are giving their masters "the silent treatment," what we call passive resistance. The servants have no desire to carry out the requirements of the master.

We should thank the Lord we do not have the slave/master relationship today in our land! However, we can still see an application if we think of an employer/employee relationship. A demanding and unreasonable boss may get the silent treatment. Expressed or implied threats of being fired may result in grudging, minimal obedience on the part of the employee.

The proverb thus tells us of what won't work (words). But what will work? If those in authority in the workplace will be respectful and ask for reasonable outcomes, then usually the employees will respond with a job well done. The principle is simple: receive respect by being respectful. It works both ways for the employer and employee. Since we spend much of our time at work, this principle is essential for a well-ordered life.

❧ WHAT SECULAR CULTURE REALIZES ❧

Aretha Franklin recorded the Otis Redding song "Respect" in 1967. As secular feminism gained steam, the Franklin version became a signature song for the movement. *Rolling Stone* magazine placed Franklin's version fifth in its 2004 list "500 Greatest Songs of All Time." The popularity of the opposite word *disrespect,* often used as a verb, shows that secular culture understands both sides of the concept, even if it does not practice it.

We may wonder if Christians understand the concept of respect as well as the secular culture does. Think about your driving habits. Think about how you treat your colleagues at school or in the workplace. Think about your manner of speech, whether person-to-person or in blogs.

Lack of respect is usually (always?) traceable to a "me oriented" attitude. Shifting to a "God oriented" attitude is the cure. Respect for God should be the foundational principle in a respectful society. Are we Christians speaking and practicing that message loudly enough?   —C. R. B.

D. Avoiding Haste (v. 20)

20. Seest thou a man that is hasty in his words? there is more hope of a fool than of him.

Haste is considered a bad thing in the book of Proverbs (see Proverbs 19:2; 21:5; 25:8). Even good words must be spoken at the right time (see 15:23; 25:11). To speak too quickly can lead to foolish talk because the words are not thought out (see 15:28). The issue is one of discretion—not just in speaking the right words, but also in saying those right words at the right time.

Such wisdom is found in the New Testament: "Wherefore, my beloved brethren, let every man be swift to hear, slow to speak" (James 1:19). When we combine "swift to hear" with "slow to speak," we have a great principle to live by. We

would all have a better-ordered life if we listened more and held our tongues before speaking.

Part of the problem in failing to do so is seeing ourselves as "wise" and wanting to share our "wisdom" as quickly as possible (see Proverbs 26:12, which is the other *more hope of a fool* passage in Proverbs). Not only should we listen more, but we should listen more intently; then we will learn to speak the right words at the right time.

What Do You Think?
  What are some specific things we can do in various areas to avoid haste in our words?
Talking Points for Your Discussion
  ▪ In the rapid pace of modern culture
  ▪ In the anonymity of certain communication media (Internet forums, etc.)
  ▪ In dealing with pride
  ▪ In being uncomfortable with silence

E. Instructing Properly (v. 21)

21. He that delicately bringeth up his servant from a child shall have him become his son at the length.

This proverb is difficult to translate because it contains a word that is used nowhere else in the Old Testament. Thus, there is nothing to compare this word with as a "translation control." The *King James Version* translates this rare word as *shall have him become his son.*

To move toward a proper understanding, the best place to begin is with what is not in doubt: the verse is referring to a slave or servant born in a household (see Exodus 21:4) and how this slave or servant is reared during childhood.

To bring up such a child *delicately* carries the idea of "being indulgent." Most children are indulged to varying degrees, but there is such a thing as a child having too much free rein. In that light, one commentator believes that the rare word translated *shall have him become his son* carries the negative idea of "trouble," as in "shall have him become his troubled son."

Only proper instruction gives hope for such a situation. The warning of this verse must be balanced with what we have read in verses 17, 19, above.

F. Understanding Anger (v. 22)

22. An angry man stirreth up strife, and a furious man aboundeth in transgression.

Anger or wrath is mentioned in Proverbs 15:1, 18; 19:19; 22:24; 27:4; 30:33. Anger is a God-given emotion, and becoming angry is not a sin in and of itself. Jesus himself became angry (Mark 3:5; 11:15). What this proverb speaks to, rather, is the person whose life is characterized by anger. Have you ever known someone like that? This is the person who is always "on edge." One little word or even a gesture can set off an angry tirade. The result is *strife* and *transgression*.

In order to turn this proverb into a positive principle for living, we must look at the opposite trait: self-control (Proverbs 17:27). The self-controlled (temperate) person bears much good fruit (see Proverbs 14:29; 16:32; 29:11; etc.). For the Christian, being self-controlled is a good trait (2 Peter 1:6; etc.), but being Spirit-controlled yields the best fruit—the fruit of the Spirit (Galatians 5:22, 23). To be self- and Spirit-controlled is to live the ordered life.

What Do You Think?
 How can you do better at keeping anger from leading you to sin?
Talking Points for Your Discussion
 ▪ In controlling situations you allow yourself to be in
 ▪ In development of spiritual disciplines
 ▪ In having an accountability partner
 ▪ In evaluating deeper issues such as unresolved grief

G. Having Honor (v. 23)

23. A man's pride shall bring him low: but honour shall uphold the humble in spirit.

This is one of those proverbs where you have to stop and think. The person who pridefully lifts himself or herself up will be brought low, but the person who is already low will be lifted up. What a paradox! Yet it is true. Human pride is always a bad trait in the book of Proverbs (see 8:13; 11:2; 13:10; 15:25; 16:5, 18, 19; 21:4, 24). The New Testament also speaks of the danger of pride (Luke

1:51; 2 Timothy 3:2; 1 Peter 5:5). It was the pride of humankind that caused God to scatter people from Babel (Genesis 11:1-9). The humble person realizes that he or she doesn't know everything and is therefore teachable. The prideful person is much less teachable.

What Do You Think?
 Which Scripture do you find most helpful in convicting you about humility? Why?
Talking Points for Your Discussion
 ▪ 1 Samuel 9:21
 ▪ 2 Samuel 7:18
 ▪ Matthew 3:14
 ▪ Matthew 8:8
 ▪ 1 Corinthians 15:9

H. Staying Honest (v. 24)

24. Whoso is partner with a thief hateth his own soul: he heareth cursing, and bewrayeth it not.

This proverb is difficult to understand in its original setting, but it seems to be describing an ethical dilemma. Assume that a thief is caught and is put on trial for a crime. Then his partner or accomplice is called to testify against him. If the partner is silent *(bewrayeth it not)*, then he is in violation of Leviticus 5:1. But if the partner "rats out" the thief, then the partner points a finger of guilt at himself for having been an accomplice! The phrase *he heareth cursing* is the translator's conclusion that profanity is directed against the guilty parties.

In essence, we have a warning against being enticed by the ungodly (see Proverbs 1:8-19). Once again, we must turn this negative proverb into a positive principle: "Honesty is the best policy"—a well-known modern proverb! One cannot live the well-ordered life without honesty.

I. Trusting God (v. 25)

25. The fear of man bringeth a snare: but whoso putteth his trust in the LORD shall be safe.

Upon whom do we lean for approval—man or God? In whom do we trust—man or God? Certainly, we try to do what is right in the eyes of both (2 Corinthians 8:21). But having too much anxiety about "what people think" will only bring us into a snare, a trap of some kind.

Humankind cannot be trusted for approval or security. *Trust in the Lord* is the only kind of trust that leads to safety. The word *safe* literally is "to be set securely on high," presumably above all danger (see Job 5:11; Psalm 69:29; Proverbs 18:10).

There is a true fear that one should have toward God (see Proverbs 1:7). It is the theme of wisdom literature in general. Instead of worrying too much about what others think, we should be concerned mainly about what God thinks. So will our private and public worlds be ordered.

J. Receiving Justice (v. 26)

26. Many seek the ruler's favour; but every man's judgment cometh from the LORD.

When a person needs justice done, he or she goes to the one who has the power to bring it about. In both ancient and modern times, that is the governing authority. Sometimes the result can be good (see 1 Kings 3), sometimes bad (see Isaiah 5:23). Consistently true justice comes only from the Lord himself. People should be flocking to His throne in prayer.

III. Final Proverb
(PROVERBS 29:27)

27. An unjust man is an abomination to the just: and he that is upright in the way is abomination to the wicked.

In something of a parallel with our opening proverb of this lesson, we have come full circle to the contrast between *the just* (the righteous) and *the wicked*. Thus we have the second of our two bookends we mentioned earlier.

However, this proverb has a twist to it in that it expresses what is common about the righteous and the wicked: each is *an abomination* to the other. The righteous find the wicked repulsive, while the straight path of the righteous is despised by the wicked.

Abomination is an emotional reaction that the Lord himself has against the wicked and their lifestyle (see Proverbs 3:32; 11:1; 12:22; 15:9, 26;

16:5; 17:15; 20:10). The righteous are only imitating their God when they perceive the wicked as an abomination. This makes a fitting close to the last proverb of Solomon in the book of Proverbs.

What Do You Think?
 What are some specific examples of how hatred toward the people of God is evidenced by the unjust today?
Talking Points for Your Discussion
 ▪ In how Christians are portrayed in media
 ▪ In how company employee manuals are written
 ▪ In the workplace from colleagues
 ▪ In laws that are enacted

Conclusion
A. The Ordered Life in Christ

Let us group these 10 principles for simplification. Group 1 consists of verses 18, 25, 26 in that they teach us to trust the Lord for our security and to look to Him for true justice.

Group 2 consists of verses 19, 20, 22, 23, 24 in dealing with personal characteristics that enhance life. This grouping teaches us to maintain a humble spirit, be self-controlled, and have a listening ear. Respecting another's humanity and dealing honestly with everyone is vital to relationships.

Group 3 consists of verses 17 and 21. This grouping teaches us that discipline in family and work relationships is very important for the peace and rest it will provide. The New Testament teaches us all these principles and more. Let us practice these principles and thus live the ordered life in Christ.

B. Prayer

Our Father, teach us to trust in You for our security and not in man, to look to You for justice and not to human courts. May our relationships with others be honest, humble, and wise. Help us to live the ordered life according to Your Word. In the name of Jesus we pray, amen.

C. Thought to Remember

Make living an ordered life a priority.

INVOLVEMENT LEARNING

Some of the activities below are also found in the helpful student book, Adult Bible Class.
Don't forget to download the free reproducible page from www.standardlesson.com to enhance your lesson!

Into the Lesson

Bring to class five random objects of your choice (for example: a book, a shirt, a child's toy, a gardening tool, a candy bar). Display the objects on a table and ask the class to help you put them in order—whatever they think that means, without suggestions from the teacher.

Once they have put them in order, ask if they can think of any different ways to organize the objects. The class might decide to arrange them according to increasing or decreasing size, color, or value. Ask, "How can we know the right order for the objects, given that there are so many different options and opinions?" After discussion, suggest that the only real way to know is if the teacher describes for us what constitutes a "good" order. Say, "In the same way, we cannot know the right way to order our lives unless we look at the intent of the master teacher, as expressed in the Bible."

Alternative: Ask a series of unanswerable questions. Examples: Why is a boxing ring square? When sign makers go on strike, do they carry blank signs? Why does rain *drop* but snow *falls*? Why do we park on a driveway and drive on a parkway? Why is *abbreviated* such a long word?

Ask the class to suggest some serious examples. Examples: Why do bad things happen to good people? How can I get through to my teenager? Is there any justice in this world? Say, "While people of other cultures and time periods would not have understood our humorous questions, these more serious questions are of universal relevance and interest. This is what gives the book of Proverbs its timeless appeal."

Into the Word

Explain to the class that Hebrew poetry is often characterized by *parallelism*. Write on the board *antithetical parallelism = opposite* and *synthetic parallelism = continue*. Explain that in the first type of parallelism the lines of the proverb are set in con-

trast, whereas in the second type, the second line continues the thought of the first line.

Divide the class into two groups. *Group A* will identify all the examples of antithetical parallelism in today's text, while *Group S* searches for all examples of synthetic parallelism. *(Answers for Group A: Proverbs 29:16, 18, 23, 25, 26, 27; answers for Group S: Proverbs 29:17, 19, 20, 21, 22, 24.)* If your class is large, you can form more than two groups and give duplicate assignments.

Ask Group A if they noticed any one recurring word that can serve as a signal of antithetical parallelism. They may have noticed the second line of most of their proverbs begins with *but*. However, verse 27 does not follow this pattern, so this is not a hard-and-fast rule. Ask group members to read again the proverbs they identified and suggest contemporary examples that either confirm the principle expressed in that proverb or seem to be an exception.

After the groups have had time to discuss their proverbs, have each group share with the whole class its best example that confirms a proverb and the most difficult-to-explain example that serves as an exception. Discuss these examples as a class, consulting the commentary for clarification. For exception examples, particular areas to consider are whether in some cases the negative or positive consequences of behavior are not fully realized until after death, or if there are negative consequences during life that are not readily visible.

Into Life

Download the reproducible page and distribute copies of the Jesus the Living Proverb exercise. Your learners can complete it either individually or in small groups (you can make this into a good-natured contest to see who can finish first). Finally, ask learners to suggest specific ways they can keep their focus on Christ this week in order to follow His example.

VALUING TRUE WISDOM

DEVOTIONAL READING: Psalm 33:13-22
BACKGROUND SCRIPTURE: Ecclesiastes 9:13–10:20

ECCLESIASTES 9:13-18

13 This wisdom have I seen also under the sun, and it seemed great unto me:

14 There was a little city, and few men within it; and there came a great king against it, and besieged it, and built great bulwarks against it:

15 Now there was found in it a poor wise man, and he by his wisdom delivered the city; yet no man remembered that same poor man.

16 Then said I, Wisdom is better than strength: nevertheless the poor man's wisdom is despised, and his words are not heard.

17 The words of wise men are heard in quiet more than the cry of him that ruleth among fools.

18 Wisdom is better than weapons of war: but one sinner destroyeth much good.

ECCLESIASTES 10:1-4

1 Dead flies cause the ointment of the apothecary to send forth a stinking savour: so doth a little folly him that is in reputation for wisdom and honour.

2 A wise man's heart is at his right hand; but a fool's heart at his left.

3 Yea also, when he that is a fool walketh by the way, his wisdom faileth him, and he saith to every one that he is a fool.

4 If the spirit of the ruler rise up against thee, leave not thy place; for yielding pacifieth great offences.

KEY VERSE

Wisdom is better than strength: nevertheless the poor man's wisdom is despised, and his words are not heard. —Ecclesiastes 9:16

TRADITION AND WISDOM

Unit 1: Teaching and Learning

LESSONS 1–8

LESSON AIMS

After participating in this lesson, each student will be able to:

1. List one foolish behavior and one wise behavior.

2. Describe how wisdom and folly are contrasted in today's text.

3. Identify a life choice he or she is currently facing and describe why one path is wiser than another.

LESSON OUTLINE

Introduction
  A. Full, Yet Empty
  B. Lesson Background
I. Sample of Wisdom (ECCLESIASTES 9:13-16)
  A. Circumstance Recounted (vv. 13-15)
  B. Conclusion Reached (v. 16)
    Learning from (Someone Else's) Life
II. Sayings About Wisdom (ECCLESIASTES 9:17–10:4)
  A. Wisdom: An Asset (9:17, 18)
    The Need for Wiser Heads
  B. Folly: A Liability (10:1-3)
  C. Wisdom Illustrated (v. 4)
Conclusion
  A. Measuring Wisdom
  B. Prayer
  C. Thought to Remember

Introduction

A. Full, Yet Empty

Shel Silverstein (1930–1999) was a popular author of stories and poems geared toward children. But much of Silverstein's writing also conveyed meaningful messages to adults. In his poem entitled "Never," Silverstein pictures someone recounting all the various heroic acts that he has *never* accomplished in life. In the last two lines of the poem, the would-be hero laments his depression about all the things he *hasn't* done.

The book of Ecclesiastes pictures an individual (most likely Solomon) who was able to do and have virtually anything he wanted. Yet, unlike Silverstein's imaginary character, Solomon became depressed and frustrated over what he *could* do and have. All of his many achievements and possessions left him empty and miserable. No matter what new direction he took in his efforts to find meaning in his life, he returned to the same tired refrain of "Vanity of vanities; all is vanity."

B. Lesson Background

Like the book of Proverbs, from which the previous five lessons in this quarter are drawn, the book of Ecclesiastes is part of the wisdom literature of the Old Testament. It is the fourth in the group of what is often called the Old Testament's Books of Poetry (that is, Job, Psalms, Proverbs, Ecclesiastes, and Song of Solomon).

While the author of Ecclesiastes is not specifically named, traditionally it is believed to be Solomon. This is because of the phrases "son of David" and "king in Jerusalem" that are found in Ecclesiastes 1:1. In addition, the person's intense interest in wisdom (1:13-18; 2:12-16; 7:1–8:1; 8:16, 17; 9:13-18) along with his ability to obtain most anything he wanted (2:1-11) fit well with both Solomon's renowned wisdom and his abundant wealth.

The title *Ecclesiastes* comes from the Greek translation of the Old Testament known as the Septuagint. The Hebrew title is rendered in English letters as *Koheleth* (sometimes spelled *Qoheleth*), which comes from a verb meaning "to call." The Greek title includes the word *ekklesia*, which is the primary word translated as "church" in the New Testament. That word means "called out ones." Thus the terms *Koheleth* and *Ecclesiastes* describe "one who calls out"; this results in the common English translation of "the Preacher" in Ecclesiastes 1:1.

As you read Ecclesiastes, try not to think of Solomon as the wise and dignified king whose wisdom drew audiences and acclaim from throughout the world of his time (1 Kings 10:23-25). Rather, think of Solomon as divesting himself of all the trappings of royalty and addressing us simply as a fellow human being trying to make sense of a puzzle called *life*. Think of Ecclesiastes as this man's spiritual journal, recording his quest for clarity and meaning. And think of his quest as being answered, ultimately and decisively, in the one who declared himself to be "greater than Solomon" (Matthew 12:42)—the Lord Jesus Christ.

I. Sample of Wisdom
(ECCLESIASTES 9:13-16)
A. Circumstance Recounted (vv. 13-15)

13. This wisdom have I seen also under the sun, and it seemed great unto me.

One of the key phrases in the book of Ecclesiastes is *under the sun*, appearing nearly 30 times. The term describes life from the perspective of this world only—its values, priorities, and aims—without any acknowledgment that there is someone "above" the sun, namely God. While some of what this world has to offer is good and satisfying, other features are far from that. In fact, they

HOW TO SAY IT

apothecary	uh-***paw***-thuh-*care*-ee.
Assyrian	Uh-*sear*-e-un.
Ecclesiastes	Ik-*leez*-ee-***as***-teez.
ekklesia *(Greek)*	ek-lay-*see*-uh.
Hezekiah	Hez-ih-*kye*-uh.
koheleth *(Hebrew)*	ko-*hel*-eth.
Micaiah	My-*kay*-uh.
Pharaoh	*Fair*-o or *Fay*-roe.
Qohelet *(Hebrew)*	Koe-*hel*-it.
Sennacherib	Sen-*nack*-er-ib.
Septuagint	Sep-*too*-ih-jent.

can be quite disheartening and frustrating. Thus at certain places Solomon seems rather positive about life *under the sun* (Ecclesiastes 5:18-20). But that optimism can turn quickly into a dour, glass-half-empty (or completely empty) attitude (6:1-12).

Let's be honest: most of us can relate very easily to such thinking—even as we freely acknowledge God as Creator. Some of what we see going on under the sun is quite satisfying to us; other situations leave us rather discouraged or even depressed. Some days we find ourselves eager to get out of bed; other days we would just as soon not see or hear from anyone.

In the section of Scripture before us, Solomon proceeds to comment on an example of wisdom that he initially finds quite impressive. But upon further reflection, he wonders . . .

14. There was a little city, and few men within it; and there came a great king against it, and besieged it, and built great bulwarks against it.

Whenever we see the word *city* in the Old Testament, we should not think in terms of what we consider to be a city today. Both the population and the territory covered are rather limited in ancient times. Towns in Old Testament Israel are usually very small, with about 150 to 250 houses and a population of perhaps 1,000. The city cited by Solomon in this verse, while not specifically named, is described as *little* with *few men* living there. The total number of residents, including women and children, may have been no more than 500. Thus there was little hope when *there came a great king against it, and besieged it, and built great bulwarks against it.*

Warfare is, unfortunately, a common part of life in the Old Testament world. The siege is a standard way of attacking a walled city. The bulwarks used in such a procedure include a siege ramp, constructed with a foundation of trees and large stones and mixed with earth and whatever other resources are at hand. At some point, battering rams are used to break down the city's walls, allowing the enemy to enter. The Old Testament records several instances of such sieges and attacks (Judges 9:50; 2 Samuel 20:15; 2 Kings 6:24; 17:5; 25:1-4).

15. Now there was found in it a poor wise man, and he by his wisdom delivered the city; yet no man remembered that same poor man.

In 2 Samuel 20:14-22, we are told of a certain wise woman who saves her city from a siege through her wise advice to the residents. In the case described in our text, a *poor wise man* is responsible for saving his city from a similar attack.

Yet no man remembered that same poor man. Apparently nothing has been done to commemorate the wise man's heroic efforts; thus future generations will lose this vital link to their past. Sadly, many people treat God in much the same manner as this wise man has been treated: they accept His blessings each day and even call on Him for help in time of need, but when the crisis has passed, so has their faith.

What Do You Think?

What was a time you forgot what God had done for you? What was the result?

Talking Points for Your Discussion
- The intensity of the problem at the moment
- Distinguishing between a cause and a symptom

B. Conclusion Reached (v. 16)

16. Then said I, Wisdom is better than strength: nevertheless the poor man's wisdom is despised, and his words are not heard.

In the situation described by Solomon, military strength and preparedness had nothing to do with rescuing the city from destruction. The rescue happened because of the exercise of wisdom. Thus, concludes Solomon, *wisdom is better than strength*—at least that's the ideal that one would like to see acknowledged on a regular basis.

In reality, such acknowledgment does not always happen. In the example cited, *the poor man's wisdom is despised;* his wise counsel to the people is forgotten. In today's world, the accomplishments that highlight physical strength (such as those in sports) quite often generate far more interest and receive much more publicity than those that reflect wisdom, especially the wisdom that is grounded in a firm faith in the Lord.

What Do You Think?

What was a time when you made the mistake of relying on some kind of strength instead of wisdom? How did you grow spiritually as a result?

Talking Points for Your Discussion
- On the job
- In church
- In the home

❧ LEARNING FROM (SOMEONE ELSE'S) LIFE ❧

A godly woman lived to the age of 97. For the last decade of her life, members of the succeeding four generations of her family would gather on her birthday to honor her wise contributions to their lives. Prior to each of those birthdays, one of her daughters would transcribe the woman's "lessons learned" from life. At the celebration, the great-grandchildren would take turns reading aloud from the memories.

A few years after the woman's death, one of her grandsons had a health scare that made him realize that he would not always be around to advise his grandchildren. So he began writing down what he had learned from life. These recollections were then placed in what was called a *21 Box.* Each grandchild was to receive one of the boxes on reaching age 21. So, once again, the wisdom of one generation was passed on to a succeeding generation.

The wise ponderings of Ecclesiastes can work in a similar way. If we listen to the godly writers of the Bible, it will save us a lot of grief because we will learn from someone else's mistakes rather than our own. A key lesson of the Old Testament is that God's people are always just one generation away from apostasy (Judges 2:10).   —C. R. B.

II. Sayings About Wisdom
(ECCLESIASTES 9:17–10:4)
A. Wisdom: An Asset (9:17, 18)

17. The words of wise men are heard in quiet more than the cry of him that ruleth among fools.

Consider for a moment the people whom you would view as the wisest you have ever known. In many cases, you will be thinking of people who are not loud, brash, or arrogant, but whose quiet, humble disposition reflects a rock-solid commitment to biblical truth. Often such individuals will not immediately speak up in a time of crisis or uncertainty, but when they do their words usually merit the utmost respect and attention.

The Scriptures include several illustrations of rulers *among fools*—rulers whose arrogance and brashness are eventually silenced by the Lord, in His own way and time. Think of Pharaoh and his sneering defiance of the Lord (Exodus 5:1, 2). The plagues and the destruction of Pharaoh's army at the Red Sea left his kingdom shattered. Read the words of the Assyrian ruler Sennacherib, who brazenly boasted of his superiority over God and King Hezekiah of Judah (2 Kings 18:17-35). Overnight, his mighty army was annihilated by the angel of the Lord; Sennacherib himself returned in disgrace, eventually to be murdered by two of his sons (2 Kings 19:35-37).

Tragically, even God's people are not immune from the consequences of being ruled by such men. King Ahab of Israel (the northern kingdom) thought he could outsmart God's prophet Micaiah. By disguising himself before battle, Ahab thought he could escape the prophet's prediction of death. The ruse failed; Ahab died exactly as the man of God foresaw (1 Kings 22:26-38).

> **What Do You Think?**
> Who displays a quiet wisdom that you would like to emulate? How will you do so?
> *Talking Points for Your Discussion*
> - A coach
> - A relative
> - A spiritual giant

18a. Wisdom is better than weapons of war.

Again, the virtue and value of wisdom is praised. The assertion *wisdom is better than weapons of war* is not necessarily saying that weapons of war are therefore wrong to employ. But clearly if the rulers of this world set a goal of living by God's wisdom, the need for weapons of war will decrease

Choose the way of wisdom.

Visual for Lesson 6

Point to this visual as you ask, "How do we know when we're at a crossroads like this?"

dramatically. It is because world leaders throughout history have rejected God's wisdom (or have exercised their own wisdom and called it God's) that reliance on weapons of war has escalated.

❧ THE NEED FOR WISER HEADS ❧

During the U.S. presidential campaign of 1860, Abraham Lincoln spoke against the expansion of slavery. As a result, seven states in the South seceded even before Lincoln was inaugurated. America's Civil War began on April 12, 1861, when Confederate forces attacked Fort Sumter. President Lincoln's subsequent Emancipation Proclamation made the end of slavery one of the objectives of the war.

The war lasted 4 long years. The carnage was horrendous: together, the 2 sides experienced over 600,000 deaths of those in uniform. Counting an unknown number of civilian casualties, the country lost perhaps 3 percent of its population.

If wiser heads had prevailed at the outset—heads with an understanding of the biblical teaching on human worth and dignity—the practice of slavery may have been brought to an end without resorting to weapons of war (as happened in Great Britain). What areas of life today call for the application of biblical wisdom?   —C. R. B.

18b. But one sinner destroyeth much good.

This statement forms a transition to the next theme covered in our printed text: the danger of ignoring wisdom and embracing folly as one's pattern for living. One of the most discouraging realities of life in a fallen world is that a person can work faithfully and diligently—for years in some cases—to establish a ministry, only to see his or her efforts set back or altogether ruined in a relatively short amount of time by one person's sinful and destructive words or actions.

But this principle applies to other areas of life as well: destruction takes far less time to achieve than construction. An imposing structure that took months or years to erect can be destroyed quickly by an explosion or by fire. Solomon provides his own example of this principle in the next verse.

B. Folly: A Liability (10:1-3)

1. Dead flies cause the ointment of the apothecary to send forth a stinking savour: so doth a little folly him that is in reputation for wisdom and honour.

Solomon now expands on the point made at the conclusion of the previous verse. In the Hebrew text, the phrase *the ointment of the apothecary* is literally "the oil of the mixer." The mixer is one who combines the oils that are used to make the perfumes of biblical times.

These perfumes serve a purpose similar to deodorants today. Oil (such as olive oil) is rubbed into one's body to soothe the skin, which is almost a necessity in the hot, dry climate of biblical lands. Perfume, added to the oil, helps disguise body odor where there is not much water for washing. These perfumes are usually extracted from flowers, seeds, or fruit. They may also come from various gums or resins of certain trees or bushes.

Many of the perfumes used in ancient Palestine are imported and are therefore quite a luxury. And yet, notes Solomon, the presence of a few *dead flies* can cause even the most pleasing fragrance to become foul—and when it becomes so, the foulness cannot be reversed easily.

So it is with the negative impact of just *a little folly* on one's *reputation for wisdom and honour*. It takes years for someone to establish a reputation for wisdom and integrity. Yet he or she can lose it all because of one indiscretion. Once lost, that reputation can take years to rebuild.

2. A wise man's heart is at his right hand; but a fool's heart at his left.

One should avoid thinking of *right* and *left* in modern "conservative" or "liberal" terms on a political spectrum. That is a misapplication of Solomon's point. He is simply observing that wisdom and folly involve two totally different ways of thinking about and approaching life.

At the same time, we should note that the position on one's *right* in biblical times is associated with a place of power and influence or of special treatment (Psalm 110:1, 5; Matthew 26:64; Acts 7:56). In His description of the final judgment, Jesus pictures His followers (the sheep) on His right hand and everyone else (the goats) on His left (Matthew 25:31-33). We still refer to a leader's close associate or adviser as a "right-hand man."

> *What Do You Think?*
> Which Scripture convicts you most about the need to develop a wise heart and proper ways of thinking? Why?
>
> *Talking Points for Your Discussion*
> - Old Testament: Joshua 1:8; 1 Kings 3:7-14
> - New Testament: Romans 12:3; Philippians 2:5-8; 4:8

3. Yea also, when he that is a fool walketh by the way, his wisdom faileth him, and he saith to every one that he is a fool.

In some instances, it may appear that folly yields more results than wisdom, with less effort expended. Why live by wisdom's standards, when all that you accomplish while seeking to follow it can be reversed by just "a little folly" (v. 1)?

But one should not look only at the results of wise versus foolish living, which in certain instances may seem to prove that the foolish path is the preferred one. The daily routine of the fool (here represented by the phrase *walketh by the way*) reveals that lifestyle to be anything but the carefree, glamorous experience that is often portrayed in various media outlets. Seldom displayed is the degree of guilt and heartache that accompany those who choose to live as if there were no God and as if, to use Paul's phrase, their "God is their belly" (Philippians 3:19).

C. Wisdom Illustrated (v. 4)

4. If the spirit of the ruler rise up against thee, leave not thy place; for yielding pacifieth great offenses.

Our printed text concludes with a practical piece of advice on how to exercise wisdom. It is given in the form of a hypothetical situation, yet one that can be encountered at some point: *If the spirit of the ruler rise up against thee.* This is the picture of someone who becomes the target of a ruler's anger. The individual is counseled not to leave his or her place, perhaps implying that such a person is an official of some kind in the ruler's administration. Fleeing might, in this instance, be taken as a sign of guilt of some wrongdoing.

Yielding (thus remaining submissive) in response to the ruler's rage (while doing nothing to agitate it further) is a better reaction. That such an approach *pacifieth great offenses* may mean that once the ruler's anger has abated, the ruler may come to realize that the official in question is innocent of wrongdoing. In that case, the ruler will no longer find any cause to take offense in the official.

As is the case with almost any proverbial kind of statement, one can think of exceptions to what this verse says. With certain rulers, no amount of yielding or submission can pacify their rage or deter them from carrying out their murderous intentions (see 1 Samuel 19:11, 12). As Solomon goes on to observe, not everyone in a place of authority deserves to be there (Ecclesiastes 10:5, 6).

As a general rule, though, the statement in the verse before us is true and echoes the sentiments of Proverbs 15:1: "A soft answer turneth away wrath: but grievous words stir up anger." Sometimes it's a good idea to confront a ruler (2 Kings 5:13), sometimes not (Ecclesiastes 8:4).

What Do You Think?
What was a time you had to stand in the place of opposition? How did things turn out?
Talking Points for Your Discussion
- On an issue in the workplace
- On moral issues
- On an issue of biblical doctrine

Conclusion

A. Measuring Wisdom

The title of today's study is "Valuing True Wisdom." How do we measure wisdom? What criteria should we use to determine its value or worth? It is interesting to consider how wise Solomon was (assuming he is the author of Ecclesiastes) as a result of God's gracious gift to him (1 Kings 3:5-14), yet wrestling with the real value of this gift. In today's text we have seen Solomon regret the fact that wisdom, in spite of its positive contributions (even saving a city from destruction), is in some cases forgotten and "despised."

And yet, Solomon is not ready to cast aside wisdom totally. It is "better than strength" (Ecclesiastes 9:16). It is "better than weapons of war" (9:18), in spite of the fact that its fruits can be negated so easily by a small amount of folly. Wisdom—God's wisdom—is the right way, the true way.

The rightness and the truth of that way are not affected in the least by how others respond to it or by whether its impact is forgotten the next day by the general public. Because wisdom's ultimate source is God, it is His response that ultimately matters; and it is abundantly clear from Scripture that He does not and will not forget the person who has made wisdom the pattern for life.

This is the ultimate conclusion reached by Solomon (Ecclesiastes 12:13, 14). That is why it is so important to read Ecclesiastes all the way through to the very end, where Solomon states the conclusion of his search for life's meaning. We will examine his conclusion in more detail in the next study.

B. Prayer

Father, sometimes we wrestle intensely with trying to live for You in a fallen world. Remind us at those times of struggle that although this world is fallen, You are still in control, and that this world's so-called wisdom is still folly compared with Yours. Keep us faithfully walking in wisdom's way, and help us not to be distracted by lesser concerns. In Jesus' name, amen.

C. Thought to Remember

To live by God's wisdom means
trusting Him to bless those who do so.

INVOLVEMENT LEARNING

Some of the activities below are also found in the helpful student book, Adult Bible Class.
Don't forget to download the free reproducible page from www.standardlesson.com to enhance your lesson!

Into the Lesson

Download the reproducible page and distribute copies of the Wise or Wrong? activity. Ask learners to take turns reading the Ben Franklin maxims aloud, then give learners a few seconds to circle "wise" or "wrong," depending upon whether they think the statement is biblically sound or not. Challenge learners to recall relevant passages of Scripture to support their opinions.

Suggested answers with relevant biblical references are provided on the answer key, but note that these answers are not hard and fast—in some cases learners may interpret the statement differently and be able to support their perspective biblically. Use such opportunities to reflect with the learners on the fact that wisdom requires discernment about how to apply God's Word in specific life circumstances. Say, "Without knowledge of the circumstances, we may not always be able to reach a definite conclusion."

Into the Word

Share with the class a summary of the Lesson Background material provided by the lesson writer in the Introduction. Emphasize the idea of Ecclesiastes as a "journal" of the author's quest for clarity and meaning in life. Ask learners to share whether they are in the habit of keeping a journal and whether they find this to be a spiritually productive activity.

Even if the learners do not journal, ask them to consider whether they were more optimistic or pessimistic at an earlier stage of life. If they had kept a journal, how different would their entries have looked at age 14 than at age 40? Discuss some of the reasons people grow either in cynicism or hopefulness as life moves along. Is a cynical attitude wrong, or is it realistic? Is optimism the biblical virtue of hope, or is it naiveté?

After this discussion, invite the learners to look at today's lesson text. Allow learners to take turns reading verses of the text aloud, then ask the following questions to review the content. The verse with the answer is listed in italics after each question; do not read the verse number aloud. You may wish to rearrange the order of the questions.

1. Where was the author when he saw a great example of wisdom? *(v. 13)* 2. What crisis did the city face? *(v. 14)* 3. Who saved the city, and how? *(v. 15)* 4. What was the result for the person who saved the city? *(v. 15)* 5. What did the author conclude about the value of wisdom versus strength? *(v. 16)* 6. Who does the author say destroys much good? *(v. 18)* 7. What gives perfume a bad smell? *(v. 1)* 8. What outweighs wisdom and honor? *(v. 1)* 9. What does the fool show people as he walks down the road? *(v. 3)* 10. What should you do if the ruler rises against you? *(v. 4)*

Although this passage contains references to cultural situations that most of us do not face today (siege warfare, flies in our perfume, serving a king), its value is nonetheless timeless. Engage the class in a discussion of situations in families, church, school, or workplace that give opportunities to apply the message of this passage. Refer to the lesson writer's commentary and add your own examples as appropriate.

Into Life

Distribute copies of the My Legacy activity from the reproducible page. Give learners time to reflect and compose an answer to the question. Ask volunteers to share their wise statements with the group.

Finally, have the group suggest practical ways to pass on these words of wisdom to younger generations. Examples may include living consistently with our words, writing a meaningful letter, looking for teachable moments to repeat the message, including the statement every year on birthday cards, engraving key words on a keepsake, or writing it in the cover of a gift book or journal.

Valuing True Wisdom

GROWING OLD WITH WISDOM

DEVOTIONAL READING: Psalm 71:1-12
BACKGROUND SCRIPTURE: Ecclesiastes 11:7–12:14

ECCLESIASTES 11:9, 10

9 Rejoice, O young man, in thy youth; and let thy heart cheer thee in the days of thy youth, and walk in the ways of thine heart, and in the sight of thine eyes: but know thou, that for all these things God will bring thee into judgment.

10 Therefore remove sorrow from thy heart, and put away evil from thy flesh: for childhood and youth are vanity.

ECCLESIASTES 12:1-7, 13

1 Remember now thy Creator in the days of thy youth, while the evil days come not, nor the years draw nigh, when thou shalt say, I have no pleasure in them;

2 While the sun, or the light, or the moon, or the stars, be not darkened, nor the clouds return after the rain:

3 In the day when the keepers of the house shall tremble, and the strong men shall bow themselves, and the grinders cease because they are few, and those that look out of the windows be darkened,

4 And the doors shall be shut in the streets, when the sound of the grinding is low, and he shall rise up at the voice of the bird, and all the daughters of musick shall be brought low;

5 Also when they shall be afraid of that which is high, and fears shall be in the way, and the almond tree shall flourish, and the grasshopper shall be a burden, and desire shall fail: because man goeth to his long home, and the mourners go about the streets:

6 Or ever the silver cord be loosed, or the golden bowl be broken, or the pitcher be broken at the fountain, or the wheel broken at the cistern.

7 Then shall the dust return to the earth as it was: and the spirit shall return unto God who gave it.

· ·

13 Let us hear the conclusion of the whole matter: Fear God, and keep his commandments: for this is the whole duty of man.

KEY VERSE

Fear God, and keep his commandments: for this is the whole duty of man. —**Ecclesiastes 12:13**

TRADITION AND WISDOM

Unit 1: Teaching and Learning
LESSONS 1–8

LESSON AIMS

After participating in this lesson, each student will be able to:

1. List some of Solomon's contrasts between youth and old age.

2. Describe some challenges and blessings that accompany seeking to obey God in both youth and old age.

3. Recite Ecclesiastes 12:13 from memory.

LESSON OUTLINE

Introduction
  A. No Age Discrimination Here
  B. Lesson Background
I. Warnings About Youthfulness (ECCLESIAS-TES 11:9, 10)
  A. Future Accountability (v. 9)
  B. Present Action (v. 10)
II. Warnings About Aging (ECCLESIASTES 12: 1-7)
  A. In General Terms (v. 1)
  B. In Specific Terms (vv. 2-7)
    What Death Results in
III. Wisdom for All (ECCLESIASTES 12:13)
    Doing Our Duty
Conclusion
  A. Solomon and Scrooge
  B. Prayer
  C. Thought to Remember

Introduction

A. No Age Discrimination Here

Chuck Swindoll, in his book *The Tale of the Tardy Oxcart*, offers some observations on aging:

Your dreams are reruns;
The stewardess offers coffee, tea, or Milk of Magnesia;
You sit in a rocking chair and can't get it started;
Everything hurts, and what doesn't hurt doesn't work;
A pretty girl prompts your pacemaker to lift the garage door;
You sink your teeth into a juicy steak, and they stay there.

We may add that another sign of aging is not knowing that the obsolete word *stewardess* has been replaced by *flight attendant*!

Yes, changes do occur with growing older; quite honestly, many of them are not welcome! Solomon, the probable author of Ecclesiastes, describes in today's Scripture text some of the losses one experiences in growing older. Yet one important item does not have to be lost: wisdom. If anything, wisdom should become more precious as the changes that accompany aging become all too personal. God's wisdom does not discriminate; it's meant for all ages and all seasons of life.

B. Lesson Background

Today's lesson is the second from the book of Ecclesiastes. Thus, the background is the same as the previous lesson, and that material need not be repeated here. We recall that Ecclesiastes is a kind of journal from Solomon, documenting his quest for the meaning and significance of life. The portion of Ecclesiastes covered in today's printed text comes from the conclusion of the book.

I. Warnings About Youthfulness
(ECCLESIASTES 11:9, 10)

A. Future Accountability (v. 9)

9. Rejoice, O young man, in thy youth; and let thy heart cheer thee in the days of thy youth, and

Growing Old with Wisdom

walk in the ways of thine heart, and in the sight of thine eyes: but know thou, that for all these things God will bring thee into judgment.

The *young man* addressed in this verse probably is not any specific individual. Solomon's counsel is applicable to any young man reading or hearing these words, regardless of the time or place, when or where, he is living. Typically, wisdom is seen in Old Testament times as something to be passed on from a father to his son (note the reference to "my son" in Ecclesiastes 12:12) or from teacher to student. But one should not therefore exclude young women from what Solomon is saying. Much of the wisdom found within Ecclesiastes (or within a book such as Proverbs) is applicable to either sex.

Here Solomon not only encourages a young man to rejoice in his youth, he also seems to advocate a very carefree, lackadaisical approach to life. To walk according to *the sight of thine eyes* reminds us of the description of the moral chaos of the time of the judges, when "every man did that which was right in his own eyes" (Judges 21:25).

But just as one must read to the conclusion of the book of Ecclesiastes to capture its intended, overall message, the same must be done with this particular verse. Yes, people have the freedom to do what they choose to do, but everyone will face the Day of Judgment. At that time, all will give an account before God of their actions (see also Romans 14:10-12; 2 Corinthians 5:10).

> *What Do You Think?*
> When you think back on your youth, what song title best sums up your approach to life at the time? Why?
>
> *Talking Points for Your Discussion*
> - "I've Gotta Be Me"
> - "My Way"
> - "Que Sera, Sera (Whatever Will Be, Will Be)"
> - "Only the Good Die Young"

B. Present Action (v. 10)

10. Therefore remove sorrow from thy heart, and put away evil from thy flesh: for childhood and youth are vanity.

There are two keys to the enjoyment of one's youth, according to Solomon, and they involve the *heart* and the *flesh*. The Hebrew word translated *sorrow* carries with it the idea of anxiety or fretfulness. Youth can be a time of restlessness, of yearning to experiment with life, to have the "things" others have, or—in the modern environment—to try all the pleasures promoted through all the media outlets. A better alternative is a contentment of spirit. That will allow one to use his or her time in much more productive activities than daydreaming the hours away.

Whereas *heart* may describe one's inner self, the term *flesh* could refer to one's actions or conduct. Again, with youth always seems to come the temptation to live on the edge or push the envelope—to sample all that this world has to offer while one has the physical capacity to do so. Yet that capacity can be greatly compromised and diminished by a love for the world and all it offers (1 John 2:15).

In truth, says Solomon, *childhood and youth are vanity.* The word *vanity,* in singular and plural, is used nearly 40 times in Ecclesiastes. It translates a Hebrew word that means "vapor" or "breath." This word describes something transient or swiftly passing, and therefore unable to provide genuine satisfaction (compare James 4:14). Of course, most young people will claim that life seems to drag along at a snail's pace. But youth passes all too quickly; and if one disregards Solomon's advice in this verse, the result will be an adulthood filled with remorse and regret. Thus the counsel of the next verse.

> *What Do You Think?*
> What sorrow or anxiety weighs heavily on your heart right now? How will you remove this?
>
> *Talking Points for Your Discussion*
> - Concerns about your church
> - Concerns about family members
> - Concerns about community or nation

II. Warnings About Aging
(Ecclesiastes 12:1-7)
A. In General Terms (v. 1)

1. Remember now thy Creator in the days of thy youth, while the evil days come not, nor the

years draw nigh, when thou shalt say, I have no pleasure in them.

The word *remember* means much more in the Old Testament than simply recalling something that has slipped one's mind. The word implies awareness of a person or a situation accompanied with a desire to act on behalf of the person or the situation. For example, Exodus 2:24 describes God's response to the cries of the Israelites in bondage with the word *remembered.* One should not think of God as suddenly "remembering" something He has forgotten: the enslaved Israelites after 400 years of bondage. Rather, the idea that He "remembered" indicates that He is on the verge of doing something to remedy their plight.

Here Solomon urges any young person to get serious about God early in life, *while the evil days come not.* The word translated *evil* in this context carries with it the idea of suffering or misfortune (as opposed to evil in a moral sense as in Ecclesiastes 11:10). Age brings with it numerous aches, pains, and limitations that are not present in one's younger days. The pleasure that one could receive from certain experiences is no longer attainable because the restrictions of age prevent participation in those experiences.

However, if a person chooses to "remember" the Creator while young, the discouragement that may result from the outward person growing weaker is offset by the reality that the inward person is being "renewed day by day" (2 Corinthians 4:16).

Remember your Creator.
— ECCLESIASTES 12:1, NIV

Visual for Lesson 7. *Point to this visual as you ask your learners to share ways they have found useful for remembering the Creator.*

B. In Specific Terms (vv. 2-7)

2. While the sun, or the light, or the moon, or the stars, be not darkened, nor the clouds return after the rain.

At this point, Solomon begins to employ a series of word pictures to describe the onset of old age. The end of a typical day is used to depict the end of a person's life. That *the clouds return after the rain* suggests circumstances in which one "storm" follows another; that is, old age tends to be characterized by increasing afflictions and challenges that can make even the sunniest day seem foreboding and difficult.

3a. In the day when the keepers of the house shall tremble.

Solomon's word picture changes. The coming of old age now is compared with a house showing signs of aging. Likening the human body to a building is done elsewhere in the Scriptures (Job 4:18, 19; 2 Corinthians 5:4; 2 Peter 1:13, 14). Solomon's descriptions suggest how aging affects various parts of the body. *The keepers of the house* may refer to hands and arms, which are crucial for defending one's self. Now they tremble, unable to provide the steadiness that they once did.

3b. And the strong men shall bow themselves, and the grinders cease because they are few, and those that look out of the windows be darkened.

Other physical consequences of old age complete this verse. That *the strong men shall bow themselves* likely pictures the loss of upright posture that often accompanies growing old. *Grinders* are teeth, which become *few* as time goes on (the correctives provided by modern dentistry are of course not available in Old Testament times). The increasing loss of eyesight is captured by the phrase *those that look out of the windows be darkened.*

4. And the doors shall be shut in the streets.

The doors of the house being *shut* likely pictures the decreased activity of old age. Older people may not go out in public, out *in the streets,* as often as they once did for several reasons. Besides the aforementioned physical limitations, which make such activity ever more difficult, there is a hesitancy to venture out in inclement weather or after dark when one's vision is not as clear.

4b. When the sound of the grinding is low, and he shall rise up at the voice of the bird.

The sound of the grinding is low may refer to how one's hearing weakens with age. At the same time, an older person *shall rise up at the voice of the bird*. This may describe how the slightest noise during the night may awaken an individual. Then, perhaps because of uncertainty as to the source of the sound, the individual finds it nearly impossible to go back to sleep. The phrase may also describe how early some older people awaken (as in the phrase "waking up with the chickens").

4c. And all the daughters of musick shall be brought low.

Daughters of musick is literally, in the Hebrew, "daughters of song." This may be another way of describing increased loss of hearing, or it may refer to the weakening of one's voice with age.

The limitations that Solomon portrays should be kept in mind by today's church in its ministry to "senior saints." For example, those up front should make certain that they speak loudly enough to be heard or are provided with voice amplification. Activities specifically for seniors should usually not be scheduled after dark because many seniors hesitate to go out at night.

5a. Also when they shall be afraid of that which is high, and fears shall be in the way.

With increased age often comes an apprehension about doing risky things, such as climbing *that which is high* (a fear of heights). The phrase *fears shall be in the way* describes anything that may make older people reluctant to venture outdoors in public. These can include the fear of falling or of embarrassment at being unable to see or hear something going on around them.

> **What Do You Think?**
> What risks are you less likely to take as you grow older? Does this indicate a lack of faith? Why, or why not?
> *Talking Points for Your Discussion*
> - Physical risks
> - Work-related risks
> - Financial or investment risks
> - Emotional risks

Bathsheba	Bath-*she*-buh.
Ebenezer	*Eb*-en-***ee***-zer.
Ecclesiastes	Ik-*leez*-ee-***as***-teez
Eos	*Heh*-ohs.
Solomon	*Sol*-o-mun.
Tithonus	Tith-oh-*nus*.
Zeus	Zoose.

5b. And the almond tree shall flourish, and the grasshopper shall be a burden.

Solomon resumes his description of the physical characteristics that come with age. Blossoms of the almond tree have a silvery-gray appearance, perhaps symbolic of the gray hair of old age. The phrase *the grasshopper shall be a burden* likely pictures the slower, stiffer movements of the elderly.

5c. And desire shall fail.

The Hebrew text here reads literally, "the caperberry fails." This fruit is considered in Old Testament times to stimulate sexual desire. That too may diminish with age.

5d. Because man goeth to his long home, and the mourners go about the streets.

Once the various stages of aging have occurred in a person's life, death cannot be far away. At that point, says Solomon, *man goeth to his long home*, a phrase that describes the permanence of death. As David so touchingly stated after the death of his and Bathsheba's infant son, "I shall go to him, but he shall not return to me" (2 Samuel 12:23).

A statement such as Solomon's in this verse can be seen as highly pessimistic, offering little hope of life beyond the grave. But that is not part of Solomon's concern here. His primary focus is on making this present life count the most—before a person has no more opportunity to do so. Mourners will lament an individual's passing, but they cannot bring him or her back from the grave.

6. Or ever the silver cord be loosed, or the golden bowl be broken, or the pitcher be broken at the fountain, or the wheel broken at the cistern.

Solomon returns to the imagery he has been using to describe the effects of aging, although here the meaning of the figures of speech is a bit harder to determine. Some students suggest that certain bodily functions are being pictured (as in the previous verses). If so, the *silver cord* may represent the spinal cord, the *golden bowl* is the brain, the *pitcher* is the heart, and the *wheel* stands for the circulatory system.

On the other hand, the terms may be describing items that are valuable or useful but also fragile. Some suggest that the golden bowl refers to the reservoir of oil in a lamp that allows the flame to burn. The lamp is pictured as suspended by a silver cord or chain. If that cord is broken, the lamp in turn will break and be useless. The terms *pitcher* and *wheel* depict the process of obtaining water in Old Testament times. The wheel is attached to a rope, serving as a kind of pulley that, when attached to a bucket, allows a person to lower the bucket into a cistern and fill it with water. When either the pitcher or the wheel is broken, one cannot draw water.

Still other commentators suggest that Solomon's words in this verse depict the cessation of daily activities that accompanies death. The dead do not light lamps or gather water. Whatever the specific meaning of Solomon's words, the gist of his message is in keeping with the overall thrust of this passage: this life will end at some point. One must prepare now so that he or she will have no regrets when that day comes.

7. Then shall the dust return to the earth as it was: and the spirit shall return unto God who gave it.

It is at death that *shall the dust return to the earth*. Such a statement reminds us of the creative act that brought humanity into existence (Genesis 2:7) and also of the punishment that God pronounced upon humanity following the sin in the Garden of Eden (Genesis 3:19). It is at death that *the spirit shall return unto God who gave it*. Apparently this is for the purpose of facing the judgment that Solomon has already alluded to in our text (Ecclesiastes 11:9) and to which he will refer at the book's conclusion, as we will see shortly.

We should not be overly concerned about the lack of any reference here to a resurrection of the body. One must remember that this statement is made *before* the time of Jesus and the impact of

His death and resurrection. The New Testament offers a clearer understanding of these matters—one that Solomon, despite his legendary wisdom, did not possess. It will be up to the one "greater than Solomon" (Matthew 12:42) to shed additional light on the afterlife.

What Do You Think?
Is it possible or realistic to "live each day as if it were your last"? Why, or why not?
Talking Points for Your Discussion
- In terms of sharing your faith
- In terms of "making arrangements"
- In terms of employment

❧ *WHAT DEATH RESULTS IN* ❧

Greek mythology tells a story of Eos, the goddess of the dawn. According to the myth, Eos loves Tithonus, a human, so she asks Zeus to allow Tithonus to live forever. The wish is granted, and they have a happy life for a time.

But as Tithonus grows older, his human body becomes so feeble he can no longer move. Yet he cannot die because Zeus has given him the gift of immortality. Eos forgot to ask Zeus to grant eternal youth to Tithonus along with eternal life! Such are the errors and foibles of mythical "gods."

Death is a sad reality. It is a punishment imposed by God for sin (Genesis 2:17). We appreciate modern medicine, which helps us live longer, healthier lives. But modern medicine cannot halt the aging process entirely. And is there anyone who really would like to live forever in a body that never stops aging, a body that becomes ever more frail with the passing years? Death must happen so that our spirits can return to God.

—C. R. B.

III. Wisdom for All
(ECCLESIASTES 12:13)

13. Let us hear the conclusion of the whole matter: Fear God, and keep his commandments: for this is the whole duty of man.

With this, the next to last verse in Ecclesiastes, comes *the conclusion of the whole matter*—the last word after all of Solomon's experiences, questions,

Growing Old with Wisdom

and reflections. Our duty, our purpose or reason for living on this earth, is to *fear God, and keep his commandments*. Apart from God, life has no purpose or reason.

The book's final verse, though not a part of today's printed text, reaffirms the reality of final judgment. Those who choose to ignore their Creator and live this life on their own terms will be confronted with their deeds on the Day of Judgment. It is an appointment all must keep.

> **What Do You Think?**
> How does a healthy fear of God influence your daily decisions? How will you improve in this area?
> *Talking Points for Your Discussion*
> - Attitude (Matthew 18:33; 1 Peter 4:1)
> - Discernment (Matthew 12:33; John 2:24)

❧ *Doing Our Duty* ❧

When you hear or see the word *duty,* is your immediate reaction positive or negative? My guess is that most people see this word in a negative light. Doing one's *military duty* can result in getting killed. Serving *jury duty* may involve a lot of waiting around in a courthouse, hoping you won't get called to hear a case that involves one of society's bottom-feeders. Being assigned to *kitchen clean-up duty* at church camp is, well, just that!

In such cases, the word *duty* implies an obligation to do something—an obligation imposed on us by someone else. A "what's in it for me?" culture has a negative attitude toward duty. But when we fulfill our duty to "fear God, and keep His commandments," there is indeed something in it for us: the approval of God!

Jesus himself had something to say about duty (see Luke 17:10). He himself lived a life of duty, as witnessed by the surrender of His will to the Father as the reality of the cross loomed (Luke 22:42). At the end of the Preacher's (Solomon's) quest for truth, he came to the realization that we are made to glorify God and live by His standards. Although this is a duty, it is not burdensome (Matthew 11:30). And there is definitely "something in it for me"!   —C. R. B.

Conclusion
A. Solomon and Scrooge

Solomon's warnings about the coming of old age and eventual death may be compared with the warnings Ebenezer Scrooge received from Jacob Marley's ghost in the Charles Dickens classic *A Christmas Carol*. Scrooge, a selfish, miserly wretch, is warned one night by the ghost of Marley (his former business partner) that three spirits were to visit him. Scrooge encounters these visitors as promised. As a result of what the visitations tell Scrooge about himself, he becomes a changed man and learns how to "keep Christmas" truly.

Solomon's warnings at the close of Ecclesiastes do not include promises of any visits by spirits. But the warnings he does give should be sufficient to cause us to take stock of our lives and acknowledge our Creator while we are still in a position to do so. The fact is, someday I will come face to face with an individual who will remind me of the choices I made in life, whether good or bad. And that individual will be—me! Unless something happens to prevent me from reaching old age, I will experience the physical changes described by Solomon in today's text. Modern medical advances may help to slow down some of the processes, but those problems will come my way just the same.

What will it be like when I face that future version of me? Will I be grumpy or gracious, crabby or congenial, a burden or a blessing? The answer depends on whether I daily face someone else: the Creator in whose image I was made and who alone knows what is best for me. Only when I follow His directions will I be able to look my future self in the eye—with no regrets.

B. Prayer

Father, thank You that no matter what age or stage of life we are in, Your promises remain true. As changes come, keep us focused on what is changeless. Keep us fixed, not on what is seen, but on what is unseen. In Jesus' name, amen.

C. Thought to Remember
Growing old gracefully is possible only with the help of God's grace.

INVOLVEMENT LEARNING

Some of the activities below are also found in the helpful student book, Adult Bible Class.
Don't forget to download the free reproducible page from www.standardlesson.com to enhance your lesson!

Into the Lesson

Write *LOSE* and *GAIN* as headings on the board. Ask learners to give examples of things we lose and gain as we get older. Jot their suggestions under the appropriate heading. Examples of losses: hair, teeth, mental sharpness; examples of gains: knowledge, weight, and debt.

If no one else does so, be sure to mention *wisdom*. Ask learners which column wisdom fits under. This should lead the class to reflect on whether it is true that wisdom comes with age. Ask, "Do some people make increasingly unwise decisions as they age?" To enhance discussion, describe a scenario where a seemingly stable man reaches midlife and begins to make inappropriate, sinful decisions, such as abandoning his wife for a younger woman. Ask, "Why do some people have the quality of wisdom and others lack it?"

Into the Word

Say, "In today's lesson, the writer of Ecclesiastes reflects on the effects of aging and tells us how to age with wisdom. The author will use some vivid imagery to compare the effects of aging on the human body with pictures from nature and daily life." Read through the text verse by verse, pausing to ask for learners' suggestions of what each image refers to; see the lesson commentary for probable references. Ask, "What alternative images could Solomon have used if he were writing today?" (Examples: difficulty getting a cell phone signal for loss of hearing; bald tires for unsteady legs.)

Focus the learners' attention on the writer's instructions to the young in verse 9. Ask these discussion questions: What is your reaction to the broad license the writer apparently gives to young people to follow their hearts wherever they lead? Would you feel comfortable giving your own children and grandchildren this much freedom? If judgment were not taken into account, what would be the results of this degree of liberty?

Tie the answers together by noting that at the end of the verse the writer tries to limit the negative repercussions by reminding young people that they will face judgment for how they use this freedom. Discuss with your class the merits of establishing rules-and-punishments versus motivating people to behave morally out of a personal sense of conscience. Compare and contrast the approaches that are appropriate for different age levels, for different relationships (one's own children versus others), and for different levels of spiritual maturity.

Into Life

Option 1. Download the reproducible page and distribute copies of The Bucket List activity. Give learners time to fill out their lists. If time allows, have learners share an item from their list with the class, but don't let this drag out. The discussion at this point may be lighthearted and humorous. Next, ask for volunteers to give their reactions to the "honesty check" that is part of this exercise. The discussion at this point may be serious and reflective. Encourage learners to share specific ideas of how they can make their bucket lists more meaningful in an eternal sense.

Option 2. Download the reproducible page and distribute copies of the Weak or Strong? activity. Have one volunteer read 1 Corinthians 1:27 and another read 2 Corinthians 12:10. As a class, brainstorm how each of the weaknesses listed in the activity (and from today's text) can be used by God as a strength. Learners who have already begun to experience some of these conditions may be able to share personal examples of how they have grown spiritually or have had opportunities for service they otherwise would not have had.

Follow up with a discussion about how you can ensure that older people in your church have opportunities to bless others with the unique gifts and perspectives that age brings.

FINDING TRUE LOVE

DEVOTIONAL READING: Genesis 2:18-24
BACKGROUND SCRIPTURE: Song of Solomon 4:1–5:1

SONG OF SOLOMON 4:8-16

8 Come with me from Lebanon, my spouse, with me from Lebanon: look from the top of Amana, from the top of Shenir and Hermon, from the lions' dens, from the mountains of the leopards.

9 Thou hast ravished my heart, my sister, my spouse; thou hast ravished my heart with one of thine eyes, with one chain of thy neck.

10 How fair is thy love, my sister, my spouse! how much better is thy love than wine! and the smell of thine ointments than all spices!

11 Thy lips, O my spouse, drop as the honeycomb: honey and milk are under thy tongue; and the smell of thy garments is like the smell of Lebanon.

12 A garden inclosed is my sister, my spouse; a spring shut up, a fountain sealed.

13 Thy plants are an orchard of pomegranates, with pleasant fruits; camphire, with spikenard,

14 Spikenard and saffron; calamus and cinnamon, with all trees of frankincense; myrrh and aloes, with all the chief spices:

15 A fountain of gardens, a well of living waters, and streams from Lebanon.

16 Awake, O north wind; and come, thou south; blow upon my garden, that the spices thereof may flow out. Let my beloved come into his garden, and eat his pleasant fruits.

SONG OF SOLOMON 5:1A

1a I am come into my garden, my sister, my spouse: I have gathered my myrrh with my spice; I have eaten my honeycomb with my honey; I have drunk my wine with my milk.

KEY VERSE

How fair is thy love, my sister, my spouse! how much better is thy love than wine! and the smell of thine ointments than all spices! —**Song of Solomon 4:10**

TRADITION AND WISDOM

Unit 1: Teaching and Learning
LESSONS 1–8

LESSON AIMS

After participating in this lesson, each student will be able to:

1. Describe how love is expressed in today's text.

2. Explain how the Song of Solomon helps us appreciate God's perspective on the love between husband and wife.

3. Write a prayer of commitment to accept the biblical perspective on love and reject the secular perspective.

LESSON OUTLINE

Introduction

A. A Song to Remember

It's happened to all of us. We hear a song on the radio or a jingle that goes with a TV commercial, and we just can't get it out of our heads. The tune keeps coming back to the point of being a nuisance. At some point, however, the melody gets pushed aside, replaced by more pressing matters.

The Song of Solomon (or Song of Songs as it is titled in the Hebrew text) has no melody to it. All we have are the words recorded in Scripture. The problem with this song, though, is not keeping it out of our minds, but getting it into our minds and giving proper attention to its message.

Because of the rather frank language within the book, Christians in many cases have avoided close study of it, and the church has been hesitant to teach or preach from it. One congregation's preacher decided he would prepare a series of messages from this book. He wanted the announcement in the bulletin to read, "Pray that God will help us to treat this book in a sacred manner." But a "typo" occurred (one of those that the spell-checker can't catch), and the announcement came out, "Pray that God will help us to treat this book in a *scared* manner."

The Song of Solomon is indeed a part of *sacred* Scripture. And there is nothing to be *scared* of. A close look at the Song's contents will reveal that its message is desperately needed in today's church and society.

B. Lesson Background

The Hebrew title "Song of Songs" identifies this song as the best or most outstanding song composed by Solomon. Since Solomon wrote 1,005 songs (1 Kings 4:32), to call this the "Song of Songs" is quite a commendation!

The theme of this book is the very special bond, designed by God, that exists in marriage between a man and a woman, particularly in the area of physical intimacy. Some interpreters have attempted to "spiritualize" the book's message, suggesting that the book is meant to portray God's love for His people and thus Christ's love for His bride, the church. There may be some applications of that kind that are warranted; whether these comprise the primary purpose of the book is subject to question. The greatest benefit from the Song of Solomon will be gained when Christians (particularly Christian couples) allow it to speak concerning that sacred relationship that God in His wisdom created a husband and wife to enjoy.

The authorship by Solomon, whose name appears several times in the book, may spark the question of how someone infamous for his 700 wives and 300 concubines (1 Kings 11:3) could know anything about genuine love. The answer depends in large part on one's interpretation of what is happening within the Song.

Commentators differ as to how many main characters are presented in the book. Some believe there are two: Solomon and the Shulamite maiden (Song of Solomon 6:13). Others suggest three: Solomon, the Shulamite maiden, and a young man (a shepherd) from whom Solomon is trying to woo the Shulamite so that she may become part of his harem. Under this second viewpoint, the Shulamite refuses Solomon's offer and chooses to give her devotion to the man she knows she loves. This "three-character view" is the position that will be reflected in the comments on today's Scripture text.

In many editions of the Song of Solomon, the reader will find headings throughout the text that designate a certain individual or individuals as speaking. Usually there are three such parties: the "beloved" (the woman), the "lover" (the shepherd whom she loves, in keeping with the suggested interpretation above), and a group of "friends"

HOW TO SAY IT

Abana	*Ab*-uh-nuh or Uh-*ban*-uh.
Deuteronomy	Due-ter-*ahn*-uh-me.
Hermon	*Her*-mun.
Jerusalem	Juh-*roo*-suh-lem.
Lebanon	*Leb*-uh-nun.
Naaman	*Nay*-uh-mun.
Pharpar	*Far*-par.
Shenir	*She*-nur.
Shulamite	*Shoo*-lum-ite.
Solomon	*Sol*-o-mun.

who may be viewed as members of Solomon's court. We should keep in mind that such headings are not part of the original Hebrew text. They simply reflect efforts on the part of translators or editors to identify a specific speaker or speakers. In truth, it is sometimes hard to know when one speaker's words end and another's begin.

The fact that the Shulamite refuses Solomon's overtures means that Solomon has recorded an account of a romantic failure on his part. Why would he do that? What would there be within such an account to merit it becoming the "Song of Songs" or the greatest of Solomon's songs? Perhaps one could consider the Song of Songs as similar in message to the book of Ecclesiastes. While Ecclesiastes teaches that life is best lived by recognizing and honoring one God, the Song teaches that the most satisfying human relationship is one man and one woman bound to each other for life (not in having many spouses as Solomon did).

I. Expressions of Love
(SONG OF SOLOMON 4:8-15)
A. Love's Longing (vv. 8, 9)

8. Come with me from Lebanon, my spouse, with me from Lebanon: look from the top of Amana, from the top of Shenir and Hermon, from the lions' dens, from the mountains of the leopards.

The previous verses of this chapter are filled with imagery used by the shepherd in complimenting the external beauty of his spouse (the Shulamite maiden). One cannot be certain if the shepherd and the Shulamite are indeed married at this point, or whether only a betrothal has occurred (which in biblical times is considered as binding as marriage).

Our first picture is that of the shepherd beckoning the woman he loves to *come . . . from Lebanon*. Lebanon is located in northern Palestine, some distance from Solomon's palace in Jerusalem. Mount Hermon is located in that region. Some believe that this was the mountain on which Jesus was transfigured.

Amana and Shenir are other mountain peaks in the same region. Shenir is equated with Hermon in Deuteronomy 3:9, though Shenir may be a part of the Mount Hermon range.

It is important to read a verse like this as love poetry. The woman is not literally located in these distant regions. The purpose of the language is to convey a sense of distance. The shepherd longs to be near the woman he loves; it seems she is miles away from him, and he wants that separation to end. Furthermore, he senses danger where the woman is; there are lions and leopards dwelling in the mountains. The shepherd longs to protect the Shulamite from any threats to her safety. Simply put, this man wants to be with the woman he loves so deeply.

❧ *AMANA* ❧

Amana is the name of a mountain, as noted above. From this peak come the sources of the Abana River, one of the two rivers to which Naaman referred when he resisted dipping in the Jordan River (2 Kings 5:12). He said that the waters of Abana and Pharpar were "better," probably with the idea of "purer."

Perhaps because of this association, a German religious colony that settled in Iowa in the 1850s called itself *Amana*. A communal colony, Amana practiced a close discipline over the lives of its members, bringing prosperity to its six villages. In the 1930s, the group formed a corporation to manufacture refrigerators, freezers, and later air conditioners. Thus the name *Amana* lives on in many modern homes.

But what about the biblical imagery of *Amana* living on in your heart? The reference in the text is to look from the heights of Amana. Views from mountaintops are exciting. One can get the sensation of being closer to God when on a mountaintop. Without "spiritualizing" the current verse too much, Jesus longs for His bride (the church) to be with Him. Can you think of a way to have a mountaintop experience with Him today, even without standing on a literal mountain?

—J. B. N.

9. Thou hast ravished my heart, my sister, my spouse; thou hast ravished my heart with one of thine eyes, with one chain of thy neck.

The shepherd now gives the reason why his beloved should descend from the mountainous regions and come to him: *Thou hast ravished my heart, my sister, my spouse.* He is smitten by her "ravishing" beauty—and it doesn't require much for that to happen! Just a glance from one of her eyes or at one chain of her neck, and he is overcome. James E. Smith notes that it is customary for an Eastern woman to unveil one of her eyes when addressing someone. "This would render visible some of the ornaments worn about the neck. The idea is that only a portion of her beauty has overpowered him."

The reference to the bride as a *sister* does not imply a sibling relationship, any more than terms like *father* or *son* necessarily imply a direct family relationship in Scripture. In some cases, *father* can be a term of respect or can be used to mean "ancestor," while *son* can mean "descendant." Here *sister* is simply a term of endearment or affection.

> *What Do You Think?*
> What are some "visual stimulations" you experience that result in your heart being captured by something? How do we distinguish between healthy and unhealthy visual stimulations?
> *Talking Points for Your Discussion*
> - Things made by God
> - Things made by people
> - Psalm 101:3; Luke 11:34

B. Love's Language (vv. 10-15)

10. How fair is thy love, my sister, my spouse! how much better is thy love than wine! and the smell of thine ointments than all spices!

The shepherd gives full expression to his emotions. The pleasure of the love that he and his spouse share outweighs any other earthly delight. Wine in Old Testament times is a source of refreshment (Psalm 104:15; Zechariah 10:7), though it certainly can be abused (Proverbs 23:29-35; Isaiah 5:11, 22). The fragrance of ointments or perfumes worn by the woman contributes to the shepherd's being overwhelmed. Fragrances have always been associated with romance, and it is so in biblical times.

11. Thy lips, O my spouse, drop as the honeycomb: honey and milk are under thy tongue; and the smell of thy garments is like the smell of Lebanon.

Kissing has always been part of the expression of romantic feelings. Here the shepherd uses the sweetness of the honeycomb to describe the pleasure experienced from the lips of his spouse. The mention of lips first, then the tongue, describes the increased intimacy shared by a romantic kiss.

The words *honey and milk* are associated with the description of the blessings found in the promised land (Deuteronomy 6:3, among many others). Here they reflect the shepherd's desire to enjoy the blessings that are experienced through shared intimacy with the woman he loves. One might say that just as arrival in the promised land ended the Israelites' wandering in the wilderness, the degree of love shared by this man and woman indicates that each has found true contentment in the other. No more searching or "wandering" is necessary.

The territory of Lebanon is often associated in Scripture with its renowned cedars (Psalm 92:12; 104:16; Ezekiel 27:5). That may be the fragrance described here.

12. A garden inclosed is my sister, my spouse; a spring shut up, a fountain sealed.

Garden imagery is frequently used within this book. This may be a way of affirming that romantic love reverses the disruption of the relationship between a man and a woman that is a consequence of what happened in the Garden of Eden (Genesis 3:16-19). To pick and eat the fruits of the garden represents the enjoyment of physical intimacy.

Also used in this verse is the picture of *a spring shut up, a fountain sealed*. The satisfaction of quenching one's thirst at a spring or fountain represents the satisfaction of one's longing for the kind of loving relationship that is possible only through the marriage of one man and one woman as designed by the Creator (Genesis 2:24). The spring being shut up and the fountain sealed likely implies a state of virginity. The shepherd will be the only one to "open" and "drink from" the fountain.

13. Thy plants are an orchard of pomegranates, with pleasant fruits; camphire, with spikenard.

These verses also picture the enjoyment of romantic love in terms of tasting *pleasant fruits* or savoring aromatic spices. The variety described highlights the abundance of pleasures to be experienced as the shepherd contemplates the beauty of his beloved. *Pomegranates* are mentioned in Song of Solomon 4:3 to describe the "temples" of the Shulamite (see also 6:7, 11; 7:12; 8:2). The fact that this fruit contains many seeds may represent an abundance of fruitfulness, thus once more calling attention to the many delights this woman has to offer.

Point to this visual as you ask learners to share examples of lifetime love in Christian marriages.

Camphire is a shrub whose flowers yield both a highly valued perfume and a dye that ranges in color from orange to yellowish red. It should not be confused with camphor, which has been used for medicinal purposes. Camphire is mentioned also in Song of Solomon 1:14.

Spikenard is a very costly perfume; its source is an aromatic oil extracted from the roots and stems of a plant that grows in northern India. This is the spice that Mary poured on Jesus' feet. The fact that it was contained in an alabaster box reflects the typical way to transport it in order to preserve its fragrance (Mark 14:3; John 12:3). It is mentioned earlier in Song of Solomon 1:12.

14. Spikenard and saffron; calamus and cinnamon, with all trees of frankincense; myrrh and aloes, with all the chief spices.

Perhaps this second mention of the costly spice *spikenard* reflects the exceptional nature of the pleasures the shepherd finds in the woman he loves. *Saffron* is a plant from the crocus family, valued for its aroma and its orange dye. *Calamus* describes a fragrant cane or reed found in India; the name also refers to the aromatic oil extracted from it. *Cinnamon* is a spice that is more familiar to us than most of the other items listed. In Old Testament times, it is imported from India.

Frankincense and *myrrh* are well known because of their association with the wise men who came to see Jesus. Frankincense is a fragrant gum obtained from the bark of a tree native to northern India

and Arabia (also mentioned in Song of Solomon 3:6; 4:6). Myrrh is a gum resin extracted from the bark of an Arabian shrub-like tree. The gum has been used as a perfume, for embalming, and as incense. Myrrh, cinnamon, and calamus are all used in making holy oil for the tabernacle (Exodus 30:22-25). Myrrh is also mentioned in Song of Solomon 1:13; 3:6; 4:6; 5:5, 13; Mark 15:23; and John 19:39.

Aloes comes from a tree that is native to India. Its wood contains a resin that has been prized for centuries. Aloes are used as a perfume for garments (note Psalm 45:8, where the context indicates its use for wedding garments). Like myrrh, aloes are used by Nicodemus in preparing the body of Jesus for burial (John 19:39). *All the chief spices* apparently describes other fragrances in addition to the ones listed; the phrase adds to the thought that the woman whom the shepherd loves is the source of an abundance of pleasures.

15. A fountain of gardens, a well of living waters, and streams from Lebanon.

Once more the imagery of water is used to picture the quenching of love's "thirst." *Streams from Lebanon* result from the melting snow on the mountains (referred to earlier in verse 8). These waters are especially cool and refreshing, as is the love that binds the shepherd with the Shulamite.

❧ THE POWER OF THE FIGURATIVE ❧

Garden is an interesting word in light of its cultural implications. As an American, when I hear the word *garden,* I first think of a vegetable garden. Yet when the British refer to a *garden,* they normally are talking about a flower garden. There is nothing inherently wrong in either reference, of course. It is just another reminder of the old observation that the British and Americans are two peoples separated by a common language!

The text refers to a garden (v. 12), to fruit trees and spices (vv. 13, 14), and to "a fountain of gardens" (v. 15). But to import into the text either an American or British sense of *garden* is to take things too literally. The figurative sense, which is what the author intends, is far more powerful. If you think about it, you'll understand why!

—J. B. N.

II. Excitement of Love

(Song of Solomon 4:16)

16. Awake, O north wind; and come, thou south; blow upon my garden, that the spices thereof may flow out. Let my beloved come into his garden, and eat his pleasant fruits.

These words are addressed by the Shulamite to her beloved (the shepherd). She is pictured as responding to the shepherd's pleas by calling on the winds to *blow upon my garden* so that the bounty of spices listed previously may yield their fragrance and attract the shepherd to be by her side. As her beloved one, he alone is to have access to her garden and to all of its aromas and fruits, all of which represent the intimacy that he and the Shulamite will share.

III. Experience of Love

(Song of Solomon 5:1a)

5:1a. I am come into my garden, my sister, my spouse: I have gathered my myrrh with my spice; I have eaten my honeycomb with my honey; I have drunk my wine with my milk.

Now the shepherd speaks again, responding to the invitation offered by the woman he loves. He is pictured as preparing to enjoy to the maximum all that his beloved has to give. She in turn is prepared to give it only to him and to no one else—not even to Solomon. Solomon, with his 700 wives and 300 concubines, can never know anything of this kind of one-man to one-woman relationship.

What Do You Think?

Which secular sources most influence modern understandings of what marriage and relationships should be? How can Christians be taught to evaluate these sources?

Talking Points for Your Discussion
- Evaluation of the source's worldview
- Evaluation of outcome
- Evaluation of consistency

Conclusion

A. Finding a Balance

The topic of sex seems to move toward one of two extremes. On the one hand, certain sectors of today's culture glorify sex to the point of making it a god. Sexual themes permeate television and movies, and very seldom is sex portrayed in the way God intended. A Christian perspective on sex is ridiculed as out of touch and restrictive to personal freedom.

On the other hand (and often this has been the case in Christian circles), the subject of sex is avoided out of embarrassment. As a result, young people who have legitimate questions about their bodies and emotions go to the secular world for insights after finding the church ill-equipped or unwilling to address such matters. The outcome is that often Christian relationships, marriages, and homes end up looking like their secular counterparts. An important means of witnessing to the world is therefore lost.

Consider that today's lesson is part of a quarter of studies that is dedicated to the theme of wisdom. In Proverbs 1:20, wisdom is described as proclaiming her voice "in the chief place of concourse, in the openings of the gates: in the city." Biblical wisdom is clearly not something restricted to men and women of great learning, locked inside their hallowed halls of ivy. Wisdom is "street smart"!

The Song of Solomon, as part of the Old Testament's "wisdom literature," fits perfectly with this perspective on wisdom. Biblical wisdom is not just for the "religious" setting; it is for the workroom, the classroom, and, says the Song of Solomon, the bedroom. In fact, all "rooms" of our lives (the bedroom included) are meant to reflect God's wisdom and in that way to be sanctuaries just as much as the places where we worship on Sunday.

B. Prayer

Father, help us not to compartmentalize our lives in such a way that we leave certain areas untouched by the lordship of Jesus. May we submit every area of life, even the most intimate, to Him whose beloved bride is the church. In Jesus' name, amen.

C. Thought to Remember

Seeking God's way first
makes a marriage last.

INVOLVEMENT LEARNING

Some of the activities below are also found in the helpful student book, Adult Bible Class.
Don't forget to download the free reproducible page from www.standardlesson.com to enhance your lesson!

Into the Lesson

Display pictures of men and women of different cultures and historical periods who are (or were) considered attractive. Good sources include books of classical art or sculpture, travel and fashion magazines, pictures from the Internet, or old high school yearbooks. Distribute these resources to the class and have them select humorous examples showing the extremes of human concepts of beauty. Ask the learners to describe their own hair or clothing styles that they thought looked good at one time, but remember today with a cringe.

Say, "We have all heard that 'beauty is in the eye of the beholder.' Is that statement true, or are there some things that are considered universally beautiful?" Learners might discuss spiritual qualities, dispositions of character, or healthy physical characteristics (lack of disease, physical functionality, etc.). Be sensitive in this discussion to those present who may not live up to all of these characteristics. Ask if class members can identify scriptural descriptions of timelessly beautiful characteristics (example: 1 Peter 3:4-6).

Into the Word

Share background commentary on Song of Solomon from the lesson writer's Introduction. Say, "Because the book is written in the form of a poetic dialogue between a man and a woman, we will read the text responsively with male and female speaking parts. The class will help decide which verses each gender will read." Divide the class into two groups, male and female. (If your class is solely male or female, ask for volunteers to read the part of the other gender.)

Before the responsive reading, each group should decide which verses are intended to be spoken by the male and which are by the female. Do not allow the two groups to coordinate with one another—each group must decide independently which verses it thinks it is to read.

After this deliberation, ask the class to begin reading the text aloud in unison. Group members will read the verses they believe are for their gender as the class gets to them. Expect confusion or hesitation at points as the two groups begin to speak at the same time.

Use the outcome as a launching point for a class discussion of such issues as the need for communication between the genders; the confusion and hurt that results from one spouse "speaking over" the other; the need to respect the different ways individuals express romantic feelings; etc.

Go back through the lesson text to share elements of the lesson commentary that your class will find of interest. *Option:* Bring to class samples of the various spices mentioned in the text, if you have access to them. Allow smelling and tasting as appropriate. Using objects that appeal to a variety of senses will assist your kinesthetic learners (people who learn best by engaging in a tactile activity).

Into Life

Download the reproducible page and distribute copies of The Spice of Life! activity. Allow learners time to find the hidden words. (*Option:* Turn this into a contest between small groups.) Invite learners to discuss whether they tend to see the good or the bad in others. Ask, "In what ways might we help bring out and emphasize the best in others this week?"

Alternative: Download the reproducible page and distribute copies of the Isn't She Lovely? activity. Allow learners time to complete their drawings. You may wish to do your own humorous drawing on the board. Allow learners to compare drawings. Ask, "Based on the text's description, does this woman sound beautiful or bizarre?" Follow this activity with a discussion about how to use art and poetic descriptions as aids for Bible study, worship, expressing love and appreciation, etc.

Finding True Love

SEEKING TRUE HAPPINESS

DEVOTIONAL READING: James 5:7-11
BACKGROUND SCRIPTURE: Matthew 5:1-16

MATTHEW 5:1-12

1 And seeing the multitudes, he went up into a mountain: and when he was set, his disciples came unto him:

2 And he opened his mouth, and taught them, saying,

3 Blessed are the poor in spirit: for theirs is the kingdom of heaven.

4 Blessed are they that mourn: for they shall be comforted.

5 Blessed are the meek: for they shall inherit the earth.

6 Blessed are they which do hunger and thirst after righteousness: for they shall be filled.

7 Blessed are the merciful: for they shall obtain mercy.

8 Blessed are the pure in heart: for they shall see God.

9 Blessed are the peacemakers: for they shall be called the children of God.

10 Blessed are they which are persecuted for righteousness' sake: for theirs is the kingdom of heaven.

11 Blessed are ye, when men shall revile you, and persecute you, and shall say all manner of evil against you falsely, for my sake.

12 Rejoice, and be exceeding glad: for great is your reward in heaven: for so persecuted they the prophets which were before you.

KEY VERSE

Blessed are they which do hunger and thirst after righteousness: for they shall be filled. —**Matthew 5:6**

TRADITION AND WISDOM

Unit 2: Jesus Teaches Wisdom

LESSONS 9–13

LESSON AIMS

After participating in this lesson, each student will be able to:

1. Identify key emphases of Jesus' teaching on blessedness.

2. Contrast the idea of "being blessed" with "being happy."

3. Identify one area where he or she has pursued "being happy" rather than "being blessed" and make a plan for change.

LESSON OUTLINE

Introduction

A. Defining Success

Have you ever attended a class reunion? Most of us feel nervous about seeing people from our past. We want to show that we are successful and happy. Sometimes people lose weight, buy a new car, etc., to make a better impression at a reunion. For a few hours they hope to create the impression that they have achieved the good life.

There is a big difference between looking successful for an evening and being successful in all of life. At the core of that difference is our definition of success. Only God, the creator of human life, can rightly define what a successful human life is. He defines our purpose, and so He declares what it means to achieve that purpose.

We can fairly say that the Bible's teaching on God's view of success comes to its climax in Jesus' teaching. As God's Son, Jesus lived out the epitome of a successful life on God's terms. His teaching reflected God's wisdom.

Nowhere do we see that better than in Jesus' statements about being *blessed,* the passage that we often call the Beatitudes. What Jesus describes does not necessarily make a good impression at a class reunion. But it describes the heart of success from God's point of view.

B. Lesson Background

Today's text comes near the beginning of Jesus' ministry in Matthew's Gospel. Matthew has presented Jesus as the great king who fulfills God's promises to His people (chapters 1, 2), declared to be God's own Son at His baptism (3:17), and victorious over the devil in His temptation (4:1-11). As Jesus returned from His temptation in the desert, He began to preach to the people with the message "Repent: for the kingdom of heaven is at hand" (4:17).

In Matthew, "the kingdom of heaven" means much more than being in God's presence after death. With this phrase Jesus was declaring that God was about to establish His reign over the whole world. The world's people had been in rebellion against God. God had allowed their rebellion, but Jesus declared that He was establishing God's rule on earth, where God's will is done just as it is in Heaven (Matthew 6:10).

So what does it mean to live under God's reign? That is the question answered by Jesus' Sermon on the Mount. For those ready to submit to His reign, this sermon describes how life is to be lived. It begins a description of a person who leads a successful life on God's terms in God's kingdom.

I. The Setting
(MATTHEW 5:1, 2)
A. Wide Angle (v. 1)

1. And seeing the multitudes, he went up into a mountain: and when he was set, his disciples came unto him.

Matthew describes the scene in a way that conveys its importance. Jesus' preaching about the coming of God's kingdom has already gathered large crowds that include hundreds or even thousands of people. A mountain setting may remind Jesus' hearers of God's giving the Law to Moses on Mount Sinai (Exodus 19). Now Jesus is presenting something like the Law of Moses, yet greater. This site may provide a natural amphitheater so that people can hear Jesus teach.

Matthew calls the crowd Jesus' *disciples*. This word means "follower" or "learner." Here it applies to all who seek to follow Him, not just to those such as Peter, Andrew, James, and John, to whom Jesus has extended a special invitation to follow (Matthew 4:18-22).

What Do You Think?

Why does God often seem to draw people out of their routines and into special settings to teach them spiritual truths? What personal example of this can you cite?

Talking Points for Your Discussion

- Avoiding distractions of life (Matthew 13:22)
- More receptive in crisis?
- God's qualities visible in nature (Romans 1:20)

B. Narrow Focus (v. 2)

2. And he opened his mouth, and taught them, saying.

HOW TO SAY IT

Babylon	*Bab*-uh-lun.
Hebrews	*Hee*-brews.
Isaiah	Eye-*zay*-uh.
Jerusalem	Juh-*roo*-suh-lem.
Judah	*Joo*-duh.
Moses	*Mo*-zes or *Mo*-zez.
Pietism	*Pie*-uh-*tih*-zim.
Sinai	*Sigh*-nye or *Sigh*-nay-eye.

This little phrase acts like a camera zooming in on one character in a movie. It focuses our attention closely on what Jesus is about to say. To this point in Matthew, readers have heard Jesus utter only a sentence or two at a time. Now He will speak continuously over three chapters.

II. Favor on the Needy
(MATTHEW 5:3-6)
A. Poor People (v. 3)

3. Blessed are the poor in spirit: for theirs is the kingdom of heaven.

Jesus begins the sermon with a series of statements about being *blessed*. We may find it hard to describe confidently what this word means. Some modern translations render it with the more familiar term "happy." But being blessed is more than happiness. It is to experience the approval and favor of God, to receive God's good gifts.

Thus, it makes sense for Jesus to begin His sermon about God's kingdom with statements about blessedness. Jesus' statements in this regard fall into three main categories: neediness, godliness, and persecution. Concerning the first of these, we may wonder how a person can be poor and at the same time be the recipient of God's blessing!

The answer seems to lie in the way that *the poor* are presented in the Old Testament. There we find repeated statements that God will act on their behalf (Psalms 35:10; 69:33; 113:7); at the same time, those who call on God for deliverance present themselves as "poor and needy" (40:17; 70:5; 86:1; 109:22). God promises deliverance to those who know their need and call out to Him for help.

Jesus' statement of blessing is specifically for *the poor in spirit*. They may indeed be poor materially: being in material need can teach us our helplessness. But their outlook is utter reliance on God's power regardless of their material circumstances. These are the people God has always promised to bless. Jesus' statement is an announcement that God's blessing on the needy is about to happen.

B. Sorrowful Sinners (v. 4)

4. Blessed are they that mourn: for they shall be comforted.

The theme sounded in the first beatitude is repeated in the second. To be in mourning seems to us the opposite of blessing, as does the poverty of verse 3. Again, we need to understand the Old Testament to understand the statement.

Six centuries before Jesus delivers the Sermon on the Mount, the Babylonians destroyed Jerusalem. God's prophets had warned Judah that this disaster was God's judgment for rebellion against God. But they promised that God would restore the nation after the exile (Isaiah 61:2, 3).

Babylon was conquered, and the exiled Jewish people were allowed to return to their homeland. But in many ways their captivity continued. Their nation remained weak. They were ruled by pagan empires. And the promised king had not appeared. This is the very situation of the Jewish people in Jesus' time, living under Roman rule.

What Jesus' audience mourns, then, is the ongoing "exiled" condition of the Jewish people. The loss that they grieve is the loss of nationhood that means the loss of God's favor on them. But if they truly understand their exile, then they mourn the sin that gave rise to it, the sin that is at the root of all that is wrong in the human condition. Yet the faithful still wait for God to bring the restoration that He has promised. That restoration will mean the reversal of sin and its effects.

Jesus' statement is an announcement that this promised restoration is beginning. God is about to change the exiled condition of His people. But He is about to do it not in outward political circumstances, but within their own lives and hearts. This will address the sin that makes people alienated from the life that God wants for them.

C. Humble and Hungry Humans (vv. 5, 6)

5. Blessed are the meek: for they shall inherit the earth.

The promise we see here, like the two before it, obviously depends on God's action. The only way that the meek, who by definition have no power, can *inherit the earth* is for God to give it to them.

Psalm 37:11 tells us that what Jesus says is not new. Neither is Jesus' statement about the meek a statement about a kind of personality. Rather, it is about a position that we voluntarily take. In God's kingdom, Jesus is king. But as king, Jesus surrenders His life. And by doing that, Jesus brings God's greatest power to bear on the world's greatest problem. No wonder, then, that Jesus promises those who willingly decline to assert their own rights or power that they will share God's rule!

> *What Do You Think?*
> What can we do if we realize we have pursued our Christian life in a self-reliant way?
> *Talking Points for Your Discussion*
> - 2 Chronicles 14:11
> - Psalm 27:14
> - Isaiah 50:10
> - 2 Corinthians 1:9

6. Blessed are they which do hunger and thirst after righteousness: for they shall be filled.

The focus on people in need continues. *Hunger and thirst* remind Jesus' Jewish audience of their ancestors' experience in the wilderness after God liberated them from slavery. God provided manna and brought water out of rocks. Their need was filled by God's own action. In generations since, Israel suffered times of drought and famine. Doubtless many in Jesus' audience know what it is to be hungry and thirsty.

But there is something beyond ordinary hunger and thirst of which Jesus speaks. Jesus had been tempted to provide food for himself miraculously, but had replied, "Man shall not live by bread alone, but by every word that proceedeth out of the mouth of God" (Matthew 4:4). In the wilderness, God had sought to teach Israel what Jesus repeated to Satan in the temptation and what

Jesus says in this beatitude: the thing for which we ought to be most hungry and most thirsty is not food and water but God's right way. Those who have longed to see God's way triumph in the world, beginning with their own lives, are those whom God will now bless.

III. Favor on the Godly
(MATTHEW 5:7-9)
A. Merciful Manner (v. 7)

7. Blessed are the merciful: for they shall obtain mercy.

God's mercy has an implication for those who receive it: they too must show mercy. If they don't, God's mercy can be withdrawn from them (James 2:13). Those who do not show mercy may thereby reflect that they have never really grasped God's mercy to them. Those who live under God's rule in His kingdom are under the mandate to become like the God who rules over them. Because God has been merciful to them, it is unthinkable that they should be unmerciful to others.

What Do You Think?

Why do some Christians find it easier to judge others rather than show mercy? How do we correct this problem?

Talking Points for Your Discussion

- Realizing one's own need for mercy (Matthew 7:3; 18:21-35)
- Oversimplifying the problems of others
- Thinking that mercy implies acceptance of sin (Luke 7:34)

B. Pure Heart (v. 8)

8. Blessed are the pure in heart: for they shall see God.

The Mosaic Law's rules about "clean" and "unclean" govern the lives of those in Jesus' audience. These regulations are designed to teach the people that their God, unlike the pagan gods, is utterly pure. So those who belong to Him must be pure themselves (Psalm 24:3, 4).

Now Jesus is stressing the real meaning of purity before God. In God's kingdom, God rules

Blessed!

Visual for Lesson 9. *Point to this visual as you ask each learner to state one way that he or she is blessed by God.*

both over things that can be seen by all and over things that God alone can see. Men may judge by outward appearances, but God judges the heart (1 Samuel 16:7). So in God's kingdom, purity must be not just on the outside but on the inside—in the heart where God alone sees (Mark 7:1-23).

That kind of purity is the goal of everyone who belongs to God's kingdom. People who know their own neediness will realize that they have not measured up to that standard of purity. So Jesus' statement reminds His followers that they continue to need mercy. Ultimately, their hearts will be pure only because God will make them pure by His gracious power. The blessing pronounced on the pure in heart is that they will *see God*.

❧ *PIETISM AND PURITY* ❧

Philip Jacob Spener was a Lutheran minister in the 1660s when he became concerned about the superficial level of Christianity among his congregants. He began to encourage them to attend home Bible studies during the week. Spener wanted people to realize that Christianity was something more than what was done one hour a week in the church building.

His weekly Bible study groups were soon called "pious groups." Out of this concept came the development of Pietism. Spener emphasized that the Bible ought to be the guidebook for daily living, not just a lucky talisman placed on the coffee table and dusted once a month. Christianity is more than head knowledge. Christianity is best exemplified in the practice of love. Even intellectual arguments ought to be geared toward winning the heart of the other person, not just scoring an intellectual victory over bad doctrine.

Spener was talking about a lifestyle focused on practical Christian living, a lifestyle reflected in purity of heart. This kind of purity is not just for outward show—it is for inward renewal. Those who experience it will have an outward demonstration of it, to be sure. But the major result will be that the person will see God in eternity.

—J. B. N.

C. Peace-loving Approach (v. 9)

9. Blessed are the peacemakers: for they shall be called the children of God.

From the beginning, God's promise has been to bring peace between himself and His rebellious people. That in turn means that His people will live at peace with each other (Hebrews 12:14). Describing this future, the prophets pictured a kingdom of harmony (Isaiah 11:1-9).

As Jesus announces the coming of God's kingdom, that promised peace is about to become real. God is establishing peace among His people, and so His obedient subjects must themselves become peacemakers (James 3:18). Their goal is harmony with one another just as God has established harmony between himself and them.

The blessing of this beatitude is to be called God's child. As God's people become the agents of His peace in the world, they reveal to the world who God really is. Being known as His children is their greatest honor.

> *What Do You Think?*
> What does it take to become a peacemaker? Are the secular techniques of "conflict resolution" useful? Why, or why not?
> *Talking Points for Your Discussion*
> - Psalm 51:17
> - Proverbs 15:1
> - Ephesians 4:2, 3
> - 1 Corinthians 1:10
> - Galatians 5:22-26

IV. Favor on the Persecuted
(MATTHEW 5:10-12)
A. Rejected and Attacked (v. 10)

10. Blessed are they which are persecuted for righteousness' sake: for theirs is the kingdom of heaven.

If God's kingdom is truly coming into the world, we would expect His people to enjoy complete tranquillity, right? After all, they are now blessed, are they not? But what Jesus offers here is blessing in the midst of persecution for following God's right way (1 Peter 3:14).

Even so, we wonder how those who pursue righteousness can be maltreated if God genuinely rules over His kingdom. The answer is part of the mystery that Jesus is revealing. The arrival of God's kingdom does not mean that the world is changed suddenly and dramatically. God establishes His rule in the human heart, calling people into His kingdom with the good news of Jesus. Yet evil remains active in the presence of such a kingdom. Thus, those who pursue righteousness may find themselves abused. Jesus reminds them that they are no less a part of God's kingdom when that happens.

After all, Jesus' own suffering and death are the pivotal acts that bring God's kingdom into the world. Jesus' followers can expect to experience similar treatment (John 15:20). But they have the assurance that God's kingdom will be victorious.

> *What Do You Think?*
> If someone does not experience persecution for the faith, does that mean something is lacking in his or her witness? Why, or why not?
> *Talking Points for Your Discussion*
> - Different kinds of persecution
> - The issue of different callings (1 Corinthians 12:4-11)
> - Testing that may or may not result in persecution (Esther 4:14)

B. Reviled and Accused (v. 11)

11. Blessed are ye, when men shall revile you, and persecute you, and shall say all manner of evil against you falsely, for my sake.

This verse expands the description of persecution in the previous one. But the description of the reason for the persecution shifts. In verse 10, Jesus spoke of persecution for the sake of righteousness. Here He speaks of persecution *for my sake*.

As far as Jesus is concerned, to be persecuted as His follower and to be persecuted for God's right way are exactly the same thing. Jesus is very clear on this point: He is the one who announces, defines, describes, and inaugurates God's kingdom. He is the king of God's kingdom. Those who heed His words will enjoy the blessings He describes. Those who do not will be excluded.

C. Rejoicing and Rewarded (v. 12)

12. Rejoice, and be exceeding glad: for great is your reward in heaven: for so persecuted they the prophets which were before you.

The statement about persecution is so surprising that Jesus responds with a special call to rejoice. No one wants to face persecution, but Jesus gives two reasons to understand it as a cause for rejoicing.

One reason is a great *reward in heaven*. No matter what happens to us in this present age, even death itself, God can overcome it with blessing as we enter His presence in the life to come.

The second reason to rejoice is that the persecuted followers of Jesus are like the persecuted prophets of the past (2 Chronicles 36:16; Acts 7:52). As we look at the great figures of the Bible, we notice that God's people have always suffered for their faith. Yet we see that God worked through their difficulties to accomplish His work (Hebrews 11:32-38). When we experience suffering for our faith, we have the same assurance that God can work through us as He did through them (James 5:10).

When we are ostracized or ridiculed because of our faith, we can remember Jesus' words. We can remember what we have in common with Christians around the world, many of whom suffer for their faith much more than we. We can remember what we have in common with the saints of old. And we can remember that we stand with the Lord himself, who was despised and rejected, dying on the cross on our behalf.

We may think of religious persecution as a thing of the distant past. In the early church, Christians were killed by the Romans. During the Reformation, Protestants were killed by Catholics, and to a somewhat lesser extent Catholics were killed by Protestants. Anabaptists were killed by both.

But not all religious killings took place in the distant past. Recently, Christians have been killed in India by fanatic Hindus. We see violence directed against Christians who live in countries dominated by Islam. At the time of this writing, major news sources are telling the story of a teenager who has converted to Christianity from Islam. She is afraid to return to her parents because under Islamic law they are expected to kill her.

The ultimate hope in this ugly picture is that those who experience persecution will also experience the blessedness of God's provision and His peace. Great will be their reward. —J. B. N.

Conclusion
A. The Good Life

If you or I were defining what makes for a good life, we probably would not begin with the qualities that Jesus names. Neediness, godliness, and persecution are not common signs of success. But in God's kingdom, these are the very things to which His people are called. We belong to Him because we know our need, not because we are strong. As those who belong to Him, we want to be like Him and act like Him. And we know that suffering in His cause simply marks us as people who genuinely belong to Him.

But a life like this is not easy! Were it not for the fact that we are led in this life by the Lord Jesus, we could not begin to undertake it. But by His power we can move out with confidence.

B. Prayer

Lord, we thank You for Your grace that calls us Your people and for Your power that enables us to live as Your people. In Jesus' name, amen!

C. Thought to Remember

Seek God's blessings as He defines them.

INVOLVEMENT LEARNING

Some of the activities below are also found in the helpful student book, Adult Bible Class.
Don't forget to download the free reproducible page from www.standardlesson.com to enhance your lesson!

Into the Lesson

Purchase a sheet of the inexpensive smiling-face stickers. Give one to each learner as he or she arrives; greet each with a cheery, "Happy Day to You!" Expect amused reactions. *Option:* Cut out a yellow circle large enough for a mask; prepare it as a "smiling face" and wear it as you do the above.

As class begins, ask, "Is this what happiness is—a smiling face, a cheery greeting?" Ask class members to give their own definitions of happiness. Some will comment on such matters as financial success, good health, absence of anxiety and distress.

Note that some translations of today's text use the word *happy* instead of *blessed.* Ask for explanations of the distinctions. If no one else does so, you can point out that the word more commonly translated *blessed* involves God's favor—favor that is not typically associated with the word *happy.*

Into the Word

Down the left-hand side of a handout, list each of the nine "Blessed are" statements of Matthew 5:3-12 (today's text) with its accompanying clause. Down the right, have the nine concluding statements in this order: "for they shall obtain mercy"; "for they shall inherit the earth"; "for they shall be called the children of God"; "for great is your reward in heaven"; "for theirs is the kingdom of heaven"; "for theirs is the kingdom of heaven"; "for they shall be comforted"; "for they shall see God"; "for they shall be filled." Ask learners to match the statements in the two columns without using their Bibles. When finished, invite everyone to check their accuracy using their Bibles. This will give a quick look at the wording of the familiar text.

Next, distribute handouts with the following paraphrases:

1. Blessed are those who are uncomfortably discontent in this world of sin and sinners, for they will know absolute righteousness.

2. Blessed are those who seek to reconcile men to one another and to God, for they will hear Him say, "My child!"

3. Blessed are those who sense the depth of their personal unworthiness, for they will be privileged to walk through the gates of Heaven.

4. Blessed are those who suffer indignity and harm because of their relationship to me, for they will one day have opportunity to laugh and be glad.

5. Blessed are the ones who grieve over personal and societal sin and the destruction it brings, for they will know the abiding presence of my Spirit.

6. Blessed are those who forsake spitefulness and cruelty to adopt grace and love, for they will be shown the full extent of God's mercy.

7. Blessed are those who show the strength of self-control in all things, for they will know the full joys of physical life . . . and of eternal life.

8. Blessed are those whose core values are untainted by guile and self-centeredness, for they will one day stand face to face with their Father.

9. Blessed are those who demonstrate holy behavior and are rebuked and attacked for it, for they will one day enter a place where holy behavior is all that will be seen, and it will be blessed.

Ask learners to match each paraphrase with the beatitude that comes closest to it. There are no exclusively "right" answers; your learners will probably make a good case for more than one answer for each. Go back through the paraphrases and ask how each may be inadequate in light of what Scripture actually says. Again, your learners may make a good case for more than one answer each.

Into Life

Download the reproducible page and distribute copies of the Blessed Am I activity. After learners fill it out, ask each to verbalize one of their entries. Distribute copies of the Blessed I Will Be activity as take-home work.

LIVING IN HARMONY WITH OTHERS

DEVOTIONAL READING: Psalm 32:1-5
BACKGROUND SCRIPTURE: Matthew 5:17-37

MATTHEW 5:17-26

17 Think not that I am come to destroy the law, or the prophets: I am not come to destroy, but to fulfil.

18 For verily I say unto you, Till heaven and earth pass, one jot or one tittle shall in no wise pass from the law, till all be fulfilled.

19 Whosoever therefore shall break one of these least commandments, and shall teach men so, he shall be called the least in the kingdom of heaven: but whosoever shall do and teach them, the same shall be called great in the kingdom of heaven.

20 For I say unto you, That except your righteousness shall exceed the righteousness of the scribes and Pharisees, ye shall in no case enter into the kingdom of heaven.

21 Ye have heard that it was said of them of old time, Thou shalt not kill; and whosoever shall kill shall be in danger of the judgment:

22 But I say unto you, That whosoever is angry with his brother without a cause shall be in danger of the judgment: and whosoever shall say to his brother, Raca, shall be in danger of

the council: but whosoever shall say, Thou fool, shall be in danger of hell fire.

23 Therefore if thou bring thy gift to the altar, and there rememberest that thy brother hath ought against thee;

24 Leave there thy gift before the altar, and go thy way; first be reconciled to thy brother, and then come and offer thy gift.

25 Agree with thine adversary quickly, whiles thou art in the way with him; lest at any time the adversary deliver thee to the judge, and the judge deliver thee to the officer, and thou be cast into prison.

26 Verily I say unto thee, Thou shalt by no means come out thence, till thou hast paid the uttermost farthing.

KEY VERSES

If thou bring thy gift to the altar, and there rememberest that thy brother hath ought against thee; leave there thy gift before the altar, and go thy way; first be reconciled to thy brother, and then come and offer thy gift. —**Matthew 5:23, 24**

Photo: SWP, incorporated

TRADITION AND WISDOM

Unit 2: Jesus Teaches Wisdom

LESSONS 9–13

LESSON AIMS

After participating in this lesson, each student will be able to:

1. Describe Jesus' teaching on anger and reconciliation as fulfillments of God's purpose for humanity.

2. Relate Jesus' teaching on anger and reconciliation to the gospel theme of forgiveness.

3. Explain how he or she plans to place a high priority on practicing reconciliation.

LESSON OUTLINE

Introduction
  A. Extrovert or Introvert?
  B. Lesson Background
 I. Fulfilling the Law (MATTHEW 5:17-20)
  A. No Part Contradicted (v. 17)
  B. Every Part Completed (v. 18)
   Amending the Law
  C. Obedience Commanded (v. 19)
  D. Righteousness Commended (v. 20)
 II. Obeying the Law (MATTHEW 5:21, 22)
  A. What You Have Heard (v. 21)
  B. What I Say (v. 22)
 III. Pursuing Reconciliation (MATTHEW 5: 23-26)
  A. Harmony Restored (vv. 23, 24)
   Be Reconciled
  B. Conflict Resolved (vv. 25, 26)
Conclusion
  A. Mercy Received; Mercy Offered
  B. Prayer
  C. Thought to Remember

Introduction

A. Extrovert or Introvert?

Do you consider yourself an extrovert or an introvert? Do you prefer to be around other people or alone? Does being with other people give you energy, or does it sap your energy?

Psychologists say that most people are introverts: interacting with others tires them out. Even many who earn their living by working directly with other people—teachers, managers, counselors, ministers—are often introverts. Those of us who think of ourselves as introverts probably secretly envy the extroverts. We wish that we had their ability to deal easily with people.

But if we hear from the extroverts, they will confess that they have just as much friction and conflict with others as do the introverts. In fact, extroverts may have more intense conflicts than do introverts!

The success of our relationships with others is not just a matter of our personality type. It goes much deeper. The Bible shows us what our daily experience shows us: that where people interact, they experience conflict. As far as the Bible is concerned, that conflict exists as a result of human sin. Our rebellion against God puts us in conflict not just with God, but with each other.

Jesus' message in the Sermon on the Mount (Matthew 5–7) is that God's kingdom, the establishment of God's reign over the entire world, changes all our most important values and experiences. High on that list is human relationships. Just as God is reconciling the rebellious world to himself through Jesus, so those who have been reconciled to Him will bring an end to their conflicts with others and seek genuine reconciliation.

B. Lesson Background

Jesus' Sermon on the Mount answered the question prompted by Jesus' declaration regarding the nearness of God's kingdom: How are people to live under God's rule? As part of that sermon, this passage follows Jesus' statements about who receives blessing in God's kingdom (Matthew 5:1-12, last week's lesson) and His famous sayings about His disciples being salt and light in the world (5:13-

Living in Harmony with Others

16). These statements tell us that God is taking weak, lowly people and transforming them to become His agents to change the world, bringing the world into submission to His will.

Of prime importance under God's rule are human relationships. So Jesus turns to that theme in this passage as the first example of how God's will is to be put into practice in His kingdom.

I. Fulfilling the Law
(Matthew 5:17-20)

A. No Part Contradicted (v. 17)

17. Think not that I am come to destroy the law, or the prophets: I am not come to destroy, but to fulfil.

Jesus' Sermon on the Mount sounds radical to His audience, just as it does to us today. Some of His statements seem to contradict common sense, and many directly contradict ideas taught by respected religious leaders of the first century. To some, His teaching sounds like a contradiction of God's Word as expressed in the Law of Moses and the books of the prophets.

So Jesus assures us that He offers no contradiction of God's Word. Jesus affirms that God's Word given through Moses and the prophets is indeed sacred and good. In fact, Jesus says that He personally brings real fulfillment of God's Word.

B. Every Part Completed (v. 18)

18. For verily I say unto you, Till heaven and earth pass, one jot or one tittle shall in no wise pass from the law, till all be fulfilled.

The Law and the Prophets are books given to Israel in their ancient language of Hebrew. The Hebrew alphabet is very different from our own. The *jot* refers to a certain small character formed

HOW TO SAY IT

Aramaic	*Air*-uh-**may**-ik.
Gehenna	Geh-*hen*-uh (G as in get).
Hinnom	*Hin*-um.
Raca	*Ray*-kuh or Ray-*kah*.
Sanhedrin	*San*-huh-drun
	or San-*heed*-run.

out of a single line; the *tittle* is a tiny, horn-shaped curve on the corner of a letter. These are the smallest strokes of a pen one finds in a scroll of the Scriptures (compare Luke 16:17).

Jesus' point is to picture vividly the fulfillment of everything that God has placed in His Word. Nothing that God has planned or promised in His Word will fail to be fulfilled. In light of the previous verse, Jesus' implication is that He himself is the one who will bring all to fulfillment.

The nature of that fulfillment, however, may be very different from what people are expecting. Jesus is challenging His listeners to set aside their preconceptions and hear what He has to say, considering it as the true fulfillment of God's law.

❧ *Amending the Law* ❧

I am amused by some people's argument that the U.S. personal income tax is unconstitutional. They point out that the original U.S. Constitution, drafted in 1787, declares in Article I, Section 2, clause 3 that direct taxes are to be apportioned among the states according to population. This is seen as prohibiting a tax on personal incomes, since all direct taxes are to be apportioned among the states based on population, not income levels.

However, the Sixteenth Amendment, ratified in 1913 per provisions of Article V, allows congress to levy a tax on incomes without respect to apportionment among the states. Since the amendment follows the procedures in the Constitution, it is just as constitutional as the rest of the document.

That's how human law works. Sometimes we add, sometimes we subtract. Article V of the U.S. Constitution specifies the process for making such changes to that document. But there is no such amendment process when it comes to God's law. Jesus declared that nothing was to be subtracted from that law. But do we, in effect, end up "adding to" or "subtracting from" God's law by the way we rationalize our conduct? —J. B. N.

C. Obedience Commanded (v. 19)

19. Whosoever therefore shall break one of these least commandments, and shall teach men so, he shall be called the least in the kingdom of heaven: but whosoever shall do and teach them,

the same shall be called great in the kingdom of heaven.

As we read through Old Testament biblical history, we see that God's will is continually disobeyed by rebellious humans. The breaking of God's commandments began in the Garden of Eden, and it continues in every age and every place.

But under God's promised rule within *the kingdom of heaven* (as it is called in Matthew), God's will, expressed in His commandments, will be obeyed truly. What God has always intended people to be and to do is to be realized under His promised rule. So those who do and teach the true will of God are the greatest under God's rule. They are putting into practice what God's will is, and they are enabling others to do so as well.

By contrast, those who teach otherwise are least in God's rule. Jesus is subtly but clearly warning that His teaching about the fulfillment of God's commandments is going to sound very different from what people hear from other religious teachers. He is challenging them—and us—to listen to Him instead of to others. After listening to Him, we are to join Him in making known to others what the true will of God is.

What Do You Think?

What does Jesus' declaration tell us about how or if we should teach the Old Testament law in the New Testament era?

Talking Points for Your Discussion

- Purpose of the Old Testament law (Galatians 3:19-25)
- Relationship between the Old Testament law and the law of Christ (Galatians 6:2)
- Relationship between the Old Testament law and the law of the Spirit (Romans 8:2)

D. Righteousness Commended (v. 20)

20. For I say unto you, That except your righteousness shall exceed the righteousness of the scribes and Pharisees, ye shall in no case enter into the kingdom of heaven.

Now Jesus draws the contrast even more sharply between His teaching and the teaching of others. And those "others" are among the most prominent religious figures of His time! *Scribes* are experts in the Law of Moses and the Prophets; their knowledge of the law is regarded as unsurpassed. *Pharisees* are members of a particular Jewish religious party in Jesus' day; they emphasize a set of traditions about observing the Law of Moses, saying that if people follow those traditions, they will be protected from violating God's commandments.

Of all Jesus' contemporaries, the Pharisees are probably the most widely respected religiously. Their meticulous development of traditions about the law marks them as very devoted to it—as especially "righteous" as people observe them. But Jesus says that those who belong to God's kingdom need a righteousness even greater than that of the most meticulous observers of God's Word! How can such a thing be possible?

Jesus' statement is a double-edged sword: it cuts two ways. First, He has just informed everyone that their greatest need is for God's mercy (Matthew 5:7). If belonging to God's kingdom demands righteousness greater than that of the most respected people, then no one can belong to God's kingdom on the basis of personal righteousness (otherwise mercy would not be needed). Realizing that, people can turn only to God and ask for mercy. They must become "poor in spirit" (Matthew 5:3).

But the statement cuts another way. The scribes and Pharisees have studied the law carefully and seek to obey it meticulously. But in doing so, do they really understand what God wants? The "seven woes" of Matthew 23 establish that they do not. God wants not just outward obedience that everyone can see, but also inward obedience, where God alone can see. If God truly rules in God's kingdom, then He rules even where others cannot see: within the human heart.

What Do You Think?

How do Christians try to achieve spirituality today? Which methods are legitimate and which are not?

Talking Points for Your Discussion

- The issue of sincerity
- The issue of zeal

Living in Harmony with Others

II. Obeying the Law
(MATTHEW 5:21, 22)

A. What You Have Heard (v. 21)

21. Ye have heard that it was said of them of old time, Thou shalt not kill; and whosoever shall kill shall be in danger of the judgment.

Jesus now turns to an example of true righteousness and fulfillment of God's law. We might think that Jesus is about to contrast His teaching with the Law of Moses itself. After all, Jesus quotes the commandment, "Thou shalt not kill" (Exodus 20:13; Deuteronomy 5:17).

But the way Jesus introduces this statement is important: *Ye have heard,* not "it is written." Jesus is not making a contrast between His teaching and the Law of Moses, but between His teaching and what others teach or practice about the Law of Moses. It is the interpretation of the law, not the law itself, with which Jesus makes a contrast.

B. What I Say (v. 22)

22a. But I say unto you, That whosoever is angry with his brother without a cause shall be in danger of the judgment.

What Jesus says in this verse is not that the Law of Moses is wrong to condemn murder. Rather, what is seriously wrong is thinking that merely avoiding murder guarantees that one is righteous. Since God rules over everything in His kingdom, then He rules over both what can be seen (murder, violence, etc.) and over what cannot be seen (attitudes of the heart, like anger and hatred).

Jesus develops His statement in three parts. In the first, the issue is to be *angry . . . without a cause.* Of course, most people who are angry believe that they have a very good cause! But in the Sermon on the Mount, Jesus' warning is based on the truth that judgment ultimately belongs to God alone (Matthew 7:1, 2). To be angry "with cause" means to reflect the wrath of the holy God against the sinful world. But as we do that, we also recognize that we are sinners and so are subject to that same judgment ourselves. If our anger is "with cause," we realize that we are not in a position to condemn others, and so our anger is tempered. Passages such as Matthew 7:15-20 and 1 Corin-

Point to this visual as you ask, "How is true righteousness different from legalistic righteousness?"

thians 5 imply a legitimate judging function. But to judge others of things we ourselves are guilty is to see the mote in another's eye while ignoring the beam in our own (Matthew 7:3).

What Do You Think?

What issues should we become angry about, if any? How should that anger be expressed?

Talking Points for Your Discussion

- Things that make God angry (Exodus 4:14; Hebrews 3:10)
- Biblical guidelines for anger (Ephesians 4:26; James 1:19, 20)
- Speaking truth in love (Ephesians 4:15)

22b. And whosoever shall say to his brother, Raca, shall be in danger of the council.

The second part of the statement uses an expression from the Aramaic language. *Raca* is nearly a swear word in that language, implying "empty-headed." Jesus notes that when we insult another person with such a term, we are speaking of someone who, like us, is created in God's image. The person who speaks this way is said to be subject to *the council.* That term suggests the Sanhedrin, which in Jesus' time is the chief religious and judicial body of Judaism. The implication is that a person who speaks of another this way is as guilty before the court as if committing murder.

22c. But whosoever shall say, Thou fool, shall be in danger of hell fire.

The third part of the statement brings Jesus' saying to a climax. To call someone a fool in Jesus' culture is to imply that the person is ignorant of God (Psalm 14:1). In other words, it is to stand in judgment of another's relationship with God and pronounce the person excluded from God's people.

Jesus turns the tables on this statement: the person who presumes to judge what only God can judge is subject to the severest form of judgment. *Hell fire* translates an expression that had become a byword in Jesus' time. The Valley of Hinnom (or Gehenna) is a place near Jerusalem where garbage is dumped and where fires burn it constantly. That image had become a way of describing the punishment that God brings on the wicked.

Jesus does not argue His points from Israel's Scriptures, although He could do so. He simply says, "But I say unto you." In God's kingdom, Jesus speaks with all authority. Those who recognize that fact will seek to be righteous inside and out. They will put their confidence in God's perfect judgment to bring justice where it is due.

III. Pursuing Reconciliation
(MATTHEW 5:23-26)

A. Harmony Restored (vv. 23, 24)

23. Therefore if thou bring thy gift to the altar, and there rememberest that thy brother hath ought against thee.

If judging others presumptuously is excluded in God's kingdom, then what should people do with conflict? The answer is to do what God has done: seek reconciliation and restored harmony. God has made it His first priority to be reconciled to rebellious people. So those who have been reconciled to Him are to have that same priority and seek reconciliation with others.

Jesus makes this priority clear with a comparison that begins in this verse. A person with a gift on the altar is making a sacrifice to honor God, even to seek forgiveness of sin. For the people of Israel, there is no more solemn and sacred act. But Jesus imagines that a person who is doing this realizes at that very moment that he is in conflict with another person, one who bears the image of God and whom God loves. That realization changes

the priorities. Now the most solemn and sacred act becomes something else (next verse).

24. Leave there thy gift before the altar, and go thy way; first be reconciled to thy brother, and then come and offer thy gift.

Jesus' surprising instruction is that reconciliation is even more important to God than sacrifice. The subject of God's kingdom wants most of all to do God's will. The focus of God's will is reconciliation. Other matters have their importance, but reconciliation comes first.

> *What Do You Think?*
> Whose responsibility is it to initiate the reconciliation process, the perpetrator or the victim? Why do you say that?
>
> *Talking Points for Your Discussion*
> - Abimelech's initiative (Genesis 20:9)
> - The Lord's instructions (Numbers 5:5-7)
> - David's initiative (1 Samuel 24:11)
> - God's initiative (Romans 5:8)
> - Paul's initiative (2 Corinthians 7:2)
> - John's initiative (3 John 9)

❧ BE RECONCILED ❧

A friend of mine is a junior-high history teacher. Early each year, his students construct a timeline of world events from the ancient history up to about the year 1500. The students then can see how various events in different parts of the world overlap one another.

Recently, he was putting the details together before the students began work. The art teacher found out about this and said he could not use the long wall in the gym because she was planning on putting student art works on it. It was the only unbroken long wall in the building. He pointed out he planned to have the timeline up for only a week, but she was adamant: she needed it for the entire year. Some harsh words were spoken, and they separated, both feeling rather aggrieved.

Over the weekend, however, the art teacher called him and said she had been reconsidering. Since he needed the wall only for a week, she would delay the hanging of her students' art work until he was through with the wall. Her attitude created harmony. This is what Jesus wants. Even better, however, would have been the absence of harsh words in the first place. Then there would have been no need for reconciliation.   —J. B. N.

B. Conflict Resolved (vv. 25, 26)

25. Agree with thine adversary quickly, whiles thou art in the way with him; lest at any time the adversary deliver thee to the judge, and the judge deliver thee to the officer, and thou be cast into prison.

Reconciliation is not just supremely important; it is also supremely urgent. It cannot be put off, because the time available for it is limited.

To make this point, Jesus borrows from a situation familiar to His audience and probably familiar to us as well. He pictures two people about to go to court, where one is suing the other. The person who is being sued has only a short time to reach a settlement before the trial. So that person asks his adversary for terms of settlement while there's still time. Otherwise, he may be subject to the judge's verdict against him. In Jesus' time, people who owe debts can be thrown into prison until they pay up (compare Matthew 18:34).

Jesus uses this story to stress the urgency of acting before judgment is final. In our situation, God is our judge, and He calls us to reconciliation. If we fail to pursue it, we show ourselves as people who do not truly know God, who sacrifices His own Son to be reconciled to us. Reconciliation is urgent because it is at the heart of our relationship with God, and we do not know how much time we have left to be reconciled.

What Do You Think?
What is Jesus implying about people who do not reconcile with one another?
Talking Points for Your Discussion
▪ Matthew 5:22, 23
▪ Romans 12:18
▪ 2 Corinthians 5:12-15
▪ Philippians 4:2, 3

---

26. Verily I say unto thee, Thou shalt by no means come out thence, till thou hast paid the uttermost farthing.

Debtors' prisons in Jesus' time are harsh places. The purpose of the imprisonment is to hold the person in custody until his debt is paid. But it is obviously difficult to earn even a little money while in prison! So working one's way out of debt is often impossible.

Jesus does not make this comparison to provide an allegory of eternal punishment. His idea is not that after God's judgment we slowly work our way out of punishment. Rather, Jesus is comparing the harshness of the debtors' prison with the reality of God's coming judgment. If we truly believe that we can escape God's judgment only because God has reconciled us to himself, then we will follow Him by seeking reconciliation with other people urgently.

Conclusion
A. Mercy Received; Mercy Offered

Is God's ideal person an extrovert or an introvert? The answer is neither. What God wants is for His people to fulfill His will by being reconciled to each other under the authority of Jesus. Throughout Scripture, we see God bringing rebellious people back to Him, reconciling sinners to himself. When we realize that, we can no longer stand in angry judgment of other people. We must seek reconciliation with others because God has brought about reconciliation with us.

Of course, our efforts at reconciliation may not be successful. Reconciliation requires a willingness from both parties. But when we remember the cost to God to be reconciled to us, we cannot be content to remain adversaries with others.

B. Prayer

O God, we come to You as former enemies. By the gracious gift of Your Son, we have become reconciled. Empower us by Your Spirit to break down the divisions among us, to be united with our brothers and sisters as we are united with You. In the name of Jesus, who reconciles us, amen!

C. Thought to Remember

Be reconciled not just to God,
but to others too.

INVOLVEMENT LEARNING

Some of the activities below are also found in the helpful student book, Adult Bible Class.
Don't forget to download the free reproducible page from www.standardlesson.com to enhance your lesson!

Into the Lesson

As class members arrive, hand each a card on which you have written either *SALT* or *LIGHT,* an equal number of cards each. This will be the basis for the two-group activities to follow.

Read the verses occurring between last week's study and today's: Matthew 5:13-16, in which Jesus characterizes the citizens of His kingdom as *salt* and *light.* Say, "Remember these two images for their relevancy to the truths in today's lesson as you ponder what being salt and light have to do with the theme of reconciliation emphasized today." Ask learners to hold their answers until later.

Into the Word

Note that Jesus uses "polar-opposite imagery" in Matthew 5:17-20. Ask your two groups to alternate in identifying these opposites: one group will identify an image, then the other group will identify the polar-opposite image. Possible opposites that your learners will point out are these: abolish/destroy➤fulfill; least➤greatest; break➤keep; God-righteous➤self-righteous; disappear/pass➤be accomplished/fulfilled; heaven and earth➤the kingdom of heaven; truth➤lie.

After each pair of opposites, ask, "What is it that Jesus is suggesting causes or promotes this opposition of imagery?" For example, for "truth➤lie," some claim that Jesus is denying the Law of Moses, but He says (v. 17) the truth could not be any more different! Let your learners respond freely. If they overlook a choice that you see, give the first option and let them give the opposite.

For verses 21-26, tell the class you are going to name some of the sins Jesus mentions in the text. As you come to each one, you will ask two questions: "What has salt got to do with it?" and "What has light got to do with it?" The two groups are to respond to the question based on their assigned word. Give this example: Jesus says murder is sin. Salt says, "My job is to preserve, not kill; to make

worthwhile; not to end possible usefulness, but to extend it"; Light says, "My role is to show the way, not take away the possibility of proceeding!"

Use the following affirmations, or create your own: (1) Jesus says showing contempt in word to another is sin; (2) Jesus says calling another worthless—a fool—is a sin; (3) Jesus says worship should be delayed until slights toward a friend are resolved; (4) Jesus says going to court over a disagreement may be a sinful mistake.

Here are possible responses (by previous numbering). (1) Salt: "My goal is to improve, not lessen"; Light: "My task is to help one grow, not cause one to wither." (2) Salt: "If I don't do what God designed me for, I'm the worthless one"; Light: "What am I for if not to lift the pall of darkness?" (3) Salt: "How can I experience the joy of worship before I've done my 'preserving' job?" Light: "The shadow of sin on a bowed head keeps me out." (4) Salt: "If I'm locked inside a salt shaker, what good am I?" Light: "My role is to let the truth be seen, even if I show my own sins!"

Into Life

Download the reproducible page and use one or both activities. If you use the If It's Broken, Fix It! exercise, divide the class into three groups. Have each group evaluate one of the images and propose a "fix." Then ask one of the other groups to disagree and give a reason why "that won't work." Finally, allow a rejoinder from the third group to suggest why the fix *will* work. Rotate through your groups so that each group has one chance to propose a positive solution, one chance to be contrary, and one chance to offer a rejoinder.

If you use the "Well, I Thought . . ." exercise, have learners work in small groups of no more than three to complete it. Rotate through the groups to glean answers for the whole class. As each answer is offered, ask, "What difference will this make in your life in the coming week?"

LOVING
UNCONDITIONALLY

DEVOTIONAL READING: Matthew 22:34-40
BACKGROUND SCRIPTURE: Matthew 5:38-48

MATTHEW 5:38-48

38 Ye have heard that it hath been said, An eye for an eye, and a tooth for a tooth:

39 But I say unto you, That ye resist not evil: but whosoever shall smite thee on thy right cheek, turn to him the other also.

40 And if any man will sue thee at the law, and take away thy coat, let him have thy cloak also.

41 And whosoever shall compel thee to go a mile, go with him twain.

42 Give to him that asketh thee, and from him that would borrow of thee turn not thou away.

43 Ye have heard that it hath been said, Thou shalt love thy neighbour, and hate thine enemy.

44 But I say unto you, Love your enemies, bless them that curse you, do good to them that hate you, and pray for them which despitefully use you, and persecute you;

45 That ye may be the children of your Father which is in heaven: for he maketh his sun to rise on the evil and on the good, and sendeth rain on the just and on the unjust.

46 For if ye love them which love you, what reward have ye? do not even the publicans the same?

47 And if ye salute your brethren only, what do ye more than others? do not even the publicans so?

48 Be ye therefore perfect, even as your Father which is in heaven is perfect.

KEY VERSES

Love your enemies, bless them that curse you, do good to them that hate you, and pray for them which despitefully use you, and persecute you; that ye may be the children of your Father which is in heaven.

—Matthew 5:44, 45

TRADITION AND WISDOM

Unit 2: Jesus Teaches Wisdom

LESSONS 9–13

LESSON AIMS

After participating in this lesson, each student will be able to:

1. Summarize Jesus' teaching on love for enemies.

2. Relate Jesus' instructions on love between people to God's love for people.

3. Demonstrate one tangible act of love in the coming week.

LESSON OUTLINE

Introduction

A. Love in the Abstract and the Concrete

A generation ago, Charles Schulz (1922–2000) ended one of his beloved *Peanuts* cartoons with a line that became famous: "I love mankind; it's people I can't stand." That remark became famous because it matches so well with our experience. Everyone, it seems, wants to live up to the ideal of loving other people. That's easy to do when we think of other people in the abstract. Lump all human beings together, and no one would say that it is good to be indifferent, uncaring, or hostile to them. We all want to love "mankind."

But talk about individuals, and it is quite a different matter! We can find all kinds of reasons not to love specific people we know. Sometimes we find them annoying. Harder still to love are people who have done us harm, whether deliberately or accidentally. Then there are those who seem to be focused on their resentments toward us, who seem constantly to try to hurt us. Sadly, some of those people are close to us; they may even be family members.

In today's passage, Jesus tackles this vital subject. In addressing it, He lays out some of His most challenging teaching on how we are to live. What He says seems unnatural to us, even impossible to carry out. But when we understand what God has done for us, we see that what Jesus says is our only possible response.

B. Lesson Background

Today's text is part of Jesus' Sermon on the Mount, which is His great exposition of what it means to be a subject in God's kingdom. God's kingdom, or *the kingdom of heaven* as it is called in Matthew's Gospel, is the establishment of God's promised rule over the world. The world is in rebellion against God, as human beings express their desire to be free of God by disobeying Him. Sin has made us God's enemies. But in God's kingdom, God reestablishes His reign over all. He overcomes sin and invites sinners—His enemies—to become His friends.

Jesus' audience was very much looking forward to the coming of God's kingdom. Jesus'

Loving Unconditionally

announcement that the kingdom was "at hand" (Matthew 4:17) had led a large crowd to follow Him and listen to His teaching (5:1). But many in that crowd probably understood God's kingdom to be a political, military entity—like other kingdoms of which they knew.

More particularly, Jesus' Jewish audience likely understood that when God's kingdom came, it would mean the end of their being ruled by pagan empires, like the Romans under whom Israel lived in Jesus' time. People anticipated that the coming of God's kingdom would mean that the enemies of His people, their pagan overlords, would be utterly defeated. After all, God had worked in the past through military leaders, had He not?

But God was to establish His kingdom not with the sword, but with the cross. Those who are subjects of a kingdom established in this manner must live out God's grace as they deal with their own enemies.

I. Not Retribution but Generosity
(MATTHEW 5:38-42)

A. Personal Revenge Forbidden (vv. 38, 39)

38. Ye have heard that it hath been said, An eye for an eye, and a tooth for a tooth.

Jesus begins this section with a famous—and widely misunderstood—passage from the Law of Moses. Found repeatedly in the books of the law (Exodus 21:24; Leviticus 24:20; Deuteronomy 19:21), the *eye for an eye* statement had a very specific meaning in its original context, one that for many has been forgotten in Jesus' time.

When God gave Israel His law, Israel's neighbors followed law codes that assessed different criminal penalties depending on who did the crime and who was the victim. In one ancient law code, for example, if a nobleman killed a slave, the nobleman's punishment was payment to the slave's owner for the slave's value. But if a slave did even

minor physical harm to a nobleman, the slave was punished with death. So when the Law of Moses specified "an eye for an eye," God was stating that the punishment must fit the crime for all, with no favoritism. No punishment was to exceed the severity of the crime that was committed.

As time went on, however, some understood this statement to mean that people are authorized to seek personal revenge whenever they have been harmed. Rather than understanding these words as a limitation on what punishment the community could exact for a crime, they were taken as permission to "get even."

For Jesus' audience, the words about *an eye for an eye* seem to address their present situation under the Roman Empire. Roman soldiers and officials make demands on their lives for taxes and all kinds of services. The Romans enforce their authority with brutality. Thus many in Israel look forward to the coming of God's rule, when they expect that the tables will be turned on the Romans. Then they can exact revenge on their former overlords.

Jesus does not take issue with the Mosaic Law's instructions. Instead, He takes issue with people's abuse of the law (next verse).

39. But I say unto you, That ye resist not evil: but whosoever shall smite thee on thy right cheek, turn to him the other also.

In contrast with seeking personal retribution, Jesus says that the subject of God's kingdom does the opposite. If "an eye for an eye" gives permission for revenge, then the proper response to a slap on the cheek is to slap back. To turn the other cheek puts everything backward: instead of striking back, the person allows himself or herself to be struck again.

This statement is powerful and challenging, but it must be understood in its context. For Jesus' audience, the kind of abuse described here most commonly comes from the Romans. In that setting, Jesus is challenging those who believe that God's kingdom is to arrive through the violent overthrow of the Roman Empire. Yet what Jesus speaks of allows nothing of the kind. God's kingdom will be established to be sure, but not by armed force.

HOW TO SAY IT

Mahatma Gandhi	Muh-*hot*-muh *Gon*-dee.
Mosaic	Mo-*zay*-ik.
pagan	*pay*-gun.

Some wonder whether Jesus is forbidding all forms of self-defense. We should note that the subject at hand is not self-defense, but revenge. A slap to the face is painful and a sign of great disrespect, but it is not a significant threat to one's life. To strike back would simply be trying to get even vengefully.

Jesus' statement becomes clearest when we consider its reason. Much later in Matthew, Jesus will be struck, but He will not respond in kind (Matthew 26:67, 68; 27:27-31). Rather, He waits for God to bring vindication at His resurrection. Jesus brings God's kingdom into the world by submitting to this abuse. To turn the other cheek is to trust in God as Jesus does, to count on God to protect us, and to punish our enemies if that is what they deserve.

Jesus' followers belong to God's kingdom even though they deserve punishment for their sins. Knowing that, we are compelled to act with the same mercy toward those who do wrong to us.

What Do You Think?
How would your life be different if you consistently "turned the other cheek" when insulted?
Talking Points for Your Discussion
- Ways your life would become better or easier
- Ways your life would be more difficult

❧ NONVIOLENCE ❧

Mahatma Gandhi (1869–1948) was an inspiring figure of political significance in India. In the first half of the twentieth century, India was part of the British Empire, and the British treated it as a colony to be exploited. The British overlords tended to treat the Indians as inferiors, discriminated against them, and burdened them with excessive taxes. Gandhi was determined to rid India of the British, but he was also convinced that nonviolence was the only way to do it.

Combining nonviolence with civil disobedience, Gandhi experienced jail terms and brutality. He also experienced times of frustration when many of his followers did not follow precisely in his ideals of nonviolence. His efforts for a free India were rewarded in 1947, although he was assassinated five months later. Probably more than any other person, Gandhi was the one responsible for Indian independence.

Gandhi's ideals of nonviolence influenced others, including Martin Luther King, Jr. Whether Jesus would have approved civil disobedience is debatable. But He certainly would have approved Gandhi's nonviolence, since He (Jesus) was the one who proposed this approach in the first place.

—J. B. N.

B. Resistance Discouraged (vv. 40, 41)

40. And if any man will sue thee at the law, and take away thy coat, let him have thy cloak also.

With a different setting, this saying makes much the same point as the previous one. A lawsuit pits two people against each other as adversaries. The normal response when one is sued is to resist. Again, Jesus' instruction is to do the opposite.

As Jesus describes it, the object of the lawsuit is something very important. The *coat* for which the person is being sued is a garment worn next to the skin by people in Jesus' culture. Because people often have only one set of clothes, this is a precious possession, well worth protecting. But Jesus says not to protect that inner garment, but to give it away along with the outer garment, the *cloak,* as well.

Again, the point is to suggest the opposite of what one would naturally do. And doing this opposite thing is both necessary and possible because of what God does for His people. God does not give us what we deserve, but instead sacrifices His very Son for us. If God's people have been given such a generous gift, then they are compelled to act in the same way toward others. We can do this in the confidence that the God who gives His Son for us will also supply all our needs.

Jesus' words do not call for an uncritical generosity that gives anything to anyone who asks. In our time, if a person asks us for money to buy narcotics, for example, we are not showing that person God's love by enabling his or her addiction. But Jesus is calling for a radical, selfless generosity that is concerned not about hoarding for ourselves, but about imitating God's own generous love to us.

> **What Do You Think?**
> Under what circumstances, if any, should a Christian defend himself or herself in a legal proceeding as opposed to merely "giving in"?
>
> *Talking Points for Your Discussion*
> - Civil lawsuits (1 Corinthians 6:1-11) vs. criminal charges (Acts 18:12-16)
> - The "lesser of two evils" concept
> - Paul defended himself in criminal court (Acts 24:1–25:12)

41. And whosoever shall compel thee to go a mile, go with him twain.

Jesus now describes a third situation, much like the first one. Roman soldiers can compel members of the local populace to carry the Romans' gear as they march. Some sources suggest that the limit to such a command is one mile. Of course, people resent being forced to bear burdens for the occupying soldiers and seek ways to avoid it. But Jesus instead says that His followers should voluntarily go the second mile.

The message is clear. God's kingdom does not come by resisting the Romans. Rather, it comes through the radical gift of God, given for rebellious sinners. If God is so generous as to give His Son to die on the cross for the sake of those who are His enemies, then His people need to show similar generosity toward those who are their enemies.

C. Sharing Encouraged (v. 42)

42. Give to him that asketh thee, and from him that would borrow of thee turn not thou away.

This saying sums up what Jesus says previously. Loans in Jesus' day are not as common as in our modern economy. They are emergency measures that allow someone without any means to continue to eat. But it is not just the person's desperate circumstances that matter here. For those who know the gracious generosity of God, the only right response is one of generosity, like their Lord's.

> **What Do You Think?**
> How do we give to people who ask without causing more harm than good?
>
> *Talking Points for Your Discussion*
> - Evaluating genuine need (Acts 6:1-6; 1 Timothy 5:3)
> - Not fostering laziness (1 Thessalonians 4:11, 12; 2 Thessalonians 3:12)
> - The issue of reciprocity (2 Corinthians 8:13-15)

II. Not Hatred but Love
(MATTHEW 5:43-48)

A. New Approach (vv. 43, 44)

43. Ye have heard that it hath been said, Thou shalt love thy neighbour, and hate thine enemy.

Once again Jesus draws a contrast between what He is teaching and what people are accustomed to hearing about God's law. The command to love one's neighbor is very clear in the law found in Leviticus 19:18. But nowhere does the biblical law command one to hate an enemy. That is the idea that Jesus is about to challenge.

How does someone get the impression that God commands hatred of enemies? To hate one's enemies is, of course, a perfectly natural thing to do. But it is easy for the people of God to conclude that their enemies are also God's enemies and to justify hating them on that basis. For many in Jesus' time, this outlook justifies hatred for the Roman occupiers. Yet as far as Jesus is concerned, God's people must do something very different from hating their personal enemies, whether they are truly God's enemies or not.

44. But I say unto you, Love your enemies, bless them that curse you, do good to them that hate you, and pray for them which despitefully use you, and persecute you.

What Jesus describes here is the opposite of hatred and sums up much of what He has said in this section. The natural thing to do is hate one's enemies, but Jesus says to love them. When we are treated abusively, we are to respond with prayer. Instructions regarding a kind response to enemies also are found in the Old Testament (Exodus

23:4, 5; Proverbs 25:21), but the people of Jesus' day seem to have forgotten about them!

Again, what Jesus says defies what we like to call common sense. But Jesus has a clear reason for what He instructs. All this strange treatment of enemies makes sense when we know what God has done for us.

We note in passing that the statements about *bless, curse,* and *do good* do not occur in the earliest available Greek manuscripts of Matthew's Gospel. But these statements do occur in those manuscripts for Luke 6:27, 28, so we are certain that the thoughts are original to Jesus.

What Do You Think?

What are some practical ways to love, bless, do good for, and pray for our enemies?

Talking Points for Your Discussion

- Things we say about them publicly
- Thoughts we think about them privately
- How we interpret their behavior

❧ *Too Difficult?* ❧

During the War of 1812, Oliver Hazard Perry led a squadron of American ships against the British in the Battle of Lake Erie (otherwise called the Battle of Put-in-Bay, which is located near Sandusky, Ohio). After the Americans emerged victorious, Perry sent his famous message, "We have met the enemy and they are ours."

About 150 years later, the comic-strip character Pogo announced, "We have met the enemy and he is us." The irony of this humorous statement is not lost on us; we all know that we are our own worst enemy at times. We defeat ourselves. We know our weaknesses, yet we succumb to them anyway. We plan our work, and then we fail to work our plan. We shoot ourselves in the foot without even trying. We don't even have to aim! We know in certain situations we ought to keep our mouth shut, and then we open it anyway and make fools of ourselves.

Jesus says we are to love our enemies. Before we object on the grounds that that is too difficult, think about how unlovable we are at times!

—J. B. N.

B. Divine Outreach (v. 45)

45. That ye may be the children of your Father which is in heaven: for he maketh his sun to rise on the evil and on the good, and sendeth rain on the just and on the unjust.

A person can justify hating an enemy if such a person is also God's enemy. But what if God treats His enemies with generosity, kindness, and grace? That, of course, is exactly what Jesus reminds us that God does.

The blessings of nature are not reserved for "good people" alone. God has ordered His world so that it provides for all, whether they obey Him or not. God's gracious treatment *on the evil and on the good* (and, of course, we know that none of us is truly good) is what compels us not to hate our enemies, but to be generous, loving, and forgiving with them.

Such an attitude marks us as children of the heavenly Father. Above all, our God is the God of grace, who gives people better than they deserve. If we genuinely belong to Him as children belong to their father, then we will show the family resemblance in the way we treat our enemies. Jesus pronounces blessing on "peacemakers" as God's children (Matthew 5:9) for this very reason.

The kingdom of a gracious God comes into the world only with grace. As subjects of God's kingdom and agents of its expansion, we must act toward others with the same grace that God has shown us. As we do, God's enemies will be defeated not by our aggression, but by our godly love.

C. Extra Dimension (vv. 46-48)

46. For if ye love them which love you, what reward have ye? do not even the publicans the same?

Jesus now reminds His audience that simply loving those who love them shows no special connection with God. Even those thought to be furthest from God know how to love those who love them. *Publicans* are the tax collectors of the Roman Empire. In Jesus' time, the Romans allow local people to bid for the right to collect taxes. The tax collector can then keep everything he collects above his bid.

Loving Unconditionally

In the eyes of the public, the tax collector has "sold out" his own people to make a profit. So tax collectors are among the most despised people of Jesus' culture, thought to have given up their membership in God's kingdom. (Matthew, who records Jesus' words, had been one of these and notes himself as such; see Matthew 9:9; 10:3). Jesus plays off that concept: if someone so far from God knows how to love those who love him, there is no sign of godliness in that.

47. And if ye salute your brethren only, what do ye more than others? do not even the publicans so?

In Jesus' culture, offering greetings to people in public is an important and elaborate duty. But there are those who are excluded from the social circle. A person indicates who is a friend and who is an enemy by offering or not offering greetings.

Again, Jesus points out that such behavior does not mark one out as God's person but as someone who does not know God. God invites all to come to Him, no matter how they have rejected Him in the past. His people have to do the same.

48. Be ye therefore perfect, even as your Father which is in heaven is perfect.

This statement sums up everything that Jesus has said about love for other people. For subjects of God's kingdom, our actions are determined not by our own best interests, our emotions, or the practices of our culture. Rather, our actions toward others are to be determined by God's actions toward us. God loves us despite our rebellion. We are compelled to love others, especially the unlovely, in the same way.

Followers of Jesus do not compare their behavior toward others with the imperfect standards set by humans. Their standard is the complete, unfailing love of God himself. This is Jesus' point in calling His followers to be *perfect* like God (also Deuteronomy 18:13). Only by looking to God's love can we really see what our behavior toward others must be like.

Of course, it is a byword that none of us is perfect. This statement also reminds us that in our imperfection we rely on the gracious forgiveness of a perfect God. That in turn reminds us to treat others as God has treated us.

Conclusion

A. Loving the Unlovely

Someone once made the observation that we all find it easy to love a certain kind of person—the YAVIS person: "Young, Attractive, Verbal, Intelligent, and Sophisticated." Who would not love someone like that? But the truth is that most of us are HOUNDs: Homely, Old, Unsophisticated, Nonverbal, and Dumb! We are all hard to love. But God, who knows better than anyone how unlovable we are, has loved us. His love transforms us to learn to love others in the same way, even those who have hurt us most deeply.

B. Prayer

Father, strengthen our love for others so that the world will see You in us. In Jesus' name, amen.

C. Thought to Remember

God's love is perfected in us (1 John 4:12).

Visual for Lesson 11. *Point to this visual as you ask your learners to give examples of how this statement is true.*

INVOLVEMENT LEARNING

Some of the activities below are also found in the helpful student book, Adult Bible Class.
Don't forget to download the free reproducible page from www.standardlesson.com to enhance your lesson!

Into the Lesson

Hand to each learner arriving a coin-like disc (can be light cardboard) onto which you have written *C of G?* on one side and *C of D?* on the other. Assign the following references to four of your best readers: John 8:44; Acts 13:10; 1 John 3:10; Matthew 5:45a.

As class begins, ask what the learners think the letters stand for. Do not indicate the correct answers yet. (The letters stand for *Child of God* and *Child of the Devil.*) Have the assigned texts read aloud in the order given above. The answers should be obvious to everyone. Comment: "Jesus says that the point of behavior that shows uncommon love—as He pictures it in today's text—is to demonstrate whose child we are."

Into the Word

Let the class read through the text, or have it read aloud. Then say, "I am going to affirm several key attributes of God. After each, think of an idea from today's text that implies that same characteristic in the one who is in the kingdom, 'a child of God.'" The point is to emphasize that responding and reacting as Jesus requires is the way we show that we are a child of God.

Next, affirm the following truths, pausing after each one: God is just; God is gracious; God is love; God is generous; God is forgiving; God is impartial; God is perfect. As you pause, ask learners to suggest connections to the text.

Allow the class the freedom of its matches, but here is an example for each truth: God is just—He does punish when punishment is due, as seen in the "eye for an eye" commands (v. 38). God is gracious—He provides sustaining rain for everyone, the good and the bad (v. 45). God is love—He loves even those who are His enemies and is ready to forgive (v. 44). God is generous—He blesses even those who curse Him, and He will give beyond what is needed to those who ask

of Him (v. 41). God is forgiving—His "second cheek" is turned (v. 39). God is impartial—He "greets" friend and foe, insider and outsider alike with His call (v. 47). God is perfect—His holiness and power are complete (v. 48).

As you introduce each of the truths and receive your learners comments, stop to discuss the implications for one who would be a "child of the heavenly Father." You can ask, "How can the specific actions Jesus described and calls for be generalized to everyday living in the twenty-first century?" This discussion will lead into the Into Life segment.

Into Life

Display this puzzle:

The __ __ __ __ __ __ __ __
of the __ __ __ __ __ __ __ __.

Ask learners to suggest fill-in letters. (The phrase you want is "The opposite of the expected.") As correct letters are suggested, write in all occurrences of the letter.

Once the phrase is deciphered, say, "In today's text, Jesus commonly prescribes doing the opposite of what is normally expected." Review the expectations of Jesus as noted in today's text. After you do, lead your learners in repeating aloud your phrase in unison three times. Then challenge your learners to look for occasions this week where they can act as Jesus desires. Remind learners that the model is the perfect love and grace of God.

Download the reproducible page and distribute copies of the Pattern of Perfection activity. Have learners work in pairs to complete this. Suggest that they think about the "coin" you gave them as they do. Ask for volunteers to share answers, but do not put anyone on the spot. Distribute copies of the Hair Pulls activity from the reproducible page as a take-home reminder as learners depart. Suggest that they post the completed exercise where they can see it often in the week ahead.

PRAYING SINCERELY

DEVOTIONAL READING: Isaiah 12
BACKGROUND SCRIPTURE: Matthew 6:1-18

MATTHEW 6:5-15

5 And when thou prayest, thou shalt not be as the hypocrites are: for they love to pray standing in the synagogues and in the corners of the streets, that they may be seen of men. Verily I say unto you, They have their reward.

6 But thou, when thou prayest, enter into thy closet, and when thou hast shut thy door, pray to thy Father which is in secret; and thy Father which seeth in secret shall reward thee openly.

7 But when ye pray, use not vain repetitions, as the heathen do: for they think that they shall be heard for their much speaking.

8 Be not ye therefore like unto them: for your Father knoweth what things ye have need of, before ye ask him.

9 After this manner therefore pray ye: Our Father which art in heaven, Hallowed be thy name.

10 Thy kingdom come, Thy will be done in earth, as it is in heaven.

11 Give us this day our daily bread.

12 And forgive us our debts, as we forgive our debtors.

13 And lead us not into temptation, but deliver us from evil: For thine is the kingdom, and the power, and the glory, for ever. Amen.

14 For if ye forgive men their trespasses, your heavenly Father will also forgive you:

15 But if ye forgive not men their trespasses, neither will your Father forgive your trespasses.

KEY VERSE

When thou prayest, enter into thy closet, and when thou hast shut thy door, pray to thy Father which is in secret; and thy Father which seeth in secret shall reward thee openly. —**Matthew 6:6**

Photo: SWP, incorporated

TRADITION AND WISDOM

Unit 2: Jesus Teaches Wisdom

LESSONS 9–13

LESSON AIMS

After participating in this lesson, each student will be able to:

1. Identify key features of the Lord's Prayer.

2. Relate Jesus' teaching on prayer to His teaching on God as Father and the coming of God's kingdom.

3. Recite the Lord's Prayer from memory.

LESSON OUTLINE

Introduction

A. Prayers That Get Past the Ceiling

Have you ever realized that you were talking but no one was listening? Maybe you were on the telephone and did not realize the connection had dropped. Maybe you were speaking to someone whom you thought was in the next room, but the person was not actually there. Maybe you were speaking to someone who turned out to be asleep. Or maybe you were just being ignored!

Prayer, of course, is talking to God. When we pray, how can we know that God is listening? That is a natural question for people of faith. Sometimes when we pray, we may feel as if our prayers never make it past the ceiling.

Jesus addresses that very question in the text we will study today. It includes one of the best known passages in the entire Bible. But as we study this familiar text, we need to listen to it carefully because it can answer some of our most crucial questions, questions wrapped up in what it means to pray as a subject of God's kingdom.

B. Lesson Background

Today's passage is near the center of Jesus' Sermon on the Mount. Overall, this sermon is Jesus' exposition of what it means to live under the reign of God, the *kingdom of heaven* as it is called in Matthew's Gospel. Early in that sermon, Jesus had pronounced blessing on the "pure in heart" (Matthew 5:8) and those who "hunger and thirst after righteousness" (5:6). A little later, He warned that those who belong to God's kingdom must have righteousness greater than that of the scribes and Pharisees (5:20). The middle section of Jesus' sermon provides an explanation of those challenging ideas.

Jesus stressed that true righteousness means righteousness not just on the outside, but on the inside. Obedience to God means not just avoiding murder, but controlling anger (Matthew 5:21-24), not just avoiding adultery, but controlling lust (5:27-30). Real purity is to be pure in heart. Those who live obediently under the rule of God are obedient not just where everyone can see, but where God alone can see.

In Matthew 6:1-18, Jesus reinforces this point by talking about three acts of devotion to God: fasting, praying, and giving alms (gifts to the poor). His Jewish audience understood these actions to be important parts of their obedience to God. But Jesus stresses a difference between the subjects of God's kingdom and the religious leaders of His day in the way that they perform these acts of devotion. Our text is the middle part of this discussion, and the longest part of it.

I. Sincere Prayer Described
(MATTHEW 6:5-8)

A. Directed to God Alone (vv. 5, 6)

5. And when thou prayest, thou shalt not be as the hypocrites are: for they love to pray standing in the synagogues and in the corners of the streets, that they may be seen of men. Verily I say unto you, They have their reward.

Prior to the time of Jesus, the word *hypocrite* was used to describe actors on the stage, people who pretend to be what they are not. That is Jesus' point: there are people who are respected in their community for their devotion to God, but in fact they are not devoted to God at all. Rather, they want other people's attention and approval. They want to *be seen of men*. Ironically, these people already *have their reward*: it comes from the human approval that they seek. Because they are not actually talking to God but to other people, God "answers" their prayers by not listening!

Jesus' words are not a condemnation of public prayer as such, since He himself prayed publicly (Matthew 14:19; John 11:41). Rather, He condemns hearts that *love to pray* as a means of gaining a standing with other people. True prayer is pointed in a very different direction.

❧ *LIKE KISSING MY WIFE IN PUBLIC?* ❧

One of the challenges I experienced when I was a young preacher was the task of leading in prayer during the Sunday morning worship service. It wasn't the praying that was the problem. It was having the right attitude.

I wanted to pray in such a way that I could lift up my concerns before God. But the small church where I was preaching did not have a microphone system, so I had to be sure to raise my voice enough to be heard by the people sitting in the rear of the church building. I felt it was difficult to be sincere in my prayers when I actually was concerned about the volume level of my voice.

In addition, I always thought of prayer as a private thing; yet there I was leading a public prayer. My purpose was not to voice my private thoughts to God; I was to lead the thoughts of other people in prayer. I thought that that was a little bit like kissing my wife in public as a demonstration to others of how it ought to be done. With all due respect, I would rather kiss my wife in private. Ideally, I thought I should say things in my prayer that would be spiritually helpful to others; yet I found myself being more concerned about crafting the right words and phrases than communicating honestly with God.

Offering sincere public prayer remains a challenge for me. But perhaps the fact that I struggle with this issue is part of the solution!   —J. B. N.

6. But thou, when thou prayest, enter into thy closet, and when thou hast shut thy door, pray to thy Father which is in secret; and thy Father which seeth in secret shall reward thee openly.

In contrast with those who pray to be seen by other people, the subject of God's kingdom prays to God alone. Jesus describes such a prayer with an outward, humanly observable action: the praying person goes to a place where no other person can see him or her. But in light of the previous verse, Jesus is obviously stressing not where a person prays physically, but how a person prays from the heart. A true prayer is directed to God alone and has no concern with whether others notice or not.

God, of course, sees everything, including the human heart. The insincere person who wants human approval may receive it for now, but the time will come when God will reveal to all what is true of the heart. Realizing that God knows all and will reveal all forces us to be honest with God in our prayers, to focus on talking to Him and not on fulfilling the expectations of others.

But sincere prayer is offered not primarily out of fear of God's punishment, but with confidence in His goodness. Jesus refers to God as *Father* here. God is the kind of Father who gives His children what they need at the time that they need it (Matthew 7:9-11).

> *What Do You Think?*
> What are some pitfalls to avoid in public prayer? How do we avoid them?
> *Talking Points for Your Discussion*
> - The issue of edification (Ephesians 4:29)
> - Identifying issues appropriate only for private prayer
> - Planned vs. spontaneous prayers

B. Trusting in God's Faithfulness (vv. 7, 8)

7. But when ye pray, use not vain repetitions, as the heathen do: for they think that they shall be heard for their much speaking.

Now Jesus makes a second contrast: between true prayer and prayer of the person who is ignorant of the true God. Prayer is different depending on whom we understand God to be. If we know God as a good Father, we will pray to Him differently from those who do not know Him that way.

In the cultures that surround Israel in Jesus' time, the "gods" are often thought to be unpredictable and selfish, like powerful human rulers. Praying to such gods is a matter of begging them not to do harm or nagging them for some gift.

Further, many pagans think of their gods less as personal beings and more like unseen forces that can be manipulated. For these pagans, prayer is a matter of saying magic words and phrases that are thought to have the power to make those forces bend to one's will.

In either case, such prayer is a matter of *vain repetitions,* of saying the same thing over and over.

HOW TO SAY IT

heathen	*hee*-thun.
Lamentations	Lam-en-*tay*-shunz.
Thessalonians	*Thess*-uh-*lo*-nee-unz
	(*th* as in *thin*).

This is not the kind of prayer that acknowledges the God who acts toward His people as a loving Father does toward His children.

> *What Do You Think?*
> How can we pray in a way that eliminates modern "vain repetitions"?
> *Talking Points for Your Discussion*
> - Avoiding "filler words"
> - Approaching prayer as a true conversation

8. Be not ye therefore like unto them: for your Father knoweth what things ye have need of, before ye ask him.

In praying, we are not telling God things that He does not know already (also Matthew 6:32). Rather, we are approaching Him humbly to ask Him to supply our needs, honoring Him as our good Father, and expressing that we depend on Him completely.

In that attitude, we may pray persistently (Luke 18:1). We may indeed pray often for the same thing. But persistent prayer, expressing constant reliance on God, is different from repetitious prayer that seeks to manipulate or persuade God to do something that He is otherwise unwilling to do.

II. Sincere Prayer Modeled
(Matthew 6:9-13)

A. Devoted to God's Reign (vv. 9, 10)

9. After this manner therefore pray ye: Our Father which art in heaven, Hallowed be thy name.

The attitudes of prayer that Jesus has just articulated He now models in the prayer He gives to His disciples. Before beginning the prayer itself, Jesus uses the word *ye* to emphasize the contrast between the subjects of God's kingdom and the pagans who pray with empty words over and over.

The prayer itself begins with the very point that Jesus has just raised: prayer means expressing our understanding of and devotion to God as *our Father*. He is a good, kind Father who provides what His children need. Further, He is a powerful Father in that He is *in heaven,* the supreme place of authority over creation. *Hallowed* means "treated as holy or sacred." The first request of the prayer is that God's name—His identity, reputation, and authority—should be honored everywhere by all.

10. Thy kingdom come, Thy will be done in earth, as it is in heaven.

God's kingdom-coming means that His reign will be full. In God's kingdom, what God wants will be done by all. In Heaven, in the presence of God, His will is done perfectly. For the subject of God's kingdom, the greatest desire is that God's will be done here as it is there.

God's name being honored, His kingdom coming, and His will being done are three ways of stating the foundation of sincere prayer. We ask God to rule over all as king, beginning with us but including all that exists.

What Do You Think?
  How would your life change if your prayers began to focus more on God himself rather than on your own problems and desires?
Talking Points for Your Discussion
  ▪ Changes in how much you worry
  ▪ Changes in your attention to God's will
  ▪ Changes in the "depth" of your prayer

B. Reliant on God's Provision (vv. 11-13)

11. Give us this day our daily bread.

It is no accident that this prayer begins with a request that God's will be done. That is the foundation of the disciple's relationship with God. But part of God's will is that His people should have what they need. So the second half of the prayer consists of requests for God to supply our needs in three crucial areas.

The first of these is physical provision: *daily bread* on *this day.* That language reminds us of what God did for Israel in the wilderness, supplying food each day through the manna that appeared on the ground each morning. The people were commanded to gather only enough for one day. Taking more only meant that the leftover manna would spoil by the next day. That was

true except on the sixth day, when the people were to collect two days' worth. On the Sabbath, there was no manna, but the leftovers stayed good for that day (Exodus 16).

God had a lesson for Israel through this process: regardless of their situation, they had to depend on God to provide their needs. In the wilderness, they had only enough for a day, but every day they had enough. God gave them what they needed and taught them clearly that it came from Him alone.

Jesus now calls for subjects of God's kingdom to pray in that same way. They pray in confidence that God will supply their needs constantly, day by day. They do not seek a surplus, only what they need for now. They trust God for the future as well as the present.

Many of us probably may prefer to pray for bread for several years, not just bread for a day. When we have a surplus, we feel confident about the future. But the prayer that Jesus teaches shows us that our confidence in the future is not based on what we have accumulated. It is based on God's faithful provision for our needs, day by day.

What Do You Think?
  What are some ways to make the idea of praying for "daily bread" meaningful if we always have several days' food supply in the pantry?
Talking Points for Your Discussion
  ▪ Prayers to be contented
  ▪ Switching from "asking" to "thanking"
  ▪ Identifying other daily needs

❧   *THE PROBLEM OF ABUNDANCE*   ❧

The level of abundance in America (and in other western democracies) completely dwarfs the standards of most of the world's population. Halloween reminds me of this. Every year at that time we get numerous flyers at our house advertising costumes, candy, and various games suitable for Halloween parties. The ethical nature of Halloween aside, I am amazed at the availability of all this stuff. Obviously, I live in a society that has more money than commonsense. We come to expect the abundance that we experience.

A few years ago, our church hosted a young man from eastern Europe. He spoke briefly in one of our worship services. The gist of his comments was to express his sorrow regarding the wealth that Americans have.

By contrast, the Christians of eastern Europe have experienced repression, punishment, persecution, and sometimes even martyrdom. Many Christians there had relatives who were killed for their faith during the Communist times. Even today, Christians there experience a level of poverty that Americans consider unacceptable. I still remember his comment: "I have been to your large grocery stores. You do not know what it means to pray for your daily bread."

His words are true. If we find it hard to pray to receive something we already have, perhaps we can offer prayers of thanks for the fact that we do indeed have such provisions. This will keep our thoughts focused on the God who is the source of all blessings.   —J. B. N.

12. And forgive us our debts, as we forgive our debtors.

From material needs the subject turns to our need for forgiveness. Subjects of God's kingdom know that they belong to that kingdom only because God has mercifully forgiven them of their rebellion and invited them to belong to His people. That forgiveness gets them in and keeps them in God's kingdom. They rely on it always, so they express that reliance always as they ask for God's forgiveness (1 John 1:9).

Jesus uses *debts* as a vivid figure of speech for our sins. We know what it is like to forgive something that has a cost, like a debt. God's forgiveness of our sin is like that. God forgives freely, but His forgiveness is costly to Him: He pays the price of the life of His Son on the cross.

Realizing that fact compels us to act differently toward others. If God has forgiven us, we ought to forgive others, those who are debtors to us. That includes all who have harmed us, but again the term *debtors* reminds us that this is costly. Forgiving others is hard, but it is absolutely necessary if we know God's forgiveness. If God's forgiveness does not compel us to forgive others, we show that

we have never really received it seriously. Those who cannot find it in their hearts even to try to forgive others may in fact demonstrate that God's forgiveness has never found its way into their own hearts.

13a. And lead us not into temptation, but deliver us from evil.

This half-verse provides the third request for our need to be supplied, this one for strength and protection in temptation. As Jesus proclaims the coming of God's kingdom, He describes a paradox. God's rule is breaking into the world, but the adversary, Satan, remains active and dangerous. The subjects of the kingdom must therefore be prepared for His attacks.

The expression *lead us not into* in Jesus' language is a way of saying "protect us from" or "give us power over." Jesus is not suggesting that God is the source of temptation (see James 1:13). Rather, He is reminding His followers to rely on God's power to overcome the temptation that continues in the world.

Deliver us from evil likely emphasizes not just evil in the abstract but also the evil one himself: the devil, who tempts people to do evil. Here we see part of the prayer's assurance. Powerful as he is, Satan is no match for Almighty God (see John 17:15; 2 Thessalonians 3:3; 2 Timothy 4:18).

> *What Do You Think?*
> What was a time when God answered your prayer for deliverance from temptation in an unexpected way? How did things turn out?
> *Talking Points for Your Discussion*
> - A time when God led you to do something
> - A time when God led you to avoid doing something

13b. For thine is the kingdom, and the power, and the glory, for ever. Amen.

This half-verse is not found in the earliest manuscripts of Matthew's Gospel. But with echoes of 1 Chronicles 29:11-13, it nevertheless expresses a biblical idea based on biblical language, and is very fitting for the themes of Jesus' prayer. In fact, the phrase repeats the emphasis on God's reign with which Jesus' prayer began.

Praying Sincerely

III. Sincere Prayer Applied

(Matthew 6:14, 15)

A. Good Results (v. 14)

14. For if ye forgive men their trespasses, your heavenly Father will also forgive you.

Jesus follows His model prayer with a reemphasis of one of its key implications: those who have received God's forgiveness, who continue to rely on God's forgiveness, must also forgive others. To do otherwise is to dishonor God's forgiveness of us. This is why Jesus states that God's forgiveness of us is conditioned on our forgiveness of others. He knows that the sincere heart that receives His forgiveness will inevitably extend the same to others.

This is not to say, of course, that extending forgiveness is easy for those who have been truly forgiven. It remains costly, and so it is always a struggle. But it is a struggle that those who know God's forgiveness will gladly engage in (Ephesians 4:32; Colossians 3:13).

B. Bad Consequences (v. 15)

15. But if ye forgive not men their trespasses, neither will your Father forgive your trespasses.

The passage ends with a solemn warning: to refuse to forgive others is to dishonor the forgiving God. One cannot pray for God's will to be done and at the same time refuse to submit to His will by learning to forgive in turn.

In Matthew 18:21-35, Jesus tells a story of a man who is forgiven an enormous debt by his master. But then the forgiven man refuses to forgive someone who owes him a much smaller sum. Learning of this, his master summons him and revokes his forgiveness. That is the same warning that Jesus gives here.

Of course, when we are honest with ourselves, we will realize that our forgiveness of others is far from perfect. Does that mean that we have lost our forgiveness from God? No, but it does remind us how much we rely on God's forgiveness moment by moment. And with that reminder, we realize again how important it is that we grow in our forgiveness for others.

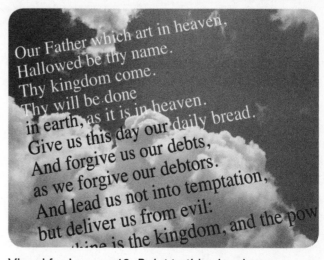

Visual for Lesson 12. *Point to this visual as you challenge your learners to look heavenward as they pray the Lord's Prayer in the week ahead.*

Conclusion

A. Evaluating Our Prayer Life

So, do your prayers get past the ceiling (Lamentations 3:44)? Jesus' teaching shows us how we can assess our prayer life. We need to acknowledge God as our king and our Father, who loves us and gives us what we need. In that light, we need to be completely honest before Him, concerned about His will and power, not our own standing with others. Moment by moment we need to rely on Him to provide what we need for life and for spiritual wholeness.

When we close our eyes in prayer, we remind ourselves that we stand before God alone. But when we open them again, we see other people. As we ask God confidently to forgive us, we realize that we are compelled to forgive others. We do not pray to be seen by other people, but if we do not treat other people differently because of our prayer, then we have not prayed at all.

B. Prayer

Father, rule in our lives and over the world. Please give us just what we need. Please strengthen us to forgive others as You have forgiven us. In the name of Jesus, who taught us to pray, amen!

C. Thought to Remember

"You can't pray a lie—I found that out" (in *The Adventures of Huckleberry Finn* by Mark Twain).

INVOLVEMENT LEARNING

Some of the activities below are also found in the helpful student book, Adult Bible Class.
Don't forget to download the free reproducible page from www.standardlesson.com to enhance your lesson!

Into the Lesson

Download the reproducible page and place copies of the Bad Doctrine and Bad Prayer activity in chairs. Learners can begin working on this as they arrive.

Recruit two learners to have the following short, dramatic conversation as they stand before the class, as if walking by.

First: "Say, _____, you know me well. What do you think of my prayer life? Second: "Well, _____, I don't know much about it. I've heard you pray a few times, but overall, how would I know?" First: "That's what I wanted to hear, _____. My prayer life is . . . well, my prayer life!"

Note that this is much of the point of Jesus' teaching on prayer in today's study: prayer is both personal and private. But also note that prayer is not self-centered, not "all about me."

Into the Word

Create a handout titled *What Prayer Isn't* with the following list of entries, with a small box (for check marks) to the left of each: letting God know your needs; a display of eloquence; all about "me"; an affirmation of not trusting God; limited to earthly concerns; an expression of personal worthiness; a public show of spirituality; measured by amount of time spent; an occasion to be noticed by others; talking to oneself. Say, "Put a check mark by each entry you believe is a true response to the heading *What Prayer Isn't.*"

After a few minutes, briefly discuss responses. Expect that most learners will mark most of the entries. Comment: "In today's text, Jesus clearly delineates what prayer is not, but He also indicates what it is when best understood."

When you come to the verses revealing Jesus' model for effective and proper prayer, say, "I want you to see Jesus' prayer as a *Today Prayer,* that is, it carries elements we should be expressing every day." Ask, "What are the TODAY elements?"

Let learners respond freely, but certainly they will include such elements as (1) worship of God (6:9b); (2) a concern for God's kingdom (6:10); (3) physical sustenance (6:11); (4) forgiveness (6:12, 14); (5) spiritual warfare (6:13). Say, "These are the things that matter every day." *Option:* Distribute copies of the A Prayer Chart for TODAY activity from the reproducible page; have learners fill it out as part of this section of the lesson.

Assign the five elements above (or those suggested by class members) one each to small groups of three or four. (If your class is too small to have five groups of three, give two elements to some groups; if your class is large, give duplicate assignments.) Say, "Make a quick statement of phrases and clauses appropriate to be included in daily prayer, as related to your theme."

Let each group share its expressions. Such ideas as the following may by included: for *worship,* "Great is Your name, O God, and great is our praise"; for *kingdom concern,* "Show Your grace and power to those preaching and teaching in difficult cultures"; for *physical sustenance,* "Strength for today, Father, as You provide my food"; for *forgiveness,* "My sins are small and great, O Lord, but all are an affront to Your holiness"; for *spiritual warfare,* "Help me strike a blow against the devil today, O God."

Into Life

Say, "Prayer must acknowledge God's supremacy and power; it must plead for the success of His kingdom; it must appeal for personal, physical well-being, and even more importantly it must concern itself with spiritual well-being, especially regarding the need for forgiveness and forgiving, dealing with temptation, and confronting Satan. Do you see all those in Jesus' model?" Assuming a *yes* answer, ask, "Do you incorporate all those elements in your daily prayers? Will you?" Conclude by leading in a recitation of the model prayer.

FACING LIFE
WITHOUT WORRY

DEVOTIONAL READING: Psalm 37:1-8
BACKGROUND SCRIPTURE: Matthew 6:19-34

MATTHEW 6:25-34

25 Therefore I say unto you, Take no thought for your life, what ye shall eat, or what ye shall drink; nor yet for your body, what ye shall put on. Is not the life more than meat, and the body than raiment?

26 Behold the fowls of the air: for they sow not, neither do they reap, nor gather into barns; yet your heavenly Father feedeth them. Are ye not much better than they?

27 Which of you by taking thought can add one cubit unto his stature?

28 And why take ye thought for raiment? Consider the lilies of the field, how they grow; they toil not, neither do they spin:

29 And yet I say unto you, That even Solomon in all his glory was not arrayed like one of these.

30 Wherefore, if God so clothe the grass of the field, which to day is, and to morrow is cast into the oven, shall he not much more clothe you, O ye of little faith?

31 Therefore take no thought, saying, What shall we eat? or, What shall we drink? or, Wherewithal shall we be clothed?

32 (For after all these things do the Gentiles seek:) for your heavenly Father knoweth that ye have need of all these things.

33 But seek ye first the kingdom of God, and his righteousness; and all these things shall be added unto you.

34 Take therefore no thought for the morrow: for the morrow shall take thought for the things of itself. Sufficient unto the day is the evil thereof.

KEY VERSES

Seek ye first the kingdom of God, and his righteousness; and all these things shall be added unto you. Take therefore no thought for the morrow. . . . Sufficient unto the day is the evil thereof. —**Matthew 6:33, 34**

TRADITION AND WISDOM

Unit 2: Jesus Teaches Wisdom

LESSONS 9–13

LESSON AIMS

After participating in this lesson, each student will be able to:

1. List things Jesus says not to worry about.

2. Explain how seeking God's kingdom first helps one deal with the problem of worry.

3. Identify one area of worry in his or her life and write a prayer to release that worry to God.

LESSON OUTLINE

Introduction

A. Who Needs This Lesson?

There may be people in the class today who do not need to hear this lesson. If you have never experienced any of the following, you do not need what we are studying today: sleepless nights, sweaty palms, nervous restlessness, feelings of panic.

I suspect that not one of your learners will say that he or she has experienced none of those! But in case you have such a person, today's lesson is not something he or she needs . . . yet.

Eventually, everyone experiences what we are talking about today. Call it stress, call it anxiety, call it worry—we all go through it, and no one wants it. Learning to cope with stress, learning not to worry, overcoming anxiety: these are topics that fill lots of books, seminars, and videos. They keep selling because people keep worrying.

Does God want us to worry? Jesus says that the answer is *no*. Because God's kingdom has arrived, God's people can be confident, not worried, about their future. God, who rules as king over all, promises to meet our needs. We can replace worry with calm, stress with peace, anxiety with tranquillity.

But what Jesus says is more than just "don't worry, be happy." He provides a new perspective that enables us to free ourselves from worry. When we recognize God's promise to care for His people under all circumstances, we can surrender our worry and find peace in God's provision.

B. Lesson Background

Today's text is from Jesus' Sermon on the Mount, His great exposition of what it means to be a subject under God's kingdom, His promised reign. Before the opening point of today's lesson, Jesus has already stressed that God's reign has two major implications.

The first implication is that God's people will submit to Him, doing His will both on the outside and on the inside. They will pursue a life in which God's will is done "in earth, as it is in heaven" (Matthew 6:10). They will honor Him as king in all that they do.

The second major implication is about what God does for His people under His reign. The subjects of God's kingdom are not powerful people, but needy people (Matthew 5:3-6). They look to God to rescue them because they know that they cannot help themselves.

These two implications are summed up in the verse just preceding our text, Matthew 6:24: "No man can serve two masters: for either he will hate the one, and love the other; or else he will hold to the one, and despise the other. Ye cannot serve God and mammon." God is king, so His people must serve Him, not the false God of mammon (money). We do not need to serve mammon because we have the promise of the king's provision.

We should remember that Jesus delivered this teaching to a people who lived a very simple lifestyle under a powerful, military empire. Most people in Jesus' audience were farmers, simple tradesmen, etc. They made just enough in a good year to feed their families. In a bad year, they probably went hungry. They lived constantly under the shame and threat of Rome's domination of their land. Jesus spoke to their very deep vulnerability as poor people. He did not promise a political change, but a change in their hearts.

I. Call to a Worry-free Life
(MATTHEW 6:25-30)
A. Matter of Focus (v. 25)

25. Therefore I say unto you, Take no thought for your life, what ye shall eat, or what ye shall drink; nor yet for your body, what ye shall put on. Is not the life more than meat, and the body than raiment?

Jesus begins with a strong call to abandon worry. Food, water, and clothing are the most essential needs for life. For Jesus' audience, much of their time is devoted to work simply to obtain

HOW TO SAY IT

Galilee	*Gal*-uh-lee.
Gentiles	*Jen*-tiles.
Solomon	*Sol*-o-mun.
Thessalonians	*Thess*-uh-**lo**-nee-unz (*th* as in *thin*).

basic necessities. But Jesus says that they are now free from *thought*, which here means anxiety or worry, about those needs.

By saying that life is *more than meat* (food) and the body more *than raiment* (clothing), Jesus is pointing to a larger purpose for our existence. In God's kingdom, people exist for more than just the sake of existing. They live as God's people dedicated to His will. And for God, they are precious, the objects of His love and the focus of all that He has done.

❧ *TAKE NO THOUGHT* ❧

Recently, my wife and I have had the pleasant experience of becoming grandparents. At the time of this writing, our granddaughter is 15 months old, and she is a joy to us as well as to her parents.

She shows no concern about what we call the necessities of life. When she gets hungry, she gets fed. Clothing is put on her—sometimes with her assistance, sometimes against her efforts. When she bumps her head, someone is there to give her comfort. When she gets cranky, someone puts her down for a nap. When it is time to go to bed at night, her clothing is removed and fuzzy pajamas are put on so she can be warm and comfortable. All her needs are supplied, and she doesn't even think about them.

That's the picture Jesus paints. We sometimes think we have provided for our own needs, but unemployment, natural disasters, etc., remind us of how powerless we are. Oh, to have the faith of little children that God will supply our needs!

—J. B. N.

B. Illustration of Birds (v. 26)

26. Behold the fowls of the air: for they sow not, neither do they reap, nor gather into barns; yet your heavenly Father feedeth them. Are ye not much better than they?

Jesus here offers a comparison from the lesser to the greater. Birds are understood by His audience to have little value (Matthew 10:29). They are common and prolific. Although humans work through the farming cycle of sowing, harvesting, and storing, worthless birds do none of that. Yet

BEHOLD THE FOWLS OF THE AIR . . .
YOUR HEAVENLY FATHER FEEDETH THEM.

ARE YE NOT MUCH BETTER THAN THEY?
—MATTHEW 6:26

Visual for Lesson 13. *Point to this visual as you introduce the discussion question that is associated with verse 26.*

God cares for them. So if God cares for birds enough to see that they are fed without farming (the lesser thing), then surely He will see to it that His people are fed with the benefit they have of agriculture (the greater thing).

In reading this text, we note that Jesus is not encouraging people to stop growing food. He assumes, rather, that sowing, harvesting, and storing are what people ought to do. After all, God created humans to work in a garden (Genesis 2:15) and commanded Israel to work (Exodus 20:9). Rather, Jesus is pointing out that if worthless birds, who do not farm, are fed by God, then how much more valuable are humans who do farm and do other useful work.

> *What Do You Think?*
> What was the last time you worried excessively about something? How do you break the worry cycle?
> *Talking Points for Your Discussion*
> ▪ Worry about self
> ▪ Worry about loved ones
> ▪ Worry about cultural issues

C. Illustration of Life (v. 27)

27. Which of you by taking thought can add one cubit unto his stature?

To the comparison with birds, Jesus adds the observation that worry can add nothing to our lives. He illustrates this with a point about one's length of life. The word *thought* again refers to worry and anxiety. The cubit is a measure of length, the distance from a man's elbow to the tip of the finger—about 18 inches. The term translated *stature* likely refers to the length of life. So we might paraphrase Jesus' statement in our setting as, "Which of you by worrying can make your life span longer by even half a yard?"

Clearly, it is not worry that keeps us alive and well for even a moment. Today we know that excessive worry and stress actually can shorten a person's life. Only God's provision can sustain us through the trials of life, and certainly only God can give us life that triumphs over death.

> *What Do You Think?*
> When do we cross the line between making prudent decisions about the future and engaging in undue worry about the future?
> *Talking Points for Your Discussion*
> ▪ In the purchase of insurance
> ▪ In retirement planning
> ▪ In "saving for a rainy day"
> ▪ In how we define "good stewardship" (Matthew 25:14-30)

D. Illustration of Plants (vv. 28-30)

28. And why take ye thought for raiment? Consider the lilies of the field, how they grow; they toil not, neither do they spin.

This third illustration is like the first one in being an argument from the lesser thing (common wildflowers and grasses) to the greater thing (human beings). Where the comparison with birds focused on food, this one focuses on *raiment* (clothing).

In Jesus' time, most people make their own clothes and grow/raise their own food. Making clothing starts with the growing and harvesting of flax and/or the raising and shearing of sheep. The fibers of linen or wool are spun into thread, then the thread is woven into cloth. Finally the cloth is cut and sewn to become garments. All those steps, done by hand, means considerable *toil*. By contrast, wildflowers do none of that.

Facing Life Without Worry

29. And yet I say unto you, That even Solomon in all his glory was not arrayed like one of these.

In biblical history, the greatest material glory is associated with King Solomon (2 Chronicles 9:13-28). None can expect to surpass his possessions and adornments. Yet nothing in Solomon's treasure could rival a field of wildflowers for beauty.

30. Wherefore, if God so clothe the grass of the field, which to day is, and to morrow is cast into the oven, shall he not much more clothe you, O ye of little faith?

This verse makes clear the force of Jesus' comparison. Wildflowers and grasses grow commonly in the countryside of Galilee where Jesus speaks. Because wood is not common there, it is not often burned for fuel. So cooking fires often are made with dried plants gathered from the countryside. Thus, the wildflowers that are adorned so finely might end up the next day in an oven. So if God adorns nearly worthless plants so beautifully, how much more will He provide clothing for His people, His most precious possession?

Jesus stresses some key ideas through these illustrations. One is that God has supreme control over even the smallest matters of nature. Another is that people are of supreme value to God; from God's vantage, humans have more value than anything else in God's creation. A third is that though humans work for their living, it is ultimately God who provides all that they have. That leads to a magnificent conclusion: because of God's power and the value He places on His people, we are free from worry over our needs.

II. Call to Depend on God
(MATTHEW 6:31-34)
A. No Anxiety for Needs (v. 31)

31. Therefore take no thought, saying, What shall we eat? or, What shall we drink? or, Wherewithal shall we be clothed?

This verse repeats the phrases of verse 25, stressing again Jesus' central point to be free from worry. The questions asked are those of a person who does not know where the food, water, and clothing will come from in the future. Those who

ask such questions rightly realize that they cannot guarantee for themselves a supply of necessities. Health may be ruined, business may fail, savings may give out. What then?

> *What Do You Think?*
> What was a time when you had God's priorities reversed? How did you get into that mode of thinking? What helped you correct the situation?
>
> *Talking Points for Your Discussion*
> - Media messages (clever advertising jingles, etc.)
> - The lure of earthly pleasures (James 4:3)
> - The need to "prove something" to others

B. Reasons for Confidence (v. 32)

32. (For after all these things do the Gentiles seek:) for your heavenly Father knoweth that ye have need of all these things.

Jesus now makes two distinct but related points. These put in perspective our powerlessness to guarantee that we will have what we need.

The first is that getting what is needed for the future is the priority of the Gentiles, that is, of people who do not know God. If we are ignorant of who God really is, if we do not know Him as a loving, generous, and powerful Father who values His people supremely and uses His power to supply their needs, then we have nowhere to turn for help. The future, which we cannot control, also is not under anyone else's control. That outlook, of course, is the opposite of the one that God's people have. Our knowledge of God casts out fear of the future.

The second point is that God is completely aware of His people's needs. He has not forgotten His people or failed to note that they require food, drink, and clothing. As Jesus has said, if God feeds worthless birds and clothes worthless plants, He knows what His people need.

Jesus made the same point back in Matthew 6:7, 8. If we genuinely know God, if we genuinely believe what Jesus says about Him, we can be confident that He will supply our needs, even though we have no control over the future whatsoever.

C. God's Daily Provision (vv. 33, 34)

33. But seek ye first the kingdom of God, and his righteousness; and all these things shall be added unto you.

Jesus brings the discourse to a climax. The discourse is preceded by a contrast between serving God and serving mammon (Matthew 6:24); it ends with a contrast between worry and our need to seek God's kingdom.

The pagans struggle first and foremost to have physical provisions. They believe that they must give their primary attention to survival. By contrast, Jesus' followers are to seek God's kingdom first. We want above all for God to reign, for His will to be done everywhere. We are to be focused not on providing for ourselves, but on serving God, obeying God, and sharing God. It is what we are to do first and constantly.

In seeking God's kingdom, Jesus' followers are also to seek God's righteousness. The Sermon on the Mount begins with a blessing for those who "hunger and thirst after righteousness" (Matthew 5:6) and the warning that in God's kingdom one's righteousness must be greater than the outward-only righteousness of the religious leaders (5:20). What Jesus expresses here, the active pursuit of righteousness, complements those earlier statements. For those in the kingdom of God, nothing matters as much as having God's righteousness, His right way, prevailing in the world.

For kingdom people, that means we pursue God's right way for ourselves, seeking first to do God's will personally. But it also means that we seek to bring the rest of the world into conformity with God's right way. Matthew will end his Gospel with Jesus' command to make disciples of all nations (Matthew 28:19, 20). God's kingdom is more than just a matter of my personal standing with God. God's purpose is that the whole of humanity should come to know and serve Him.

Jesus promises that those who seek the kingdom will receive *all these things*. In the context this obviously refers to basic needs: food, drink, and clothing. Without trust in the God who rules over the kingdom, we would think that those necessities demand our primary attention. We would fear that if we stopped pursuing them, we might not obtain them, or at least not enough of them. That fear is especially real for people like Jesus' audience, who live on the smallest of margins as they raise their own food and make their own clothing. But as Jesus has stressed, God promises to provide those things. By giving first attention to God's kingdom, Jesus' followers acknowledge that they do not hold ultimate power over their survival. God does! And God promises that He provides for His people under His rule.

We cannot stress enough that this promise has to do with God meeting our needs, not our wants. Many have distorted this text and others like it to suggest that if people pursue God's kingdom vigorously enough, then God will grant material abundance, whatever we ask for. That obviously ignores the emphasis of this passage. Jesus speaks entirely of basic needs. The whole emphasis of His teaching in this section is on trust in God and submission to God's will. People who do that realize that they are not in a position to specify the precise amount of material goods that they require. Rather, they trust God to give them what they need in the right amount. They express faith not by demanding more, but by believing that what God supplies is sufficient.

It is also important to note that Jesus' teaching does not imply that people do nothing for their own support. They seek the kingdom first, but they continue to obey God's purpose for humanity as expressed in creation: to do useful work in the world (2 Thessalonians 3:12). The issue is not whether or not to work, but in how we approach our work. Pursuing God's kingdom frees us from anxiety as we work because we trust God. We see our work not as the means of providing for ourselves, but as God's provision for our needs. Further, we are to see our work as a way of serving God and pursuing God's right way.

> *What Do You Think?*
> How do we harmonize Jesus' promise with the reality of famine we see in the world?
> *Talking Points for Your Discussion*
> - Resources lacking vs. resources not shared
> - Cause vs. effect

34a. Take therefore no thought for the morrow: for the morrow shall take thought for the things of itself.

The closing remarks remind us again that God is in control of the future over which we have no power at all. Again, to *take no thought* means to have no worry. Jesus does not exclude planning or saving, but His words do remind us that our planning and saving ought not be motivated by fear but directed by trust in God.

The expression *the morrow shall take thought for the things of itself* is ironic but clear. "The future," an inanimate entity, obviously does not worry. But the God who controls the future promises to care for His people in the future. Even if the worst happens to them, God's people can be confident that God will provide for them, in this life and the life to come.

> *What Do You Think?*
> Is it God's will that some Christians remain in a continual state of poverty? Why, or why not?
> *Talking Points for Your Discussion*
> ▪ What God causes vs. what God permits
> ▪ 1 Timothy 6:9; James 2:5
> ▪ The issue of taking a voluntary "vow of poverty"

❧ NEGLECT AND OBSESSION ❧

In the movie *Gone with the Wind*, Scarlett O'Hara neglects the future by saying, "I'll think about that tomorrow." That turns out to be irresponsible! But the opposite can also be true. We can become so obsessed with the future that we fail to enjoy God's blessings today.

Some time ago, I read the story of a woman who wrote of certain experiences that she had when she was a little girl. Three carnivals would come to her town at various times of the year. Normally, she had enough money to go to all three and enjoy the rides. But things were tough for her family one particular year. Her father told her she would have enough money only for one carnival. She chose to go to the first. As the months passed, however, her family's finances improved, so her father said she could go to another. She chose the second rather than wait

for the third. By the time the third carnival came to town, her family could afford all three.

Think of what would have happened if she had obsessed about the future and hoarded her money to go only to the third carnival: she would have missed the fun of at least one of the other two. Neglecting the future can be irresponsible; obsessing about it can be punitive. Trusting God for the future keeps us from doing either.   —J. B. N.

34b. Sufficient unto the day is the evil thereof.

Why worry about tomorrow when there are sufficient problems today? For the follower of Jesus, the focus is not the uncertain future, but the concrete present. If today has trouble, how does God call us to address that trouble as subjects of His kingdom? Jesus calls His people to be obedient in "the now," not anxious about "the later."

Conclusion
A. Making Our Lives Easier

Few passages of the Bible challenge us as much throughout our lives as does this one. Do you see all the ways it makes us think about our lives? Trusting God for the future, seeking His kingdom constantly as the first priority, makes us think about how we use our time, where we place our efforts, how we relate to the people around us, and how we feel inside.

Jesus gives His followers a great responsibility in this passage. But we are missing the point if we feel burdened by that responsibility. When we listen carefully, we realize that Jesus is not making our lives harder with these words. Rather, He is making our lives easier. We are free from the burden of worry when we submit to God.

B. Prayer

Our Father, we thank You that You value us above all things, so much that You gave Your Son for us. Teach us to be at peace because we rest in Your care. In the name of Jesus, amen!

C. Thought to Remember
Jesus removes worry—if we let Him.

INVOLVEMENT LEARNING

Some of the activities below are also found in the helpful student book, Adult Bible Class.
Don't forget to download the free reproducible page from www.standardlesson.com to enhance your lesson!

Into the Lesson

Download the reproducible page and place in chairs copies of the Why Worry? exercise. Learners can work on this as they arrive.

Play a game of "word association of opposites" with your class. Say, "Call out the first 'opposite word' that comes to mind as I read the following list."

Use the following list or one of your own choosing; possible responses are in parentheses: happy (sad); smart (ignorant); sleepy (rested); miserly (generous); rude (polite); thrilled (disappointed); hungry (filled); indifferent (enthusiastic); compassionate (callous). Make this the final word: *worried*. The responses made to this last entry will allow you to make a transition to today's study of "Facing Life Without Worry."

Into the Word

Comment to your class, "Worry is another sign of bad doctrine!" Remind the class that in last week's study you saw that bad prayer bespeaks bad doctrine. Then say, "What one believes about who God is sets the boundaries around his or her concept of prayer. Likewise, what one believes about who God is sets the tone for her or his inner sense of peace or anxiety, contentment or frantic fretting."

Write these two questions on the board to begin a discussion: "In today's text, how does Jesus picture God with regard to His person and character? What is there about God's person and character that speaks to your sense of contentment and calm?" (*Option:* Put these on a handout and assign them to small groups for discussion.)

Let the learners answer freely, but expect these truths to be noted: (1) God is characterized as *your* Father (vv. 26, 32), implying a Father's love and care for His children; (2) God's creation is such that animals are fed, so He will provide for His people, whom He values more than ani-

mals (v. 26); (3) God clothes plants with beauty, so He will make certain His children are clothed (vv. 28-30); (4) God will not overlook our needs, which He knows so well—thus we have no need to panic in worry (v. 32); (5) God knows what really matters (v. 33), and we get bogged down in things that do not ultimately matter; (6) God has a perfect understanding of the relationship of time and eternity (v. 34), and our worries are almost always related to the temporal and the temporary.

If you hear no reflections on the contrasts between God's power and our limited powers, ask these questions as follow-up: "How do these attributes of God contrast with us and our own 'powers'? What does that contrast have to do with our choice between anxiety and peace of mind?"

Suggest that learners look at each attribute of God in their earlier answers to discover parallel elements in their own status. As related to the six responses above, the following are samples: (1) God is Father and fully in control; our worries are almost always of things we do not or cannot control; (2 and 3) God is a provider of unlimited resources, so our success does not depend solely on resources we "own"; (4) God's focus on needs is in sharp contrast with our lists of comforts and wants; (5) God wants us to prioritize His kingdom, and often we put other, lesser things on our "worry lists"; (6) God is not limited by time, but we let the constraints of time haunt and hassle us into worry.

Into Life

Download the reproducible page and distribute copies of the Foolishness of Worry activity. Allow about three minutes for learners to complete this. Call for volunteers to share answers, but don't put anyone on the spot since their answers will be quite personal in some cases. Your learners may be more willing to share answers in small groups or study pairs.

GOD ESTABLISHES A FAITHFUL PEOPLE

Special Features

Lessons

Unit 1: God's Covenant

Unit 2: God's Protection

Unit 3: God's Redemption

QUARTERLY QUIZ

Use these questions as a pretest or as a review. The answers are on page iv of This Quarter in the Word.

Lesson 1

1. How old was Abram when he set out for the land of Canaan? (55, 65, 75?) *Genesis 12:4*

2. Abram took along his nephew _____ on the trip to Canaan. *Genesis 12:5*

3. When Abram arrived in Canaan, he built a temple to the Lord. T/F. *Genesis 12:7*

Lesson 2

1. The Lord was Abram's "shield" and "great _____." *Genesis 15:1*

2. When Abram believed God's promise, God counted this to him as what? (obedience, opportunity, righteousness?) *Genesis 15:6*

Lesson 3

1. Abraham and Isaac led a live ram as they climbed the mountain. T/F. *Genesis 22:6-8*

2. Abraham was prevented from killing his son by the _____ of the Lord. *Genesis 22:11, 12*

Lesson 4

1. Mary sang that her what magnified the Lord? (soul, voice, offering?). *Luke 1:46*

2. Julius Caesar was the emperor when Jesus was born. T/F. *Luke 2:1*

Lesson 5

1. Potiphar's wife used Joseph's sandal as evidence against him. T/F. *Genesis 39:15*

2. Because of Potiphar's wife's false accusation, Joseph was sent to _____. *Genesis 39:20*

Lesson 6

1. What did Pharaoh give Joseph to express pleasure and approval? (pick three: ring, house, boat, linen robe, gold necklace, silver bowl?) *Genesis 41:42, 43*

2. What were the names of Joseph's sons? (pick two: Ephraim, Judah, Benjamin, Manasseh, Potiphera, On?) *Genesis 41:51, 52*

Lesson 7

1. How many years was the famine in Joseph's day to last? (one, two, seven?) *Genesis 45:6*

2. Joseph allowed his family to live in the land of _____. *Genesis 45:10*

Lesson 8

1. When Jacob died, Joseph's brothers feared that he would exact revenge. T/F. *Genesis 50:15*

2. Joseph asked that his bones remain in Egypt, his adopted home. T/F. *Genesis 50:25*

Lesson 9

1. Aaron's sister _____ celebrated the demise of Pharaoh's chariot army. *Exodus 15:20*

2. The water of Marah was bitter. T/F. *Exodus 15:23*

Lesson 10

1. Paul said that he must be what for the law? (attuned to, aware of, dead to?) *Galatians 2:19*

2. Paul said, "I am _____ with Christ." *Galatians 2:20*

Lesson 11

1. Paul said that people of faith are children of whom? (Adam, Abraham, Moses?) *Galatians 3:7*

2. From what effect of the law did Christ redeem us? (cure, curse, curtain?) *Galatians 3:13*

Lesson 12

1. God sent His Son when the fullness of _____ had come. *Galatians 4:4*

2. Through faith in Christ, we become heirs. T/F. *Galatians 4:7*

Lesson 13

1. "Peace" is a fruit of the Spirit. T/F. *Galatians 5:22*

2. When we bear one another's burdens, we fulfill the _____ of Christ. *Galatians 6:2*

by Mark S. Krause

Do you ever doubt? Many Christians feel as if they are persons of doubt rather than persons of faith. Perhaps you wonder how to be a person of faith, how to put faith into action. This is where Scripture comes in.

Much of what Scripture teaches us about faith comes through stories of faithful people. In this quarter, we learn about the actions of some of the great heroes of our faith. Each stands on the faithful shoulders of those who have gone before him or her. Let's look at our quarter in reverse chronological order to see how that happened.

The Result of Abraham's Faith

The quarter ends with a careful study of Paul's teaching on faith in Galatians. But as wonderful as Galatians is in and of itself, Paul's teachings don't "come out of thin air." Paul draws heavily on the example of Abraham (who predates Paul by some 2,000 years) as the central example to our understanding of faith in Christ.

Paul's argument combines the promise God made to Abraham with that man's faithfulness to show us how we become heirs of Abraham's promise. We do so through Christ, the promised blessing to Abraham. Christ is the one who redeems the faithful from the curse of the law. Thus we do not have to be physical descendants of Abraham to be heirs of the promise.

Between Paul and Abraham

There are important people of faith between Paul and Abraham. Moving back in time some 60 years from the writing of Galatians, we are privileged to witness the obedient faith of Mary and Joseph (Lesson 4), the parents of Jesus. Mary accepted the news of her miraculous pregnancy with faithful words of praise that expressed trust in God for her future.

Joseph trekked with Mary to Bethlehem at an inconvenient time. This allowed prophecy to be fulfilled regarding the place of Jesus' birth. The road to Bethlehem was the road of obedience as the two traveled in faith as Abraham had done.

Many centuries before Mary and Joseph, Moses walked his road of faith as well. We often think of Moses in relation to "the law," but he was a man of great faith too. After the miraculous deliverance of Israel from Egyptian bondage, Moses and his sister Miriam led the nation in a celebration that acknowledged God as deliverer (Lesson 9). Our faith celebrations should do likewise.

Four centuries before Moses there was Joseph. He was a man who faithfully maintained his integrity even when it caused him to be thrown in prison. God worked through Joseph to rescue his family from starvation in a time of famine. The faithfulness of Joseph is important to us not only as an example, but also because his actions preserved the line of the ancestors of our Lord Jesus.

Abraham, the Forefather of Faith

Joseph's great-grandfather was Abraham. He trusted God to the extent that he ventured to an unknown country as an old man and eventually risked his son's life. He did both in faithful obedience to God's direction.

> ### We are God's true children.

The Christian community of faith is made possible by Abraham's faith and Jesus' redemptive death for us. We are truly changed, a community that lives by faith in the Son of God, who loved us and died for us.

An important part of that change is the fact that we are given the Spirit of God's Son. This "seals the deal," giving us the complete assurance that we are God's true children. May that fact cause us to walk as Abraham did!

GET THE SETTING

by John Nugent

THIS QUARTER'S LESSONS begin and end with God's promise to Abraham. God called Abraham out of Ur around 2000 BC. Ur was an important Babylonian city located between the Tigris and Euphrates Rivers. In the preceding millennium, this area of Babylonia, known as Sumer, was embroiled in a prolonged power struggle with an area known as Akkad, to the north. Sumer thrived from 2850 to 2360 BC, but the Akkadians dominated from 2360 to 2180 BC. This dominance came to an end when barbarians from the Zagros Mountains crippled the Akkadian Empire. As a result, the Sumerians regained power from 2060 to 1950 BC under the Third Dynasty of Ur.

Those were glorious days for southern Babylonia. Commercial and social activity thrived. The oldest known and highly influential legal code of Ur-Nammu, the dynasty's founder, was established. Architectural wonders like the marvelous multitiered ziggurat were erected to testify to the grandeur of this booming metropolis.

Yet this prosperity did not last. Elamites stormed down from the mountains and brought an end to the splendid Kingdom of Ur. The resulting power vacuum attracted Arabian Semites, who overran the area and sought to establish dynasties of their own.

Exactly when in this turbulent history did God call Abraham? Was it at the peak of Sumerian civilization, or was it during a low point when greedy hoards battled to establish their own glory and prestige? Scripture is not clear about this.

It is clear, however, that God chose not to forge His people in the crucible of Babylonian power-mongering. God could have taken advantage of an impending power vacuum and positioned Abraham to be the next great king of Ur, but He didn't. Instead, He called Abraham to leave the region altogether.

The reason was simple: God was moving Abraham not simply from one land to another, but from one way of being in the world to another. God called Abraham away from the social network, lifestyle, and worldview of Babylon to live in a territory where no kingdom had thrived. God called Abraham from the apex of human power politics to a place where only God himself could make a name for His people.

The new direction in world history that God initiated through Abraham involved neither a change in rulership over Babylon nor a mere territorial shift away from Ur. Rather, it was for the creation of a people in a place where they were to trust in God and God alone.

This divine strategy was not a one-time thing. It is the pattern we see throughout Scripture and throughout this quarter's lessons. As God led Abraham's descendents into Egypt, His purpose was not to infiltrate the Egyptian power base and use its resources to build a righteous political order in that territory. Rather, God was using Egypt temporarily to preserve His people during a famine and to bide time while the wicked inhabitants of Canaan ripened themselves for divine judgment.

God then led His people out of Egypt on a renewed journey of faith. The apostle Paul found himself on a similar journey as he served with an Abraham-like faith as an ambassador for the kingdom of Christ. Paul's service was *within* the mighty transcontinental Roman Empire—the new Babylon of the time (1 Peter 5:13)—but it was not *for* that empire. That's a continuing lesson for us!

THIS QUARTER IN THE WORD

Answers to the Quarterly Quiz on page 114

Lesson 1—1. 75. 2. Lot. 3. false. **Lesson 2**—1. reward. 2. righteousness. **Lesson 3**—1. false. 2. angel. **Lesson 4**—1. soul. 2. false. **Lesson 5**—1. false. 2. prison. **Lesson 6**—1. ring, linen robe, gold necklace. 2. Manasseh, Ephraim. **Lesson 7**—1. seven. 2. Goshen. **Lesson 8**—1. true. 2. false. **Lesson 9**—1. Miriam. 2. true. **Lesson 10**—1. dead to. 2. crucified. **Lesson 11**—1. Abraham. 2. curse. **Lesson 12**—1. time. 2. true. **Lesson 13**—1. true. 2. law.

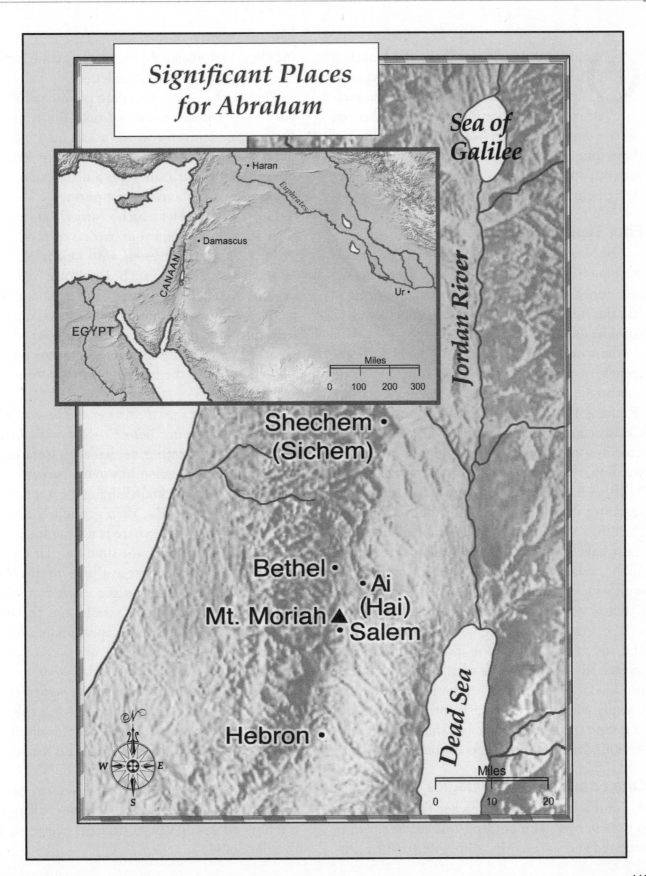

Significant Places for Abraham

Haran

Euphrates

Damascus

CANAAN

EGYPT

Ur

Miles

0   100   200   300

Sea of Galilee

Jordan River

Shechem (Sichem) •

Bethel •

• Ai (Hai)

Mt. Moriah ▲

• Salem

Dead Sea

Hebron •

N
W   E
S

Miles

0   10   20

TEACHING THE BARRIER

Teacher Tips by Brent L. Amato

Our Teacher Tips for Fall 2011 launched us on a consideration of four types of "problem students" who make their presence felt in the classroom: *the bored, the barrier, the boss,* and *the bomber.* We addressed the first of these four last time, and for this installment we turn our attention to the second. We will consider the remaining two in later quarters.

Four Types, More Imperatives

The New Testament offers imperatives regarding how Christians are to relate to each other. We mentioned the imperative of intercessory prayer last quarter. But there are other imperatives to consider as well.

Many imperatives are found in the New Testament's "one another" passages. We are to love one another (John 13:34). We are to honor one another (Romans 12:10). We are to accept one another as Christ accepted us (Romans 15:7). If you take some time to scan through the "one another" passages, you'll see that this just scratches the surface!

These passages serve to remind us that good teaching involves much more than mastery of teaching techniques. To reach your students, you must have a Spirit-filled relationship with them. Such a relationship will have much more to do with your effectiveness as a teacher than the brilliance of your lesson plan and presentation.

The Master's teaching was always relational, and you can tailor the "one anothers" specifically to each student, no matter what category they fall in. The fact that the teacher communicates relationally with the students beyond the lessons per se is a powerful antidote for all that would otherwise hinder the effectiveness of your teaching.

One Focus, Three Strategies

For this installment of Teacher Tips, we'll focus on *the barrier.* This student, unlike *the bored,* is engaged and sincerely has something to offer during class. Unfortunately, the barrier's contribution has nothing to do with your lesson!

Picture this: You're making good headway as you teach a lesson on devotional life from the Psalms. Suddenly, *the barrier* asks a question that deals with the end times! We call this kind of question a "rabbit trail"; it is a distraction from your lesson and should not be pursued.

How do we deal with such a barrier? Let's explore three strategies to keep your barriers on task.

First, know your lesson plan and stick to it. Granted, there will always be legitimate "detours" or some need to be attended to. But detours should be the exception and not the rule. Lesson outlines help not only you but also the students in this regard. Use your lesson plan as a litmus test for the relevancy of the barrier's issues, comments, and questions.

Second, affirm both the barrier and the rest of the class when confronted with a rabbit trail. Rather than ignoring, rejecting, or challenging the barrier's comment or question, affirm the barrier before the class by briefly acknowledging the importance of his or her point. But then graciously remind the barrier that while there is a time for everything (Ecclesiastes 3:1), the time for that topic is not now, but that you are available to discuss it after class. Affirm the class as a whole by quickly moving on and sticking with the lesson. The apostles dealt with detours in an appropriate manner (Acts 6:2), and so must we.

Third, address the barrier's point with him or her personally right after class or as soon as possible thereafter. Again, it is your relationship with the barrier and not the detour or even your lesson that is paramount. Your positive action in this regard will speak volumes to these students.

As with the other three types, I hope my barrier students show up! May you rise to the challenge of teaching all your problem students effectively for the glory of God.

THE LORD CALLS ABRAM

DEVOTIONAL READING: Hebrews 6:13-20
BACKGROUND SCRIPTURE: Genesis 11:27–12:9

GENESIS 12:1-9

1 Now the LORD had said unto Abram, Get thee out of thy country, and from thy kindred, and from thy father's house, unto a land that I will shew thee:

2 And I will make of thee a great nation, and I will bless thee, and make thy name great; and thou shalt be a blessing:

3 And I will bless them that bless thee, and curse him that curseth thee: and in thee shall all families of the earth be blessed.

4 So Abram departed, as the LORD had spoken unto him; and Lot went with him: and Abram was seventy and five years old when he departed out of Haran.

5 And Abram took Sarai his wife, and Lot his brother's son, and all their substance that they had gathered, and the souls that they had gotten in Haran; and they went forth to go into the land of Canaan; and into the land of Canaan they came.

6 And Abram passed through the land unto the place of Sichem, unto the plain of Moreh. And the Canaanite was then in the land.

7 And the LORD appeared unto Abram, and said, Unto thy seed will I give this land: and there builded he an altar unto the LORD, who appeared unto him.

8 And he removed from thence unto a mountain on the east of Bethel, and pitched his tent, having Bethel on the west, and Hai on the east: and there he builded an altar unto the LORD, and called upon the name of the LORD.

9 And Abram journeyed, going on still toward the south.

KEY VERSE

I will make of thee a great nation, and I will bless thee, and make thy name great; and thou shalt be a blessing. —**Genesis 12:2**

Photo: Jupiterimages / Photos.com / Thinkstock

GOD ESTABLISHES A FAITHFUL PEOPLE

Unit 1: God's Covenant
LESSONS 1–4

LESSON AIMS

After participating in this lesson, each student will be able to:

1. Summarize God's initial call of Abram (Abraham).

2. Describe the faith of Abram in his reaction to God's call.

3. Adopt Abram's faith response as a model for carrying out a ministry in the week ahead.

LESSON OUTLINE

Introduction
  A. What This World Needs
  B. Lesson Background
 I. Promises to Abram (GENESIS 12:1-3)
  A. Place (v. 1)
  B. People (v. 2)
  C. Purpose (v. 3)
    A Life of Purpose
 II. Journey of Abram (GENESIS 12:4, 5)
  A. Clouds (v. 4)
    Troubles Along the Way
  B. Success (v. 5)
 III. Arrival of Abram (GENESIS 12:6-9)
  A. Promise Threatened (v. 6)
  B. Promise Reaffirmed (v. 7)
  C. Movements in the Land (vv. 8, 9)
Conclusion
  A. What This World Wants
  B. Prayer
  C. Thought to Remember

Introduction

A. What This World Needs

When God created this world, it was exactly how He wanted it to be. The heavens and earth were perfectly aligned. The ground was fertile, and humans enjoyed an undefiled garden. God was pleased with His creation, repeatedly calling it good and ultimately declaring it very good.

Yet things did not stay that way. Adam and Eve disobeyed God, ate the forbidden fruit, and propelled this world into a state of corruption (Genesis 3). Cain followed with murder (4:8), Lamech escalated revenge (4:23, 24), and eventually every human thought was evil, all the time (6:5). Things were so bad that God decided to cleanse the earth with a flood (6:7, 13; 7:4).

Though the flood brought a necessary end to a dreadful past, it would not be God's means of bringing the future. God signaled a decisive end to globally destructive floods by hanging His bow in the clouds (Genesis 9:7-13). In choosing not to destroy the earth every time human sin got out of control, God placed the burden on himself to find some other way to meet the world's need. Somehow He would right the world's wrong.

God could have done this with a reign of terror that would strike fear and obedience into the human race. He could also have done it by depriving the race of free will, programming it for involuntary obedience. But He did not. Instead, God chose a route that respected human freedom and showcased both His love and His justice. That route culminated in the death of His Son on the cross, but it began with a man named Abram.

B. Lesson Background

God's solution for the world's problem began with an ordinary man. Genesis 11:27-32 furnishes important background information for our text and for God's strategy to redeem His world. Three facts from this text are important for the plot of our story today.

First, we meet Abram, the son of an ordinary man from an extraordinary city. Ur was one of the leading cities of Mesopotamia, the place where civilizations thrived and where humans sought to

The Lord Calls Abram

make a name for themselves. It was the same land in which humans began building the Tower of Babel against God's wishes (Genesis 11:1-9).

Second, we learn that Abram's brother has died and left behind a son named Lot. Lot will factor significantly in Abram's story. Third, we learn that Abram was married to a barren woman named Sarai. Her infertility would become the occasion for God to show His power through this family.

I. Promises to Abram
(Genesis 12:1-3)
A. Place (v. 1)

1. Now the Lord had said unto Abram, Get thee out of thy country, and from thy kindred, and from thy father's house, unto a land that I will shew thee.

God's positive solution for this world's need begins with a directive to Abram (later renamed Abraham in Genesis 17:5). Thus it is God who takes the initiative to redeem the world. Humans cannot engineer their own salvation. It must begin with God because it can be accomplished only by His power.

Abram's role is thus not to plan how the world will be saved, but to obey God's command. Abram must leave his homeland and his father's family and go to an unspecified place. The town of Abram's departure is Haran (Genesis 11:31). In

HOW TO SAY IT

Ai	*Ay*-eye.
Babel	*Bay*-bul.
Babylon	*Bab*-uh-lun.
Beth-aven	*Beth-**ay**-ven.*
Bethel	*Beth*-ul.
Canaan	*Kay*-nun.
Canaanites	*Kay*-nun-ites.
Hai	*Hay*-eye.
Mediterranean	*Med*-uh-tuh-**ray**-nee-un.
Mesopotamia	*Mes*-uh-puh-**tay**-me-uh.
Moreh	*Moe*-reh.
Sarai	*Seh*-rye.
Sichem	*Sigh*-kem.
Terah	*Tair*-uh.

English, this town seems to have the same name as Abram's dead brother (11:28), but the Hebrew spelling is different.

On the surface, Abram's departure from Haran seems to contradict Genesis 15:7, which states that God calls Abram out of Ur. However, a careful reading shows otherwise. We note in 11:31 that Terah (Abram's father) left Ur in order to go to Canaan. Then we learn in 12:5 that the place that God promises to take Abram is this same land of Canaan. This means that God is taking responsibility for bringing Abram out of Ur through the earlier move of Terah. Perhaps Terah was called by God to leave Ur and go to Canaan, but for some reason decided to stop part way. Thus Abram has to finish what Terah started. Or perhaps God called Terah to make the first part of the trip and then Abram to complete it.

What is important is not the precise way that God brings about Abram's departure from Ur, however. What is most important is that God's plan for the world requires Abram to step out on faith and leave the center of human prosperity—to leave the place where he is most likely to flourish. In so doing, Abram is to go to Canaan, where civilization has not prospered to the extent it has in Mesopotamia. God cares not where humans have achieved greatness for themselves. He calls people to serve Him in unexpected places, places where any greatness will be entirely dependent on Him.

Also significant is the fact that Abram is called to leave his *father's house* behind. When Terah departed Ur, he took with him his son Abram and his grandson Lot, whose father was deceased (Genesis 11:28, 31). We also know from Genesis 24 that Abram's other brother, Nahor, settled there at some point. So for Abram to leave his father's family behind entails leaving behind not only his aging father, but other close relatives as well. Thus God calls Abraham to leave behind family security. This will teach Abram how to trust in God's strength alone (Acts 7:2-5).

B. People (v. 2)

2. And I will make of thee a great nation, and I will bless thee, and make thy name great; and thou shalt be a blessing.

God's strategy for Abram begins to take shape. We wonder what goes through Abram's mind when he hears the promise to have a great nation and a great name. There are no specifics regarding how this will happen. Will Abram become a mighty warrior-king to rule the world? What about the fact that Abram's wife is barren (Genesis 11:30)? No plan is specified, only the general promises of being blessed and being a blessing.

> **What Do You Think?**
> In what ways has God blessed you to be a blessing to others?
> *Talking Points for Your Discussion*
> - Through experiences
> - Materially

C. Purpose (v. 3)

3. And I will bless them that bless thee, and curse him that curseth thee: and in thee shall all families of the earth be blessed.

Verse 2 indicates that Abram will be a blessing, and the verse before us begins to address how. Abram's state of being blessed, like his name's greatness, is to be rooted in God's action. Wherever Abram's descendants will go, God will look after them. He will take note not only of their actions but also of the interactions of others with them. Those who treat Abram's descendants well will receive God's blessing; those who treat them poorly will incur God's judgment.

> **What Do You Think?**
> When was the last time someone cursed you? How did you react?
> *Talking Points for Your Discussion*
> - While driving
> - At work
> - At home
> - Proverbs 26:2

Such blessing is not, however, merely for the sake of Abram's biological family. God shines His favor on one family so that they may be His instrument of blessing to *all families of the earth*. God's strategy is to begin small. Abram's forthcoming offspring are the pilot project for what God intends (Gala-tians 3:7-9). We should note that God gives the same or similar promise to each of the three great patriarchs: across six chapters to Abram (Genesis 12:1-3, 7; 13:14-18; 15:4, 5, 13-18; 17:1-8; 18:17-19; 22:15-18), twice to Isaac (26:4, 23, 24), and twice to Jacob (28:14, 15; 35:9-12).

❧ *A Life of Purpose* ❧

The Purpose Driven Life by Rick Warren—leader of a California megachurch—is one of the best-selling nonfiction books of all time. More than 30 million copies were in print four years after its publication in 2002. The book raises a very important question: *What on earth am I here for?* Secular voices say that there is no overarching purpose to the universe, since everything exists by chance evolutionary processes. But then those same voices will irrationally claim that it's up to each of us to create our own little islands of purpose within the vast, purposeless universe.

If Abram ever believed his life had no purpose, God destroyed that notion by calling him to get out of his comfort zone, leave his homeland, and become the father of a nation through which all the world would be blessed. From the perspective the New Testament affords us, we can see that this blessing comes through Jesus, the Savior.

As Christians, each of us should be asking ourselves the question posed by Rick Warren: *What on earth am I here for?* We should ask ourselves that question while we read Matthew 28:19, 20. That's the passage that tells us how we best can be a blessing to others.   —C. R. B.

II. Journey of Abram
(GENESIS 12:4, 5)
A. Clouds (v. 4)

4. So Abram departed, as the LORD had spoken unto him; and Lot went with him: and Abram was seventy and five years old when he departed out of Haran.

The good news in this verse is that Abram exhibits great faith and accepts God's commission to leave his homeland for an unknown destination. But this verse also introduces a couple of complications. First, Abram is 75 years old. Comparing this figure with the age we see in Genesis 17:17, we can compute the age of Sarai, Abram's wife, to be about 65. Their ages will have a major impact on how the story unfolds.

> **What Do You Think?**
> What attitudes and practices make trusting God's promises more difficult at age 75 than at, say, 35?
> *Talking Points for Your Discussion*
> - In the workplace
> - In family life
> - In the church

The second complication is the fact that Abram brings his nephew Lot along. Some students think that Lot, as a member of Abram's father's household, should have been left behind according to God's instructions in Genesis 12:1 for Abram to leave his father's house. It is customary, however, for brothers of a deceased man to take responsibility for the deceased's household. So perhaps Abram considers Lot to be of his own household.

Whatever the reason, the inclusion of Lot hangs like a cloud over the narrative to follow. In Genesis 13, there is a dispute between the servants of Abram and Lot over the land, with the result that Abram and Lot part ways. In Genesis 14, Abram risks his life and reputation to rescue Lot from neighboring kings. The offspring of Lot's daughters eventually grow to become the nations of the Moabites and the Ammonites (19:37, 38), enemies of Israel centuries later. Seemingly small decisions can have massive ripple effects as time goes on!

❧ TROUBLES ALONG THE WAY ❧

My father, with tears in his eyes, tried to smile as one friend after another grasped his hand in a last farewell. Mama was overcome with grief. At last we were all in the wagons. The drivers cracked their whips. The oxen moved slowly forward and the long journey had begun.

Those are the words of Virginia Reed telling how a fabled journey started. James Reed, her father, led a band of pioneer settlers from Illinois toward California in 1846. After reaching Wyoming, the settlers chose George Donner as their new leader. It

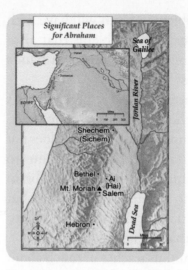

Visual for Lesson 1

Post this map for the lessons of Unit 1 so your learners can have a geographical perspective.

was a fateful decision, as Donner's name would forever be attached to the disaster to follow.

The party arrived at the eastern base of the Sierra Nevada just as winter arrived with a vengeance. They couldn't make it through the deep snow to safety. When food ran out, the settlers began eating their oxen. Members of the Donner party even began to eat their own dead. Nearly half of the group died from starvation, disease, or the effects of the bitter winter weather.

Abram's journey was also beset by troubles. Like some of the trials the Donner party faced, the troubles came as a result of unwise decisions. God doesn't always rescue us from our self-imposed problems, but in Abram's case God's eternal purpose was working to bring good out of bad. May we learn, as Abram did, that it's always better to listen to God's wisdom than to our own ideas!

—C. R. B.

B. Success (v. 5)

5. And Abram took Sarai his wife, and Lot his brother's son, and all their substance that they had gathered, and the souls that they had gotten in Haran; and they went forth to go into the land of Canaan; and into the land of Canaan they came.

God does not intervene to keep Abram from bringing Lot along. Neither does God inform Abram how two elderly childless people will become a great nation. Our comments on verse 4 above sketch the problems Abram will have with Lot. Genesis 16 reveals the problems that arise when Abram takes matters into his own hands regarding his childless state.

Throughout the narrative, God respects Abram's decisions even when those decisions result in heartache and needless complications. Yet God does not prosper Abram's mistakes. He allows Abram to make and learn from his mistakes. He gives Abram enough information to embark on his journey, but not enough information for Abram to be able to walk by sight rather than by faith.

The story of Abram thus teaches us much about the Christian life. As followers of Christ, we know that God has big plans for us. But He may not give us all the details of those plans, thus allowing us to complicate matters by our own questionable decisions. There are clouds hanging over all of our heads—some that are beyond our control and others that we have brought on ourselves. But God is faithful to continue with us on our journey as He does with Abram.

The destination of Canaan is repeated from Genesis 11:31. Canaan is located between the Mediterranean Sea and the Jordan River. For centuries after Abram's time, Canaan will not serve as the seat of any great nation. It serves more as the crossroads between larger empires like that of Egypt and Babylon. So God chooses "the land of the not great" to form a people "whose name is great." Only with God's help can a great people flourish in a backwater place like Canaan.

III. Arrival of Abram
(Genesis 12:6-9)
A. Promise Threatened (v. 6)

6. And Abram passed through the land unto the place of Sichem, unto the plain of Moreh. And the Canaanite was then in the land.

The journey from Haran is almost 400 miles. The fact that Abram travels *unto the plain of Moreh* means that Abram does not stop his journey once he reaches the outer perimeter of Canaan, since Sichem is southeast of the Sea of Galilee. Sichem is a place of importance in Old Testament history (Genesis 33:18; Joshua 24:1, 25; etc.).

Most important in this passage is the reference to the Canaanites who are in the land. The term *Canaanites* is rather generic. As such, it is likely not a reference to a specific race or people group, but to the total population of that portion of Palestine. Many of these people are descended from Canaan, a grandson of Noah (Genesis 9:18; 10:6, 15-19). But the land is also occupied by people such as the Philistines who have settled along the Mediterranean coast (21:32-34). If God is going to make Abram's name great, God will have to overcome not only Sarai's barrenness and Lot's problematic presence, but also the land's inhabitants.

What Do You Think?

What are some figurative "Canaanites" that may hinder us from doing what God wants? How will you overcome these?

Talking Points for Your Discussion
- Time pressures
- Wrong priorities
- Poor spiritual nutrition

B. Promise Reaffirmed (v. 7)

7. And the LORD appeared unto Abram, and said, Unto thy seed will I give this land: and there builded he an altar unto the LORD, who had appeared unto him.

Abram is the starter seed for the people that God is forming for himself. They will become a great nation, and their name will be great because of God's blessing. This is in direct contrast with the tower builders in Genesis 11, who sought to make a great name for themselves. The unique people God forms through Abram will (or should) know that any greatness they achieve they will owe to God. Galatians 3:16 establishes the importance of the singular *thy seed* (see Lesson 12).

Abram may feel intimidated when he sees the land's inhabitants. He has already agreed to relocate his family in obedience to God, but Abram may not have anticipated that God is leading him into a place that is already occupied. In order to reassure Abram that this is indeed the right place, the Lord appears to Abram (we are not told how) and confirms it. Abram's bold response is to build

The Lord Calls Abram

an altar unto the Lord—bold because pagan altars undoubtedly are already in the area.

C. Movements in the Land (vv. 8, 9)

8. And he removed from thence unto a mountain on the east of Bethel, and pitched his tent, having Bethel on the west, and Hai on the east: and there he builded an altar unto the LORD, and called upon the name of the LORD.

Abram continues his southward trek and settles temporarily between Bethel and Hai. Bethel means "house of God." It will later become an important, even sinful, place of worship for Abram's descendants (Genesis 28:16-22; 35:1-7; redesignated *Beth-aven,* "house of wickedness," in Hosea 4:15; 5:8; 10:5). Hundreds of years later, Hai (called *Ai*) will be the site of an Israelite defeat and victory (Joshua 7:4, 5; 8:1-29). The altar Abram builds is likely similar to the one he built in the previous verse.

9. And Abram journeyed, going on still toward the south.

We are not told why Abram continues traveling southward. Perhaps it is because God wants to show him the full extent of the land that Abram and his descendants will possess. It may also be to prepare Abram for the next step: a temporary stay in Egypt to survive a famine (Genesis 12:10). God will keep His promise, but His plan has many layers, and it spans many generations.

What Do You Think?
When was a time when someone's step of faith inspired you to take one of your own?
Talking Points for Your Discussion
- In a new way of serving
- In giving
- In evaluating God's leading

Conclusion
A. What This World Wants

The people of this world know that something is wrong. Though they may not call it sin and may not acknowledge the corruption of God's good creation, they have developed numerous habits and practices to insulate themselves from the pain and disorder brought about by human selfishness. They immerse themselves in the false reality of television and the big screen. They numb their senses with alcohol, drugs, or prescription medications. They buy more stuff to try to fill the void in their lives that results from rejecting God's solution to their real needs.

But God's solution remains the same. He has called into existence a people who are to know better. He has revealed His will and His Son to them so they can show and tell a hurting world about His kingdom. God wills to bless the world, and His Son sends us out into the world by the power of His Spirit to do this. But we, like Abram, must leave "Ur" behind us (compare Mark 10:28-30).

We cannot proclaim God's kingdom while we seek the kingdoms of this world. Like Abram, we do not always know what the next step will be, and we may even make mistakes that will blow up in our faces. Like Abram, we may have to wait a long time. We may have to tarry in an "Egypt," while God continues to prepare our hearts.

The world wants a quick and cheap fix. May God grant us the grace not to settle for giving the world what it wants. May we instead truly bless the world by giving it what God knows it needs.

B. Prayer

God, we thank You for forming a people to show Your love to this fallen world. We thank You for sending Jesus to gather, atone for, and empower this people to be a blessing to all nations. We confess that Your plans are higher than ours, and we ask Your forgiveness when we fail to execute Your plan Your way. Please give us a faith like that of Abram. In Jesus' name, amen.

C. Thought to Remember
God still calls His people to step out in faith.

VISUALS FOR THESE LESSONS

The visual pictured in each lesson (example: page 125) is a small reproduction of a large, full-color poster included in the *Adult Resources* packet for the Winter Quarter. That packet also contains the very useful *Presentation Helps* on a CD for teacher use. Order No. 020029211 from your supplier.

INVOLVEMENT LEARNING

Some of the activities below are also found in the helpful student book, Adult Bible Class.
Don't forget to download the free reproducible page from www.standardlesson.com to enhance your lesson!

Into the Lesson

Download the reproducible page and put copies of the Abram's Call activity in chairs for learners to work on as they arrive.

Form groups of three to five. Give each group a handout with the following instructions: "Write at the top the name of a place where no one in your group has visited nor lived. Then list the preparations needed (1) to move *from* their present location and (2) to move *to* the new location." After five minutes, ask each group to share three "moving from" and "moving to" preparations.

Say, "Moving can be complicated, difficult, and expensive. The fact that Abram obeyed God's command to move is a great demonstration of faith. He continues to be a model for us."

Into the Word

Form the class into five study teams for the following assignments. Smaller classes can form fewer teams, with some teams having more than one assignment. Give each team a piece of poster board, a marker, and the photocopies of relevant portions of the lesson commentary as noted.

Team 1: Create a map of the places Abram visited in today's text. Draw that map on the poster board and be prepared to share it with the class. (Provide two colors of markers and a Bible atlas or map of Abram's travels.)

Team 2: List some practical "faith issues" faced by Abram in leaving Ur. (Provide a photocopy of the commentary on verse 1.)

Team 3: List the seven promises God made to Abram in verses 2 and 3 of today's text. Also share how these promises would be fulfilled. (Provide a photocopy of commentary on verses 2, 3.)

Team 4: Read today's printed text and Hebrews 11:8-10. List qualities in Abram that demonstrated his great faith and leadership strengths. Illustrate these qualities in his behaviors or responses to the Lord. (Provide a copy of the lesson commentary.)

Team 5: List lessons that you see surfacing in the lives of Abram and Sarai that teach us something about living a Christian life. (Provide a photocopy of the lesson commentary on verse 5.)

Allow each team to report. However, before Teams 4 and 5 report, caution the class that this lesson is not simply history. The Old Testament record exists to direct our lives in right paths (1 Corinthians 10:6-11).

Into Life

Recruit a volunteer to record responses on the board as you pose the following questions.

1. What are some "basic calls" that come to all Christians—calls to behaviors, activities, and values? *(Possible responses: to follow Him, to worship, to commune, to practice responsible stewardship, to endure hardship).*

2. How would you explain to an 18-year-old about how God may wish to direct his or her life? How do "calls" from God come about today? How may the teen catch a glimpse of God's will for his or her life?

3. Is there anyone here who has experienced a call for a particular direction in life or who has recently sensed God's tugging to make an adjustment in life's direction? Would you be willing to share that experience with us?

Alternative. Download the reproducible page and distribute copies of the Key Lessons in Faith activity. Discuss as a class or in small groups. This can be a take-home assignment if time is short.

Conclude with three prayers. First, ask for a volunteer to thank God for Abram's wonderful model of faith. Second, ask another volunteer to pray on behalf of parents and youth leaders in your church for God to help them discover the joy and adventure of following God's direction in all of life. The third prayer will be for class members always to be willing to respond to God's direction and will in life.

THE LORD GIVES HIS PROMISE

DEVOTIONAL READING: **Hebrews 11:8-12**
BACKGROUND SCRIPTURE: **Genesis 15**

GENESIS 15:1-6, 12-18

1 After these things the word of the LORD came unto Abram in a vision, saying, Fear not, Abram: I am thy shield, and thy exceeding great reward.

2 And Abram said, LORD God, what wilt thou give me, seeing I go childless, and the steward of my house is this Eliezer of Damascus?

3 And Abram said, Behold, to me thou hast given no seed: and, lo, one born in my house is mine heir.

4 And, behold, the word of the LORD came unto him, saying, This shall not be thine heir; but he that shall come forth out of thine own bowels shall be thine heir.

5 And he brought him forth abroad, and said, Look now toward heaven, and tell the stars, if thou be able to number them: and he said unto him, So shall thy seed be.

6 And he believed in the LORD; and he counted it to him for righteousness.

· ·

12 And when the sun was going down, a deep sleep fell upon Abram; and, lo, an horror of great darkness fell upon him.

13 And he said unto Abram, Know of a surety that thy seed shall be a stranger in a land that is not theirs, and shall serve them; and they shall afflict them four hundred years;

14 And also that nation, whom they shall serve, will I judge: and afterward shall they come out with great substance.

15 And thou shalt go to thy fathers in peace; thou shalt be buried in a good old age.

16 But in the fourth generation they shall come hither again: for the iniquity of the Amorites is not yet full.

17 And it came to pass, that, when the sun went down, and it was dark, behold a smoking furnace, and a burning lamp that passed between those pieces.

18 In the same day the LORD made a covenant with Abram, saying, Unto thy seed have I given this land, from the river of Egypt unto the great river, the river Euphrates.

KEY VERSE

[Abram] believed in the LORD; and he counted it to him for righteousness. —**Genesis 15:6**

GOD ESTABLISHES A FAITHFUL PEOPLE

Unit 1: God's Covenant

LESSONS 1–4

LESSON AIMS

After participating in this lesson, each student will be able to:

1. List the key features of God's promises to Abram.

2. Describe how Genesis 15:6 is used in Romans 4:3, 9, 22; Galatians 3:6; and James 2:23.

3. Write a prayer of commitment to produce spiritual offspring for Christ.

LESSON OUTLINE

Introduction

A. Cruel God?

Marcion of Sinope (AD 85–160) was the first acknowledged heretic of the early church. He said that the teachings of Jesus of Nazareth were fundamentally different from those of the Old Testament. He therefore concluded that the God of the Old Testament must be different from the God of the New Testament.

Marcion then assembled the Scriptures in a way that reflected Christianity as he saw it. His truncated Bible contained only one Gospel and no books from the Old Testament. It is little wonder that the church of his day soundly rejected his teaching.

It is surprising, then, that some of Marcion's key principles and arguments are alive and well today. Some folks who want to discount the God of Scripture often point out the so-called contradiction between His display of love to the whole world through Jesus and His extermination of the Canaanites in the time of Joshua. The Israelite conquest of the promised land is sometimes interpreted as racial genocide, with God "playing favorites" with the Israelites. Thus some Christians are at a loss to explain why the God of the New Testament seems to be a God of peace and love, whereas the God of the Old Testament seems to be a God of violence and wrath.

This kind of thinking does justice neither to the Old Testament nor the New. A careful reading of both testaments demonstrates that the truth is more complicated than the simplistic portrait above. One way to clarify matters is to perform a careful study of the conquest of Canaan to note exactly what did and did not happen. Another way is to read the Joshua narrative in its wider biblical context in order to note the original purpose behind the conquest and God's timing of the conquest. In today's lesson we are studying this important biblical context, beginning with God's promise to Abram in Genesis.

B. Lesson Background

In last week's lesson we learned that Abram made a questionable move by taking Lot with him after God called Abram to leave behind both his land and his father's household (Genesis 12:1-5). As the men traveled together, they accumulated such great possessions that they could not dwell in the same region. Quarreling among their herdsmen eventually led the two to part ways (13:5-12). Lot and his family settled in the region of Sodom.

Subsequently, certain kings waged war against the city of Sodom and the surrounding area (Genesis 14:1-16). Lot and his family were captured. This put Abram in the difficult position of attempting a rescue mission. Failure and death would have meant the collapse of the promise from God that all nations would be blessed through Abram.

Yet God prospered Abram, and the rescue mission succeeded. Lot and his family returned to their homes, and Abram was established as a powerful man throughout the region. But such power could be threatening to the local populace. By flexing his power, Abram became exposed to the jealous eye of his neighbors. By securing Lot, Abram imperiled his own position. But God knew how to respond to this situation.

I. Promise Restated
(GENESIS 15:1-6)
A. Abram's Concern (vv. 1-3)

1. After these things the word of the LORD came unto Abram in a vision, saying, Fear not, Abram: I am thy shield, and thy exceeding great reward.

God's first words *fear not* imply that Abram is afraid of something—perhaps the jealous neighbors noted in the Lesson Background. God can respond to Abram's insecurity in a variety of ways. He can reprimand Abram for bringing Lot along in the first place. He can give Abram the silent treatment and allow him to stew in his own juices of insecurity. He can congratulate Abram for his great military potential and encourage him to accomplish whatever he puts his mind to. But God does none of these things. Instead, He calms Abram's fears with a reminder that God alone is the source of Abram's protection *(shield)* and prosperity *(great reward)*.

In identifying himself as Abram's shield, God informs Abram that his security is not rooted in military prowess or in strategic alliances with neighboring peoples. This is an important lesson that the Israelites of the future will forget. In identifying himself as Abram's reward, God is affirming Abram's decision in Genesis 14:21-24 not to keep the spoils of war that were rightfully his according to ancient custom. In that act, Abram showed his trust in God as his source of prosperity.

> *What Do You Think?*
> What was a time when focusing on God's promises helped alleviate your fear?
> *Talking Points for Your Discussion*
> - A health issue
> - A financial issue
> - A workplace issue
> - A family issue

❧ OUR ONLY CERTAIN PROTECTION ❧

After America's Great Depression of the 1920s and '30s, the U.S. government enacted numerous regulations for the nation's financial structure. The idea was to reassure Americans that "it can't happen again."

But it did happen again! The Great Recession that began in 2007 came in spite of those regulations. We learned (once again) that no matter how

HOW TO SAY IT

Abram	*Ay*-brum.
Amorites	*Am*-uh-rites.
Babylon	*Bab*-uh-lun.
Canaan	*Kay*-nun.
Canaanites	*Kay*-nun-ites.
Damascus	Duh-*mass*-kus.
Eliezer	El-ih-*ee*-zer.
Euphrates	You-*fray*-teez.
Haran	*Hair*-un.
Marcion	*Mahr*-shuhn.
Mediterranean	*Med*-uh-tuh-**ray**-nee-un.
Sinope	Suh-*no*-pea.
Sodom	*Sod*-um.
Wadi el-Arish	Wah-dee el-Uh-*rish*.

many rules we make, bad things can still happen. We found that neither the stock nor housing markets go up forever, and that looking to them for security is an exercise in vain faith. We found that no job is secure, no investment is certain, and no one is safe from the ingenuity of greedy people.

Many Christians who thought they were prepared to sail through rough economic seas found their boats taking on water. Many also found that their faith in God and help from their church family kept them afloat when the collapsing economy threatened to swamp them. Even in the midst of economic downturns, God shows himself to be our shield and great reward.

Abram lived a life of vulnerability. God did not remove that vulnerability, but reassured him that his vulnerability was not as great as God's ability to protect him. It's a lesson most of us have to keep learning over and over. —C. R. B.

2, 3. And Abram said, Lord God, what wilt thou give me, seeing I go childless, and the steward of my house is this Eliezer of Damascus? And Abram said, Behold, to me thou hast given no seed: and, lo, one born in my house is mine heir.

Protection and possessions are not Abram's only concerns. He takes advantage of this unique opportunity to converse with God by raising a larger issue: it appears that the heir to his possessions and the promise will be a household steward, a certain *Eliezer of Damascus*.

What Do You Think?
Which biblical promises are hardest to believe and trust? Why?
Talking Points for Your Discussion
▪ For nonbelievers
▪ For Christians in general
▪ For you in particular

B. God's Affirmation (vv. 4-6)

4. And, behold, the word of the Lord came unto him, saying, This shall not be thine heir; but he that shall come forth out of thine own bowels shall be thine heir.

God makes it clear that Eliezer will not be Abram's successor. On the contrary, Abram's own child-to-be will be the heir. Notice, however, what God does not say: He does not say who will be the mother. In ancient society, it is common practice that if a man's wife cannot have children, then a man may have children through one or more of his wife's servants (as in Genesis 30:1-6). This possibility will indeed be tried by Abram and Sarai before God later reveals that Sarai will be the mother (17:15, 16).

What Do You Think?
What was a time when God expanded your idea of what you thought possible? How did He do it?
Talking Points for Your Discussion
▪ Through Scripture
▪ Through another person
▪ Through events and circumstances

5. And he brought him forth abroad, and said, Look now toward heaven, and tell the stars, if thou be able to number them: and he said unto him, So shall thy seed be.

God uses a visual aid to remind Abram of the massive scope of the future that God has planned for him. Earlier, God used the illustration of the dust of the earth to show how many descendants will come from Abram (Genesis 13:16). Now God shows him the stars of the sky.

Abram has no telescope, of course. In that respect, we can see many more stars than he could. But Abram has the advantage of not having artificial lighting to block his view. It is difficult for modern city-dwellers to see just how many stars Abram can see in his day!

6. And he believed in the Lord; and he counted it to him for righteousness.

Since God originally made His promise to Abram, that man has relocated to a distant country, avoided a drought by laying over in Egypt, and secured an improbable military victory. Yet Abram still seems no closer to having an heir. Even so, Abram believes God! The God who has taken him thus far will finish what He began. This kind of faith is an example for God's people in all generations (Romans 4:3, 9, 22; Galatians 3:6).

The Lord Gives His Promise

Abram's righteousness is not based on the number of sacrifices he offers, prayers he prays, victories he wins, or deeds he performs. His right standing before God is rooted in his unswerving faith that God keeps His promises. This does not mean, of course, that Abram's deeds are irrelevant. If Abram had never put one foot in front of the other in response to his beliefs, had he not packed up and headed for Canaan to begin with, then his belief in God's faithfulness would have proven hollow (James 2:20-24).

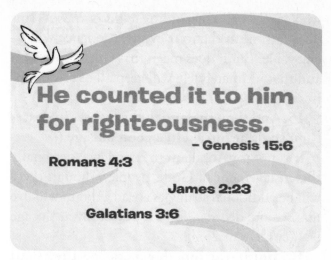

He counted it to him for righteousness.
– Genesis 15:6
Romans 4:3
James 2:23
Galatians 3:6

Visual for Lessons 2 & 11. *Point to this visual as you relate Genesis 15:6 to its three uses in the New Testament.*

> **What Do You Think?**
>
> How does this story help you better understand the relationship between faith and works for the Christian?
>
> *Talking Points for Your Discussion*
> - "Actual" vs. "imputed" righteousness
> - How faith is "credited" as righteousness under the old and new covenants
> - How belief and trust are different but connected

II. Enslavement Predicted

(Genesis 15:12-16)

A. Darkness (v. 12)

12. And when the sun was going down, a deep sleep fell upon Abram; and, lo, an horror of great darkness fell upon him.

After God confirms His promise and acknowledges Abram's faith, Abram asks how he can be sure (Genesis 15:8, not in today's text). In response, God initiates a ceremony to affirm the covenant. This involves animal sacrifice (15:9-11).

Yet the ceremony is not quite complete. God brings *a deep sleep* on Abram, perhaps one like Adam experienced before God fashioned Eve from his rib (Genesis 2:21, 22). But Adam's "deep sleep" is not described as coming with the horror we see here. The language used perhaps reflects that what Abram is about to learn may not be pleasant.

B. Mistreatment (v. 13)

13. And he said unto Abram, Know of a surety that thy seed shall be a stranger in a land that is not theirs, and shall serve them; and they shall afflict them four hundred years.

Indeed, the news is not pleasant. Abram's descendants will not possess the land of Canaan in any real sense for hundreds of years. First, they will be strangers in someone else's land. Not only that, their hosts in that land will subjugate them for four centuries.

This is an important lesson for Abram to learn: he must show patience with God. Abram must operate on God's timetable. God has long-term plans. Sadly, Abram won't learn this lesson fully, as we see him try to "push" God's plan along with regard to having an heir (Genesis 16).

C. Vindication (vv. 14-16)

14. And also that nation, whom they shall serve, will I judge: and afterward shall they come out with great substance.

Abram probably does not welcome this news of long-term enslavement. Yet God's justice and concern for His people will be made evident when He resolves this ominous development. God will bring justice on the oppressors and will use those oppressors to prosper His people with material abundance. At the end of Genesis and beginning of Exodus, we learn that the Egyptians are those oppressors.

Abram is learning what Paul affirms many centuries later in Romans 8:28: "All things work together for good to them that love God, to them who are the called according to his purpose." This does not mean that our every experience will be enjoyable. But it does mean that God is sovereign and that ultimately He will keep all of His promises to us.

15. And thou shalt go to thy fathers in peace; thou shalt be buried in a good old age.

It is not for Abraham to experience personally the enslavement of God's people. Though there will be additional struggles ahead, Abram will live many more decades and die peacefully at the age of 175 (Genesis 25:7).

16. But in the fourth generation they shall come hither again: for the iniquity of the Amorites is not yet full.

The reason that God allows His people to suffer prolonged hardship is stated in this verse. Apparently, the sin of those currently inhabiting the promised land has not yet reached a point that warrants their removal from the land. We should note that the term *Amorites* is used interchangeably with *Canaanites* in Joshua 7:7-9. Canaan is described as the father of the Amorites in Genesis 10:15, 16.

Here again God shows His justice. It is a mistake to assume that God so favors His people that He is willing to bulldoze whoever may be in their way in order to accomplish what He wants. God so honors the dignity of the people living in Canaan that He refuses to punish them prematurely. Even though God knows He will eventually drive them from the land, He does not "cut to the chase" in order to execute His edict before it is justified.

Thus God is in no rush with Abram and Sarai. God has a long time to work out His plans for His people. Of course, God could simply leave Abram and his descendants in Ur or Haran for another 400 years before the time is ripe. But God deems this faith-building process, this long, drawn out struggle, as essential to their formation as a people.

God has infinite wisdom. God knows that a people that wanders without a home and that suffers the shackles of slavery will be best suited to be the kind of blessing to all nations that He is calling them to become.

III. Covenant Made
(GENESIS 15:17, 18)
A. Sign (v. 17)

17. And it came to pass, that, when the sun went down, and it was dark, behold a smoking furnace, and a burning lamp that passed between those pieces.

God now provides Abram the sign he requested in Genesis 15:8. According to ancient practice, the two parties of a covenant or treaty split animals in two, and then both pass through the middle of the animals as a sign to one another that they will not forsake their commitment. In passing between the parts, each party is essentially saying, "If I drop my end of the bargain, may I become like these animals here" (compare Jeremiah 34:18).

It is noteworthy that Abram does not pass between the pieces; only the symbols of God's presence do so. The symbol of *a smoking furnace* resembles the oven used for baking offerings in Leviticus 2:4. The symbol of *a burning lamp* might reflect God's judgment as in Job 41:19 and Zechariah 12:6.

Though Abram has an important part to play, the primary role for him and his descendants is to bear witness to God's fulfillment of His promises for His people and the world. This serves as an important reminder to Abram that it is not his job to engineer the fulfillment of God's promise to him, but to wait on God's timing and God's strategy for fulfilling it.

God and Abram are not equal partners, as in human-to-human covenants. And so it is yet today: our primary role is to respond faithfully to the tasks that God has given us and not try to remake the Great Commission (Matthew 28:19, 20) according to our liking.

B. Promise (v. 18)

18. In the same day the LORD made a covenant with Abram, saying, Unto thy seed have I given this land, from the river of Egypt unto the great river, the river Euphrates.

God reiterates His commitment to Abram: God will give the promised land to Abram's seed. This is all that Abram needs to know. Though he may want more, he will have to take God at His word—first spoken orally and now enacted in human terms with the kind of covenant ceremony with which Abram is familiar.

Directly to the east of the promised land is a massive desert that separates Babylon from Canaan. Directly to the west is the Mediterranean Sea. So the only two borders Abram needs in order to identify the land of promise is one to the north, which is *the river Euphrates,* and one to the south, which is *the river of Egypt.*

The river mentioned likely does not refer to the Nile River, but to a smaller, seasonal river. This is perhaps Wadi el-Arish, which serves as the traditional Egyptian border (see also Numbers 34:5; Joshua 15:4).

❧ *"WHAT WOULD HAPPEN IF . . . ?"* ❧

Curiosity is what causes us to wonder, "What would happen if . . . ?" A search of the Internet for "stupid tricks" or something similar will result in numerous videos of people making painful discoveries to the above question as they exercise more curiosity than good sense.

Considerably higher on the "satisfying curiosity" scale is Discovery Channel's *Mythbusters* program. It has been called "the best science program on television." The program is centered on the question, "What would happen if . . . ?" But in this case, it involves somewhat more mature people actually testing and demonstrating scientific principles to separate myth from scientific fact, such as, "What would happen if we actually *tried* to slip on a banana peel?"

The result of such inquiries can either get us into trouble or keep us out of it. Sometimes our curiosity is greater than our need to know. God's response to Abram's desire to know was to make a covenantal promise. Abram didn't need to ask,

"What would happen if God doesn't keep His promises to me?" Neither Abram nor we need to know all the "ifs, ands, or buts," as the saying goes. Insisting on such knowledge before proceeding means that we are walking by sight, not by faith. Trusting in God's proven faithfulness is sufficient.

—C. R. B.

Conclusion

A. Long-suffering God

Any special privilege that God's chosen people experienced in Old Testament times was to serve the greater good of the human race in preparation for Jesus' arrival. God's people were not protected and treasured for their own sake, but for the sake of the nations, so they may become a blessing to all nations.

Yet sometimes being a blessing meant that God's chosen people had to suffer. The Israelites had to suffer in Egypt, the prophets had to suffer at the hands of the wicked, and God's only Son had to suffer and die on the cross. In light of this bigger biblical picture, all notions of a God who "plays favorites" so that only this or that people group experiences pain and judgment should be dismissed.

Followers of Christ are especially aware of this. When Christ bids us to follow Him, He first bids us to take up our cross (Luke 9:23). This includes suffering in various ways, but it is the kind of suffering that pales in light of the eternal joy set before us in Christ.

B. Prayer

Patient Lord, please teach us Your patience. It is so difficult for us to submit our busy schedules to Your timetable. We desire instant results, visible progress, and tangible guarantees.

Yet, out of Your grace You rescue us from our faithless, "walk by sight" desires. Instead of giving us what we want, You give us what we need and what is best. Thank You for this gift. In Jesus' name, amen.

C. Thought to Remember

Embrace the Lord's timing.

INVOLVEMENT LEARNING

Some of the activities below are also found in the helpful student book, Adult Bible Class.
Don't forget to download the free reproducible page from www.standardlesson.com to enhance your lesson!

Into the Lesson

Option 1. Ask the class to give examples of covenants or contracts people enter into. List these on the board. Discuss the nature of some of those listed. For example, in a contract to purchase a car, one party agrees to provide the automobile and a warranty while the other party agrees to terms of payment. Be sure *will* or *last will and testament* is included in the list.

Make the transition to Bible study by saying, "The last will and testament may include the giving of inheritances. However, it also may include conditions upon which that inheritance rests. We'll see that issue as one of Abram's dilemma's in today's study."

Option 2. Display a genealogy chart or book. Tell the class, "Genealogies always cite the past. They list persons who have existed before you. However, in our study today, one man has a rare glimpse of what we might call his 'future genealogy' or 'forward genealogy.'"

NOTE: If you decide to do both options, after the first option tell the class you are focusing on two issues today: covenants and genealogies. Then after the second option say, "Last week we detailed the covenant between God and Abram. In today's study we'll see that covenant reemphasized. However, we'll especially see it come to fruition in Abram's genealogy."

Into the Word

Have three learners read today's printed text aloud in the parts of the narrator, the Lord, and Abram. Give each reader a copy of the text with his or her portion highlighted in color.

After the reading, show the following visuals one at a time. As each is shown, ask the class to retell the part of the story the visual highlights in today's account in the life of Abram. The visuals are (1) a shield (v. 1); (2) a last will and testament (vv. 3, 4); (3) the night sky with many stars (v. 5);

(4) a beautiful sunset (v. 12); (5) slaves (v. 13); and (6) a tombstone (v. 15). These images are easy to find on the Internet. Use the lesson commentary to explain the ancient practice of the covenant ceremony described in verse 17.

Say, "Genesis 15:6 is a wonderful compliment to Abram." Ask three learners each to have one of the following sets of Scriptures ready to read to the class: Romans 4:3, 9, 22; Galatians 3:6; and James 2:23. Ask the learners to describe how each of these New Testament passages reinforces the verse in Genesis. After discussing all three sets, summarize by saying, "Abram's right standing before God was rooted in his unswerving faith that God keeps His promises."

Into Life

Option 1: Lead a discussion by asking the following groups of questions.

1. Why should we study today's passage? Why did God record and preserve it for people in 2011? What lessons should we be learning from Abram's experience? (List responses on the board.)

2. Tell the class that one important idea often overlooked is that of pondering our own "forward genealogy." Abram's genealogy looked forward to how he would bless many people and nations. Ask, "What are some practical ways we can be a blessing to our spiritual descendants?" (Jot responses beside the previous list on the board.)

3. Who in our "forward genealogy" will we bless? (Distribute index cards. Ask each learner to name someone whom they will encourage during the new year.)

Option 2: Download the reproducible page and distribute copies of the Emotions, Emotions! activity. Have learners work in small groups to complete this. Ask a volunteer to pray for the class to follow Abram's example in trusting God. Distribute copies of the Dear Lord activity from the reproducible page as a take-home activity.

THE LORD PROVIDES

DEVOTIONAL READING: Philippians 4:15-20
BACKGROUND SCRIPTURE: Genesis 22:1-19

GENESIS 22:1-14

1 And it came to pass after these things, that God did tempt Abraham, and said unto him, Abraham: and he said, Behold, here I am.

2 And he said, Take now thy son, thine only son Isaac, whom thou lovest, and get thee into the land of Moriah; and offer him there for a burnt offering upon one of the mountains which I will tell thee of.

3 And Abraham rose up early in the morning, and saddled his ass, and took two of his young men with him, and Isaac his son, and clave the wood for the burnt offering, and rose up, and went unto the place of which God had told him.

4 Then on the third day Abraham lifted up his eyes, and saw the place afar off.

5 And Abraham said unto his young men, Abide ye here with the ass; and I and the lad will go yonder and worship, and come again to you.

6 And Abraham took the wood of the burnt offering, and laid it upon Isaac his son; and he took the fire in his hand, and a knife; and they went both of them together.

7 And Isaac spake unto Abraham his father, and said, My father: and he said, Here am I, my son. And he said, Behold the fire and the wood: but where is the lamb for a burnt offering?

8 And Abraham said, My son, God will provide himself a lamb for a burnt offering: so they went both of them together.

9 And they came to the place which God had told him of; and Abraham built an altar there, and laid the wood in order, and bound Isaac his son, and laid him on the altar upon the wood.

10 And Abraham stretched forth his hand, and took the knife to slay his son.

11 And the angel of the LORD called unto him out of heaven, and said, Abraham, Abraham: and he said, Here am I.

12 And he said, Lay not thine hand upon the lad, neither do thou any thing unto him: for now I know that thou fearest God, seeing thou hast not withheld thy son, thine only son from me.

13 And Abraham lifted up his eyes, and looked, and behold behind him a ram caught in a thicket by his horns: and Abraham went and took the ram, and offered him up for a burnt offering in the stead of his son.

14 And Abraham called the name of that place Jehovahjireh: as it is said to this day, In the mount of the LORD it shall be seen.

KEY VERSE

I know that thou fearest God, seeing thou hast not withheld thy son, thine only son from me.

—Genesis 22:12

GOD ESTABLISHES A FAITHFUL PEOPLE

Unit 1: God's Covenant

LESSONS 1–4

LESSON AIMS

After participating in this lesson, each student will be able to:

1. Retell the story of Abraham's testing.

2. Explain the significance of God's testing of Abraham.

3. Make a plan to sacrifice something to or for God in the week ahead.

LESSON OUTLINE

Introduction

A. Test for the Best

A bright student of mine recently applied for admission into a rigorous graduate-school program. There was no doubt in my mind that this student was capable of excelling in this program. He possessed extraordinary intellectual power, he was a strong leader on campus, and he was respected by his peers.

So we were all taken aback when this student received a rather cold letter from the academic dean of the graduate school asking him to rethink whether he truly wanted to be admitted. The letter further required him to write an additional essay in order to convince the admittance committee that he was the kind of student they could accept. As they looked over the student's records, they apparently saw a considerable gap between his potential and his production. Though the student's experiences were impressive and his references solid, his academic marks were not nearly as high as they should have been given his ability.

The admittance committee thus put him to the test. They knew that he could succeed in their program, but they wanted more—they wanted him to excel. They wanted him to bring his best self to their program. The student could have been put off by this test. He could have been insulted by their request and applied his money and energies elsewhere, but he didn't. Instead he wrote a solid response that confessed his lack of effort in the past and committed to excelling in his academic future should they give him that opportunity.

When executed properly and with the right motive, tests bring out our best. In today's passage God puts Abraham to the test, and Abraham's performance is exemplary for us all.

B. Lesson Background: The Issue of Faith

Abraham's faith journey began well. He (as Abram) obeyed God's call to pack his bags and head into the unknown. Though he and his wife were well advanced in years, Abraham trusted that God would somehow make them into a great nation—a nation through which all nations would be blessed.

But Abraham's journey was not easy, and his faith showed fault lines at multiple points. Twice Abraham tried to save his own skin by passing his wife off as his sister—once to the Pharaoh of Egypt (Genesis 12) and once to the king of Gerar (Genesis 20). Abraham tried to engineer the fulfillment of God's promise of offspring by fathering a child through his wife's handmaid, Hagar (Genesis 16). Some students think that the decision to bring along Lot, the son of Abraham's deceased brother, was Abraham's attempt to ensure offspring in a legal sense.

These mistakes blew up in Abraham's face. Even so, God did not forsake him. Instead, God gently taught Abraham the lessons he needed to learn along the way. But did Abraham truly learn from these lessons, or did Abraham merely harden his heart? Since God had kept His promise of providing Abraham with a son through his aged wife, Sarah (Genesis 21:1-7), would Abraham trust God in an ultimate test?

C. Lesson Background: An Issue of Names

In our previous two lessons, God's chosen patriarch was called by his birth name, Abram. Today he is referred to as Abraham. God had made a covenant with Abram in Genesis 17, and that covenant involved changing his name. Thus Abram, which means "exalted father," became Abraham, which means "father of a multitude."

Similarly, his wife Sarai's name was changed to Sarah. Both Sarah and Sarai mean "princess." So the change was only a matter of pronunciation. However, the change was still significant. It meant

HOW TO SAY IT

Beersheba	Beer-*she*-buh.
Gerar	*Gear*-rar (G as in get).
Hagar	*Hay*-gar.
Isaac	*Eye*-zuk.
Ishmael	*Ish*-may-el.
Jehovahjireh	Jeh-*ho*-vuh-*jye*-ruh.
Moriah	Mo-*rye*-uh.
Nebuchadnezzar	*Neb*-yuh-kud-**nez**-er.
Pharaoh	*Fair*-o or *Fay*-roe.
Solomon	*Sol*-o-mun.

for both Abraham and Sarah that God was beginning a new phase in their lives. They were turning a corner together as God gifted them with the child of promise, whose name was Isaac.

Isaac's name also has significance. It means "laughter," for both Abraham and Sarah laughed when they heard that infertile Sarah was going to have a son in her old age (Genesis 17:17; 18:12; 21:5, 6). What God was about to ask Abraham to do, however, was no laughing matter.

I. God Tests
(GENESIS 22:1, 2)
A. Call (v. 1)

1. And it came to pass after these things, that God did tempt Abraham, and said unto him, Abraham: and he said, Behold, here I am.

The phrase *after these things* indicates a certain passage of time, but how much time we do not know. Abraham was 100 years old when Isaac was born (Genesis 21:5), and now Isaac is old enough to carry on a conversation and carry wood (22:6-8, below). Thus *after these things* indicates the passage of several years since Isaac's birth. The word *tempt* implies that a test is coming, not a temptation to do evil (James 1:13). As God calls on His servant, Abraham's response *Behold, here I am* is as elegantly simple as it is proper.

B. Requirement (v. 2)

2. And he said, Take now thy son, thine only son Isaac, whom thou lovest, and get thee into the land of Moriah; and offer him there for a burnt offering upon one of the mountains which I will tell thee of.

God's test for Abraham is quite startling: the sacrifice of his son Isaac. It is interesting that Isaac is referred to as Abraham's *only* son, since Abraham had previously fathered Ishmael through Hagar (Genesis 16). Yet in Genesis 21:9-12 we learn that Ishmael is not the son of promise. He is the son that results from Abraham and Sarah's seeking to fulfill God's promise of an heir through ancient custom rather than divine provision. So God has made it clear that Ishmael is not "the son" for whom Abraham is waiting.

God does not, however, reject Ishmael altogether. On account of Abraham, God blesses Ishmael and makes a great nation of his offspring as well (21:13). But there is only one son of promise to Abraham, and he is Isaac.

It may seem scandalous that God would ask Abraham to sacrifice his child (compare Deuteronomy 18:9-12). But God is not going to allow Abraham to slay his son, as we shall see. Though God is willing to test his servant using the practice of child sacrifice, God is unwilling to sacrifice the child.

It almost goes without saying that Abraham does not want to offer up Isaac as a sacrifice! But what is probably the most scandalous aspect of God's request to Abraham is that God previously had told him that Isaac is to be the heir to carry forth God's intention to bless all nations. Since his call, Abraham's life has revolved around this promise. Is God now taking it away? Thus God's test is whether Abraham trusts God enough to fulfill His promise should the fulfillment of that promise be taken out of the reach of Abraham's own ability. If Abraham passes this test, then he has clearly become the great man of faith that God knew he could be when he called him from Ur.

The location of the sacrifice is also significant. Moriah is in the vicinity of Jerusalem and in the precise spot where Solomon later builds the temple (2 Chronicles 3:1). So the place where God asks Abraham to offer his son is the same place where the Israelites will later sacrifice their offerings and very close to where God will offer up His own Son, Jesus.

❧ TEACHING TO THE TEST ❧

Should a child be promoted from one grade to another regardless of academic progress? This question has been argued for as long as most Americans can remember. In 2002, President George W. Bush signed into law what has come to be known as the *No Child Left Behind Act*. Federal aid to school districts is based on how well each district's students perform on standardized tests.

Advocates of the measure emphasize the importance of standards-based education. Critics argue that the practical result of the act is the temptation for teachers to "teach to the test"—that is, to teach primarily the information the test will focus on rather than giving the students a broader, more widely applicable education. The argument will no doubt continue into the foreseeable future.

God has His standards, and He may decide to test our obedience to those. But Abraham discovered that God's tests are not always predictable: we must face life's tests as they come. Abraham failed in some of his earlier tests, but his faith grew. When the test in today's lesson came, the depth of his faith was clear. Each moral test we pass makes us stronger and prepares us to pass whatever tests still lie ahead.   —C. R. B.

> *What Do You Think?*
> What objections might some raise about God's testing of Abraham? How would you respond to those objections?
> *Talking Points for Your Discussion*
> - Regarding the need for such a test given God's foreknowledge
> - Regarding the morality of such a test
> - Regarding the precedent that such a test sets

II. Abraham Acts
(GENESIS 22:3-10)

A. Journey and Preparation (vv. 3-6a)

3. And Abraham rose up early in the morning, and saddled his ass, and took two of his young men with him, and Isaac his son, and clave the wood for the burnt offering, and rose up, and went unto the place of which God had told him.

Abraham wastes no time carrying out his assignment. Early the next day, he makes preparations and sets out to perform this dreadful task. There is no haggling with God as we see in Genesis 18:22-33.

4. Then on the third day Abraham lifted up his eyes, and saw the place afar off.

If we assume that Abraham's point of departure is Beersheba according to Genesis 21:22-34, then the trip to Moriah is one of about 50 miles. This three-day journey must seem like an eternity to Abraham! It gives him plenty of time to get cold feet, to devise an excuse, or otherwise maneuver his way out of this terrible assignment. In building such time into this test, God makes sure that Abraham's compliance will not be an impulsive act. Abraham's faith is tested in the crucible of time.

5, 6a. And Abraham said unto his young men, Abide ye here with the ass; and I and the lad will go yonder and worship, and come again to you. And Abraham took the wood of the burnt offering, and laid it upon Isaac his son; and he took the fire in his hand, and a knife.

When the party comes within sight of the destination, Abraham quickly dismisses the servants and moves forward with Isaac only. Having the servants stay behind will prevent them from interfering with what is about to happen. It is interesting to note that Abraham tells the servants that both he and Isaac will worship and then return (the verb *come again* is plural in the Hebrew).

B. Question and Answer (vv. 6b-8)

6b. And they went both of them together.

This short segment of the journey with Isaac must be doubly awkward. Abraham undoubtedly is engrossed in thought about what God has asked him to do. We wonder if Abraham drags his feet a bit as the moment of truth approaches.

❧ *Don't Run!* ❧

Runaway Bride was a 1999 film about a bride who got cold feet at several weddings. In 2005, a real-life runaway bride was in the news for several days. Jennifer Wilbanks disappeared a week ahead of her scheduled wedding. It was to have been an extravagant affair, with 28 attendants and 600 guests. She reported that she had been abducted, but actually she had taken a bus from Georgia to Las Vegas to New Mexico of her own volition.

Psychologists speculate that a major cause for prewedding jitters is the expectation the bride has to "be happy." However, they may experience tremendous pressure as they try to put together an event that is supposed to be "the perfect wedding." The result may be a groom left standing alone at the altar as the bride attempts to cope by fleeing.

Abraham wasn't dreaming of a perfect social event as he headed to the mountain. There is no indication that Abraham expected to "be happy" regarding what was to happen there. Yet Abraham's faith caused him to move steadfastly toward the mountain. The same kind of faith will pull us through life's challenges. To run away from God is never the solution. See Jonah 1:3.   —C. R. B.

7. And Isaac spake unto Abraham his father, and said, My father: and he said, Here am I, my son. And he said, Behold the fire and the wood: but where is the lamb for a burnt offering?

This verse indicates that Abraham has not yet told Isaac what is about to happen. Isaac has a question to be answered. One does not carry wood to worship unless one plans to build a fire and sacrifice an animal. The animal is normally taken from one's own flock, since sacrifices are intended to represent the best of what one has.

So perhaps Isaac has been wondering why there is no animal with them. Later in Israel's history, long-distance travelers can bring money to purchase an animal to sacrifice on site in Jerusalem. But no such provision is in place in Abraham's day. Thus Isaac's question is not surprising.

8. And Abraham said, My son, God will provide himself a lamb for a burnt offering: so they went both of them together.

Abraham's response is remarkable because he does not know that God will provide an animal soon. God has not told him so at this point, otherwise it would not be a true test. Some think that Abraham misleads his son to avoid scaring him away. A better idea is that Abraham is so convinced by God's past provision that he is confident in God's miraculous provision for the present. Abraham has learned that God's promise does not depend on human planning. Abraham has learned to wait expectantly on God to provide.

> *What Do You Think?*
> How do Abraham's *words* reveal the growth of his faith since Genesis 12? How is this a model?
> *Talking Points for Your Discussion*
> - His responses to God, his servants, and Isaac
> - His discretion in revealing things to others at the right time

C. Arrival and Intention (vv. 9, 10)

9. And they came to the place which God had told him of; and Abraham built an altar there, and laid the wood in order, and bound Isaac his son, and laid him on the altar upon the wood.

We easily imagine both Abraham and Isaac to be nervous at this point. God has not (yet) provided an animal. Perhaps Isaac feels duped, that his father has misled him this entire time, and now he is going to die.

Abraham may have similar feelings. God has said that Isaac is to be his heir. Now Abraham has followed God's instructions to the letter, probably hoping all the while that God will provide an alternative before it is too late.

10. And Abraham stretched forth his hand, and took the knife to slay his son.

But now it seems to be too late. So Abraham begins the unthinkable and raises the knife to take his son's life.

> **What Do You Think?**
> How do Abraham's *actions* reveal the growth of his faith since Genesis 12? How can this be a model for you?
> *Talking Points for Your Discussion*
> - His speed of obedience
> - His attention to detail

III. God Intervenes
(Genesis 22:11-14)

A. Sacrifice Halted (vv. 11, 12)

11. And the angel of the LORD called unto him out of heaven, and said, Abraham, Abraham: and he said, Here am I.

At the last second, God intervenes through *the angel of the Lord.* The repetition of Abraham's name underscores the urgency. Like a parent screaming to a child who is chasing a ball into oncoming traffic, God's heavenly messenger stops Abraham in his tracks.

According to the book of Hebrews, this is not what Abraham expects to happen. Hebrews 11:17-19 tells us that Abraham concludes that God will raise Isaac from the dead. This means that Abra-

ham is truly prepared to take his son's life. The test is real, and Abraham really passes.

12. And he said, Lay not thine hand upon the lad, neither do thou any thing unto him: for now I know that thou fearest God, seeing thou hast not withheld thy son, thine only son from me.

Having successfully stilled Abraham's stabbing hand, the angel reveals God's desire for this situation. God never intended Abraham to harm Isaac; He has been testing Abraham's fear of God. As noted in the introduction, Abraham's faith has not always been rock solid. When it came to producing an heir, he had tried to force matters his own way rather than submit fully to God.

But in this pivotal movement, with knife held overhead, it is clear that Abraham's faith has matured and that he is prepared to surrender his plans and ideas to the Lord. Likewise, Jesus endures pivotal moments in the desert (Matthew 4:1-11) and in the garden (Mark 14:32-36). In both, He demonstrates absolute dependence on God. These are models for us.

> **What Do You Think?**
> What are some things you need to "sacrifice" (not withhold from God)? How will you do this?
> *Talking Points for Your Discussion*
> - Certain thinking processes
> - Priorities in activities
> - Things you hold dear

B. Sacrifice Provided (vv. 13, 14)

13. And Abraham lifted up his eyes, and looked, and behold behind him a ram caught in a thicket by his horns: and Abraham went and took the ram, and offered him up for a burnt offering in the stead of his son.

God does indeed provide for the sacrifice. The ram was not provided when Abraham began his three-day journey. It was not provided along the way. It was not provided at the foot of Mount Moriah. It is provided only after Abraham demonstrates his willingness to go all the way in carrying out God's instructions. This is an important lesson for Christians. God's provision does not mean

His people will never suffer, face tough choices, or stare at dead ends. It means that God will provide when we find ourselves in these kinds of situations. Sometimes He provides a way out and sometimes a way through. But God will provide.

Abraham did not know when his ram-in-a-thicket would appear, and seldom do we. We must trust God with an Abraham-like faith that our ram will be there at just the right time.

14. And Abraham called the name of that place Jehovahjireh: as it is said to this day, In the mount of the LORD it shall be seen.

Not only does Abraham pass his faith test, he also learns more about God. The designation *Jehovahjireh* literally means "the Lord sees." The Hebrew *jireh* ("sees") is the term Abraham uses in responding to Isaac's question about the animal. Abraham tells Isaac, in essence, that the Lord will "see to it" that an animal is provided. This is why many versions of the Bible offer the translation "the Lord will provide."

When we cannot see how God will provide, God sees what we need. If we remain faithful, we will see His provision.

Visual for
Lesson 3

You can use this visual to relate Genesis 22:13 with God's provision of Jesus as the sacrificial Lamb.

> **What Do You Think?**
> How have tests helped stretch your faith?
> *Talking Points for Your Discussion*
> - Tests of obedience
> - Tests of patience
> - Tests of endurance
> - Tests of God's saying no in answer to prayer

Conclusion

A. Moments of Decision

Abraham faced moments of decision, and so will we. Such a moment may be a lucrative job offer that can compromise our ability to keep faith commitments. It may be a chance to advance ourselves at the expense of others. It may be starting a friendship for short-term happiness that we know will bring long-term trouble. Whether through money, prestige, or relationship, it is God's good pleasure to test our faith.

We must remain alert to the significance of such moments of decision. Abraham's story ends happily. He passes the test, receives God's blessing, and becomes a model to us all. Yet not all such stories end happily. In the moment of decision, some decide to lean on their own strength and understanding—people like Nebuchadnezzar (Daniel 4:30) and the 10 fearful spies (Numbers 13:26-32).

Such moments of testing are helpful indicators of where we truly are in our faith. Abraham had been growing in his faith for years. That growth began with his decision to pack everything and head to the unknown. It was tested on a smaller scale with famine and local conflicts. Sometimes Abraham passed, other times he slipped up, but he never allowed his mistakes to consume him. Likewise, we do not pass our faith tests by cramming overnight the day before the exam. We pass because God has matured our faith through countless acts of faithfulness along life's journey.

B. Prayer

Lord God, we call on You to be in our life what You have been for our forefathers and foremothers of the faith. Give us the faith to trust in Your provision and to stand in the midst of testing. Please forgive us when we fail, and continue to test us in our faith that we may grow in strength and in witness. In Jesus' name we pray, amen.

C. Thought to Remember

Expect God to test you.

INVOLVEMENT LEARNING

Some of the activities below are also found in the helpful student book, Adult Bible Class.
Don't forget to download the free reproducible page from www.standardlesson.com to enhance your lesson!

Into the Lesson

Say, "Sometimes adults feel called to make huge sacrifices for a high and noble purpose. The word *sacrifice* usually implies a loss of some sort to the person involved." Ask class members to pair off and list circumstances when people might be driven or asked to make significant sacrifices. The loss that is implied in the sacrifice should be included in the list. After a few minutes, ask volunteers to share their examples while a scribe lists the responses on the board.

Make the transition to Bible study by saying, "Today's study will examine one of history's greatest demonstrations of a willingness to sacrifice. But this sacrifice, while supported by great faith in God, was also a test."

Into the Word

Scripture Reading. Ask four people to assist you in reading the printed text. Give each person a photocopy of the text with the parts for Abraham, Isaac, God, and the angel of the Lord highlighted. You will read the part of the narrator.

Option 1: Dialogue. During the week prior to this study, ask two learners to prepare a brief skit. They are to portray an imaginary conversation between Abraham and Isaac as they returned from Abraham's testing on the mountain. The skit should include the following questions.

Abraham to Isaac: "I'm sorry I frightened you; will you forgive me?"

Isaac to Abraham: "Why did you do it, Dad?" "Why did God want to test you?" "Why did you call the place 'the Lord will provide'?" "What should we tell Mom?"

Other dialogue may be added as the team deems appropriate. Ask your class to discuss the impact this event may have had on Abraham and Isaac's relationship.

Option 2: Discussion. Ask the class what questions come to their mind as they read of the dif-

ficult test that God gave Abraham. List these questions on the board. Some possible questions that may be proposed are, "Why would God make such a shocking request of Abraham?" "What is the purpose of divine testing?" "What lessons do we learn about God's expectations of us?" "What lessons about faith are demonstrated in Abraham?" "What is the significance of the name Abraham gave to that place of sacrifice?"

After listing several questions, take time to discuss each. If there are many questions, select key questions from the list to discuss.

Option 3: Sharing in Pairs. Download the reproducible page and distribute copies of the Sacrifices as Tests activity. Ask learners to pair off and work through the questions. You may wish to ask for volunteers to share stories of sacrifices they made for God and what they learned from the experience.

Into Life

Download the reproducible page and distribute copies of the My Sacrifice activity. Say, "God still calls His people to live sacrificial lives. Is He the Lord of our lives, or is He not?" Ask each learner to write on the beam of the cross some sacrifice that he or she will make this week for God's glory. It may be in the form of a material gift or the gift of time for a ministry task. Ask how this gift "hurts" to the point of being a genuine sacrifice.

Alternative. Give each team that you used in the opening activity a piece of paper with the word *provide* printed vertically in large letters. Also have the following key words printed at the bottom: *sacrifice, divine testing, faith, obedience.*

Ask the teams to write an acrostic prayer of commitment across the word *provide.* Say, "Make sure to use each of the four words at the bottom somewhere in your prayer." Give each team the opportunity to read its prayer to the class as a whole as you close.

The Lord Provides

THE LORD KEEPS HIS PROMISE

DEVOTIONAL READING: 2 Corinthians 1:18-22
BACKGROUND SCRIPTURE: Luke 1:26–2:7; Galatians 3:6-18

LUKE 1:46-55

46 And Mary said, My soul doth magnify the Lord,

47 And my spirit hath rejoiced in God my Saviour.

48 For he hath regarded the low estate of his handmaiden: for, behold, from henceforth all generations shall call me blessed.

49 For he that is mighty hath done to me great things; and holy is his name.

50 And his mercy is on them that fear him from generation to generation.

51 He hath shewed strength with his arm; he hath scattered the proud in the imagination of their hearts.

52 He hath put down the mighty from their seats, and exalted them of low degree.

53 He hath filled the hungry with good things; and the rich he hath sent empty away.

54 He hath helped his servant Israel, in remembrance of his mercy;

55 As he spake to our fathers, to Abraham, and to his seed for ever.

LUKE 2:1-7

1 And it came to pass in those days, that there went out a decree from Caesar Augustus that all the world should be taxed.

2 (And this taxing was first made when Cyrenius was governor of Syria.)

3 And all went to be taxed, every one into his own city.

4 And Joseph also went up from Galilee, out of the city of Nazareth, into Judaea, unto the city of David, which is called Bethlehem; (because he was of the house and lineage of David:)

5 To be taxed with Mary his espoused wife, being great with child.

6 And so it was, that, while they were there, the days were accomplished that she should be delivered.

7 And she brought forth her firstborn son, and wrapped him in swaddling clothes, and laid him in a manger; because there was no room for them in the inn.

KEY VERSES

My soul doth magnify the Lord, and my spirit hath rejoiced in God my Saviour. —**Luke 1:46, 47**

Illustration: Dynamic Graphics / Liquidlibrary / Thinkstock

GOD ESTABLISHES A FAITHFUL PEOPLE

Unit 1: God's Covenant
LESSONS 1–4

LESSON AIMS

After participating in this lesson, each student will be able to:

1. List some ways that the birth of Christ demonstrates God's faithfulness to His promises.

2. Identify some surprising things about the birth of Jesus.

3. Personalize Mary's song.

LESSON OUTLINE

Introduction

A. Not What You'd Expect

Have you ever had to wait a long time for a promise to be fulfilled? Do you remember as a child wondering if a special day would ever come? Can you remember a time when a promise was fulfilled in an unexpected way? Maybe you got what you wanted, but not from the anticipated source. Or maybe what you received was better than what you expected.

The Bible is filled with situations where God kept His promises in unexpected ways and when His blessings came at unexpected times. The Christmas season is the ultimate example of a promise fulfilled in an unexpected way at an unanticipated time.

B. Lesson Background

Over the past several weeks, we've looked at God's covenant promises to Abraham. In Genesis 12, God promised to make Abraham a great nation if he would leave his home country and follow God's leading. Years later, God reaffirmed this promise by telling Abraham that he would have numerous descendants, even though at that time he had no children (Genesis 15:1-6). Last week, we saw how God tested Abraham's trust by asking him to sacrifice his promised son, Isaac. Because Abraham was willing to obey even this mystifying command, God promised once more that all people would be blessed through him (22:18).

By the days of Mary and Joseph, over 2,000 years had passed since the time of Abraham. The hope of the promise seemed to be nowhere in sight. The Jews had indeed become a large people group, but centuries of internal strife, political turmoil, and idolatry had resulted in generations of exile and domination by foreign nations.

At the time of Jesus' birth, the Roman Empire, under the brilliant leadership of Emperor Octavian (Augustus), was just entering the apex of its power and had taken control of almost the entire Mediterranean world. The only chance for freedom lay in the ancient hope that God would remember His covenant with Abraham. The promise had been a long time coming by human standards.

The Lord Keeps His Promise

I. Exuberant Praise

(LUKE 1:46-55)

The context of "Mary's Song" in today's text largely explains its content. Luke's Gospel opens with the story of Zacharias and Elisabeth, the parents of John the Baptist. After years of infertility, the aged couple are enabled to conceive a child and are promised that their son will turn many people back to the Lord (Luke 1:13-17). This is the first of many surprises in God's plan to fulfill His promises to Abraham.

Six months into Elisabeth's pregnancy, the angel Gabriel appears to Mary and informs her that she will give birth to a child who will reign on the throne of David—this despite the fact that she is a virgin (Luke 1:26-35). Mary then leaves her home in Nazareth to visit her close relative Elisabeth. As the two women greet each other, John leaps in his mother's womb, inspiring Elisabeth to praise God and to bless Mary and her child (1:41-45). Mary's hymn of praise follows this incredible sequence of events. The song focuses on how God often acts in unpredictable ways.

A. Worship (vv. 46, 47)

46. And Mary said, My soul doth magnify the Lord.

Luke 1:46-55 is often referred to as "Mary's Song." A more traditional designation is the "Magnificat" on the basis of the verb *magnify* that Mary uses here. *Magnify* means to "glorify" God, to praise Him for who He is and what He has done.

47. And my spirit hath rejoiced in God my Saviour.

HOW TO SAY IT

Bethlehem	*Beth*-lih-hem.
Caesar Augustus	*See*-zer Aw-*gus*-tus.
Cyrenius	Sigh-*ree*-nee-us.
Davidic	Duh-*vid*-ick.
Herod	*Hair*-ud.
Magnificat	Mag-*nif*-ih-cot.
Nazareth	*Naz*-uh-reth.
Octavian	Ok-*tay*-vee-an.
Sepphoris	*Sef*-uh-ris.

This verse sets a tone for the remainder of the passage. The term *Saviour* highlights God's ability to rescue people from difficult circumstances. In this immediate context, this may include Mary's amazement that God has healed the pain of Elisabeth's infertility. The theme of God's salvation and His ability to do what seems impossible underlies the entire passage.

> *What Do You Think?*
> What was a time when you praised God when a blessing of God brought big challenges with it?
> *Talking Points for Your Discussion*
> - A pregnancy
> - A financial windfall
> - A job offer

B. Status (vv. 48, 49)

48. For he hath regarded the low estate of his handmaiden: for, behold, from henceforth all generations shall call me blessed.

Mary's Song is similar to the prayer of Hannah, the mother of the prophet Samuel, uttered over 1,000 years previously at this point (1 Samuel 2:1-10). Hannah had been unable to conceive, so she prayed urgently for God to remove her shame.

The Lord granted her request, and Hannah gave birth. In gratitude, she dedicated her son to God's service (1 Samuel 1:11, 22, 27, 28). After presenting young Samuel at the temple, Hannah offered a lengthy prayer of thanks to God that anticipated many of the themes that appear in Mary's Song. Like Hannah, Mary begins by expressing joy for the special blessing she has received.

Mary's prayer is characterized by a spirit of humility, evident in Mary's description of herself as God's *handmaiden*. Hannah twice refers to herself this way (1 Samuel 1:16, 18). A handmaiden is literally a female slave. Mary's use of the term recalls her earlier response to the angel Gabriel after being told that she was to conceive miraculously (Luke 1:38). This is a response of complete submission of one who recognizes her unworthiness to be blessed in such a manner.

49. For he that is mighty hath done to me great things; and holy is his name.

The description of God as *mighty* is commonly used in the Bible to highlight things that God has done to display His power (examples: Psalm 132:5; Isaiah 49:26; Jeremiah 32:19). The phrase *to me* indicates that Mary is thinking particularly of the special blessing that she herself has received. The remainder of her hymn covers other cases where God intervenes mightily on behalf of the faithful. The Bible often connects God's holiness with His might (example: Revelation 4:8).

C. Mercy (v. 50)

50. And his mercy is on them that fear him from generation to generation.

Emphasizing God's power is a good thing to do. But we should not allow an emphasis on God's power to cause us to overlook His love and grace. Mary's prayer offers a balanced approach by following the recognition of God's might with praise for His mercy. *Fear* in this verse does not refer to "terror," but rather to the awe and respect that come from a recognition of God's ability and willingness to save His people. Several psalms combine the ideas of fear/respect and mercy/love to highlight the fact of God's gracious care for those who trust Him (see Psalms 103:11, 17; 118:4; 147:11).

Generation to generation emphasizes God's ongoing faithfulness to His promises. In the context of the previous three lessons of this quarter, the phrase reminds us of God's promise to Abraham and his descendants. Mary, as a descendant of Abraham, is now reaping the benefits of a promise that was made to that forefather many centuries before she was born.

D. Deeds (vv. 51-53)

51. He hath shewed strength with his arm; he hath scattered the proud in the imagination of their hearts.

We now begin a section of the Magnificat that illustrates what becomes a key refrain in Jesus' teaching: "the last shall be first" (see Matthew 19:30; 20:16). God, in the mighty strength of His arm, certainly has the power to send His Son into the world in any way He chooses. Thus many expect the Christ to arrive through a king's house. We remember that the wise men come to Herod's palace in search of the newborn "King of the Jews" (Matthew 2:1-3). Logically, the Christ should be the son of royalty, not the son of a peasant girl. Mary's words reflect proud Herod's agitated reactions to the wise men's visit (2:3, 16).

52. He hath put down the mighty from their seats, and exalted them of low degree.

Commentators are divided on the specific references of verses 51-53. The nature of the Greek verbs in this section can mean that Mary is referring to ways that God has surprised people in the past by preferring the humble over the proud. Thus Mary may be thinking of specific stories from the Old Testament, such as Joseph's rise from prison to be ruler over Egypt, Hannah's miraculous pregnancy, and David's being chosen as king.

On the other hand, the verb tenses as used here may describe future realities. If this is the case, Mary may be predicting what her son, the Messiah, will accomplish when He grows up and begins to reign. Jesus does indeed exalt those *of low degree*. Jesus humbles himself to become a man and die on the cross, only to be exalted above all (Philippians 2:6-9).

> *What Do You Think?*
> What are some examples of God bringing down the high and mighty? What should be our reaction when this happens?
> *Talking Points for Your Discussion*
> ▪ Politicians
> ▪ Professional athletes
> ▪ Religious leaders

53. He hath filled the hungry with good things; and the rich he hath sent empty away.

If wealth were a sign of faithfulness and blessing, then Mary would not be chosen to bear the Messiah. Many ancient people conclude that wealthy and powerful people have been blessed, while those less fortunate do not enjoy God's favor. Yet role reversal is a key feature of God's kingdom (Matthew 5:3; Luke 6:24-26; 16:25). Of course, God doesn't reject rich people just because they have money, and He does not accept poor people merely because they don't enjoy worldly wealth. God looks at the heart.

"Let me tell you about the very rich. They are different from you and me. . . . They think, deep in their hearts, that they are better than we are." That was F. Scott Fitzgerald's pointed observation about a small, but influential part of the human race. We may also muse on the flip side of that statement: those who are not rich may agree that the very rich are better than they (the not rich) are.

But as Mary says in her reflections, God isn't impressed by the movers and shakers of the world nearly as much as we humans are. The pages of Scripture tell us how God deals with "the proud," "the mighty," and "the rich"—to use Mary's terms. He cuts them down to size while lifting up the humble and filling the hungry.

The world may think it knows who really counts, but God judges by a different standard. Have you adopted God's standard as your own?

—C. R. B.

E. Remembers (vv. 54, 55)

54. He hath helped his servant Israel, in remembrance of his mercy.

Mary moves her song toward its conclusion with a key term from Hannah's story. After prayer and a conversation with Eli, the Lord "remembered" Hannah and enabled her to conceive (1 Samuel 1:19, 20). Throughout the Old Testament, God is frequently described as "remembering" His covenant with His people and acting to save them (see Genesis 8:1; 19:29; 30:22; Exodus 2:24; 6:5; Psalm 105:8, 42). When God remembers His promises, He takes action. The reference to *his servant Israel* indicates that what God has done will benefit not only Mary, but the entire nation.

55. As he spake to our fathers, to Abraham, and to his seed for ever.

This verse connects the coming of Christ with the promises *to Abraham,* noted in the Introduction. Jews think of themselves as Abraham's physical and spiritual descendants (see John 8:33, 37) and thus heirs of God's promises. That the promises to Abraham and his descendants extend *for ever* is explicitly stated at Genesis 17:7. In Mary's day those promises have been a long time coming, but God never forgets. We are truly blessed to be

counted as "Abraham's seed, and heirs according to the promise" (Galatians 3:29).

> *What Do You Think?*
> What adjustments do you think Mary might have thought about making to her "song" as time progressed?
> *Talking Points for Your Discussion*
> ▪ At the manger (Luke 2:1-7, 16-19)
> ▪ In the temple when Jesus was age 12 (Luke 2:41-52)
> ▪ At the cross (Luke 23:26-56)

II. Surprising Fulfillment
(LUKE 2:1-7)

Our Lesson Background noted briefly the reign of the Roman Emperor Octavian (Augustus). He ruled from 27 BC to AD 14. Thus his rule is firmly established as the events of today's text are narrated.

A. Decree and Journey (vv. 1-5)

1. And it came to pass in those days, that there went out a decree from Caesar Augustus that all the world should be taxed.

Those days refers to the period immediately following the birth of John the Baptist (Luke 1:57-79). It is during this time frame that the Roman government announces a new tax census that requires Jews to register in their home villages.

2. (And this taxing was first made when Cyrenius was governor of Syria.)

Luke's dating of Jesus' birth has generated considerable controversy. Historically, the "first" tax census known to be conducted during the governorship of Cyrenius does not take place until AD 6. This is a controversial census, marked by considerable political unrest (see Acts 5:37). Jesus, however, could not have been born after 4 BC, the year of King Herod's death.

There are two possible ways to resolve this problem. One theory is that Cyrenius serves as governor at a date earlier than the nonbiblical sources suggest. Another proposal is that the word *first* here carries the idea of "former." In that case, Luke means something like, "at the time of the census that was taken *before* the one when Cyrenius became governor—that is, before the one I mention in Acts 5:37."

In any case, we do not want to miss the point of these verses. Since the authors of the Gospels rarely date events from Jesus' life to Roman history, Luke's dating may have more to do with doctrinal symbolism than the political calendar. Luke 1 stresses again and again that God fulfills His promises in unexpected ways at unexpected times. What could be more surprising, then, than to bring the Messiah into the world at the very time when Rome is reaching the apex of its power?

While a tax census seems to symbolize Caesar's authority over the Jews, Mary's Song has already shown that a new world order is emerging—one where the last will be first. Luke's reference to the census, then, not only explains why Jesus of Nazareth is born in Bethlehem, but also clarifies that worldly powers cannot stop God's eternal promises.

3. And all went to be taxed, every one into his own city.

Because it is common for people to move from place to place in search of work, they are typically required to register for a tax census in their ancestral homes. This simplifies record keeping. In modern terms, people must return to the county where birth certificates are registered with the court.

What Do You Think?

What was a time when a secular event or requirement pushed your service for God in a particular direction? How did things turn out?

Talking Points for Your Discussion

- Jury duty
- Court appearance
- Secular holiday

4, 5. And Joseph also went up from Galilee, out of the city of Nazareth, into Judaea, unto the city of David, which is called Bethlehem; (because he was of the house and lineage of David:) to be taxed with Mary his espoused wife, being great with child.

Joseph apparently has migrated from Bethlehem to Nazareth. As a carpenter, he may be working on the new Roman administrative center at Sepphoris, four miles from Mary's home (Luke 1:26). Since Mary and Joseph are at least legally betrothed at this point, it is natural for Mary to accompany Joseph to his hometown to register.

Jesus' coming not only fulfills God's promises to Abraham that all nations will be blessed through him, it also fulfills God's promise to David that one of his descendants will reign over Israel forever (2 Samuel 7:16). Although Joseph is not Jesus' biological father, Joseph is Jesus' legal father. This is part of the fulfillment of Jesus' Davidic lineage (Luke 3:21-31). Bethlehem was David's hometown (1 Samuel 17:12, 58).

On the basis of Micah 5:2, ancient Jews understand that the Christ is to be born in Bethlehem (see also Matthew 2:3-6). This prophecy leads many to doubt Jesus' messianic identity, since it becomes widely known that Jesus actually grows up in Nazareth (see Luke 4:16; John 7:41-52).

B. Birth and Circumstances (vv. 6, 7)

6, 7. And so it was, that, while they were there, the days were accomplished that she should be delivered. And she brought forth her firstborn son, and wrapped him in swaddling clothes, and laid him in a manger; because there was no room for them in the inn.

When Mary and Joseph arrive in Bethlehem, the natural thing to do is first to seek lodging with some of Joseph's relatives. The text doesn't say they did that, but it's a natural thing to suppose. With no room available among relatives, the next step is to try the inn, but there's no room there either. Of course, there is always room to crowd in two more people, but Mary needs privacy for her delivery. The number of people present at the inn must be too great for that.

Ancient Christian tradition suggests that Jesus is born in a cave. Such a cave in this context would most likely be a makeshift root cellar in a natural crevice below or near a house. These small caves are used to store grain and other perishable goods, and also to shelter domestic animals at night.

There is nothing unusual about *swaddling clothes*. But Luke places particular significance on the fact that Jesus is laid *in a manger*. When the

The Lord Keeps His Promise

angel appears to the shepherds to announce the Savior's birth, the only identifying "sign" mentioned is that the child is to be found in a manger (Luke 2:12, 16). This is unusual even for the poorest families: a manger is a feed trough for animals, usually made of scrap wood and generally dirty and unfit for a baby. Even so, the manger makes a convenient crib for Jesus. The symbolism is obvious: God's Son comes into the world in the most unexpected way imaginable, in utter humility rather than royal glory.

What Do You Think?

What is gained by retelling the Christmas story when we have heard it many times already?

Talking Points for Your Discussion

- Gains within your church family
- Gains in witnessing to nonbelievers
- Gains within your own family

❦ DIFFERING MOTIVES ❦

Octomom is the catchy nickname (with a biting edge to it) that was given to Nadya Suleman in 2009. She gained notoriety by giving birth to octuplets, conceived by means of fertility treatments. A wide variety of critics joined the public debate: members of the general public, medical professionals, and even Suleman's own mother! They raised questions about the morality—or at least the advisability—of the fertility treatment that enabled her to carry so many babies.

Other facts contributed to the debate: Suleman was a single mother living on public assistance, and she already had 6 children—also conceived by fertility treatments. Much of the debate appropriately centered on how she would be able to care for all 14 of her youngsters.

We easily imagine that Mary also was judged by a chattering public. One difference (among many) between the two is that Mary did nothing to become pregnant other than submit to God's offer to bless the world through the child she would carry. Unlike the Octomom, Mary's decision was not about her. Rather, it was about allowing God to use her as an agent in His plan to save the world. Do you have Mary's attitude?   —C. R. B.

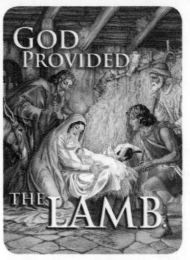

Visual for Lesson 4

Post this visual alongside the visual from Lesson 3 so your learners will see an important connection.

Conclusion

A. Mysterious Ways

Nothing about the way that the Savior came into the world was what first-century Jews expected. Some expected that the Christ would be a rebel leader and great warrior to drive the Gentiles out of the land. Others thought the Messiah would be a great priestly prophet, who would reform corruptions of the temple system. Some believed that God himself would appear on earth to destroy evil suddenly. As far as we can tell, none imagined that the Messiah would be born to an unknown peasant girl and laid in a manger!

If somehow Abraham could step into a time machine and visit our world, we can only imagine what he would think about the way that God finally fulfilled His promise to bless all nations! No doubt he would be more than a little surprised by God's methods and timing. The Lord really has worked in mysterious ways. He still does.

B. Prayer

Father, we are thankful that You remember Your promises and are faithful to them. Please teach us to be patient as we wait for You to work out Your perfect plans in our lives. Thank You for surprising us! In Jesus' name, amen.

C. Thought to Remember

God is still fulfilling His promises.

INVOLVEMENT LEARNING

Some of the activities below are also found in the helpful student book, Adult Bible Class.
Don't forget to download the free reproducible page from www.standardlesson.com to enhance your lesson!

Into the Lesson

Ask class members to pair off and discuss a time they desired something but had to wait a long time to receive it. It may have been something from childhood, such as a particular toy. Ask for volunteers to share with the class what it felt like to wait for the object of their desire.

Make the transition to Bible study by saying, "Waiting for a promise or hope to be fulfilled can be very difficult. But imagine waiting your whole life! The Jewish nation waited centuries for their promised Messiah to come. Today, let's share Mary's joy as she anticipates the Messiah's arrival."

Into the Word

Start with a very brief lecture of the Lesson Background. List in advance the following phrases on the board:

1. Genesis 12—a great nation
2. Genesis 15—numerous descendants
3. Genesis 22—testing Abraham's faith
4. 2,000+ years
5. Mary's *Magnificat*

Cover each point with paper, removing the appropriate cover as you deliver your talk. Point to #5 as you say, "The first part of our printed text is often called 'the *Magnificat*,' or 'Mary's Song.'"

Form five study teams. Provide a piece of poster board for all teams except Team 1. Distribute handouts with instructions as follows.

Team 1: Write interview questions for Mary at age 60, asking her to reflect on her experiences as revealed in today's text. Be prepared to conduct this "interview" for the class. *Team 2:* Review Mary's song in Luke 1:46-55 and compare it with Hannah's song in 1 Samuel 2:1-10. List similarities and differences on the poster board. *Team 3:* Make two lists: one about surprising features regarding the birth of Jesus, the other about ways that this birth demonstrates God's faithfulness to His promises. *Team 4:* Imagine that you are challenged to defend the truth of the virgin birth of Jesus. What answers or arguments would you use? See Isaiah 7:14; Matthew 1:18-25. *Team 5:* Sketch out a homepage for a Web site that celebrates the birth of Jesus. Be sure to include a heading for the homepage, appropriate tabs, subject headings under the various tabs, links, and photos.

Allow time for teams to present to the class as indicated by their assignments.

Into Life

Remind the class that Christians celebrate Christmas because what happened in Bethlehem is at the core of our beliefs. God has done great things in our lives through Jesus. Ask, "What are the blessings God has brought to us through Jesus?" List the answers on the board.

Then say, "Now we're going to consider how we can best allow God to use us for praising Him for His work in our lives." Distribute copies of a two-column handout you have prepared in advance. The first column will be headed "Mary's Song," with that text reproduced underneath. The second column will be headed "My Song." In that column, list the verse numbers 46b to 55 along with the first three words of each verse (except for v. 55). Ask learners to write a completion to those three words of each verse in the second column. The completions are to express praise for how God has blessed them through Jesus. Allow each learner to share his or her completed work with the same person they interacted with in the opening activity.

Alternative. Download the reproducible page and distribute copies of the Mary's *Magnificat* . . . and Mine Too! activity. Have students work in small teams to complete the exercise. Close by having the class sing "Hark, the Herald Angels Sing."

Distribute copies of the O Little Town of Bethlehem activity from the reproducible page activity as a take-home exercise.

The Lord Keeps His Promise

JOSEPH SHOWS CHARACTER

DEVOTIONAL READING: **1 Corinthians 10:1-13**
BACKGROUND SCRIPTURE: **Genesis 37, 39**

GENESIS 39:7-21A

7 And it came to pass after these things, that his master's wife cast her eyes upon Joseph; and she said, Lie with me.

8 But he refused, and said unto his master's wife, Behold, my master wotteth not what is with me in the house, and he hath committed all that he hath to my hand;

9 There is none greater in this house than I; neither hath he kept back any thing from me but thee, because thou art his wife: how then can I do this great wickedness, and sin against God?

10 And it came to pass, as she spake to Joseph day by day, that he hearkened not unto her, to lie by her, or to be with her.

11 And it came to pass about this time, that Joseph went into the house to do his business; and there was none of the men of the house there within.

12 And she caught him by his garment, saying, Lie with me: and he left his garment in her hand, and fled, and got him out.

13 And it came to pass, when she saw that he had left his garment in her hand, and was fled forth,

14 That she called unto the men of her house, and spake unto them, saying, See, he hath brought in an Hebrew unto us to mock us; he came in unto me to lie with me, and I cried with a loud voice:

15 And it came to pass, when he heard that I lifted up my voice and cried, that he left his garment with me, and fled, and got him out.

16 And she laid up his garment by her, until his lord came home.

17 And she spake unto him according to these words, saying, The Hebrew servant, which thou hast brought unto us, came in unto me to mock me:

18 And it came to pass, as I lifted up my voice and cried, that he left his garment with me, and fled out.

19 And it came to pass, when his master heard the words of his wife, which she spake unto him, saying, After this manner did thy servant to me; that his wrath was kindled.

20 And Joseph's master took him, and put him into the prison, a place where the king's prisoners were bound: and he was there in the prison.

21a But the LORD was with Joseph.

KEY VERSE

How then can I do this great wickedness, and sin against God? —**Genesis 39:9**

GOD ESTABLISHES A FAITHFUL PEOPLE

Unit 2: God's Protection

LESSONS 5–9

LESSON AIMS

After participating in this lesson, each student will be able to:

1. Describe the temptations of Joseph by Potiphar's wife and the outcome.

2. Compare and contrast the temptation of Joseph by Potiphar's wife with that of Judah by Tamar (Genesis 38).

3. Write a skit of a modernized version of the story of Joseph and Potiphar's wife.

LESSON OUTLINE

Introduction

A. The Ninth Commandment

He was in prison, and he functioned as the unofficial assistant to the chaplain. He was always willing to pray, to read portions of the Bible during any of the regular or special services, or to help in any way he could. He said that he had been an elected county official and an active member of his church. He claimed that two others had embezzled funds and then testified against him. They had the money, and he received the prison sentence. To know this humble, quiet man tended to give credence to his account.

False accusations have ruined lives, shattered families, ended careers, and caused the guiltless to have prison records. A scheming individual may bump into a coworker, fall to the floor, and then accuse the innocent person of assault. A teenager may concoct a false account of sexual misconduct against a youth sponsor. Children whose whims are not satisfied may call a social service hotline to lodge charges of child abuse. The motivations behind such charges are varied: vengeance, power, greed, jealousy, or covetousness.

When the people of Israel made their exodus from Egypt and reached Mt. Sinai, one of the first things God did for this new nation was to provide the Ten Commandments (Exodus 20; Deuteronomy 5). These were given about 450 years after the events of today's lesson. The Ninth Commandment is expressed in these words: "Thou shalt not bear false witness against thy neighbour" (Exodus 20:16; compare Deuteronomy 5:20). The lesson today provides a memorable example of why such a commandment is necessary. Principles of right and wrong are always true, regardless of the culture or century involved (Romans 1:18-32). But God can bring good out of evil.

B. Lesson Background

The first three lessons of the quarter featured Abram/Abraham to introduce the theme "God Establishes a Faithful People." Abraham is the first person in the Bible about whom it is said that he believed God (Genesis 15:6). The writer of the book of Hebrews, however, cites three others who lived before Abraham whose lives exemplified faith (Abel, Enoch, and Noah, per Hebrews 11:4-7).

Abraham died at age 175. At that time, grandsons Jacob and Esau, the only children of Abraham's son Isaac, were 15 (Genesis 21:5; 25:7, 8, 26). The fact that Abraham had only two grandsons through Isaac may have caused Abraham to wonder about the rate at which God was moving to fulfill the promise that his descendants would be as many as the stars (15:5). These grandsons began to change things, for Jacob became the father of 12 sons (35:23-26), and Esau had 5 sons (36:4, 5).

It is Joseph, the eleventh son of Jacob, who is featured in this lesson and the next three. Joseph was the first son of Jacob's favorite wife (Rachel), and Jacob demonstrated favoritism in giving Joseph a multicolored robe, the kind worn by persons in places of royalty (Genesis 37:3). The same word is used in 2 Samuel 13:18 for a robe worn by a daughter of King David.

This preferential treatment produced jealousy on the part of Joseph's older brothers (Genesis 37:4). This intensified when Joseph related two of his dreams that depicted family members paying homage to him (37:5-9). When the brothers had an opportunity, they mistreated Joseph and sold him into slavery. As Jacob had once deceived his own father (27:5-33), so he was deceived in turn by his sons: they dipped Joseph's robe in the blood of an animal, presented it to Jacob, and asked him to identify the robe. This caused Jacob to believe that his favorite son was dead (37:31-35).

HOW TO SAY IT

Esau	*Ee*-saw.
Hagar	*Hay*-gar.
Ishmael	*Ish*-may-el.
Ishmaelites	*Ish*-may-el-ites.
Judah	*Joo*-duh.
Keturah	Keh-*too*-ruh.
Les Misérables	Lay Mee-zay-*rah*-bl.
Midian	*Mid*-ee-un.
Midianites	*Mid*-ee-un-ites.
Potiphar	*Pot*-ih-far.
Reuben	*Roo*-ben.
Sinai	*Sigh*-nye or *Sigh*-nay-eye.

Joseph was taken to Egypt by a caravan of Ishmaelites and Midianites. Both groups were relatives of Jacob and his family, for Abraham was the progenitor of each (Ishmael as a son of Hagar [Genesis 16:15], and Midian as a son Keturah, Abraham's wife after Sarah died [25:1, 2]). In Egypt, Joseph was sold to Potiphar, the captain of Pharaoh's bodyguard (37:36). Based on Genesis 37:2, it is usually assumed that Joseph was 17 years old when he was sold by his brothers. The date was about 1899 BC when Joseph arrived in Egypt.

Genesis 39:6 describes Joseph as "a goodly person, and well favoured." This is a comment on Joseph's physical attractiveness. Perhaps he is blessed with the good looks of his mother, since the same Hebrew words are used to describe both mother and son in 29:17 and 39:6. This factor is combined with a strong work ethic, wisdom, and God's blessing. Potiphar determines that it is prudent to make Joseph the overseer of all he owns (39:4).

I. Choices by Joseph
(GENESIS 39:7-12)
A. First Temptation (vv. 7-9)

7. And it came to pass after these things, that his master's wife cast her eyes upon Joseph; and she said, Lie with me.

The hero of this narrative is about to be tempted. Those qualities that enable him to do well make him attractive to *his master's wife*. It is not unusual for a hero to be tempted, and similar accounts exist in the literature of Egypt and throughout history. Joseph has not yet risen to be a famous leader; he is simply a handsome, capable servant at this point.

It is tempting to assign motives to Potiphar's wife for her proposal to Joseph. Is she lonely, neglected, desirous of power, or seeking revenge for something her husband has done or not done? Her statement to Joseph is in the form of a command. Regardless of her motive, she is violating her marriage commitment and jeopardizing Joseph's life in the process.

8. But he refused, and said unto his master's wife, Behold, my master wotteth not what is with me in the house, and he hath committed all that he hath to my hand.

Joseph's response to her command is stated very succinctly: he refuses. Sexual immorality is often rampant among slaves who do not have the benefits of marriage. It is therefore very likely that Joseph has been challenged in this type of temptation frequently.

One preacher advises couples whom he is marrying on how to resist such temptations. He suggests that they probably will be tempted at some time in the future, and that they should have a predetermined plan in mind that can be put into operation to resist the temptation successfully. It is very possible that previous comments or actions by Potiphar's wife have already prepared Joseph for such a situation.

Joseph's first line of defense is to affirm that his submission to her would break the trust that his master has placed in him. Joseph states that his master trusts him so completely that he is not concerned with what happens *in the house*. The Hebrew behind the antique word *wotteth* speaks to "knowledge" or "awareness."

What Do You Think?
  In what ways can greater success result in greater temptation?
Talking Points for Your Discussion
  - How others gravitate toward the successful person
  - Access to power, resources
  - Codependencies
  - Lack of accountability

9. There is none greater in this house than I; neither hath he kept back any thing from me but thee, because thou art his wife: how then can I do this great wickedness, and sin against God?

Joseph continues his resistance by putting the situation into its proper perspectives as it relates to his master, his master's wife, and God. As stated above, it will be almost 450 years before God will proclaim the Ten Commandments at Mt. Sinai. It is the Seventh Commandment that will forbid adultery. It is remarkable that Joseph has a sense of morality that many today seem not to have achieved!

The sources of Joseph's concepts about God and holiness are unknown. His grandfather Isaac is still living, at age 168, when Joseph is sold by his brothers; Isaac lives to be 180 (Genesis 35:28). Joseph therefore may have been taught about God and righteousness by both his father and his grandfather. The sin of adultery by Reuben, Joseph's oldest brother, has made Joseph aware of the devastation that such sin can cause in a family (35:22). It is interesting to see that the biblical author puts the sexual sin of Judah, one of Joseph's brothers, in close proximity to the narrative of Joseph's temptation (38:15-26).

What Do You Think?
  What are some ways that you have found to be helpful for resisting temptation? Does your answer depend on the type of temptation being faced? Explain.
Talking Points for Your Discussion
  - Considering earthly consequences
  - Considering eternal consequences
  - Considering "collateral damage" to loved ones
  - Bringing Scripture to mind
  - Running away

B. Frequent Temptations (v. 10)

10. And it came to pass, as she spake to Joseph day by day, that he hearkened not unto her, to lie by her, or to be with her.

The temptations for Joseph become a matter of willpower. Potiphar's wife seems determined to win this war, and she propositions Joseph on a daily basis. Joseph's response is to become resolute in righteousness. He ignores her pleadings, and he is careful not even *to be with her*. Many centuries later, Solomon will warn about the adulteress and say that a young man should keep far from her (Proverbs 5:8).

C. Final Test (vv. 11, 12)

11. And it came to pass about this time, that Joseph went into the house to do his business; and there was none of the men of the house there within.

How does Joseph end up alone with Potiphar's wife, given Joseph's practice of refusing to be with her? Joseph must have a responsibility in the house that cannot be delegated to others. Thus it is necessary for him to risk entering his master's house. It is also possible that others are present when he enters, but then they leave. The intent here is to show how Joseph becomes the target of the false accusations that will be made, in spite of his precautions.

> **What Do You Think?**
> What is an example of a situation in which a Christian may not be able to avoid *being* tempted (realizing that God will always provide a way out from *yielding* to the temptation)?
> *Talking Points for Your Discussion*
> - Unexpected events
> - Unavoidable people
> - Initial emotional reactions

12. And she caught him by his garment, saying, Lie with me: and he left his garment in her hand, and fled, and got him out.

Potiphar's wife not only seizes the opportunity, she also seizes Joseph's clothing to try to force him to submit to her advances. It is sometimes said that the best defense against this type of temptation is to use your two legs to run away, and that is what Joseph does. The apostle Paul says the same thing 2,000 years later when he writes that a person should "flee fornication" (1 Corinthians 6:18). In 2 Timothy 2:22, Paul also suggests alternatives: pursue instead such things as righteousness, faith, love, and peace.

II. Charges Against Joseph
(GENESIS 39:13-18)
A. To the Household (vv. 13-15)

13. And it came to pass, when she saw that he had left his garment in her hand, and was fled forth.

Joseph's triumph is short-lived, for he makes the mistake of leaving a part of his apparel behind. The schemes of Potiphar's wife have been frustrated, but she quickly cooks up a plan to turn the situation to seek revenge. The evidence that is *in her hand* will be the "proof" for the charges that are forming in her mind.

Visual for Lesson 5. *Point to this visual as you ask, "What are some techniques you use to resist surrendering to temptation?"*

14. That she called unto the men of her house, and spake unto them, saying, See, he hath brought in an Hebrew unto us to mock us; he came in unto me to lie with me, and I cried with a loud voice.

The devious woman immediately launches her plan for revenge. Her desire for Joseph becomes fury against him. The plan needs an audience, so she assembles people to serve as witnesses, and she provides a false account on how the garment has come to be in her hands. In addition, the attack on Joseph is subtly stated so as to refer to him simply as *an Hebrew*, thus exploiting the differences between Joseph and the others.

15. And it came to pass, when he heard that I lifted up my voice and cried, that he left his garment with me, and fled, and got him out.

Mrs. Potiphar also changes the order of the events, for her scream actually took place after Joseph had already made his escape from her presence. Thus we have her official revision of the facts. The scenario that she presents sounds very reasonable, and the servants know that it is in their best interest to support the wife of their master.

B. To Her Husband (vv. 16-18)

16. And she laid up his garment by her, until his lord came home.

The last phrase is interesting in the way it refers to Potiphar. The first part of this verse gives what Potiphar's wife does, but the arrival of Potiphar to his home centers on Joseph's relationship to Potiphar—*his lord*. In the meantime, she guarantees that the evidence will be available by keeping it with her until Potiphar arrives.

17. And she spake unto him according to these words, saying, The Hebrew servant, which thou hast brought unto us, came in unto me to mock me.

The carefully contrived scheme is repeated by using the imagery Potiphar's wife has already devised. First, the fact that Joseph is a Hebrew is emphasized. Second, she subtly puts the blame on Potiphar for bringing such a person into the household. Third, she indicates how she is the innocent party because Joseph came to her to make the advances.

Finally, she describes Joseph's actions in words that are used to provide a smear against him for his attitude toward her. This is a new element in her fabricated account. The word given as *mock* can carry the idea of "laugh," but in this context it means to laugh at someone with scorn. Or it may be that she is insulted by his actions more than his words.

18. And it came to pass, as I lifted up my voice and cried, that he left his garment with me, and fled out.

The imaginary scene is described in the same way it is given to the servants. She tells how she uses one of the defensive devices that people can use in such situations—a loud voice. This is given as having had the desired effect: Joseph fled from the scene. At this point the offended housewife rests her case.

❧ *FALSE TESTIMONY* ❧

A young attorney, just out of law school, was given assignments in various departments of the firm that hired him. The idea was to find out where his greatest skills lay. His apprenticeship in the criminal law department was particularly interesting. A state prison inmate had filed a suit against some of the prison guards, alleging mistreatment. The young attorney took depositions first from the prisoner and his cell mate, then from the guards.

The two sets of testimony were so different, according to the attorney, that one would

have thought the testimonies concerned different cases! Testimony on each side seemed to be so well rehearsed as to make the listener question whether truth and justice even had a chance of being served when the case went to court. We wonder what level of disillusionment the young attorney experienced as a result!

In the case against Joseph, it seems that Potiphar's wife had rehearsed her allegations quite well. Joseph had no chance for justice. His only hope lay in the justice that God would provide. Some folks reading this account have also felt the sting of false allegations. When that happens, our hope in God's ultimate justice can be our greatest source of strength.   —C. R. B.

What Do You Think?

How should a Christian respond when falsely accused of wrongdoing?

Talking Points for Your Discussion

- Remain silent? (Matthew 26:61-63)
- Answer charges? (Acts 22:1)
- Make countercharges? (Luke 11:14-20)

III. Changes for Joseph
(GENESIS 39:19-21A)

A. Master's Anger (vv. 19, 20)

19. And it came to pass, when his master heard the words of his wife, which she spake unto him, saying, After this manner did thy servant to me; that his wrath was kindled.

The natural flow of the words indicates that Potiphar believes his wife. We don't know if Joseph has an opportunity to give his version of what happened. The circumstances demand that Joseph be punished; thus Potiphar becomes angry. It is also possible that Potiphar realizes that he has lost a very responsible servant, and he may have to resume the supervision of his affairs personally.

20. And Joseph's master took him, and put him into the prison, a place where the king's prisoners were bound: and he was there in the prison.

The fact that *Joseph's master* only puts Joseph in a prison has caused some to think that Joseph is able to give his version of what happened. The treatment that he receives is harsh, but it could be worse. The personal regard that Potiphar has for Joseph may temper the punishment. One ancient source indicates that the laws of Egypt demand "1,000 blows" for an attempt at adultery, and the punishment for rape is even more severe.

Psalm 105:18 states that Joseph's feet and neck are shackled in some way. Joseph later describes his situation as being put into a dungeon (Genesis 40:15). It also seems that this prison is connected with the captain of the guard, where political prisoners are confined.

What Do You Think?
How does resisting temptation make life both easier and harder for the Christian?
Talking Points for Your Discussion
- Rewards
- Punishments
- Reputation
- Open and closed doors of opportunity

B. Lord's Kindness (v. 21a)

21a. But the LORD was with Joseph.

The same words are used in Genesis 39:2 when Joseph is being sold to Potiphar. The emphasis is that God is always present. Stephen, the first Christian martyr, echoes the same thought in Acts 7:9. The genuine believer is always comforted by the fact that the Lord is present—in the pleasures and pains of life, and in death.

❧ *REDEMPTION OR VINDICATION?* ❧

Stories of redemption warm our hearts. Just one example comes from *Les Misérables,* one of the greatest novels of the nineteenth century. The historical setting is the years between 1815 and the Paris Uprising of 1832. The complicated plot centers on Jean Valjean, an ex-convict, whose life is turned around by a priest. Valjean becomes a successful businessman and mayor. He also becomes a compassionate man who works to bring grace into the lives of the downtrodden. Thus, the story is one of redemption.

There is a difference, however, between *redemption* and *vindication.* Valjean had a criminal past

and a criminal mind-set from which he was redeemed. That was not true of Joseph, who had committed no crime. Even in the darkest days of his life, he knew God was with him. Even if he had never been released from prison, the fact that "the Lord was with Joseph" was vindication.

In life's dark hours, does our faith in God allow Him to provide us with that same vindicating gift of His presence? —C. R. B.

Conclusion

A. Overcoming Temptations

A person may overcome some temptations by avoiding the places or persons delighting in causing a Christian to sin. But it is also helpful to know some tips on handling or overcoming the temptations that are certain to come.

1. Flee. To run from temptation is what Joseph did, and it is recommended by the apostle Paul (see the comments on verse 12 above).

2. Know your Bible. When Jesus was tempted, He used biblical passages against Satan (Matthew 4:1-11).

3. Be confident. Every temptation has a way of escape, so plan to look for it and use it (1 Corinthians 10:13).

4. Call a friend. Have a friend available to whom you may go, or such a person can come to you and help you to overcome your trial.

5. Rejoice. This seems strange, but James provides the assurance that to overcome a test develops the attribute of steadfastness or endurance for Christ (James 1:2, 3).

6. Be stubborn. Commit yourself to be firm about not yielding. Determine not to allow Satan to use you to discredit the kingdom of Christ (Romans 6:13; Ephesians 6:13).

B. Prayer

Lord, You taught us to pray about not being led into temptation. That is my prayer now as I begin another week with its tests, trials, and temptations. In Jesus' name, amen.

C. Thought to Remember

Flee temptation.

INVOLVEMENT LEARNING

Some of the activities below are also found in the helpful student book, Adult Bible Class.
Don't forget to download the free reproducible page from www.standardlesson.com to enhance your lesson!

Into the Lesson

Prepare 10 large cards for display. Put the following two-letter pairs on the cards, one pair per card (without the word *and*): *T* and *R; O* and *C; E* and *E; M* and *S; I* and *N; P* and *I; T* and *A; T* and *S; A* and *T; N* and *E*. Using masking tape, affix the 10 cards vertically to the board, in a single column in the order given. When your display is complete, say, "If we rearrange these pairs properly, we will see two words that are keys to today's lesson." Help the class by putting the *T* and *R* at the top, with the *N* and *E* at the bottom.

After some guessing and rearranging, you will end up with the word *TEMPTATION* (vertically on the left) and the word *RESISTANCE* (vertically on the right). Say, "Today we will study what happens when temptation meets resistance."

Into the Word

Read Genesis 37:36 and 39:1 aloud. Identify these as "back-to-back verses with a slight interruption: Genesis 38, the story of Judah's sexual sin with his daughter-in-law." Continue: "It is interesting that the arrangement serves to contrast Judah's impurity with Joseph's purity. Which son is more worthy to move God's promises forward?"

Option: Download the reproducible page and distribute copies of the activity titled The Lord Was with Joseph. You can have individual learners read aloud the seven passages noted, with each reading followed by the class saying in unison *but the Lord was with Joseph!* This will establish the context for the study.

Say, "Recognizing the elements of temptation and resistance is the first step to maintaining holiness. From today's text, those on my left are to identify elements of temptation, while learners on my right identify elements of resistance." After time for reading and reflection, call for responses.

Learners may see a variety of elements, but here are several for each. *Elements of temptation* often come through the eyes (vv. 6b, 7a); suggest things that sound pleasurable (v. 7b); are persistent (v. 10a); strike at moments of easy access (v. 11); can involve lies (vv. 14, 15); may draw in those in authority (vv. 16-19). *Elements of resistance* can involve simple refusal (v. 8a); clear thinking (vv. 8, 9); recognizing the presence of wickedness (v. 9b); knowing that God's will is the most important thing; (v. 9b); avoiding tempting situations (v. 10b); fleeing from tempting occasions (vv. 12b, 13); accepting that the consequences for doing right may be necessary (v. 20). Allow your class to suggest other truths they see.

Into Life

Give the following incomplete case studies to two groups.

Case Study 1: Sue had risen like a rocket in the publishing company she worked for. No one in her church was surprised; everyone knew her character and work ethic. She went from office assistant, to editorial assistant, to editor, to acquisitions editor in only eight years. Her sterling performance was all a boss could ask for. Her stunning good looks and fashion sense were only pluses. The problem was that the publisher was a womanizer. From touching to lewd remarks, he had become increasingly aggressive, demanding that she accompany him on business trips as his "personal assistant."

Case Study 2: Lee's work in the auto assembly plant matched his skills and personality perfectly. His work ethic was solid and godly. But his handsome face and physique caught the eye of a vice president. She looked for occasions to call him to her private office for "business" that turned out to be hopes for sexual encounters.

Say, "Read your story and complete it in 50 words or less. We'll hear several." After hearing a few, read 1 Corinthians 10:11-13 to conclude the class. The Too Strong? You're Wrong! activity on the reproducible page will help apply the truths.

JOSEPH FINDS FAVOR

DEVOTIONAL READING: Genesis 49:22-26
BACKGROUND SCRIPTURE: Genesis 41

GENESIS 41:37-46, 50-52

37 And the thing was good in the eyes of Pharaoh, and in the eyes of all his servants.

38 And Pharaoh said unto his servants, Can we find such a one as this is, a man in whom the Spirit of God is?

39 And Pharaoh said unto Joseph, Forasmuch as God hath shewed thee all this, there is none so discreet and wise as thou art:

40 Thou shalt be over my house, and according unto thy word shall all my people be ruled: only in the throne will I be greater than thou.

41 And Pharaoh said unto Joseph, See, I have set thee over all the land of Egypt.

42 And Pharaoh took off his ring from his hand, and put it upon Joseph's hand, and arrayed him in vestures of fine linen, and put a gold chain about his neck;

43 And he made him to ride in the second chariot which he had; and they cried before him, Bow the knee: and he made him ruler over all the land of Egypt.

44 And Pharaoh said unto Joseph, I am Pharaoh, and without thee shall no man lift up his hand or foot in all the land of Egypt.

45 And Pharaoh called Joseph's name Zaphnathpaaneah; and he gave him to wife Asenath the daughter of Potipherah priest of On. And Joseph went out over all the land of Egypt.

46 And Joseph was thirty years old when he stood before Pharaoh king of Egypt. And Joseph went out from the presence of Pharaoh, and went throughout all the land of Egypt.

. . . .

50 And unto Joseph were born two sons before the years of famine came, which Asenath the daughter of Potipherah priest of On bare unto him.

51 And Joseph called the name of the firstborn Manasseh: For God, said he, hath made me forget all my toil, and all my father's house.

52 And the name of the second called he Ephraim: For God hath caused me to be fruitful in the land of my affliction.

KEY VERSE

Pharaoh said unto his servants, Can we find such a one as this is, a man in whom the Spirit of God is?
—**Genesis 41:38**

God Establishes a Faithful People

Unit 2: God's Protection

Lessons 5–9

Lesson Aims

After participating in this lesson, each student will be able to:

1. Summarize Joseph's change in status.

2. Explain the interrelationship between faith and advance planning.

3. Explain to an unbeliever how the story of Joseph inspires the Christian.

Lesson Outline

Introduction

A. Cream Rises to the Top!

The familiar idiom *cream rises to the top* is not used as much as it once was. In a literal sense, it refers to the butterfat in milk. In a figurative sense, it refers to those individuals in groups who rise to the top because of their outstanding abilities. To use the expression is usually a compliment.

But "rising cream" can create challenges. A church in a southern U.S. town had a new associate minister for music and youth. He was very capable in both areas, and soon he was making a solid impact for Christ. Young people were being baptized, and the church was growing. The students at the high school voted him to be their baccalaureate speaker.

The senior minister had never been selected for such an honor. He could have been very pleased to have such a wonderful associate rise to the top so quickly, but the green-eyed monster of jealousy reared its ugly head and dissension resulted. Handling the favors that others receive can create difficulties.

The situations Joseph found himself in had their origin in sibling jealousy and envy (Genesis 37:11). Yet Joseph managed to rise to the top in ancient Egypt in three different areas. His dedication and efficiency prompted his rise (1) in the household of Potiphar, (2) in the prison where he had been placed because of a false accusation, and (3) in the leadership of the nation of Egypt. This lesson develops the third of these occasions.

B. Lesson Background

The final verses of the previous study depicted how Joseph, the eleventh and favorite son of Jacob the patriarch, came to have a prison record. Even so, the last phrase of that lesson affirmed that the Lord was with Joseph.

Joseph always tried to live honorably before God, but he also experienced the dishonor of being sold by his brothers, becoming a slave, and being placed in prison on a false charge. An ordinary man may have resigned himself to these things, surrendered all hope, and given in to bitterness. But Joseph was not an ordinary man.

Joseph's conduct in prison caused history to repeat itself. Previously he had risen in the sight of Potiphar to be in charge of his household. In prison, Joseph found himself functioning as an assistant to the warden, in charge of the prison and the prisoners (Genesis 39:22, 23).

Joseph was then given a new responsibility—to be the personal attendant for two political prisoners (Genesis 40:4). They were the cupbearer and baker for the Pharaoh of Egypt. The two held very important places of service, for they oversaw what the king drank and ate. One ancient Jewish source conjectures that there was a plot against Pharaoh, and the reaction was to imprison any possible culprits until the situation was investigated. The Hebrew simply states that this arrangement continued for "days," an indefinite period of time.

Both of the special prisoners had dreams, but there was no one to interpret them. Dreams were considered to be very important in ancient times, and manuals or dream books were used to provide meanings. In Egypt, such books were guarded closely so as to preserve the importance of the priests. Joseph's viewpoint was that valid interpretations belong to God. So Joseph asked for the prisoners to tell their dreams to him (Genesis 40:8). Joseph supplied the interpretations, and what he said was fulfilled exactly (40:9-22).

Up to that point, four dreams are associated with the life of Joseph: the two he had as a youth that caused his brothers to resent him (Genesis 37:5-11) and then a dream by each of these two officials. Two years later, Pharaoh had two dreams (41:1-7). The wise men of Egypt were not able to provide an interpretation. The cupbearer, who was out of prison, suddenly remembered Joseph. This provided an opportunity to tell how the interpretations given by Joseph came to pass (41:9-13). Joseph was summoned to come from the prison into the presence of Pharaoh, where Pharaoh related the contents of his two dreams (41:14-24). Joseph provided the interpretation, gave God the credit, and suggested a plan of action for the pending years of abundance and drought (41:16, 25-36). Pharaoh's reaction is where today's lesson begins.

I. Joseph's Plan
(GENESIS 41:37, 38)
A. Proposal Evaluated (v. 37)

37. And the thing was good in the eyes of Pharaoh, and in the eyes of all his servants.

Pharaoh likes what he hears! Joseph has provided a detailed and decisive approach to deal with the coming years of famine (Genesis 41:33-36). This king of Egypt is very impressed with the straightforward approach that Joseph proposes. Joseph does not offer the kind of vague proposals that are subject to more than one interpretation that royal counselors often give.

What Do You Think?
What differences should there be, if any, in the ways we advise Christians and non-Christians?
Talking Points for Your Discussion
- In our use or nonuse of Scripture
- In using the language of the recipient's worldview

B. Man Evaluated (v. 38)

38. And Pharaoh said unto his servants, Can we find such a one as this is, a man in whom the Spirit of God is?

The response required by Pharaoh's rhetorical question here is obvious. At this time, the leaders of Egypt are still very "multi-god" in their outlook. The question by Pharaoh is interpreted by some to show that he is acknowledging the God of Joseph. It is also possible that he is saying Joseph has "the spirit of the gods." The latter view minimizes the impact of what Pharaoh understands.

HOW TO SAY IT

Asenath	*As*-e-nath.
Ephraim	*Ee*-fray-im.
Manasseh	Muh-*nass*-uh.
Pharaoh	*Fair*-o or *Fay*-roe.
Potiphar	*Pot*-ih-far.
Potipherah	*Pot*-i-**fee**-ruh.
vizier	veh-*zir*.
Zaphnathpaaneah	**Zaf**-nath-*pay*-uh-nee-uh.

It is very likely that Joseph has or will offer some of his concepts about the one God to Pharaoh, and that this information is implied in Pharaoh's response. The next verse tends to confirm this view.

II. Joseph's Position
(Genesis 41:39-46)
A. Praised (v. 39)

39. And Pharaoh said unto Joseph, Forasmuch as God hath shewed thee all this, there is none so discreet and wise as thou art.

Pharaoh's praise of Joseph begins by affirming that he understands that God is the one who has revealed these matters to Joseph. Pharaoh's observations about Joseph are a tribute to him. Joseph evidently exhibits poise and confidence when he makes his presentation to Pharaoh, who may not expect this from a prisoner.

In Genesis 41:33 (not a part of the printed verses for the lesson), Joseph describes the desirable attributes of the person who should be appointed as the administrator for the ambitious program that will be needed. Pharaoh uses exactly the same words and applies them to Joseph. The statements by Pharaoh show that he is a person who has accurate recall of what is said. He demonstrates that he wants what is best for his country, and he is able to assess Joseph and his abilities correctly and quickly. He concludes that Joseph is the right person for the task.

What Do You Think?

What characteristics of the Christian are especially attractive to the world? Why do you think these stand out?

Talking Points for Your Discussion

▪ Intrapersonal qualities
▪ Interpersonal qualities
▪ 2 Corinthians 8:21

B. Promoted (v. 40)

40. Thou shalt be over my house, and according unto thy word shall all my people be ruled: only in the throne will I be greater than thou.

Joseph is now the prime minister or vizier of the country of Egypt. Two very important areas are assigned to him: (1) managing the household of the king in the palace and (2) ruling over all the people of Egypt. The phrase *only in the throne will I be greater than thou* essentially means that Joseph is second-in-command (compare Daniel 2:48; 5:29; 6:1, 2).

Joseph's assignment to be over the household of the king makes us wonder if Potiphar provides any testimony of endorsement for Joseph by relating how his household prospered when Joseph served him (see last week's lesson). There is also curiosity concerning the matter of Mrs. Potiphar—does Joseph have any confrontation with her after his promotion? We can only wonder about such things, but they are intriguing possibilities.

C. Place (vv. 41-43)

41. And Pharaoh said unto Joseph, See, I have set thee over all the land of Egypt.

Pharaoh immediately clarifies the tremendous scope of the position that he has just assigned to Joseph. To be placed over *all the land of Egypt* speaks volumes to any and all persons who are witnessing what has just transpired. They know with certainty that Joseph is to be obeyed in every matter. They may seek information about certain details, but the final decisions belong to Joseph.

No record is given about any verbal response that Joseph makes, but it is almost certain that he acknowledges in an appropriate way what is being said. Joseph has been in Egypt for 13 years by this time, and he has had time to become fluent in the language. He probably is coached in proper protocol before entering the presence of Pharaoh.

What Do You Think?

Should Christians seek political office? Why, or why not?

Talking Points for Your Discussion

▪ Temptations of power
▪ Possibilities of good
▪ Conflicts with ministry

---

42. And Pharaoh took off his ring from his hand, and put it upon Joseph's hand, and

arrayed him in vestures of fine linen, and put a gold chain about his neck.

Three symbolic actions confirm what is said. First, the transfer of the official ring from Pharaoh's hand to Joseph's means that Joseph now has the authority to validate policy and decisions by the use of this ring. Its distinctive design is pressed into the wax seal of official documents.

Joseph has already changed out of his prison clothes (Genesis 41:14), but these garments *of fine linen* are an additional improvement. Linen is made from flax, and its qualities are its strength and sheen. Egypt is renowned for the quality of its linen (see Ezekiel 27:7).

Lastly comes *a gold chain* to adorn Joseph's neck (compare Daniel 5:29). This type of chain usually has a precious stone, set in gold, attached to it.

43. And he made him to ride in the second chariot which he had; and they cried before him, Bow the knee: and he made him ruler over all the land of Egypt.

The three items of the previous verse are personal in nature. Now Pharaoh takes care of Joseph's public recognition by having him ride in a chariot that demonstrates to others that Joseph is second only to Pharaoh. Men are assigned to go before Joseph and to give a command that alerts people along the way that the one who is passing is Joseph. *Bow the knee* is a possible translation, although the exact meaning of what they say is uncertain. It is similar to a Hebrew word meaning "to kneel"; and it can also be an Egyptian word meaning "attention."

D. Power (v. 44)

44. And Pharaoh said unto Joseph, I am Pharaoh, and without thee shall no man lift up his hand or foot in all the land of Egypt.

Joseph is at the center of this account as it tells of his sudden transformation from prison to be the prime minister for *all the land of Egypt*. We should not overlook the fact that this Pharaoh is able to evaluate and make decisions. The actions by Pharaoh leave no doubt about his intentions for Joseph's place in the kingdom. His statement to Joseph emphasizes Joseph's authority in that no one is to do anything unless Joseph approves it.

E. Spouse (v. 45)

45. And Pharaoh called Joseph's name Zaphnathpaaneah; and he gave him to wife Asenath the daughter of Potipherah priest of On. And Joseph went out over all the land of Egypt.

Joseph's new position brings with it changes in his personal life. First, his name is changed (compare Daniel 1:6, 7), and his new name seems to be Egyptian in origin. The exact meaning is uncertain. Older sources suggest "savior of the world," and more recently it is thought that the name might mean "God speaks, and this one lives."

Second, Joseph's new life needs to be complete by his having a wife. So Pharaoh provides one from a respected family of Egypt. The city of On is located in northern Egypt, about seven or eight miles from the present city of Cairo.

Joseph's father-in-law, Potipherah, is probably a priest for the sun god, Ra. References to this god go back to about 2800 BC, several centuries before Joseph's time. The Egyptians have the concept that Ra created and rules the world, and Pharaoh rules Egypt. We caution that *Potipherah* is not the same as *Potiphar*, although the names are similar.

What Do You Think?

Why do some "unequally yoked" marriages (2 Corinthians 6:14) seem to be blessed, as Joseph's apparently was?

Talking Points for Your Discussion
- God's ability to redeem situations
- What is seen vs. what is unseen
- Long-term consequences

❧ TRAPPINGS OR TOOLS? ❧

Before the financial meltdown of 2007–2008, many Americans lived as if they were wealthier than their financial situation permitted. For example, it was possible to lease a car that was much more expensive than one would have been able to purchase. Easy credit persuaded many that they could afford an impressive home. Cruises, designer clothes, and dining at expensive restaurants became other trappings of success. When the meltdown came, the trappings disappeared.

Joseph himself ended up with many of the symbols of success when the king gave him the royal ring, royal clothing, a chariot, and even what today we might call a "trophy wife"! But Joseph did not allow himself to become "trapped by the trappings." The things the king gave him became Joseph's tools to accomplish an important task: the saving of many (Genesis 50:20).

To live a life of prosperity is a double-edged sword. The "stuff" of prosperity we possess can either be trappings or tools to us. If we make the mistake of becoming trapped by the trappings, God may do us a favor by taking those things away!

—C. R. B.

F. Survey (v. 46)

46. And Joseph was thirty years old when he stood before Pharaoh king of Egypt. And Joseph went out from the presence of Pharaoh, and went throughout all the land of Egypt.

When we compare Joseph's age of 30 here with his age of 17 on being sold into slavery (see Genesis 37:2), it means that Joseph has been in Egypt 13 years by this time. He will be here another 80 years, dying at age 110 (50:22).

Joseph has a new name, a new wife, and new responsibilities—indeed, it seems that he has an entirely new life! It is time for him to begin his service. His previous places of service probably did not include any travel. Now he needs to conduct his personal survey throughout Egypt in order to know how to organize the people and the places in preparation for the coming years of famine.

Verses 47-49 (not in today's text) summarize Joseph's work during the seven years of plenty. Every city has storage facilities for the grain, and the quantity of grain is so great that keeping records of the amount is not practical.

III. Joseph's Offspring
(GENESIS 41:50-52)
A. Sons Noted (v. 50)

50. And unto Joseph were born two sons before the years of famine came, which Asenath the daughter of Potipherah priest of On bare unto him.

Verse 53 tells us that *the years of famine* are preceded by seven years of abundance. Thus Joseph and Asenath become parents of two sons during the first seven years of their marriage.

Joseph probably travels much of the time, so there is concern about his wife's being qualified to give instruction to her sons about the one true God. No one knows for certain, but it is usually assumed that she has accepted the faith that Joseph demonstrates so well in his life. Since her father is a pagan *priest of On,* we wonder what strains this causes in the wider family!

B. Sons Named (vv. 51, 52)

51. And Joseph called the name of the firstborn Manasseh: For God, said he, hath made me forget all my toil, and all my father's house.

At this time in history, children's names are given because of the meaning, not because the sounds of the syllables are pleasant to the ears. The name *Manasseh* comes from a Hebrew verb meaning "forget." The joys of having a wife and a son help Joseph forget the mistreatment that he has experienced. He cannot totally forget them, of course, but the new situations in his life cause them to fade.

> **What Do You Think?**
> Should Christian parents give names to their children that "mean something"? Why, or why not?
> *Talking Points for Your Discussion*
> - Cultural fads
> - Unisex names
> - Given names vs. nicknames

52. And the name of the second called he Ephraim: For God hath caused me to be fruitful in the land of my affliction.

The name *Ephraim* has the meaning of "being fruitful" or "becoming fruitful." Joseph's situation has changed since he came to Egypt, but he keeps the proper perspective by giving the glory to God. He recognizes that it is God who has enabled him to become *fruitful in the land* where he first endured mistreatment. It's easy to forget God when times are good. But Joseph doesn't forget. God is the cause of his prosperity.

Joseph's sons will be significant in the history that unfolds. The tribe of Ephraim will produce Joshua, who will be Moses' assistant, general, and successor. Jeroboam, also of this tribe, will be the first king of the northern nation after the nation divides into two: Israel to the north and Judah to the south (1 Kings 11:26).

The tribe of Manasseh is distinctive in that it will be the only tribe to receive two land allotments when the nation begins to take possession of the promised land. Half the tribe will settle on the eastern side of the Jordan (Joshua 1:12-14). The other half will be assigned land adjacent to Ephraim on the western side of that river (Joshua 16, 17).

❧ VICTORS, NOT VICTIMS ❧

We are fascinated by abduction cases that result in the victim's being rescued months or even years later. Famous cases that come to mind include those of Jaycee Lee Dugard, Elizabeth Smart, and Shawn Hornbeck.

The state of the victim's mental health becomes a primary concern after the rescue. Over the course of a captivity, kidnap victims may make psychological adjustments that are necessary to maintain some level of emotional stability. Sometimes these adjustments take the form of "Stockholm Syndrome," where the victims become emotionally attached to their captors.

Before coming to Christ, we were captives of the devil and sin (2 Timothy 2:26). During that captivity, perhaps we became comfortable with sin. We may have identified with it. We may have become emotionally attached to it. The example of Joseph can help us here. He rejected sin during his captivity (see last week's lesson). After his captivity ended, he continued to focus steadfastly on God; the names Joseph gave to his two sons are evidence of this. With God's help, we too can be victors!

—C. R. B.

Conclusion

A. Handling Favor

Up to the point of this lesson, Joseph was able to handle successfully the trials and adversity that came his way. He handled adversity without blam-

Visual for Lesson 6. *Turn this statement into a question as you ask, "In what ways have you experienced God's perfect timing?"*

ing God, and he resisted sexual temptation without yielding. But at the age of 30, Joseph was confronted with his greatest challenge: how to handle position, power, and wealth. To become exceedingly powerful and wealthy brings with it a temptation to wallow in luxurious decadence. It may be a blessing for some not to receive great wealth, lest they be unable to handle the temptations that come with it!

One preacher cited the example of an acquaintance who regularly made statements about what he would do for his church if he just had the money. Then oil was discovered on the man's land. The preacher's observation was this: "He became rich overnight, and he went to Hell just as fast."

Many events of the Old Testament serve as negative examples so that we will not desire the evil things that the people of Israel did (see 1 Corinthians 10:6-11). But the story of Joseph is a positive example, for his life is worth emulating.

B. Prayer

Almighty God, I come to You in Jesus' name to thank You for the favors You have given to me. Please grant me the maturity to handle my blessings successfully, to recognize that they are from You, and to use them wisely for Your glory. In Jesus' name, amen.

C. Thought to Remember

Handle favor with care!

INVOLVEMENT LEARNING

Some of the activities below are also found in the helpful student book, Adult Bible Class.
Don't forget to download the free reproducible page from www.standardlesson.com to enhance your lesson!

Into the Lesson

Have the following sequence of letters on display as learners arrive: *B A F D A T V I O M R E S*. Hand five additional letter cards with the letters *F, A, V, O, R* (one letter per card) to five learners, one each. As class begins, say, "Those with a letter card, bring it up and tape it blank side out over a corresponding letter." (Have masking tape available.) If the one holding the *A* starts to cover the first *A*, quickly say, "Cover the second." What remains will read *BAD TIMES*.

Say, "Finding favor in bad times is Joseph's secret and the theme of his life." Read Genesis 39:23 aloud. Emphasize the second half of the verse as the key idea. Refer to last week's study. Assign these four verses to be read: Genesis 37:28; 37:36; 39:20; and 40:23. Note: "These were Joseph's 'bad times': being sold into slavery, being falsely imprisoned, being forgotten by one he had helped. All these set the stage for Joseph's 'good times'—the subject of today's lesson."

Into the Word

Form five groups or study pairs. Assign one of these letters to each group or pair: *P, H, A, R, O*. (Note that these are the letters of the title *Pharaoh*.) Establish a competition with these directions: "Identify words or concepts from today's text of Genesis 41:37-46, 50-52 (you may include the omitted verses 47-49, if you choose) that begin with the letter you have. Single words only, please. Be ready to explain words you suggest."

Here are sample responses that your teams may offer: *P*—Pharaoh, people, Potipherah, priest, put, presence; *H*—hand, house(hold), handfuls, heirs (Joseph's sons); *A*—Asenath, according, all, arrayed, affliction; *R*—records (v. 49), ruled/ruler, ring, ride, renamed (v. 45); *O*—officials (of Egypt), orders (Joseph's word), over, only, On (city). Move from letter to letter, asking for one word at a time; make a list for each letter.

When a group no longer can suggest an entry, say, "You're out of the competition." When you have one letter-group left, declare it the winner, using Pharaoh's words to Joseph (v. 39) regarding being so discreet and wise. (*Option:* Call each member of the winning group forward and put a "10-cent" ring on his or her finger, as Pharaoh gave Joseph his signet ring in verse 42.) This humorous exercise will provide a good overview of the text.

To help your learners appreciate Joseph's exalted position, say, "Name at least five blessings Joseph received from Pharaoh." Anticipate such answers as public commendation (v. 38), personal praise of Joseph (v. 39), being placed over Pharaoh's household (v. 40), making Joseph's word authoritative (v. 40), putting his signet ring on Joseph's finger (v. 42), giving him fine garments and jewelry (v. 42), providing a chariot (v. 43), giving him attendants (v. 43), giving him a wife from the noble class (v. 45), and trusting him to survey the land independently (v. 46). Stress that Pharaoh's blessings came because he found Joseph to be "such a one . . . in whom the Spirit of God is" (v. 38).

Download the reproducible page and distribute copies of the One in Whom the Spirit of God Is exercise. This can be a small-group activity.

Into Life

To help your learners personalize today's study, download the reproducible page and distribute copies of the God's Gifts and Personal Responsibility activity. To keep from putting learners "on the spot," you can generalize the discussion by asking "What is a way for Christians to improve their service in the area of _____?" (Fill in the blank with one of the categories on the activity.)

After learners offer suggestions, ask, "What service responsibility comes with God's gifting in that area?" Address each category listed on the activity in this manner.

GOD PRESERVES
A REMNANT

DEVOTIONAL READING: Psalm 81:1-10
BACKGROUND SCRIPTURE: Genesis 42:1–46:7

GENESIS 45:3-15

3 And Joseph said unto his brethren, I am Joseph; doth my father yet live? And his brethren could not answer him; for they were troubled at his presence.

4 And Joseph said unto his brethren, Come near to me, I pray you. And they came near. And he said, I am Joseph your brother, whom ye sold into Egypt.

5 Now therefore be not grieved, nor angry with yourselves, that ye sold me hither: for God did send me before you to preserve life.

6 For these two years hath the famine been in the land: and yet there are five years, in the which there shall neither be earing nor harvest.

7 And God sent me before you to preserve you a posterity in the earth, and to save your lives by a great deliverance.

8 So now it was not you that sent me hither, but God: and he hath made me a father to Pharaoh, and lord of all his house, and a ruler throughout all the land of Egypt.

9 Haste ye, and go up to my father, and say unto him, Thus saith thy son Joseph, God hath made me lord of all Egypt: come down unto me, tarry not:

10 And thou shalt dwell in the land of Goshen, and thou shalt be near unto me, thou, and thy children, and thy children's children, and thy flocks, and thy herds, and all that thou hast:

11 And there will I nourish thee; for yet there are five years of famine; lest thou, and thy household, and all that thou hast, come to poverty.

12 And, behold, your eyes see, and the eyes of my brother Benjamin, that it is my mouth that speaketh unto you.

13 And ye shall tell my father of all my glory in Egypt, and of all that ye have seen; and ye shall haste and bring down my father hither.

14 And he fell upon his brother Benjamin's neck, and wept; and Benjamin wept upon his neck.

15 Moreover he kissed all his brethren, and wept upon them: and after that his brethren talked with him.

KEY VERSE

So now it was not you that sent me hither, but God. —Genesis 45:8

GOD ESTABLISHES A FAITHFUL PEOPLE

Unit 2: God's Protection

LESSONS 5–9

LESSON AIMS

After participating in this lesson, each student will be able to:

1. Summarize the account of Joseph's revealing his identity to his brothers.

2. Describe the nature of forgiveness in the story of Joseph and his brothers.

3. Make a plan to forgive someone in the week ahead.

LESSON OUTLINE

Introduction
  A. Unexpected Joy!
  B. Lesson Background
 I. Revelation (GENESIS 45:3-8)
  A. Identity Confirmed (vv. 3, 4)
  B. Providence Affirmed (vv. 5-8)
   All by Myself?
 II. Recommendations (GENESIS 45:9-11)
  A. For Joseph's Father (vv. 9, 10)
  B. For Joseph's Family (v. 11)
 III. Recognition (GENESIS 45:12-15)
  A. Testimonial by Joseph (vv. 12, 13)
  B. Tears with Benjamin (v. 14)
  C. Talking with Brothers (v. 15)
   The Power of Forgiveness
Conclusion
  A. Lessons from Joseph
  B. Prayer
  C. Thought to Remember

Introduction

A. Unexpected Joy!

Two brothers lived about 300 miles from each other. Ordinarily they saw each other only on holidays, and those were good times.

Almost exactly midway between them was a large city with a major league baseball team. On one occasion, both brothers and their families attended the same baseball game. Neither knew that the other family had planned to be there. The chances of their selecting the same day were quite remote, of course, but what about the chances of their acquiring seats in the same section of the stadium? Yet that is what happened.

The game was not very far along when one brother noticed the back of the head of the other brother—just a few rows in front of him. He called to him, and a joyful reunion took place that was much more rewarding than the outcome of the game.

Many have had similar experiences—the unexpected thrill that comes from finding a neighbor or friend when both are many miles from home. It brings a surge of surprise and joy that is difficult to put into words. "Virtual reunions" are becoming common today given the existence of social networking sites such as Facebook. Today's lesson is about a startling reunion in the ancient world: that of Joseph and his brothers.

B. Lesson Background

The previous lesson ended with Joseph being blessed with two sons. The seven years of plenty were in progress, and the interpretations of Pharaoh's dreams were being fulfilled.

Nothing was said about the reactions of the Egyptians at that time. Some probably questioned Joseph's administrative decisions, and there undoubtedly were skeptics who ridiculed his dire prediction of seven years of famine. After all, everyone knew of the agricultural prosperity brought by the Nile River as it flooded each year. Egypt was the breadbasket of the world! Nothing was stated about anyone's taking personal responsibility for storing the abundance of grain. After all, that was a government program (Genesis 41:48, 49).

But the years of famine began as predicted, and the people went to Pharaoh with their problem. Pharaoh told them to do whatever Joseph said. In the first year, Joseph sold grain to the Egyptians (Genesis 41:53-57).

The region affected by the famine extended beyond Egypt—to areas that were not dependent on the flooding of the Nile. The famine reached to Canaan to Joseph's father and brothers, who were over 200 miles away. Jacob (Joseph's father) heard that there was grain in Egypt, and he sent 10 sons to Egypt to buy grain. He did not send Benjamin, his youngest son. In Jacob's mind Joseph was dead, and Benjamin was the only surviving son of his favorite wife, Rachel (Genesis 42:1-5).

Joseph recognized his brothers, but he spoke to them through an interpreter (Genesis 42:7, 23). Joseph spoke harshly to them and imprisoned them for three days. He mandated that they bring Benjamin on a return trip. Joseph also arranged things so his brothers looked like thieves (42:25-35). Some see Joseph's actions as a type of revenge. Others say that he was simply testing them.

At first Jacob did not want to permit Benjamin to go to Egypt, but he eventually surrendered to the inevitable (Genesis 42:36–43:14). The brothers then went back to Egypt to buy more grain. The arrival in Egypt was marked by a banquet, more questioning by Joseph, and another "set up" to make the brothers appear dishonest (43:26–44:34).

Jacob's fourth son, Judah, became the spokesman for the brothers in their defense. He gave a thrilling, emotional speech that some regard as one of the finest speeches of all time. The brothers still assumed that Joseph was dead (Genesis 44:20). They explained how Jacob would be greatly grieved if Benjamin did not return.

The defense delivered by Judah had a profound effect on Joseph. This supposedly dispassionate lord of Egypt lost control, and he suddenly commanded all his Egyptian staff to leave (Genesis 45:1). Undoubtedly, the brothers were stunned into silence, wondering what this meant for them. It is at this point that today's study begins.

I. Revelation
(GENESIS 45:3-8)
A. Identity Confirmed (vv. 3, 4)

3. And Joseph said unto his brethren, I am Joseph; doth my father yet live? And his brethren could not answer him; for they were troubled at his presence.

Joseph abandons his use of an interpreter (Genesis 42:23), since all the Egyptian attendants have been asked to leave (45:1). Thus Joseph now speaks to his siblings in Hebrew.

This language has no word for *am*, so Joseph's first declaration is just two words: "I Joseph!" There is an escalating emotional impact that ripples through the room as the brothers hear this high Egyptian official claim, in their native tongue, to be their long-lost brother. Joseph's dramatic statement is followed immediately by a question about his father. This serves to steer the emotional flow toward a subject in which they are all vitally concerned—the welfare of Jacob.

But the brothers are speechless. They simply cannot comprehend what is happening and what is in store for them as they cower in the presence of the second most powerful man in Egypt.

4. And Joseph said unto his brethren, Come near to me, I pray you. And they came near. And he said, I am Joseph your brother, whom ye sold into Egypt.

If the brothers are frozen in fear, then the physical action of coming closer, at Joseph's invitation, provides a partial release from the torrent of emotions that engulf them. No verbal responses are described at this point, but the brothers dare not disobey. Joseph confirms his identity by stating

HOW TO SAY IT

Canaan	*Kay*-nun.
Egypt	*Ee*-jipt.
Egyptians	Ee-*jip*-shuns.
Goshen	*Go*-shen.
Judah	*Joo*-duh.
patriarch	*pay*-tree-ark.
patriarchal	pay-tree-*are*-kul.
Potiphar	*Pot*-ih-far.
Zoan	*Zo*-an.

something that only he and they know—that they are the ones who sold him into Egypt.

B. Providence Affirmed (vv. 5-8)

5. Now therefore be not grieved, nor angry with yourselves, that ye sold me hither: for God did send me before you to preserve life.

Joseph now tries to put things in their best light, providing a positive spin on the flow of events. On the first trip to Egypt, the 10 brothers (Benjamin had not come along) commented among themselves about their abuse of Joseph, and Joseph heard them although they did not realize it (Genesis 42:21-23). Joseph knows that his brothers need assurance about what is happening. In one sense Joseph is simply stating in his own way what Paul says in Romans 8:28: "that all things work together for good to them that love God, to them who are the called according to his purpose."

Joseph also cautions his brothers about their reactions toward each other. He knows that through the years they have carried the burden of guilt and remorse for what they did. We find it amazing that they have been able to keep this secret for so long from their father, Jacob.

What Do You Think?

What was a time when you found it difficult to avoid beating yourself up over a sin or mistake? What was the source of your difficulty, and how did you resolve the problem?

Talking Points for Your Discussion
- Doubting God's forgiveness
- Sense of self-reliance
- Seeing consequences of the sin
- Cultural expectations

6. For these two years hath the famine been in the land: and yet there are five years, in the which there shall neither be earing nor harvest.

Joseph continues by placing events on a timeline of sorts. The bottom line is that things will get worse before they get better.

The *King James Version* has an antique word in this verse: the word *earing.* This is a noun in the Hebrew, and the noun form is used only three times in the Old Testament (here, plus Exodus

34:21 and 1 Samuel 8:12). The verbal root means "to cut," "to inscribe," or "to engrave"; therefore the idea here is one of plowing (that is, cutting into the ground).

7. And God sent me before you to preserve you a posterity in the earth, and to save your lives by a great deliverance.

Joseph explains why and how the various events of the past are being used by God. They have two purposes, and they are stated in reverse chronological order. The ultimate purpose (stated first) is to guarantee that there will be future generations in this family that are descended from Abraham. The words indicate that there will be difficult times ahead, but not a total destruction.

The transition to Egypt by Jacob and his family is the beginning of the fulfillment of the prophecy made to Abraham that his people are to be enslaved in a foreign land for 400 years (Genesis 15:13). Exodus 12:40, 41 states that the total time in Egypt is 430 years; thus the prediction of a 400-year enslavement is a round number (compare Acts 7:6; Galatians 3:17).

But for the 400-year prophecy to happen, the lives of the current generation must by saved *by a great deliverance.* Combining Genesis 41:46 with 45:6, we calculate Joseph's age to be about 39 at this point. This means that the year is about 1877 BC. Their father, Jacob, is now age 130 (47:9); grandfather Isaac has been dead for about 10 years (35:28); and great-grandfather Abraham has been dead 115 years (25:7). God made the initial promise to Abraham at age 75 (12:1-5), so the promise itself is about 215 years old at this point. The entire family will move to this foreign land shortly, and the slavery will develop later.

What Do You Think?

What purposes has God had for suffering in your life? How have those purposes become clearer in hindsight?

Talking Points for Your Discussion
- Results of personal spiritual growth
- Results of spiritual growth of others
- Results of salvation of others
- 1 Peter 5:10; Revelation 1:9; 2:10

8. So now it was not you that sent me hither, but God: and he hath made me a father to Pharaoh, and lord of all his house, and a ruler throughout all the land of Egypt.

God is able to work through wrong attitudes and actions, and this is one example of that. The brothers are not absolved from guilt, but good has resulted. One outstanding thing that has happened is that Joseph is the primary advisor to Pharaoh. A father might ordinarily serve in this role, so it is customary in this part of the world to describe any such advisor as *a father.*

Joseph, however, is more than a counselor; he is the lord of Pharaoh's house and a ruler over *all the land of Egypt.* He therefore has the authority to make provisions for his family. Whatever Joseph decides will be accomplished.

❧ ALL BY MYSELF? ❧

Claiming credit is a common thing to do. Think of the strutting "look at me" end-zone display of a football player who has just scored a touchdown. He acts as if he did it without anyone else's help! When a business prospers, a savvy CEO may get the credit, but what about all the help from dedicated employees throughout the organization? Even in the realm of individual sports, the record-setting athlete owes much of the success to coaches, trainers, and the gift of athletic prowess that God has granted.

Even at a human level, Joseph's rise to success in Egypt owed much to the servant who had testified to Pharaoh about Joseph's divine gift of interpreting dreams (Genesis 41:9-13). However, Joseph wisely recognized the primary source of his success was God's providential direction of his life (contrast Daniel 4:28-32). Joseph is unwavering in this regard. Are we?   —C. R. B.

II. Recommendations
(GENESIS 45:9-11)
A. For Joseph's Father (vv. 9, 10)

9. Haste ye, and go up to my father, and say unto him, Thus saith thy son Joseph, God hath made me lord of all Egypt: come down unto me, tarry not.

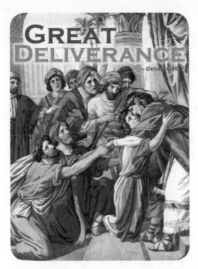

Visual for Lesson 7

Point to this visual as you ask, "When was a time you experienced God's deliverance?"

Joseph has provided astounding information, but now it is time for action. He has had time to develop the plan in his mind, and he knows that his brothers immediately need an activity that will help them to overcome the mental shock they have just experienced. This capable and experienced administrator knows what they must do: hurry back to Canaan with the message for Jacob that it is Joseph who is asking him to come to Egypt.

Joseph provides an enduring example by giving the credit to God for the things that have happened in his life. Joseph may be good-looking, intelligent, capable, and the *lord of all Egypt,* but he knows that it is God who deserves the glory.

What Do You Think?
Under what circumstances should adult children make decisions for their aging parents? How can the church assist in this regard?
Talking Points for Your Discussion
▪ Issues of health
▪ Issues of danger, to self or to others
▪ Exodus 20:12; 1 Timothy 5:4

10. And thou shalt dwell in the land of Goshen, and thou shalt be near unto me, thou, and thy children, and thy children's children, and thy flocks, and thy herds, and all that thou hast.

It will not be easy for Jacob to leave the land of Canaan, since his grandfather Abraham migrated to Canaan over 200 years prior. Joseph makes the new situation attractive by telling them that they will settle *in the land of Goshen*. That is a very desirable place for a group that depends heavily on flocks and herds for support (Genesis 46:28–47:6).

Joseph makes the situation attractive for himself and his father by stating that they will be living near each other. Jacob will be able to see his favorite son frequently. Goshen, also called "Zoan" in Psalm 78:12, 43, is probably in northern Egypt.

> *What Do You Think?*
> What dangers and opportunities present themselves when extended family members live very close to one another?
> *Talking Points for Your Discussion*
> ▪ Dangers and opportunities for a church
> ▪ Dangers and opportunities for a neighborhood
> ▪ Dangers and opportunities for the family itself

B. For Joseph's Family (v. 11)

11. And there will I nourish thee; for yet there are five years of famine; lest thou, and thy household, and all that thou hast, come to poverty.

Joseph makes a transition from Jacob to the entire family. Jacob's sons are grown and have children of their own (see Genesis 46:8-27), but this is a patriarchal society, and the patriarch has the final say in the decisions that are made. Jacob needs to understand that the famine will continue. A sojourn to Egypt will have long-term benefits, while remaining in Canaan will be disastrous.

III. Recognition
(GENESIS 45:12-15)

A. Testimonial by Joseph (vv. 12, 13)

12. And, behold, your eyes see, and the eyes of my brother Benjamin, that it is my mouth that speaketh unto you.

Joseph has finished telling his brothers the detailed plan he has for them and the extended family. Now he resumes the reunion celebration. He assures them again that he is indeed Joseph. Benjamin, more than anyone else, is able to vouch for his identity. Being full-blood to each other,

Benjamin and Joseph probably spent the most time together before Joseph was sold. The loss of their mother when Benjamin was born (Genesis 35:17-20) probably had helped them to feel closer to each other.

It seems reasonable that Rachel's handmaid, Bilhah, could have been assigned to care for them, but she and the others wives of Jacob had children of their own. So it could be that by default Jacob found himself providing sole care for them—and more favoritism in the process.

13. And ye shall tell my father of all my glory in Egypt, and of all that ye have seen; and ye shall haste and bring down my father hither.

Joseph's responsibilities probably prevent him from making a trip to Canaan. So it is his brothers' task to tell their father about his position and responsibilities in Egypt. The trip probably will take at least two weeks. Even so, Joseph expresses an urgency to see his father again, so he wants them to depart as soon as possible.

B. Tears with Benjamin (v. 14)

14. And he fell upon his brother Benjamin's neck, and wept; and Benjamin wept upon his neck.

Joseph and Benjamin are grown men, but the people of this time and place do not hesitate to show their emotions in ways that many today might not. This is a time for the tears of a joyful reunion to flow freely.

Joseph previously honored Benjamin when the brothers feasted with him. This was before Joseph had identified himself. The portion of food that was distributed to Benjamin was five times greater than to the others (Genesis 43:34). We can only wonder how the other brothers interpreted that event at the time. Similar preferential treatment takes place as the brothers leave to go back to Canaan. They will be given changes of clothing by Joseph, but Benjamin will receive 5 changes of clothing and 300 pieces of silver (45:22).

C. Talking with His Brothers (v. 15)

15. Moreover he kissed all his brethren, and wept upon them: and after that his brethren talked with him.

The displays of emotion continue for each brother. It may be somewhat awkward for the ones who had been the leaders in the effort in selling Joseph, but at this point they are all glad for the happy ending that they are enjoying. They are able to be united with Joseph again, and Joseph has dispelled (for now) any thoughts of retribution (compare Genesis 50:15).

These exchanges of mutual affection are followed by conversation. The 11 brothers undoubtedly have much to tell Joseph about what has happened in the 22 years since they last saw each other. No one can produce pictures of their children, of course, but vivid word pictures and excited gestures can provide understanding of the changes in their lives.

What Do You Think?
How can Christian men show godly love for one another in ways that will not be misinterpreted in modern culture?
Talking Points for Your Discussion
- In words
- In gestures
- In emotions
- In physical contact

❧ THE POWER OF FORGIVENESS ❧

Three cathedrals have been built in Coventry, England. The first dates back to the twelfth century. The current one is built on the ruins of the second, which was destroyed by Nazi fire-bombs on the night of November 14, 1940. Dick Howard, the cathedral's provost at the time of its destruction, vowed that its rebuilding would not be an act of defiance.

As one enters the new cathedral through the ruins of the old, one's eyes are drawn to the words *Father Forgive* on the wall. The words *Never Forget,* or something similar, could have been used instead. But that alternative would have served to keep open the wounds of that terrible night. Thus those who designed the rebuilt sanctuary decided to use Jesus' words from the cross.

Joseph's family reunion could not have taken place as it did had it not been for the fact that he found the power to forgive his brothers. Recognizing how God has forgiven us is a key to being able to forgive others in turn. —C. R. B.

Conclusion

A. Lessons from Joseph

The narratives about Joseph and the dramatic reversals in his life can be used to teach abiding lessons about changes, choices, and forgiveness.

Changes. Joseph's life was full of extraordinary changes. He went from being his father's favorite to being sold as a slave. His life changed in the household of Potiphar from that of a servant to that of a supervisor. He had a similar experience in the prison where Potiphar placed him. The most outstanding change in his position was going from the prison to becoming the prime minister of Egypt. Joseph knew how to adjust and make the most of changes.

Choices. The regular temptations by Potiphar's wife did not weaken Joseph, but they seemed to make him stronger and more determined to avoid what he knew to be sin. Joseph chose righteousness rather than suffering the remorse that would surely have followed. He did not rationalize why he should sin against God. Joseph chose God's way, and thus became an example for us.

Forgiveness. Joseph is an excellent example of forgiving others. His life is in harmony with what Jesus taught in the Sermon on the Mount (Matthew 6:14), and again when He encouraged extending forgiveness to what seems to be an impossible degree (see Matthew 18:21, 22). It is never stated, but Joseph also probably forgave Potiphar for doing what he did—imprison Joseph.

B. Prayer

God in Heaven, it is my resolve this day to be even more faithful, to be fervent in serving, and to find joy in forgiving family, friends, and even enemies. Help me to imitate the forgiveness that You provided for me. In Jesus' name, amen.

C. Thought to Remember

All things work together for good
to those who love God.

INVOLVEMENT LEARNING

Some of the activities below are also found in the helpful student book, Adult Bible Class.
Don't forget to download the free reproducible page from www.standardlesson.com to enhance your lesson!

Into the Lesson

Have Beethoven's "Ode to Joy" from his Ninth Symphony playing as learners arrive. Ask, "Can anyone identify this musical piece?" Identify it if no one else does. Say, "This is appropriate music for today's study."

Alternative: Before class, give to several learners noisemakers, confetti, and streamers. These are to be concealed until your signal, which may be the word *Amen* at the end of an opening prayer. At the signal, those involved are to shout "Surprise!" and blow their noisemakers while tossing confetti and/or streamers.

As the class recovers from being startled, say, "Joseph did not need noisemakers or confetti, but today's text reflects one of the biggest *Surprise!* moments in literature." (*Option:* Download the reproducible page and distribute copies of the Surprise! activity at this point to open a discussion on the possible consequences of being surprised.)

Into the Word

Form small groups of no more than six, and put a life-size outline of a human male Bible-times figure on display. Say, "Today's text continues to reveal Joseph's character and skill. Look at the lesson text and think of one thing that impresses you about Joseph. I'll start." Write, as a sample, "He expresses concern for his elderly father."

Allow time for groups to deliberate. Encourage each group to agree on one entry, then come forward and write it on the outline. Anticipate entries such as "He shows discretion by revealing his identity in private"; "He sees God's hand in human events"; "He attempts to allay his brothers' fears"; "He wants his family near him"; "He is not afraid to display emotion."

Once the activity is complete, say, "What a man! Joseph reveals that he was indeed one in whom the Spirit of God resided, as we saw Pharaoh affirm in last week's study."

Say, "Next, I am going to ask several questions, but I do not want oral answers. I only want you to ponder, then word a silent prayer related to your response. I call this an *Introspection Quiz*. It is based on Joseph's words and behaviors in today's text."

Use the following questions, but do not include the italicized verse numbers as part of your question. 1. Do you have a vital concern for members of your family (*v. 3, etc.*)? 2. Are you willing to reestablish broken relations, even if confrontation is necessary (*v. 3*)? 3. Do you sense the hand of God in ordinary events, even when there are negative circumstances (*v. 5*)? 4. Does it seem as if you have been "sent ahead" in some sense to preserve the physical or spiritual lives of others (*v. 7*)? 5. Do you truly want to be near your family, even with the possibility of bad relationships (*v. 10*)? 6. Are you willing to share the blessings and prosperity you have by God's hand with those in need (*v. 11*)? 7. Are you ready to show emotion in the presence of those you care about (*vv. 14, 15*)? 8. Can you forgive others when they have wronged you, even grievously (*whole text*)?

At the end, reiterate that Joseph said *Yes* to all these questions in the events of today's text.

Alternative. Download the reproducible page activity and distribute copies of the Brothers and Other Strangers activity. Use this instead of the above, according to the directions on the exercise.

Into Life

Provide a handout of your eight questions. Give one to each learner, with this challenge: "All of us can think of individuals—both family and nonfamily—whom we need to forgive (or seek forgiveness from) and make an effort to reestablish good relationships with. Use these questions this week in your devotional life, as you ponder whom you need to forgive. Make a plan to work toward the godliness of 'forgive and relate.'"

God Preserves a Remnant

Joseph Transmits Abraham's Promise

DEVOTIONAL READING: Deuteronomy 7:6-11
BACKGROUND SCRIPTURE: Genesis 50

GENESIS 50:15-26

15 And when Joseph's brethren saw that their father was dead, they said, Joseph will peradventure hate us, and will certainly requite us all the evil which we did unto him.

16 And they sent a messenger unto Joseph, saying, Thy father did command before he died, saying,

17 So shall ye say unto Joseph, Forgive, I pray thee now, the trespass of thy brethren, and their sin; for they did unto thee evil: and now, we pray thee, forgive the trespass of the servants of the God of thy father. And Joseph wept when they spake unto him.

18 And his brethren also went and fell down before his face; and they said, Behold, we be thy servants.

19 And Joseph said unto them, Fear not: for am I in the place of God?

20 But as for you, ye thought evil against me; but God meant it unto good, to bring to pass, as it is this day, to save much people alive.

21 Now therefore fear ye not: I will nourish you, and your little ones. And he comforted them, and spake kindly unto them.

22 And Joseph dwelt in Egypt, he, and his father's house: and Joseph lived an hundred and ten years.

23 And Joseph saw Ephraim's children of the third generation: the children also of Machir the son of Manasseh were brought up upon Joseph's knees.

24 And Joseph said unto his brethren, I die: and God will surely visit you, and bring you out of this land unto the land which he sware to Abraham, to Isaac, and to Jacob.

25 And Joseph took an oath of the children of Israel, saying, God will surely visit you, and ye shall carry up my bones from hence.

26 So Joseph died, being an hundred and ten years old: and they embalmed him, and he was put in a coffin in Egypt.

KEY VERSE

As for you, ye thought evil against me; but God meant it unto good, to bring to pass, as it is this day, to save much people alive. —**Genesis 50:20**

GOD ESTABLISHES A FAITHFUL PEOPLE

Unit 2: God's Protection

LESSONS 5–9

LESSON AIMS

After participating in this lesson, each student will be able to:

1. List the elements of the suppressed fear of Joseph's brothers and Joseph's reactions when it was expressed.

2. Compare and contrast the seeking and granting of forgiveness in today's text with the ideal of seeking and granting forgiveness in the New Testament.

3. Ask forgiveness of someone he or she has wronged.

LESSON OUTLINE

Introduction

A. Last Words

"Last words" are what a person utters just before dying. Sometimes these are treasured by family members. Sometimes those final utterances have an unusual twist. Such was the situation when a man's last words to his wife were to tell her that in the garage loft was a can full of silver dollars. He was the only one who knew about this treasure, and he wanted to make sure that she did not sell the property without knowing about it.

The study for today is based on the final 12 verses of the book of Genesis. Many people are able to recite the opening phrase of Genesis 1, but only a few know the final words of the book. The first four words in Genesis are "In the beginning God." Those four words are very important. If a person understands that phrase and governs his or her life accordingly, then other things fall into place.

The last phrase of Genesis is rather sobering: "in a coffin in Egypt." These words cause contemplation, because death is our destiny. Few of us will be buried in Egypt, but we will have a grave somewhere unless Jesus returns before we die.

"In the beginning God . . . in a coffin in Egypt." Those phrases mean much. Words, as well as actions, have great significance.

B. Lesson Background

At the conclusion of our previous study, we saw that Egypt was in its second year of famine. Joseph was 39 years old, having become the administrator of Egypt at age 30 (Genesis 41:46). Jacob and his family were entering Egypt. Jacob was then presented to Pharaoh, and he stated that he was 130 years old (47:9). Those facts allow us to calculate that Jacob was 91 when Joseph was born.

Interesting things take place as the book of Genesis comes to a close. As the famine dragged on, we see the Egyptians purchase their grain from the government. But when their funds were depleted, they sold their livestock to buy grain (Genesis 47:16). The next step was to sell their land and themselves to have food (47:19).

Jacob, for his part, lived 17 years in Egypt before he died (Genesis 47:28). He did two things in his final days. First, he had special blessings for the sons of Joseph, giving the primary blessing to the younger son (48:19). Second, Genesis 49 tells us that Jacob provided inspired prophecies for the sons and their descendants as they were to become the tribes of Israel. Jacob sometimes used animals as figures of speech to typify the characteristics of each tribal group. Judah was Jacob's fourth son (29:35). It was through him that the Messiah would be born, and the five verses for Judah (49:8-12) indicate that it was the tribe of royalty.

Jacob had requested that he be taken back to Canaan for burial in the same cave where others of the patriarchal families were buried. He died at age 147 (Genesis 47:28). After the necessary days for embalming and mourning, Joseph and others honored the request of Jacob, escorting his body to Canaan so that he could be buried with his fathers (49:29–50:14).

There is a coincidence in the number 17 for Jacob and Joseph. Jacob was able to be with Joseph for the first 17 years of Joseph's life before he was sold by brothers (Genesis 37:2). It was in Jacob's final 17 years that father and son were together again.

I. Brothers' Fear
(GENESIS 50:15-18)
A. Concern Expressed (v. 15)

15. And when Joseph's brethren saw that their father was dead, they said, Joseph will peradventure hate us, and will certainly requite us all the evil which we did unto him.

HOW TO SAY IT

Abraham	*Ay*-bruh-ham.
Canaan	*Kay*-nun.
Dothan	*Doe*-thun (*th* as in *thin*).
Ephraim	*Ee*-fray-im.
Isaac	*Eye*-zuk.
Machir	*May*-ker.
Manasseh	Muh-*nass*-uh.
patriarchs	*pay*-tree-arks.
Pharaoh	*Fair*-o or *Fay*-roe.
sarcophagus	sar-*coff*-uh-gus.
Shechem	*Shee*-kem or *Shek*-em.

Joseph's siblings apparently have suppressed a fear for 17 years. They are concerned that Joseph has restrained himself from vengeance against them only because of the influence of Jacob, the father. Joseph had assured his brothers previously that he understood how God had brought about good from what they had done (Genesis 45:5-8).

However, the brothers apparently have not forgiven themselves for what they did in selling Joseph as a slave (Genesis 37:28). Now that Jacob is dead, they reason among themselves that Joseph may feel free to get even with them. They also may be expressing how they would react if they were in Joseph's shoes.

Some have difficulty in accepting forgiveness, and feelings of guilt continue through the years. Joseph's spiritual maturity is validated by how he extends forgiveness to those who have injured him and then demonstrates that forgiveness by his subsequent actions. Joseph does not hold a grudge, but the brothers have trouble believing that.

B. Communicated to Joseph (vv. 16, 17)

16a. And they sent a messenger unto Joseph, saying.

These men demonstrate another character weakness by using a third party to deliver their apprehensions to Joseph. Ideally, they should go to express their concerns personally. Even so, what they do provides an opportunity for them to determine how Joseph reacts to what is said.

16b. Thy father did command before he died, saying.

The last part of verse 16 raises questions, and there are no positive answers. It is not recorded elsewhere that Jacob ever made such a statement that we see in verse 17 (next) *before he died*. There are at least three possibilities.

One possibility is that Jacob indeed did make such a comment, and it is given here for the first time. It is also possible that the concerns of the brothers have been stated to Jacob, and that he has tried to provide assurance by telling his sons that they should personally ask Joseph to forgive them for what they did.

However, many read this verse, combine it with what is known about these men, and suggest that the brothers are not truthful in what they say. The message is then a fabrication. To make such an accusation against them is wrong if either of the other options is true. But we simply don't know.

17. So shall ye say unto Joseph, Forgive, I pray thee now, the trespass of thy brethren, and their sin; for they did unto thee evil: and now, we pray thee, forgive the trespass of the servants of the God of thy father. And Joseph wept when they spake unto him.

Jacob's (supposed) words for Joseph are that he is to forgive his brothers, for they also are *servants of the God* whom Jacob worships. Joseph's response to the message is tears. He is overwhelmed to think that they can even have such thoughts after all that he has done for his family during the famine and the years since that time. Surely they know his heart in these matters!

But the brothers' feelings of guilt and remorse are still strong. They receive many blessings through Joseph as God works through him. This means that they owe much to Joseph. Some people try to cancel such debts by finding or imagining character flaws in the ones to whom they are indebted.

What Do You Think?
What are some things you should resolve before you pass away?
Talking Points for Your Discussion
- Relationship issues
- Property and asset issues
- Spiritual issues

C. Commitment to Joseph (v. 18)

18. And his brethren also went and fell down before his face; and they said, Behold, we be thy servants.

The text does not say how many of the brothers present themselves to Joseph. Some students think that Benjamin is not present. But those who come fall down before Joseph as a group and make the dramatic affirmation we see here. It has been 39 years since Joseph was sold as a slave by his brothers. Now those who sold him offer themselves to Joseph in the same capacity.

II. Joseph's Fidelity
(Genesis 50:19-21)
A. Reassuring His Brothers (v. 19)

19. And Joseph said unto them, Fear not: for am I in the place of God?

The initial words of Joseph are designed to remove the fears of his brothers. He will say the same thing again in verse 21. For 17 years, Joseph has been faithful to what he said he would do for these men and their families. He is not going to change now.

Joseph has an understanding of personal vengeance and judgment that is impressive. He recognizes that such things are reserved for God. He therefore states what Moses will say 450 years later—that vengeance belongs to God (Deuteronomy 32:35). This verse from Deuteronomy is quoted in Romans 12:19 and Hebrews 10:30.

What Do You Think?
What was a time you put yourself in the place of God? How did you grow spiritually as a result?
Talking Points for Your Discussion
- Issues of judging
- Areas of control
- Feeling responsible for someone else's conversion

B. Reviewing the Past (v. 20)

20. But as for you, ye thought evil against me; but God meant it unto good, to bring to pass, as it is this day, to save much people alive.

The brothers' mistreatment of Joseph was done with improper motives. But the things that happened 39 years before were used to bring about good. The two little words *but God* are very important in the ebb and flow of the biblical record and the events of history (examples: 1 Samuel 23:14; Acts 13:29, 30).

Joseph not only saved the lives of his family, but also the lives of Egyptians and others during the famine. The brothers seem to be concerned only about themselves at this point, but Joseph reminds them of the bigger picture: God has used Joseph as a man of faith to provide food for thousands.

Sometimes we plan something for good only to have it turn out to be a disaster. Sometimes the reverse happens. In the thirteenth century, Pope Innocent was struggling with Holy Roman Emperor Frederick II. Through his father, Frederick had inherited Germany and most of northern Italy; through his mother, he had inherited southern Italy. He hoped to pull these together into one tight political rule. But Pope Innocent saw that this would make the Papal States in central Italy completely surrounded by the Empire, and he feared this would become a vise that would squeeze the Papal States out of existence.

So Innocent began to meddle in German politics to keep Frederick off balance so he could never give full attention to Italy. The policy, as continued by the pope's successors and German princes, was successful. But the popes did not count on the fact that Germany became so decentralized that later emperors were not able to exert complete control over the German princes. In the early sixteenth century, Martin Luther challenged the teachings of the papacy. The popes tried to silence Luther, but he was protected by his prince, Frederick of Saxony. Protestant ideas flourished as a result.

Pope Innocent wanted to save the Papal States. But in so doing he created the conditions that led to the elimination of Catholic dominance in Europe. Unintended consequences are a fact of life. That's why it's important to pray! —J. B. N.

C. Reassurance Repeated (v. 21)

21. Now therefore fear ye not: I will nourish you, and your little ones. And he comforted them, and spake kindly unto them.

The repetition from verse 19 helps assure Joseph's brothers of the sincerity of his words. The death of their father should not be a source of alarm. Joseph uses the opportunity to remind them that he will continue to make sure that they and their families receive what they need. This will be in addition to what they provide for themselves through their own efforts. All the events of recent years should convince them that God cares. There will be suffering in the future, but God will use it to take His people back to Canaan.

The word *kindly* does not carry the full impact of what is written. The original language literally says that Joseph is speaking "to their heart." That makes it more meaningful.

III. Joseph's Final Days
(GENESIS 50:22-26)
A. Dwelling in Egypt (v. 22)

22. And Joseph dwelt in Egypt, he, and his father's house: and Joseph lived an hundred and ten years.

This verse summarizes Joseph's final days. With Joseph now at age 110, simple arithmetic reveals that it has been 54 years since Jacob died. Thus it has been 54 years since Joseph renewed his promise that he would do his part to provide for others in Jacob's family. Joseph was 39 when the family came from Canaan to Egypt, and he was 56 when his father died 17 years later (Genesis 37:2; 41:46; 45:6; 47:9, 28). It is an interesting coincidence that Joseph's most famous descendant, Joshua, lives to be the same age of 110. Joshua will be a descendant of Ephraim, Joseph's younger son.

The famine ended many years before, and the Israelites are flourishing as they live in the land of Goshen (Exodus 1:7). The prophecy to Abraham that his descendants will spend 400 years in a foreign land is moving along the road to fulfillment (Genesis 15:13). At this time there is no oppression or other reason to leave Egypt, but that will change as the centuries pass (Exodus 1:8).

> **What Do You Think?**
> In what ways is a long life both a blessing and a burden in today's world?
> *Talking Points for Your Discussion*
> ▪ Ecclesiastes 12:1-7
> ▪ Philippians 1:22-24
> ▪ Philemon 9

B. Descendants of Joseph (v. 23)

23. And Joseph saw Ephraim's children of the third generation: the children also of Machir the son of Manasseh were brought up upon Joseph's knees.

Joseph's longevity allows him to see his great-grandchildren through his sons, Ephraim and Manasseh. Joseph's great-grandchildren through Manasseh have a distinctive figure of speech used about their being on *Joseph's knees*. This means that Joseph is treating them as his adopted children. The same figure of speech is used by Jacob's wife Rachel as she gives her handmaid to Jacob (Genesis 30:3); this is very plain in the *King James Version*. The same language is used for Jacob's "adoption" of Joseph's sons when Jacob pronounces blessings on them (48:5, 12).

C. Promise to Patriarchs (v. 24)

24. And Joseph said unto his brethren, I die: and God will surely visit you, and bring you out of this land unto the land which he sware to Abraham, to Isaac, and to Jacob.

Abraham died 76 years before Joseph was born, so Abraham was a great-grandfather whom Joseph never saw. The promise that the Lord made to Abraham about giving the land of Canaan to his descendants is still being passed down almost three centuries later. It is vividly remembered, and it will serve to give hope to future generations when they leave Egypt under the leadership of Moses (Exodus 6:4, 8).

Joseph is convinced that that promise will be fulfilled. In his final moments, he encourages his family and reminds them of the promise that the Lord had made. The promise about the land of Canaan was given to the patriarchs on several occasions—to Abraham (Genesis 12:7; 13:15, 17), to Isaac (26:3) and to Jacob (35:12; 48:3, 4). The title that has been selected for this study is based on the cumulative impact of these promises.

What Do You Think?
As we age, how can we maintain an optimistic outlook that will encourage those of a younger generation?
Talking Points for Your Discussion
▪ Things we read
▪ What we focus on
▪ What lessons we learn from our own time of youth

D. Pledge to Joseph (v. 25)

25. And Joseph took an oath of the children of Israel, saying, God will surely visit you, and ye shall carry up my bones from hence.

Joseph does more than just remind his kinsmen of the promise. He has them enter into *an oath* that when God is ready for them to go to Canaan they will carry his bones with them as they go.

This commitment to Joseph is passed down to future generations, and at the time of the exodus someone fulfills what Joseph has committed them to do; Exodus 13:19 states that Moses takes the bones of Joseph as the Israelites leave Egypt. Joshua 24:32 records that Joseph's bones are buried at Shechem, a part of Canaan that is assigned to Joseph's older son Manasseh (Joshua 17:7). This vow is also mentioned in Hebrews 11:22, and there it is given as an example of Joseph's faith in believing that there would be an exodus from Egypt.

Thus Joseph's final resting place is where he, at age 17, had been sent to check on his brothers. At that time, he had been informed that they had moved on to Dothan, just northwest of Shechem (Genesis 37:12-17). Joseph's initial destination as given to him by his father, Jacob, becomes Joseph's burial site.

❧ *SURPRISE!* ❧

Yogi Berra is a legendary baseball figure. He is also famous for his misuse of the English language. A collection has been made of some of his outrageous sayings. One in particular is interesting in light of today's study. His wife once asked, "Yogi, you are from St. Louis, we live in New Jersey, and you played ball in New York. If you go before I do, where would you like me to have you buried?" He replied, "Surprise me."

One's final resting place is seen as significant. For example, think of Arlington National Cemetery. Most people believe that it is important to have an identifiable final resting place even for the nonfamous. We have all seen the reports of strenuous attempts—sometimes years in the process—to "bring home" the remains of a loved one so the deceased can "finally" be laid to rest.

But, surprise! There is no final resting place in this world. No matter where we are buried, it

Joseph Transmits Abraham's Promise

is temporary because of the promise of resurrection of both the good and the evil (John 5:28, 29). It's where we end up after that that's "final."

—J. B. N.

E. Placed in a Coffin (v. 26)

26. So Joseph died, being an hundred and ten years old: and they embalmed him, and he was put in a coffin in Egypt.

The word used for *coffin* refers to a wooden box. (It is the same word that is used for the ark of the covenant, Exodus 25:15.) The practice of the Egyptians at this time is to place the embalmed body in a coffin that is made to resemble the shape of a person. Perhaps you have seen such a coffin (also referred to as a *sarcophagus*) in a museum display that features Egyptian mummies.

What Do You Think?

In terms of Christian morality, what difference does it make, if any, in how we treat dead bodies?

Talking Points for Your Discussion

- Image of God issue (Genesis 1:27)
- Comfort for mourning family
- Confidence in resurrection
- Embalming
- Cremation

Conclusion

A. Standing on the Promises

A preacher once developed a sermon in which he said that the Christian faith rests on several pillars, and one of the pillars is the promises of God. There are promises to individuals and nations that were made and fulfilled, and there are promises that are still waiting to be fulfilled. Since God has always kept His promises in the past, we can have assurance that He will keep the promises that are yet to be fulfilled.

The promises about the birth, ministry, and death of the Messiah are found throughout the Old Testament. For example, Jesus was born of the seed of a woman per Genesis 3:15, and He was born in Bethlehem as Micah 5:2 prophesied. Jesus was a descendant of David (Psalm 89:3, 4;

COMPARISON OF JOSEPH AND JESUS

JOSEPH		JESUS
GENESIS 37:8	Hated for his testimony	JOHN 7:7
GENESIS 37:28	Taken to Egypt under stressful circumstances	MATTHEW 2:13-15
GENESIS 37:28 LEVITICUS 27:5	Sold for the price of a slave	MATTHEW 26:15 EXODUS 21:32
GENESIS 39:4	A servant	PHILIPPIANS 2:7
GENESIS 39:6B-12	Resisted strong temptations	MATTHEW 4:1-17
GENESIS 39:14	Falsely accused	MARK 14:56
GENESIS 40	Associated with two criminals, one who was blessed and one who was not	LUKE 23:39-43
GENESIS 41:41-43	Exalted by God after suffering	PHILIPPIANS 2:9-11
GENESIS 41:46	Began most important work at age 30	LUKE 3:23
GENESIS 41:57	Fed the hungry	MARK 6:41
GENESIS 42:8	Not recognized by his own	JOHN 1:10
GENESIS 45:7	Sent by God to save people	JOHN 3:16

Visual for Lesson 8. *As you work your way through this chart, ask your learners if they can think of other similarities between these two lives.*

132:11), and this is shown in the first chapter of the book of Matthew. Many of the things that are a part of Jesus' ministry are given in the book of Isaiah, and that great prophet also wrote about the suffering Messiah who bore our sins (Isaiah 53).

The theme of promise is developed by the apostle Peter in 2 Peter 3. He emphasizes the fact that the great Day of the Lord will happen. Jesus will return, just as He promised. The final words of this great apostle warn that there will be those who scoff at God's promises, but they forget that the promises made in the past were fulfilled. Peter gives the flood in the days of Noah as one example of God's keeping His promises.

Peter also includes a warning about being carried away with the errors of the wicked (2 Peter 3:17). Peter then concludes his epistle with two commands: The Christian is to grow in grace and to grow in the knowledge of Jesus Christ. To grow in Christ is an imperative, and growing in knowledge involves having faith in the promises of Jesus—that He will return, just as He said.

B. Prayer

Almighty God, Your love and forgiveness are more than I can comprehend. Help me to forgive others, just as You have forgiven me. In Jesus' name, amen.

C. Thought to Remember

Anticipate the fulfillment of God's promises.

INVOLVEMENT LEARNING

Some of the activities below are also found in the helpful student book, Adult Bible Class.
Don't forget to download the free reproducible page from www.standardlesson.com to enhance your lesson!

Into the Lesson

Download the reproducible page and place in chairs copies of the Relationships and Pivotal Moments activity. Learners can begin working on this as they arrive. Discussing results is optional.

Have this question on display as learners arrive: "Which is easier: to forgive another who has wronged you, or to ask and accept forgiveness from one you have wronged?" Take a vote of class members; insist that each choose an option. Allow your learners to discuss their decisions and disagreements. Wrap up by reminding your class that both are necessary to godly living as learners will see in today's study.

To make a bridge to today's study, hold up a sign that says *THE END.* Say, "Keep a mental list through today's study of things that are coming to an end." You may want to point to the sign at random times during the hour. (You will return to the issue, as noted below, to let class members list their results.)

Into the Word

Recall occasions in elementary school when the teacher used "flash cards" to highlight and reinforce key words, concepts, dates, and names. Use strips of poster board to prepare flash cards for the following words: *fear, favor, flashback, opportunity, offers, repentance, retribution, realization, guilt, grudge, grace, intention, if, initiative, volition, vision, voluntary, entreaty, egotism,* and others you choose using the same beginning letters.

Introduce all the words to your class in a "flash card" procedure, revealing then hiding each quickly in succession. After all are seen, ask, "What does each of these words have to do with the events of today's study?" If necessary, have the text read aloud, reintroduce the words one at a time, and let learners comment.

At some point—if no one notices as you post each word—tell the class that the words form a beginning-letter acrostic on the word *forgive.* Most of the terms obviously can be related to the concept of forgiveness, but for any that stump the class, you may need to explain. For example, *egotism* refers to the self-centeredness that makes forgiveness both necessary and difficult. Explain any others the class questions.

Download the reproducible page and distribute copies of the Bridging the Gap activity. This will foster a discussion of the various emotions involved in forgiveness, such as the fear the brothers express in verse 15 and the peace of mind Joseph offers in verse 21.

Remember to question your learners about *THE END* as suggested in Into the Lesson. (Possible suggestions: the ends of Jacob's life, Joseph's life, the book of Genesis, the brothers' fear of retribution, of Israel's time in Egypt, the class's study of Joseph.) Conclude with a statement that "Now God wants you to stamp *THE END* to the broken relationships you have allowed to exist."

Into Life

Hand each learner a small sheet of paper that is divided into four equal parts, with the word *GIVE* on each part. Smile as you say, "Here, I am giving you 'four gives.' I want you to consider in the week ahead four opportunities you have to ask forgiveness from another. Each time you take advantage of the opportunity, tear off and throw away one *give.* Perhaps this will help you begin a habit of seeking forgiveness in matters large and small."

Include on the back side of the same sheet (perhaps two or three per segment), some of these New Testament references to forgiveness that need to be considered and applied: Matthew 6:12; Matthew 6:14, 15; Matthew 18:21, 22; Mark 11:25; Luke 6:37; Luke 7:47; Luke 23:34; Ephesians 4:32; 1 John 1:9. Draw attention to the references and recommend reading the selections previous to the occasion of seeking forgiveness.

Joseph Transmits Abraham's Promise

ISRAEL IS DELIVERED FROM EGYPT

DEVOTIONAL READING: Psalm 77:11-20
BACKGROUND SCRIPTURE: Exodus 1–15

EXODUS 15:1-5, 19-26

1 Then sang Moses and the children of Israel this song unto the LORD, and spake, saying, I will sing unto the LORD, for he hath triumphed gloriously: the horse and his rider hath he thrown into the sea.

2 The LORD is my strength and song, and he is become my salvation: he is my God, and I will prepare him an habitation; my father's God, and I will exalt him.

3 The LORD is a man of war: the LORD is his name.

4 Pharaoh's chariots and his host hath he cast into the sea: his chosen captains also are drowned in the Red sea.

5 The depths have covered them: they sank into the bottom as a stone.

. . . .

19 For the horse of Pharaoh went in with his chariots and with his horsemen into the sea, and the LORD brought again the waters of the sea upon them; but the children of Israel went on dry land in the midst of the sea.

20 And Miriam the prophetess, the sister of Aaron, took a timbrel in her hand; and all the women went out after her with timbrels and with dances.

21 And Miriam answered them, Sing ye to the LORD, for he hath triumphed gloriously; the horse and his rider hath he thrown into the sea.

22 So Moses brought Israel from the Red sea, and they went out into the wilderness of Shur; and they went three days in the wilderness, and found no water.

23 And when they came to Marah, they could not drink of the waters of Marah, for they were bitter: therefore the name of it was called Marah.

24 And the people murmured against Moses, saying, What shall we drink?

25 And he cried unto the LORD; and the LORD shewed him a tree, which when he had cast into the waters, the waters were made sweet: there he made for them a statute and an ordinance, and there he proved them,

26 And said, If thou wilt diligently hearken to the voice of the LORD thy God, and wilt do that which is right in his sight, and wilt give ear to his commandments, and keep all his statutes, I will put none of these diseases upon thee, which I have brought upon the Egyptians: for I am the LORD that healeth thee.

KEY VERSE

The children of Israel went on dry land in the midst of the sea. —**Genesis 15:19**

GOD ESTABLISHES A FAITHFUL PEOPLE

Unit 2: God's Protection

LESSONS 5–9

LESSON AIMS

After participating in this lesson, each student will be able to:

1. Describe how the Israelites celebrated their crossing of the Red Sea.

2. Outline the song of Moses and Miriam.

3. Write a prayer of commitment to listen carefully to the Lord (Exodus 15:26).

LESSON OUTLINE

Introduction

A. "Praise the Lord . . ."

"Praise the Lord and Pass the Ammunition." The older generation remembers those words as the title to a song based on a real happening at Pearl Harbor on December 7, 1941. A chaplain aboard the *USS New Orleans* used that phrase to encourage the men as he walked along their line.

Every nation has its military songs that commemorate heroes and battles. Some people do not care for such songs, for it is said that they glorify war. Whether they glorify war or not, it seems that they are here to stay. And such songs are not new. In Israel's earliest days, Moses composed a song of victory over the Egyptians. They had lost their lives as a result of following the Israelites into the Red Sea. Portions of that song are to be studied in this lesson.

B. Lesson Background

The Israelites entered Egypt as a family in the days of famine when Joseph was prime minister over the land (see Lessons 7 and 8). Over the centuries, the Israelites witnessed significant leadership changes in Egypt, from native Egyptians, to Asiatics who came into the land, and then back to the Egyptians again. The Asiatics are sometimes called Hyksos or "shepherd kings," but the word more likely just means foreigners who ruled Egypt. This caused the Egyptians to develop an even greater dislike for shepherds (compare Genesis 46:34), something that becomes very significant in the history of the emerging nation of Israel.

A new Pharaoh who did not know Joseph started a campaign against the people of Israel (Exodus 1). Oppressive measures were taken to subdue the people and slow their population growth. It was during this time that Moses was born. It is well-known that he was adopted by a princess of Egypt, but he had to flee Egypt at age 40 after killing an Egyptian (Exodus 2; the age factor for this event is found only in Acts 7:23).

Forty years later Moses encountered the Lord at Sinai. Thus began Moses' special ministry as the leader of slaves who wanted freedom. But Pharaoh resisted the demands made by God through

Moses. The result was a series of plagues that came on Egypt. Among other things, the plagues demonstrated the powerlessness of the gods of Egypt. As the plagues progressed, Pharaoh offered four compromises to Moses, but these were rejected. The tenth plague, which resulted in the loss of all the firstborn of the Egyptians, caused the Egyptians to thrust the Israelites out of Egypt. It had been 430 years to the day since Jacob and his family entered Egypt (Exodus 12:40, 41).

But Pharaoh had a change of heart, and he decided to give chase with 600 chariots (Exodus 14:5-7). The Israelites crossed the Red Sea safely after the waters parted, but the Egyptians drowned when they tried to follow. The God of Israel was superior to any of the gods of Pharaoh! The crossing of the Red Sea was pivotal in the history of ancient Israel. The slaves were free, beyond reach of Pharaoh. It was an event remembered in song.

I. Moses' Praise
(EXODUS 15:1-5, 19)
A. Cause for Jubilation (vv. 1-3)

1. Then sang Moses and the children of Israel this song unto the LORD, and spake, saying, I will sing unto the LORD, for he hath triumphed gloriously: the horse and his rider hath he thrown into the sea.

The first song in the history of this new nation is a song of rejoicing because of the victory that the Lord has obtained for the people. The defeat of Pharaoh's host is distinctive, for it is certainly not the norm for a cavalry force to be *thrown into the sea* during battle! Exodus 14:25 adds that the Lord caused problems for the Egyptians by disabling

HOW TO SAY IT

Asiatics	A-zhee-*ah*-tiks.
Bede	Beed.
Caedmon	*Kad*-mun.
Canaanites	*Kay*-nun-ites.
Hyksos	*Hik*-sus.
Miriam	*Meer*-ee-um.
Pharaoh	*Fair*-o or *Fay*-roe.
Sinai	*Sigh*-nye or *Sigh*-nay-eye.

the wheels of the chariots. Any speedy escape to the shore was made impossible.

This same event is cited in another song—in Psalm 136:13-15. It is also mentioned in the New Testament as a decisive time for the Israelites, for it has the effect of baptizing them into Moses and his leadership (1 Corinthians 10:1, 2). At this point, the Israelites are committed to following the Lord through Moses, but the people will fail often in obeying God's leader.

We also note in passing that there is a minor difficulty in finding an appropriate designation for this song. It is sometimes called a Song of Moses and Miriam (compare Exodus 15:20) or a Song of Moses and Israel (15:1). A Song of Moses already exists in Deuteronomy 32 (see Deuteronomy 31:30, which introduces the next chapter as a "song" of Moses).

> **What Do You Think?**
> How do modern worship songs compare and contrast with the two songs noted above?
> *Talking Points for Your Discussion*
> - Ways they are similar
> - Ways they are different

❧ SING OUT! ❧

The father of English church history is a man known as Bede, an English monk who died about AD 735. His book *A History of the English Church and People* is a classic. He is the best source for much of early British history. One of the most charming tales he relates has to do with Caedmon, an early monk.

In his early adult life, Caedmon followed a secular vocation. Whenever he attended a feast and people started to sing, he left because he had no musical ability whatsoever. In his sleep one night a man came to him in a dream and asked him to sing. "I can't," replied Caedmon. "That's why I left the feast."

"But you shall sing for me," the man said.

"What shall I sing?" asked Caedmon.

"Sing of creation," the man replied.

And so Caedmon began to sing. The next morning he told his experience to a local official,

Visual for Lesson 9

Point to this visual as you ask, "When do you most feel like singing praise to the Lord?"

who in turn told it to the abbess of a monastery. She had Caedmon sing, and all agreed to its quality. He became a monk and soon was singing of creation, the exodus, Israel's coming into the promised land, the coming of Christ, His crucifixion, His ascension, the Holy Spirit, etc. Caedmon became well-known for his poetry and his songs.

Singing and giving praise to God seem to go hand in hand. It was true for the song of Moses in today's passage, for Caedmon, and for the twenty-first century church. Sing out!   —J. B. N.

2. The LORD is my strength and song, and he is become my salvation: he is my God, and I will prepare him an habitation; my father's God, and I will exalt him.

Moses realizes that it is the Lord who is behind all the things that he (Moses) is able to accomplish. This also sounds like the apostle Paul when he says that he can do all things through Christ who strengthens him (Philippians 4:13).

Approximately 700 years after Moses, Isaiah writes about the boastful Assyrians. They boast that their conquests come about by their own strength (Isaiah 10:12-14). The Assyrians refuse to acknowledge that it is the Lord who is the source of their strength. A comparison is made to an axe that begins to boast of what it has done, failing to understand that the arm that swings it is the real strength for the axe (Isaiah 10:15; compare Daniel 4:28-33).

Those who compare translations will see that the phrase *I will prepare him an habitation* is unique to the *King James Version*. A few ancient Jewish writings are the source for this idea of habitation or "sanctuary." It is true that the Israelites will construct the tabernacle within the next year in the form of a portable tent. Exodus 15:17, which is part of the song under consideration, speaks of a place of the Lord's dwelling—the sanctuary. However, the Hebrew words are different from the habitation in view here.

3. The LORD is a man of war: the LORD is his name.

Moses is aware that the victory over the Egyptians belongs completely to the Lord. The Israelites had nothing to do with it except that they were running from the Egyptians.

The name of God became important to Moses at the place of the burning bush (Exodus 3:13-15). At that time, God affirmed His name and identified himself as the one who revealed himself to the patriarchs—Abraham, Isaac, and Jacob. The imagery of the Lord as *a man of war* is expressed later by the phrase "Lord of hosts," with *hosts* referring to angelic armies (particularly in 1 and 2 Samuel).

B. Catastrophe for Egypt (vv. 4, 5)

4. Pharaoh's chariots and his host hath he cast into the sea: his chosen captains also are drowned in the Red sea.

Chariots had been introduced into Egypt as instruments of war by the Hyksos, who ruled Egypt for a time. Previously, chariots were used for ceremonial purposes. The Egyptians quickly learned of their military usefulness and added many chariots to their armies.

The number of chariots the Egyptians lost totals 600 (see the Lesson Background). The language used to describe the Lord's throwing the chariots into the sea is very strong. It was not a gentle action, but a decisive act that has made Israel victorious.

In a subsequent battle several years after the event described here, the Egyptians will capture almost 900 chariots from northern nations, so they secure replacements of their losses at the

Israel Is Delivered from Egypt

Red Sea. We may also note the 900 iron chariots mentioned in Judges 4:3, which form the power by which the Canaanites oppress the Israelites roughly two centuries later. A song is also written about their defeat (Judges 5).

What Do You Think?

How would you explain to a skeptic how a God of love could take action that results in so much loss of life such as we see here?

Talking Points for Your Discussion

- Issues of justice
- The error of trying to fit all of God's actions and attitudes under the umbrella concept of *love*
- Issues of "fair warning"

---

5. The depths have covered them: they sank into the bottom as a stone.

The imagery described by Moses in these verses is very graphic. The chariots had difficulty with their wheels (Exodus 14:25). As indicated above, the waters returned and covered the officers and their chariots (14:26-29). The Egyptian army that had been in hot pursuit disappeared. It is now no more. It has been conjectured that some weapons may float to the eastern shore, and that these are later used by the Israelites in their battles. This is a possibility, but a miracle probably would be required for the weapons to float (compare 2 Kings 6:1-6).

C. Contrast for Israel (v. 19)

19. For the horse of Pharaoh went in with his chariots and with his horsemen into the sea, and the LORD brought again the waters of the sea upon them; but the children of Israel went on dry land in the midst of the sea.

The rest of the song, which continues through verse 18, is not part of today's printed text. The verse before us is a summary statement that follows the song. It describes the contrast in the outcomes for the two groups. Both the Egyptians and *the children of Israel* experience the depths of the sea. For God's people, the depths are just dry ground. But those same depths become the final resting place for the Egyptians, who had been their taskmasters.

II. Miriam's Praise
(EXODUS 15:20, 21)
A. Methods (v. 20)

20. And Miriam the prophetess, the sister of Aaron, took a timbrel in her hand; and all the women went out after her with timbrels and with dances.

Miriam is designated in two ways: as *the prophetess* and as *the sister of Aaron* (who is Moses' brother). Regarding the first, a prophet or prophetess is one who speaks a message that has been received from God. Based on her comments in Numbers 12:2, the term *prophetess* is appropriate, for she indicates that the Lord has also spoken through her. Exodus 7:1 provides an illustration of the function of a prophet. The second designation helps Moses, as the author, to make certain that his brother is also mentioned.

Miriam and *all the women* use their small drums and rhythmic dance to provide a refrain to the song of Moses. How that refrain is worded is our next verse.

❧ *SHALL WE DANCE?* ❧

My "coming of age" time was in the 1950s. That was a time when many people of strong religious convictions believed that it was a sin to dance. In Sunday school classes, youth group lessons, as well as from the pulpit on Sunday, we were often told how wrong it was to dance.

I must confess that I was not the perfect example of purity in this regard. In high school I actually went to a couple of sock hops. I also remember a Wednesday night Bible study when our preacher mentioned that there were some young men in the church who expected to go to Bible college, but he would not be giving them letters of recommendation. I thought he was looking right at me when he said that. I never went to another sock hop.

I always wondered, however, why regular dancing was so wrong, but square dancing was acceptable. I suppose it had to do with the fact that in regular dancing male and female bodies get much closer to each other than in square dancing. But I always felt that there was something inconsistent with the general condemnation of dancing.

Divided opinions on dancing are not new. King David's wife expressed strong displeasure when he danced before the Lord (2 Samuel 6:14, 20). Is there any place for "praise dancing" in the church today?   —J. B. N.

B. Message (v. 21)

21. And Miriam answered them, Sing ye to the LORD, for he hath triumphed gloriously; the horse and his rider hath he thrown into the sea.

The vocal response by Miriam echoes words in Exodus 15:1, which opens the song. The implication is that Miriam is the one who leads the other women in a type of antiphonal singing. (That's when one group answers another.)

III. Marah's Waters
(EXODUS 15:22-25a)
A. Movement (v. 22)

22. So Moses brought Israel from the Red sea, and they went out into the wilderness of Shur; and they went three days in the wilderness, and found no water.

We now move from singing back to historical narrative, which reports a journey of *three days*. During this time, the people of Israel move from the Red Sea to an arid region, and the mood of the people changes from jubilation to deep concern. Water is a necessity, and they do not find any.

B. Murmuring (vv. 23, 24)

23. And when they came to Marah, they could not drink of the waters of Marah, for they were bitter: therefore the name of it was called Marah.

Moses may have known about this site from his having been a shepherd in the region for 40 years during his exile from Egypt (Exodus 2:15). The Hebrew word *Marah* means "bitter," and it is an appropriate name for what the Israelites discover when they arrive.

24. And the people murmured against Moses, saying, What shall we drink?

The people vent their frustration by complaining *against Moses*. The recent song of praise to the

Lord has changed quickly to a criticism of the person whom the Lord has chosen to lead Israel.

> **What Do You Think?**
> What was a time you experienced a sense of "let down" after a great victory? Why does this happen?
> *Talking Points for Your Discussion*
> - Focus on self (1 Kings 18:1–19:10)
> - Difficulty of maintaining "spiritual highs" (Matthew 17:1-20)
> - Issue of humility (2 Corinthians 12:7)

This is the second occasion of complaining since the departure from Egypt. The first such event is given in Exodus 14:10-12, when the army of Pharaoh approached. Numbers 14:22 states that the people complain 10 times during the wilderness sojourn, and the Lord is not appreciative of those who murmur and gripe.

> **What Do You Think?**
> What are some ways to present legitimate concerns to our leaders without being guilty of faithlessness?
> *Talking Points for Your Discussion*
> - Proposing solutions (Acts 6:1-5)
> - Imposing burdens (Hebrews 13:17)
> - Examining motives first
> - Evaluating when to take concerns only to God

C. Miracle (v. 25a)

25a. And he cried unto the LORD; and the LORD shewed him a tree, which when he had cast into the waters, the waters were made sweet.

Moses, the special servant of the Lord, takes the appropriate action. He prays, and the Lord responds by directing him how to remedy the problem. The word translated *tree* can refer to anything from a tree. One thing is certain: to obey the commands of the Lord can produce the unusual! In the past, Aaron's wooden staff changed into a serpent when he threw it on the ground (Exodus 7:8-10). This time the throwing of wood produces another wonder that will long be remembered.

Israel Is Delivered from Egypt

Alternative views are sometimes presented to explain what happens. Some think that putting certain long sticks in a spring sweetens the water. Others think that the type of wood used is known to accomplish this purpose, and that the Lord merely tells Moses where to find it. The flow of the words indicates a miracle, however, and God is certainly capable of producing one.

What Do You Think?

What was a time God answered a prayer in an unusual or unexpected way? Why do you think he sometimes chooses to work like that?

Talking Points for Your Discussion

- In a spiritual crisis
- In a family crisis
- In a financial crisis
- In a church crisis

IV. Mandate by the Lord
(Exodus 15:25b, 26)

A. Demand for Obedience (vv. 25b, 26a)

25b, 26a. There he made for them a statute and an ordinance, and there he proved them, and said, If thou wilt diligently hearken to the voice of the LORD thy God, and wilt do that which is right in his sight, and wilt give ear to his commandments, and keep all his statutes.

The miracle at Marah has more than one purpose. In addition to providing potable water, it also serves to establish *a statute and an ordinance* that has special significance. A blessing is promised, but first there are two requirements. The first is that the people are to obey the Lord—to do that *which is right in his sight*. A simple definition of "righteousness" is to do that which is right.

The second demand emphasizes that obedience to the Lord is not to be a cafeteria approach in which a person may pick and choose what to obey. The requirement is that the people are to *keep all* the ordinances that the Lord gives.

B. Diseases Restricted (v. 26b)

26b. I will put none of these diseases upon thee, which I have brought upon the Egyptians: for I am the LORD that healeth thee.

Diseases may refer to the sixth plague (boils) that came on the Egyptians (Exodus 9:8-10). This is mentioned as a punishment by the Lord in Deuteronomy 28:27, but the word *diseases* in the printed text is much more comprehensive. Similar wording is found in Deuteronomy 7:15, where the word *evil* is used to describe the diseases. Deuteronomy 28:60 says that the Israelites are fearful of "the diseases of Egypt." The promise before us is therefore very meaningful to the people.

Conclusion
A. Prayer or Protest!

When any group encounters problems, there is a tendency to blame the leadership. This can lead to rebellion (again, Numbers 14:22). We see a major rebellion organized by three men in Numbers 16. God expressed His displeasure to this in dramatic ways. Yet before the chapter ends, the people complain about leadership again, with the penalty of a severe plague as a result.

The experiences of Israel in the wilderness confirm that the Lord is displeased when people take His blessings for granted and grumble when things are not to their liking. People who complain often do so to try to control situations in which they are involved. They have difficulty when others are in charge. The better way is to pray for the leaders and trust them to lead unless they prove to be unfaithful. Yes, there are corrupt leaders. Such situations must be handled, but many do not give God's plan an opportunity to work.

Make prayers for leaders part of your daily devotion—and tell your leaders that you are praying for them. Both they and the Lord will be pleased.

B. Prayer

Almighty God, today I am grateful for those who have leadership roles in the church. I pray for them now that they may walk uprightly before You, and that they may have wisdom in the decisions that they make. In Christ's name, amen.

C. Thought to Remember

Before protesting, pray!

INVOLVEMENT LEARNING

Some of the activities below are also found in the helpful student book, Adult Bible Class.
Don't forget to download the free reproducible page from www.standardlesson.com to enhance your lesson!

Into the Lesson

Option: Download the reproducible page and put copies of The Great Escape activity in chairs for learners to work on as they arrive.

Recruit a musically talented class member to bring in a keyboard to play the following songs as simple one-note melody lines in an activity based on the old television game show *Name That Tune.* Songs: "Praise God, from Whom All Blessings Flow"; "Praise Him, Praise Him, All Ye Little Children"; "Sing Your Praise to the Lord"; "O For a Thousand Tongues to Sing"; "Let's Just Praise the Lord"; and "Praise Him! Praise Him!" Feel free to substitute and/or add other praise songs and choruses at discretion.

Have your musician start with only five notes, wait for responses (guesses!), then replay adding a sixth note, and so on, until someone guesses the song correctly. If your class enjoys competition, divide them into two groups and alternate between the two until someone guesses the song. Learners should quickly see that the theme of praising the Lord for what He has done is the emphasis; this introduces the theme of today's lesson.

Into the Word

Write on the board the following as potential song titles, one at a time, as you ask the class to identify a verse in today's text on which it might be based. Suggested verses are given in parentheses, but don't write those on the board. Allow learners to justify their choices. "Sweet Water" (v. 25); "Swimming Like a Rock" (v. 5); "Drowning in the Blues of the Red Sea" (v. 4); "Dancing Fever" (v. 20); "God of My Father" (v. 2); "Walking on Dry Ground" (v. 19); "Warrior" (v. 3); "In over Their Heads" (v. 19); "Going Dry" (v. 22); "Grumbles, Murmurs, and Complaints" (v. 24); "Stirring with a Sweet Stick" (v. 25). You can research titles of actual songs and use those instead if you think that approach will work well with your class.

Option: Have a good oral reader read Exodus 15:6-18, which is not included in today's printed text. Then ask, "Which exclamation of Moses in these verses most speaks to you?" Allow free responses. As certain titles or descriptions are introduced, ask, "What hymns and choruses come to mind when you hear such a truth about God?" For example, if someone notes the great power in God's arm, verse 16, someone else may suggest "Leaning on the Everlasting Arms."

Ask your class to help you make a list of designations for God from today's text. As learners voice their ideas, write them on the board. Expect these answers: my strength (v. 2), my song (v. 2), my salvation (v. 2), my Father's God (v. 2), a man of war (v. 3), healer (v. 26). Have the goal of discovering all six of these designations. If learners mention more than these six, ask for justification. Use this list as a transition to the Into Life segment.

Into Life

Referring to the list of designations you have just made, say, "Now you have some ways to address God in your daily devotions in the week ahead. You can do so as you reflect on the wonders of His name and character. Which designation will you use most often? Why?" Allow responses.

Point out the grand truth of verses 25b, 26. Have someone introduce the contemporary chorus "I Will Sing of the Mercies of the Lord Forever." Then suggest these alternative lyrics: "I will listen to the voice of the Lord forever; I will heed; I will heed." Have the class sing the alternate lyrics. Then say, "This would be an ideal chorus to use at the waking of each day. Try it this week as your morning prayer of commitment."

Download the reproducible page and distribute copies of the I Will Sing to the Lord activity as learners depart. Say, "This is also designed for your devotional times in the coming week. Fill it out as you use it."

JUSTIFIED BY FAITH IN CHRIST

DEVOTIONAL READING: Luke 18:9-14
BACKGROUND SCRIPTURE: Galatians 1, 2

GALATIANS 2:15-21

15 We who are Jews by nature, and not sinners of the Gentiles,

16 Knowing that a man is not justified by the works of the law, but by the faith of Jesus Christ, even we have believed in Jesus Christ, that we might be justified by the faith of Christ, and not by the works of the law: for by the works of the law shall no flesh be justified.

17 But if, while we seek to be justified by Christ, we ourselves also are found sinners, is therefore Christ the minister of sin? God forbid.

18 For if I build again the things which I destroyed, I make myself a transgressor.

19 For I through the law am dead to the law, that I might live unto God.

20 I am crucified with Christ: nevertheless I live; yet not I, but Christ liveth in me: and the life which I now live in the flesh I live by the faith of the Son of God, who loved me, and gave himself for me.

21 I do not frustrate the grace of God: for if righteousness come by the law, then Christ is dead in vain.

KEY VERSE

I am crucified with Christ: nevertheless I live; yet not I, but Christ liveth in me: and the life which I now live in the flesh I live by the faith of the Son of God, who loved me, and gave himself for me. —**Galatians 2:20**

Photo: SWP, Incorporated

GOD ESTABLISHES A FAITHFUL PEOPLE

Unit 3: God's Redemption

LESSONS 10–13

LESSON AIMS

After participating in this lesson, each student will be able to:

1. State why salvation by law-keeping is impossible.

2. Explain what Paul's opponents in Galatia were teaching that nullified salvation by grace.

3. Use one of the seven verses of today's text as the focus of personal devotions in the week ahead, a different verse for each day.

LESSON OUTLINE

Introduction
  A. Living by the Rules
  B. Lesson Background: Judaizing
  C. Lesson Background: Recipients
I. Justified by Christ (GALATIANS 2:15-19)
  A. Keeping Law, Falling Short (vv. 15, 16)
    On What Basis?
  B. Seeking Righteousness, Finding Sin (v. 17)
  C. Dying to Sin, Living for God (vv. 18, 19)
    Dead to the Law
II. Crucified with Christ (GALATIANS 2:20, 21)
  A. Dying and Living (v. 20)
  B. Leaving and Grasping (v. 21)
Conclusion
  A. Crucified with Christ
  B. Prayer
  C. Thought to Remember

Introduction

A. Living by the Rules

Rules and laws—they are everywhere. When we drive, we see signs posting speed limits and no parking areas, lights indicating stop or go, and painted lines showing us lanes and turns. All of these reflect the laws and rules of the road. Workplace rules are legion as well. Companies may have thick employee manuals with page after page of rules. In addition, workplaces have unwritten rules, and the learning curve for these may be quick and brutal.

Most churches seem to have rules too, often evolved from traditions and opinions, and most of these are unwritten. These may be simple things like when to stand and sit during the worship service. More than once in my church we have had visitors get up and come to the Communion table during the Lord's Supper, even though we pass trays in the pews. The visitors come to the table because their church background taught them that those who want to participate in Communion are to do so. Other unwritten church rules may cover appropriate dress. Such rules may be awkward, but they are inevitable. Unintentional violation of these rules by visitors is usually tolerated graciously.

Much more serious, however, are church rules that give the false impression that God "owes us something" when we keep the rules. The Bible is a very ethical book, and rules are central to ethics, but we cannot earn God's favor by keeping rules. This does not mean that keeping God's rules is a bad thing! It means, rather, that if our relationship with God is no more than keeping rules, then we have left no room for God's grace. We cannot earn God's grace; we can only receive it as a gift. When we accept God's grace, we willingly follow the teachings of the Bible. We know God's rules, and we "play by them" because we love Him and have a deep desire to obey Him.

This unit of lessons comes from Paul's letters to the Galatians. In this book, Paul addresses a serious danger to the Galatian churches: the idea that keeping the law is the key to being a Christian. Although written over 1,900 years ago under

Justified by Faith in Christ

very different circumstances, this threat is as near today as any church that teaches rule-keeping as the key to salvation.

B. Lesson Background: Judaizing

The dating of Galatians is uncertain. We know, however, that it was written after the Jerusalem Conference of AD 51, as described in Acts 15, because Galatians 2:1-10 is Paul's account of that conference. A date of AD 57 or 58 is a reasonable guess for the writing of the letter.

The Jerusalem Conference was a meeting of church leaders to come to agreement over the biggest issue of the first-century church: whether Gentiles needed to be circumcised in order to be accepted into the fellowship of the church. Circumcision for religious purposes seems like a remote issue to us today, but it was hotly debated in Paul's day. The underlying issue was the role of the Jewish law in salvation.

Since the earliest church was made up entirely of Jews, this was not an issue for the first years of the church's existence. All male Christians had been circumcised already, because they were all Jews. As Peter, Paul, Barnabas, and others began to evangelize Gentiles (that is, non-Jews), circumcision emerged as a divisive issue. The question can be boiled down to this: Must a Gentile become a Jew before becoming a Christian?

There were those who said, *Yes!* and their voices were loud. The pivotal problem was the Jewish practice of circumcising all males. To be a Jew was to be circumcised, and there were no gray areas in this regard. Consequently, some Jewish Christians reasoned that all Gentile men must submit to circumcision in order to be recognized as Christians.

This issue boiled over when some of these men traveled from Jerusalem to Antioch and taught, "Except ye be circumcised after the manner of Moses, ye cannot be saved" (Acts 15:1). Paul and Barnabas disagreed and went to Jerusalem in order to gain consensus on this issue. In both Acts 15 and Galatians 2, we are told that the leaders of the church agreed not to require circumcision of Gentiles. This was a great day for the church, for it freed the gospel from the shackles of the Jewish law and allowed the church to grow rapidly among Gentiles.

The circumcision party based in Jerusalem did not give up easily, however. They continued to teach in Jerusalem the necessity of circumcision. They also appear to have spread their teaching to the churches Paul had planted in Gentile cities. We refer to these people as *Judaizers* and their teaching as *Judaizing* because they were still teaching that all Christians were obligated to keep the customs of the Jews and the Law of Moses.

The influence of these Judaizers extended even to Peter. This led to a confrontation between Paul and Peter in Antioch as related in Galatians 2:11-14. Paul's disappointment with Peter plus Paul's determination not to yield an inch to the Judaizers form the immediate background of this week's lesson text. Paul, therefore, wrote this letter to the churches of Galatia to condemn this Judaizing heresy.

C. Lesson Background: Recipients

A second background issue for studying Galatians is the identity of the recipients. Galatia was not a city, but a region. Therefore, Paul addressed the "churches of Galatia" (Galatians 1:2) rather than an individual congregation. Galatia was generally seen as the south central section of Asia Minor (modern Turkey). Probable intended recipients of this letter included churches at Antioch of Pisidia, Iconium, Lystra, and Derbe. Paul visited these cities on his first missionary trip, prior to the Jerusalem Conference (Acts 13:13–14:20).

HOW TO SAY IT

Antioch	*An*-tee-ock.
Barnabas	*Bar*-nuh-bus.
Derbe	*Der*-be.
Gentiles	*Jen*-tiles.
heresy	*hair*-uh-see.
Iconium	Eye-*ko*-nee-um.
Judaizers	*Joo*-duh-*ize*-ers.
Lystra	*Liss*-truh.
Pisidia	Pih-*sid*-ee-uh.
rabbi	*rab*-eye.

He revisited them on his second trip (Acts 15:36, 41; 16:1, 2).

Before we begin our study, we should note the harsh tone of the letter. Galatians is bereft of anything "warm and fuzzy." It begins abruptly and has no opening prayer or personal greetings. Paul's first statement after his preliminary items is his astonishment ("I marvel") at his readers' willingness to abandon the gospel he taught them. Paul calls doubly for false teachers to be accursed (Galatians 1:8, 9). This is strong language indeed!

I. Justified by Christ
(GALATIANS 2:15-19)

A. Keeping Law, Falling Short (vv. 15, 16)

15. We who are Jews by nature, and not sinners of the Gentiles.

In Paul's day, there is a marked difference in the moral behavior of Jews and Gentiles. The Greek societal rules that dominate Gentile culture have few restrictions on sexual promiscuity, drunkenness, and idolatry. While Roman traditions were originally more moralistic than those of the Greeks, by Paul's day the indifferent morality of the Greeks had become widespread in the empire. Therefore, a common Jewish designation for Gentiles (that is, non-Jews) is *sinners*.

Here, Paul is drawing a contrast between the cultural immorality of the Gentiles and the higher moral standards of the Jews. The *Jews by nature* are Paul's people. He is not saying this to be judgmental, but to set up his next point that neither Jews nor Gentiles are saved by keeping the law.

What Do You Think?
Which sinful cultural trends are most alluring to Christians today? How do we resist while still keeping lines of communication open to culture?
Talking Points for Your Discussion
- In the world of entertainment
- In the business world
- 1 Corinthians 5:9, 10

16. Knowing that a man is not justified by the works of the law, but by the faith of Jesus Christ, even we have believed in Jesus Christ, that we might be justified by the faith of Christ, and not by the works of the law: for by the works of the law shall no flesh be justified.

The key word for our understanding of this passage is *justified*, used three times in this verse alone. While we may be familiar with the religious implications of this word, its background is in the legal world. To be justified in a legal sense is to be declared innocent by a judge. In the context of our relationship with the divine judge, to be justified means that God does not intend to give us the deserved punishment for our sins.

Paul points out the ultimate weakness of the Judaizing approach, which relies on *the works of the law*. This means that the Judaizers teach that justification is determined, at least in part, by how faithfully a person follows the many points of the Law of Moses.

Paul does not condemn law-keeping as such, but he is uncompromising in his claim that this cannot be a means to justification. Paul knows that with this approach it is "all or nothing." A person who keeps the law 99.9 percent of the time is still guilty. Such a person falls short of a righteous standing before God (see Romans 3:23).

Paul's understanding of the gospel is based on the alternative to any attempt to be justified by keeping the law: the only possible way to be justified is through *the faith of Jesus Christ*. Some variation of this phrase occurs three times in this verse. Christians are justified in the eyes of God the judge because they have placed their faith in Christ. This passage is ground zero for the doctrine of justification by faith as opposed to works—one of the foundational tenets of Christianity.

Paul insists here and elsewhere that there are not two ways of salvation, one for Jews and one for Gentiles (see Romans 3:9). Jews may decide to keep the law for various valid reasons, but law-observance as a means to salvation is futile. Paul is an accomplished, educated Jew, with deep knowledge of the law and the technicalities of its observance (see Philippians 3:4-6). He speaks with great authority when he says there can be no justification through *works of the law*. If anyone could be justified by the law, it would be Paul! But he acknowledges the impossibility of this approach. In so doing, he undermines the credibility of the Judaizers who have been preaching another gospel to the Galatians (see Galatians 1:7, 8).

What Do You Think?

What modern traditions or works might Christians trust in for justification? How do we perpetuate such an attitude, and what can we do to fix the problem?

Talking Points for Your Discussion

- The area of church attendance
- The area of giving
- The area of prayer
- The area of the Lord's Supper

❧ ON WHAT BASIS? ❧

Some time ago I read a novel about a young man who was left as an infant on the steps of a hospital. He grew up in an orphanage and foster homes, and he never really "knew who he was." He learned to be tough in order to survive. As a result, he became successful and wealthy. But he still felt the need to know his roots. He hired an investigator, who learned that he was born on a ranch in Texas.

He went to the ranch to learn his background, but he arrived as a drifting ranch hand. He got a job on the ranch and worked hard. His work ethic earned him the respect of others on the ranch, including the elderly owner. He also fell in love with the ranch. Within a short period of time, he began to assume management responsibilities for the ranch.

Eventually, the man disclosed that he was wealthy and offered to buy the ranch, but the owner refused. He had determined that it would only go to his blood relatives. It turned out, however, that the owner was actually the man's father, who ended up giving him the ranch. The man gained possession of the ranch not by his works, but by his lineage. Works of fiction are always good at hitting us with such twists! But this twist has a real-life counterpart: "If ye be Christ's, then are ye Abraham's seed, and heirs according to the promise" (Galatians 3:29).   —J. B. N.

B. Seeking Righteousness, Finding Sin (v. 17)

17. But if, while we seek to be justified by Christ, we ourselves also are found sinners, is therefore Christ the minister of sin? God forbid.

Paul now turns to a major objection from the Judaizer perspective: If keeping the law is not a requirement for Christians, do we not open a door for all the sinful vices of the Gentile world? In other words, if we reduce the law's power, are we not saying that "anything goes"? If this is the case, are we then presenting Christ as a *minister of sin*? A very literal translation of this would be "Is Christ a server of sin?" The implication of such a hypothetical situation is not so much that Christ is in service to sin, but that He is serving sin to us like a waiter serves his customers food.

Paul raises the same question from a different perspective in Romans 6:1: "Shall we continue in sin, that grace may abound?" In both cases, he is using an argument we call *reduction to the absurd*. This is where we press a mistaken notion to its logical extreme, and the consequences of the error become obvious. In Galatians, it is absurd to think that Christ is a servant of sin. In Romans, it is absurd to think that sinning is a good thing if it allows additional grace to be given to us.

In both cases, Paul's answer is the same: *God forbid*. This is very strong language, actually a two-word prayer. Paul is saying, "God, may you never let this happen!"

C. Dying to Sin, Living for God (vv. 18, 19)

18. For if I build again the things which I destroyed, I make myself a transgressor.

Having established that it is ridiculous to believe that Christ somehow condones sinful behavior, Paul moves to address the central issue: What, then, is the answer to ongoing sin in the life of a Christian believer?

Paul's says here that winking at sin is not possible for the consistent believer. As Paul will go on to explain, Christ has set us free from the bondage of sin (see Galatians 5:1). If I have been freed from the tyrant of sin, why would I want it to enslave me anew? Why, under any circumstances, would I willingly *make myself a transgressor*?

19. For I through the law am dead to the law, that I might live unto God.

Paul makes a remarkable admission here, perhaps a pre-Christian conclusion he arrived at while still a young rabbi. He says that *through the law* (meaning through his attempts to keep the Jewish law) he realizes he is *dead to the law* (meaning that keeping the law leads to death, not life). Paul explains this similarly in Romans 7, where he says that his attempts to keep the law sometimes serve only to inflame his passions for sin, thereby putting him on the road of death.

If our focus is on keeping rules rather than serving God, we will be unsuccessful. We will find that our attempts are imperfect and bear only the "fruit unto death" (Romans 7:5).

❧ *Dead to the Law* ❧

When I finished graduate school, I went to teach in a small Christian college. There I met a young woman on staff who had come from a very legalistic background. The church she attended as a young girl and the whole movement of which it was a part were very strict in moral and ethical teachings. Girls were not allowed to wear makeup or have short hair. They were not allowed to wear slacks or jeans except for recreational or work pur-poses. Members of that church were not to go to movie theaters or to dances. They could not go to restaurants where alcoholic beverages were sold. They were not to listen to modern music (rock music was just coming into vogue back then).

Then this girl went off to college. She was soon faced with numerous temptations to her strict way of life. She knew this was coming, of course, and many of those "temptations" were not tempting to her at all. But she also was exposed to a broader understanding of Christianity. She learned that her legalistic background was just that—a legalism that was supposed to win favor with God. She came to see that it was the sacrifice of Christ, not her legalism, that won God's favor.

We must wonder if her church had ever studied the book of Galatians. Has yours?   —J. B. N.

II. Crucified with Christ
(GALATIANS 2:20, 21)
A. Dying and Living (v. 20)

20. I am crucified with Christ: nevertheless I live; yet not I, but Christ liveth in me: and the life which I now live in the flesh I live by the faith of the Son of God, who loved me, and gave himself for me.

In one of the most memorable passages in the New Testament, Paul presents an alternative to the deadly path of law-keeping. This alternative involves a symbolic death, but it is this death that defines our relationship to Christ. Paul says, *I am crucified with Christ.*

In Romans, Paul uses the symbolism of Christian baptism to illustrate this parallel dying between the believer and Christ: we "were baptized into his death" (Romans 6:3). When we accept Jesus Christ as the Lord of our lives and trust Him for salvation, we are killing off any claims and rights we have to live the way we please. We are "dead indeed unto sin" (6:11), and the pursuit of sinful desires is no longer the controlling factor of our lives. Instead, we are made alive by a new presence in our souls: Christ living in us (compare Galatians 5:24; 6:14).

When I read these words, I tremble at the depth of emotion being expressed by the apostle. How can Paul do anything but offer his life in submissive service when he realizes that Christ loved him so much that He died for him? Christ gave His life for helpless sinners. Should we not give our lives back to Him in service?

When we reach this point, the Judaizing questions about law and sin begin to seem trivial. The Christian life is not a matter of how well we keep the rules. It is a matter of ongoing submission to the will of God, serving Him with all we do and say.

What Do You Think?

How does your life reflect the fact that Christ is living in you? Or would answering this question indicate a lack of humility? Explain.

Talking Points for Your Discussion

- Stands you are willing to take (Esther 4:16)
- Sacrifices you are willing to make (2 Corinthians 11:25)
- Service you are willing to do (Galatians 2:10)

B. Leaving and Grasping (v. 21)

21. I do not frustrate the grace of God: for if righteousness come by the law, then Christ is dead in vain.

Paul summarizes dramatically. If the claims of the Judaizers are correct—that we gain a right standing before God by keeping the rules of the law—then there was no reason for Christ to die. If the Judaizers are right, then the central message of the gospel is rendered ineffective, and all things Christian sink back into the legalism of Judaism.

Paul, however, will not stand for this. To yield to the Judaizing heresy would be to *frustrate the grace of God,* meaning to reject God's gracious offer of salvation through Jesus Christ. If we seek to be saved by good works—by our attempts at self-righteousness—then we must realize we are still in our sins and have no promise of life.

Conclusion

A. Crucified with Christ

I was once speaking for a youth rally where we did something unusual. A member of the church had constructed a very large, rough-lumber cross.

Visual for Lesson 10. *Point to this visual as you ask, "In what ways will others see Christ living in you in the week ahead?"*

It was approximately 10 feet long and 6 feet wide. We laid this cross on the floor of the stage in the church auditorium. Then we invited the young people to come forward, one by one, to lie on the cross in the position of a crucified person. It was very quiet as we did this, and we all watched as several came and laid themselves in the position of Jesus just before He was nailed to the cross.

After this, we asked each to share what it felt like to be in that position. One girl said it brought to mind the verse, "I am crucified with Christ" (Galatians 2:20). She shared that for the first time she began to understand that faith in Christ meant complete surrender.

When we confess Jesus as Lord, we do not sign up to earn His favor by keeping a set of rules. Instead, we submit our whole beings to Him, and we willingly do obey Him. We no longer live for ourselves. We live for Him.

B. Prayer

God of grace and mercy, we offer our hearts to You anew. Forgive us for the times we have attempted to gain Your favor by our deeds. Allow us to serve You with all of our hearts, our souls, and our minds from love and gratitude for Your gracious salvation. We pray this in the name of the Lord Jesus, amen.

C. Thought to Remember

Trust Christ, not rules.

INVOLVEMENT LEARNING

Some of the activities below are also found in the helpful student book, Adult Bible Class.
Don't forget to download the free reproducible page from www.standardlesson.com to enhance your lesson!

Into the Lesson

Download the reproducible page and place in chairs copies of the No Other Gospel activity for learners to work on as they arrive. This activity requires learners to scan the portion of Galatians that precedes today's text, thus providing background context.

Conduct a quick childhood game of Simon Says with your class. You may wish to remind your class how Simon Says works: if "Simon says" precedes a direction, it is to be followed; if not, then the direction is to be ignored. Make it difficult, if not impossible, to carry out the instructions. Here are a few sample directions: "Stand on one foot and close your eyes"; "Put your fist in your ear"; "Turn around three times with your hands clasped behind you."

As learners fail, they are to sit. After a few minutes, ask all to sit, and then ask, "Who is this Simon, and what authority does he have to tell us what to do? There is always someone who will want to tell you what to do. That was a problem in the first century also." Discuss the Judaizing influences in the early church (use the introductory comments on "Living by the Rules" and "Lesson Background: Judaizing").

Into the Word

Give each learner a card with a large *YES* on one side and a large *NO* on the reverse. Tell the class you are going to give them a simple but personal *Yes-No* quiz on today's text. They are to hold up their card toward you to reflect their response to each statement. Use the following statements or some of your own composition:

1. I am Jewish by birth. 2. I am a sinner. 3. I expect to be saved by keeping God's laws. 4. My justification before God is in my faith in His Son. 5. No one will be right before God by observing the Old Testament law. 6. If I must depend on Christ for my justification, He is—in a sense—

promoting my sin. 7. Law in and of itself leads only to disobedience and death. 8. In a sense, I have been crucified—put to death—in Christ. 9. Christ lives in and through me. 10. Jesus loved me enough to die for me. 12. If righteousness could be attained by law-keeping, it would negate God's grace. 13. If the law had the power to save, then Christ died for no good reason.

These statements follow the order of the text for the lesson (Galatians 2:15-21). You may use them to open a discussion on the text as each question is asked in turn. *Alternative:* Ask all the questions without stopping for discussion between them, then open the floor to discussion only after learners have responded to all questions.

Use the following questions to tie the affirmations of the preceding activity directly to Paul's teaching. 1. Why is salvation by keeping the law impossible? 2. How did Paul's opponents nullify grace? 3. What do modern teachers say that nullifies God's grace? 4. Why is sin not an option for the one saved by God's grace? 5. What is it that dies when one is crucified with Christ? 6. In what ways does my trying to be "good enough" for Heaven insult and dishonor God?

With each response press for a truth from the text for support. *Option:* Download the reproducible page and distribute copies of the Preaching and the Gospel exercise. This can be a small-group activity requiring learners to ponder Paul's flow of thought. There is no one right "answer" to this, since some learners may focus on nuances in the flow while others take a broader look.

Into Life

Reproduce the seven verses of today's text on handouts. Arrange the verses in such a way that they can be detached easily (torn or cut). Say, "Every day this week, remove one verse, read it, and highlight one key word. Then use that one word as a basis for your devotional focus."

Justified by Faith in Christ

BLESSED WITH ABRAHAM

DEVOTIONAL READING: Matthew 19:16-23
BACKGROUND SCRIPTURE: Galatians 3:1-14

GALATIANS 3:1-14

1 O foolish Galatians, who hath bewitched you, that ye should not obey the truth, before whose eyes Jesus Christ hath been evidently set forth, crucified among you?

2 This only would I learn of you, Received ye the Spirit by the works of the law, or by the hearing of faith?

3 Are ye so foolish? having begun in the Spirit, are ye now made perfect by the flesh?

4 Have ye suffered so many things in vain? if it be yet in vain.

5 He therefore that ministereth to you the Spirit, and worketh miracles among you, doeth he it by the works of the law, or by the hearing of faith?

6 Even as Abraham believed God, and it was accounted to him for righteousness.

7 Know ye therefore that they which are of faith, the same are the children of Abraham.

8 And the scripture, foreseeing that God would justify the heathen through faith, preached before the gospel unto Abraham, saying, In thee shall all nations be blessed.

9 So then they which be of faith are blessed with faithful Abraham.

10 For as many as are of the works of the law are under the curse: for it is written, Cursed is every one that continueth not in all things which are written in the book of the law to do them.

11 But that no man is justified by the law in the sight of God, it is evident: for, The just shall live by faith.

12 And the law is not of faith: but, The man that doeth them shall live in them.

13 Christ hath redeemed us from the curse of the law, being made a curse for us: for it is written, Cursed is every one that hangeth on a tree:

14 That the blessing of Abraham might come on the Gentiles through Jesus Christ; that we might receive the promise of the Spirit through faith.

KEY VERSE

[Christ hath redeemed us] that the blessing of Abraham might come on the Gentiles through Jesus Christ; that we might receive the promise of the Spirit through faith. —**Galatians 3:14**

GOD ESTABLISHES A FAITHFUL PEOPLE

Unit 3: God's Redemption

LESSONS 10–13

LESSON AIMS

After participating in this lesson, each student will be able to:

1. Identify "the children of Abraham" (Galatians 3:7)

2. Relate Galatians 3:6 with Genesis 15:6 (Lesson 2).

3. Confess to God a personal "human effort" that is inconsistent with the idea of salvation by grace.

LESSON OUTLINE

Introduction

A. Bewitched Believers

Bewitched was a popular television show in the 1960s. Some Christians objected to the show as promoting witchcraft and other unbiblical practices. Others saw it as no more than a silly situation comedy built on a premise that was sheer fantasy. To those in the latter camp, the show was merely "cute."

In Paul's day, however, there was nothing cute or harmless about being "bewitched." Paul asked the Galatian Christians, "Who hath bewitched you?" This strong language indicates his deep frustration and puzzlement concerning their predicament. These believers had accepted the idea that salvation could be earned by their good works. This was so opposed to the gospel preached by Paul that he could not see a rational reason for their change. That the Galatians would exchange the promise of salvation by God's grace for a false hope of being saved by their works was beyond explanation. Thus, he labeled them as bewitched believers.

B. Lesson Background

The connections between Paul's letters to the Galatians and to the Romans run very deep. In both cases Paul presents his gospel in the context of the Jewish religion. Both letters do this with frequent quotes from and allusions to various Old Testament passages.

The two are different in purpose, however. Romans presents Paul's gospel to show that Jews and Gentiles alike are under the condemnation of the law, for all fall short of its perfection and have earned a judgment of death (Romans 3:23). Because of this universal condemnation, our only hope for salvation is through faith in Jesus Christ (5:9). Paul wrote Romans to the Christians in Rome without having visited the city personally. Thus Romans gives a broader, more general picture of salvation by faith.

Galatians, on the other hand, arose from a real-life crisis. Paul was confronting a menace to the churches he had helped plant in Galatia. This danger was the false teaching that it was necessary to keep the Jewish law in order to be saved. This was the Judaizing heresy (as discussed in last week's lesson). Paul's argument against this heresy necessarily involved exposition of Scripture. We could say that Romans is intended as *explanation* whereas Galatians is intended for *correction*. Since Paul is the author of both, it is not surprising that his basic premise is the same in both books.

Some Christians, however, may be surprised to learn that Paul's great truth of our justification by faith is grounded in the Old Testament itself. Paul's case for salvation by grace through faith is based on two key Old Testament passages, which he quotes in both Romans and Galatians. As we shall see today, the Old Testament is a vital background to Galatians.

The effect of Paul's masterful and inspired use of Old Testament passages is to show that the gospel is not a radical departure from the Old Testament. If properly understood, the Old Testament also teaches a relationship to God based on faith rather than works. Thank God for Paul, the champion of salvation through faith!

I. Questions to Ponder

(Galatians 3:1-5)

A. Bewitched by Others (v. 1)

1. O foolish Galatians, who hath bewitched you, that ye should not obey the truth, before whose eyes Jesus Christ hath been evidently set forth, crucified among you?

Paul hits his readers with a series of six rhetorical questions in our first five verses for today. We see the first such question here. The language is harsh. He is not merely chiding, but scolding. In

HOW TO SAY IT

Galatia	Guh-*lay*-shuh.
Galatians	Guh-*lay*-shunz.
Habakkuk	Huh-*back*-kuk.
heretics	*hair*-uh-tiks.
Judah	*Joo*-duh.
Judaizers	*Joo*-duh-*ize*-ers.
Lystra	*Liss*-truh.
Nadia Comaneci	*Nah*-dee-yuh Koh-muh-*neech*.

a forceful manner, he draws to the readers' attention the fact that their disregard for his teachings has led them to disobey the truth.

For Paul, the heart of this truth is *Jesus Christ . . . crucified* (see 1 Corinthians 1:23; 2:2). Paul reminds his readers of the vividness of his previous presentation of Christ's sacrificial death—so vivid he can describe it as having been done before their eyes. Paul is not allowing for any lack of clarity in his personal presentation to the Galatians. The error is not in misunderstanding the truth, but in abandoning it.

The Greek verb for *bewitched* is found only in Galatians 3:1 in all of the New Testament. Its root is the Greek word from which we get our term *fascinate*. This word has a deeper meaning than being fascinated in the sense of "enthralled" or "entertained," though. In Paul's day, it means to cast an evil spell on someone. There is no doubt among the people of Paul's world that there are magicians and witches able to do just this (see Acts 8:9; 13:6; 19:19). In Galatians 3:1, however, Paul's question about bewitching is not intended to be taken literally. He does not think that those who have fed the Galatians false teachings are magicians, sorcerers, or witches. But the false teachers have indeed been mesmerizing!

B. Abandoning the Spirit (vv. 2-5)

2, 3. This only would I learn of you, Received ye the Spirit by the works of the law, or by the hearing of faith? Are ye so foolish? having begun in the Spirit, are ye now made perfect by the flesh?

Paul presses his discussion by asking bluntly *Received ye the Spirit by the works of the law, or by the hearing of faith?* One of the major distinctions between the Old Testament people of God and the New Testament people of God is the presence of the Holy Spirit. It is true that mention of the Holy Spirit can be found in the pages of the Old Testament, but the actual phrase *Holy Spirit* occurs only three times there: Psalm 51:11; Isaiah 63:10, 11. And only in Psalm 51:11 is there a sense of the Holy Spirit indwelling a believer (in that instance, King David). While the Spirit of God is often present (see Genesis 1:2), there is no description of the Holy Spirit being given to the people of Israel individually in the "indwelling" sense of the New Testament.

Paul's point is that the Old Testament laws do not promise anything like the Spirit. It is not "keep the Sabbath and you will receive the gift of the Holy Spirit." The gift of the Holy Spirit, experienced by the Galatian believers, is a part of the new covenant. This gift is seen only prophetically in the Old Testament (see Ezekiel 37:14). Therefore, Paul is warning his readers that reverting to the old covenant is to disregard and endanger this precious gift. It is to buy the lie that we can be *made perfect* by our own efforts apart from faith.

4. Have ye suffered so many things in vain? if it be yet in vain.

Paul is aware that the acceptance of his gospel has come at a cost. In Lystra, a likely target city for this letter, Paul himself was nearly killed when some Jews stoned him (Acts 14:19). He knows that the rejection of the law as a means to salvation is not without consequences. There have been some nasty accusations flying around, and others may have suffered physical violence from this decision. Now if there is a return to the law by Jewish Christians or even Gentile Christians, this suffering will all have been *in vain*, both for the Galatians and for Paul himself (see Galatians 4:11).

5. He therefore that ministereth to you the Spirit, and worketh miracles among you, doeth he it by the works of the law, or by the hearing of faith?

Paul asks another pointed question: did the Galatians witness miracles when he preached to them or when the Judaizers taught them the law? Paul's reference to the one who *ministereth to you the Spirit* is not to himself, but to God. God's miraculous activity occurred during Paul's ministry among the Galatians when he proclaimed salvation through faith.

There is no record that the false teachers had brought anything miraculous along with their message. In Lystra, Paul had healed a man who could not walk (Acts 14:10). Paul himself had survived a brutal stoning in a way that may be seen as miraculous (Acts 14:19, 20). If miracles are a sign of God's confirmation (see Hebrews 2:4), shouldn't the Galatians follow the teacher whose message had been accompanied by signs from God?

What Do You Think?
What was a time when the presence of the Holy Spirit served as a comfort to you personally in a time of need? How did things turn out?
Talking Points for Your Discussion
- In a physical distress
- In a spiritual distress
- In an emotional distress
- At a crossroad of life

II. Example to Consider
(GALATIANS 3:6-9)
A. Counted as Righteous (v. 6)

6. Even as Abraham believed God, and it was accounted to him for righteousness.

One might think that the Jews of Paul's day look to Moses as their ancestral leader, especially the law-promoting Judaizers. But this is not the case. They do not consider themselves to be children of Moses, but children of Abraham (see John 8:39). Paul will have much more to say about Abraham in the rest of Galatians, but he begins his presentation at this point by quoting Genesis 15:6 (also quoted in Romans 4:3).

The gist of this quotation is to show that Abraham's relationship with God was built on faith at the deepest level. Abraham's obedient works were not motivated by wanting to earn a reward, but by his confidence in God. The ultimate act of faith for Abraham was his willingness to kill his son Isaac as a sacrifice in accordance to God's directions. The author of Hebrews tells us that Abraham obeyed this directive because he believed God had the power to raise Isaac from the dead (Hebrews 11:17-19).

Paul makes the important point in Romans 4:9-11 that Genesis 15:6 comes before the Law of Moses, and even before the command to Abraham to have all the males of his household circumcised. Thus, to hold up Abraham as the main example of a person blessed and justified by God necessarily excludes circumcision from the discussion—and this is the lynchpin of the Judaizers' demands.

B. Considered Children (vv. 7-9)

7, 8. Know ye therefore that they which are of faith, the same are the children of Abraham. And the scripture, foreseeing that God would justify the heathen through faith, preached before the gospel unto Abraham, saying, In thee shall all nations be blessed.

Paul continues to fight the Judaizing heretics on their own turf: the Old Testament Scriptures. In the great covenant statement to Abraham found in Genesis 12:1-3, there is a promise that all nations of the earth would be blessed. The blessings promised to Abraham are not reserved for his physical descendants alone. There is a much broader intent: inclusion of all the peoples of the earth. Since this promise, too, comes long before any practice of circumcision or the Law of Moses, Paul interprets it as a promise of faith.

Since being made righteous through faith is the foundation of Paul's gospel, he can go so far as to say that the message to Abraham 2,000 years before Christ is effectively the message of the gospel. Although not fully understood, perhaps not even by Abraham, God's intent all along was to have a faith relationship with His children. Paul explains that this promise to Abraham was prophetically foreseeing that *God would justify the heathen through faith*. Thus Paul is not preaching some new or misguided gospel, but the oldest and truest gospel message of all.

❧ *Spiritual DNA* ❧

One of the wonders of modern medical science is the decoding of DNA, the "blueprint" of life. The news media is filled with various stories of the influence of this relatively new science. Many prisoners who have lived behind bars for years have been released because DNA ("genetic fingerprinting") proved their innocence. Use of DNA to find cures for diseases shows great promise. And, of course, we all know that DNA can be used to prove or disprove paternity.

Paul certainly was not aware of DNA and its modern usage. But Paul was an expert on what we might call *spiritual paternity*. The Jews of Paul's day placed great importance on being descended from Abraham (John 8:33, 39). But Paul affirms

He counted it to him for righteousness.
– Genesis 15:6
Romans 4:3
James 2:23
Galatians 3:6

Visual for Lessons 2 & 11. *Point to this visual as you relate Galatians 3:6 to the three other passages noted here.*

that faith is what makes a person a child of Abraham. Their spiritual DNA is the same. No biological connection needed!　　　　　—J. B. N.

9. So then they which be of faith are blessed with faithful Abraham.

So there is no mistake, Paul draws a summary conclusion. Abraham should be remembered as *faithful Abraham*. All men and women, whether Jew or Gentile, are offered the blessing of righteousness through their faith, and therefore can join the company of Abraham. There is no second option given, no possibility for being saved through circumcision or other observances of the law.

III. Basis of Salvation
(Galatians 3:10-14)
A. Fruitless Works (vv. 10-12)

10. For as many as are of the works of the law are under the curse: for it is written, Cursed is every one that continueth not in all things which are written in the book of the law to do them.

Having established the priority of faith, Paul now addresses the faulty teaching that presents law-keeping as a means to righteousness. The problem is that either you keep the law perfectly in every aspect for a lifetime, or you are cursed. Paul does not make this bold claim just on his own authority. He quotes Moses himself, from Deuteronomy 27:26 (compare Romans 3:19, 20).

PAUL, JAMES, AND LUTHER

There have been many "compare and contrast" studies between what Paul and James have to say about works of law and faith. One of the most famous is that of Martin Luther (1483–1546). But Luther's analysis has led to one of the classic misunderstandings of church history: that Luther was so opposed to the epistle of James that he left it out of his German translation of the Bible.

It simply isn't true. Luther translated James into German, and it has been in every German Bible since Luther's day. Luther found resonance in Paul, but Paul and James do not disagree. In Galatians 3:10 and James 2:10, the sense is the same: if you follow the law but miss one point, you are guilty of breaking the law.

But this is not to throw *works* out the window. James 2:20 says, "Faith without works is dead." Luther agrees and presses even harder: "Faith without works is not even faith." As Paul says, we are "created in Christ Jesus unto good works" (Ephesians 2:10). Paul, James, and Luther are all on the same page. Are we on that page as well?—J. B. N.

11. But that no man is justified by the law in the sight of God, it is evident: for, The just shall live by faith.

Paul now uses his second major Scripture that teaches justification by faith: Habakkuk 2:4 (see also Romans 3:20; Galatians 2:16). Habakkuk is unique among the prophets for his presentation of dialogue with God (some call it arguing). Habakkuk worked in a time when evil, selfish men controlled the nation of Israel, and their dishonesty and injustice seemed to go unpunished. When Habakkuk complained about this, God told him that He was sending the Babylonians to wipe out the nation of Judah for this evil. Habakkuk objected to this in strong terms. He did not think it fair for God to use a "more evil" nation like Babylon to punish his own "less evil" nation.

God's answer to Habakkuk was that it was not for that prophet to know or understand all of God's dealings, particularly on the international level. Habakkuk's job was to trust God. In the end, it was the prophet's faith that would save him, for *the just shall live by faith*. Paul's point is that as the old nation of Judah was powerless to save itself from the mighty Babylonians, so sinful men and women cannot save themselves through their own efforts. Their salvation can come only from God; this is based on faith, not on works of law.

12. And the law is not of faith: but, The man that doeth them shall live in them.

Paul returns to the theme of the law as condemning rather than saving. The law has a valuable function, and that is to define what actions constitute sin (see Romans 7:7). There is no room for grace or faith in this approach to God, however.

Under a law system, our righteousness before God becomes a transaction, a payment for good deeds. This will never work, however. It didn't work for Abraham. It doesn't work for Paul. It won't work for the Galatians. Life from the law is found only in perfection, as Paul's quotation from Leviticus 18:5 shows, and none of us is able to attain perfection. Because of our sin, our just reward is death (see Romans 6:23). There is no middle ground between law-keeping and faith-living as means for salvation. Thus, Paul's stark statement: *the law is not of faith*.

B. Promised Spirit (vv. 13, 14)

13. Christ hath redeemed us from the curse of the law, being made a curse for us: for it is written, Cursed is every one that hangeth on a tree.

If we are all cursed, condemned for failing to keep the law perfectly, how is this curse overcome? Paul has made a strong case to show that we cannot lift this curse ourselves. Therefore, he turns to Christ and the power of His atoning death for us.

Paul again uses the Old Testament to make his case, in this instance the teaching that anyone who is executed by hanging on a tree is cursed (Deuteronomy 21:22, 23; see Acts 5:30; 10:39). To be killed in this manner is a death reserved for the vilest of criminals. The law teaches that this manner of death is used to shame the one being executed.

The execution of Christ on a tree (cross) was not because God had cursed Him, but because He had willingly taken upon himself the curse for the sins of the world (see John 1:29). The curse of sin that results from our law-breaking was therefore transferred to Jesus, the sinless one.

14. That the blessing of Abraham might come on the Gentiles through Jesus Christ; that we might receive the promise of the Spirit through faith.

Paul ties it all together in the final verse for this section. It is through the atoning death of Jesus Christ that the promised blessing of Abraham lives and is actualized. Even the Gentiles can receive this blessing, best seen in the gift of the Spirit. All of this is based on faith rather than law-keeping. The arguments and teachings of the Judaizers are put to rest, and Paul has done this by using Scriptures from the law itself.

Conclusion

A. Almost Perfect

In Olympic gymnastic competitions, the judges traditionally have scored each contestant's efforts on a scale from 1 to 10. Occasionally, an outstanding performance has been awarded a "perfect 10," as was the case with Nadia Comăneci in 1976.

Advanced technology in slow-motion video is now able to show that a supposedly flawless performance still has small imperfections, perhaps unnoticeable to the eyes of the judges in real time. This and other factors caused a change in gymnastics scoring for the 2008 Beijing Olympics, and some believe we will never see another "perfect" performance given a 10. The truth is, though, that none of them were ever perfect in the first place. They were "almost" perfect.

In the same way, one instance of failing to keep the law makes a person imperfect and unrighteous. We can never be justified by our works. We experience heartbreak whenever a believer abandons the faith. This is especially difficult when a believer quits trusting the Lord and only trusts himself or herself. If we understand the big picture, our utter inability to save ourselves is absolute, and any attempts to do so are futile. May we not be "bewitched" by this distortion of the gospel.

B. Prayer

Father of Abraham, may we too be Your children through faith. We thank You that Christ's death has redeemed us from the penalties of breaking Your law. May we live each day in gratitude to You, as we enjoy the Holy Spirit's presence in our lives. We pray in Jesus' name, amen.

C. Thought to Remember

Our connection with Abraham is based on faith.

INVOLVEMENT LEARNING

Some of the activities below are also found in the helpful student book, Adult Bible Class.
Don't forget to download the free reproducible page from www.standardlesson.com to enhance your lesson!

Into the Lesson

Arrive at class wearing a "sandwich board"; fashion this from two large pieces of poster board that are attached at the shoulders with strips of cloth. Put a large question mark on the front and back. As each learner arrives, say to him or her, "I have a question for you" as you hand the learner a small card with a large question mark on it. When learners act confused, say, "We'll get to the question later."

As class begins, say, "In today's text Paul in effect says, 'Galatian Christians, I have some questions for you.'" Ask the class what thoughts come to mind when someone approaches them with such a statement. Expect remarks such as, "I would be thinking, *Uh, oh—I wonder what he/she wants?* and *I hope I don't embarrass myself with the wrong answer!*"

Into the Word

Say, "If you identify one of Paul's questions in today's text aloud to our group, I will take your question card, and you'll be 'off the hook.'" The first five verses include the questions that your learners will identify. After learners identify all the questions, note that Paul's technique is designed to elicit right thinking in his readers.

Once all Paul's questions from verses 1-5 are given, tell your other learners (the ones still holding question cards), "I want you to word a question for us based on verses 6 through 14 of our text. This will be like playing *Jeopardy,* where you look at the 'answer' found in a verse and come up with a question. For example, for verse 6 the question could be, 'On what basis was Abraham considered righteous by God?'" Take questions until all your learners have "redeemed" their question cards. This procedure will allow a close look at the verses and enable you to add commentary as necessary.

Use the "Almost Perfect" illustration from the Conclusion of the lesson commentary to lead a discussion of how impossible it is for anyone to be perfect by his or her own efforts. Make the point of how thankful we should be that our salvation doesn't depend on our being perfect, but on our faith in Jesus' death on the cross on our behalf.

Into Life

Option 1: Download the reproducible page and distribute copies of the Questions with Answers activity. Have learners form study pairs to share responses.

Option 2: Give each learner a badge with the letters *I T B J D.* (Badge-making kits are available at office supply stores, or perhaps your church already has one. A volunteer might welcome the job of preparing these for you. If the badge idea is not feasible, use peel-and-stick labels instead.) Explain that the letters stand for *I tried, but Jesus died.* Explain that this is the essence of today's study; our efforts are not what saves us—it is Jesus' death and His grace that does. Suggest that at some point this week the badge/label be worn to elicit inquiries as to its meaning. The explanation will provide an opportunity for speaking the gospel to another or simply provide a personal affirmation in the efficacy of Christ's death.

Option 3. Distribute markers and strips of paper. Write the following mottoes on the board: "Works Don't Work"; "Busy or Believing?"; "Faith or Foolishness?"; "Cursed or 'Crossed'?"; "Blessed or Burdened?" Briefly discuss the relationship of each to today's study. Then ask learners to choose one and write it on the strip. They can post their "bumper stickers" somewhere at home for a few days to remind themselves of the truth of today's lesson. The strips of paper need not be the peel-and-stick kind. You may choose to use smaller strips that can be used as Bible bookmarks.

Finally, download the reproducible page and distribute copies of the "Curses! Foiled Again" activity as a take-home exercise.

Blessed with Abraham

INHERITING ABRAHAM'S PROMISE

DEVOTIONAL READING: Romans 4:1-8
BACKGROUND SCRIPTURE: Galatians 3:15–5:1

GALATIANS 3:15-18

15 Brethren, I speak after the manner of men; Though it be but a man's covenant, yet if it be confirmed, no man disannulleth, or addeth thereto.

16 Now to Abraham and his seed were the promises made. He saith not, And to seeds, as of many; but as of one, And to thy seed, which is Christ.

17 And this I say, that the covenant, that was confirmed before of God in Christ, the law, which was four hundred and thirty years after, cannot disannul, that it should make the promise of none effect.

18 For if the inheritance be of the law, it is no more of promise: but God gave it to Abraham by promise.

GALATIANS 4:1-7

1 Now I say, That the heir, as long as he is a child, differeth nothing from a servant, though he be lord of all;

2 But is under tutors and governors until the time appointed of the father.

3 Even so we, when we were children, were in bondage under the elements of the world:

4 But when the fulness of the time was come, God sent forth his Son, made of a woman, made under the law,

5 To redeem them that were under the law, that we might receive the adoption of sons.

6 And because ye are sons, God hath sent forth the Spirit of his Son into your hearts, crying, Abba, Father.

7 Wherefore thou art no more a servant, but a son; and if a son, then an heir of God through Christ.

KEY VERSE

Wherefore thou art no more a servant, but a son; and if a son, then an heir of God through Christ.

—Galatians 4:7

GOD ESTABLISHES A FAITHFUL PEOPLE

Unit 3: God's Redemption

LESSON AIMS

After participating in this lesson, each student will be able to:

1. Identify the seed of Abraham.

2. Explain the connection between the terms *son, slave/servant,* and *heir.*

3. Construct a simple timeline of the events noted in today's text.

LESSON OUTLINE

Introduction

A. Wills

The history of making wills extends back into antiquity. In the Greek/Gentile world in particular, there were strict laws governing wills, and not all of these were like our current regulations. One of these ancient customs made it very difficult to alter a legally posted will. In that male-dominated world, a will was usually drawn by the father of a family. Once he had written his will, it was considered irrevocable.

Paul, in writing to the Galatians, is in this Greek/Gentile environment. A central point of today's lesson is that God's "will" as promised to Abraham is not annulled by the laws of Moses, which came later. This would be in keeping with Paul's readers' understanding of a will. Once God made His promise to Abraham, Paul's readers would expect it only to be supplemented, not changed.

B. Lesson Background

A key to understanding the Old Testament is comprehending the position of Abraham in the history of the nation of Israel. His story begins in Genesis 11:26 (where he is called *Abram*) and continues through 25:10. Abraham's story is that of a journey of faith as he set out for a new home and homeland.

When the Lord commanded Abram to go to Canaan, he was given a promise of blessing, and this promise is repeated several times in Genesis in various forms. Central to the promise was the idea that this man's descendants would one day become a "great nation" (Genesis 12:2).

This promise tested Abram's faith in two dramatic ways. First, Abram had no son for many years, no legitimate male heir through whom the promise could be fulfilled. God's commitment to keeping the promise was so strong, however, that He changed Abram's name to *Abraham,* meaning "father of many" (Genesis 17:5). God fulfilled the promise through the miraculous conception and birth of Abraham's son Isaac (21:1-3), so Abraham's crisis of faith was resolved.

Another crisis presented itself when Abraham was commanded to kill his son Isaac as a sacrifice

Inheriting Abraham's Promise

to God. The death of this only son would ruin the promise of Abraham's descendants becoming a great nation as effectively as if he had never been born. (Although Abraham had another son, Ishmael, through Hagar, God refers to Isaac as Abraham's "only son" in Genesis 22:2.) God intervened and provided an alternative (22:13). In these and other actions throughout his life, Abraham was vindicated as the exemplary man of faith, the one whose relationship with God was based on trust, no matter the circumstances.

The Old Testament understands Abraham's "great nation" as coming to fruition by the descendants of Jacob, Abraham's grandson. Jacob's name was changed to *Israel* after an encounter with God (Genesis 32:28). Through Jacob, the "great nation" of Abraham was the nation of Israel.

The New Testament recognizes an even greater role for Abraham: he is more than the father of Israel; he is the father of all who have faith in the true God. This is seen in the opening verses of the New Testament, where Matthew carefully shows Jesus to be a descendant of Abraham (Matthew 1:1, 2, 17). Even before Jesus' birth, Mary sang a song of praise to God that included her belief that the birth of the Messiah was a fulfillment of God's promise to Abraham (Luke 1:55).

All of this was an important backdrop for Paul's discussion of Abraham in Galatians. In his doctrinal battle with the heretical Judaizers, Paul used the promises given to Abraham. The life story of Abraham was Paul's means to show the priority of faith rather than works as the way to be justified before God.

I. Single Seed
(GALATIANS 3:15-18)
A. Covenant Stands (v. 15)

15. Brethren, I speak after the manner of men; Though it be but a man's covenant, yet if it be confirmed, no man disannulleth, or addeth thereto.

To *speak after the manner of men* is to take an example from the general sphere of humanity, not the Bible. Paul intends to build his argument on common assumptions that everyone can accept.

In this case, Paul uses the example of a covenant. In doing this, Paul is playing on the broad meaning of this word. A covenant can be a binding agreement between two parties. This is the word used for the agreements between God and various persons in the Old Testament (examples: Genesis 6:18; 17:21; Psalm 89:3).

The word *covenant* can also be used to describe a human document that outlines the disposition of a person's assets at death. In this sense, it is roughly equivalent to our practice of drafting a last will and testament. Paul's example is along this line. He lifts up the understanding of wills in the ancient world: once confirmed, they cannot be disannulled.

What Do You Think?
How are secular covenants similar to God's covenants? How are they different?
Talking Points for Your Discussion
- Regarding purchase contracts
- Regarding marriage vows
- Regarding conditions of employment
- Regarding community covenants
- Regarding warranties

B. Christ Promised (v. 16)

16. Now to Abraham and his seed were the promises made. He saith not, And to seeds, as of many; but as of one, And to thy seed, which is Christ.

The connection between the promise of a future blessing for all nations and the seed of Abraham is made several times in Genesis. One of the clearest is this: "And in thy seed shall all the nations of the earth be blessed; because thou hast obeyed my voice" (Genesis 22:18). In carefully noting this promise, Paul brings to bear his great rabbinical training as an expert in Scripture. He battles the Judaizers on their own ground: Genesis. Both Paul and his opponents believe this book to have been written by Moses, and it therefore is part of the law.

Paul notes the detail that the word *seed* in this promise is singular, not plural. Those readers who check his observation will find this to be true in both the original Hebrew text and in the Greek translation of Genesis commonly used in places like Galatia. Although Abraham was promised that his descendants would number as the stars in the heavens or the sand on the beach (Genesis 22:17), there is also a specific individual in mind for God's promise. It is not the millions of Israelites who are to bless all nations, but one particular descendant of Abraham: *which is Christ.*

We should remember that Paul's opponents are not Jews who have rejected Jesus. Rather, Paul's opponents are Christian Jews who have accepted Jesus as the promised Messiah. There is no disagreement over the truth of the resurrection or the deity of Jesus as the Son of God. The disagreement has to do with the necessity of keeping the Law of Moses in the Christian era.

C. Confirmation Effective (vv. 17, 18)

17. And this I say, that the covenant, that was confirmed before of God in Christ, the law, which was four hundred and thirty years after, cannot disannul, that it should make the promise of none effect.

The strands of Paul's argument become a single rope. First, Paul makes the obvious point of the validity of the covenant promise with Abraham in light of its having been *confirmed before of God.* Paul uses language that reminds his readers of the process of having a last will legally confirmed by the proper authorities. For both Paul and the readers, there is no higher authority than God, so there should be no quibbling over this point.

Second, Paul brings in his point from the previous verse that the promise to Abraham finds its fulfillment *in Christ.* The promises given to Abraham are both valid in his day and anticipatory of Christ. Paul and his readers (and we) are in the Christian era, the historical period of the full realization of these promises.

Third, Paul again uses his great knowledge of Scripture to bring a chronological point to bear: the law was given to Moses 430 years after the promise to Abraham. This factoid is taken from Exodus 12:40, 41, where the time of Israel in Egypt is given as exactly 430 years. The nation of Israel was in existence, albeit as slaves in Egypt, for more than four centuries without having the Law of Moses.

This leads to Paul's concluding historical point: the law, coming much later, *cannot disannul* the promise given to Abraham. Abraham's covenant and promises are still in effect.

18. For if the inheritance be of the law, it is no more of promise: but God gave it to Abraham by promise.

Paul brings all of this to a simple conclusion: among people of honor, promise always trumps law. For example, if I promise to pay you $25 to mow my lawn, I am bound by that promise. If you cut my grass and then I claim I need not pay because there was no written contract, I would be breaking my promise. I may or may not be legally in the clear, but I have not kept my word. God always keeps His word. He always keeps His promises. Humanly, there are times when I may be unable to keep a promise due to circumstances beyond my control. There are no circumstances beyond God's control. The Lord God always keeps His promises.

Paul adds another element to the argument that he will use more fully in the next chapter: that our share of the promise to Abraham comes through inheritance (see Galatians 4:7, below). An heir always has more rights and expectations than does a contract employee or an indentured servant. Relationships based in law are shallow compared with the family relationships between a father and child.

At this point, we may wonder, if the promise system is superior to the law system, then why did God ever give the law to Moses? Answering this question is the focus of Paul's discussion in Galatians 3:19-29, not in today's text.

HOW TO SAY IT

Abraham	*Ay*-bruh-ham.
Abram	*Ay*-brum.
Galatia	Guh-*lay*-shuh.
Hagar	*Hay*-gar.
Isaac	*Eye*-zuk.
Ishmael	*Ish*-may-el.
Judaizers	*Joo*-duh-*ize*-ers.
rabbinical	ruh-*bin*-ih-kul.

Inheriting Abraham's Promise

What Do You Think?

How do people react when they know they are going to inherit something? How should that reaction be like and unlike our reaction to our heavenly inheritance?

Talking Points for Your Discussion

- Psalm 61:5
- Luke 12:13
- Luke 15:12
- Colossians 1:11-14

II. Sent Son

(GALATIANS 4:1-7)

A. Children in Bondage (vv. 1-3)

1. Now I say, That the heir, as long as he is a child, differeth nothing from a servant, though he be lord of all.

Paul uses another illustration from the everyday life of his readers. In the households of Paul's world, *a child* and a *servant* are treated the same. Neither is independent of the commands and whims of the father of the house. It makes little difference that one of the household children might be the oldest son, the eventual heir and head of the family. As a child, this son's inheritance is only a potential that awaits future realization.

2. But is under tutors and governors until the time appointed of the father.

According to Roman law of the time, a son reaches adult status at age 14. But we do not know if the Galatians follow this tradition. Paul indicates that the age of majority for an inheriting son may be *appointed of the father* of the household. During childhood, the male heir is under the supervision of *tutors and governors*. In a prosperous household, the father may employ various adults who have direct control over the children. These are in the same category as the "schoolmaster" of the household (Galatians 3:24, 25, not in today's text) and represent the function of the law before Christ.

❧ *TEMPORARY TUTOR* ❧

Wealthy families in the ancient world usually had their children educated by private tutors. The tutor was well educated himself, and it was his responsibility to supervise the learning activities of the youngster(s). This included study in academic subjects as well as social graces and royal obligations. This tutoring might be only for a few years, or it could last all through childhood. But whether few years or many, the tutoring was temporary.

For example, the great philosopher Aristotle (384–322 BC) was hired as the tutor for Alexander, age 13, the son of King Philip of Macedon. Aristotle taught Alexander medicine, philosophy, religion, morals, logic, and art. Three years later, Aristotle was dismissed because Philip went off to war, and Alexander took over the regency of Macedon. Aristotle's job had been to prepare the person later known as Alexander the Great for the responsibilities of government, and the time came when that period of preparation ended.

So it is with the Law of Moses. Paul says the law was a tutor to bring us to Christ (compare Galatians 3:24). With that function now fulfilled, the tutor is no longer our master.   —J. B. N.

3. Even so we, when we were children, were in bondage under the elements of the world.

Paul moves from the household to the spiritual realm. He teaches that when the law is the controlling factor for the people of God, they are actually *in bondage* to *the elements of the world*. The contrast could not be greater. The household custodians (the law) are controlling while being beneficent in purpose and intent. The true bondage is to something far more sinister and malevolent. When Paul uses the terminology *elements of the world,* he is referring to the spiritual forces that attack the people of God.

In drawing this comparison, Paul widens his application from Jews-under-the-law to all people in bondage to sin, which includes everyone without Christ. These *elements of the world* are understood to be the various forces of nature represented by pagan deities (see Colossians 2:8, 20). To be under their control is to be a slave to sin (see Romans 7:25).

B. Redemption in Adoption (vv. 4, 5)

4. But when the fulness of the time was come, God sent forth his Son, made of a woman, made under the law.

In simple, beautiful words, Paul injects Jesus into this story of human bondage. At the right time, God sent His answer to the world. This was *his Son,* the Word become flesh (John 1:14). His arrival into the human realm was unlike anything from Gentile religions and myths. This Son was truly human, *made of a woman.* He did not appear fully-grown on a cloud or walking out of the sea.

> *What Do You Think?*
> What was an instance when God worked at just the right time in your life? How did this increase your faith?
> *Talking Points for Your Discussion*
> - In an area of health
> - In an area of finances
> - In an area of relationships
> - In a spiritual struggle

❧ FULLNESS OF TIME ❧

My study of history has given me a great appreciation for God's planning. God carefully chose the right moment in time for Jesus to be born. He worked through three groups of people to do this.

The Jews. When the Jews were scattered because of foreign oppression, they had to develop a system of worship that didn't depend on access to the temple in Jerusalem. They came up with the synagogue. Synagogues eventually appeared in almost every city in the eastern Mediterranean region.

The Greeks. Alexander the Great (356–323 BC) conquered much of the known world of his day. As a result of the spread of Greek culture, the Greek language became something of a common language.

The Romans. A succession of emperors conquered even more of the known world and built a network of highways. From Scotland to Egypt, from the Atlantic Ocean to the Persian Gulf, there were no awkward border crossings. Everyone could travel easily, without hindrance in this unified empire.

As a result, Paul and other missionaries in the first century could travel easily, on well-known highways, to major cities in the Empire to preach about Christ. In every city they could go to the synagogue to spread the gospel. They could speak in a language understood by all educated people. The birth of Jesus was not an accident of history. God coordinated all the pieces. In the fullness of time, He sent His Son.   —J. B. N.

5. To redeem them that were under the law, that we might receive the adoption of sons.

God's Son was sent with a clear mandate: *to redeem them that were under the law.* This continues the language of slavery and bondage. To redeem a slave is to buy the slave's freedom. But the redeemed are not just freed slaves; they are adopted as children into the household of God.

Paul's point is that Jesus was necessarily born a Jew because He was to enter the household of those under bondage to the law and set them free. As a Jew, Jesus was under the law (v. 4, above), but not a slave to the law, for He was without sin. He did not need to be freed from law or sin himself, and thus was able to serve as our Redeemer.

C. Heirs in the Spirit (vv. 6, 7)

6. And because ye are sons, God hath sent forth the Spirit of his Son into your hearts, crying, Abba, Father.

Being a person of faith has immediate consequences. As adopted children, Christians receive the benefits of the unadopted Son. Foremost of these is the *Spirit of his Son,* sent into our innermost beings. It is the presence of God's Spirit in the life of the believer that marks him or her as truly a child of the king (see 2 Corinthians 1:22).

Paul never understands the gift of the Holy Spirit to be an afterthought in the plans of God. The mission of the Son was more than the cross and atonement for sins. By solving the sin problem of believers, the Holy Spirit may come and dwell in our hearts. It is then that we truly begin to act like children of God. We can pray, *Abba, Father!* The word *Abba* is a term from Paul's childhood, an affectionate term like "Daddy" or "Poppa." To say *Father* is to claim the status of a son. We can imagine a scene when a fatherless boy is legally adopted, and realizing his new status says, "Father!"

7. Wherefore thou art no more a servant, but a son; and if a son, then an heir of God through Christ.

The progression is clear for Paul and the readers. We all start as slaves, serving law and sin without any hope of freedom. *Through Christ* we are adopted as sons and daughters, full members of the household of God (see Ephesians 2:19). Our status is changed from slave to son. Since we are true sons, we become heirs, and the first installment of our inheritance is already given: the Spirit of God (Ephesians 1:13, 14).

Conclusion

A. From Slave to Son

Even though slavery is illegal in almost every nation today, it is estimated that millions of people are enslaved in underground economies worldwide. Even so, slavery is not something most of us have experienced firsthand. The idea of being a slave owner is repugnant to us. The thought of being a slave is horrifying. We want nothing to do with slavery, even though we have not encountered it personally.

Paul's teaching on how we transition from slave to son may be difficult for some to understand. Don't let it be. We have all experienced oppression

Visual for Lesson 12

Point to this visual as you discuss the marvel of God's accepting us into His family.

and lack of control in our lives, whether that might be in our employment, relationships, or experiences with government agencies. Expand those experiences to this: to never, ever being in control and always being oppressed. This was the lot of the slave in Paul's day. He or she had no meaningful rights or privileges, except those provided by the slave owner. While a "good" slave owner may have made this tolerable, the life of a slave was a day-to-day existence without hope for the future.

Now imagine being the son or daughter of a perfect father. This is the parent who never loses his temper, who never gets drunk and wastes his paycheck, who never abandons you. This perfect father is our heavenly Father. He gives us His most precious gifts: His Son as a sacrifice for our sins, His Spirit as a comfort to our souls, and His inheritance of eternal life with Him. Through God's provision in Christ, we gain the spirit of adoption, and we can legitimately cry to God with our loudest voice: *Abba, Father!*

B. Prayer

God of Abraham, we thank You for Your promise of blessing fulfilled. We thank You that we are no longer bound by the law, but free to live in Your grace. We thank You that we have become heirs with Christ. We pray in His name, amen.

C. Thought to Remember

God's promises to Abraham are ours in Jesus.

INVOLVEMENT LEARNING

Some of the activities below are also found in the helpful student book, Adult Bible Class.
Don't forget to download the free reproducible page from www.standardlesson.com to enhance your lesson!

Into the Lesson

Write the following on the board: "Describe one item you have received as an inheritance and tell what it means to you" and "Have you ever received an inheritance from someone who wasn't a relative? Explain how that happened." Ask learners to get in small groups of two to four and discuss.

After five minutes, get everyone's attention as you say, "Did you know that all Christians have an inheritance from Abraham even though very few are biologically descended from him? Let's find out how that works."

Into the Word

Alternative 1: Object Lesson. Divide the class into two or more larger groups. Give each group the following objects: a single seed in a clear plastic bag, an alarm clock (or a picture of a clock), several cut-out hearts, a paper chain, and a picture of Little Orphan Annie. Ask each group to see how many of the items they can relate to today's text.

After several minutes, hold up each item and ask for one of the groups to suggest an explanation. Expect these answers: the single seed refers to the seed promised to Abraham (Christ); the alarm clock relates to the "fullness of time" when God sent His Son; the hearts relate to the fact God has sent His Spirit into our hearts; the paper chain relates to our status as slaves to the rudiments of worldliness; Little Orphan Annie relates to our need to be adopted into God's family. Discuss the corresponding verse(s) for each item.

Alternative 2: Chart. Have students stay in the groups from the opening activity. Give each group a sheet that is divided boldly into four horizontal rows that intersect three vertical columns. On the first row have the names *Paul, Moses, Abraham,* one per block; on the second row have the digits 3, 0, 4, one per block; on the third row, have the words *heir, servant, son,* one per block; on the fourth row, have the verbs *made (born), redeem, sent.*

Tell your class this is a "tear and arrange" activity. Direct them to tear off the top row (the names), then tear it into the three individual blocks. Say, "Now put these three names in proper order." Once they see the sequence is Abraham, Moses, Paul, ask, "What does this sequence have to do with today's text?"

Proceed to the second row (the numerals) and have learners do the same thing. The idea is that Paul emphasizes the 430-year period between God's promise to Abraham and giving the law. After learners arrange the elements of row three, say, "When children, we were just like *servants*, but we became *sons* with all the relationship rights, but ultimately we are *heirs* of all the Father's wealth and blessings. Row four relates to Galatians 4:4, as Christ is *sent* by God, is *made (born)* into flesh, to *redeem* us by His death. *Option:* The Which Came First? activity on the downloadable reproducible page is an abbreviated version of this alternative; you may wish to use it instead if time is short.

Into Life

Give each learner an image of a traditional clock face that has the hour and minute hands at noon, but with a cross bar (ideally in red) that makes the hands resemble a cross. Put the word *Abraham* at the number 3, the word *Moses* at 9. Have learners read Galatians 4:4, 5 in unison. Continue: "By God's blessing we were born into an opportune time, a time God calls *full.* Christ's coming occurred at the most opportune time, from God's perspective." Recommend that learners post their clock faces where they will see it often this week as a reminder of the special privilege we enjoy by having been "born into God's right time."

Download the reproducible page and distribute copies of the In the Will activity. If time allows, have learners complete it in class and name some of the blessings of inheritance they wrote down. Otherwise, distribute it as a take-home activity.

BEARING THE FRUIT OF REDEMPTION

DEVOTIONAL READING: 2 Peter 1:3-8
BACKGROUND SCRIPTURE: Galatians 5:2–6:18

GALATIANS 5:22-26

22 But the fruit of the Spirit is love, joy, peace, longsuffering, gentleness, goodness, faith,

23 Meekness, temperance: against such there is no law.

24 And they that are Christ's have crucified the flesh with the affections and lusts.

25 If we live in the Spirit, let us also walk in the Spirit.

26 Let us not be desirous of vain glory, provoking one another, envying one another.

GALATIANS 6:1-10

1 Brethren, if a man be overtaken in a fault, ye which are spiritual, restore such an one in the spirit of meekness; considering thyself, lest thou also be tempted.

2 Bear ye one another's burdens, and so fulfil the law of Christ.

3 For if a man think himself to be something, when he is nothing, he deceiveth himself.

4 But let every man prove his own work, and then shall he have rejoicing in himself alone, and not in another.

5 For every man shall bear his own burden.

6 Let him that is taught in the word communicate unto him that teacheth in all good things.

7 Be not deceived; God is not mocked: for whatsoever a man soweth, that shall he also reap.

8 For he that soweth to his flesh shall of the flesh reap corruption; but he that soweth to the Spirit shall of the Spirit reap life everlasting.

9 And let us not be weary in well doing: for in due season we shall reap, if we faint not.

10 As we have therefore opportunity, let us do good unto all men, especially unto them who are of the household of faith.

KEY VERSES

The fruit of the Spirit is love, joy, peace, longsuffering, gentleness, goodness, faith, meekness, temperance: against such there is no law. —**Galatians 5:22, 23**

Photo: Hemera Technologies / Photos.com / Thinkstock

GOD ESTABLISHES A FAITHFUL PEOPLE

Unit 3: God's Redemption

LESSONS 10–13

LESSON AIMS

After participating in this lesson, each student will be able to:

1. Identify what is reaped by those who sow to the flesh and those who sow to the Spirit.

2. Explain the sowing and reaping principle.

3. Recite from memory "the fruit of the Spirit."

LESSON OUTLINE

Introduction

A. Farming, Ancient and Modern

Technology has improved crop yields dramatically for the modern farmer. Technology also has decreased the man hours needed to attain those yields. Even so, the basics of farming have not changed over the centuries. For a crop like wheat, the field must be prepared by breaking up the dirt (plowing), seed must be spread (sowing), moisture must be provided (watering), invasive plants must be removed (weeding), and time must be given for the wheat to mature (growing).

These steps had been largely unchanged for centuries when Paul wrote to the Galatians. The small cities and towns of the intended recipients for his letter were not distant from the agricultural world of wheat, barley, etc. Many of the church members who heard his letter read undoubtedly were involved in farming on a seasonal or full-time basis. It is not surprising, then, that Paul and other Bible authors used farming activities to illustrate truths about God and the kingdom of God (for examples, see Proverbs 26:1; Hosea 6:11; Mark 4:26-29). Such is the case in this week's lesson, as Paul uses the concepts of sowing and reaping to illustrate spiritual truths within the church.

B. Lesson Background

Paul's letter to the Galatians is a masterful presentation of the Christian message, a message unfettered by the legalism of first-century Judaism. Paul's immediate concern was to refute false teachers who claimed that Gentiles had to become Jews if they were to be Christian. In this view, the Jewish law was binding on Christ's followers, and the synagogue was the gateway to the church. Paul shows in the first two chapters of Galatians that this was never his message and was not the consensus he reached with the leaders of the church in Jerusalem (Acts 15; Galatians 2:9).

In Galatians 3 and 4, Paul argues that Abraham was never under the Law of Moses, for he predated the lawgiver, Moses, by hundreds of years. Abraham's relationship with God was based on faith, and his true heirs are people of faith, whether Jews or Gentiles. Paul equates law-keeping as a

Bearing the Fruit of Redemption

type of slavery and living by faith as freedom. He implored the Galatians to remain free in Christ and not to submit again to the bondage of the law (Galatians 5:1; compare 2 Corinthians 3:17).

In the final two chapters of Galatians, Paul expands on one of the greatest promises of living by faith: the blessings of the Holy Spirit. After discussing some obvious sins in Galatians 5:19-21, this is where today's lesson opens.

I. Traveling with the Spirit
(GALATIANS 5:22-26)
A. Spiritual Crop (vv. 22-24)

22, 23. But the fruit of the Spirit is love, joy, peace, longsuffering, gentleness, goodness, faith, meekness, temperance: against such there is no law.

Paul wants his readers to understand that Christian behavior transcends any law. The Bible often pictures the results of our actions as *fruit* (examples: Proverbs 11:30; Micah 7:13; Matthew 12:33). Christians are to exhibit certain fruit, and these are the finest human qualities. The nine qualities listed are similar to other lists of virtues found in the New Testament (see Philippians 4:8; Colossians 3:12; James 3:17). Here, the nine may be divided conveniently into three groups of three.

Love, joy, peace are inner attitudes that manifest themselves in the way we live. Love is a godly quality, the attitude of the Father toward His wayward children (Romans 5:8). Elsewhere Paul advises that when we act with genuine love we are fulfilling the intent of the law (Romans 13:10). Paul sees love as the motivation for serving one another within the church (Galatians 5:13).

Joy is often connected with the Holy Spirit (examples: Acts 13:52; Romans 14:17). Joy is godly

HOW TO SAY IT

Cézanne	Say-*zahn*.
Isaiah	Eye-*zay*-uh.
Judaism	*Joo*-duh-izz-um or *Joo*-day-izz-um.
Judaizing	*Joo*-duh-*ize*-ing.
reciprocity	reh-suh-*prah*-suh-tee.

happiness, caused by the awareness of our blessedness in the Lord (see Psalm 21:6). The Bible sees joy as a natural reaction to the one who is allowed to be in the presence of the Lord (Psalm 16:11), so we should expect joy in the life that is filled with the presence of God's Spirit.

Peace is also a central feature of the character of God (Romans 16:20; Philippians 4:7). This peace of God should be present in the life of the believer who trusts that God reigns supreme (Isaiah 52:7).

Longsuffering, gentleness, goodness, the second triad of spiritual fruit, can be understood as ways in which we are to relate to other people. All three serve as a witness to unbelievers in a way that may bring them to believe in God.

Longsuffering describes a person who is willing to wait. This too is a quality of God. Peter even sees the patience of God as a core element of Paul's letters (2 Peter 3:15). The longsuffering patience of God serves to give men and women an opportunity for salvation. Spiritual persons should be patient with both the saved and the unsaved. If we are not in the business of earning salvation by keeping the law, then we can patiently trust our futures to God through the Holy Spirit.

Gentleness is the opposite of harsh treatment. We as sinners deserve to be treated harshly by God, yet He treats us kindly as a means of leading us to repentance (Romans 2:4). Likewise, Christians should treat others kindly, trusting that this will help lead unbelievers to a repentance.

Goodness may be seen as "good actualized." It is more than abstractly wanting to be good; it is *being* good. This is goodness in relationship with others. It is not being good to yourself (as in "I love to spoil myself"). It is doing things that benefit others. Goodness is defined by a giving spirit, another quality of God (see Nehemiah 9:35).

Faith, meekness, temperance, the third triad, are personal virtues that should characterize people who have placed their trust in God. In this context, faith is not so much "faith in God," but the quality of personal faithfulness. Faithful people are those who keep their word, who do not give up, who are loyal to their friends and family. This, again, is a primary way of understanding God, for He is always faithful (see Isaiah 49:7; 1 Corinthians 1:9).

Visual for
Lesson 13

*Display this poster prominently as you work through
the Into the Lesson segment on page 224.*

Meekness is a quality blessed by Jesus (Matthew 5:5) and was central to the personality of Jesus himself (11:29). Meekness is a kind of submissiveness, but not the weak, "milquetoast" kind. True meekness comes from deep inner strength, in this case fueled by the presence of the Holy Spirit.

Temperance often has been applied to limiting the use of alcoholic beverages, but the original Greek word has many more applications than that. For an interesting study, see Acts 24:25; 1 Corinthians 7:9; 9:25; Titus 1:8; and 2 Peter 1:6, where this same word occurs in both noun and verb forms.

What Do You Think?

When you consider how well you are producing the fruit of the Spirit, how would you describe your crop? How will you improve?

Talking Points for Your Discussion

- Parched—dry, in need of nourishment
- Tender shoots—just starting to break through
- Weather distressed—contrary winds have wreaked havoc; in need of support
- Firmly planted—growing and maturing

---

24. And they that are Christ's have crucified the flesh with the affections and lusts.

This verse refers back to the "works of the flesh" as listed in Galatians 5:19-21, a list of horrible vices. To be Christ's means we have the presence of the Holy Spirit. We have been crucified with Him (see Galatians 2:20), and this means we have

left our sinful desires and passions behind. We are no longer controlled by our own selfish wants, but by the Spirit of God and the desire to serve Him.

B. Spiritual Journey (vv. 25, 26)

25. If we live in the Spirit, let us also walk in the Spirit.

What is the difference between "living in" and "walking in" the Spirit? For Paul, to *live in the Spirit* refers to our salvation. As believers we receive God's Holy Spirit as a gift (Acts 2:38). We do nothing to earn this gift, as we do nothing to earn our salvation. We do have choices to make, however, regarding how we live our lives as believers. Paul is saying that if the Holy Spirit lives in you (and He does), then you are to conduct yourself in a way that honors this holy presence.

26. Let us not be desirous of vain glory, provoking one another, envying one another.

We should be on guard against slipping back into patterns of selfishness. Even if we are not engaging in the heinous "works of the flesh," we may fall to more insidious behaviors that are not pleasing to God.

Paul's short list includes things that are all too common in churches and may have been characteristic of his Judaizing opponents. *Desirous of vain glory* is the empty smugness of a boastful person. *Provoking* and *envying* refer to the constant rivalries and fussing that are found in some churches. None of these is consistent with a person walking by the Spirit of Christ.

II. Restoring in the Spirit
(GALATIANS 6:1-5)
A. Burdens of Others (vv. 1, 2)

1. Brethren, if a man be overtaken in a fault, ye which are spiritual, restore such an one in the spirit of meekness; considering thyself, lest thou also be tempted.

A foundational principle in the church is that those who are stronger should help those who are weaker (see Acts 20:35). Christian leaders should be stronger in their spiritual walk and maturity, and this strength is to be extended to help restore a wayward brother or sister (compare Jude 23).

Paul offers a warning, though, of two pitfalls that the one who undertakes a ministry of restoration should be aware. One danger is being too rough on the one who has fallen. If the restoration process is too firm (lacking *the spirit of meekness*) for the context of the problem, then the erring brother or sister could be driven away permanently (compare 2 Corinthians 2:5-11).

The second danger is that the restorer might be tempted and fall into the same sin. As a firefighter is endangered when entering a house fire to rescue a child, so the spiritual leader who attempts to restore a fallen member may be burned.

❧ *RESTORATION IN MEEKNESS* ❧

When I was in graduate school many years ago, I attended a church that was a delight to my wife and me spiritually, a church that encouraged us in Christian maturity. We gained many friends there, some of whom we still have contact with some 40 years later.

But there was one woman in that church who was rather forthright in her ways of Christian confrontation. If she became aware that someone in the congregation had slipped from the high standard of spiritual purity, she would write that person a letter of rigorous chastisement. The letters were often abrasive and hurtful. She probably caused more spiritual harm than good. The leaders of the congregation tried to tone down her strident corrections, but she was adamant that she was only trying to remind people of their higher calling.

In retrospect, it seems that this woman herself was misguided. Paul's admonition to the Galatians is that the process of restoration ought to be done with meekness. The woman's letters came across as "holier than thou," causing hurt and alienation as a result. We are to speak the truth in love (Ephesians 4:15), not in rage or denunciation.—J. B. N.

2. Bear ye one another's burdens, and so fulfil the law of Christ.

Although not stated, *the law of Christ* is usually understood as the Golden Rule taught by Jesus: that we should do to others as we would have them do to us (Luke 6:31). This is called *the principle of loving reciprocity*. When a fellow Christian

has burdens, life issues that are weighing heavily, those who are spiritually mature should help that person as they would want to be helped.

It is this mutual burden-bearing that gives strength to the body of Christ. If those in need are neglected or ignored, then the church is not fulfilling its purpose of being a refuge from the storms of life. As Martin Luther said, "Christians must have strong shoulders and mighty bones" when it comes to helping weaker brothers and sisters.

> *What Do You Think?*
> When do you most find it difficult to bear the burdens of others? How do you distinguish between when it is appropriate and inappropriate to bear the burden of another?
> *Talking Points for Your Discussion*
> - Culture of "rugged individualism"
> - Desire to avoid promoting laziness (2 Thessalonians 3:10)
> - Pride (Luke 10:31, 32)
> - Desire to avoid risking self (Matthew 25:7-9)

B. Burdens of Our Own (vv. 3-5)

3. For if a man think himself to be something, when he is nothing, he deceiveth himself.

This verse describes what is perhaps the biggest danger to spiritual leaders. Some may develop an inflated view of themselves, thinking they are *something*. Paul is implying that this may even lead to the neglect of the needs of others, since such leaders might think themselves too good for such ministry. This is self-deception, for we are all equal in the sight of God (remember Galatians 3:28). In that sense, we are all *nothing*, unable to save ourselves without help. We cannot be saved from damnation without the grace of God, and we likewise need the help of fellow believers to make it through life's troubles.

4, 5. But let every man prove his own work, and then shall he have rejoicing in himself alone, and not in another. For every man shall bear his own burden.

It may seem contradictory for Paul to command us to share in the burdens of others (v. 2, above) and then call each person to *bear his own bur-*

den. Paul is speaking specifically to spiritual leaders here, reinforcing the danger of arrogance in church leaders. Paul commands each such leader to *prove his own work.* Sadly, some find pleasure in leadership only when they are being praised by others. Paul assures them that such praise is empty; as each strives to prove his own work, the leader will not look to another for evaluation.

A frequent theme of Paul is that his ministry is not based on human approval. His job is to be a servant of God, not to be a people pleaser (Galatians 1:10; compare 1 Thessalonians 2:4). Leaders must have a higher standard than crowd approval, else they risk disaster for themselves and great collateral damage for their flock.

It is in this context that each must bear his or her own burden. Leaders are not leading if their actions result in a downward spiral of sin. They must watch their own lives carefully, for they are surely being watched by others.

III. Harvesting from the Spirit
(GALATIANS 6:6-10)
A. Bumper Crop of Life (vv. 6-8)

6. Let him that is taught in the word communicate unto him that teacheth in all good things.

The word *communicate* is not used here in the sense of talking with others (or, in our day, texting others). It means to share materially, to provide monetary or other support for the teachers of the church (see 1 Corinthians 9:14).

Some Christians contend that it is wrong for a church to pay a person who does the tasks of ministry. This is not the attitude that Paul reflects here. Yet this is not a roundabout way of Paul asking the Galatians to send him money. It is more likely an admonition for them to take care of those who have given up their jobs in order to serve the church full-time. If they have received good, solid teaching, they are obligated to share with their teachers.

7, 8. Be not deceived; God is not mocked: for whatsoever a man soweth, that shall he also reap. For he that soweth to his flesh shall of the flesh reap corruption; but he that soweth to the Spirit shall of the Spirit reap life everlasting.

The word Paul uses to refer to mocking God is very descriptive. It is based on the word for *nose* and implies to "turn up one's nose" to God. While the danger of such an action is obvious, Paul indicates that some do this in the way they *soweth,* or invest their lives. If they have turned up the nose to God and invested in gratification of their sinful passions and lusts, the return on investment will be *corruption.* Lest we misunderstand what is meant by this, Paul includes the parallel opposite (antithesis): the one who invests in the things of the Spirit will be rewarded with *life everlasting.*

> *What Do You Think?*
> When was the most recent time you were spiritually deceived? How did things turn out?
> *Talking Points for Your Discussion*
> - Genesis 3:6, 13
> - Obadiah 3
> - Ephesians 5:6
> - Titus 3:3

The import of these contrasting results is not to say that some thumb their nose at God and then go their merry way in sin. It is saying, rather, that yielding to our sinful passions *is* to mock God. What type of harvest do we want? Do we want the bountiful harvest of salvation or the poison crop of destruction?

> *What Do You Think?*
> In what way can you best "sow to the Spirit" today?
> *Talking Points for Your Discussion*
> - In the way you spend money
> - In the way you invest quiet time with God
> - In the way you invest in the life of the church
> - In the way you invest yourself one on one with another Christian

B. Bumper Crop of Good Deeds (vv. 9, 10)

9. And let us not be weary in well doing: for in due season we shall reap, if we faint not.

The instant news coverage of every worldwide disaster has caused many to give up helping. Social scientists describe this problem as *compassion fatigue.* Every church is in danger of coming down with compassion fatigue, even in relation to its own community. Those in need, sometimes dire need, are always with us (compare John 12:8).

Paul gives us hope when this gets us down: there will be a reward for those many good deeds, those acts of compassion. It may come back in the form of someone attracted to a church where compassion is practiced. It may come back many years later when we learn of our help being a turning point in someone's life. Or it may not be rewarded until we face God and hear Him say, "Well done!"

❧ *BEING NOT WEARY* ❧

John Wesley (1703–1791) was one of the major leaders of the eighteenth century Evangelical Revival in England. He had a single-minded devotion to the cause of Christ. His long life gave him opportunities of service few have matched. He rode his horse over most of England, as well as Scotland along with numerous trips to Ireland, as a traveling evangelist. It is estimated that he rode about 8,000 miles a year during his active ministry, totaling over 250,000 miles during his lifetime.

He wrote thousands of letters, many of them while riding his horse. He also edited many of his books while riding. No one has been able to estimate the total number of his sermons. He often preached every day, sometimes as many as eight times a day. It is certain that he often preached over a thousand sermons a year.

If there is anyone since the time of the apostles who was not weary in well doing, it was John Wesley. He continues to be an example to us.

—J. B. N.

10. As we have therefore opportunity, let us do good unto all men, especially unto them who are of the household of faith.

Paul finishes this section by recognizing a certain priority in our acts of kindness and burden-bearing. While we are called to have compassion upon *all men,* our attention should be given first to those *of the household of faith.* As would be the case with any normal family, limited resources are given first to close relatives. If a church truly functions as a family, it will be aware when a brother or sister is in need, even if such a person is too proud to ask for help. This is the time to step up and "bear the burdens of others," as a testimony to all. In so doing, we are truly walking in the Spirit and showing the fruit of the Spirit.

Conclusion

A. Fruit on Display

In a famous art museum near my home, there is a painting by the French painter Paul Cézanne (1839–1906). A central feature of this painting is a bowl of fruit, as in many of the still-life works of this artist. I have spent many minutes pondering this painting, and one thing always impresses me: if taken very literally, Cézanne's perspective seems off-kilter. This is because the artist attempts to provide a level of depth perception for the viewer. The bowl of fruit is presented as if you are looking down on it and looking at if from the side at the same time.

When we consider the spiritual fruit of a Christian, we should expect tangible, observable results. It should not be a flat, lifeless view. It should have depth and vitality. The fruit of our lives should provide nourishment and encouragement to others. Unlike the painter's unchanging still-life bowl of fruit, however, our lives should be ever blossoming and providing seed for fruitful work of ministry.

B. Prayer

O Lord, we are weary and burdened. May we find refuge in Your arms. In so doing, may we shoulder some of the stress of others who are overwhelmed. May Your Spirit give us the strength we need for this ministry. In Jesus' name, amen.

C. Thought to Remember

Ours is a journey of faith and growth in the Holy Spirit.

INVOLVEMENT LEARNING

Some of the activities below are also found in the helpful student book, Adult Bible Class.
Don't forget to download the free reproducible page from www.standardlesson.com to enhance your lesson!

Into the Lesson

Have one or more bowls of fruit on display as learners arrive. Have a note by each: "Please choose and take one." Include exactly nine kinds of fruits. Do not comment as learners select. (If you can't afford to purchase actual fruit, display pictures of fruit instead.)

As class begins say, "From verses 22, 23 of today's text, decide which fruit of the Spirit you can best relate—in some way—to the fruit you chose. There are no 'correct' answers." If you need to give an example, hold up an orange and say, "I relate my orange to longsuffering because this kind of fruit must be peeled at the pace of patience before it can be eaten." Anticipate interesting responses as you allow an explanation of the nature and value of each fruit.

Into the Word

Note that you have nine fruits and that there are nine in Paul's list. If a fruit that Paul names is not included in your class's choices from Into the Lesson, say, "Well, Paul's fruit _____ was not named. Which literal fruit can we liken it to?"

Samples responses by your class can include (1) "apples are like joy, because they bring to mind all the good occasions apples are related to, such as apple pie as part of a celebration," (2) "bananas are like temperance (self-control) because they come in crowds (bunches) where restraint is often needed," (3) "grapes are like faith(fulness) because they give us the 'fruit of the vine' that reminds of the Lord's Supper and the heart of our faith in Christ," (4) "pears are like gentleness, because such an attitude is necessary when we are 'paired' in dealing gracefully with one another," (5) "tangerines are like peace in that differing persons (segments) are held together by the bond of unity."

Undoubtedly, some of your learners will groan as certain analogies seem to be "a bit of a stretch." To those who groan you can offer a good-natured challenge to think up a better way to describe the connection.

Direct learners' attention to verse 24 as you refer back to verses 19-21 (not in today's text), which contain Paul's list of acts of the flesh. Erect a simple wooden cross you have prepared (sturdy enough for the following) and say, "I want volunteers to come, select a sin from this bag [display as you mention], read it aloud, and nail it to this cross." Have a small hammer, tacks, and a bag with slips of paper that bear the sins Paul lists in 5:19-21. Once all are nailed, say, "That's what Paul means: if we are in Christ, all these behaviors and mind-sets are crucified, dead!" (*Alternative:* If you can't use a wooden cross and nails, draw a cross on the board and have learners "nail" the sins to it with masking tape.)

Next, give each learner a large-print copy of Galatians 5:25–6:10, with this direction: "Search these verses for examples of the nine attributes we've studied. Write the words over the text." If learners need an example, point out that both gentleness (in correcting sinners) and self-control (guarding self from the same sin) is seen in 6:1.

Into Life

Download the reproducible page and distribute copies of the Sowing the Spirit activity. Use this to brainstorm class projects that have the nine entries as themes. Begin by asking the class as a whole, "What can we do as a class that will sow and reap the fruit of *joy* in the weeks ahead for our congregation (or our community, etc.)?" Ask this question eight more times, substituting one of the other fruits in each case.

Form "prayer pairs" for a time of reflection; write *Prayer Pears* on the board as a play on words. Distribute copies of the An Inadequate Orchard exercise from the reproducible page. Have learners complete it according to the directions. Ask the pairs to pray for one another.

GOD'S CREATIVE WORD

Special Features

Lessons

Unit 1: In the Beginning Was the Word

Unit 2: Jesus' Powerful Words

Unit 3: I Am . . .

QUARTERLY QUIZ

Use these questions as a pretest or as a review. The answers are on page iv of This Quarter in the Word.

Lesson 1

1. Proverbs presents wisdom as a human tradition that begins after creation. T/F. *Proverbs 8:22*

2. Proverbs promises that keeping the ways of wisdom results in blessing. T/F. *Proverbs 8:32*

Lesson 2

1. The first three words of the Gospel of John are the same as the first three words of the book of _____. *John 1:1*

2. John 1 first presents John the Baptist in what role? (baptizer, prophet, witness?) *John 1:6, 7*

Lesson 3

1. The wedding celebration in Cana ran out of what? (cake, wine, bread?) *John 2:3*

2. Who informed Jesus of the wedding's problem? (His mother, John, the groom?) *John 2:3*

Lesson 4

1. Jesus met with Nicodemus during lunch, the midday meal. T/F. *John 3:2*

2. What did God send His Son *not* to do to the world? (forsake, redeem, condemn?) *John 3:17*

Lesson 5

1. Which celebration was underway when the Jews took Jesus to Pilate? (Passover, Day of Atonement, Tabernacles?) *John 18:28*

2. _____ asked, "What is truth?" *John 18:38*

Lesson 6

1. The first person recorded by John to enter Jesus' empty tomb was _____. *John 20:5, 6*

2. The disciples saw "the linen clothes" and "the napkin" used for Jesus' burial lying together. T/F. *John 20:5-7*

Lesson 7

1. When Jesus spoke of restoring the destroyed temple, He was referring to His _____. *John 2:21*

2. Jesus found what being sold in the temple? (pick three: oxen, goats, sheep, dogs, doves, cats, fish?) *John 2:14*

Lesson 8

1. John was with Jesus when He met the Samaritan woman at the well. T/F. *John 4:7, 8*

2. Jesus said that true worshipers must worship in _____ and in _____. *John 4:24*

Lesson 9

1. The man healed by Jesus had become blind in an accident. T/F. *John 9:1*

2. Some Pharisees were upset because Jesus healed the blind man on the _____. *John 9:16*

Lesson 10

1. Jesus said that it was not _____ who gave bread from Heaven. *John 6:32*

2. Jesus said that He was the bread of what? (of life, of death, of judgment?) *John 6:35*

Lesson 11

1. The good shepherd gives his life for the sheep. T/F. *John 10:11*

2. Hirelings of Jesus' day were known for their bravery in defending sheep. T/F. *John 10:12, 13*

Lesson 12

1. Jesus told Martha that He was the resurrection and the what? (truth, life, spirit?) *John 11:25*

2. Lazarus took off his burial clothes before he came out of the tomb. T/F. *John 11:44*

Lesson 13

1. Thomas confidently affirmed that he knew where Jesus was going. T/F. *John 14:5*

2. Jesus revealed to His disciples that He was one of two ways to the Father. T/F. *John 14:6*

3. Which disciple asked Jesus to "show us the Father"? (Philip, Thomas, Peter?) *John 14:8*

QUARTER AT A GLANCE

IN THE satiric novel *The Hitchhiker's Guide to the Galaxy*, highly intelligent space aliens design a computer program to answer the question of "life, the universe and everything." After eons of time, the computer offers an answer: 42.

Author Douglas Adams was grimly poking fun at the human longing to understand our existence. For him, the best answer—a meaningless number—was really no answer at all. Adams thought that if life even has a meaning, we humans could never understand it. Followers of Jesus see this differently. By ourselves, we could never figure out the meaning of "life, the universe and everything." But God has revealed what we could never have discovered on our own.

The Eternal Word

This quarter's lessons focus on the Gospel of John, which vividly presents Jesus as the answer to life's riddles. Proverbs 8:22-35 provides the background, presenting God's wisdom in personal terms as one who acts with God to create the world and instruct God's people. From there we consider the epic presentation of the eternal Word, who is both eternally present with God and himself God, gives life and light, and becomes flesh to dwell among us (Lesson 2). In this Word is everything that God's wisdom represents—and more.

At His every appearance this Word-become-flesh demands allegiance. He is the worker of mighty signs (Lessons 3 and 9). He is the authoritative ruler (Lesson 7). He is the great teacher who confounds a religious leader (Lesson 4) and an imperial governor (Lesson 5), yet reaches out to a marginalized woman (Lesson 8). He routinely makes claims to be on a par with God himself. Uttering the pregnant phrase "I am," He calls himself "the light of the world" (Lesson 9), "the bread of life" (Lesson 10), "the good shepherd" (Lesson 11), "the resurrection and the life" (Lesson 12), and "the way, the truth, and the life" (Lesson 13).

The God of Life

Who can say and do such things? Is He indeed the eternal Word—who was with God and even was God from eternity, who created everything, even life itself? Could God have become flesh and lived in the world as one of us?

The key to our answer comes in the middle of the quarter, at Easter (Lesson 6). The greatest of Jesus' mighty signs, securing all His claims, is His resurrection. Just as He said, He is the shepherd who gives his life for the sheep (Lesson 11). Just as He said, He raised up the temple of His body, destroyed by His enemies (Lesson 7). Here all the mighty signs reach their climax. Here every bold *I am* has its demonstration. At His resurrection, Jesus, the author of life, defeats death for all time.

Receiving the Answer

So there is an answer to the question of "life, the universe and everything." The answer is Jesus, the Word made flesh.

But there remains a difference between *hearing* the answer and *receiving* the answer. We can ignore the wisdom of God who pleads for our hearts. Like those who saw and heard the Word made flesh, we can know of Jesus' mighty signs and bold claims

> *At His every appearance this Word-become-flesh demands allegiance.*

—even His empty tomb—and still reject Him. Though the Word comes to His own world, we may still refuse to receive Him (John 1:11).

God's own answer to the question of existence is a hard answer. It is hard not because it lies beyond our understanding, but because it demands our lives. As students of the Bible, we face the same challenge as the witnesses of the Word-made-flesh: will we genuinely accept the answer that God has given to that most important question of all?

by Mark S. Krause

CLEMENT OF ALEXANDRIA (about AD 150– 215) called John's Gospel the "spiritual Gospel." By this he meant that John was more concerned with internal, spiritual, and intellectual matters than the other three were. How so?

Engagement with Philosophy

Interest in philosophy ran high in John's day (Acts 17:18-21). Greece had enjoyed a golden age of philosophy several centuries earlier, and we still remember the names Socrates, Plato, and Aristotle today. The Romans were developing their own thinking traditions. The Stoic philosopher Marcus Aurelius became emperor in AD 161, using his philosophical understandings to rule the empire.

The Jews had their own philosophical traditions. We see this in their "wisdom" documents. The books of Job, Proverbs, and Ecclesiastes, in our Bibles today, are examples. The Jews had many nonbiblical wisdom writings as well. Philo (20 BC–AD 50), a Jewish teacher living in Egypt, attempted to harmonize the principles of Greek philosophy with Scripture. Many writers since Philo, both Jewish and Christian, have attempted to blend philosophy with the teachings of the Bible.

John and Philosophy

The apostle John lived into the second and third generations of Christianity. Tradition tells us that he migrated to Ephesus in his old age, dying there about AD 100.

Ephesus was a crossroads for many religions and philosophies. Paul had founded a church there in about AD 54. He used "the school of one Tyrannus" (Acts 19:9) to preach the gospel and engage in debate. This location was likely a place where philosophy was taught. We can say, then, that the Ephesian church was birthed in an environment of Greek philosophy. Paul may have been well versed in such philosophy, but he never allowed it to control his message. He even warned the Colossian church (about 120 miles east of Ephesus) to be wary of philosophy (Colossians 2:8).

The Ephesian church to which John came decades later was still surrounded by this philosophical jungle. The temptation to incorporate pagan Greek ideas into the teachings of Christianity was great, for this could show the faith to be a completion of earlier thought rather than a contradiction. John, like Paul, would not tolerate this. Yes, John sought to engage some of the ideas of the Greeks, but he would not yield to anything that compromised the gospel. John's understandings were controlled by his grounding in the Jewish Scriptures and by his firsthand acquaintance with the teachings of Jesus.

Philosophy and John

All this helps us understand why Clement would label John's Gospel the "spiritual gospel."

John answers certain philosophical questions on the basis of Christian doctrine. John wants his readers to understand the role of the Christ in creation as the pre-existing Word of God (the *logos*, chapter 1). John desires that they understand spiritual rebirth (chapter 3), the role of God's Holy Spirit in the human sphere (chapters 4, 13–16), and spiritual blindness (chapter 9). Readers even are given the Christian perspective on the nature of truth, which is the core of any philosophical system (chapters 8, 14, 19). All of these issues would have been seen as philosophical questions as much as they were religious questions in John's environment.

The questions of philosophy have not changed much over the centuries, only the proposed answers. This quarter we will see that although historical circumstances may change, the answers of the Christian faith remain true and trustworthy.

Answers to the Quarterly Quiz on page 226

Lesson 1—1. false. 2. true. **Lesson 2**—1. Genesis. 2. witness. **Lesson 3**—1. wine. 2. His mother. **Lesson 4**—1. false. 2. condemn. **Lesson 5**—1. Passover. 2. Pilate. **Lesson 6**—1. Simon Peter. 2. false. **Lesson 7**—1. body. 2. oxen, sheep, doves. **Lesson 8**—1. false. 2. spirit, truth. **Lesson 9**—1. false. 2. Sabbath. **Lesson 10**—1. Moses. 2. of life. **Lesson 11**—1. true. 2. false. **Lesson 12**—1. life. 2. false. **Lesson 13**—1. false. 2. false. 3. Philip.

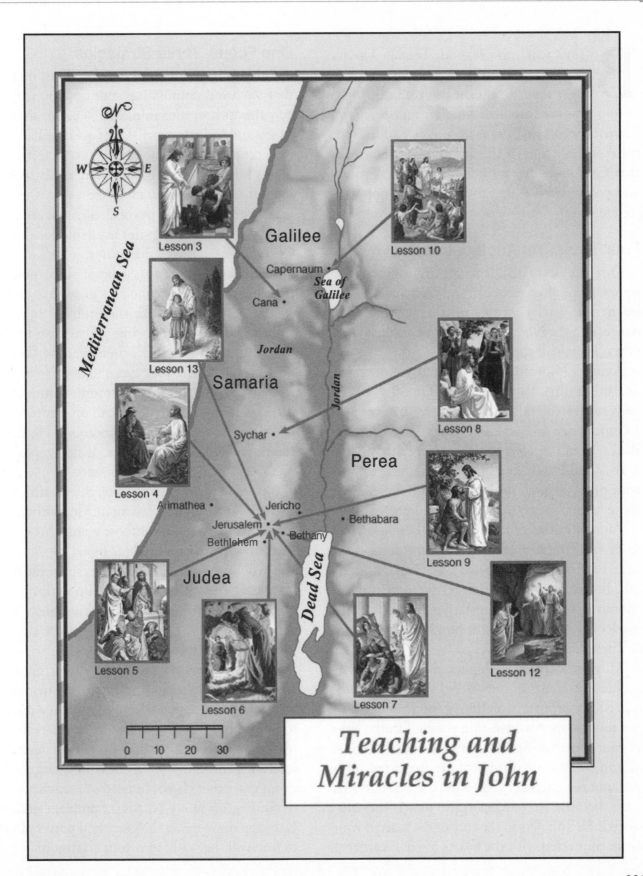

Teaching and Miracles in John

TEACHING THE BOSS

Teacher Tips by Brent L. Amato

B
Y NOW you know that our Teacher Tips for 2011–12 are considering classroom challenges that present themselves in the form of four types of "problem students": *the bored, the barrier, the boss,* and *the bomber.* As we address the third of these four in this installment, remember that God loves every student in His classroom, and you've been called to be an equal opportunity teacher!

Four Types, Yet Another Imperative

Our previous installments highlighted two imperatives: intercessory prayer on behalf of your learners and relating to your learners in accordance with the New Testament "one another" passages. These still apply!

Another imperative is to "parent" your learners as Paul did his. Paul described Timothy as "my own son in the faith" (1 Timothy 1:2; see also 1 Corinthians 4:17 and 2 Timothy 1:2); Titus was Paul's "own son after the common faith" (Titus 1:4). Would your attitudes and actions toward your problem students be different if you viewed those learners as your spiritual children?

Parents know, of course, that there is a time to be confrontational with their children (compare 1 Corinthians 4:14-16; Galatians 3:1; 4:19, 20). But surely a gentle, nurturing mother or an encouraging, comforting father is the primary model for making the most progress with a child (1 Thessalonians 2:11, 12)!

All your learners—whether you view them as problem students or not—need spiritual parenting. Paul's spiritual parenting of the Thessalonians is a touchstone for investing yourself in the lives of your learners: "So being affectionately desirous of you, we were willing to have imparted unto you, not the gospel of God only, but also our own souls, because ye were dear unto us" (1 Thessalonians 2:8). This gets to the core of the matter: your heart connected with the hearts of your learners.

One Focus, Three Strategies

For this installment of Teacher Tips, imagine that *the boss* is dominating your classroom. Can't you almost hear him thinking, "I've got so much to say and so little time!" Can't you see her grabbing center stage and holding on for dear life? *The boss* is lurking in every classroom, ready to stifle the learning process for everyone.

As with the other types of challenging students, there are certain strategies available for dealing with *the boss.* Let's consider three.

First, control the boss. As he or she expounds, take heart that everyone has to take a breath. When that occurs, seize the moment by interrupting with a terminating affirmation by saying, "Interesting point!" Then exercise "benign neglect" by moving your eyes and body away from *the boss* to others in the classroom. Immediately direct your attention and/or call on someone else in a different section of the classroom. Hopefully the boss will get the message. If not, repeat the method as many times as necessary.

Second, connect with the boss. Spend time with *the boss* outside of the classroom. Get with him or her one-on-one and utter those words this kind of student loves to hear: "Tell me more!" By doing so, you will save precious class time, spare the other learners, develop your relationship with *the boss,* and even sharpen your listening skills. Such "overtime" will earn you the right to confront the boss lovingly about the issue.

Third, channel the boss. Like directing water along a strategic path, find other forums for *the boss.* It is desirable to replicate yourself as a teacher, so be mindful that *the boss* may be another effective teacher in disguise. Perhaps this person deserves a teaching platform. Try team-teaching with *the boss* or suggest other classes in need of a teacher.

Never grow weary because of problem students! Just keep drawing on the grace and power of God to teach all that walk into your classroom.

WISDOM'S ORIGIN

DEVOTIONAL READING: Psalm 8
BACKGROUND SCRIPTURE: Proverbs 8

PROVERBS 8:22-35

22 The LORD possessed me in the beginning of his way, before his works of old.

23 I was set up from everlasting, from the beginning, or ever the earth was.

24 When there were no depths, I was brought forth; when there were no fountains abounding with water.

25 Before the mountains were settled, before the hills was I brought forth:

26 While as yet he had not made the earth, nor the fields, nor the highest part of the dust of the world.

27 When he prepared the heavens, I was there: when he set a compass upon the face of the depth:

28 When he established the clouds above: when he strengthened the fountains of the deep:

29 When he gave to the sea his decree, that the waters should not pass his commandment: when he appointed the foundations of the earth:

30 Then I was by him, as one brought up with him: and I was daily his delight, rejoicing always before him;

31 Rejoicing in the habitable part of his earth; and my delights were with the sons of men.

32 Now therefore hearken unto me, O ye children: for blessed are they that keep my ways.

33 Hear instruction, and be wise, and refuse it not.

34 Blessed is the man that heareth me, watching daily at my gates, waiting at the posts of my doors.

35 For whoso findeth me findeth life, and shall obtain favour of the LORD.

KEY VERSE

Hear instruction, and be wise, and refuse it not. —**Proverbs 8:33**

GOD'S CREATIVE WORD

Unit 1: In the Beginning Was the Word

LESSONS 1–6

LESSON AIMS

After participating in this lesson, each student will be able to:

1. List some of the images used to describe wisdom and its origin.

2. Explain the advantages and limitations of using poetic language to describe wisdom.

3. Identify one way he or she can obey the command of Proverbs 8:33.

LESSON OUTLINE

Introduction
   A. Wisdom in Our World
   B. Lesson Background
I. Wisdom's Pedigree (PROVERBS 8:22-31)
   A. Preexistence (vv. 22-26)
      God's Wisdom . . . and Ours
   B. Participation (vv. 27-31)
      Wisdom and Human Life
II. Wisdom's Plea (PROVERBS 8:32-35)
   A. Listen! (vv. 32, 33)
   B. Be Blessed! (vv. 34, 35)
Conclusion
   A. Wisdom and Intelligent Design
   B. Wisdoms Compared
   C. Prayer
   D. Thought to Remember

Introduction

A. Wisdom in Our World

How do we recognize wisdom today? How do we identify wise people? All religions stake some type of claim to wisdom. This is sometimes justified by nothing more than a claim to antiquity: "Our traditions are really old, so they must hold some secret wisdom."

Tradition that has weathered the test of time is certainly an alluring characteristic. But the assumption that teachers of the distant past had a better handle on wisdom than moderns do has no rational basis. In fact, we could argue that later teachers should be wiser because they benefit from the accumulation of learning over the centuries.

Christians believe that while we may find strands of wisdom in many places, the Bible has priority in helping understand the nature of wisdom. The Bible also has priority in showing us what constitutes wise actions as opposed to foolishness. Genuine wisdom is not a human invention, open to endless innovation and modification. Rather, it has its origin in God himself and played a role in the creation of the universe.

B. Lesson Background

The Bible has a lot to say about wisdom, for it is mentioned in about half of its books and discussed extensively in a half dozen. Chief among these is the famous book of Proverbs. Proverbs is a collection of "wise sayings" from King Solomon and other authors. But what makes them "wise"? In order to understand this, we must understand the concept of wisdom from a biblical perspective. Here are three things to keep in mind.

First, true wisdom cannot be divorced from faith in God. Wisdom depends on discerning between good and evil, and these are issues of morality. There is no morality without faith. Therefore, there is no true wisdom without faith. The one who denies God's existence (a person without faith) is the opposite of a wise person (Psalm 14:1).

Second, wisdom is related to knowledge but is not the same thing. Knowledge is recognition and retention of facts. The opposite of knowledge is ignorance. A person with a brain crammed full of facts is not ignorant, but he or she is not necessarily a wise person either. The winner of all the trivia games may live foolishly in almost every aspect of his or her life. Accumulation of knowledge does not make one wise.

Third, then, wisdom is the just and righteous use of knowledge. Once we have learned what God's will is, what God's standards of justice and personal righteousness are, we are counted wise when we choose to obey God.

The book of Proverbs teaches us these things. The book itself falls into three major sections: (1) a long introduction to the collections of the proverbs (Proverbs 1–9); (2) the collections of the proverbs themselves (10:1–31:9); and (3) an acrostic conclusion (31:10-31). Proverbs 8, from which today's lesson comes, thus falls within the introduction.

Solomon, the author of Proverbs 8 (see 1:1), treats wisdom as a person in a poetic way to explain its (in the text, "her") characteristics and source. In using this literary technique (called *personification*), the author is not creating or recognizing another god or goddess. The Egyptians saw Isis as a goddess of wisdom. The Greeks worshipped Athena in this way, and the Romans revered Minerva as a wisdom deity. There is no sense of this here. For the Bible, there is no wisdom apart from God. So while this author uses personification, he is not recognizing or promoting a separate deity.

I. Wisdom's Pedigree
(PROVERBS 8:22-31)
A. Preexistence (vv. 22-26)

22, 23. The LORD possessed me in the beginning of his way, before his works of old. I was set up from everlasting, from the beginning, or ever the earth was.

We should be careful not to take the figurative expressions of these verses (and others) in a casual way that assumes God is like us; even so, we are given insight into wisdom's relationship with God. First, we are told that God *possessed [wisdom] in the beginning*. The language is reminiscent of Genesis 1:1, "In the beginning God . . ."

Second, the wisdom of God was present before *the earth was*. God's wisdom is unlike our own,

which grows by our accumulation of knowledge through trial and error, experimentation, or chance discovery. No one gave wisdom to God, for He already had it at the beginning. Wisdom is part of the nature of God and is therefore uncreated.

> *What Do You Think?*
> In what ways do you see God's eternal wisdom at work?
> *Talking Points for Your Discussion*
> - Within creation (Psalm 8:3)
> - Within family life
> - Within the plan of salvation (Acts 2:38; Ephesians 2:8, 9; etc.)

24. When there were no depths, I was brought forth; when there were no fountains abounding with water.

The preexistence of wisdom continues to be stressed. This time the comparison is with two features of nature that are sources of amazement for ancient people: the seemingly limitless oceans *(depths)* and the sources of water on land coming directly out of the ground *(fountains)*.

For a man with an inquisitive mind like Solomon, there are no answers to the questions that are raised by the existence of these phenomena. How deep are the oceans? How does water bubble out of a natural spring in the desert? The point here is not to explain these wonders, however, but to assert that the wisdom of God is already there at their creation. God does not "get wiser" as a result of trial and error in creating oceans and bubbling springs. God was fully wise all along.

> *What Do You Think?*
> How do people grapple with things that seem to be unexplainable today?
> *Talking Points for Your Discussion*
> - Approaches that include God in the explanation
> - Approaches that exclude God from the explanation

❧ GOD'S WISDOM . . . AND OURS ❧

God's wisdom guided the creation of water as an essential element of life. Its formulation is exactly right. Both fresh water and seawater play vital roles in allowing life to flourish.

We humans often act unwisely in the use of this vital substance. We use it to make beverages that are less than healthy for our bodies. Industrial societies pollute ground water with dangerous chemicals. Primitive societies use "slash and burn" agricultural techniques that contribute to silt buildup in streams, making pure drinking water scarce. The list goes on.

In the case of our water supply, it is abundantly clear that God's wisdom is superior to ours. If our lack of wisdom is so evident with something as basic as water, can we hope that our wisdom will approach God's in any other area?   —C. R. B.

25, 26. Before the mountains were settled, before the hills was I brought forth: while as yet he had not made the earth, nor the fields, nor the highest part of the dust of the world.

This description of creation is continued for the dry parts of the earth. As with the wet parts of oceans and springs (v. 24), wisdom was present at their creation.

Earth's geographical features seem unchanging and eternal to us. Yet the Bible's doctrine of creation assumes that even these seemingly eternal things are not without a beginning, however long ago that might have been. The created physical universe came into being as an act of God at a point in time. When we come to grips with this, we must also accept that wisdom was not created alongside the rest of creation, but was already present and active before creation. The pedigree of wisdom for us is its eternal, uncreated nature.

B. Participation (vv. 27-31)

27. When he prepared the heavens, I was there: when he set a compass upon the face of the depth.

In this verse and the next, the author makes a slight shift from his emphasis on the preexistence of wisdom to the role of wisdom in creation. He does this with a dramatic assertion while describing the creation of the heavenly realm: *I was there.*

The *compass* on the ocean is the horizon, the point at which the heavens and the seas meet

visually. This is another source of wonder for the ancient world, a point that is visible to them, but immeasurably distant. We feel the same amazement today, even with our maps and satellite photo images of the earth. When we stand on the beach and look out at the seemingly limitless ocean, it makes us feel small and vulnerable. Yet God's wisdom not only comprehends this immensity, it rules over it. *I was there.*

28. When he established the clouds above: when he strengthened the fountains of the deep.

This verse alludes to the creative acts of God on the second day of creation (Genesis 1:6-8). People of this time believe that there are sources of water in the oceans that gush continually to keep the seas full (see Genesis 7:11; 8:2). They are well aware that clouds are the source of water from the sky. While they may not have had all the geological and meteorological knowledge we possess today, they understand that nature maintains equilibrium in its water through rain, rivers, and oceans (compare Ecclesiastes 1:7). How this all works is another demonstration of the wisdom of the Creator. God knows exactly how to fine-tune these factors for the benefit of the earth.

29. When he gave to the sea his decree, that the waters should not pass his commandment: when he appointed the foundations of the earth.

This verse reflects the creative acts of God on the third day of creation, when the Creator caused dry land to appear (Genesis 1:9, 10). This separation was necessary in the order of creation so that God could create appropriate life forms for the dry land and for the water (1:20-26). For these vari-

HOW TO SAY IT

Aquinas	Uh-*kwi*-nuss.
Aristotle	*A*-reh-*stot*-tuhl.
Athena	Uh-*thee*-nuh.
Corinthians	Ko-*rin*-thee-unz (*th* as in *thin*).
Isis	*Eye*-sus.
Minerva	Meh-*nur*-vuh.
Ponce de León	Pont-suh day Lee-*own*.
Solomon	*Sol*-o-mun.

ous life forms to have continuity into the future, it was necessary that this division between dry land and sea remain fixed by God's decree (Job 38:8-11). All of this is seen as evidence of the magnificent wisdom of God.

The division between dry land and ocean was removed in the flood of Noah's day. The result was that the living creatures of the earth were destroyed. The only exceptions were those in the ark, which God used as a temporary separator between land and water (Genesis 7:23). While Proverbs does not mention the flood, it too is evidence of the providential wisdom of God acting to preserve His creation as He destroys the irredeemable majority of the human race.

30, 31. Then I was by him, as one brought up with him: and I was daily his delight, rejoicing always before him; rejoicing in the habitable part of his earth; and my delights were with the sons of men.

The personification of wisdom is played up in this picture. The result is that wisdom is seen as a companion and coworker with God in creating the world. We should again remember that this is not intended to teach that there was another god or goddess alongside the Lord God Almighty.

Many Christians believe, however, that this reflects a Trinitarian sense upon the acts of creation. Genesis speaks of the presence of the Spirit of God at creation (Genesis 1:2). The New Testament pictures the Son of God as an active agent of creation (Colossians 1:16; compare John 1:1-3). While the passage before us does not speak directly of the Messiah, the personification of wisdom does bear resemblance to the New Testament's understanding of the Son of God as the Word of God (John 1:1; Hebrews 11:3). Next week's lesson will explore this more fully.

> **What Do You Think?**
> When you view creation, what feelings do you have and why?
> *Talking Points for Your Discussion*
> ▪ Things that cause joy
> ▪ Things that cause humility
> ▪ Things that cause hope

Earth's axis is tilted 23.5 degrees from vertical. It is this tilt that gives us our seasons. For example, the axis is pointed away from the sun during winter in the northern hemisphere, so that solar radiation must travel through about twice the atmosphere as it does in the summer.

The tilt causes the seasonal effects of warmer and cooler weather along with the trade winds circling the globe that bring us our weather. The climatic effects of the axial tilt on the landmass of the earth have made some parts more habitable than others throughout most of human history.

Today we have the ability to heat and cool buildings and vehicles efficiently and conveniently. Thus we can say that "the habitable part of his earth" is somewhat larger today than it was in ancient times. But we dare not allow our technological achievements to result in arrogance, a modern Tower of Babel. When we are no longer able to see God's wisdom in how the world is constructed, then we are in big trouble!   —C. R. B.

II. Wisdom's Plea
(PROVERBS 8:32-35)
A. Listen! (vv. 32, 33)

32, 33. Now therefore hearken unto me, O ye children: for blessed are they that keep my ways. Hear instruction, and be wise, and refuse it not.

Visual for Lesson 1. *Start a discussion by turning this statement into a question: "How is wisdom a gift from God?"*

This section puts a practical spin on the magnificence of God's wisdom, as wisdom speaks directly to the reader. Wisdom is not something to be marveled at and then ignored. Wisdom demands to be heard and obeyed. If godly, wise instruction is received and realized in actions, the student will be counted *wise* and will be *blessed*. Other proverbs warn of the consequences of being a fool, that is, one who rejects wisdom (Proverbs 10:8, 10, 14, etc.).

We do not become wise by pondering our own navels or getting wrapped up in our own musing. Proverbs is written for the express purpose of providing godly wisdom to those willing to listen. Our wisdom comes from listening to a proven source of wisdom (see Proverbs 4:1). The one who has access to a wise teacher but refuses to listen is a "scorner" (see Proverbs 13:1), the same as the "fool."

Many cultures have used the owl as a symbol for wisdom. For example, Athena, the Greek goddess of wisdom, is often depicted with an owl perched on her arm as a sign of wisdom. Owls have been accorded this status because they have been observed watching and listening patiently for their prey. The old nursery rhyme expresses it this way:

A wise old owl lived in an oak,
The more he saw, the less he spoke.
The less he spoke, the more he heard.
Why can't we all be like that wise old bird?

The moral of the rhyme is that we are not wise because we do not listen (Proverbs 18:13).

> **What Do You Think?**
> In what areas do you need to listen more to God and thus gain godly wisdom?
> *Talking Points for Your Discussion*
> - Proverbs 16:16
> - Proverbs 19:8
> - 2 Corinthians 1:12
> - James 3:17

B. Be Blessed! (vv. 34, 35)

34. Blessed is the man that heareth me, watching daily at my gates, waiting at the posts of my doors.

This verse encourages us to be more than mere passive receivers of wisdom. We should be seekers of wisdom. We should be like the man watching for a visitor at the gates of the city or the doors of his house. We should have a thirst for the righteous wisdom of God as it has been revealed to us (compare Matthew 5:6).

King Solomon's reputation for wisdom spread throughout the world of his day, and many journeyed to hear him (1 Kings 4:29-34; 2 Chronicles 9:22). The most famous of these was the Queen of Sheba, who came to Jerusalem with riches and questions for the wise king (1 Kings 10:1, 2); she was not disappointed (10:6-9). We do well to heed his wisdom (1 Kings 4:32; Proverbs 1:1; 10:1; etc.).

> **What Do You Think?**
> What do you do to seek wisdom from God? What should you do?
> *Talking Points for Your Discussion*
> - In your prayer life
> - In private worship
> - In corporate worship
> - In serving

35. For whoso findeth me findeth life, and shall obtain favour of the LORD.

This section ends with two promises related to wisdom. They should motivate us to seek wisdom. First, the one who finds wisdom will find life, an allusion to the quest for the supernatural tree of paradise (compare Revelation 2:7). Wisdom is said to be a "tree of life" in Proverbs 3:18, evoking the images of the tree of life that exists in Paradise (see Genesis 2:9; Revelation 22:2).

Access to the tree of life brings happiness to those who find it (again, Proverbs 3:18). But we do not need to tramp through the swamps of Florida like Ponce de León did in search of the Fountain of Youth. The effects of wisdom begin to give us life as soon as we incorporate them into our lives. Our lives are better and more fulfilling the more they are aligned with the wisdom of God as revealed in Proverbs and the other books of the Bible.

Second, the seeker of wisdom will also find the *favour of the Lord.* The word *favor* in this context is related to our word *will* in the sense of what one desires to be done. If we walk in the ways of wisdom, we find ourselves squarely in the will of God. We are living as God wants us to live, and therefore in harmony with our created nature and purpose.

Living wisely (according to God's will) is not a ticket to Heaven, for we cannot earn our salvation. Salvation is a gift received by the grace and mercy of God. However, living wisely has benefits for the present. When we live in wise obedience to God, we will find many blessings. On the other hand, living foolishly brings a host of self-inflicted hardships and pain. Not every unfortunate thing that comes upon us is the result of our bad choices. But we are stubbornly foolish to deny the damage of our bad, unwise decisions. The wise person is not exempt from suffering in this life, for bad things can and do happen to righteous people (see Ecclesiastes 9:11, 12). But wise living is the best course.

Conclusion

A. Wisdom and Intelligent Design

Efforts to require the teaching of the theory of intelligent design alongside the theory of evolution have made headlines in recent years. The proponents of intelligent design claim that the complexity and integration of the universe make it impossible to suppose it came into being through a random process (as atheistic evolutionists claim).

This actually is an old argument, dating back to Thomas Aquinas (1225–1247), even to Aristotle (384–322 BC). If there is a design to the universe, there must be a designer. While such a proposal seems modest to many, it has been attacked by secularists as a veiled attempt to teach religion in public schools as well as by some Christians as a watered down, unacceptable version of the biblical account of creation.

In today's lesson, however, we are taught more than that the order of the universe is a created design. God's creation is more than complexity and more than beauty. The wisdom of God is displayed in His creation. It is not just that God is the skilled Creator; He is the wise Creator. We could even say that the universe as created by God is a wise creation, for it is a reflection of its Creator.

This is a profound insight, not easily dismissed or comprehended. We are wise to ponder it.

B. Wisdoms Compared

About AD 52, the apostle Paul came to the Greek cities of Athens and Corinth. The Greeks were famous for their desire to hear the newest teachers (Acts 17:19-21). Many such teachers spouted their philosophies as self-credentialed experts. This gave Paul an instant audience. They were ready to hear what he had to say.

But when Paul preached, he proved that he was not like the other traveling teachers. He did not portray himself as a fount of wisdom as the Greek teachers did. And he did not demand that his adoring hearers lavish him with money and gifts.

Paul found that some wanted to be astounded by words of philosophical wisdom. Paul recognized these itching ears (compare 2 Timothy 4:3). He said, "The Greeks seek after wisdom" (1 Corinthians 1:22). But Paul just preached the gospel—he preached "Christ crucified" (1:23). This seemed like foolish talk to the more sophisticated pagans. Paul's profound and ironic comment is, "The foolishness of God is wiser than men" (1:25). As we seek to be wise in the way of godly, biblical wisdom, may we also be humble and grateful for wisdom we may gain through God's Word.

C. Prayer

All-knowing, all-wise God, nothing is hidden from You. Forgive us when we try to be wise without You. Give us Your holy wisdom so we may know Your will and obey it. May we truly build the houses of our lives on the rock that is higher than we are. In the name of Jesus, amen.

D. Thought to Remember

Wisdom apart from God—isn't.

VISUALS FOR THESE LESSONS

The visual pictured in each lesson (example: page 237) is a small reproduction of a large, full-color poster included in the *Adult Resources* packet for the Spring Quarter. That packet also contains the very useful *Presentation Helps* on a CD for teacher use. Order No. 020039212 from your supplier.

INVOLVEMENT LEARNING

Some of the activities below are also found in the helpful student book, Adult Bible Class.
Don't forget to download the free reproducible page from www.standardlesson.com to enhance your lesson!

Into the Lesson

Have the hymn "Immortal, Invisible" playing in the background as learners arrive. As class begins, ask if anyone can identify the song and sing or recite the first stanza. If no one does, read it: "Immortal, invisible, God only wise, / In light inaccessible hid from our eyes, / Most blessed, most glorious, the Ancient of Days, / Almighty, victorious, Thy great Name we praise."

Ask, "How do these words speak to wisdom's origin?" Someone may note the phrase, "God only wise." Point out that ultimate wisdom issues only from Him, the true source of wisdom, as today's text affirms and clarifies. Have someone read James 3:17, which characterizes godly wisdom.

Alternative: Establish study pairs to look at 1 Corinthians 1:17-31. Say, "The Spirit's words through Paul in 1 Corinthians are essential in a study of wisdom from God's perspective." Ask each pair to write "Simple and Profound Truths About Wisdom" in five words or less. Ask volunteers to read their lists. Expect statements such as the following to be offered: (1) Human wisdom ignores the cross; (2) God overwhelms human wisdom; (3) God makes worldly wisdom foolish (4) Christ crucified is God's wisdom; (5) God chooses the "unwise"; (6) Christ Jesus is God's wisdom.

Comment: "Anything that purports to be wisdom that does not issue from the wisdom of God is not wisdom at all."

Into the Word

Distribute handouts with the following observations. The verse notations in italics are from Proverbs 8; do not include these on the handouts. 1. Wisdom is seen as one who rejoices with God in His creation *(vv. 30, 31)*. 2. Water from rain maintains equilibrium in the rivers and oceans; God fine-tuned these factors for the benefit of the earth *(vv. 28, 29)*. 3. If we walk in the ways of wisdom, we will find life and favor with God *(v. 35)*.

4. Blessings come to those who watch and listen daily for God's wisdom *(v. 34)*. 5. Wisdom is part of the nature of God—always has been *(vv. 22, 23)*. 6. Before the mountains and hills were created, there was wisdom *(vv. 25, 26)*. 7. Wisdom was involved in setting the boundaries of the heavens and the earth *(v. 27)*. 8. Our wisdom comes from listening to a proven source *(vv. 32, 33)*. 9. Even the most mysterious marvels of nature are a reflection of God's wisdom *(v. 24)*.

Include these directions on the handouts: "Identify one or two verses from Proverbs 8:22-35 that relate best to each. Make sure to use all 14 verses exactly once each." After giving time for reading and responding, go through the items. Disagreement on verse(s) will stimulate discussion and a close look at the text.

Into Life

Give your learners copies of the following fill-in-the-blank sentence:

"W _ _ _ I _ _ W _ _ _,
I L _ _ _ _ _ _ T _ G _ _;
W _ _ _ I _ _ N _ _,
I I_ _ _ _ _ H _ _!"

Ask learners to suggest fill-in letters. With each correct suggestion, indicate where it goes at every point. The answer is *When I am wise, I listen to God; when I am not, I ignore Him!* After a few letters, someone probably will decipher the whole thought. Challenge learners to let this thought, drawn from Proverbs 8:33, be their motto.

Alternative: Download the reproducible page and distribute copies of the Where Do You Get Your Wisdom? activity. Allow learners time to complete it individually, then discuss it as a class or in small groups.

Distribute copies of the Making Time to Listen activity from the reproducible page as learners depart.

THE WORD BECAME FLESH

DEVOTIONAL READING: Isaiah 40:21-26
BACKGROUND SCRIPTURE: John 1:1-18

JOHN 1:1-14

1 In the beginning was the Word, and the Word was with God, and the Word was God.

2 The same was in the beginning with God.

3 All things were made by him; and without him was not any thing made that was made.

4 In him was life; and the life was the light of men.

5 And the light shineth in darkness; and the darkness comprehended it not.

6 There was a man sent from God, whose name was John.

7 The same came for a witness, to bear witness of the Light, that all men through him might believe.

8 He was not that Light, but was sent to bear witness of that Light.

9 That was the true Light, which lighteth every man that cometh into the world.

10 He was in the world, and the world was made by him, and the world knew him not.

11 He came unto his own, and his own received him not.

12 But as many as received him, to them gave he power to become the sons of God, even to them that believe on his name:

13 Which were born, not of blood, nor of the will of the flesh, nor of the will of man, but of God.

14 And the Word was made flesh, and dwelt among us, (and we beheld his glory, the glory as of the only begotten of the Father,) full of grace and truth.

KEY VERSE

The Word was made flesh, and dwelt among us, (and we beheld his glory, the glory as of the only begotten of the Father,) full of grace and truth. —**John 1:14**

Photo: Medioimages / Photodisc / Thinkstock

GOD'S CREATIVE WORD

Unit 1: In the Beginning Was the Word

LESSONS 1–6

LESSON AIMS

After participating in this lesson, each student will be able to:

1. List some identifying characteristics of "the Word."

2. Tell how the incarnation of the Word is important.

3. Suggest at least one way he or she can bear witness to the light (the Word).

LESSON OUTLINE

Introduction
  A. Creation Accounts
  B. Lesson Background
 I. Creation by the Word (JOHN 1:1-5)
  A. With and Was (vv. 1, 2)
  B. Life and Light (vv. 3-5)
 II. Witness to the Word (JOHN 1:6-11)
  A. Forerunner to the Light (vv. 6-8)
  B. The True Light (vv. 9-11)
   Lighting the Way
III. Incarnation of the Word (JOHN 1:12-14)
  A. Power of Faith (vv. 12, 13)
  B. Visitation of Glory (v. 14)
   Bringing New Life
Conclusion
  A. Why the God-Man?
  B. Prayer
  C. Thought to Remember

Introduction

A. Creation Accounts

Where do you turn in the Bible to learn about creation? Most students go to Genesis, and this is an excellent place to start. The first book in our Bible begins with a broad, panoramic description of the days of creation (Genesis 1:1–2:3). A second telling of creation follows immediately (2:4-25). But other books in the Old Testament include creation references too (see Exodus 20:11; Job 38:4-11; Psalm 8:3; 90:2; Isaiah 40:26; 45:7, 12, 18; and Amos 4:13). A consistent theme is that creation is to be understood as an intentional plan, skillfully and powerfully executed by God the Creator.

The New Testament also has many references to God's work of creation. The central argument of Paul's address to the Greek philosophers in Athens was based on a common knowledge of God as the Creator of the world, and therefore of all humans (Acts 17:24-28). In Romans, Paul's account of the progression of sin among humans begins with praise of God's creating and creation (Romans 1:20; compare Genesis 1:31; 1 Timothy 4:4).

Unlike the writers of the Old Testament, the New Testament authors find a place for Christ in their references to creation (compare Colossians 1:15-17; Hebrews 1:2). The greatest of these "Christ as Creator" texts is the first part of the Gospel of John, our lesson text for this week.

B. Lesson Background

Although the author is not named, we credit the fourth Gospel to the apostle John. There are several reasons for this, including certain references within the book (John 13:23; 19:26; 21:7) and in early tradition outside the book. The book gives no pretense of being the dispassionate history we might expect from modern historians. John writes passionately about Jesus as teacher, friend, and Savior. John wants the reader to know the eternal significance of the being who was God in human form, who visited humanity for a brief time.

John's knowledge of Jesus and the significance of His person are unsurpassed and unique. In his zeal to give a picture of Jesus and His work, John includes information that goes beyond eyewitness

               The Word Became Flesh

recollections. Some of what he tells us could only have come to him through the insights of divine revelation. For example, he goes behind and earlier than Jesus' nativity to Christ's role in creation. That's where today's lesson—and John's Gospel itself—begins.

I. Creation by the Word
(John 1:1-5)
A. With and Was (vv. 1, 2)

1, 2. In the beginning was the Word, and the Word was with God, and the Word was God. The same was in the beginning with God.

In simple yet profound language, John lays out his explanation for Jesus' prehuman existence. The Greek term translated *Word* is famous in both the history of philosophy and doctrine. It is the word *logos,* and it has influenced the English language in many ways. From *logos* we get the word *logic,* indicating an orderly and consistent pattern of thinking. Any English term ending in *-logy* incorporates *logos* with another term and refers to the orderly and systematic study of a subject. Think of the words *psychology, biology,* and *ecology.*

The ancient Greek philosophers asked many questions about the nature of the world, a world most believed to be the creation of various "gods." Their questions were like this: Why is there a consistency to the natural world? Why does the sun rise in the east every day? Why is there an annual cycle of seasons? These philosophers were able to understand natural laws well enough to predict these phenomena with amazing accuracy, but this did not answer how these laws of nature came to be or who enforced them.

Some philosophers proposed that there is an ordering principle to the universe that is beyond human control. This they called the *logos.* For some, the *logos* was an impersonal force; for others, it was more like a god or goddess. But while these philosophers were aware of this transcendent

HOW TO SAY IT

Colossians	Kuh-*losh*-unz.
logos (Greek)	*law*-goss.

power, they had no inkling of the *logos* as a person who cared anything about men and women.

The apostle John's "one God" background from Judaism (Deuteronomy 6:4) is foundational to his Christian beliefs. He has no interest in speculating about the mythical "gods" of Greek paganism. Yet John knows that if Jesus is truly the Son of God, then there is a need to explain His existence before His human birth. Thus John chooses the term *Word (logos)* to label this state of preexistence. John is not depending on Greek thought, but on the rich creation tradition of his own Jewish Scriptures. For John, the best way to understand the mystery of God's creation is the picture found in Genesis 1, where God speaks creation into existence. This was the powerful and creative Word of God in action.

The Word *(logos)* was both *with God* and *was God* in the beginning. This makes no sense at first glance, from either a Jewish or a Greek perspective. How can the *logos* both be *with* God and *be* God at the same time? The first idea implies separation; the second implies unity. How can this be?

As a Jew, John is not going to allow for more than one God. At the same time, John wants his readers to realize that God's nature is complex. There are relationships and roles within the Godhead, and this is nothing new (compare 1 Corinthians 8:5, 6). It was the situation *in the beginning* (see Genesis 1:1). Both the *with* and the *was* are true.

B. Life and Light (vv. 3-5)

3. All things were made by him; and without him was not any thing made that was made.

The *him* of this and the following verses refers most specifically to the Word *(logos)* and more generally to God. John gives us two demanding, absolute statements here that are difficult to qualify or dilute. These two statements together mean that the Word was not a part-time assistant in the work of creation, but was the primary agent of the entire thing. Paul echoes this in Colossians 1:16. There is no created thing in the universe that does not find its source in the creative Word of God (compare Hebrews 1:2).

The two statements in the verse before us also mean that the Word himself was not created. John

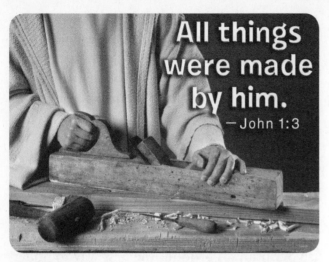

All things were made by him.
— John 1:3

Visual for Lesson 2. *Point to this visual as you introduce the discussion question that is associated with John 1:3.*

has already implied this by saying the Word was there at the beginning, but this verse adds clarity. This helps us understand Colossians 1:15, which calls the preexistent Christ "the firstborn of every creature" (compare Romans 8:29; Hebrews 1:6). To be *firstborn* does not mean the Word is a created being who was somehow *born first.* Rather, *firstborn* refers to priority in that context. As far back as our perspective allows us to imagine ("the beginning"), the Father and Son/Word were already there.

> **What Do You Think?**
> How does the fact that Christ is Creator affect you personally?
> *Talking Points for Your Discussion*
> - Regarding your thoughts
> - Regarding your actions
> - Regarding your speech patterns

4. In him was life; and the life was the light of men.

John now introduces two key concepts of his Gospel: *life* and *light* (compare John 8:12). In Genesis, "life" is not a created thing so much as it is a gift from the Creator. The creation of man is pictured as the forming of a lifeless body, then breathing "the breath of life" into it. Only then does the man become a "living soul" (Genesis 2:7).

All living beings depend on God for life. Despite outlandish claims, scientists will never create true life in a laboratory or by using computers. There is no life apart from God (compare John 5:21). The mission of the Son is to bring life that is never subject to death—eternal life (John 5:24; compare 6:47; 20:31).

Directly connected with this divine life is light. John calls this the *light of men,* but he is not talking about light that has a human source, something we turn off and on like a flashlight. We would better understand this as "light for men." This is a reference to revelation—divine enlightenment given to men and women. John will have much more to say about this topic later in the book, for he understands Jesus as the "light of the world" (John 9:5).

5. And the light shineth in darkness; and the darkness comprehended it not.

In Genesis, the creation of light involves separating it from darkness (Genesis 1:3, 4). Darkness, however, is not created. Darkness is the absence of light. From a physical standpoint, darkness has no power to overcome light. Even a small candle will produce light in a pitch-dark cave. There is no anti-candle of darkness that dims bright sunlight.

This fact is important for understanding the word *comprehended.* This word has a broad sense here. It refers to complete mastery of something and therefore control over it. For darkness to have such a power over the light would mean that the light could be extinguished by darkness. John is not saying that the forces of darkness have merely misunderstood Jesus; rather, those forces have lost any battle to control or defeat the Son of God. This is a figurative way of understanding the resurrection, for it is the triumph of both life and light.

> **What Do You Think?**
> What are some ways that you have seen the light of Christ overcome the darkness of this world?
> *Talking Points for Your Discussion*
> - In personal habits
> - In your family
> - In your church
> - Concerning a coworker or friend

The Word Became Flesh

II. Witness to the Word

(JOHN 1:6-11)

A. Forerunner to the Light (vv. 6-8)

6. There was a man sent from God, whose name was John.

Having painted a picture using a gigantic cosmic brush, John now narrows his focus to human history. He begins the events of the Gospel with *John*—not the apostle John, but John the Baptist (compare Matthew 3:1; Mark 1:4; Luke 1:13).

7. The same came for a witness, to bear witness of the Light, that all men through him might believe.

John the Baptist becomes God's witness to many important things. To him it is given to see the Spirit of God come upon Jesus at His baptism (Matthew 3:13-17; John 1:32-34). John has the insight that Jesus is the "Lamb of God," the perfect sacrifice for sins (John 1:29, 36). John also knows that Jesus will bring the Holy Spirit to His followers (John 1:33; compare 20:22).

8. He was not that Light, but was sent to bear witness of that Light.

John the Baptist ends up being a type of light in that he is a conduit or channel of revelation from God to the people of Israel. John is *not that Light,* however, for he is no more than a gifted human instrument of God. All of his information is received from God. He can pass along only that which he is told, so he is a secondary source.

The true Light comes after John the Baptist prepares the way (John 1:23). We see this when Jesus begins His public ministry, and John points some of his disciples to Jesus (1:35-37). John the Baptist recognizes that he himself must "decrease" as Jesus must "increase" (3:30).

What Do You Think?

What can you do to improve the way you bear witness to the Light, Jesus Christ?

Talking Points for Your Discussion

- Issues of preparation
- Issues of technique
- Issues of consistency between "talk" and "walk"

B. The True Light (vv. 9-11)

9. That was the true Light, which lighteth every man that cometh into the world.

Now the author introduces the Word himself into human history, for He comes *into the world.* By referring to Him as *the true Light,* the apostle John is not implying that the message of John the Baptist was a false light. Rather, the author means that any revelation that comes from John the Baptist was incomplete and limited in audience. The true Light gives light to *every man,* not just to the Jewish audiences of John the Baptist.

This is John's first use of another key category of terms: *true* or *truth.* Truth is a primary characteristic of God, and all truth comes from God (see John 3:33). A central aspect of John's portrayal of Jesus is that His life and message are a revelation (light) of truth and that this truth has the power to give freedom (8:32). This task of bringing the truth to the disciples of Jesus is continued by the Holy Spirit, the Spirit of truth (16:13).

❧ LIGHTING THE WAY ❧

In the late 1880s, the first automobile headlights were acetylene lamps. The first electric headlamps appeared in 1898. Low beam headlamps followed in 1915, but it wasn't until 1924 that high and low beams were incorporated into a single bulb. Fog lamps came along in 1938, followed by sealed beam headlamps in 1940.

The next major advance was halogen bulbs, introduced in 1962. Replaceable lamp bulbs were permitted in the U.S. in 1983. The high-intensity discharge (HID) lamps of the 1990s did not catch on in America, but may do so yet. Headlamps using light-emitting diodes (LEDs) are now under development. All of this is part of the relentless search for the most efficient, convenient, and safe way to illuminate the road at night.

How sadly ironic it is to see humans searching for a better physical light while overlooking God's solution to moral darkness. John identifies Jesus as the true source of light. We will live in earthly and eternal darkness if we reject him.   —C. R. B.

10, 11. He was in the world, and the world was made by him, and the world knew him not.

He came unto his own, and his own received him not.

The author now uses his previous point that all things were created by the Word to tell us of the greatest irony in human history. When the Word humbled himself to enter our time and space (Philippians 2:7, 8), the Creator was neither recognized nor accepted by His creatures (compare Romans 1:25). More specifically, He came to *his own,* probably a reference to the nation of Israel, God's special possession (see Exodus 19:5). John does not say why at this point, but simply notes this tragic twist of events. Later, John attributes this rejection to simple unbelief (John 3:18; 6:36; 12:37). Those who refuse to believe in Jesus have rejected light, life, and truth.

What Do You Think?

What are some reasons that people fail to "receive" Christ?

Talking Points for Your Discussion

- Reasons that never seem to change
- Reasons that seem to come and go
- Reasons that seem to be new (but maybe really aren't)

III. Incarnation of the Word
(John 1:12-14)
A. Power of Faith (vv. 12, 13)

12. But as many as received him, to them gave he power to become the sons of God, even to them that believe on his name.

Not all are unbelievers, though. The ones who receive the Son of God are the ones who *believe on his name.* This is an unusual expression for us because normally we do not speak of faith in names. In John's day, however, to place faith in a person's name is to place one's faith in that person himself in an unreserved manner.

The power of faith comes back to the believer as he or she becomes a child of God. This rings of restored creation, of reentry into the family of God (see Galatians 4:5). It is a reversal of the sin of Adam and Eve, which resulted in expulsion from the garden and, therefore, from the immediate presence of God.

13. Which were born, not of blood, nor of the will of the flesh, nor of the will of man, but of God.

A fourth key theme is now introduced: *born.* The idea of new birth is central to the message and mission of Jesus. How do we become new children of God? We must be born again (John 3:3). This cannot be some type of physical birth, however. A person cannot squeeze back into his or her mother's womb (3:4). It is not the result of a human pregnancy caused by *the will of man.* Rather, the new birth is of God. It is a spiritual birth. It is an act of new creation by the Creator of the universe (compare 2 Corinthians 5:17; James 1:18; 1 Peter 1:23).

B. Visitation of Glory (v. 14)

14a. And the Word was made flesh, and dwelt among us, (and we beheld his glory, the glory as of the only begotten of the Father,)

How can all this happen: life, light, truth, and new birth? It required that the eternal Word of God take human form *(made flesh)* and live among men and women. We refer to this as "the incarnation" of Christ, literally "the enfleshment" of God.

John introduces himself as the narrator of this marvelous story for the first time by adding a personal note: *we beheld his glory.* Some believe this is a reference to the transfiguration of Jesus (not mentioned in John, but see Matthew 17:1-9). This may be part of it, but more likely John is referring to his personal experience with the resurrected Christ. Jesus lives an extraordinary life, dies an atoning, prophecy-fulfilling death, and then comes back from the dead. To describe that as *glory,* a term reserved by the Jews for God alone, is understandable.

Having presented the Christ as the eternal agent of creation, the bringer of life and light to humankind, and God in human form, John gives a couple more ways of understanding who this person is. He is the *only begotten of the Father.* This is later expanded to the "only begotten Son" (John 3:16). This expression does not imply a time when the Word did not exist, for "the Word is God." It is better to understand this as a contrast with our new birth as children of God (1:12). We can be restored to God's family, but we will never be a

Son of God in the way Jesus is. He is the unique and eternal Son of God, and no one will ever take His place.

What Do You Think?

What spiritual advantages did those who saw Jesus in the flesh have that we don't have today, if any? What advantages do we have today that they didn't have, if any? Why are these questions important?

Talking Points for Your Discussion

- Issues concerning technology
- Issues concerning 2,000 years of church history
- Issues regarding human nature

❧ BRINGING NEW LIFE ❧

Lost limbs and battle-scarred flesh decrease the quality of life for wounded military personnel. Burn victims suffer disfigurement. Diseased hearts, kidneys, livers, and other organs cause death for many.

But hope is on the way because of the efforts of researchers at the Wake Forest Institute for Regenerative Medicine. As a result of this institute's efforts, patients have been receiving lab-grown bladders (from the patients' own cells) since 1999. Burn victims and muscular dystrophy patients have more hope because of the use of stem cells from the patients' own bone marrow. Work is progressing on regenerating heart valves and muscle tissue.

We may well consider these medical advances as gifts from God. However, we need to keep things in perspective: God's greatest gift in human flesh came not as a replacement of diseased tissue, but in the form of the incarnate Word. He came to bring us the kind of regeneration that only God can give. Unlike any medical advances, His gift results in new life for eternity.   —C. R. B.

14b. Full of grace and truth.

A final way of understanding the Christ in our lesson is found in an addition to the concept of *truth*. The Christ indeed brings life, light, and truth. But for us to understand this better, John now describes the human Jesus as *full of grace and truth*. The term *grace* emphasizes the gift nature of God's revelation to us through Christ. It is not something we deserve or earn. We can never earn the right to know anything about God. The visitation of God in human form could have been an event of terror for sinful men and women, but that was not the case. It was an act of profound grace, a central characteristic of the Son of God (see John 1:16, 17).

Conclusion
A. Why the God-Man?

One of the most significant works of medieval Christian scholars was Anselm's *Cur Deus Homo* (meaning *Why the God Man?*). Anselm's primary question is, "For what cause or necessity [did] God become man?" We can get lost in Anselm's learned argument, but his simple answer is that the incarnation of the Christ, the coming of the Son of God in human form, was the only way God could redeem sinful humanity. Our sin left us in a helpless state—lost and unable to save ourselves. Only God could provide a sacrifice to cover our sins: the spotless Lamb of God (John 1:29; compare Revelation 7:14).

Anselm sounds a note similar to the opening verses of John. The coming of the Son of God to bring salvation to the world was an act based on the gracious love of God for His creation, for His lost children. It is through our faith in the living Christ that we can be saved, we can be born again as children of God.

B. Prayer

God our Creator, we thank You for loving us so much! We thank You for Jesus, who became like us in order to save us. We thank You for ways in which Jesus revealed You to us as our gracious Father. We thank You for the life, light, and truth He has brought to us. We pray this in the name of Your only begotten Son; amen.

C. Thought to Remember

Both Christ's humanity and His divinity
are key for our salvation.

INVOLVEMENT LEARNING

Some of the activities below are also found in the helpful student book, Adult Bible Class.
Don't forget to download the free reproducible page from www.standardlesson.com to enhance your lesson!

Into the Lesson

Place in chairs copies of the Word Up activity, from the reproducible page you have downloaded, for learners to work on as they arrive.

Wear heavy galoshes to class. As learners express interest, say, "Well, we're heading into some deep ideas today!" That will allow you to introduce the concept of Jesus as Creator and Word, both significant doctrinal ideas.

Randomly distribute cards with the following "deep" questions: 1. What do you think God was doing before He created the heavens and the earth? 2. How could John, mortal that he was, conceptualize things eternal? 3. Is it easier to think of eternity in the past or eternity in the future? Why? 4. How is it possible for a nonphysical God to be born into a body of flesh?

Introduce the questions by saying, "Those holding cards are going to read questions that will put your head into a spin. Those of you who have a question read them now, one at a time, but without pausing between questions." After the questions are read, exclaim, "Whew! That's more than my finite mind can deal with. Perhaps the issues raised in John 1 will be easier to grasp."

Into the Word

Say, "I want to see if you are smarter than fifth graders. I will assign a clause from today's text (John 1:1-14) to each of you. Your job is to identify the simple subject and verb of the statement given." If you think a reminder is necessary, use this example: *The Lord's Day is the first day of my week,* in which you identify the subject as *Day* and verb as *is.*

Have individual clauses from the lesson text written on separate slips of paper to distribute. For example, verse 1 has three clauses that you will write on three slips of paper, one each: "In the beginning was the Word" and "the Word was with God" and "the Word was God." John 1:1-14 can be divided into about 30 primary clauses in this manner.

After allowing time for decision, work your way through the text and allow learners to reveal their responses. The series will read something like this: *Word was / Word was / Word was / same was / things were made / thing was (not) made / life was / life was / light shineth / darkness comprehended (not) / man was sent / name was / same came / men might believe / he was (not) / [he] was sent / that was / that cometh / He was / world was made / world knew (not) / he came / own received (not) / many received / he gave / them that believe / were born / Word was made and dwelt / we beheld.*

One of the points you should make is that even though the thoughts and ideas are profound, the language is amazingly simple, since God wants us to understand these truths. Ask the class to compare and contrast the beginning *Word was* (v. 1) with the concluding *Word was made and dwelt* (v. 14)—the first speaking of His preexistence, the last of His incarnation!

Into Life

If your budget allows for an expenditure of about 50 cents per learner, purchase a carnation (live or silk) for each one. Use a marker to write a small letter *N* on the base of the flower. Hand one to each learner, and ask, "What can this flower represent to you?" Someone will notice the letter and the flower type and respond, "Incarnation!"

Suggest that learners find someone to give the flower to, adding the simple comment, "I present this to you in the name of the one who came in the flesh!" Perhaps a conversation about Jesus' deity and humanity will ensue. (If your budget does not allow for this, distribute copies of pictures of carnations downloaded from the Internet.)

Distribute copies of the 1:1 activity, from the reproducible page you have downloaded, as take-home work.

The Word Became Flesh

WATER TURNED TO WINE

DEVOTIONAL READING: John 17:1-5
BACKGROUND SCRIPTURE: John 2:1-12

JOHN 2:1-12

1 And the third day there was a marriage in Cana of Galilee; and the mother of Jesus was there:

2 And both Jesus was called, and his disciples, to the marriage.

3 And when they wanted wine, the mother of Jesus saith unto him, They have no wine.

4 Jesus saith unto her, Woman, what have I to do with thee? mine hour is not yet come.

5 His mother saith unto the servants, Whatsoever he saith unto you, do it.

6 And there were set there six waterpots of stone, after the manner of the purifying of the Jews, containing two or three firkins apiece.

7 Jesus saith unto them, Fill the waterpots with water. And they filled them up to the brim.

8 And he saith unto them, Draw out now, and bear unto the governor of the feast. And they bare it.

9 When the ruler of the feast had tasted the water that was made wine, and knew not whence it was: (but the servants which drew the water knew;) the governor of the feast called the bridegroom,

10 And saith unto him, Every man at the beginning doth set forth good wine; and when men have well drunk, then that which is worse: but thou hast kept the good wine until now.

11 This beginning of miracles did Jesus in Cana of Galilee, and manifested forth his glory; and his disciples believed on him.

12 After this he went down to Capernaum, he, and his mother, and his brethren, and his disciples: and they continued there not many days.

KEY VERSE

This beginning of miracles did Jesus in Cana of Galilee, and manifested forth his glory; and his disciples believed on him. —**John 2:11**

Photo: Stockbyte / Stockbyte / Thinkstock

GOD'S CREATIVE WORD

Unit 1: In the Beginning Was the Word

LESSONS 1–6

LESSON AIMS

After participating in this lesson, each student will be able to:

1. List the major points of the account of Jesus' turning water into wine.

2. Explain the "sign" value of Jesus' turning water into wine.

3. Tell what it means to believe on Jesus today.

LESSON OUTLINE

Introduction

A. A Wedding to Remember

As a minister who has officiated at many weddings, I can testify to wide differences in scale and cost. Some brides spend thousands of dollars on their dresses. The bill for wedding receptions can run tens of thousands of dollars. Videographers, flowers, decorations, programs, musicians, facility rental, limousines, and many other things can produce a staggering overall cost.

At the other end of the scale, some weddings are very simple and cost very little. I recently married a couple in a low-key Thursday afternoon ceremony. She wore her best dress: her high-school prom dress. He wore a borrowed sport coat and tie. The only flower was a single rose she carried. We played some recorded music for them using the church sound system. After the ceremony, the bride, groom, and a couple of friends walked down the street to a restaurant for a meal.

One thing all weddings have in common, however, is the participants' desire for the event to be memorable. As a minister, I try to help them realize their dreams. One of the things I tell them is that we do indeed want the wedding to create memories, but not the kind that end up on the funny video shows. We do not want someone to step on the bride's dress or trip on the way up the steps. We do not want the veil to catch fire from a candle or a member of the wedding party to show up intoxicated. We want positive, beautiful memories of this important event.

Today's lesson tells the story of one of the first events in the public ministry of Jesus: a miracle that took place at a wedding. Here Jesus both revealed himself as the miracle-working Son of God and saved the wedding host from potential embarrassment. That it was a wedding to remember is verified by our discussion of it some 2,000 years later.

B. Lesson Background

The Gospel of John does not speak of Jesus' birth in Bethlehem, but the author clearly presents Nazareth as the place Jesus grew up, His hometown (see John 1:45, 46; 18:5-7; 19:19). Nazareth was a village in the northern half of Palestine, an area referred to as Galilee. Nazareth was in the hill country of southern Galilee, roughly equidistant from the Sea of Galilee and the Mediterranean coast. Nearby was another Galilean village named Cana, about eight miles north of Nazareth. There were many Gentiles who lived in the Galilean region (see Matthew 4:15), so the Jews in this area tended to have their own villages.

Although John gives no details, it is likely that there were strong family ties between Nazareth and Cana. Men from Nazareth might marry women from Cana and vice versa. This may explain why Jesus, His mother, and His disciples attended a wedding in Cana. This could have been the wedding of a relative or a family friend. They were not crashing the party, nor were they invited so that Jesus could perform miracles. He was there as a guest, and there were no expectations on Him other than His participation in the celebration.

Some Christians are troubled that this story involves wine, an alcoholic beverage. We must understand two things in this regard. First, the contention that this was some type of unfermented grape juice with zero alcohol content cannot be supported by what we know of the ancient world. Wine was a common beverage for the people of that day. Good wine (meaning non-vinegary) would have been the normal, expected beverage to be served at a wedding celebration.

But, second, we must understand that the people of Jesus' day normally drank wine diluted with water. This was both an economy measure (to stretch the supply) and a health measure (to provide a moderate antiseptic for the water supply). Undiluted wine may have had an alcohol content of 10 or 11 percent. The diluted wine of Jesus' day would have had an alcohol content of 2 or 3 percent. While it was possible for heavy consumers to become intoxicated, the wedding guests who had two cups of wine per hour would have felt little effect from the alcohol.

Jewish traditions strongly condemned excessive consumption of wine and the resulting drunkenness. To be drunk in public was shameful (see 1 Samuel 1:14). The drunkard is spoken of disparagingly in both the Old and New Testaments (see Proverbs 23:20, 21; 1 Corinthians 5:11). While we therefore see Jesus at a wedding celebration where alcoholic beverages were being served, we need not think this was any type of drunken gala.

I. Hope for a Miracle
(John 2:1-6)
A. Celebration Begins (vv. 1, 2)

1. And the third day there was a marriage in Cana of Galilee; and the mother of Jesus was there.

The third day is a reference to the marriage being three days after Jesus' encounter with Philip and Nathanael (John 1:43-51). Nathanael is from Cana (21:2), so he likely is well acquainted with the family having the wedding.

We are also told that *the mother of Jesus* (Mary) is there. If there is a family connection with this wedding (which is likely), Mary may be one of the aunts or cousins helping with the wedding festivities. This would be a village-wide event, with a couple hundred people in attendance. To provide food and refreshments necessitates many helpers.

2. And both Jesus was called, and his disciples, to the marriage.

Jesus and His disciples are personally invited to this wedding, but we are not told why. There are at least five disciples in the group by this time: Andrew (John 1:40), Simon Peter (1:42), Philip (1:43), Nathanael (1:49), and the unnamed disciple that many assume to be John (1:40).

The author says nothing about the wedding ceremony or the identity of the bride or groom because our story is concerned with the festivities of this celebration. A wedding feast or banquet involves lots of food and drink (compare Matthew 22:2-4), music and dancing.

HOW TO SAY IT

Cana	*Kay*-nuh.
Capernaum	Kuh-*per*-nay-um.
Galilee	*Gal*-uh-lee.
Mediterranean	*Med*-uh-tuh-**ray**-nee-un.
Nathanael	Nuh-*than*-yull (*th* as in *thin*).
Nazareth	*Naz*-uh-reth.
Sepphoris	*Sef*-uh-ris.

Visual for
Lessons 3 & 9

Teaching and Miracles in John

Keep this map posted throughout the quarter to give your learners a geographical perspective.

Jesus refers to the latter two in Luke 7:33, 34 when He chastises the people for their unending criticism of himself and John the Baptist. Jesus uses the analogy of children "playing wedding" and "playing funeral" as He says, "We have piped unto you, and ye have not danced; we have mourned to you, and ye have not wept" (Luke 7:32). The first part of Jesus' analogy (playing wedding) gives a picture of festive music and dancing. The people of small villages such as Nazareth and Cana work hard, so they welcome a break when they can celebrate and enjoy themselves for a brief time.

B. Disaster Looms (vv. 3-6)

3. And when they wanted wine, the mother of Jesus saith unto him, They have no wine.

In the course of the celebration, the unexpected happens: the guests have consumed all the wine on hand. Whether this reflects poor planning or more guests than anticipated, we do not know.

This situation may seem like a minor thing to us. But in Jesus' day, this is a deeply embarrassing failure. Forever after the hosts will be known as "the stingy people who ran out of wine at their wedding." Some of this is based on a social obligation to have abundant food and drink at a wedding feast. It is not a place or time to economize. The families involved in this party have attended the weddings of their neighbors and were given plenty of food and drink in the process. Now it is their turn to do likewise.

There is no easy solution. A small village like Cana probably has no ready stores of wine available for purchase. It is possible that someone can go all the way to Sepphoris, some four miles away, to find a wine merchant. Taking a cart to the city, buying the wine, bringing it back to Cana, and preparing it can easily take half a day—far too long to keep everyone happy and save face.

Jesus' mother, perhaps one who is helping with the catering, decides to take matters into her own hands. She simply turns to her son and presents the dire situation to Him. She makes no demands, but we can pick up the unspoken expectation in her voice: "We need your help."

4a. Jesus saith unto her, Woman, what have I to do with thee?

Jesus' response to His mother is hard to understand. Some even have seen rudeness and disrespect in His words, but this is unnecessary.

His statement, *Woman, what have I to do with thee?* is very difficult to translate, for it involves idioms in the original Greek. A very literal translation is, "What to me and to you, woman?" If we take this as a starting point and fill in a few blanks, we can render it as "What does this have to do with me or you, mother dear?" The answer is obvious: nothing. The wine supply is certainly not Jesus' problem, and Mary's responsibility is very limited. Jesus' answer serves to say that the decision to intervene must be His, not His mother's.

4b. Mine hour is not yet come.

The next part of Jesus' response serves two purposes. First, it shows that Jesus has a plan for revealing himself as the promised Messiah, the

Water Turned to Wine

Son of God. Despite traditions and legends outside the Bible, there is no convincing evidence that Jesus has performed miracles before this time. Mary is certainly aware of the miraculous events preceding His birth, but John counts this as Jesus' first sign or miracle (see John 2:11, below).

Second, Jesus' statement that His time *is not yet come* (repeated later in John 7:6-8, 30; 8:20) implies that His time *will* come later. This coming hour is to be the time of His death (13:1) and His glorification through the resurrection (17:1). That is three years away at this point, but Jesus' display of divine power in the forthcoming miracle is a partial manifestation of the glory God has given to Him (2:11, below).

❧ *Not a Photo Op* ❧

Bruce Whelihan, an aide to Press Secretary Ron Ziegler during the Nixon presidency, is credited with coining the phrase *photo op* (short for "photograph opportunity"). At that time, the term described a situation in which the aide would invite the White House press corps into the Oval Office to take a picture of the president that would put him in a positive light.

Since then, the phrase *photo op* frequently has come to refer to a staged event—that is, a publicity stunt—that is touted as "news." This seems especially so when it is planned to get a politician's name and face before the public during an election campaign. Politicians do seem to love the camera!

When we think of what was happening at the wedding feast in Cana, we may be tempted to think, in modern terms, "What a perfect opportunity Jesus had to get His picture and a sound bite on Cana's evening infotainment TV program!" But Jesus was not one to seek the limelight to further himself (John 6:15), although others certainly pushed Him in that direction (7:4). He was following the Father's agenda and timing, not that of the world's. May we do so as well.   —C. R. B.

5. His mother saith unto the servants, Whatsoever he saith unto you, do it.

Mary does not argue with her son or give Him any directions. She operates with an amazing

degree of faith, a belief that He will come to the rescue for this looming disaster. She merely turns to the servants (probably men hired for the occasion) and advises them to do whatever Jesus asks. We can assume that Mary believes Jesus will provide more wine, but she does not know how He will do it. Perhaps even she is surprised at what He does!

> **What Do You Think?**
> What was a time when someone advised you to do what Jesus said? How did things turn out?
> *Talking Points for Your Discussion*
> - Regarding lifestyle choices
> - Regarding financial stewardship
> - Regarding taking risks for the kingdom of God

6. And there were set there six waterpots of stone, after the manner of the purifying of the Jews, containing two or three firkins apiece.

A *firkin* is an old English measure equal to about 9 or 10 gallons, so these stone jars hold roughly 20 to 30 gallons apiece. Imagine a jar that can contain the volume of five or six plastic five-gallon water jugs that are used in water coolers!

The observant Jews of Jesus' day use limestone jars for ceremonial washing purposes. They believe that natural stone is not subject to being "unclean" because of contact with Gentiles or nonkosher food. Such jars are manufactured in many places in Judea and Galilee at this time because limestone is abundant, easily worked, and durable.

The *waterpots of stone* have nothing to do with the wedding celebration. They are not used as wine containers. They are the property of the Jewish householder for the use of his family.

> **What Do You Think?**
> Thinking of the water pots, what are some things in your possession that you need to make available for use in the service of the Lord? How will you do so?
> *Talking Points for Your Discussion*
> - Home
> - Car
> - Unique skills

II. Hope from a Miracle

(John 2:7-12)

A. Crisis Averted (vv. 7-10)

7. Jesus saith unto them, Fill the water-pots with water. And they filled them up to the brim.

The fact that the jars are filled *up to the brim* shows that these containers have only water in them. Perhaps they are overfilled a bit so the excess runs down the sides. There is no possibility of someone's slipping a hidden supply of wine into them since there is no room for anything else. Depending on how much water is in the jars to begin with, it may take the servants an hour or so to carry water from the village well to complete this task.

8. And he saith unto them, Draw out now, and bear unto the governor of the feast. And they bare it.

We can well imagine the confusion of the servants at this point. They have filled the pots as directed and have no reason to think they contain anything but water.

Yet Jesus asks them to fill a small container from one of the jars and take it to the *governor of the feast.* This person is not the groom, as the next verse shows. Rather, he is the hired person in charge of catering the wedding festivities. This command of Jesus undoubtedly makes little sense to the servants, for they do not see why the head man would care to taste the purification water. We can expect that they begin to realize a miracle has taken place when they *draw* the water, though, for the aroma of fine wine is there.

9, 10. When the ruler of the feast had tasted the water that was made wine, and knew not whence it was: (but the servants which drew the water knew;) the governor of the feast called the bridegroom, and saith unto him, Every man at the beginning doth set forth good wine; and when men have well drunk, then that which is worse: but thou hast kept the good wine until now.

We are not told whether the bridegroom is aware of the wine crisis or not. It may be something the caterer is trying to manage on his own.

But that *ruler of the feast* is perplexed. Not knowing anything of Jesus or the water pots, he assumes that the groom has been keeping a stash of wine hidden from him, perhaps several wineskins in a storage area. So he questions the groom along these lines, pointing out that it is customary to begin the celebration with good wine and end with cheaper stuff. His somewhat sarcastic comment is that the guests do not notice the difference in quality after a few cups of wine.

His comments lead us to understand two things about this incident. First, the wine produced by the miracle of Jesus is excellent in quality. We expect nothing less. When God provides food miraculously, it is always superb; the manna provided for the nation of Israel while in the wilderness had the exquisite, luxurious taste of honey (Exodus 16:31). Second, the quality of the initial supply of wine was lower than that of the wine Jesus creates.

What Do You Think?

In what ways has Jesus taken the ordinary and made it extraordinary in your life or church?

Talking Points for Your Discussion

- Teaching skills
- Mercy and compassion
- Leadership skills
- Interpersonal skills

❧ *Celebrating or Impressing?* ❧

Jennifer Aniston and Brad Pitt got married on a Malibu bluff overlooking the Pacific Ocean in what the bride's father called "a spectacular wedding." It should have been spectacular—it was rumored to have cost $1 million! A string quartet, a band, and a gospel choir provided the music. Decorations included 50,000 flowers. A fireworks display closed out the celebration. (Five years later, fireworks of another kind went off as divorce papers were filed.)

It's natural for people to want their weddings to be memorable. What will people think if one's wedding is not "just perfect"? Sadly, the sky-is-no-limit approach that we see in celebrity weddings creates a cultural climate in which weddings are judged by the extravagant impressions they make.

The wedding in Cana was not as spectacular as a lot of modern weddings are, but the concern for making a good impression still seems to have been present! And we may assume that the wedding did indeed make a good impression thanks to someone we might call a reluctant hero: Jesus.

Jesus was there to share in a celebration. His mother was there for the same reason, but she developed an additional concern: to rescue the wedding from creating a bad impression. Jesus "saved the day," as the expression goes, but there is every indication that He did so only from the purest of motives. Maintaining purity of motives is a daily challenge, isn't it? —C. R. B.

B. Disciples Believe (vv. 11, 12)

11. This beginning of miracles did Jesus in Cana of Galilee, and manifested forth his glory; and his disciples believed on him.

John uses a distinctive word to describe what has happened—it is literally a miracle. Yet, Jesus' action is more than a miracle to help a family friend out of a tight spot. It is a miracle with a purpose: to reveal the divinity and power of Jesus, to show His glory (compare John 3:2). The result is that *his disciples believed on him.*

This begins to show a key conflict in the Gospel of John: the battle between belief and unbelief. For John, the key to understanding Jesus is faith in Him based on Jesus' ability to set aside laws of nature as He performs miracles (John 20:30, 31). Natural laws cannot explain water turning into wine any more than they can explain God in human form (1:14).

What Do You Think?

In what ways has Christ's work increased your faith in Him?

Talking Points for Your Discussion

- In a change in the direction of your life (compare Acts 16:6-10)
- In His provision in a time of need
- In a healing
- In His provision of peace and comfort

---

12. After this he went down to Capernaum, he, and his mother, and his brethren, and his disciples: and they continued there not many days.

John gives many location details to help us understand Jesus' traveling ministry. Capernaum figures prominently as something of a headquarters for Jesus while in Galilee. Jesus spends so much time there it is considered His second home (see Matthew 4:13; Mark 2:1). Jesus leads a group of perhaps a dozen or more from Cana to this lakeside village. They remain there until it is time to go to Jerusalem for the Passover celebration (John 2:13).

Conclusion

A. Signs of the Messiah

The changing of water into wine is the first miracle recorded by John. The immediate result of this first sign is the faith of the disciples, the core group of men that Jesus was preparing to lead the church after His departure. Later, John (one of those early disciples) explained that there were many other signs. John had chosen only certain ones to reveal aspects of Jesus' divinity (see John 20:30).

There are connections between the miraculous signs in the Gospel of John that the reader will notice. The second sign also involved Cana of Galilee (John 4:46, 54). Many have also seen a connection between the first sign (water to wine), and the feeding of the five thousand (see 6:14). This link is between fruit of the vine and bread, the symbols of the Lord's Supper. Certainly, the sign of the raising of Lazarus (11:38-44) foreshadowed the resurrection of Jesus himself. These signs still serve as markers for our faith in Jesus as the Son of God.

B. Prayer

Father God, You provide us necessary food and drink on a daily basis. You provide signs and reasons for our faith. And You provide the means of our salvation through Your Son, the spotless lamb. Thank You. We pray in the name of the one in whom we believe, Jesus our Savior; amen.

C. Thought to Remember

Believe on Jesus.

INVOLVEMENT LEARNING

Some of the activities below are also found in the helpful student book, Adult Bible Class.
Don't forget to download the free reproducible page from www.standardlesson.com to enhance your lesson!

Into the Lesson

Ask, "What was the most memorable wedding you ever attended, not including your own? What made it memorable?" Allow several to share. Then comment, "Today's lesson is about a small-town wedding that was so memorable, we're still talking about it 2,000 years later!"

Alternative: If your learning area is equipped with video, show some clips of wedding bloopers. Ask, "Are these the kinds of memories most people want for their wedding?" After discussion, say, "Today's lesson is about a wedding that was memorable for a more noble reason. It was so memorable that we're still talking about it 2,000 years later!"

Into the Word

Recruit three or four class members who enjoy drama to be "guests at a wedding." Ask them to sit at a table in the front of the room, to be interviewed by other class members and you. Give your "guests" copies of the following questions prior to today's study session so they can think about how to dramatize their answers. Inform the "guests" that there may be other questions they will be asked. The "guests" are to give biblical answers where possible; they can be creative but reasonable where the Bible does not reveal the answer.

These are the questions to be distributed to both the "guests" and the class members who will be asking them: 1. We know Jesus came from Nazareth for this wedding. How far did you come? 2. Were any of you members of the families of the bride and groom? 3. How many would you estimate were at the wedding? 4. How would you characterize the quality of the wine served at the wedding? 5. Was any one of you a servant at the wedding? What did you observe? 6. Those large stone jars—how had you seen such jars used in times past? 7. How long did it take to fill those jars—if you observed the process? 8. Which of you was the "master of the wedding feast"? Exactly what was your role? 9. Who noticed that the wine supply was low? What were you thinking? 10. I don't understand the words about "good wine first and worse wine later." How did that work exactly? 11. How did the bridegroom react when he was questioned about the best wine being served last?

Have someone read today's text aloud before you start the interview. The speculation involved at points in the answers given by the "guests" will allow you to comment as you see necessary, possibly adding your own follow-up questions.

Continue by saying, "John reveals that this changing of water to wine was the first of Jesus' miraculous signs." As you reveal a sign that says *SURPRISE!* ask your class these questions: 1. What surprises you about the fact Jesus had not performed miracles before this occasion? 2. What is surprising about the fact that *this particular one* was His first? 3. Who do you suppose was most surprised when this miracle was performed? 4. Are you surprised that Jesus' disciples put their faith in Him as a result of this event? Why, or why not?

Distribute copies of the Wedding Surprise! activity from the reproducible page that you have downloaded. Have learners discuss their conclusions in small groups.

Into Life

Say, "The phrase *and his disciples believed on him* from John 2:11 summarizes the point of Jesus' miracles: when His glory is seen, the only logical reaction is to put faith in Him." For the week ahead, ask learners to meditate daily on this question: *What is it about Jesus that causes me to believe in Him?*

Suggest that learners keep a spiritual journal for the week ahead; each day they are to write one thing that reveals Jesus' glory to them personally. Distribute copies of the Glory! activity from the reproducible page as learners depart. Suggest that learners complete this as an enhancement to their journaling.

Water Turned to Wine

NICODEMUS LEARNS OF NEW BIRTH

DEVOTIONAL READING: Matthew 5:13-16

BACKGROUND SCRIPTURE: John 3:1-25; Numbers 21:4-9

JOHN 3:11-21

11 Verily, verily, I say unto thee, We speak that we do know, and testify that we have seen; and ye receive not our witness.

12 If I have told you earthly things, and ye believe not, how shall ye believe, if I tell you of heavenly things?

13 And no man hath ascended up to heaven, but he that came down from heaven, even the Son of man which is in heaven.

14 And as Moses lifted up the serpent in the wilderness, even so must the Son of man be lifted up:

15 That whosoever believeth in him should not perish, but have eternal life.

16 For God so loved the world, that he gave his only begotten Son, that whosoever believeth in him should not perish, but have everlasting life.

17 For God sent not his Son into the world to condemn the world; but that the world through him might be saved.

18 He that believeth on him is not condemned: but he that believeth not is condemned already, because he hath not believed in the name of the only begotten Son of God.

19 And this is the condemnation, that light is come into the world, and men loved darkness rather than light, because their deeds were evil.

20 For every one that doeth evil hateth the light, neither cometh to the light, lest his deeds should be reproved.

21 But he that doeth truth cometh to the light, that his deeds may be made manifest, that they are wrought in God.

KEY VERSE

God so loved the world, that he gave his only begotten Son, that whosoever believeth in him should not perish, but have everlasting life. —**John 3:16**

GOD'S CREATIVE WORD

Unit 1: In the Beginning Was the Word

LESSONS 1–6

LESSON AIMS

After participating in this lesson, each student will be able to:

1. Summarize what Jesus told Nicodemus about light, life, and faith.

2. Explain the significance of the word pictures in today's text.

3. Recite John 3:16 from memory.

LESSON OUTLINE

Introduction

A. Night Visitors

My city has been embroiled recently in controversy concerning electronic billboards. These advertising innovations are powered by LEDs, and their messages change every few seconds via computer control. Some of these billboards are enormous, measuring over 40 feet in length. At night they create a multicolored brightness that lights up the sky. Opponents cite these bright billboards as part of a larger problem: light pollution. Artificial light seems to be everywhere these days. Some long for a darker environment at night.

Whatever one's opinion concerning light pollution, we should realize that bright lighting at night (indoors or outdoors) is a recent phenomenon on the time line of human history. In Jesus' time, daily life cycles were controlled by the light of the sun. Oil lamps and candles were available, but they were expensive and provided dim light at best. Business, travel, teaching, and other activities generally were done during daylight hours out of practical necessity. It would have required many candles or oil lamps to equal the light output of a single 100-watt incandescent light bulb of today. Sunset was the time for one to be at home, preparing for bed.

It was unusual, then, for Nicodemus and Jesus to meet at night (John 3:2). The Gospel author does not say why, although there are many theories. A common idea is that Nicodemus wanted to keep his interest in Jesus a secret, fearing damage to his reputation if it were known that he associated with this controversial young teacher. Others think an evening meeting allowed for a more leisurely discussion since the crowds that followed Jesus during the day would be absent.

Whatever the reason, we can imagine Jesus and Nicodemus outdoors in the cool of the evening, perhaps sharing a light meal. They may have benefited from the light of a bright moon, enough for them to see each other's face clearly and read unspoken messages as part of their conversation. The words of Jesus were of high importance when He spoke them to Nicodemus that night, and they remain so for us today.

B. Lesson Background

Nicodemus is mentioned only in the Gospel of John. His training was that of a Pharisee (John 3:1), a strict adherent of the Law of Moses. This was very helpful in his vocation as a teacher. And he was no ordinary teacher! Jesus calls him "a master of Israel" (3:10). All this signifies that Nicodemus was well educated and respected. He was surely a cut above the other teachers of his time.

Additionally, Nicodemus is identified as "a ruler of the Jews" (John 3:1). This means he was a member of the Sanhedrin ("being one of them," 7:50), the high council of the Jewish people (see 7:47-50). That was a select group of 70 priests, elders, and scribes of the people plus the presiding high priest (71 total; compare 11:47). These men were the elite of the elites in Israel—wealthy, influential, and admired. It is ironic, then, that this Jewish leader had a Greek name: *Nicodemus* means "victory of the people" in Greek. Perhaps his parents were Hellenistic Jews, that is, they were Jews who had adopted some Greek ways. But his status as a Pharisee and his membership on the Sanhedrin means that we should understand him to have been a very loyal, observant Jew.

Nicodemus spoke up for Jesus in the Sanhedrin (John 7:50, 51). After the crucifixion, Nicodemus assisted Joseph of Arimathaea in the burial of Jesus (19:39). Some believe that John wants us to understand Nicodemus as a secret disciple of Jesus, as was Joseph of Arimathaea (19:38). This may be true, but John never says this explicitly. We like to think that Nicodemus became a follower after the resurrection, though. In fact, there is an early Christian writing known as the *Gospel of Nicodemus*, although it was not written by the man in today's lesson. Even so, this is a testimony to the man's reputation in the early church that such a book would be attributed to him.

HOW TO SAY IT

Arimathaea	*Air*-uh-muh-***thee***-uh (*th* as in *thin*).
Nicodemus	*Nick*-uh-***dee***-mus.
Sanhedrin	*San*-huh-drun or *San*-***heed***-run.
Zeus	Zoose.

I. Believers and Unbelievers
(JOHN 3:11-17)
A. Regarding the Witness (vv. 11-13)

11. Verily, verily, I say unto thee, We speak that we do know, and testify that we have seen; and ye receive not our witness.

A characteristic expression of Jesus in the Gospel of John is *verily, verily* (25 times). Jesus often uses this expression to begin an important section of teaching. The actual term behind this expression is the word we use to end our prayers: *amen.* This word comes from Hebrew and means "this is true" (see Revelation 3:14). When we say *amen,* we are asserting our agreement with a speaker. When Jesus says *verily* (amen), He means that what follows is a truth that requires special attention.

This verse draws together several things from earlier sections of the book. Nicodemus is well aware of the miraculous signs Jesus has been performing (John 3:2). Yet we also know that witnessing these signs does not necessarily result in a faith that Jesus finds acceptable (2:23-25). Nicodemus has just been told that he must be "born again," referring to a spiritual birth, if he is to be part of the "kingdom of God" (3:3). He has tripped on this directive, however, unable to understand birth in anything but physical terms (3:4). When Jesus explains the spiritual nature of this new birth, Nicodemus seems confused (3:9).

In the verse before us, Jesus takes a more direct approach. Jesus' comments serve to say that He has been honest and straightforward in His actions and words, yet Nicodemus has not accepted Him or His message. What follows is one of the most important explanations of Jesus' person and mission in all of Scripture.

12. If I have told you earthly things, and ye believe not, how shall ye believe, if I tell you of heavenly things?

Some people seem to have been born with "an incredulous bone"—they have trouble believing. Despite Nicodemus's status as a leader of a very religious people, he has a problem conceiving of things on the spiritual level. Yet this he must do, for the treasure in Jesus' words is to be found in *heavenly things,* not in *earthly things.*

13. And no man hath ascended up to heaven, but he that came down from heaven, even the Son of man which is in heaven.

The key to believing Jesus' message is knowing His origin: He is the one who *came down from heaven*. Jesus is able to teach about God because He knows God intimately (John 1:18). It is through Jesus that Heaven is revealed (1:51). This is because Jesus is the Son, who is able to give Nicodemus direct knowledge of the Father. This is more than information about the nature of the Father. In the following verses, Jesus reveals the Son's part in God's plan for human salvation.

B. Regarding the Cross (vv. 14, 15)

14. And as Moses lifted up the serpent in the wilderness, even so must the Son of man be lifted up.

Knowing that Nicodemus is an expert in Jewish history, Jesus draws on Numbers 21:5-9: the story of how God punished the grumbling, disobedient nation of Israel by sending a plague of poisonous snakes into their camp, causing many deaths. The terrified Israelites came to Moses and admitted their sin, begging him to save them. According to directions received from the Lord, Moses made a brass snake and raised it high above the camp on a pole. If anyone bitten by a snake looked at the brass serpent, that person was saved from death. This was God's way of saving the people.

Jesus uses that story as a powerful analogy to explain His mission of salvation. For Jesus to *be lifted up* is a reference to His being raised on the cross (see John 12:32, 33), although how this results in salvation is not made clear until later.

The serpent in the wilderness, then, is a type of prophecy of the saving power of the cross.

❧ NO MORE FEAR ❧

Some psychologists suggest that our distant ancestors had an instinctive dislike of snakes because some species are venomous. Even today, some folks can't even tolerate a picture or video of a snake. A movie that features one of these cold-blooded creatures oozing its way along the ground—sometimes obscured by the undergrowth, suddenly appearing in view—can make our hearts pound and our skin crawl.

The Bible itself offers a negative view of snakes. Genesis 3 depicts "the serpent" as the tempter that introduced sin into the world. The serpents of Numbers 21 brought terror and death to the Israelite encampment. Paul was bitten by a viper (Acts 28:3). Passages such as Psalm 58:4; Proverbs 23:32; Ecclesiastes 10:8; Matthew 3:7; and Luke 11:11 offer further negative images of snakes.

Isn't it interesting, then, that God used a serpent of brass as the symbol to which Israel could look for salvation? More interesting yet is how that symbol prefigured the cross of Christ by which we are saved! We need not fear the bite of the serpent, the devil. Christ has indeed interceded on our behalf. See Genesis 3:15.   —C. R. B.

15. That whosoever believeth in him should not perish, but have eternal life.

As those who took a step of faith and looked at the brass serpent were saved, so those who look on Jesus in faith will be saved. The serpent-salvation of Moses' day was temporary, for those people eventually died. The Son's salvation is forever, for those who place faith in Him have *eternal life.*

While this text speaks to everyone, it is originally a direct challenge to Nicodemus. If he is to be part of the eternal kingdom of God, then he must be born anew. This spiritual rebirth is not put into effect by a ritual observance of the law, by secret knowledge, or by magical incantations. Today we might say it is not actualized by counseling therapy, by a personal makeover, or by a fresh start. It comes through belief in Jesus, the place where Nicodemus is falling short (John 3:12). This verse leads to the high point of the chapter, perhaps the most famous verse in the Bible: John 3:16.

C. Regarding the Son (vv. 16, 17)

16. For God so loved the world, that he gave his only begotten Son, that whosoever believeth in him should not perish, but have everlasting life.

If there is such a things as the gospel in a nutshell, this verse is the leading candidate. It gives both the "what's so" and the "so what?" of the Christian message of salvation. God works to save us because He loves the world. God saves by sending the one closest to His heart: the Son. We must believe in Him, placing our trust in the Son of God. The result is that we no longer have to fear death, for we will not perish. Instead, we have the gift of everlasting life.

As mentioned in the second lesson of this quarter, for Jesus to be referred to as the *only begotten Son* does not force us to conclude that the Son is a created, finite being. The single Greek word translated "only begotten" was the subject of intense study in the twentieth century by Bible scholars. We now think its meaning is something like "unique" or "one of a kind."

Even though the language of parenthood and childhood is used here, we should not think that John wants us to understand this in physical terms. Jesus as God's Son is not like the semidivine men of pagan mythology—heroic men like Hercules, who was the son of Zeus and a human mother. Before the Word became flesh as the human Jesus, the Word was eternal and uncreated. The eternal Word and the Son of God are the same for John.

What Do You Think?
How should God's love for the world influence the way you live? Where do you need to improve most in this regard?
Talking Points for Your Discussion
- 1 Corinthians 6:20
- James 1:21
- 1 John 4:7, 8

17. For God sent not his Son into the world to condemn the world; but that the world through him might be saved.

This verse begins with a restatement of John 1:14, for "the Word was made flesh" is another way of saying "God sent His Son." In this case, though, we are told what God did *not* intend by sending His Son: He was not sent to *condemn the world.*

The word *condemn* has the sense of being judged, found guilty, and sentenced to death. Jesus is not sent to Israel as a judge, a fact He repeats at a later time (see John 8:15), even though He has the authority to judge (5:22). His mission is salvation, and He is not to be both Savior and condemner at the same time. He promises to come again and take His saved ones home (14:3). It is this second coming that will reveal the Christ as judge (compare Matthew 25:31-33).

II. Doers and Haters
(JOHN 3:18-21)

A. Truth About Darkness (vv. 18-20)

18. He that believeth on him is not condemned: but he that believeth not is condemned already, because he hath not believed in the name of the only begotten Son of God.

There is a warning in these verses for Nicodemus and for anyone who chooses not to believe: the nonbeliever will not escape condemnation. The nonbeliever has no promise or hope for eternal life. The nonbeliever is *condemned already.* His or her lack of faith is a self-condemning choice. And a general belief in God (as Nicodemus and his fellow Jews have) is not sufficient.

The kind of belief necessary is a specific, focused belief: it is faith in the Son of God. There is no

Visual for Lesson 4

Start a discussion by asking learners to personalize both statements on this visual.

substitute, no other way. Jesus alone is the way to salvation (John 14:6; compare Acts 4:12).

19. And this is the condemnation, that light is come into the world, and men loved darkness rather than light, because their deeds were evil.

Jesus seems now to appeal to Nicodemus to have the necessary, saving faith. Jesus' words and deeds reveal Him to be the light that the ancient Jewish people are looking for (see John 1:9; 8:12; 9:5). Nicodemus is not one who loves spiritual darkness if he is a genuine seeker of truth. We have no reason to think that Nicodemus is one whose deeds are evil. Even so, he must make a choice: faith or unbelief.

Everyone must make this choice. Those who dismiss the gospel as ancient, superstitious nonsense are condemning themselves, choosing darkness rather than light. Those who admire Jesus but reject His claim to be the Savior of the world, the Son of God, are choosing unbelief. They will perish eternally. There is a harsh reality here. Jesus' words do not leave any wiggle room.

❧ *DABBLING IN DARKNESS* ❧

Batman—also known as "the Caped Crusader" or "the Dark Knight"—began his fictional life in 1939 as a comic-book character. His story has now run for over 70 years through two television series and numerous feature films. Batman is "really" Bruce Wayne, wealthy socialite of Gotham City. His parents were murdered when he was 8 years

old, and he decided to avenge their deaths by fighting the city's criminal element personally. Since "criminals are a superstitious cowardly lot," he saw the need to adopt a disguise that would "strike terror into their hearts." So he became "a creature of the night, black, terrible." Thus Bruce Wayne adopted the bat as his crime-fighting persona.

As a vigilante, Wayne ends up participating to a degree in the lawlessness against which he fights. Christopher Nolan, director of the 2008 Batman film *The Dark Knight,* said, "When you're dealing with questionable notions like people taking the law into their own hands, you have to really ask, where does that lead? That's what makes the character so dark, because he expresses a vengeful desire."

Is that a parable of your life? Do you ever adopt a "the ends justify the means" approach? Remember Paul's words: "Have no fellowship with the unfruitful works of darkness, but rather reprove them" (Ephesians 5:11). Do we really hate the darkness? —C. R. B.

20. For every one that doeth evil hateth the light, neither cometh to the light, lest his deeds should be reproved.

If anyone is confused as to his or her status, Jesus advises an examination of life. If it is full of evil, that person has rejected the light and the life it brings (John 1:4). Acts of wanton evil are a denial of any claim to faith (1 John 1:6). Faith is something we live, not just a one-time statement of belief.

The word *reproved* here has the sense of "uncovered." In the end, the evil life of the false believer will be revealed. Nothing is hidden from the true light of the Son, for His is the living Word that pierces to the depth of our souls and lays them bare (Hebrews 4:12).

This reproving power of God is also seen in the ministry of the Holy Spirit. The same Greek word is used in John 16:8 to say that the coming Spirit will "reprove the world of sin." One of the continuing functions of the Holy Spirit is to convict unbelievers of their sin. The church has an obligation to take moral stands in an immoral world, but the ultimate power to convince sinners of their guilt is in the hands of God.

B. Truth About Light (v. 21)

21. But he that doeth truth cometh to the light, that his deeds may be made manifest, that they are wrought in God.

This verse offers one of the most remarkable concepts in the Bible: that truth is more than something to be accepted mentally. Truth is also something we do and live. The lovers of darkness will be exposed by their evil deeds. The lovers of light will also be exposed by their deeds of truth. The actions of light do not come about by mere human effort. Rather, they are *wrought in God,* accomplished according to God's power and will.

What does it mean to do the truth? In the Gospel of John, Jesus is revealed as the personified truth of God (John 1:14; 14:6). It is this truth-nature in the life of Jesus that is rejected by unbelievers, for they choose to believe the father of lies, the devil (8:44, 45). Jesus came to save us for eternal life, but He also came to show us how to live in this life (10:10). We are living the truth when we follow Jesus as our Lord and seek to live like Him (compare 1 Corinthians 11:1). And it is by knowing the truth in our lives we are truly set free from sin and condemnation (John 8:32). In this sense, eternal life begins now.

Conclusion

A. What Is "Eternal Life"?

John 3:15 is the first time we encounter the expression *eternal life* (or its parallel *everlasting life*) in the Gospel of John. Over half of the New Testament occurrences of these phrases are in John and 1 John. What does it mean?

We should recognize that there is a difference between *eternity* and *eternal life.* The word *eternity* has the sense of unending time; therefore, time is an endless continuity of both past and future. Time is part of God's creation, but when God creates a new heaven and a new earth, time will be affected too. As the old hymn states, "The trumpet of the Lord shall sound and time shall be no more."

Eternal life, for its part, means we will survive this end of time and continue to have life beyond that. *Eternal life* is a much bigger concept than *eternity.* No single verse in the Gospel of John explains this, but we learn many things when we look at the various places where *eternal/everlasting life* appears in John's writings. Let us consider four of the most significant.

First, the one who does not have eternal life will be subject to the wrath of God (John 3:36; compare 5:24). Second, believers will be raised to the ultimate aspect of eternal life on the last day, a future time (John 6:40). Third, eternal life is a gift of God; it cannot be taken away by any who seek to harm us (John 10:28; compare 17:2; 1 John 5:11). Fourth, believers can know for sure that they have the gift of eternal life (1 John 5:13). Eternal life is a hope, a promise, a comfort, and a reality for the one who believes in the Son of God and has followed the plan of salvation.

B. Prayer

Precious Lord, we marvel at Your love for us. We wonder at the gift of eternal life through Jesus. We pray that You will guide us to be lovers of the light in all things, to live the truth in everything. We pray this in the name of the one whom You sent for us, Jesus Your Son; amen.

C. Thought to Remember

Our salvation is the result of God's love.

INVOLVEMENT LEARNING

Some of the activities below are also found in the helpful student book, Adult Bible Class.
Don't forget to download the free reproducible page from www.standardlesson.com to enhance your lesson!

Into the Lesson

Ask, "Did you ever have a teacher who asked you a question you could not answer, perhaps a question that humbled and embarrassed you because you should have known the answer?" Let several recall such occasions. Then comment, "Nicodemus, a learned Pharisee, found out he didn't really 'know it all.' And he embarrassed himself with a foolish remark."

Into the Word

Tell the class you want them collectively to speak as Nicodemus. Distribute copies of the following to be read responsively. You read the Jesus (J) statements, and the class will read the Nicodemus (N) responses/questions. (This is a very free rephrasing of today's text, John 3:11-21.)

୧୨ ୧୨ ୧୨

J: You and your people seem to be rejecting the truth I reveal. **N:** Reject? I am here, am I not?

J: I speak of simple things like human birth and the wind, but you seem confused and disbelieving. **N:** Confused perhaps, but I certainly believe in birth and the weather. But "born again"?

J: Will you ever be able to believe the spiritual principles I am teaching? **N:** I don't get your point. Am I dense?

J: Like Moses' brass snake, when the Son of Man is lifted on display, all who honor Him will be saved from death. **N:** At least I know about Moses' snake. But what's that got to do with me right now?

J: Those who were saved by obeying Moses have all died, but those saved by the Son will live forever. **N:** I do believe in resurrection, Rabbi. Is that what you're talking about?

J: God's love for all is so great that He is willing to give His only Son. All who accept Him will never die, but will live forever. **N:** Wait! I haven't made the jump from a snake-on-a-pole to . . . well, what exactly is it the Son of Man will do?

J: God isn't giving His Son as a condemning judge, but as a Savior. **N:** I'm not sure who you're talking about yet.

J: The issue is always about belief, Nicodemus, not works. Disbelief condemns. Belief in the Son will save. **N:** You keep on speaking of belief, Rabbi. What am I to believe?

J: Light or darkness—which do you love, Nicodemus? **N:** I have come in the dark of night, Master, but I am seeking light.

J: Living the truth will bring one into the light, teacher of Israel. May you find it to be so.

୧୨ ୧୨ ୧୨

When finished, lead a discussion of the above dialogue, comparing it with today's text. You can use the following questions: 1. Why was Nicodemus having such a hard time understanding what Jesus was saying? 2. How is Moses' snake-on-a-pole similar to the cross of Christ? 3. What are some differences between people who love the light and those who love the darkness?

Into Life

Say, "John 3:16 is a good answer to many spiritual inquiries." Ask your class to quote the verse in unison response after you make each of the following statements: 1. "I've never really understood Christianity—God demanding human sacrifice to appease Him." 2. "Jesus was certainly a good man and marvelous teacher, but 'God in the flesh'? I'm doubtful." 3. "It seems to me that what we do here on earth is all that matters."

Alternative: As a class, work through the questions in the Gospel in a Nutshell activity from the reproducible page, which you have downloaded.

Option: If time allows, distribute copies of the Nicodemus, with a Capital *I* activity from the reproducible page, which you have downloaded. Have students pair off and come up with the characteristics of pride and belief. Allow time for volunteers to share their discoveries.

JESUS TESTIFIES TO THE TRUTH

DEVOTIONAL READING: John 8:28-38
BACKGROUND SCRIPTURE: John 18, 19

JOHN 18:28-38

28 Then led they Jesus from Caiaphas unto the hall of judgment: and it was early; and they themselves went not into the judgment hall, lest they should be defiled; but that they might eat the passover.

29 Pilate then went out unto them, and said, What accusation bring ye against this man?

30 They answered and said unto him, If he were not a malefactor, we would not have delivered him up unto thee.

31 Then said Pilate unto them, Take ye him, and judge him according to your law. The Jews therefore said unto him, It is not lawful for us to put any man to death:

32 That the saying of Jesus might be fulfilled, which he spake, signifying what death he should die.

33 Then Pilate entered into the judgment hall again, and called Jesus, and said unto him, Art thou the King of the Jews?

34 Jesus answered him, Sayest thou this thing of thyself, or did others tell it thee of me?

35 Pilate answered, Am I a Jew? Thine own nation and the chief priests have delivered thee unto me: what hast thou done?

36 Jesus answered, My kingdom is not of this world: if my kingdom were of this world, then would my servants fight, that I should not be delivered to the Jews: but now is my kingdom not from hence.

37 Pilate therefore said unto him, Art thou a king then? Jesus answered, Thou sayest that I am a king. To this end was I born, and for this cause came I into the world, that I should bear witness unto the truth. Every one that is of the truth heareth my voice.

38 Pilate saith unto him, What is truth? And when he had said this, he went out again unto the Jews, and saith unto them, I find in him no fault at all.

KEY VERSE

Pilate therefore said unto him, Art thou a king then? Jesus answered, Thou sayest that I am a king. To this end was I born, and for this cause came I into the world, that I should bear witness unto the truth. Every one that is of the truth heareth my voice. —**John 18:37**

GOD'S CREATIVE WORD

Unit 1: In the Beginning Was the Word

LESSONS 1–6

LESSON AIMS

After participating in this lesson, each student will be able to:

1. Tell what "truth" Jesus testified to in the court of Pilate.

2. Tell how Jesus' kingdom/kingship and truth are related.

3. Tell how he or she "hears" Christ's voice, and what he or she does as a result.

LESSON OUTLINE

Introduction

A. Those in Authority

For our twenty-fifth wedding anniversary, my wife and I returned to the site of our honeymoon: Victoria, British Columbia. After we checked into our hotel, we were surprised to learn that Queen Elizabeth II was in town and would make a public appearance the next day on the steps of the parliament building.

As Americans, we owed no allegiance to the queen, but were curious nonetheless. So we walked from our hotel to the parliament building lawn and were lucky enough to be quite close to the speaker's platform. We observed the queen to be impeccably dressed and coiffed, well spoken, and a little shorter than we expected. She was a person of great dignity and commanded respect. But she also was just a human being like the rest of us.

Most reading this lesson are like me, having very little experience with kings or queens. Royals seem out of place in our modern world; often they serve in ceremonial ways with little actual authority. Such was not the case in the days of the New Testament. Almost everyone in the ancient world had a king of some type, whether a tribal chieftain, a city king, or the Roman emperor.

B. Lesson Background: Kings and Governors

Both the Greeks and Romans had a history of republics (forms of democracy with no king), but those days were long gone by the time Jesus came on the scene. Palestine in the time of Jesus was ruled by the Roman Caesar (sometimes called a *king,* see John 19:15) and his proxies.

The Jewish people also had a long history of kings. That history began with King Saul in 1050 BC and ended when Jerusalem was conquered by the Babylonians in 586 BC. There was no king in Jerusalem for quite a while after that. Judas Maccabee and members of his family were considered to be kings after that man liberated Jerusalem in 165 BC, although this was done with the approval of the rising world power of the period, the Romans.

The title of king over the Jews was taken from the Maccabean dynasty by Herod the Great in 37 BC. Herod, however, served only at the pleasure of the Romans. The reign of Herod ended rather badly, and his kingdom was divided among his sons. The son given the reign over Judea, Herod Archelaus (Matthew 2:22), was such a poor ruler that the Romans exiled him and installed a Roman governor in his place.

Because of this history, there were great tensions between the Jews and the Romans when it came to kings. The Jews of Jesus' day hated their Roman overlords and longed for a savior like David or Judas Maccabee who could raise an army and oust the Romans from their land. They wanted their own king, someone who would restore their sovereignty and keep their holy covenant with the Lord. The wary Romans were not about to tolerate any such thing, however.

As the Roman Empire grew, many provinces were added. Those areas under the direct control of the Roman senate were called *senatorial provinces*. The governors of senatorial provinces were from the ranks of the senators themselves and were usually called *proconsuls*. Two such proconsuls are named in Acts 13:7 and 18:12.

Other Roman provinces were under the supervision of the emperor and were known as *imperial provinces*. Imperial provinces were less stable and usually had Roman legions stationed within them. The governors of these provinces were known as *prefects* or *procurators*. These imperial governors were usually from the equestrian class, a citizen class below the noble senatorial class.

A Roman governor, whether proconsul or prefect, had two main, interrelated responsibilities.

First, he was expected to keep order within his province, using military force if necessary. Second, he was charged with keeping the stream of tax revenue flowing. The threat of revolt was also a threat to the tax income, and these threats were not taken lightly by the governors.

C. Lesson Background: Pilate

Pontius Pilate was one of the imperial governors. Bible scholars at one time identified him as a procurator. But an inscription uncovered in 1961 at the ruins of Caesarea Maritima lists Pilate as a prefect, a lesser title than procurator. Pilate was the fifth Roman governor of Judea, serving AD 26–36. That was an unusually long term. This indicates Pilate had little motivation to return to Rome, although we do not know why. Perhaps his prospects for enrichment were greater in the province, so he stayed.

We think the Roman governors of Judea spent most of their time in the beautiful little seaside city of Caesarea Maritima. Roman governors did not stay in Jerusalem any more than necessary, but tended to be there during the time of Passover and other festivals. This was a precautionary measure in case the large crowds of Jews got out of hand. The Romans wanted to nip any rebellion in the early stages. The Romans had a fortress headquarters in Jerusalem where their troops were garrisoned; it was near the temple. Pilate and the other governors, however, stayed in Herod's palace on the west side of the city when they were in town.

I. Pilate Listens
(JOHN 18:28-32)

A. Seeking Audience (v. 28)

28. Then led they Jesus from Caiaphas unto the hall of judgment: and it was early; and they themselves went not into the judgment hall, lest they should be defiled; but that they might eat the passover.

There are two high priests involved in Jesus' trials (see Luke 3:2). Annas served as high priest until AD 15, when he was deposed by the Romans. By the time of Jesus' arrest, Caiaphas, the son-in-law of Annas, had become the high priest (John

HOW TO SAY IT

Annas	*An*-nus.
Babylonians	Bab-ih-*low*-nee-unz.
Caesarea Maritima	Sess-uh-*ree*-uh Mar-uh-*tee*-muh.
Caiaphas	*Kay*-uh-fus or *Kye*-uh-fus.
Essenes	*Eh*-seenz.
Herod Antipas	*Hair*-ud *An*-tih-pus.
Herod Archelaus	*Hair*-ud Are-kuh-*lay*-us.
Judas Maccabee	*Joo*-dus *Mack*-uh-bee.
Pontius Pilate	*Pon*-shus or *Pon*-ti-us *Pie*-lut.
praetorium	*pree*-tor-ee-um.

18:13). Some Jews do not recognize the Romans' authority to demote Annas, and therefore consider him still to be the high priest.

Rather than becoming rivals, Annas and Caiaphas work together as joint high priests in certain respects. After His arrest, Jesus is first taken to the house of Annas (John 18:13) and then to the house of Caiaphas (18:24). Since Caiaphas is the one recognized by Rome, any request for Roman judgment has to come from him.

The hall of judgment is the Jerusalem residence of the governor, probably the former palace of Herod the Great, who has been dead for more than 30 years. John's actual term for this place is *praetorium,* a Latin word used to refer to a military headquarters (see this word in Mark 15:16).

This place has an inner hall where the governor can receive audiences. But the Jewish leaders accompanying Jesus do not enter. To do so would put them in contact with Gentiles, resulting in ceremonial uncleanness. Such a defilement would render them unfit to continue participating in the Passover festival. The day of the week is Friday, and the next day is particularly important to the Jews (John 19:31).

> *What Do You Think?*
>   Why can it be dangerous for the church to seek
>   help from a secular governing authority?
> *Talking Points for Your Discussion*
> - Issues of law enforcement
> - Issues of law enactment
> - Issues involving matters internal to the church

B. Accusing Jesus (vv. 29, 30)

29. Pilate then went out unto them, and said, What accusation bring ye against this man?

Pilate accommodates the Jewish leaders by going *out unto them.* This may be to a balcony or platform overlooking an open courtyard below, as this scene is often depicted by artists. If so, it means that Pilate has the upper hand psychologically, as the Jews are forced to look up at him while he looks down on them.

Pilate offers no polite small talk, but begins business talk immediately, almost rudely: *What accusation bring ye against this man?* The Greek word translated *accusation* is where we get our word *category.* So Pilate is asking for formal, categorized accusations based on written legal code. Perhaps Pilate already has the charges, but he wants the Jewish leaders to speak them publicly.

It is unlikely that this scenario has been played out many times in the past. To ask for Pilate's help would be very humbling to these proud men, a reminder that they are not the masters of their land, but are living under Roman occupation.

> *What Do You Think?*
>   Which accusations that were leveled against
>   Jesus throughout His ministry are still leveled
>   against Him today? Which of these are Jesus'
>   followers charged with as well and why?
> *Talking Points for Your Discussion*
> - Matthew 9:11; 11:19
> - Matthew 26:63-66
> - John 7:12
> - John 8:48

30. They answered and said unto him, If he were not a malefactor, we would not have delivered him up unto thee.

The Jews may be trying to make things easier for Pilate, as in, "We've already convicted this person; all you have to do is sign the death warrant."

❧ *Justice and Agendas* ❧

Many have grown cynical about the administration of justice today. Sometimes the guilty seem to go free because they could afford excellent lawyers. Sometimes the innocent are convicted, as DNA evidence proves their innocence years later. Sometimes the infamy of the crime and the nature of the media coverage make the selection of impartial jurors a near impossibility; this was one factor in play in January 2010 when authorities began contemplating a "change of venue" away from New York City for the trial of the alleged mastermind of the 9/11 terrorist attacks.

Jesus himself received more than one change of venue, but not out of a sense of fairness or impartiality. The accusers who took Jesus from the courtroom of the high priest to the judgment hall

Jesus Testifies to the Truth

of Pilate had already decided His guilt, as their statement in John 18:30 proves. They had a vested interest in the outcome (see John 11:48).

Pilate was appropriately skeptical of the Jewish leaders' claim to be seeking justice. But his own vested interests put him on the path to implementing history's greatest injustice. How do we make sure that we don't have a bit of Pilate or the Jewish leaders in us today?   —C. R. B.

C. Demanding Death (vv. 31, 32)

31. Then said Pilate unto them, Take ye him, and judge him according to your law. The Jews therefore said unto him, It is not lawful for us to put any man to death.

The Romans allow the Jews a great deal of authority in the rule of the city of Jerusalem. For example, the Jews are allowed to collect a "temple tax" for support of the religious establishment. The Jews also have their own courts and judges, including the Sanhedrin, a type of supreme court.

The decision of the Sanhedrin in the case of Jesus is that He is guilty of blasphemy in claiming to be the Son of God (see Matthew 26:63-65; Mark 14:61-64). The crime of blasphemy carries the death penalty according to Leviticus 24:16. But the Sanhedrin has no authority to execute anyone because of the restrictions imposed by the Romans. Thus the need to approach Pilate.

Pilate is likely aware of the charge of blasphemy already, for he doubtlessly maintains an efficient network of spies. Thus his suggestion *judge him according to your law* is a taunt, and both sides know it (compare Acts 18:15). Later, however, the charge of blasphemy that is voiced to Pilate is played like a trump card (John 19:7).

32. That the saying of Jesus might be fulfilled, which he spake, signifying what death he should die.

If the Jews themselves could execute Jesus, it would be by stoning (again, Leviticus 24:16). But this would not fulfill Jesus' prophecy concerning His death: that He must "be lifted up" (John 12:32), a reference to being raised on a cross (12:33). This lifting up on a cross fits the pattern established by the brass snake of Moses, which saved those who looked upon it (see 3:14, 15, last

week's lesson). Elsewhere, Jesus foretells His death by a Gentile court, which also indicates that He is not to be stoned by the Jews (see Matthew 20:18, 19; Mark 10:33, 34).

II. Pilate Questions
(John 18:33-38)

A. Are You the King? (vv. 33, 34)

33. Then Pilate entered into the judgment hall again, and called Jesus, and said unto him, Art thou the King of the Jews?

Jesus is being kept inside in the judgment hall. The Jewish leaders have no concern for His own ritual cleanliness, for no one expects Him to continue participating in the weeklong festival.

John pictures Pilate as roaring back into the hall and barking at Jesus, voicing the charges at the heart of the matter. He does this by asking a series of questions. His first question—*Art thou the King of the Jews?*—is an accusation. He is saying, in effect, "You claim to be the Jewish king? Don't you know I have been warned to move quickly against anyone trying to reestablish the Jewish monarchy?" The Romans have zero tolerance for the idea of a Jew sitting on a royal throne in Jerusalem.

We don't know how much Pilate knows about Jesus. Pilate's spy network probably keeps him informed, but there is no record of his showing any interest in investigating Jesus or His disciples before (unlike Herod Antipas, per Luke 23:8).

34. Jesus answered him, Sayest thou this thing of thyself, or did others tell it thee of me?

Jesus calmly responds with a question of His own. This presents a marked contrast with Pilate's abruptness. Jesus knows the answer, but He wants Pilate's manipulations out on the table. Jesus is asking, "Who accused me of being a king?"

What Do You Think?
What do people say about Jesus today, and how can we respond to these statements?
Talking Points for Your Discussion
- Statements that are outright false
- Statements that are true as far as they go, but they don't go far enough

---

B. Am I a Jew? (vv. 35, 36)

35. Pilate answered, Am I a Jew? Thine own nation and the chief priests have delivered thee unto me: what hast thou done?

Pilate's second question—*Am I a Jew?*—is a complaint. He wishes he had not been dragged into this mess. Perhaps he sees no way out at this point; it's a losing situation no matter what he does. If he protects Jesus, he enrages and further alienates the most powerful leaders in his province. If he executes Jesus, he allows them to manipulate him in a way that may cause problems in the future. He does not want to be their pawn.

Therefore, Pilate wants Jesus to be straight with him: *what hast thou done?* Pilate must know.

36. Jesus answered, My kingdom is not of this world: if my kingdom were of this world, then would my servants fight, that I should not be delivered to the Jews: but now is my kingdom not from hence.

Jesus' answer indicates that He is not a threat to Rome, since Jesus' *kingdom is not of this world*. Jesus does not intend to challenge the Romans in any political or military way (see Mark 12:17; John 6:15). As evidence to this effect, Jesus points out that His followers did not put up a fight at His arrest to keep Him from being *delivered to the Jews* (with the minor exception of Peter's swordsmanship, quickly corrected; see John 18:10, 11).

Pilate likely has received a report about the arrest and knows that what Jesus says is true. But Jesus' answer does not solve Pilate's dilemma. If Jesus has no designs on a political kingdom and is not resisting arrest and trial, then He is even more of a puzzle. Why are others so angry with Him?

> **What Do You Think?**
> Since we are part of a kingdom that is not of this world, what impact should this have on the way we live?
> *Talking Points for Your Discussion*
> - Concerning attitude (Matthew 5:3)
> - Concerning perseverance (Luke 9:62)
> - Concerning the power in which we live (1 Corinthians 4:20)
> - Concerning vigilance (1 Corinthians 14:20)

C. Are You a King? (v. 37)

37a. Pilate therefore said unto him, Art thou a king then?

Pilate's next question is similar to the first with a slight twist. This time he asks Jesus if He is *a king* rather than "the King of the Jews" (John 18:33, above). We might interpret this as a follow-up question to Jesus' last answer, His claim to be something other than an earthly king. Pilate is asking, "What sort of king are you? Help me understand."

37b. Jesus answered, Thou sayest that I am a king. To this end was I born, and for this cause came I into the world, that I should bear witness unto the truth. Every one that is of the truth heareth my voice.

Jesus' answer may confuse Pilate. Perhaps Pilate is expecting Jesus to say that He is the king of some small, nonviolent group of holy people. Maybe such a group intends to found some kind of monastic community in the desert, as the Essenes have done.

But that is not the implication of what Jesus says. He is directing the discussion away from politics (even away from religion) to *the truth*. Jesus says, in effect, that He is the king of those who love the truth. We note in passing that Paul refers to Jesus' response to Pilate as "a good confession" (1 Timothy 6:13).

> **What Do You Think?**
> What can you do to be more "of the truth"?
> *Talking Points for Your Discussion*
> - In your walk (Psalm 26:3; 86:11; Ephesians 4:25; 3 John 3; contrast 1 John 1:6)
> - In your desire to hear the truth (Acts 10:33; contrast Acts 7:57; 2 Timothy 4:4)
> - In personal study (Acts 17:11; 1 Timothy 6:20)
> - In cooperating with other Christians (3 John 8)

D. What Is Truth? (v. 38)

38. Pilate saith unto him, What is truth? And when he had said this, he went out again unto the Jews, and saith unto them, I find in him no fault at all.

Pilate's final question—*What is truth?*—is one of the most ringing queries in all of human history. Sadly, Pilate is not interested in Jesus' answer. Pilate has all the answers he wants and is tired of this game. So he returns to the Jewish leaders and announces that he has found *no fault at all* in Jesus. Thus he presents the Jewish leaders with a logjam, and the next move is theirs.

The resulting dialogue between Pilate and the Jewish leaders is tragically ironic. Pilate should be enraged by Jesus' claim to be a king, and the Jews should be encouraged by it. Instead, the Jews want Jesus dead, while Pilate wants to let Him go. Pilate continues to taunt the Jews, presenting Jesus as a broken, helpless man while still naming Him as their king. This pushes the Jewish leaders to exclaim "We have no king but Caesar" (John 19:15). The very men who chafe under Rome's oppressive rule claim loyalty to the emperor! All this would be comical if it were not so tragic, cruel, and unjust.

❧ *A VERY POSTMODERN QUESTION* ❧

Postmodernism is the controlling attitude in Western culture today. This attitude says that truth is subjective and personal to each individual. Gone are the days when biblical concepts were the basis for society's attitudes about government, business, or morality. Now everyone is said to have his or her own truth.

The result is that anyone who dares question someone else's personal truth is dismissed as intolerant. Anyone attempting to state the logic of the objective truth of Christianity risks derision. As one advocate of postmodern thought put it, "Logic can no longer be seen as either/or. You can't say either Christianity is true or it's false. Reality is also/and." The result of this kind of thinking: "every man did that which was right in his own eyes" (Judges 21:25). Anything goes.

Pilate's question "What is truth?" was designed to shut down a dialogue, to end a discussion. Today's Christian who tries to say "Here is truth" is likely to be shut down by the postmodern listener. But there's a brighter side: people still seek relationships with those whose lives model genuine care and concern for others—in other words, the kind of life Jesus lived! Postmodern culture may yet find the truth when it sees us living the way Jesus tells us to live. "By this shall all men

STAND UP FOR THE TRUTH

Visual for Lesson 5

Point to this visual as you ask, "What are some ways you will stand up for the truth in the week ahead?"

know that ye are my disciples, if ye have love one to another" (John 13:35).   —C. R. B.

Conclusion

A. "What Is Truth?"

When we get to this point in John's Gospel, the question "What is truth?" is asked of us almost as a quiz to test what we have learned in reading this book. The Bible does not separate truth from God. All truth is God's truth, and all truth comes from God. A few hours before appearing in front of Pilate, Jesus had prayed to the Father to "Sanctify them [His disciples] through thy truth: thy word is truth" (John 17:17). The readers of the Gospel of John know that the Word is personified in Jesus (1:14). He is the truth (14:6).

A better question for Pilate to have asked would have been, *"Who* is truth?" for Pilate was in the presence of the Son of God, the Word of truth. So are we.

B. Prayer

Father, we pray that You sanctify us in Your truth. May we not be like Pilate, who missed the blessing of Your Son. May we listen to Jesus' voice of truth and trust Him with all of our lives. We pray this in Jesus' name; amen.

C. Thought to Remember

Never compromise the truth of the gospel.

INVOLVEMENT LEARNING

Some of the activities below are also found in the helpful student book, Adult Bible Class.
Don't forget to download the free reproducible page from www.standardlesson.com to enhance your lesson!

Into the Lesson

Ask the class if anyone has fallen victim to or pulled off a successful "April Fool's Day" prank so far today. Allow several to share. Then ask, "What would you say is the most essential ingredient to get someone to fall for a prank?" After discussion, say, "It's ironic that our lesson titled 'Jesus Testifies to the Truth' falls on April Fool's Day. Let's see what Jesus had to say about truth."

Alternative: Have these letters on display as learners arrive: *C W H H A O R I G S E ?* Ask if anyone has the puzzle figured out. (Playing on the idea of *in* meaning "inside of," the solution is "Who is in charge?" C **W** H H **A O** R **I** G **S** E.) Indicate that today's text is a study of who's really in charge: the Jewish leaders, Pilate (representing the Roman Empire), or Jesus.

Into the Word

Divide your class into small groups. Instruct each group to read John 18:28-38 and work together to write five statements for a true/false quiz. After about eight minutes, have one person from each group read one of his or her group's statements aloud; then ask for a volunteer from another group to answer it. Cycle through the groups until each group has had a chance to read at least two of its statements. Then say, "What was the reason Jesus gave for why He came into the world?" After receiving the answer that He came to bear witness to the truth (John 18:37), say, "If we are followers of Jesus, then we will always want to stand on the side of truth."

Alternative: Establish three discussion groups. Give each group a handout with its instructions.

The Power Grab Group is to look at today's text for examples of both power and lack of power. Who has what power? How do they use it?

The Contentious Questions Group is to list the questions asked in the text and indicate the importance of both the answers and nonanswers.

The Moral Conflicts Group is to analyze the moral conflicts (political and spiritual) in the events described and compare them with current dilemmas faced by government and religious leaders.

Give your groups six to eight minutes to ponder and decide. Then ask each to report. During the reports, you will have opportunity to introduce ideas and questions from the lesson commentary.

Next, display these three words: *POWER, CONTENTION, CONFLICT.* Note that these were the three key words in the discussions of the three groups; affirm that these are the central issues in the so-called trials of Jesus. Ask, "In what sense does gain or loss of power affect the other two behaviors?" After responses ask, "In what way is Jesus' life is related to the three terms?"

You can also ask, "Can someone quote some of Jesus' declarations anywhere in the Gospels that deal with these three?" Responses may include the following: "I came not to send peace, but a sword" (Matthew 10:34); "I am come to set a man at variance against his father" (Matthew 10:35); and the promise to the apostles of "power from on high" (Luke 24:49).

Option: You can use the Power Struggle activity from the reproducible page, which you have downloaded, to provide another series of questions about the text. You can use it in addition to the above questions.

Into Life

Display a simple line drawing of the human ear. Impose the words "I'm All Ears" over it; below the figure insert "Every one that is of the truth heareth my voice" (John 18:37). Ask the class to brainstorm ways to "hear" Jesus in the week ahead. Also ask what can interfere with hearing Jesus and how this "static" can be overcome.

Download the reproducible page and distribute copies of the All Ears activity as learners depart.

JESUS LIVES!

DEVOTIONAL READING: Psalm 31:1-5
BACKGROUND SCRIPTURE: John 20:1-23

JOHN 20:1-10, 19, 20

1 The first day of the week cometh Mary Magdalene early, when it was yet dark, unto the sepulchre, and seeth the stone taken away from the sepulchre.

2 Then she runneth, and cometh to Simon Peter, and to the other disciple, whom Jesus loved, and saith unto them, They have taken away the Lord out of the sepulchre, and we know not where they have laid him.

3 Peter therefore went forth, and that other disciple, and came to the sepulchre.

4 So they ran both together: and the other disciple did outrun Peter, and came first to the sepulchre.

5 And he stooping down, and looking in, saw the linen clothes lying; yet went he not in.

6 Then cometh Simon Peter following him, and went into the sepulchre, and seeth the linen clothes lie,

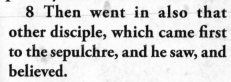

7 And the napkin, that was about his head, not lying with the linen clothes, but wrapped together in a place by itself.

8 Then went in also that other disciple, which came first to the sepulchre, and he saw, and believed.

9 For as yet they knew not the scripture, that he must rise again from the dead.

10 Then the disciples went away again unto their own home.

. . . .

19 Then the same day at evening, being the first day of the week, when the doors were shut where the disciples were assembled for fear of the Jews, came Jesus and stood in the midst, and saith unto them, Peace be unto you.

20 And when he had so said, he shewed unto them his hands and his side. Then were the disciples glad, when they saw the Lord.

KEY VERSE

Then were the disciples glad, when they saw the Lord. —**John 20:20**

GOD'S CREATIVE WORD

Unit 1: In the Beginning Was the Word

LESSONS 1–6

LESSON AIMS

After participating in this lesson, each student will be able to:

1. Retell John's account of the empty tomb.

2. Tell how the evidence of the resurrection leads one to faith in Jesus.

3. Write a prayer of gratitude for the resurrection of Jesus.

LESSON OUTLINE

Introduction

A. Shrouds and Handkerchiefs

Early in the history of the church there arose a fascination with the preservation of physical items associated with the life of Jesus. Some believed that these items possessed more than sentimental value. Some believed that the items had miraculous powers, magical properties.

The superstitious veneration of such items reached a high point during the late medieval period. That's when European crusaders and others sought the holy grail (the cup Jesus used at the last supper), the holy rood (part of the wooden cross on which Jesus was crucified), and the spear of destiny (the lance that the Roman soldier used to pierce the side of Christ to confirm His death), as well as other items. The crusaders often believed that these items would give them God's power in military conflicts. The Israelites made this mistake hundreds of years earlier with the ark of the covenant (see 1 Samuel 4:1-11).

Even today, many Christians are fascinated by claims concerning the burial cloths left in Jesus' tomb (John 19:40; 20:6, 7). Some believe that the long burial shroud was preserved and is the same as the Shroud of Turin, kept in a chapel in Italy. Books have been written, television documentaries produced, and Web sites have been devoted to the question of the authenticity of the Shroud of Turin. Less well known is the Sudarium (Latin for "sweat cloth"), a small piece of linen cloth with bloodstains that some claim to be the head cloth that John saw in the empty tomb. The alleged Sudarium is kept in a church in Oviedo, Spain.

Some have thought it desirable for churches or cathedrals to have collections of "relics," often the bones of saints. The fame and prestige of a church or cathedral was evaluated on its relic collection. Pilgrims came to these places, hoping the relics would bring them miraculous results when the devout person prayed (compare Acts 19:12). This gave great financial incentive for the unscrupulous to create forgeries of items that would be venerated. Such is probably the origin of the Shroud of Turin and the Sudarium, although we do not know this for sure.

Jesus Lives!

While artifacts from the ancient world are interesting and may help us understand the Bible better, we should not expect them to have miraculous powers. They should not be prayed to or worshiped in any way, for this is idolatry. We do not find Peter, John, or Mary going back to the empty tomb to collect these items, saying, "We had better save this stuff!" Our faith is in the risen Lord, not His grave clothes.

B. Lesson Background

The honorable disposition of dead bodies has been a concern since very ancient times. One common concern was that the corpse of a loved one not become carrion for wild animals. Some cultures, therefore, burned the bodies. Others buried the bodies in the ground or placed them in specially constructed rooms that could be sealed from animals.

In Jesus' day, the wealthier families of Jerusalem had tombs carved into the limestone hills and rock faces of the region. Such tombs would have several bed-like shelves where bodies could be placed as if asleep. The entrance to these stone rooms could be sealed, sometimes by using a separate stone carved into a disk shape so that it could be rolled in front of the entrance using tracks carved in the stone (see Matthew 27:60).

After sufficient time had passed, someone would return to the tomb, have it opened, and collect the bones. These would be placed in an ossuary (bone box), also carved out of limestone and left in the tomb. Several sets of bones could be placed in an

HOW TO SAY IT

Arimathaea	*Air*-uh-muh-***thee***-uh (*th* as in *thin*).
Coenaculum	Ken-*ock*-you-loom.
Magdala	*Mag*-duh-luh.
Magdalene	*Mag*-duh-leen or Mag-duh-*lee*-nee.
medieval	me-*dee*-vuhl.
Nazareth	*Naz*-uh-reth.
Oviedo	Oh-vee-*a*-doh (*a* as in *day*).
sepulchre	*sep*-ul-kur.
Sudarium	Sue-*deh*-ree-um.

ossuary, and space would be available for the next family body to be laid to rest in the tomb.

The Romans did not normally allow the bodies of executed criminals to be buried too soon. When a person was crucified, the body was left on the cross for a long time, to be pecked at by birds. This was a graphic, public reminder that lawbreakers suffered horrible, dishonorable deaths. But in this instance, Jesus' body and those of the thieves were taken down from the crosses quickly because the coming Sabbath "was an high day" (John 19:31).

Jesus' body was given a hasty but honorable burial in a nearby tomb. That tomb was not owned by Jesus' family. If they had had a family tomb, it would have been in Nazareth. The tomb was the possession of Joseph of Arimathaea, a prominent and wealthy leader of the Jews in Jerusalem. Matthew portrays Joseph as a disciple of Jesus (Matthew 27:57), and Mark adds that he was "an honourable counsellor," meaning a member of the Sanhedrin (Mark 15:43).

John is even more revealing when he calls Joseph a secret disciple (John 19:38). But his secret was out when he used his influence to obtain Jesus' body and bury it in his own, newly carved family tomb. Joseph's actions in using this new tomb set the stage for the drama of today's lesson.

I. Empty Tomb

(JOHN 20:1-10)

Jesus' body was allowed neither to rot on the cross nor to be buried in the ground of a simple graveyard. His body was placed in a stone room that could be sealed by rolling a door of stone across the entrance. This, along with the guard of Matthew 27:62-68, reduced to nil the possibility that the body could be stolen by His disciples.

A. Stone Rolled (v. 1)

1. The first day of the week cometh Mary Magdalene early, when it was yet dark, unto the sepulchre, and seeth the stone taken away from the sepulchre.

Although the original readers of the Gospel of John may be familiar with Mary Magdalene, she is not introduced until the end of this book. She is pictured as being one of the faithful women who did not desert Jesus while He was on the cross (see John 19:25). Luke tells us that she was a follower of Jesus from the early days of His ministry. Jesus delivered her from a terrifying case of demon possession (Luke 8:2). We remind ourselves that *Magdalene* is not a surname in the modern sense. Rather, it designates this particular Mary as being "from Magdala," perhaps to distinguish her from the other women named Mary in the Gospel accounts.

The first day of the week is our Sunday. The Jews of this time do not use names for the days of the week, since such names have pagan origins. For them the new day begins at sundown, what is Saturday evening for us. This ends the Passover Sabbath, so Mary is permitted to visit the tomb anytime after sundown.

It is still dark when she goes, although there is enough light for her to see that the stone blocking the entrance to the sepulchre is rolled back from the entrance (compare Mark 16:4). Mary is accompanied by some other women (16:1). Their chief concern is being able to gain access to the body, for they are not strong enough to roll away the stone (16:3). But Mary quickly sees that this is not going to be a problem. The tomb is wide open.

B. Apostles Informed (v. 2)

2. Then she runneth, and cometh to Simon Peter, and to the other disciple, whom Jesus loved, and saith unto them, They have taken away the Lord out of the sepulchre, and we know not where they have laid him.

Mary is disturbed by this open, abandoned tomb. She interprets it almost as a crime scene: someone has opened the tomb and removed (stolen?) the body of Jesus. She does not know who this might be, telling Peter it was *they*. She is sure, then, that neither Peter nor the other disciples have taken the body; otherwise, her report would be different. In that case, "Where did *you* take the body?" would be her question. The idea that Jesus has risen from the dead does not seem to enter her thoughts, although she may have heard Him give prophecies of His resurrection (see John 10:17, 18).

What Do You Think?
What surprises have you experienced in your own search for Christ?
Talking Points for Your Discussion
- Surprises that added to your understanding of Jesus
- Surprises that corrected your misunderstandings of Jesus

❧ TAKING AWAY THE LORD? ❧

Beginning early in the twentieth century and continuing into the twenty-first, a number of leaders within Christianity itself began to question, and then outright reject, the biblical picture of Jesus. The traditional doctrines of the virgin birth, the substitutionary atonement, the bodily resurrection, etc., became objects of doubt. Perhaps that is to be expected from atheists, but from leaders of churches traditionally committed to biblical truth?

These skeptical views gradually took hold within some denominational structures. It got to the point where one could be a leading official in a given denomination while openly denying the biblical testimony and historic confessions that supposedly governed that denomination. Such a state of confusion is traced to a rejection of the Bible as being the inspired Word of God. When that happens, everything else becomes fair game, from doctrinal clarity to moral standards for church leaders.

It's proper to raise an alarm in such instances: "They have taken away our Lord!" But some self-examination may be in order before we do too much finger-pointing. When we give lip service to Christ and fail to live up to the biblical testimony, are we not ourselves "taking away the Lord"?
—C. R. B.

C. Apostles Run (vv. 3, 4)

3, 4. Peter therefore went forth, and that other disciple, and came to the sepulchre. So they ran both together: and the other disciple did outrun Peter, and came first to the sepulchre.

The phrase *other disciple* is John's way of referring to himself (compare John 21:24). We can imagine that the daylight is now in full force.

We do not know for sure where Peter and John are in relation to the tomb when Mary Magdalene brings the news. It is possible that they are at the house where the last supper was held. This is traditionally located at a place called the Coenaculum, located in the southern end of Jerusalem. The tomb may be at the site of the current Church of the Holy Sepulchre (again, possible but not certain). This place is outside the western wall of the city in Jesus' day (compare Hebrews 13:12).

The distance from the Coenaculum to the Holy Sepulchre in modern Jerusalem is a little over one-half mile. If the speculations regarding locations are accurate, this makes for a quick morning run, perhaps of 10 minutes or less.

John arrives at the tomb first, perhaps because he is younger than Peter. The difference in arrival times is likely not more than a minute or two, but this detail indicates that they are both very concerned by Mary's news. They want to view the situation firsthand without delay.

Visual for Lesson 6

Point to this visual as you introduce the discussion question associated with verse 20.

> **What Do You Think?**
> What difference does the resurrection make in your life?
> *Talking Points for Your Discussion*
> - In your time priorities
> - In your financial priorities
> - In your conversations
> - In your relationships

D. Shroud Examined (vv. 5-8)

5. And he stooping down, and looking in, saw the linen clothes lying; yet went he not in.

John peeks through the doorway, and there is enough light now for him to make out details. He sees *the linen clothes,* but no body. The body would have been wrapped lengthwise in a long shroud with strips of cloth used to bundle it tightly. Spices had been wrapped in, but John says nothing about them at this point (see John 19:39, 40). John does not enter the tomb, though, perhaps out of deference to Peter.

6, 7. Then cometh Simon Peter following him, and went into the sepulchre, and seeth the linen clothes lie, and the napkin, that was about his head, not lying with the linen clothes, but wrapped together in a place by itself.

Peter immediately enters the tomb on arrival. He too sees what is left of the linen shroud and notices the separate *napkin* that had been wrapped around Jesus' head (compare John 11:44).

The impression we are given is that the shroud has been shrugged off and is lying in disarray on the floor, but the head cloth has been removed, folded, and stacked neatly on the ledge. There is no sign of the body. These details argue further against the body's having been stolen. Body snatchers would not take time to unwrap the shroud, and they certainly would not fold up the head cloth.

> **What Do You Think?**
> What are the potential benefits and dangers of taking a trip to see the alleged burial cloths and empty tomb of Christ?
> *Talking Points for Your Discussion*
> - The benefits of archaeology in general
> - The problem of "needing" to see such things (John 20:29; Hebrews 11:1)
> - Danger of focusing on the mystical

8. Then went in also that other disciple, which came first to the sepulchre, and he saw, and believed.

John now enters the tomb. We are not told what Peter's reaction is at this point, although Luke 24:12 notes Peter as "wondering in himself at that which was come to pass." When John takes in the scene, however, he believes.

This affirmation of John's faith does not give specific content for his belief. We are safe to say that at the least it means he believes in Jesus (see John 1:12; 19:35) because of what he has seen and experienced. John records that true faith does not require eyewitness experience, however (see John 20:29). Although John has not yet seen the risen Lord and does not fully understand what has happened, he believes.

❧ *THAT WHICH IS SEEN AND BELIEVED* ❧

After the resurrection, Jesus said to Thomas, "Because thou hast seen me, thou hast believed: blessed are they that have not seen, and yet have believed" (John 20:29). This is part of the message of Christianity that we pass on to those who have yet to accept Christ as Savior.

Unfortunately, the negative things that the world sees in Christianity often take priority over the unseen; the message of the risen Christ takes a backseat when church scandals become public. In years past, the message of Christ was harmed by the scandals involving the names Jim Bakker, Jimmy Swaggart, and Ted Haggard. At the time of this writing, the issue of pedophile priests within the Roman Catholic Church is drawing the headlines. What the world ends up believing is that Christianity doesn't really have much to offer if church leaders do not "practice what they preach."

We may have no control over what the world sees in a few errant church leaders, but we *do* have control over what our neighbor sees in us. We can argue that a few high-profile church leaders do not represent Christianity, but that millions of low-profile Christians *can* indicate what Christianity really is. Does the world see the risen Christ in you?

—C. R. B.

E. Homeward Departure (vv. 9, 10)

9, 10. For as yet they knew not the scripture, that he must rise again from the dead.

Then the disciples went away again unto their own home.

It takes some time for these earliest Christians to put all the pieces together regarding Jesus and the fulfillment of Scripture. Seven weeks later, on the Day of Pentecost, Peter will expound on Psalm 16 as a prophecy of Jesus' resurrection (see Acts 2:25-32). Decades later, Paul can state that Christ died, was buried, and rose from the dead in accordance with Scriptures (1 Corinthians 15:3, 4).

We should also understand that these deeper insights are the result of the influence of the Holy Spirit (John 14:26). John writes his gospel as much as six decades after this resurrection morning. He has had a long time to reflect and understand.

II. Risen Lord
(JOHN 20:19, 20)

In John 20:11-18 (not in today's text), Mary Magdalene remains at the tomb after the disciples depart. It is then that the risen Jesus appears to her. She reports this to the disciples, but her witness apparently does not allay their fears, as we shall see.

A. Blessing of Peace (v. 19)

19. Then the same day at evening, being the first day of the week, when the doors were shut where the disciples were assembled for fear of the Jews, came Jesus and stood in the midst, and saith unto them, Peace be unto you.

Later that day, Jesus makes a dramatic appearance to the disciples at the place they are staying (hiding). John pictures a house with doors closed tight. This reminds us of the climate of fear that they still feel. Their leader has been murdered by the men who are supposed to be the spiritual leaders of the nation. Will the disciples be next? Is there another Judas out there who will betray them too?

Yet Jesus' miraculous appearance in this secure room serves to change their fearful mind-set as Jesus declares *peace be unto you*. The fact that Jesus is able to appear inside a room without passing through an open door does not mean that He is now some type of disembodied spirit, although that is what the disciples initially think (Luke 24:37). Jesus really does have a body, as proven by the fact that He shares meals with the disciples after the resurrection (see Luke 24:42, 43; compare John 21:12, 13). We see further proof in our next verse.

B. Display of Wounds (v. 20)

20. And when he had so said, he shewed unto them his hands and his side. Then were the disciples glad, when they saw the Lord.

The reality of Jesus' body is demonstrated as He shows *his hands and his side*. This is a display of His wounds suffered on the cross, unmistakable confirmation that this is the body that was placed in the tomb (compare John 20:27, not in today's text). It is now beginning to sink in for the disciples: Jesus is risen from the dead! The reaction changes from fear and confusion to gladness and joy, the correct tone for the celebration of Resurrection Sunday.

Conclusion

A. Enduring Questions, Eternal Hope

The Gospel of John is full of pointed questions. "What seek ye?" (John 1:38). "Can there any good thing come out of Nazareth?" (1:46). "Wilt thou be made whole?" (5:6). "Will ye also go away?" (6:67). "Believest thou this?" (11:26). "Who is this Son of man?" (12:34). "Art thou the King of the Jews?" (18:33). "What is truth?" (18:38). "Simon . . . lovest thou me?" (21:16). When these questions are asked by the characters in the storyline (sometimes by Jesus himself), they usually are asked of us, the readers, too.

In particular, John includes many questions about faith. Such questions still hold today. All around us are unbelievers—men, women, and children—with no promise of forgiveness, no hope of salvation without Jesus. Their lives may hum along for a long time, but there comes a day when things fall apart, and they have no faith to sustain them.

Just as the risen Jesus Christ gave hope and peace to Mary, the sharing of the resurrection gives hope to us today. Yes, life is hard, but we know that Jesus has not abandoned us. He has gone to prepare a place for us, a heavenly abode where there will be no more tears, no more sorrow, no more heartache (Revelation 21:4).

The waiting world is looking for a Savior. It asks "Who is He? Please tell me so that I might believe" (compare John 9:36). We have the answer to that question. May we share it with all, whether they listen or not. May we proclaim *Hallelujah! Christ is risen indeed!*

B. Prayer

Father God, our Lord and Master, we are amazed at Your love for us. We are astounded that Your Son, Jesus, would willingly give His life for us. We are dumbfounded to learn that He did not stay dead, but rose to live again.

That empty tomb is the greatest news we could ever hear, for it gives us the hope that death is not the end, but the beginning of a new life with You. May we live as people of faith, trusting in You alone for our salvation. We pray in the name of our Savior, Jesus Christ; amen.

C. Thought to Remember

Only Jesus' resurrection
gives us eternal hope.

INVOLVEMENT LEARNING

Some of the activities below are also found in the helpful student book, Adult Bible Class.
Don't forget to download the free reproducible page from www.standardlesson.com to enhance your lesson!

Into the Lesson

Place in chairs copies of the Resurrection Surprise! activity from the reproducible page, which you have downloaded. Learners can begin to work on these as they arrive. After an appropriate amount of time, discuss why it was so hard for the disciples to understand what was going to happen to Jesus.

Into the Word

Give each learner a small sheet with the word *FIRST* at the top and the numerals 1 through 8 vertically down the left-hand side. Say, "I'm going to give you a quiz about the firsts of John 20." Ask for volunteers to read verses 1-20; this section includes verses 11-18, which are not included in today's printed text. Learners can have their Bibles open as you ask the following questions.

Answers are in the verses noted in italics; you can either (1) announce the verse number and have learners say what "first" they discover there or (2) not give the verse number, which will require learners to search for the correct verse in the text.

1. How does the word *first* relate to the calendar timing of the resurrection? *(day of the week, v. 1)* 2. Who arrived first at the empty tomb? *(Mary Magdalene, v. 1)* 3. What was the first explanation offered for the tomb being empty? *(body taken, v. 2)* 4. Who was the first of the two male disciples to reach the tomb? *("other disciple," John, vv. 3, 4)* 5. Which of the disciples was the first to go into the tomb? *(Peter, vv. 5, 6)* 6. Who is the first who was said to believe? *("other disciple," v. 8)* 7. Who was the first person to be confronted by the risen Lord? *(Mary, vv. 14-16)* 8. What were Jesus' first words to the disciples assembled in the locked room? *(peace be unto you, v. 19)*

As you work your way through the questions above, consider these follow-up questions, respectively: 1. In what sense did Jesus' resurrection sanctify the first day of the week? 2. Although only Mary Magdalene is named by John, who were the other women present? (Matthew 28:1; Mark 16:1; Luke 24:10) 3. Why would Mary think that someone had removed (even stolen) the body of Jesus? 4. Why do you suppose John got to the tomb before Peter? 5. How was Peter's rush into the tomb characteristic of his behavior, as we know it? 6. What exactly do you think it was that "the other disciple" (John) believed? 7. What is surprising (or not surprising) about Jesus' making His first resurrection appearance to Mary rather than one of the apostles? 8. Why do you think Jesus chose the words He did rather than, say, "Don't be afraid"?

Into Life

In advance, purchase or fabricate tiny boxes (about wristwatch size), one for each learner. Hand them out and say, "Open your box." When learners see that the boxes are empty, give each person seven strips of paper with these directions: "To focus on the joy we have because of the empty tomb, each day this week write one element of your thanksgiving and put the slip into the empty box." Have this sample ready to read and to put into your own box: "I am filled with joy because every time a Christian friend or family member dies I have this great hope: Jesus will raise that person to glory!"

Suggest that each learner open his or her box and review the seven prayer-statements at the end of the week.

Alternative: Distribute copies of the If Only . . . activity from the reproducible page, which you have downloaded. Ask learners to reflect on Paul's explanation of why Jesus' resurrection is so important to believers.

Allow time to select a verse to write and memorize. If time is short, both this and the What Do You See? activity from the reproducible page can be take-home exercises. Close with a prayer of praise for the risen Jesus.

Jesus Lives!

Temple Is Cleansed

DEVOTIONAL READING: **Psalm 122**
BACKGROUND SCRIPTURE: **John 2:13-25**

JOHN 2:13-22

13 And the Jews' passover was at hand, and Jesus went up to Jerusalem.

14 And found in the temple those that sold oxen and sheep and doves, and the changers of money sitting:

15 And when he had made a scourge of small cords, he drove them all out of the temple, and the sheep, and the oxen; and poured out the changers' money, and overthrew the tables;

16 And said unto them that sold doves, Take these things hence; make not my Father's house an house of merchandise.

17 And his disciples remembered that it was written, The zeal of thine house hath eaten me up.

18 Then answered the Jews and said unto him, What sign shewest thou unto us, seeing that thou doest these things?

19 Jesus answered and said unto them, Destroy this temple, and in three days I will raise it up.

20 Then said the Jews, Forty and six years was this temple in building, and wilt thou rear it up in three days?

21 But he spake of the temple of his body.

22 When therefore he was risen from the dead, his disciples remembered that he had said this unto them; and they believed the scripture, and the word which Jesus had said.

KEY VERSE

[Jesus] said unto them that sold doves, Take these things hence; make not my Father's house an house of merchandise. —**John 2:16**

GOD'S CREATIVE WORD

Unit 2: Jesus' Powerful Words

LESSONS 7–9

LESSON AIMS

After participating in this lesson, each student will be able to:

1. Summarize the reactions of Jesus' disciples and enemies to Jesus' cleansing of the temple.

2. Compare and contrast the literal temple with Jesus' reference to His body as "this temple."

3. State one way he or she submits to Jesus' authority as demonstrated by His cleansing of the temple.

LESSON OUTLINE

Introduction
    A. When Strange Things Make Sense
    B. Lesson Background
 I. Jesus' Actions (JOHN 2:13-17)
    A. Described (vv. 13-15)
    B. Explained (vv. 16, 17)
      The Purity of God's Temple
II. Jesus' Announcement (JOHN 2:18-22)
    A. Authority Challenged (vv. 18-20)
    B. Answer Explained (vv. 21, 22)
      Sense and Reference
Conclusion
    A. Jesus Has What We Need
    B. Prayer
    C. Thought to Remember

Introduction

A. When Strange Things Make Sense

Have you ever been in a situation like any of these?

A friend offers a strange reason why you need to be in a particular place at a particular time. When you arrive, you find out a surprise party has been planned for you.

A coworker begins acting differently on the job. You learn later that the person is experiencing a personal crisis.

You hear strange sounds from the walls or attic of your home. You eventually discover that a wild animal has decided to make your home its home.

Most of us have witnessed or otherwise experienced something that seemed strange but later made sense. Life often presents riddles that we can solve only as time passes. This is the way Jesus appeared to the people of His time, even to His closest followers. His words and actions were often unexpected, strange, even offensive. To His opponents, He appeared to be degrading everything that was sacred. To His disciples, He seemed to be a mystery, a speaker of riddles.

Because Jesus did what people did not expect —and He did *not* do what they *did* expect—His words and actions appeared mysterious. But the mystery disappears when we grasp what God was in the process of bringing about. Viewed from the end of Jesus' story, His mysterious deeds and words become astonishing indicators of what He accomplished. Things about Jesus that seemed incomprehensible become clear signs that God was at work to bring His saving work to its conclusion. Today's story, about Jesus' actions in the temple, is just such an indicator.

B. Lesson Background

The account of the temple cleansing of John 2:13-22 (today's text) connects with a series of events that show Jesus responding to the differing expectations among the people of Israel regarding God's saving work. These issues range from the Mosaic laws for purification (John 2:6), to the traditions of the Pharisees (3:1-16), to the predictions of John the Baptist (3:25-36), to the hopes of the Samaritans (4:25-42). The theme of *fulfillment* is very prominent in this section of John's Gospel, which includes our text for today.

John recounts that this temple cleansing took place near the time of the Passover observance (John 2:13). This yearly feast celebrated God's deliverance of Israel from slavery in Egypt. A major event on the Jewish calendar, Passover called for faithful Israelites to gather in Jerusalem for the observance. We can expect, therefore, that Jesus' actions in the temple at the time were witnessed by a large crowd of worshipers. This is the first of three Passovers mentioned in John (the other two are in 6:4 and 11:55). John likes to connect the storyline of his Gospel to the Jewish feasts (see 2:13; 5:1; 6:4; 7:2; 10:22; 11:55).

The temple in Jerusalem was the center of Jewish religious life. Although the faithful of Jesus' time regarded the temple as a supremely sacred place, it had also become controversial. By the time of Jesus, the temple had been led for several generations by an extended family of priests who were regarded widely as corrupt. A custom had arisen to use the outer court of the temple to sell animals for sacrifices. This was an obvious convenience for people who traveled great distances to worship there. Many people in Jesus' time probably approved of the practice, though some undoubtedly objected, especially if the corrupt temple leadership had a hand in the business.

Likewise, it had become customary that only one kind of coinage could be used to give offerings to the temple. So money changers also did business in the temple courtyard, offering the acceptable coins in exchange for whatever coins the worshipers brought with them.

The coins deemed acceptable were from the city of Tyre; ironically, such coins featured images of pagan gods. The acceptability of such coins may have been due to their high silver content. The

irony probably was not lost on the people forced to swap their money at exchange rates that were very favorable to the money changers.

As a whole, the situation suggests a combination of complacency, corruption, and controversy. While many were content with business as usual, others were anxious for reform. Those wanting reform focused on God's ancient promise to King David that David's "son" would one day build a "house" for God and establish a never-ending rule (2 Samuel 7:12-17; 1 Chronicles 17:11-14).

Some who had appeared to be the fulfillment of that promise proved to be otherwise. Solomon built the first temple, but God told him that his throne would not be established because of his idolatry (1 Kings 11:11). In the years before Jesus' birth, King Herod had begun a lavish rebuilding project for the temple, perhaps hoping to identify himself as the promised son of David.

But for Israel's faithful, the promised temple of fulfillment was yet to appear (compare Ezekiel 40–42). They looked forward anxiously to the time that God would send the one who would build the promised temple and assume the throne of an everlasting kingdom.

I. Jesus' Actions
(JOHN 2:13-17)
A. Described (vv. 13-15)

13. And the Jews' passover was at hand, and Jesus went up to Jerusalem.

The custom of Jesus' time is that every faithful Jew who is able goes to Jerusalem to observe Passover. But in John's Gospel, Jesus' visits to Jerusalem are more than mere festival observances. Each time Jesus goes from His home in the north to Jerusalem in the south, He confronts the religious leaders who perceive that His authority threatens their position.

At the end of the story, Jesus is killed at the instigation of those religious leaders in Jerusalem, during the Passover feast (John 13:1; 18:28, 39; 19:14). Today's account, near the beginning of John's Gospel, sets the stage for that coming confrontation. It especially makes the reader ponder over who will prevail in the end.

HOW TO SAY IT

Assyrians	Uh-*sear*-e-unz.
Babylonians	Bab-ih-*low*-nee-unz.
Ezekiel	Ee-*zeek*-ee-ul or Ee-*zeek*-yul.
Judah	*Joo*-duh.

The occasion of Passover focuses this idea even more. For the faithful, Passover points back to God's liberation of Israel from slavery in Egypt. But it also points forward to a second liberation. The prophets had warned Israel that disobedience would lead to God's sending them a second time into captivity in a foreign land. That had indeed happened as the Assyrians and Babylonians conquered the nation and deported its people.

But beyond those events, the prophets promised that God would lead His people out of captivity and restore them in a great second exodus (Isaiah 40:1-5). That promise had been partly fulfilled when the Persians allowed the Jews to return to the promised land. But a complete fulfillment is yet to come in Jesus' day. So His actions at Passover raise a question for those who witness them: Could this Jesus be the one who liberates and restores God's people?

14. And found in the temple those that sold oxen and sheep and doves, and the changers of money sitting.

This scene is familiar to the Jews of Jesus' day. The animals needed for sacrifice are on display for sale in the temple court. Those who exchange unacceptable coins for coins acceptable in the temple are at their tables. It is business as usual.

15. And when he had made a scourge of small cords, he drove them all out of the temple, and the sheep, and the oxen; and poured out the changers' money, and overthrew the tables.

Jesus' actions are powerful and decisive. In modern terminology, Jesus would be called *an extremist*. He does not merely protest the activities; He puts a stop to them. The overturning of tables and pouring out of money creates chaos for the money changers, now forced to gather their coins and perhaps argue over which coins belong to whom. To make *a scourge of small cords* implies that Jesus is striking the animals to get them moving.

We can imagine a crowd of anxious Passover pilgrims surrounding the scene. The actions they witness are far from normal and so are disturbing. But they also provoke thought. What do these things mean? Are they the actions of a madman or something altogether different?

B. Explained (vv. 16, 17)

16. And said unto them that sold doves, Take these things hence; make not my Father's house an house of merchandise.

Our first hint of the explanation comes from the lips of Jesus himself. His words are significant for all, but John tells us that Jesus speaks directly to those selling doves, the animals sacrificed by those too poor to afford a sheep, goat, or ox (Leviticus 5:7). Jesus orders these merchants (and presumably the others too) out of the temple.

Jesus justifies His audacious command with another audacious statement. The temple is understood to be the house of God, the sacred symbol of His presence among His people. Jesus affirms that the temple belongs to God, but in doing so Jesus makes an unexpected claim in referring to God as *my Father*.

While the people of Israel occasionally refer to God as *Father*, they do so collectively, not individually: "our Father" is the more common form of address (Isaiah 64:8; Romans 1:7; etc.). When Jesus refers to God as His Father, Jesus implies that He has a relationship as God's Son that is like no other person's. Jesus has the right to act boldly in the temple because He enters the temple as the Son of the God to whom the temple belongs.

With that authority, Jesus declares that God's house is not a place for merchandise. We can gather the reason for this statement by looking at those to whom the pronouncement is directed and the historical setting. This pronouncement is relevant to all, but it is addressed especially to those who sell to the poor. From the history of the temple's leadership, we can infer that those leaders were known for enriching themselves at others' expense.

God, by contrast, is gracious. He provides for His people's needs and protects the weak. Sacrifice in the temple is a vivid image of this: God provides His needy people with the means to approach Him in worship and to receive His forgiveness. The needy are never to be exploited, least of all in God's house! The true and right use of the temple centers on God's amazing, sacrificial grace, which will be seen most fully in Jesus' self-sacrifice.

> **What Do You Think?**
> What are some things that need to be "cleansed" from your life (1 Corinthians 3:16)? Why?
> *Talking Points for Your Discussion*
> - Destructive thought patterns
> - Inappropriate entertainment choices
> - Wrong financial priorities

❧ THE PURITY OF GOD'S TEMPLE ❧

Churches have developed different viewpoints about merchandising within the four walls of the church building. Those who see little or no connection between the temple of Jesus' day and modern church buildings may be very lenient. I know of churches that have a fish fry every Friday night; the money taken in may go to pay the church's bills. Other churches have raffles, rummage sales, or bingo games for the same purpose. Many churches have no problem with members selling Girl Scout cookies, etc., while at church.

Other churches prohibit any kind of money-making within the church building. They believe the Lord's work ought to be sustained by the free-will gifts of the members, not by the selling of merchandise. Such churches may allow the sale of tickets for, say, a father-son banquet as long as the proceeds go only to defray the costs of the dinner. Even so, the sale of tickets might be allowed only in the entryway or outside, not within the sanctuary of the church itself.

Whichever perspective we take, we must be concerned that we do not create unholiness in our corporate worship areas. Even more importantly, we should take care not to bring unholiness into the real temple for Christians: our bodies. See 1 Corinthians 3:16, 17.   —J. B. N.

Point to this visual as your class brainstorms ways to keep God's temple—our bodies—pure.

17. And his disciples remembered that it was written, The zeal of thine house hath eaten me up.

In John's Gospel, Jesus' disciples have been with Him since John the Baptist directed them toward Jesus in John 1:29-37. Having been witnesses to John the Baptist's testimony and Jesus' miracle of turning water to wine (2:1-11), they must struggle to understand what Jesus' words and actions signify. Here they are reminded of a text from the Psalms, Israel's familiar "hymnbook."

The text they remember is Psalm 69:9. Like many of the psalms, chapter 69 is a desperate call to God to protect His faithful ones from vicious enemies. The second half of Psalm 69:9 (see Romans 15:3) implies that enemies oppose and pursue God's people precisely because those people are faithful to God. As the disciples recall this verse, perhaps they see Jesus' dedication to God's temple as making Him an enemy of the temple's corrupt leaders. They no doubt wonder whether Jesus will find himself in distress like that described in the psalm.

Later, Jesus will indeed become the mortal enemy of the temple's leaders. They will plot His death, and they will appear to succeed. But just as the psalmist is confident that God will deliver him from his enemies (Psalm 69:16-18, 33-36), so Jesus will triumph through His resurrection. What the suffering people of God experience in a hostile world, Jesus takes upon himself.

II. Jesus' Announcement

(JOHN 2:18-22)

A. Authority Challenged (vv. 18-20)

18. Then answered the Jews and said unto him, What sign shewest thou unto us, seeing that thou doest these things?

Jesus' opponents keenly understand that to step into Israel's most sacred space and put an end to the conventional way of doing things requires enormous authority. They now demand some evidence of that authority, confident that Jesus can supply nothing of the kind. Specifically, they ask Jesus for a sign. But if they are given a sign, will they believe?

19. Jesus answered and said unto them, Destroy this temple, and in three days I will raise it up.

As in so many instances, Jesus' answer is indirect, like a puzzle or a riddle. It appears to present a challenge to the temple leaders: if you tear down this temple, the base of your own power, then I will build it again, and in record time, proving that I am the one with real authority over the temple.

This statement reminds the hearers of God's promise of a coming Son of David (compare Mark 12:35), who is to build the true house of God and establish an everlasting kingdom. If Jesus can do what He claims, then He is greater than Solomon, greater than Herod: Jesus is the eternal king promised by God.

20. Then said the Jews, Forty and six years was this temple in building, and wilt thou rear it up in three days?

Jesus' opponents respond to His audacious statement. Herod the Great had begun rebuilding the temple around 19 BC. The project continued long past Herod's death and is just a little past its midpoint during Jesus' ministry. Everyone knows that building the temple is taking decades. So how can Jesus possibly let it be destroyed and then rebuild it *in three days*? The statement seems preposterous.

B. Answer Explained (vv. 21, 22)

21. But he spake of the temple of his body.

Now we hear the answer to the riddle. Jesus is not speaking about the destruction and rebuilding of the literal, physical temple in Jerusalem. He is speaking of himself as the temple. Thus Jesus is making a bold claim to fulfill what God has promised regarding the temple.

The temple has profound significance for ancient Israel. It represents God's promise to be present with Israel. It is the place God provides for animal sacrifice, by which Israel is promised forgiveness for disobedience. But the temple underwent a great crisis in Israel's history. After generations of disobedience, God brought judgment on His people as the Babylonian empire destroyed Jerusalem and the temple, taking the people of Judah captive in 586 BC. But God had promised that He would restore Israel to the land and restore the temple to even greater prominence.

With His pronouncement, Jesus is implying that all this meaning associated with the temple is now coming to its focal point in Him. Jesus is the one through whom God is truly present with His people. Jesus is the one who by His own death offers the real, ultimate sacrifice that brings forgiveness. And Jesus' resurrection is what will bring the true restoration.

All of this is hidden from those who first hear Jesus' pronouncement of verse 19. That prediction is mysterious to them, but it is also memorable for its audacity. In the verse before us, it is the Gospel writer—not Jesus or any of those present with Him at the time—who explains the meaning.

❧ SENSE AND REFERENCE ❧

We often see the friends and enemies of Jesus misunderstanding His words in the Gospels. They frequently took Him literally when He was speaking figuratively. Those who study such things call this *an issue of sense and reference.*

That issue presents itself here with regard to the word *temple.* Most folks, ancient and modern, normally take the reference to be to a building used for sacred purposes. Such a building was considered the place where a divine presence resided.

By extension, the word *temple* is also used to refer to any place occupied by a divine presence. It is in this sense that the word takes on more of a spiritual than an architectural significance. The confusion of Jesus' opponents is clear to us today: when Jesus referred to the *temple,* they thought of the physical building, but Jesus was referring to His own body. Perhaps it was self-imposed spiritual blinders that prevented them from catching Jesus' real meaning. The warning of Isaiah 6:9 (repeated in Matthew 13:14; Mark 4:12; and Acts 28:26) still applies: "Hear ye indeed, but understand not; and see ye indeed, but perceive not."   —J. B. N.

22. When therefore he was risen from the dead, his disciples remembered that he had said this unto them; and they believed the scripture, and the word which Jesus had said.

The event that will reveal Jesus' meaning is His resurrection, which occurs on the third day after His death. By rising from the dead, Jesus advances the fulfillment of God's end-time promises. Through God's Spirit, Jesus will be present with His people wherever they are. Through the good news of Jesus' sacrifice, forgiveness will be available to all.

Jesus' actions and words seem outrageous at the time. But what God does in Jesus' resurrection is the demonstration that His startling claims are true. God made sacred promises in light of Israel's most sacred institution: the temple. Those promises are fulfilled in Jesus.

What Do You Think?
When was a time that a significant event made a Scripture clearer to you? What dangers lurk in relating modern events to Scripture?
Talking Points for Your Discussion
- A world or national event
- A personal or family crisis
- An issue in the church

Conclusion
A. Jesus Has What We Need

Jesus challenged some of the most powerful people and most entrenched practices of His day. He asserted authority over all of them, authority as the one who was fulfilling God's promises. Whatever people had sought from the temple and its leaders, Jesus actually delivered.

Today, people around us accept various authorities and look to various sources to supply what they need. But Jesus is the one who can supply what they actually need. To regard Jesus as having such authority and power may seem strange, even foolish, to many. But if He is truly the one whom God raised from the dead, then we have nowhere to turn but to Him.

Where do we look to be supplied with what we need? Perhaps we rely on jobs, achievement, family members, friends. All of those are good in proper contexts. But there is only one who gives what we truly need. That fact should be reflected in our thoughts and actions.

B. Prayer

Almighty God, we thank You that You have fulfilled Your gracious promises to us through Jesus. We ask that You strengthen us to live as those who have been touched by that amazing, surprising grace. In His name we pray; amen!

C. Thought to Remember
Purity in our worship expressions
is still important.

INVOLVEMENT LEARNING

Some of the activities below are also found in the helpful student book, Adult Bible Class.
Don't forget to download the free reproducible page from www.standardlesson.com to enhance your lesson!

Into the Lesson

Before class begins, outline the temple's floor plan on the classroom floor using masking tape. Drawings of the temple can be found in nearly all Bible dictionaries and certainly on the Internet. Keep the outline simple. Include the outer and inner courts, plus the large bronze altar on the inner court. Outline also the Holy Place and the Most Holy Place. Label the various courts, rooms, altars, ark of the covenant, and furnishings.

Ask the class to gather around the outline as you state that the events in today's lesson take place in the temple. (If your learning space has movable chairs, arrange them in a semi-circle around the outline.) Use a laser pointer to highlight the various areas as you briefly describe the activities that were to take place in the temple (if you need to brush up on this yourself, consult Numbers 28, 29; etc.). Also discuss the special place the temple held in the lives of Jewish people as mentioned in the Lesson Background.

Conclude: "Today's lesson involves a well-known event in Jesus' life: the temple cleansing of John 2. From what you can see of the floor plan, where would you think the merchants would have set up shop?" *(Expected answer: the outer court.)*

Into the Word

Say, "Jesus' cleansing of the temple in John 2 may be a familiar story. But are we really as familiar with it as we think we are?" Have everyone close their Bibles. Then distribute handouts of the following "What's Wrong?" quiz. Ask learners to cross out the wrong information and replace it with what is correct.

1. The festival celebration that set the stage for Jesus' temple cleansing was the Feast of Dedication. 2. Jesus found people giving away livestock freely in the temple. 3. Jesus made a scourge (whip) from links of chain. 4. Jesus burned the tables of the money changers. 5. Jesus accused the ones who sold sheep of turning His Father's house into a house of merchandise. 6. After Jesus' surprising actions, the Jews asked Jesus for money as proof of His authority. 7. Jesus' answered by saying that if the Jews would "destroy this temple," then He would raise it in four days. 8. The temple Jesus was speaking of in response to the Jews was His 12 disciples. *[Answers from John 2:13-22: 1, verse 13; 2, verse 14; 3, verse 15; 4, verse 15; 5, verse 16; 6, verse 18; 7, verse 19; 8, verse 21.]*

Discuss answers after about eight minutes. Larger classes can discuss answers in small groups.

Into Life

Write *So What?* on the board. Spend a few minutes brainstorming reasons why John 2:13-22 is important for today. Jot learner responses on the board. If no one mentions it, be sure to note the idea that Jesus used the temple cleansing to demonstrate His authority as the divine Son of God.

Let the fact of Jesus' authority lead to a discussion regarding what that authority signifies for modern culture. Write *Authority to . . .* on the board. Ask learners to complete that statement with modern-day applications. List responses on the board. Here are some possible responses you can mention if no one else does: to judge and condemn, to save and redeem, to direct behavior, to demand leaving behind wrong traditions, to expect ethical practices in government, to require truthfulness. Ask learners to select or adapt one of these answers as a resolution in his or her life for this week. Allow a brief quiet time for each person to make that commitment to God.

Alternative: Download the reproducible page and distribute copies of the Temple (and Church Building?) Purity activity. Have learners complete it in small groups, per directions. Discuss.

From the same reproducible page, distribute copies of the Complete the Bumper Sticker activity as a take-home exercise.

SAMARITAN WOMAN FINDS LIVING WATER

DEVOTIONAL READING: Revelation 22:10-17

BACKGROUND SCRIPTURE: John 4:1-42

JOHN 4:7-15, 21-30

7 There cometh a woman of Samaria to draw water: Jesus saith unto her, Give me to drink.

8 (For his disciples were gone away unto the city to buy meat.)

9 Then saith the woman of Samaria unto him, How is it that thou, being a Jew, askest drink of me, which am a woman of Samaria? for the Jews have no dealings with the Samaritans.

10 Jesus answered and said unto her, If thou knewest the gift of God, and who it is that saith to thee, Give me to drink; thou wouldest have asked of him, and he would have given thee living water.

11 The woman saith unto him, Sir, thou hast nothing to draw with, and the well is deep: from whence then hast thou that living water?

12 Art thou greater than our father Jacob, which gave us the well, and drank thereof himself, and his children, and his cattle?

13 Jesus answered and said unto her, Whosoever drinketh of this water shall thirst again:

14 But whosoever drinketh of the water that I shall give him shall never thirst; but the water that I shall give him shall be in him a well of water springing up into everlasting life.

15 The woman saith unto him, Sir, give me this water, that I thirst not, neither come hither to draw.

. . . .

21 Jesus saith unto her, Woman, believe me, the hour cometh, when ye shall neither in this mountain, nor yet at Jerusalem, worship the Father.

22 Ye worship ye know not what: we know what we worship: for salvation is of the Jews.

23 But the hour cometh, and now is, when the true worshippers shall worship the Father in spirit and in truth: for the Father seeketh such to worship him.

24 God is a Spirit: and they that worship him must worship him in spirit and in truth.

25 The woman saith unto him, I know that Messias cometh, which is called Christ: when he is come, he will tell us all things.

26 Jesus saith unto her, I that speak unto thee am he.

27 And upon this came his disciples, and marvelled that he talked with the woman: yet no man said, What seekest thou? or, Why talkest thou with her?

28 The woman then left her waterpot, and went her way into the city, and saith to the men,

29 Come, see a man, which told me all things that ever I did: is not this the Christ?

30 Then they went out of the city, and came unto him.

KEY VERSE

The water that I shall give him shall be in him a well of water springing up into everlasting life.

—John 4:14

GOD'S CREATIVE WORD

Unit 2: Jesus' Powerful Words

LESSONS 7–9

LESSON AIMS

After participating in this lesson, each student will be able to:

1. Recount the key points of the conversation between Jesus and the Samaritan woman.

2. Explain the significance of Jesus' discussion with the woman in light of the cultural, political, and religious taboos He ignored.

3. Thank God that Jesus, the Messiah, is for everyone.

LESSON OUTLINE

Introduction
    A. Awkward Conversations, "Aha" Moments
    B. Lesson Background
 I. Conversation Begins (JOHN 4:7-15)
    A. Stranger and Request (vv. 7, 8)
    B. Response and Rejoinder (vv. 9, 10)
    C. Confusion and Explanation (vv. 11-15)
      Seeking Water
 II. Conversation Climaxes (JOHN 4:21-26)
    A. True Temple (vv. 21-24)
      Proper Worship
    B. True King (vv. 25, 26)
III. Conversation's Aftermath (JOHN 4:27-30)
    A. Disciples' Amazement (v. 27)
    B. Woman's Veneration (vv. 28-30)
Conclusion
    A. Something Much Better
    B. Prayer
    C. Thought to Remember

Introduction

A. Awkward Conversations, "Aha" Moments

All of us have had awkward conversations. Perhaps a remark was misinterpreted. Or someone raised a sensitive issue that others wanted to ignore. Maybe someone said something hurtful. Or maybe we realized later that our own words made the conversation awkward. On the other hand, we also have pleasant memories of "aha" moments—those rare occasions where we suddenly realize something vitally important. Earthly "aha" moments involve sudden awareness of a truth that had been knowable but was unknown until something "clicked." Divine "aha" moments are different. These involve sudden awareness of something unknowable until God makes it known.

Sometimes in the Bible awkward conversations and divine "aha" moments come together. In Jesus' conversation with the Samaritan woman, He said things that were difficult for her, even offensive. But through the conversation she had the greatest of "aha" moments: an awareness of who Jesus was as a result of divine revelation.

B. Lesson Background

Today's text describes a conversation that took place in Samaria. That was the portion of the land of Israel between Galilee in the north and Judea in the south. Specifically, the conversation occurred at the town of Sychar (John 4:5), near Mounts Gerizim and Ebal (compare Deuteronomy 11:29, 30; 27:11-13; Joshua 8:30-33). Sychar was a historic place for the people of Israel, and the immediate area was connected with the patriarchs (Genesis 12:6; 33:18; Acts 7:15, 16). The designation *Samaria* comes from 1 Kings 16:24.

Samaria and the Samaritans were a problem for Jews in Jesus' time, for Jews and Samaritans were hostile toward each other. This hostility was rooted in a long history of conflict between the two groups. Both groups counted themselves as part of biblical Israel and so as the true people of God. The Jews were the descendants of those of the southern kingdom of Judah in the Old Testament, while the Samaritans were the mixed-race descendants of the northern kingdom of Israel (2 Kings 17:24-41).

Samaritan Woman Finds Living Water

The racial mixing resulted from the resettlement of foreigners in Samaria following the conquest by Assyria in 722 BC. When the Jews of the southern kingdom returned from Babylonian exile after 539 BC, they found the Samaritans opposed to the resettlement (Ezra 4:1-5; Nehemiah 4:1, 2). The two groups remained in conflict.

Both groups counted Abraham, Isaac, and Jacob as their ancestors. Both offered sacrifices to God—the Jews at Jerusalem's Mount Zion and the Samaritans at their temple on Mount Gerizim. The prophets had promised that both would one day be reunited as God's people under the king whom God would send (see Ezekiel 37:15-23, where *Ephraim* includes Samaria).

But neither group had any use for the other. Jews avoided traveling through Samaria. Samaritans refused hospitality to Jews who did travel through their territory (compare Luke 9:51-53). Jesus' enemies tried to discredit Him by calling Him a Samaritan (John 8:48). Any positive interaction between people from these two groups was rare.

In that culture, it also was scandalous for a man to carry on an extended conversation with a woman who was not a family member. If a man needed to communicate with a woman who was not a relative, he was expected to speak to her husband, father, or brother. These two cultural strictures regarding race and gender form important backdrops for today's lesson, as we shall see.

HOW TO SAY IT

Assyria	Uh-*sear*-ee-uh.
Babylonian	Bab-ih-*low*-nee-un.
Ebal	*Ee*-bull.
Ephraim	*Ee*-fray-im.
Galilee	*Gal*-uh-lee.
Gerizim	*Gair*-ih-zeem or Guh-*rye*-zim.
Hohokam	Huh-*hoe*-kum.
Judea	Joo-*dee*-uh.
Messiah	Meh-*sigh*-uh.
Messias	Mes-*sigh*-us.
Nehemiah	*Nee*-huh-*my*-uh.
Samaria	Suh-*mare*-ee-uh.
Samaritans	Suh-*mare*-uh-tunz.
Sychar	*Sigh*-kar.

I. Conversation Begins
(JOHN 4:7-15)
A. Stranger and Request (vv. 7, 8)

7. There cometh a woman of Samaria to draw water: Jesus saith unto her, Give me to drink.

John 4:6 notes that it is now "about the sixth hour." That means it is six hours since sunrise, or about noon. This is an unusual time to draw water from a well, since the custom is to draw water in the morning and again in the evening.

The woman, perhaps coming at this time to avoid conversation, probably is surprised to find anyone else at the well at such a time. That she finds a man is an additional surprise, since women normally draw the water in this culture (compare Genesis 24:13; Exodus 2:16). That she finds a Jewish man is more surprising still, since this location is Samaria.

Then comes an even greater surprise: Jesus asks the woman for something to drink. This level of conversation between a man and a woman might be acceptable were Jesus not a Jew. But the hostility between Jews and Samaritans is such that any remark from a Jewish man to a Samaritan woman probably is shocking.

8. (For his disciples were gone away unto the city to buy meat.)

The conversation is private, since the disciples have gone to nearby Sychar to buy food. That also is an exceptional action for Jews, who are taught not to trust food offered by Samaritans.

B. Response and Rejoinder (vv. 9, 10)

9. Then saith the woman of Samaria unto him, How is it that thou, being a Jew, askest drink of me, which am a woman of Samaria? for the Jews have no dealings with the Samaritans.

As we expect, the woman is astonished that a Jew would speak to a Samaritan, especially a Samaritan woman. The Gospel writer adds a reminder that Jews avoid interaction with Samaritans (see discussion in the Lesson Background). But Jesus is more concerned with fulfilling His mission to draw all people to himself (John 12:32) than He is with the social boundaries created by past hatreds.

10. Jesus answered and said unto her, If thou knewest the gift of God, and who it is that saith to thee, Give me to drink; thou wouldest have asked of him, and he would have given thee living water.

Jesus begins to reveal that He is interested in a much more important topic. At this point, the woman knows Jesus only as a Jewish man, forbidden by custom to speak to her. But Jesus is much more than that. He is the gift of God who provides life (John 3:16). If the woman can be made to understand this, then the roles will be reversed: she will be the one to break convention by asking Jesus to give her something. That "something" Jesus calls *living water.*

What Do You Think?

When was a time that someone crossed a boundary to reach out to you? How did things turn out?

Talking Points for Your Discussion

- A gender-based boundary
- A socioeconomic boundary
- A cultural or ethnic boundary
- A boundary you created

C. Confusion and Explanation (vv. 11-15)

11. The woman saith unto him, Sir, thou hast nothing to draw with, and the well is deep: from whence then hast thou that living water?

We sense the woman's confusion as she takes *living water* in a conventional sense of "flowing water." But seeing no nearby water source except for the well, she assumes that this stranger imagines that He can get flowing water from there, without a container and rope. The idea is preposterous, so her question may have a note of sarcasm.

12. Art thou greater than our father Jacob, which gave us the well, and drank thereof himself, and his children, and his cattle?

Samaritans and Jews claim Jacob as a common ancestor. Tradition is that Jacob dug this well centuries before. Jacob is the father of all Israel. So it is unthinkable that anyone can surpass him. So the woman phrases her question sharply, expecting a clear *no* for an answer (compare John 8:53).

13. Jesus answered and said unto her, Whosoever drinketh of this water shall thirst again.

Jesus' now begins to change the woman's understanding of the kind of water of which He speaks. More than that, He begins to change her view of who He is. Going to the well regularly to draw water, the woman is very familiar with the limitations of ordinary water.

14. But whosoever drinketh of the water that I shall give him shall never thirst; but the water that I shall give him shall be in him a well of water springing up into everlasting life.

What Jesus offers will bring permanent satisfaction (compare John 6:35). Literal water is necessary for life, but Jesus provides *everlasting life,* a key phrase in John's Gospel (3:16, 36; 5:24; 6:27, 40, 47; etc.). This life is eternal both in quantity and in quality. By quantity, it lasts forever. It is not ended by death. In quality, it is a life always in God's presence. If Jesus can deliver such life, then He truly is greater than Jacob or anyone else in history. If Jesus can deliver such life, then the woman really should ask Him for what He can give.

❧ SEEKING WATER ❧

Throughout history, people have gone to great lengths to find water and move it to different locations. Human ingenuity in this regard may amaze us. For example, the ancient Hohokam people, centered in Casa Grande in southern Arizona, developed an extensive system of irrigation ditches to provide water for their crops. Tapping into a river at higher levels, they were able to convey water dozens of miles to get it to their fields. The Romans, for their part, were experts at building sophisticated aqueducts. Many still stand today.

We who live in modern democracies often are not so much concerned with having access to water as we are with obtaining *pure* water. Thus there exists an entire industry to provide bottled water, water filtration, water-quality analysis, etc.

Just as the quantity and quality of physical water are essential to life, so proper spiritual water is essential to the soul. Do we find it amazing that some folks go to all the trouble and expense of drinking bottled water, but are rather apathetic regarding the quantity and quality of spiritual water that nourishes their souls?   —J. B. N.

15. The woman saith unto him, Sir, give me this water, that I thirst not, neither come hither to draw.

Jesus' explanation leaves some uncertainty. Is Jesus claiming to have some kind of magic water that forever ends thirst with just one drink? Jesus' claims continue to sound ridiculous. So the woman appears ready to call His bluff; essentially, she is saying, "If you have that magic water, prove it!"

Visual for Lesson 8. *Point to this visual as you ask, "What worldly substitutes for 'living water' do people embrace? How do we resist doing that?"*

tion away from herself to something controversial: the dispute between Jews and Samaritans over the proper place to worship (vv. 19, 20). The woman perhaps expects that question to end the conversation with a harsh disagreement.

Jesus' answer (which continues through verse 24) is a longer statement than He has made thus far. His announcement of the coming of an *hour* is seen elsewhere in John's Gospel to indicate a great, pivotal moment. As this Gospel develops, we realize that this coming hour is the time of Jesus' death and resurrection, or what is introduced by those events (John 2:4; 5:25, 28; 7:30; 8:20; 12:23; 13:1; 16:32; 17:1). This coming hour will transform where and how people worship God. The concept of *temple* is about to be expanded radically, fulfilling God's great purpose of salvation.

22. Ye worship ye know not what: we know what we worship: for salvation is of the Jews.

Jesus clarifies a point. He has just said that neither Jerusalem nor Mount Gerizim will be the one true place for worship in the coming time of God's salvation. But Judaism and Samaritanism are not equivalent in God's view. Samaritan worship, Jesus says, is based in ignorance, while Jewish worship is rooted in knowledge. This is not a knowledge that comes from superior human wisdom, but from the revelation of God.

Thus, says Jesus, *salvation is of the Jews.* God's salvation begins with a particular nation in a particular place at a particular time.

> **What Do You Think?**
> Which aspects of Jesus' encounter with the Samaritan woman can or should we use today in our encounters with unbelievers? Which aspects can or should we *not* use?
>
> *Talking Points for Your Discussion*
> ▪ Regarding the use of figurative language
> ▪ Regarding the nature of boundaries to be crossed
> ▪ Regarding things that only Jesus was able to do because of divine powers

II. Conversation Climaxes
(John 4:21-26)
A. True Temple (vv. 21-24)

21. Jesus saith unto her, Woman, believe me, the hour cometh, when ye shall neither in this mountain, nor yet at Jerusalem, worship the Father.

Jesus reveals His knowledge of the woman's unsavory past in verses 16-20 (not in today's text). Uncomfortable with Jesus' revelation of her shameful status, the woman shifts the conversa-

23. But the hour cometh, and now is, when the true worshippers shall worship the Father in spirit and in truth: for the Father seeketh such to worship him.

The great hour is not just on its way; it already has arrived. As the rest of John's Gospel makes clear, the hour of salvation has come because Jesus, the one who brings salvation, has come.

The place of worship will not matter in this hour. Instead, worship will be done *in spirit and in truth.* Genuine worship will be a matter of inner devotion to God. This is more than an incidental matter. The goal of God's saving action—what He truly seeks —is people who worship in spirit and truth.

We should not miss Jesus' implication. God promised salvation (1) through a particular nation, Israel, (2) through a particular part of that nation, the Jews (not the Samaritans), and (3) as connected with a particular place, the temple. Now He is fulfilling that promise in a way that makes salvation not particular, but universal. God will be wherever there are people who worship Him in spirit and in truth.

24. God is a Spirit: and they that worship him must worship him in spirit and in truth.

God's nature demands spirit-and-truth worship. God's nature is that He is Spirit (compare 2 Corinthians 3:17). He is not limited by the physical. As the life-giving Spirit, He is more powerful than any other being. As an invisible Spirit, He is mysterious. But now He has made himself known in Jesus. So those who truly worship Him do so in spirit, not just according to outward forms (compare Philippians 3:3). And they worship in the truth as revealed by God in Christ.

What Do You Think?

How do you make sure you are worshipping "in spirit and in truth"?

Talking Points for Your Discussion

- In the way you prepare your heart for corporate worship
- In the way you approach your personal devotion time
- In the way you conduct yourself as a living sacrfice (Romans 12:1)

I once read a book written by a man from a denomination that had a reputation for religious legalism. He was talking about the proper way to worship, and he insisted that worship done only in the right format was acceptable to God. Anything different from this rigid pattern was offensive to God. I knew where this writer was coming from, and I was anticipating most of his application. Yet I was surprised by one of his proof texts: "They that worship [God] must worship him in spirit and in truth" (John 4:24).

The man's emphasis on *in truth* was not surprising. But the problem was that the writer was not letting the concepts *in spirit* and *in truth* stand side by side as equals. Instead, he was placing *in spirit* underneath *in truth.* His resulting interpretation was that worship "not done in truth" was "not in the right spirit."

It would be easy to chastise this author for misreading Jesus' comment. Yet, how often do we do the same thing—emphasizing one part of Jesus' command while minimizing the other? We may feel that if our hearts are right, it doesn't make much difference what we say or do. We may sing hymns with questionable doctrine. Our worship services may feature musicians who entertain more than edify. May we not be content to follow half a commandment!   —J. B. N.

B. True King (vv. 25, 26)

25. The woman saith unto him, I know that Messias cometh, which is called Christ: when he is come, he will tell us all things.

Jesus has taken the woman away from controversy and back to what matters. The Samaritans share the Jews' belief that God will one day send a great Redeemer to fulfill God's promises and bless His people. *Messias* (or *Messiah*) and *Christ* mean "anointed one" (John 1:41). Because Israel designated its kings by anointing them with oil, these terms signify the promised king who will rule over God's people forever (2 Samuel 7:14-16).

The woman understands that this great king will *tell us all things.* Jesus has just told her more about herself than He should know and more about what is happening than she could expect.

Samaritan Woman Finds Living Water

Could this one who has revealed so much to her actually be the promised king sent by God?

26. Jesus saith unto her, I that speak unto thee am he.

Jesus' response is quite straightforward. He is indeed the promised one (compare Mark 14:61, 62; John 9:37). But His statement implies even more. What is translated *I . . . am he* is literally just "I . . . am," reminding us of the way God identified himself to Moses (Exodus 3:14; John 8:58). The implication from the whole of John's Gospel is not just that Jesus is the king whom God sends, but is God himself—visiting His people as their true Ruler and true Redeemer. In this conversation, Jesus' power to know and do what only God can know and do reveals who He truly is.

III. Conversation's Aftermath
(John 4:27-30)
A. Disciples' Amazement (v. 27)

27. And upon this came his disciples, and marvelled that he talked with the woman: yet no man said, What seekest thou? or, Why talkest thou with her?

The disciples notice Jesus' unconventional behavior on their return. What the disciples do not yet know is that what Jesus has just said is even more amazing than to whom He has said it. But the disciples hesitate to voice their amazement. They have seen Jesus' authority before, so in respect they hold their peace.

B. Woman's Veneration (vv. 28-30)

28. The woman then left her waterpot, and went her way into the city, and saith to the men.

The woman, by contrast, is more than ready to speak! She abandons the chore that brought her to the well, returns to the town where people probably hold her in contempt for her immorality, and speaks to all who will listen. (*Men* refers to both males and females.)

29. Come, see a man, which told me all things that ever I did: is not this the Christ?

Jesus has spoken to the woman about her shameful past. Yet she is joyously excited about what Jesus has said. He reveals a kind of knowledge that can come only from God. And He has promised what only God can promise. When she asks *is not this the Christ?* she asks in a way that insists the answer is *yes*.

30. Then they went out of the city, and came unto him.

The woman's message draws a crowd to see Jesus firsthand. This unlikely meeting—between a Jewish teacher and the Samaritan audience gathered by an immoral woman—will last for two days. As a result, many Samaritans will join the woman in her belief (John 4:39-42).

> *What Do You Think?*
> When was a time you encountered Jesus through someone else in a particularly important way? How did that encounter make a positive difference in your life?
> *Talking Points for Your Discussion*
> - A teacher
> - A stranger
> - A friend

Conclusion
A. Something Much Better

With disregard for social convention, Jesus opened the door for the Samaritan woman and her neighbors to learn the amazing things that God was doing. Coming to the well at an odd hour for ordinary water, she found the one who could give her what she and others truly needed.

Our situation is not much different from hers. We spend our time acquiring ordinary things. But what Jesus offers—an everlasting, spirit-and-truth relationship with the God of the universe—is what we really need and want. When we have that gift, we have everything we have ever wanted.

B. Prayer

O Lord, You have offered us more than we deserve and more than we can imagine. May we in turn be people who worship You constantly, genuinely, and truly. In Jesus' name, amen!

C. Thought to Remember

Seek living water above all else.

INVOLVEMENT LEARNING

Some of the activities below are also found in the helpful student book, Adult Bible Class.
Don't forget to download the free reproducible page from www.standardlesson.com to enhance your lesson!

Into the Lesson

Say, "We all experience *Aha!* moments in life. Earthly *Aha!* moments involve sudden awareness of a truth that had been knowable but was unknown until something 'clicked.' But divine *Aha!* moments are different. These involve sudden awareness of something unknowable until God makes it known. A person in our lesson today had one such moment. Her moment teaches us something about Jesus' work in our lives."

Into the Word

Give a three-minute summary from the Lesson Background on the relationship between the Samaritans and Jews of Jesus' day. Point to relevant places on a map of first-century Israel as you cover this information.

Give each learner a handout titled "What's So?" Include the following instructions: "Your task is to read today's story about the woman who had an *Aha!* moment with Jesus. As you do, put the key words from today's text in the list below. The first letter of each word is given." *Option:* Turn this into a contest by saying, "I have a prize for the one finishing first, but even one incorrect answer disqualifies you." The prize you will give is a bottle of water, in keeping with the lesson imagery.

v. 7 D _ _ _ and D _ _ _ _
v. 8 D _ _ _ _ _ _ _ _
v. 9 J _ _ _ and
     S _ _ _ _ _ _ _ _ _
v. 10 G _ _ _ of G _ _
v. 10 L _ _ _ _ _ _ W _ _ _ _
v. 12 G _ _ _ _ _ _ _ than
     O _ _ F _ _ _ _ _
     J _ _ _ _
v. 14 N _ _ _ _ _ T _ _ _ _ _
v. 14 L _ _ _
v. 15 G _ _ _
v. 21 W _ _ _ _ _ _ _ the
     F _ _ _ _ _

v. 21 J _ _ _ _ _ _ _ _
v. 22 S _ _ _ _ _ _ _ _
v. 23 S _ _ _ _ _ and
     T _ _ _ _
v. 25 C _ _ _ _ _
v. 26 I am H _

Answers: draw / drink (v. 7), disciples (v. 8), Jews / Samaritans (v. 9), gift / God (v. 10), living water (v. 10), greater / our father Jacob (v. 12), never thirst (v. 14), life (v. 14), give (v. 15), worship / Father (v. 21), Jerusalem (v. 21), salvation (v. 22), spirit / truth (v. 23), Christ (v. 25), He (v. 26)

Next, lead a class discussion with these questions: 1. What four surprises did this woman find at the well? *(See the lesson commentary on verse 7 for the four.)* 2. What did Jesus mean by "living water" in verses 10-14? 3. What kind of thirst was Jesus promising to relieve in verse 14? 4. Why was it important for the Samaritan woman to understand Jesus' "in spirit and in truth" declaration of verses 23, 24? 5. Why are the events in verses 28, 29 significant? *(Hint: see verse 39.)*

Into Life

On the "What's So?" handout used above, also have the heading "So What?" for the bottom half of the page. Have the following starter phrases on different lines underneath this heading: 1. The cross-cultural message is . . . 2. The doctrinal message about God is . . . 3. The impact this makes on my concept of worship is . . . Allow learners to share their "so what?" applications.

Alternative: Instead of using the five discussion questions of the Into the Word segment and the "So What?" of the Into Life segment, distribute copies of the two activities on the reproducible page, which you have downloaded. Lead your learners through the Change of Plans activity in place of the five discussion questions. Then have them complete the Thinking This Through activity in place of the "So What?" exercise.

Samaritan Woman Finds Living Water

BLIND MAN RECEIVES SIGHT

DEVOTIONAL READING: Isaiah 29:17-21
BACKGROUND SCRIPTURE: John 9

JOHN 9:1-17

1 And as Jesus passed by, he saw a man which was blind from his birth.

2 And his disciples asked him, saying, Master, who did sin, this man, or his parents, that he was born blind?

3 Jesus answered, Neither hath this man sinned, nor his parents: but that the works of God should be made manifest in him.

4 I must work the works of him that sent me, while it is day: the night cometh, when no man can work.

5 As long as I am in the world, I am the light of the world.

6 When he had thus spoken, he spat on the ground, and made clay of the spittle, and he anointed the eyes of the blind man with the clay,

7 And said unto him, Go, wash in the pool of Siloam, (which is by interpretation, Sent.) He went his way therefore, and washed, and came seeing.

8 The neighbours therefore, and they which before had seen him that he was blind, said, Is not this he that sat and begged?

9 Some said, This is he: others said, He is like him: but he said, I am he.

10 Therefore said they unto him, How were thine eyes opened?

11 He answered and said, A man that is called Jesus made clay, and anointed mine eyes, and said unto me, Go to the pool of Siloam, and wash: and I went and washed, and I received sight.

12 Then said they unto him, Where is he? He said, I know not.

13 They brought to the Pharisees him that aforetime was blind.

14 And it was the sabbath day when Jesus made the clay, and opened his eyes.

15 Then again the Pharisees also asked him how he had received his sight. He said unto them, He put clay upon mine eyes, and I washed, and do see.

16 Therefore said some of the Pharisees, This man is not of God, because he keepeth not the sabbath day. Others said, How can a man that is a sinner do such miracles? And there was a division among them.

17 They say unto the blind man again, What sayest thou of him, that he hath opened thine eyes? He said, He is a prophet.

KEY VERSE

Some of the Pharisees [said], This man is not of God, because he keepeth not the sabbath day. Others said, How can a man that is a sinner do such miracles? And there was a division among them. —**John 9:16**

GOD'S CREATIVE WORD

Unit 2: Jesus' Powerful Words

LESSONS 7–9

LESSON AIMS

After participating in this lesson, each student will be able to:

1. Retrace the sequence of events of the healing of the blind man and its aftermath.

2. Explain the significance of the healing of the blind man both in its literal reality and as a metaphor for Jesus' opening spiritually blind eyes.

3. Write a prayer that asks God's help in identifying and overcoming an area of spiritual blindness.

LESSON OUTLINE

Introduction

A. Is Seeing Really Believing?

When we need an explanation for something, we may fall back on familiar sayings as a kind of self-defense mechanism. "Seeing is believing" is a good example. But have you noticed how some common phrases seem to contradict each other? As soon as we say "Seeing is believing," someone can respond "I can't believe my eyes!"

The truth is that we do generally believe what we see, but only when it fits what we expect. Neuroscientists tell us that our brains interpret signals from the eyes according to our previous experiences and established beliefs. So if we see a dark liquid in a mug, we interpret it as coffee, not motor oil. If we see a large object in our rearview mirror, we interpret it as a truck, not a jetliner.

So when we witness something truly unusual, something outside our previous experience, we may have trouble believing our eyes. We may try to find some other explanation for what we have seen. In effect, we may trust what we have experienced in the past more than what we see in the present in an exceptional situation.

Today's passage is about such an instance. In it Jesus does something that is contrary to everyone's prior experience. Some could not believe their eyes as a result. Ultimately, Jesus proved something about those who can truly see (perceive) and those who refuse to do so.

B. Lesson Background

Like many episodes in John's Gospel, the events in today's text took place in Jerusalem. John shows Jesus in continuous conflict with the religious leaders there, a conflict that results in Jesus' death.

Another key to the story is that it occurred on the Sabbath Day. God gave Israel the Sabbath as a celebration of two great events: God's own "rest" at the end of six days of creation and His liberation of Israel from slavery in Egypt. A main feature of Sabbath observance was to rest on that day.

Sabbath observance was especially strict among the Jews of Jesus' time. The Pharisees, the most influential group among the Jews of Jesus' time. The Pharisees followed a practice of "fencing the law," that is, establishing

Blind Man Receives Sight

traditional rules that, if followed, would supposedly prevent a person from violating the laws of God. So to build a fence around the Sabbath, the Pharisees had defined 39 kinds of "work," describing them down to the smallest instances and forbidding all on the Sabbath except in a case of dire emergency.

Yet, Jesus was notable for performing healings and engaging in other activity on the Sabbath (Matthew 12:1-14; Luke 13:10-17; 14:1-6; John 5:8-18). Each instance was marked by controversy, as today's story is as well.

Controversy is an important element in the section of John's Gospel to which today's story belongs. Prior to John 9 (today's text), Jesus had engaged in sharp debate with His opponents. In the midst of that controversy, Jesus declared himself to be "the light of the world" (John 8:12). That idea is crucial to today's study.

I. Prelude to Healing
(JOHN 9:1-5)
A. Sad Situation (vv. 1, 2)

1. And as Jesus passed by, he saw a man which was blind from his birth.

In the other Gospels, we read several instances of Jesus giving sight to the blind (Matthew 12:22; 15:30, 31; 20:29-34; Mark 8:22-26; 10:46-52; Luke 18:35-43). So we expect such an action on this occasion as well. The fact that the man in question has been *blind from his birth* is an important backdrop to the query that follows.

2. And his disciples asked him, saying, Master, who did sin, this man, or his parents, that he was born blind?

The disciples do not seem to be conscious that Jesus might heal the man. They are more concerned with the doctrinal problem of the man's blindness. They do believe that Jesus, their Master, can answer such a doctrinal question authoritatively. Clearly, blindness is a curse. The curse is at work in the world because of sin. So someone's sin must have caused the man's blindness, they reason. Is the man himself the one who is responsible, or does the fault lie with his parents for his being born blind?

What Do You Think?
How would you respond to new parents who feel guilty about (or are blaming God for) their baby's birth defect?
Talking Points for Your Discussion
- Defect is due to parental sin (example: fetal alcohol syndrome)
- Defect as a result of someone else's actions or inactions (example: negligent medical care)
- No identifiable or avoidable cause of the defect

B. Authoritative Statement (vv. 3-5)

3. Jesus answered, Neither hath this man sinned, nor his parents: but that the works of God should be made manifest in him.

Jesus challenges the disciples' assumptions even as He accepts their confidence in His authority to answer. This case has nothing to do with any individual's sin, He says. Rather, it provides an opportunity to display what God is doing in the world (compare John 11:4).

This episode, like the book of Job, cautions us against jumping to conclusions about the reasons for tragedies in people's lives (compare Luke 13:1-5). The Bible teaches that the whole world has been affected by human rebellion against God, so that bad things may happen in ways that appear utterly random to us.

What Do You Think?
When was a time you saw God was glorified through difficult circumstances?
Talking Points for Your Discussion
- A death
- An illness
- A financial setback
- A natural disaster

❧ SIN IN THE CAMP? ❧

Some years ago, the school where I teach experienced a major financial difficulty. Several people were laid off, and there was a grimness around campus because of the financial belt-tightening that was necessary. One of my colleagues, filled with indignation at the difficulties, said to some of us, "This is because there is sin in the camp," referring to the situation with Achan in Joshua 7. "We need to have a campus-wide meeting of repentance," my colleague maintained, "because someone has obviously dishonored God."

I thought his comments were somewhat self-righteous. I don't think he would have agreed that his own arrogance was part of that "sin in the camp." Apparently, he was not open to the possibility that the problem may have been due to someone's poor financial judgment, inadequate funding efforts, or even churches not challenging enough young people to enroll in Christian schools to prepare for ministry vocations.

Sin in the camp? We have all sinned. Our financial difficulties at the time simply may have resulted from living in a fallen world, where poor judgment or inadequate preparation are part of our condition. Why was a man born blind? Not because any particular person sinned, but because he was born into a fallen world where such conditions exist. Even so, the man's condition became an opportunity to demonstrate God's power.   —J. B. N.

4. I must work the works of him that sent me, while it is day: the night cometh, when no man can work.

Jesus has just said that the man's blindness is an occasion for the display of God's power. Now He states that He has been sent by God to do God's work (compare John 5:17). This provokes anticipation: will Jesus perform a work of God for the blind man?

Jesus stresses the urgency of His work with His day/night analogy. The shortness of life creates urgency for all of us. For Jesus, who comes into the world to bring God's work to fulfillment, that urgency is especially sharp. There can be no delaying God's work if the time is short.

HOW TO SAY IT

Judaism	*Joo*-duh-izz-um or *Joo*-day-izz-um.
Pharisees	*Fair*-ih-seez.
Sanhedrin	*San*-huh-drun or San-*heed*-run.
Siloam	Sigh-*lo*-um.

5. As long as I am in the world, I am the light of the world.

Having declared himself to be *the light of the world* in the previous chapter, Jesus now repeats that provocative title as He stands before a man unable to perceive physical light. Again, Jesus underlines the urgency of what He does. He is *in the world* only a short time: His death, resurrection, and ascension will bring His work in the world to a conclusion. So as *the light of the world,* what shall He do as He stands before a man who is blind?

II. Actions in the Healing
(JOHN 9:6, 7)
A. Clay (v. 6)

6. When he had thus spoken, he spat on the ground, and made clay of the spittle, and he anointed the eyes of the blind man with the clay.

This action appears very curious to us, but it is vital to the development of the story. In Jesus' time, some people attribute healing powers to saliva. So here Jesus adopts what appears to be a conventional healing technique (compare Mark 8:23). However, one hardly expects such a technique to be effective to correct lifelong blindness!

A second important point is that the kneading of clay, as a potter does, is one of the kinds of "work" that has been defined as such by the Pharisees. In their view, it makes no difference how much clay one makes; the action constitutes "work." But for Jesus, doing such an action on the Sabbath (v. 14, below) is consistent with the urgency of which He has just spoken. It will not do to wait until the Sabbath is over. The time to bring God's blessing is now.

B. Command (v. 7)

7. And said unto him, Go, wash in the pool of Siloam, (which is by interpretation, Sent.) He went his way therefore, and washed, and came seeing.

Jesus has spoken of himself as sent by God (v. 4, above). Now He underlines that point by sending the man to a pool named with a Hebrew term that is also *Sent.* Looking back several decades, the Gospel writer sees significance in Jesus' instructions.

The man miraculously receives his sight when he washes. Thus the man does not see the one who has healed him as he receives his sight. That fact will create a dramatic point at the end of the story.

What Do You Think?
How can your church better minister to people with disabilities?
Talking Points for Your Discussion
- To those with hearing challenges
- To those with vision challenges
- To those with mental or developmental challenges
- To those with mobility challenges

III. Responses to the Healing
(JOHN 9:8-12)
A. Identity (vv. 8, 9)

8. The neighbours therefore, and they which before had seen him that he was blind, said, Is not this he that sat and begged?

The sight of the blind man begging is familiar to many. Now some look with wonder on the one they recognize as suddenly being able to see. Theirs is not the only opinion that appears, however.

9. Some said, This is he: others said, He is like him: but he said, I am he.

For some, this is clearly the man of whom they know. Others, however, are unwilling to believe that a man born blind can now see. So they reach for another explanation, suggesting that he merely looks like the well-known beggar, but is not the beggar himself.

Finally the man himself speaks, clearly identifying himself as the beggar formerly blind. This is the first time the man speaks in the story, and

he delivers vital testimony. As the story develops, we shall see his testimony become even more significant.

B. Question (v. 10)

10. Therefore said they unto him, How were thine eyes opened?

Once the man is identified clearly, this question follows naturally. For a man born blind to receive sight is unheard of (John 9:32). So everyone wants to know how such a thing can happen. But the answer will provoke different opinions.

C. Answer (v. 11)

11. He answered and said, A man that is called Jesus made clay, and anointed mine eyes, and said unto me, Go to the pool of Siloam, and wash: and I went and washed, and I received sight.

The man now recounts the steps that led to his healing. At this point, the only thing he apparently knows about his healer is His name. Thus the man says nothing about how Jesus was able to perform the miracle.

The description contains two things that will become controversial. If *Jesus made clay,* then He did "work." If He performed a healing, He did "work" as well. What will people do with the fact that this unprecedented miracle is done in a way that appears to violate the Sabbath (v. 14, below)?

D. Uncertainty (v. 12)

12. Then said they unto him, Where is he? He said, I know not.

We can safely assume that people have different reasons for wanting to find Jesus. On the one hand, those who begin to recognize the significance of the miracle will want to know more about the one who did it. On the other hand, those who see in Jesus' actions a violation of the Sabbath will want to confront Him with His offense.

But at this point the man has told all that he knows. He has not seen Jesus because the man received his sight only after Jesus sent him away to wash. At this stage the man can say nothing about Jesus except His name and the specific actions Jesus took to bring about the healing.

IV. Debate About the Healer

(JOHN 9:13-17)

A. Preliminaries (vv. 13, 14)

13. They brought to the Pharisees him that aforetime was blind.

The controversy begins to take shape. We wonder about the motives of those who bring the man *to the Pharisees*. Do these people believe that the man should be questioned by the religious experts because of the potential violation of the Sabbath? Do they merely seek a comment or an interpretation by the Pharisees regarding an extraordinary miracle?

It is helpful to remember that the Pharisees are regarded as the strictest party within Judaism (Acts 26:5; Philippians 3:5). While some Pharisees are members of the Sanhedrin, a governing body of Judaism, the power of the Pharisees is largely a matter of influence and respect. Even so, some Pharisees apparently have the power to exclude people from local synagogues (John 9:22, 34).

14. And it was the sabbath day when Jesus made the clay, and opened his eyes.

Now the Gospel writer makes clear the issue at hand. Jesus has done two kinds of work on the Sabbath: making clay and healing. That appears to violate the commandment not to work on the Sabbath, at least by the tradition of the Pharisees (compare Luke 13:14).

B. Interrogation (v. 15)

15. Then again the Pharisees also asked him how he had received his sight. He said unto them, He put clay upon mine eyes, and I washed, and do see.

As the interrogation begins, the man again does nothing but state what he knows. The contrast between the plain actions (applying clay and washing it off) and the startling result (being able to see) is all the more dramatic for the simplicity of the statement.

The stage is now set. On which aspect of the statement will the Pharisees focus? Will they accept the dramatic healing as a sign of God's work? Or will they focus on the actions that violate their traditions about the Sabbath?

C. Division (vv. 16, 17)

16. Therefore said some of the Pharisees, This man is not of God, because he keepeth not the sabbath day. Others said, How can a man that is a sinner do such miracles? And there was a division among them.

The crowds are divided about whether this is truly the man who was born blind (vv. 8, 9, above), and now the Pharisees are divided about what this miracle means. For some, it is a clear violation of the Sabbath law. If Jesus performs a miracle while violating the law, then they conclude that His power cannot come from God.

But for others, the miracle calls into question their interpretation of the Sabbath. Surely God alone can bring sight to a man born blind! And surely God will not empower a sinner to perform such a miracle. So since Jesus clearly has done the miracle, He must not be a sinner. Therefore what He does on the Sabbath to perform the miracle does not violate the Sabbath law. The two diverging lines of logic are clearly drawn.

What Do You Think?

How do we ensure that church "policies and procedures" result in doing good, and do not end up being burdensome, counterproductive traditions?

Talking Points for Your Discussion

- In ministries to believers
- In ministries to unbelievers
- In how church finances are handled

17a. They say unto the blind man again, What sayest thou of him, that he hath opened thine eyes?

The Pharisees continue to question the man who stands before them. He alone is a witness to the event. What can he offer as a conclusion? Although this man is not an expert in doctrine, the Pharisees challenge him to take sides. He does.

17b. He said, He is a prophet.

The man's response follows the logic of those who affirm that one who brings sight to the blind must be sent by God. In calling Jesus *a prophet*, the man affirms Jesus to be inspired by God to be God's spokesperson (compare John 4:19; 7:40).

As the story continues in subsequent verses, the Pharisees question the man further. His responses remain firm, growing in conviction as those opposed to Jesus pressure him to recant his emerging faith. Finally, he affirms that Jesus most certainly is sent by God. In response, the Pharisees "cast him out" (John 9:34). This means they exclude him from worship in the synagogue, effectively saying that he no longer belongs to God's people.

Then will come another dramatic moment. Jesus will find the man and ask him if he believes in the Son of Man (John 9:35). Putting his complete trust in the one who has healed him, the one who must have been sent from God, the man will ask Jesus to identify that Son of Man (9:36). Jesus will then affirm that He is that one (9:37). In response, the man who had been blind believes and worships Jesus (9:38).

❧ ONCE I WAS BLIND ❧

"The Light of the World Is Jesus" is a hymn that I used to sing in church when I was a youngster. The refrain contains the line, "Once I was blind, but now I can see." That's what the man who had been blind said in John 9:25. He was talking about physical blindness of course, but the same thing can apply to spiritual blindness.

My church recently hosted a speaker who gave his testimony. He had been a practicing homosexual for more than 20 years. He knew it was against God's will, but the churches he had approached for help only condemned him. Only when he finally found a church that would accept him in spite of his sin did he come to put the whole thing in perspective, find Christ's strength, repent, and overcome his lifestyle. Once he was blind, but now he can see.

I have known fathers who, blinded by ambition, sacrificed their families in their climb up the corporate ladder. I have known good students who were so blinded by their obsession to get the highest grades that they resorted to various forms of cheating. We all have read of athletes who were so blinded by the desire to achieve that they resorted to illegal drugs and steroids. The list could go on and on. Is there any blindness that you have not yet allowed Christ to remove?　　　—J. B. N.

Conclusion
A. A Higher Calling

On the first day of creation, God said, "Let there be light" (Genesis 1:3); after six days of creation, God rested (2:2). Jesus declared himself to be the light of the world (John 8:12; 9:5). He brought light to a blind man on the day of the week that celebrated the completion of God's creation. Israel had received the Sabbath as a celebration of liberation from bondage (Deuteronomy 5:15), and on the Sabbath Jesus liberated a man who had been bound with blindness. This healing was one of Jesus' signs that pointed to His greater work. By healing on the Sabbath, Jesus was demonstrating that He was bringing a new beginning to God's creation and fulfilling the Sabbath's promise of rest.

Like the man who had been blind, we will meet opposition as Jesus' followers. But as His followers, we have the high calling to carry out His work of bringing God's light and God's rest into a dark, burdened world.

B. Prayer

O Lord, You have transformed our darkness into light and our burdens into rest. Guide us to live in Your light, to rest in Your promises, and to share them in Your world. In Jesus' name, amen!

C. Thought to Remember

Bring Jesus' light and rest to the world.

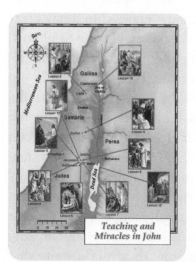

Visual for Lessons 3 & 9

Teaching and Miracles in John

Keep this map posted throughout the quarter to give your learners a geographical perspective.

INVOLVEMENT LEARNING

Some of the activities below are also found in the helpful student book, Adult Bible Class.
Don't forget to download the free reproducible page from www.standardlesson.com to enhance your lesson!

Into the Lesson

Have the following displayed on the board as learners arrive: "A Doctrinal Issue. Many ancient people held a strict cause-and-effect regarding physical disabilities: such disabilities result from divine judgment because someone had sinned. What is your viewpoint? Talk this issue through with the person sitting next to you."

After several minutes, ask learners to share their ideas with the class. Make the transition to Bible study by saying, "Jesus addresses this misconception as He heals a man who was born blind. In this act, we'll also discover a deeper application, one that goes beyond physical disabilities."

Into the Word

Early in the week, ask one of your learners to study the Lesson Background and be prepared to explain to the class why Jesus' act of performing a miracle on the Sabbath was so controversial. Ideally, the person who will give this mini-lecture will be someone who is a bit more advanced in knowledge of Scripture.

Also, prepare in advance a chart with the headings *Actors, Actions, Attitudes* to form three columns. Under the *Actors* heading, you can list the names of the various "players" in today's text (Jesus, the disciples, the blind man, the neighbors, the Pharisees); if you prefer, you can leave that column blank for your learners to complete. If you do include the names, leave a wide vertical spacing between them. Have these instructions at the top of the page: "Read John 9:1-17. Identify the main characters or groups in this passage. Then state what action(s) they took (if any) and describe any attitudes you think they held."

Form learners into small groups to complete the chart. If a group needs help getting started, suggest that on the first row they might write that the *disciples* (Actors), *asked Jesus a question about a blind man* (Actions), and *indicated a belief that "sin*

causes disabilities" (Attitudes). Discuss conclusions after an appropriate amount of time.

Option: Distribute copies of the A Blind Man Singing! activity from the reproducible page, which you have downloaded. Have learners work together in their groups to solve the puzzle. As they do, they will discover the title of a song that would have been appropriate for the man who had been blind to sing. You can turn this into a contest and award inexpensive prizes. Ask learners to suggest other songs.

Into Life

Relate the following story to your class: "The old TV quiz show *To Tell the Truth* once featured a man who had been blinded by an accident as an adult. After 10 years, doctors were able to restore his sight. When the 'actual' person was revealed and interviewed, one panelist asked him, 'So how long did it take you to get used to being blind?'

'Ten years,' he replied.

'Well, once you got your sight back, how long did it take you to adjust to not being blind?'

'Ten seconds,' he said with a big smile."

Add: "A problem more serious than physical blindness is spiritual blindness. That's when a person doesn't perceive truths about God's kingdom." Ask learners to brainstorm reasons why people are blind to spiritual truths and how such blindness can cause serious problems in their lives.

Option: If you wish to explore a deeper philosophical area, say, "Suppose I were to give each of you an index card and ask you to list a spiritual blindness of your own. Would you be able to do it?" Those answering *no* may point out that one's own spiritual blindness is, by definition, something that one is unaware of. Discuss how a spiritual blindness can be discovered and corrected.

Distribute as a take-home activity copies of the My Song! activity from the reproducible page, which you have downloaded.

THE BREAD OF LIFE

DEVOTIONAL READING: Psalm 107:1-9
BACKGROUND SCRIPTURE: John 6

JOHN 6:22-35

22 The day following, when the people which stood on the other side of the sea saw that there was none other boat there, save that one whereinto his disciples were entered, and that Jesus went not with his disciples into the boat, but that his disciples were gone away alone;

23 (Howbeit there came other boats from Tiberias nigh unto the place where they did eat bread, after that the Lord had given thanks:)

24 When the people therefore saw that Jesus was not there, neither his disciples, they also took shipping, and came to Capernaum, seeking for Jesus.

25 And when they had found him on the other side of the sea, they said unto him, Rabbi, when camest thou hither?

26 Jesus answered them and said, Verily, verily, I say unto you, Ye seek me, not because ye saw the miracles, but because ye did eat of the loaves, and were filled.

27 Labour not for the meat which perisheth, but for that meat which endureth unto everlasting life, which the Son of man shall give unto you: for him hath God the Father sealed.

28 Then said they unto him, What shall we do, that we might work the works of God?

29 Jesus answered and said unto them, This is the work of God, that ye believe on him whom he hath sent.

30 They said therefore unto him, What sign shewest thou then, that we may see, and believe thee? what dost thou work?

31 Our fathers did eat manna in the desert; as it is written, He gave them bread from heaven to eat.

32 Then Jesus said unto them, Verily, verily, I say unto you, Moses gave you not that bread from heaven; but my Father giveth you the true bread from heaven.

33 For the bread of God is he which cometh down from heaven, and giveth life unto the world.

34 Then said they unto him, Lord, evermore give us this bread.

35 And Jesus said unto them, I am the bread of life: he that cometh to me shall never hunger; and he that believeth on me shall never thirst.

KEY VERSE

Jesus said unto them, I am the bread of life: he that cometh to me shall never hunger; and he that believeth on me shall never thirst. —**John 6:35**

GOD'S CREATIVE WORD

Unit 3: I Am . . .

LESSONS 10–13

LESSON AIMS

After participating in this lesson, each student will be able to:

1. Summarize Jesus' teaching about the bread of life in its context of the feeding of the 5,000.

2. Contrast Jesus as "the bread of life" with the manna given in the time of Moses.

3. Suggest a ministry that can use bread as a means of helping people to receive Jesus, the bread of life.

LESSON OUTLINE

Introduction
    A. Bread: the Staff of Life
    B. Lesson Background
  I. Seeking Jesus (JOHN 6:22-24)
    A. Puzzling Disappearance (v. 22)
    B. Eager Search (vv. 23, 24)
  II. Seeking Answers (JOHN 6:25-30)
    A. When? (vv. 25-27)
      Motive Check
    B. What Work? (vv. 28, 29)
    C. What Sign? (v. 30)
  III. Seeking Bread (JOHN 6:31-35)
    A. Manna from God (v. 31)
    B. Bread of God (vv. 32, 33)
    C. Bread of Life (vv. 34, 35)
      Surviving the Siege
Conclusion
    A. No More Hunger; No More Thirst
    B. Prayer
    C. Thought to Remember

Introduction

A. Bread: the Staff of Life

Bread was the primary part of the diet in Bible times. Making it was a simple but time-consuming task. Barley, or occasionally wheat, was ground into flour between two stones. The flour was kneaded with water and salt into dough, which was then leavened with a piece of old dough. After the dough raised, it was baked in an outdoor oven. When severe drought caused the supply of grain to fail, people perished.

The lack of bread can change the course of history. For example, bread riots in Paris in 1789 helped foment the French Revolution. There have been other bread riots since that time. How might the world be different if people clamored for the bread of life—Jesus—as much as they desired physical bread!

B. Lesson Background

Near the beginning of Jesus' third year of ministry, He received distressing news of the death of John the Baptist (Matthew 14:3-13). Jesus took His disciples to an isolated location across the Sea of Galilee, somewhere near Bethsaida on the northeast shore (Matthew 14:13; Mark 6:31, 32; Luke 9:10; John 6:1) for a time of rest and solitude.

But the eager multitudes would not leave them alone. Thousands of people came out of the cities and ran by foot around the north end of the lake (Mark 6:33, 34; John 6:2). Jesus took compassion on the crowds, teaching them God's Word and healing their sicknesses.

At the end of the day there was nowhere for the people to get food. So Jesus took five small barley loaves and two fish and fed 5,000 men in addition to women and children (Matthew 14:21). Other than the resurrection, this is the only miracle of Jesus that is recorded in all four Gospels.

The people were so excited about a leader who could supply food miraculously that they wanted to force Him to be their king. But Jesus refused to be a bread-king, so He withdrew to a mountain to pray (John 6:15). (This opportunity to take a shortcut to kingly power bears a similarity to

The Bread of Life

the temptation by the devil in Matthew 4:8, 9). Later that night Jesus walked across the lake to join His terrified disciples in the storm-tossed boat (John 6:16-21). That is the immediate backdrop to today's lesson.

I. Seeking Jesus
(JOHN 6:22-24)

A. Puzzling Disappearance (v. 22)

22. The day following, when the people which stood on the other side of the sea saw that there was none other boat there, save that one whereinto his disciples were entered, and that Jesus went not with his disciples into the boat, but that his disciples were gone away alone.

The phrase *the day following* indicates that what comes next follows closely what is described in the Lesson Background. Although Jesus had "sent away the people" following the feeding of the 5,000 of the day before (Mark 6:45), some apparently have remained in the area *on the other side of the sea* where the miracle had taken place.

These people are puzzled by Jesus' absence since they know that (1) Jesus had not left in a boat with His disciples (again, Mark 6:45), (2) *none other boat was there* for Jesus to have used, and (3) Jesus would not have walked around the north end of the lake in the dark of night. Therefore they do not comprehend Jesus' absence. Where has Jesus gone, and how did He get there?

A storm had arisen on the Sea of Galilee the night before (John 6:18), with the wind blowing against the disciples' boat (Mark 6:48). This had kept them from making much progress toward their destination. This situation changed when Jesus walked on the water during the night and caught up with the disciples (John 6:19); they arrived "immediately" at their destination (6:21). This is what the crowd does not know.

B. Eager Search (vv. 23, 24)

23. (Howbeit there came other boats from Tiberias nigh unto the place where they did eat bread, after that the Lord had given thanks:).

Boats from Tiberias travel the other direction, since Tiberias is a city on the western edge of the

Sea of Galilee. Those who are arriving in these boats to join the search for Jesus can confirm that they have not passed Jesus traveling in the opposite direction during the daylight hours of this new day. This *place where they did eat bread* refers to the location of the miraculous feeding of the 5,000 in John 6:11.

24. When the people therefore saw that Jesus was not there, neither his disciples, they also took shipping, and came to Capernaum, seeking for Jesus.

The boats from Tiberias (v. 23, above) are put to good use: when the people realize that Jesus and His disciples are gone, they use those boats to head for Capernaum. Those not able to secure passage on a boat must travel by foot around the northern shoreline.

We are used to thinking of Nazareth as Jesus' hometown (John 1:45; Acts 2:22; etc.). But Capernaum becomes the home base for Jesus at the beginning of His public ministry (Matthew 4:13). Scripture even calls Capernaum "his own city" (Matthew 9:1; compare Mark 2:1). Thus this little fishing village, on the northwest shore of the Sea of Galilee, seems the most logical spot for the crowds to begin their search for Jesus.

What Do You Think?
What motives do people have for seeking Jesus in the twenty-first century? How are these similar to and different from the motives of those in the first century?
Talking Points for Your Discussion
- Good motives
- Bad motives
- Naïve motives

II. Seeking Answers
(JOHN 6:25-30)

A. When? (vv. 25-27)

25. And when they had found him on the other side of the sea, they said unto him, Rabbi, when camest thou hither?

The people find Jesus *on the other side of the sea.* The bookends of John 6:24 and 6:59 confirm that the location is Capernaum. The title *Rabbi* is one of honor as a student addresses a teacher. The crowd is fickle, however, for they will dispute Jesus' teaching soon enough (John 6:41, 42).

The question *when camest thou hither?* reveals puzzlement. When—and how—did Jesus arrive? At least some people had seen Him withdraw to a mountain (John 6:15), and the next day He simply was gone. He did not have a boat (6:22, above), and traveling by foot at night is extremely difficult, if not impossible. Yet here He is the next day in Capernaum! What is going on?

26. Jesus answered them and said, Verily, verily, I say unto you, Ye seek me, not because ye saw the miracles, but because ye did eat of the loaves, and were filled.

Jesus provides an answer, but not to the question the people ask. Instead of discussing His method of travel, He tells them what they really need to know. He tells them the uncomfortable truth about their real motives. They seek Him not because they have seen miracles that prove His identity and message. Rather, what motivates the people is the fact they *did eat of the loaves* and their stomachs *were filled.*

The people do not need to know when or how Jesus arrived in Capernaum. Instead, they need to confront the ugly truth that they want religion to be a means of gain (compare those denounced by Paul in 1 Timothy 6:5). Jesus has no desire to attract "soup line" Christians who follow Him only to get food. Mark 6:52 tells us that the disciples still have hard hearts at this point in Jesus' ministry.

What Do You Think?
  What do Jesus' words tell us, if anything, about how to respond to someone who seeks physical help but is not interested in spiritual nourishment?
Talking Points for Your Discussion
  ▪ Occasions to give the physical help anyway, *without* confrontation regarding spiritual need
  ▪ Occasions to give the physical help anyway, *with* confrontation regarding spiritual need
  ▪ Occasions to refuse the physical help, offering only spiritual help

---

My wife and I didn't know many people when we first moved to our city. Browsing in a bookstore one day, we met a friendly couple about our age with whom we seemed to share common interests. Just as we started to think we might be making new friends, the conversation suddenly turned toward a "business opportunity" they wanted to share. When they understood we weren't interested, they cut off the conversation and left. They said we were missing a great opportunity, but I think they missed out on the opportunity for a genuine friendship.

Jesus can perceive false motives far more clearly than any of us can. When He examines my heart, what does He find? Do I serve Him out of fear of punishment, a sense of duty or obligation, or a desire to impress others? Perhaps I see life as a big self-improvement project, and He is the one to help me reach my highest potential. I might pursue my personal relationship with Jesus in order to enjoy feelings of peace and joy without taking seriously His calling and example of self-sacrifice for the good of others.

In the final analysis, the ultimate question is *Why do I seek Jesus?* Perhaps He wants me to adjust my motives.
—A. W.

27. Labour not for the meat which perisheth, but for that meat which endureth unto everlasting life, which the Son of man shall give unto you: for him hath God the Father sealed.

It is natural to labor for food in order to stay alive. Indeed, the Bible commands that we do so (2 Thessalonians 3:12). But working for food is not to be our top priority. People are not to fill their barns just so they can take their ease—eat, drink, and be merry (see Luke 12:19). Jesus knows that the life of this present world can be snatched away at any moment. Why should people focus on what will not last?

Thus Jesus challenges His would-be followers to focus on securing the food that endures *unto everlasting life* (compare Matthew 4:3, 4). This means submitting to *the Son of man,* who can give it to them. Jesus is the one whom God the Father has sealed in this regard. Thus, He is the one who carries Heaven's own seal of approval.

The Bread of Life

B. What Work? (vv. 28, 29)

28. Then said they unto him, What shall we do, that we might work the works of God?

The crowd seems to sense that there is something available that is even better than yesterday's miracle of bread. Jesus has just said to focus on "meat which endureth unto everlasting life." So how should they do that?

The crowd's question *What shall we do, that we might work the works of God?* shows that the people have missed the point. Although they correctly see that there is a kind of food more important than ordinary food, they do not correctly see how to get it. Like the rich young ruler (see Matthew 19:16), they seem to assume that doing some kind of good work is the answer. They do not acknowledge that Jesus has just said that all this involves that "which the Son of man shall give unto you" (v. 27).

29. Jesus answered and said unto them, This is the work of God, that ye believe on him whom he hath sent.

In response to the crowd's somewhat confused question, Jesus answers clearly: the "work" God wants them to do is to *believe on him whom he hath sent.* The basis of salvation is faith in Christ (Ephesians 2:8), not works of law (Romans 3:28). It is impossible to please God without faith

HOW TO SAY IT

Bethsaida	Beth-*say*-uh-duh.
Capernaum	Kuh-*per*-nay-um.
Galilee	*Gal*-uh-lee.
Moses	*Mo*-zes or *Mo*-zez.
Nazareth	*Naz*-uh-reth.
Tiberias	Tie-*beer*-ee-us.

(Hebrews 11:6). This faith is a working faith, to be sure (James 2:14-26), but it is not the works that earn salvation. Christ calls on His hearers to believe in Him with total confidence and loyalty, and He will give them the life they seek. But will they trust that He really can do this?

C. What Sign? (v. 30)

30. They said therefore unto him, What sign shewest thou then, that we may see, and believe thee? what dost thou work?

The people are not prepared to put their trust in Jesus. Rather than submitting in humble faith, they doubt Him. The miraculous feeding of the 5,000 is not enough for them, so they request an additional sign. No longer are they seeking answers; now they are issuing demands.

Jesus has just told the crowd to do God's work by believing in Him. The people, however, throw Jesus' words back at Him. Caring nothing for what they themselves should do, they insist *What dost thou work?* They have no interest in satisfying God; the Son of God must satisfy them!

III. Seeking Bread
(JOHN 6:31-35)
A. Manna from God (v. 31)

31. Our fathers did eat manna in the desert; as it is written, He gave them bread from heaven to eat.

Israel's birth as a nation came when Moses led them out of Egypt. One of the miracles of that exodus involved *manna in the desert.* It happened just as God had promised: "I will rain *bread from heaven* for you" (Exodus 16:4). For 40 years the people of Israel could go out each morning (except

Visual for Lesson 10. *Point to this visual as you introduce the discussion question that is associated with John 6:35.*

the Sabbath) and gather manna to eat. Now, centuries later, the Jews are awaiting a Messiah who can do the same thing.

After all, Moses had promised that God would raise up a prophet in their midst, and that person would be like Moses himself (Deuteronomy 18:15). God had provided manna for six days every week, year after year, for hundreds of thousands of people during the time of Moses. Jesus has just provided a single meal for 5,000 men (plus women and children). Thus Jesus has not yet proven himself greater than Moses in the eyes (and stomachs) of the people. If Jesus really is the long-awaited prophet—even the Messiah—then He had better produce lots more bread for them!

B. Bread of God (vv. 32, 33)

32. Then Jesus said unto them, Verily, verily, I say unto you, Moses gave you not that bread from heaven; but my Father giveth you the true bread from heaven.

Jesus needs His audience to understand two vital truths. First, it was the Father—not Moses—who gave them the *bread from heaven* in the wilderness. The people do not need another Moses; they need to turn to God. Second, God has a new kind of bread that is far better than the ancient manna.

Jesus has come to be more than just another Moses. Moses was the servant of God; Jesus is the Son of God (see Hebrews 3:3-6). Moses delivered the Israelites from slavery in Egypt; Jesus can lead

them from the slavery of sin and death. Moses led the people to the entrance of the promised land; Jesus will lead believers to Heaven.

33. For the bread of God is he which cometh down from heaven, and giveth life unto the world.

Jesus himself is *the bread of God* (also John 6:41, 51). The ancient manna came down like rain from the sky (Psalm 78:24), but Jesus comes down from Heaven itself. The manna was for the body, but this bread from Heaven is for the soul. The ancient manna could keep people alive from day to day, but Jesus can keep people alive for all eternity.

Jesus comes to sustain life in ways far beyond what mere bread can do. But to accept His teaching requires faith. Later in Jesus' sermon, He will instruct the crowds about eating His flesh and drinking His blood (John 6:51-57), demands that are repugnant to them. Their forefathers had stumbled when they needed to put their faith in God; how far will this crowd go in trusting Jesus?

C. Bread of Life (vv. 34, 35)

34. Then said they unto him, Lord, evermore give us this bread.

Like the woman at the well who was eager to get an endless supply of water (John 4:15), these people are eager for the Heaven-sent bread. They cannot pass up such a good deal! But the people do not understand what Jesus is really saying. Thus the need for the next verse.

35. And Jesus said unto them, I am the bread of life: he that cometh to me shall never hunger; and he that believeth on me shall never thirst.

Jesus affirms "I am the [something]" seven times in John's Gospel. The first of these seven is right here (repeated in 6:41, 48, 51); the other six are in John 8:12 (repeated in 9:5); 10:7, 9; 10:11, 14; 11:25; 14:6; and 15:1, 5.

Here, in the first of these seven affirmations, Jesus is offering himself as God in human flesh. Jesus is the solution to all their problems. As more than a mere mortal, Jesus does not come just to *provide* the bread of life, but to *be* that bread. Anyone who comes to Jesus in trusting faith will find satisfaction for his or her deepest hunger and thirst. This is an echo of Isaiah 55:1.

The Bread of Life

As long as the people think Jesus is talking about physical bread, they are quite ready to accept it. However, when it becomes clear that Jesus is talking about something else, they back away. By the end of this story, many reject Him and leave, unable to trust Him and accept on faith what He is saying (John 6:60-66).

What Do You Think?

How has Jesus been the bread of life to you in an earthly sense?

Talking Points for Your Discussion

- A teaching of His that gave you insight on how to handle a situation
- An action of His that provided an example
- A promise of His that gave you hope

❧ SURVIVING THE SIEGE ❧

Some of the worst suffering of World War II took place during the German siege of Leningrad (modern-day St. Petersburg, Russia) from 1941 to 1944. With supplies cut off, hungry people made soup from wallpaper and shoe leather, baked bread with sawdust and cardboard, and ate pets, birds, and vermin. Some even resorted to cannibalism. Good manners required one to avoid talking about food, even as an estimated one million people starved. Some fortunate citizens successfully braved German shelling and the bitter cold to cross the "road of life"—a trail across frozen Lake Ladoga—to safety.

Though few of us will ever experience this degree of wartime suffering, in fact we do live every day under siege from the spiritual powers of a dark world that is opposed to God and His people. Under the stress of Satan's bombardment, we may try to satisfy our spiritual hunger with poor substitutes of our own devising. Material things, entertainment, educational and career achievement, even relationships can be like "shoe leather soup" that temporarily fills, but does not satisfy our real needs.

Rather than just putting on a cheerful face and trying to make ourselves as comfortable as possible in a dying world, we should focus our efforts on our pilgrimage with Christ. This is the narrow road that leads to life. As we journey, we can help others travel with us.   —A. W.

Conclusion

A. No More Hunger; No More Thirst

Deep in the soul of every person is a hunger that is more than just physical hunger. Just as our bodies have an instinct for survival, so do our souls. Only when we finally feed on the true bread from Heaven will we ever escape the gnawing dissatisfaction of spiritual emptiness.

Jesus taught us to pray, "Give us this day our daily bread" (Matthew 6:11). These words, of course, are about the physical food that we need to live from one day to the next. But are we as eager to pray each day for the bread from Heaven—the spiritual bread—that enables us to live forever? It is only when we take Jesus into our souls that the soul's deep hunger can ever be satisfied.

Jesus also said that with the true bread from Heaven we will never thirst (compare John 6:53-58). Therefore as we accept and embrace His atoning death on the cross following the plan of salvation in its entirety, we are consuming the bread that gives life. This is how we do "the work of God" as we "believe on him whom he hath sent" (John 6:29). Every time we participate in the Lord's Supper, we are remembering and proclaiming that death (1 Corinthians 11:26). As we digest the teachings of Jesus and incorporate them into our lives, we are consuming the bread that gives life (John 6:63).

Jesus is the bread of life. He is the source of life, the giver of life, the sustainer of life. His words, His atoning death, His very presence in our hearts—these make up the true bread that gives our spirits life.

B. Prayer

Father, give us this day the bread from Heaven. Help us to embrace Jesus and His teachings completely. Give us faith to follow, even when our understanding is weak. In Jesus' name, amen.

C. Thought to Remember

Focus on the most important kind of bread.

INVOLVEMENT LEARNING

Some of the activities below are also found in the helpful student book, Adult Bible Class.
Don't forget to download the free reproducible page from www.standardlesson.com to enhance your lesson!

Into the Lesson

Bring a loaf of bread to class as a visual aid. You may wish to bring several different types of bread. Ask the class, "How many varieties of bread can you name?" Answers may focus on flavors (example: garlic), ingredients (example: whole wheat), or shape (example: hot dog buns). Then ask, "What are the various ways bread is used in our culture and other cultures?" Answers may include sandwiches, dinner rolls, dipping, Communion, doughnuts, etc. Jot all answers on the board.

Make a transition to Bible study by saying, "Bread is important to modern culture, as you can see from our two lists. But bread was absolutely *vital* in ancient times, being a primary part of one's diet. Jesus used that fact to offer one of the illustrations of His nature and purpose."

Alternative: Interview a baker (or someone pretending to be a baker). Have this person wear a baker's hat while you ask him or her the two questions above. Tell this person in advance to be prepared to answer the question, "Why is bread sometimes called 'the staff of life'?" Use the same transition offered above.

Into the Word

Summarize the information in the commentary's Introduction. During your minilecture, have on display a map of the area around the Sea of Galilee in first-century Palestine. Point out, at least, the towns of Bethsaida, Tiberias, and Capernaum. (If your learning space has video projection available with Internet access, a good source is http://bibleatlas.org.) Using today's text of John 6:22-35, plus the texts noted in the Lesson Background and John 6:59, lead the class in retracing the movements of Jesus and the crowds on the map. Be prepared to help your learners sort through movements they find confusing.

Prepare in advance five poster boards with the following five questions, one each: 1. Work and don't work for what? (John 6:26, 27) 2. Do what? (John 6:28, 29) 3. Why ask for a sign, why mention manna? (John 6:30, 31) 4. What does Jesus mean by "true bread"? (John 6:32) 5. Meaning what by "bread of life"? (John 6:35)

Explain that you are going to use the questions to explore what sounded like radical teaching from Jesus. As you work your way through the questions, have a "scribe" record responses on the board.

Into Life

Post three small signs in different corners of the room. The different signs should read as follows: *Team 1: Missions and Benevolence; Team 2: Church Priorities; Team 3: Getting Real.* Say, "Please take a chair to one of the three signs." Give each team a handout with the following instructions.

Team 1: John 6:26, 27 hints at one of the challenges that missionaries and benevolent ministries often face. Explain and illustrate the problem. *Team 2:* What implications for ministry priorities do you find in John 6:26-29 and 33-35? *Team 3:* Jesus reminds believers that we must also offer the kind of bread (John 6:32) that will wipe away spiritual hunger (v. 35). Your task is to design and propose a practical way that your class can use acts of physical benevolence to introduce someone to the "bread of life."

Allow the first two teams to share their conclusions. After they report, tell the class that Team 3 faced the task of using benevolence as a way to introducing the "bread of life" to a person or group of persons. Ask the team to report on their proposal and suggest a plan to implement it. *Option:* At this point, you can distribute copies of the Two Kinds of Benevolence activity from the reproducible page, which you have downloaded. Have learners work on this either in their teams or as a whole class to enhance Team 3's conclusions.

Distribute copies of the A Seven-Day Devotional from the reproducible page as learners depart.

THE GOOD SHEPHERD

DEVOTIONAL READING: Psalm 28
BACKGROUND SCRIPTURE: John 10:1-18

JOHN 10:7-18

7 Then said Jesus unto them again, Verily, verily, I say unto you, I am the door of the sheep.

8 All that ever came before me are thieves and robbers: but the sheep did not hear them.

9 I am the door: by me if any man enter in, he shall be saved, and shall go in and out, and find pasture.

10 The thief cometh not, but for to steal, and to kill, and to destroy: I am come that they might have life, and that they might have it more abundantly.

11 I am the good shepherd: the good shepherd giveth his life for the sheep.

12 But he that is an hireling, and not the shepherd, whose own the sheep are not, seeth the wolf coming, and leaveth the sheep, and fleeth: and the wolf catcheth them, and scattereth the sheep.

13 The hireling fleeth, because he is an hireling, and careth not for the sheep.

14 I am the good shepherd, and know my sheep, and am known of mine.

15 As the Father knoweth me, even so know I the Father: and I lay down my life for the sheep.

16 And other sheep I have, which are not of this fold: them also I must bring, and they shall hear my voice; and there shall be one fold, and one shepherd.

17 Therefore doth my Father love me, because I lay down my life, that I might take it again.

18 No man taketh it from me, but I lay it down of myself. I have power to lay it down, and I have power to take it again. This commandment have I received of my Father.

KEY VERSE

I am the good shepherd, and know my sheep, and am known of mine. —**John 10:14**

GOD'S CREATIVE WORD

Unit 3: I Am . . .

LESSONS 10–13

LESSON AIMS

After participating in this lesson, each student will be able to:

1. Summarize the message of Jesus' "good shepherd" discourse.

2. Tell why a sheep-shepherd metaphor was effective in Jesus' day.

3. Suggest a twenty-first century, non-agrarian alternative to the sheep-shepherd metaphor.

LESSON OUTLINE

Introduction

A. Shepherds

"No position in the world is so despised as that of the shepherd." This was the declaration of an ancient Jewish commentator who was amazed that David would call the Lord a shepherd in Psalm 23. Similarly, the ancient rabbis included shepherding in their list of thieving and cheating occupations. To buy wool or milk directly from a hireling shepherd was forbidden, since it was assumed that he was stealing it from the owner of the flock. Shepherds were held in such contempt that they could not be admitted in court as witnesses. Shepherds were simply despised, at least in some quarters.

But the New Testament views shepherds in a favorable light. It was to shepherds that the angels announced the birth of Jesus (Luke 2:8-14). Jesus likened himself to a shepherd in His description of Judgment Day (Matthew 25:31-33). He said He had come to rescue "the lost sheep of the house of Israel" (Matthew 15:24). When the Lord built His church, the leaders were expected to be shepherds (Acts 20:28; 1 Peter 5:2) under the "chief Shepherd," Jesus (1 Peter 5:4). Today's lesson considers Jesus' declaration of himself as *the good shepherd.*

B. Lesson Background

From the Feast of Tabernacles in October (John 7:2) until the Feast of Dedication in December (10:22) in His third year of ministry, Jesus spent most of His time near Jerusalem. There was "much murmuring" and division among the people about Him (7:12). Some said He was a good man, but others said He was a deceiver. The authorities tried to arrest Him (7:30, 32, 44; 8:20); the people tried to stone Him (8:59). Even when He opened the eyes of a man born blind, the authorities refused to believe (9:13-34).

It was in this atmosphere of suspicion and disbelief that Jesus proclaimed His true identity and His divine purpose. Part of this proclamation involved comparison with sheep and sheepfolds in John 10:1-6. But the fact that "they understood not what things they were which he spake unto them" (v. 6) led Jesus to make the declaration that opens today's lesson.

The Good Shepherd

I. Not a Thief

(JOHN 10:7-10)

A. Shepherd's Aim (vv. 7-9)

7. Then said Jesus unto them again, Verily, verily, I say unto you, I am the door of the sheep.

Jesus has just been speaking about sheep and their "sheepfold" (John 10:1-6). Typically, a sheepfold consists of a small enclosure with stone walls that are topped with tangles of thorns to keep predators out. The only entrance is a doorway or gate that is guarded by a gatekeeper. (It has sometimes been suggested that a shepherd can lie down in the doorway, his own body serving as the "door.") The previous section of Jesus' comments may suggest an overnight mixture of two or more flocks, with the sheep sorting themselves out in the morning by recognizing their shepherd's voice.

As Jesus speaks *unto them again,* He changes the focus of His illustration. Rather than being the one who "entereth in by the door" (v. 2), He is now *the door of the sheep.* This is one of the seven "I am the [something]" statements in the Gospel of John that we noted in last week's lesson (see the comment there on John 6:35). The explanation of the importance of Jesus as the door of the sheep follows.

8. All that ever came before me are thieves and robbers: but the sheep did not hear them.

Many false prophets and false messiahs had come on the scene before Jesus arrived. They claimed to have the truth from God; they called for the people of God to follow them (see for instance, Acts 5:36, 37; 21:38). However, these men were not serving God as true shepherds; they were *thieves and robbers.* They were interested only in personal gain. All such men who claimed to be the Messiah were false, and the true sheep of God *did not hear them.* More false messiahs are yet to come (Matthew 7:15; 24:11, 24).

Sometimes the legitimately designated leaders of Israel were not very good shepherds. Rather than feeding and protecting God's people, they exploited and abused them (see Jeremiah 23:1, 2; Ezekiel 34:1-10). The flock of God needs someone who truly cares for the sheep; they need someone who comes to serve, not to be served. They need a shepherd, not another thief.

❧ *THIEVES OF ALL TYPES* ❧

Recently in my city, two young men came into a man's back yard, shattered his glass door with a cinder block, and barged into his house to steal a flat-screen television—all while the owner was watching it!

A homeless woman in Japan took a more subtle approach to her thievery. She sneaked into an unlocked house and hid on the top shelf of a closet for an entire year, coming down to take showers and steal food only while the owner was at work. Her thefts went undetected for a long time because they were so small. In the end, however, her long-term approach may have cost this homeowner much more than the value of one television.

Sometimes Satan launches a frontal attack, such as when he brazenly tempted Jesus to worship him (Matthew 4:9). At other times, he appears as an "angel of light" (2 Corinthians 11:14) as he brings us ideas and influences that at first appear harmless but in the end wreak havoc. This was the approach he took with Eve in the Garden of Eden (Genesis 3:1-6).

We have to be prepared for both kinds of attacks. Some Christians are well prepared to battle false doctrine or obvious cultural evils, but they leave themselves open to subtle influences that can morph into sinful attitudes. Think about self-esteem that turns into pride; a work ethic that feeds materialism; an opposite sex friendship that begins to displace feelings for a spouse. Yes, let's guard the doors to our hearts, but let's make sure the windows are secure too.   —A. W.

HOW TO SAY IT

Annas	*An*-nus.
Caiaphas	*Kay*-uh-fus or *Kye*-uh-fus.
Corinthians	Ko-*rin*-thee-unz (*th* as in *thin*).
Ephesians	Ee-*fee*-zhunz.
Ezekiel	Ee-*zeek*-ee-ul or Ee-*zeek*-yul.
Galatians	Guh-*lay*-shunz.
Messiah	Meh-*sigh*-uh.

9. I am the door: by me if any man enter in, he shall be saved, and shall go in and out, and find pasture.

Jesus does not just claim to know about the door—He *is* the door. He is not just one door among many—He is *the* door. He does not hesitate to proclaim that He is the only way to salvation (John 14:6).

Jesus offers the opportunity for anyone to enter in through this exclusive door to Heaven. The person who enters through Jesus will be saved from sin's power and penalty, but only by going through this door (compare Psalm 118:20). The goal of the good shepherd is to save His sheep.

The sheep who *go in and out* freely through this door will have security on the inside and will *find pasture* on the outside. This may serve as something of a preview of Heaven, where the gates of the holy city are never shut (Revelation 21:25). God's people will have both total security and abundant provision.

B. Contrasting Aims (v. 10)

10. The thief cometh not, but for to steal, and to kill, and to destroy: I am come that they might have life, and that they might have it more abundantly.

Some reading this lesson have had the sad experience of dealing with church leaders who were dishonest and self-centered (compare Jude 12). Such leaders may have no compassion or concern for the well-being of the sheep.

But Jesus is not a thief. He does not come to abuse the flock. Quite the opposite—He comes *that they might have life*. This kind of life is not just that of unending quantity, an unending number of days. It also has the quality of being abundant.

What Do You Think?
What does Jesus' example teach us about a church leader's accountability, if anything?
Talking Points for Your Discussion
- In terms of accountability to God
- In terms of accountability to God's people
- In terms of accountability to one another

To have life *more abundantly* does not mean that the Lord's people will always have an easy, affluent lifestyle. Neither Jesus himself, nor His apostles, nor the believers in the first-century church were exempt from hardship and persecution. What is in view, rather, is the privilege of walking daily with the Master. This privilege stretches into eternity in Heaven.

II. Not a Hireling
(JOHN 10:11-14)
A. Shepherd Risks His Life (v. 11)

11. I am the good shepherd: the good shepherd giveth his life for the sheep.

Not only is Jesus the door though which the sheep have access to salvation, He is also *the good shepherd* of the sheep (Hebrews 13:20). Centuries earlier, David demonstrated that a true shepherd risks his life to save the sheep. When a lion or a bear seized a lamb from the flock, David fought to kill the intruder (1 Samuel 17:34-37).

Jesus faces a much more dangerous foe: the devil himself. Satan is the ultimate thief and intruder. His only aim is to kill and destroy (see John 8:44). In order to free the flock from certain death, Jesus not only risks His life as a true shepherd does, He willingly lays down His life as the only way to save the flock. With the cross looming only a few months away, Jesus foresees and accepts His destiny.

What Do You Think?
What sacrifices have you seen leaders make? How does this encourage you spirtually?
Talking Points for Your Discussion
- Political leaders
- Church leaders
- Supervisors at work

B. Hireling Runs Away (vv. 12, 13)

12. But he that is an hireling, and not the shepherd, whose own the sheep are not, seeth the wolf coming, and leaveth the sheep, and fleeth: and the wolf catcheth them, and scattereth the sheep.

The thieves and robbers that Jesus has just discussed are evil. The hireling, by contrast, isn't necessarily evil; he's just someone who is interested in saving his own skin. Such a person will not risk his life for a flock of sheep. They are not his sheep, so he is not particularly concerned if they are in peril. If he sees a wolf, he runs. The hired hand rationalizes that a wolf may kill a sheep and scatter the rest, but at least the man himself is safe.

We wonder if Jesus is using the image of a hireling to refer to certain religious leaders of His day. Undoubtedly, there are religious leaders of Jesus' day, as today, who will not go out of their way to rescue someone from spiritual danger.

13. The hireling fleeth, because he is an hireling, and careth not for the sheep.

When *the hireling* flees, it is not necessarily because he is a frightened weakling. He flees for the very reason of who he is—just a hired hand making a few shekels for doing a boring job. He does not care for the sheep because they are not his sheep. If a few die, it's not his loss. Even though the people in Jesus' audience easily understand the difference between a hireling and a true shepherd, it is important to Jesus to emphasize the point again so the people can see the stark contrast between them.

After Jesus has gone to the cross, His disciples will begin to understand what Jesus has done. The good shepherd gives His life to save the flock. The shepherd has become the lamb, led to the slaughter (see Isaiah 53:7). After that happens, the lamb again becomes the shepherd (Revelation 7:17).

C. Sheep Know the Difference (v. 14)

14. I am the good shepherd, and know my sheep, and am known of mine.

If the people understand the difference between a hireling and a shepherd, it is time for them to decide which one Jesus is. Jesus knows that the true flock of God—His sheep—will recognize and follow Him. By their response to Jesus, the crowd that day will reveal whether they belong to God's flock or not. Are they, or are they not, sheep who know their true shepherd?

To know Jesus and to be known by Him is far more than a matter of mere acquaintance. The bib-

lical concept *know* signifies an active involvement and participation—a very close association. The Christian's great aim is to "know" Christ (Philippians 3:8-10). The Christian's great destiny is to "know" the only true God, and this is part of the definition of eternal life (John 17:3).

What Do You Think?
What are some specific ways that church leaders continue Jesus' shepherding work?
Talking Points for Your Discussion
- In terms of sacrifice for God's people
- As "doors" for God's people
- In providing pasture for God's people

III. Not a Coward
(John 10:15-18)
A. Faces Death (v. 15)

15. As the Father knoweth me, even so know I the Father: and I lay down my life for the sheep.

Jesus understands completely what His purpose on earth is. He knows the Father and the Father's plan to the same extent that the Father knows Him (Matthew 11:27). The road to the cross does not take Jesus by surprise; in fact, He has already told His disciples exactly what is going to happen (see Mark 8:31; 9:31). He is God's "Lamb slain from the foundation of the world" (Revelation 13:8). Now He is telling the crowd in advance: when He does lay down His life, it will be for them—the sheep (compare John 15:13; 1 John 3:16).

What Do You Think?
What are some general similarities and differences between Christian leaders and secular, political leaders?
Talking Points for Your Discussion
- In terms of priorities
- In terms of commitment
- In terms of motives

B. Brings Others (v. 16)
16. And other sheep I have, which are not of this fold: them also I must bring, and they shall

hear my voice; and there shall be one fold, and one shepherd.

At this point Jesus introduces a surprising element into the picture of the good shepherd and His sheep: He has *other sheep . . . which are not of this fold*. When He calls them, they will respond. Then the two flocks will come together as a single flock. The *other sheep* that belong to Jesus are the Gentiles. Even though they have not been part of the ancient community of God's people, now it is time to bring them in.

When the shepherd lays down His life on the cross, it will be just as He said: "And I, if I be lifted up from the earth, will draw all men unto me" (John 12:32). It is for this same reason that Jesus will commission His followers to carry the gospel to "all nations" (Matthew 28:19). When the saints circle the throne of God and the lamb in Heaven, they will be people from "all nations, and kindreds, and people, and tongues" (Revelation 7:9). Many other New Testament passages discuss the unity of the flock (examples: John 17:20-23; 1 Corinthians 12; Galatians 3:28; Ephesians 2:11-22; 4:3-6).

What Do You Think?

What should be evident in church leaders who are becoming ever more Christlike in their leadership?

Talking Points for Your Discussion

- In terms of attitude toward God's people (the flock)
- In terms of personal holiness
- In terms of personal sacrifice

❧ VOICE RECOGNITION ❧

Somehow it still seems like science fiction, but computers that recognize human speech are an increasing part of daily life. Word-processing software, medical equipment, phones, car stereos, even children's toys can respond to voice commands.

The technology is still far from perfect. To my chagrin, once we had to pull our car off the road and maintain perfect silence while my daughter yelled the name of her new virtual dog into a handheld video game until it could recognize

her voice. That may be annoying in a toy, but it's unacceptable in a fighter plane. Studies have shown that pilots simply will not use a voice recognition system in the cockpit that is less than 95 percent accurate.

Much of the problem lies in the way we speak. Our speech is grammatically inaccurate; we run our words together; our vocal tones vary; we speak in regional dialects; we use colloquialisms, emotion, and body language—in other words, we are not enough like computers. Imagine how much of our humanity we would have to sacrifice in order to simplify ourselves enough for these still-primitive machines to understand us all the time!

Jesus "made himself of no reputation, and took upon him the form of a servant" (Philippians 2:7; compare Hebrews 2:14-18) so that we would be able to recognize His voice. What a sacrifice! Though we can be maddeningly slow to understand (Mark 8:17), Jesus continues to teach and correct us until we are able to perform the tasks we were designed to do.   —A. W.

C. Obeys Willingly (vv. 17, 18)

17. Therefore doth my Father love me, because I lay down my life, that I might take it again.

Jesus is secure in the knowledge that the Father loves Him. The Father has always loved His Son, of course. But a specific reason for that love is noted here: Jesus' readiness to lay down His life, dying on the cross for the sins of the world. The good shepherd will make the ultimate sacrifice for His sheep.

But that is not all. Jesus declares the humanly impossible: after He lays down His life, He will *take it again*. In rising triumphantly from the grave, Jesus will reclaim His life. He will prove that He is not the victim of unfortunate circumstances; He is the sovereign Lord!

18. No man taketh it from me, but I lay it down of myself. I have power to lay it down, and I have power to take it again. This commandment have I received of my Father.

No one is going to take Jesus' life from Him against His will. It will not be Annas and Caiaphas who determine His fate (John 18:13, 24). It will not be Pilate who has the final say (John 19:16). Jesus lays down His life by His own choice.

Not only is Jesus in control of His death, He also has the *power to take it again*. In all this, Jesus is obeying the Father's command. This is an established theme as John's Gospel progresses (see John 12:49, 50; 14:31; 15:10).

Conclusion

A. Shepherd's Tasks

Without a shepherd, the sheep are in trouble. The familiar phrase "sheep without a shepherd" is a way of saying that people are in difficulty and cannot find the way on their own. This is an indication of how vital the shepherd is to the well-being of the sheep.

The sheep depend on the shepherd for many things. First, the shepherd must *protect* the sheep from predators; he uses a stout club (the "rod" of Psalm 23:4) to beat off wild animals. Second, the shepherd must *rescue* the lost; if even one sheep goes astray, the shepherd must risk everything to find and save it (see Luke 15:4).

Third, the shepherd must *provide* pasture and water for the sheep (see Psalm 23:2). Fourth, the shepherd must *lead* his sheep personally to ensure the previously mentioned tasks are accomplished. The shepherds of Palestine do not drive their sheep with sheep dogs; rather, they lead the sheep themselves. The sheep can feel safe only when they know their shepherd is with them.

Jesus is the perfect shepherd, "that great shepherd of the sheep" (Hebrews 13:20). He cares for our souls in all these ways. He lovingly performs every task of the shepherd, providing abundant life for His flock. Most of all, He has gone beyond what most shepherds are ever called to do: He has given His life so that we may live.

B. Sheep's Response

Sheep are often considered dumb and helpless. They wander off, get stuck in predicaments, and leave themselves open to attack. They do not know how to find the best places for pasture and water. Perhaps wild sheep know how to survive, but domesticated sheep need a shepherd.

Visual for Lesson 11. *Point to this visual as you introduce the discussion question that is associated with John 10:14.*

When the Bible says that we are like sheep, it is not a favorable comparison. As Isaiah noted, "All we like sheep have gone astray" (Isaiah 53:6). As Ezekiel 34 describes it, God's sheep were scattered on the mountains, abandoned by their shepherds. In many ways we are just like the people in crowds who came to Jesus "as sheep having no shepherd" (Matthew 9:36).

At the same time, the sheep of John 10 are not entirely stupid. They can distinguish the sound of their master's voice (vv. 4, 5), and they know who their shepherd is (v. 14). When the shepherd calls the sheep by name, they respond by following him (v. 3). We are called to respond to our shepherd. In the confusion of conflicting claims by various religions, we must recognize Jesus as the door of the sheep, the only true way to God. In spite of temptation to go elsewhere, we must choose to enter in through that door. Above the clamor of this world, we must hear the voice of the good shepherd and follow Him. We must find our security in Him alone.

C. Prayer

Our Father, we thank You for sending Jesus to be our good shepherd. Help us to be ready to hear His voice and to follow His leading. In the name of Jesus our shepherd, amen.

D. Thought to Remember

Respond to the good shepherd.

INVOLVEMENT LEARNING

Some of the activities below are also found in the helpful student book, Adult Bible Class.
Don't forget to download the free reproducible page from www.standardlesson.com to enhance your lesson!

Into the Lesson

Write the heading *My Pet(s)* on the board. As learners enter the classroom, ask them to write the kinds of pets they have had through the years. Begin class by thanking learners for listing such a wide variety of pets. Say, "Isn't it amazing how certain kinds of pets know and respond to the owner's voice?" Offer an example of your own experience with pets. Allow a few minutes for others to share humorous stories with the class in this regard, but don't let this drag out.

Make the transition to Bible study by saying, "Sheep, like certain household pets, also are capable of recognizing and responding to their master's voice. In some cultures today as during Bible times, the connection between sheep and shepherd is vital to the sheep's survival. The sheep know their master's voice. Jesus, therefore, uses the imagery of sheep and shepherds to teach a lesson about how He, the good shepherd, cares for us."

Into the Word

During the week before class, ask one class member to prepare to be interviewed as a shepherd. Give that person a copy of today's Lesson Introduction and commentary plus shepherd's attire, including a staff. (If such attire is not available, simply have your interviewee wear a sign that says *Shepherd*.) Also provide your "shepherd" a copy of the questions below in advance.

Read today's text (John 10:7-18) aloud. Then introduce your "shepherd" and ask these questions: 1. As I understand it, the reputation of shepherds wasn't very good in Jesus' day and before. Would you clarify that reputation for us? *(lesson introduction)* 2. I know that you've read the Scriptures about Jesus saying He was/is the good shepherd. I'd like your help in understanding or interpreting His teaching. When Jesus said, "I am the door of the sheep," what was He talking about? *(vv. 7, 9)* 3. Jesus said that thieves and robbers came before Him. What is He talking about? *(v. 8)* 4. How is Jesus different from those thieves? *(v. 10)* 5. Jesus contrasts himself with the hired help who take care of the sheep. How is Jesus different from the hired help? *(vv. 11-14)* 6. Jesus made an interesting statement when He said He has sheep that are not of this fold or sheep pen. How should we understand this? *(v. 16)* 7. One more clarification before you go back to your flock. When Jesus paints a picture of the special relationship with His heavenly Father in this sheep/shepherd illustration, what should that mean to us? *(vv. 15, 17)*

Ask the class, "What are the lessons Jesus wants us to learn from this sheep/shepherd metaphor?" List responses on the board; keep these posted for the following segment.

Into Life

Divide the class in teams of three or four. Say, "Jesus used a metaphor of the sheep and shepherd because it was common to the culture of His day. Your task is to create a new metaphor appropriate for our culture. The metaphor must communicate the lessons listed on the board." Call for conclusions after a few minutes.

Alternative: Use instead the Promises and Peace activity from the reproducible page, which you have downloaded. Have learners work in pairs.

Say, "Jesus expects church leaders to shepherd the church. What lessons or qualities do we find in today's passage that we can apply to those who shepherd the church?" You can use John 21:15-17; 1 Peter 5:1-3; and Jude 12 in your discussion. Conclude with a two-part/two-person prayer that (1) thanks God for the wonderful snapshot we have in Jesus as the good shepherd and (2) asks God's blessing and guidance on those responsible for shepherding today's church.

As learners depart, distribute copies of the Puzzles to Ponder activity from the reproducible page, which you have downloaded.

THE RESURRECTION AND THE LIFE

DEVOTIONAL READING: 1 Corinthians 15:50-58

BACKGROUND SCRIPTURE: John 11:1-44

JOHN 11:17-27, 41-44

17 Then when Jesus came, he found that he had lain in the grave four days already.

18 Now Bethany was nigh unto Jerusalem, about fifteen furlongs off:

19 And many of the Jews came to Martha and Mary, to comfort them concerning their brother.

20 Then Martha, as soon as she heard that Jesus was coming, went and met him: but Mary sat still in the house.

21 Then said Martha unto Jesus, Lord, if thou hadst been here, my brother had not died.

22 But I know, that even now, whatsoever thou wilt ask of God, God will give it thee.

23 Jesus saith unto her, Thy brother shall rise again.

24 Martha saith unto him, I know that he shall rise again in the resurrection at the last day.

25 Jesus said unto her, I am the resurrection, and the life: he that believeth in me, though he were dead, yet shall he live:

26 And whosoever liveth and believeth in me shall never die. Believest thou this?

27 She saith unto him, Yea, Lord: I believe that thou art the Christ, the Son of God, which should come into the world.

· ·

41 Then they took away the stone from the place where the dead was laid. And Jesus lifted up his eyes, and said, Father, I thank thee that thou hast heard me.

42 And I knew that thou hearest me always: but because of the people which stand by I said it, that they may believe that thou hast sent me.

43 And when he thus had spoken, he cried with a loud voice, Lazarus, come forth.

44 And he that was dead came forth, bound hand and foot with graveclothes: and his face was bound about with a napkin. Jesus saith unto them, Loose him, and let him go.

KEY VERSE

Jesus said unto her, I am the resurrection, and the life: he that believeth in me, though he were dead, yet shall he live. —**John 11:25**

GOD'S CREATIVE WORD

Unit 3: I Am . . .

LESSONS 10–13

LESSON AIMS

After participating in this lesson, each student will be able to:

1. Recount the sequence of events in the account of the raising of Lazarus from the dead.

2. Tell how Jesus' raising of Lazarus proves the truth of Jesus' claim in John 11:25.

3. Contrast the life lived in confidence that Jesus is "the resurrection, and the life" with the life lived without such confidence.

LESSON OUTLINE

Introduction
 A. The Point of No Return
 B. Lesson Background
 I. Faith at a Funeral (JOHN 11:17-27)
 A. Status (vv. 17-19)
 B. Frustration (vv. 20-22)
 C. Life (vv. 23-26)
  More Than a Prophet
 D. Belief (v. 27)
 II. Freed from the Grave (JOHN 11:41-44)
 A. Source of Jesus' Power (vv. 41, 42)
  Getting Indirectly to the Point
 B. Lazarus Loosed (vv. 43, 44)
Conclusion
 A. Pleasant Surprises
 B. Prayer
 C. Thought to Remember

Introduction

A. The Point of No Return

The phrase *the point of no return* originated in the early days of flight. Technically, it is that place on a flight path where the amount of fuel remaining makes it impossible to return to the airfield of takeoff. When we use that phrase in other contexts, we usually mean that we've reached a point where it is impractical or even impossible to turn back and start over.

Our Bible story today is about a person named Lazarus who seemingly had reached the ultimate point of no return: death. Death is the last stop for all our hopes and dreams in this world, the final and unavoidable end to every plan and purpose. As we've all been told, the only two things that are certain in this life are death and taxes. While we theoretically can avoid taxes, there's simply no coming back from the grave.

Or is there?

B. Lesson Background

Last week's lesson found Jesus teaching at a time within the two-month period between the Feast of Tabernacles in October (John 7:2) and the Feast of Dedication in December, in Jerusalem (10:22). This week's lesson from John 11 shows us that Jesus is back in Judea after he had withdrawn to minister in Perea, on the eastern side of the Jordan River (10:40).

Our previous two lessons focused on two of the seven famous "I am the [something]" sayings of Jesus in the Gospel of John. These are found in John 6:35; 8:12; 10:7, 9; 10:11, 14; 11:25; 14:6; and 15:1, 5. Today's lesson moves us to the fifth of those seven. It is especially significant because it comes at the climax of Jesus' public ministry.

I. Faith at a Funeral

(JOHN 11:17-27)

In the Gospels of Matthew, Mark, and Luke, the Pharisees and chief priests plot to kill Jesus after becoming enraged by His cleansing of the temple, an action that explicitly challenges the integrity and authority of their leadership. In

• The Resurrection and the Life

John's account, the plot against Jesus' life is motivated additionally by the resurrection of Lazarus (today's lesson). This is a highly dramatic and public event that the Jewish leadership cannot ignore. As today's text opens, Jesus is already aware of the sickness and death of Lazarus (John 11:1-6, 14).

A. Status (vv. 17-19)

17, 18. Then when Jesus came, he found that he [Lazarus] had lain in the grave four days already. Now Bethany was nigh unto Jerusalem, about fifteen furlongs off.

This particular Lazarus appears in the Gospels only here and in the story that immediately follows in John 12. The fact that Lazarus has been *in the grave four days already* is significant. Ancient Jews believe that the souls of the dead hover near their bodies for three days, after which time they depart. This being the belief, the Jews in this story can only assume that Lazarus has passed the point of no return, with no hope whatsoever of recovery.

Before moving on, we note that this particular Bethany is the one that is *about fifteen furlongs* distant from Jerusalem. A furlong is 202 yards, 9 inches in length. Thus the distance from this Bethany to Jerusalem is about 1.72 miles. John's note on distance thus serves to distinguish this particular town from the Bethany that is on the other side of the Jordan River (also called *Bethabara* in the *King James Version;* see John 1:28).

19. And many of the Jews came to Martha and Mary, to comfort them concerning their brother.

Lazarus, Martha, and Mary are brother and sisters per John 11:2. Mary and Martha are known from the famous story in Luke 10:38-42. In another well-known episode, Mary anoints Jesus' feet with expensive perfume (Mark 14:3-9; John 11:2; 12:1-8).

Because all of these stories seem to be set in the village of Bethany just east of Jerusalem, some scholars suggest that Jesus regularly stays with these three on His trips to Jerusalem. In support of this theory, Mark indicates that Jesus stays in Bethany during the final week of His life, perhaps at the home of His friends (Mark 11:11, 12).

Based on this information, several things may be deduced about Lazarus and his sisters. First, they seem to be strong supporters of Jesus, and they know Him well (Luke 10:38). Second, the family may be financially well off given Mary's anointing of Jesus' feet with a perfume worth 300 pence, equivalent to about a year's wages for an average person (John 12:5). For this and other reasons, we conclude that the poor beggar named Lazarus in Luke 16:19-31 is not the Lazarus in view here.

Third, the presence of the large crowd of Jews who come to mourn Lazarus's death indicates that the family is well established in the community (John 11:19, below). But death is no respecter of persons. Despite any wealth, social advantages, and close relationship with Jesus, Lazarus has succumbed to an illness (11:1).

Ancient Jewish funerals often last several days and involve large numbers of family and friends. As is often the case today, one's social status can be measured by the number of people who attend one's funeral. Wealthy Jews sometimes hire professional mourners to wail and weep at a funeral to ensure that the dead will receive a level of respect sufficient to their station in life. In this case it appears that the entire village of Bethany, and perhaps also some residents of Jerusalem (compare John 11:45, 46), have come to pay their respects.

What Do You Think?
How have others tried to comfort you when someone close to you died? What lessons did you learn from those experiences?
Talking Points for Your Discussion
▪ Proper, helpful ways
▪ Improper, unhelpful ways (even though well intended)

B. Frustration (vv. 20-22)

20. Then Martha, as soon as she heard that Jesus was coming, went and met him: but Mary sat still in the house.

This verse allows us a peek at the personality differences between Mary and Martha. As in Luke 10:38-42, Martha seems to be the more assertive of the two.

21. Then said Martha unto Jesus, Lord, if thou hadst been here, my brother had not died.

Martha meets Jesus on the road, before He gets to the house, away from the crowd of sympathizers. It seems that she wants some time with Him to express her grief privately.

Martha's words are a little difficult to interpret. Some see them as an accusation (as in, "Why weren't you here to help?"). Other students see them as a statement of faith (as in, "If you had been able to come, I know you could have helped"). We note that the sisters sent word to Jesus when Lazarus fell ill, but Jesus purposefully delayed His return by two days (John 11:3-6). But given the fact that Lazarus has been dead four days by this time (v. 17, above), Lazarus would still have been dead for two days if Jesus had not taken a two-day delay.

Of course, Jesus could have healed Lazarus supernaturally from a distance (as in Matthew 8:5-13). But Jesus has allowed Lazarus to die because Jesus is planning to raise Him from the dead (see John 11:4, 11). Naturally, Martha does not know this. Thus as is so often the case, our emotions can overwhelm us before God reveals His larger plan.

> *What Do You Think?*
> Where do you find the best help for your faith when God doesn't work on your time table?
> *Talking Points for Your Discussion*
> - Scripture
> - Prayer
> - The counsel of another Christian
> - The comfort of a group of other Christians

22. But I know, that even now, whatsoever thou wilt ask of God, God will give it thee.

At first glance, this statement may look like a veiled request: "Jesus, You can still save Lazarus if You want to." But John 11:39 suggests that Martha is not thinking along these lines. When Jesus arrives at the tomb and asks that the stone be removed, Martha tries to dissuade Him by saying that the decomposing corpse will stink. This indicates that she has no expectation that Jesus will bring Lazarus back to life.

Thus Martha's statement here should be taken as a general expression of confidence in Jesus rather than as a particular expectation regarding Lazarus. Martha still respects and believes in Jesus. She still recognizes the intimacy that Jesus has with the Father. Martha's faith during grief is noteworthy.

> *What Do You Think?*
> How have the deaths of friends and family members tested your faith?
> *Talking Points for Your Discussion*
> - Deaths that follow a long illness
> - Quick, peaceful deaths
> - Deaths from accidents
> - Murder
> - Suicide

C. Life (vv. 23-26)

23. Jesus saith unto her, Thy brother shall rise again.

In the Gospel of John, Jesus often says things that are subject to more than one interpretation. The ambiguity may be intentional on Jesus' part, as seems to be the case here. Perhaps the most well-known example of such ambiguity appears in John 3:3, 4, where Jesus tells Nicodemus that he must be "born again." The Greek word translated "again" there can also mean "from above." Nicodemus picks the wrong meaning, and Jesus has to make clear that He means "born from above."

In this and other cases, Jesus may be using ambiguity intentionally to test the other person's level of understanding. Jesus can take the discussion to a deeper level if the person latches onto the wrong meaning. How will Martha respond?

24. Martha saith unto him, I know that he shall rise again in the resurrection at the last day.

Since Jesus is Martha's rabbi and since this discussion takes place during a funeral, Martha reaches a logical conclusion: Jesus is trying to make her feel better about Lazarus's death. Those who have been to the funeral of a believer have heard a minister assure the bereaved that they will see their departed loved one again in Heaven.

Some ancient Jews do not believe in resurrection (Mark 12:18-27), but many do believe that the righteous will rise to eternal life at the end of time (Daniel 12:2; Acts 23:8). Thus the words "your brother will rise again" is a comfort in that regard. "Yes, Lord," Martha says, "I know we'll see him again one day." But this affirmation, even though it is one of faith, reveals that Martha does not detect that Jesus has something else in mind.

25a. Jesus said unto her, I am the resurrection, and the life.

Here we see the fifth of Jesus' seven "I am the [something]" sayings in the Gospel of John (see the Lesson Background). Jesus is attempting to push Martha's understanding to a deeper level. Earlier, Jesus affirmed himself to be the one who raises the dead (John 5:25). But Jesus not only has the ability to *perform* resurrections, He *is* the resurrection.

The phrase *and the life* adds even more. Whereas many may think of eternal life as something that begins after we leave this world, John's Gospel insists that eternal life begins at the moment of spiritual rebirth. This being the case, Jesus tells people that eternal life is available right now through Him; this new spiritual life then continues into eternity after death (see John 5:24).

For John, eternal life essentially refers to all the benefits that come from salvation, some of which we experience now and some of which we can experience only after physical death. Because God's eternal life—both now and forever—is available only through belief in Christ, Jesus can say *I am the resurrection, and the life,* the sole source of eternal hope.

❧ *More Than a Prophet* ❧

A few years ago, I shared a plane flight with a man from Afghanistan. During our conversation, I asked him what Muslims believe about Jesus. He told me that the Quran teaches that Jesus

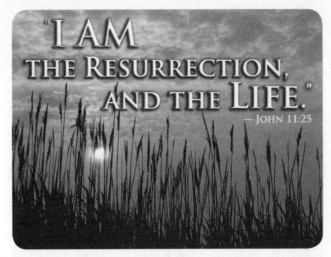

Visual for Lesson 12. *Point to this visual as you ask, "How will these two facts influence the way you live in the week ahead?"*

was born to a virgin, was a great prophet of God, worked many miracles, rose alive into Heaven, and is coming back again.

Then the man asked, "We accept your Jesus as a prophet; why won't you accept Muhammad?" I asked him what miracles Muhammad performed as proof of his claims. As it turns out, the Quran itself reports none, although later traditions attribute fantastic miracles to him.

Thinking about this conversation, I realize that the point is not simply that Jesus was able to do extraordinary feats. Some of the Old Testament prophets did spectacular wonders themselves. Only Jesus, however, presented himself as the source of life. He proved this claim not only by raising others, but by resurrecting himself.

An African man was questioned by his friends about his conversion from Islam to Christianity. He said, "It's like this. Suppose you were going down the road and suddenly the road forked in two directions, and you didn't know which way to go. But there at the fork in the road were two men, one dead and one alive—which one would you ask which way to go?" —A. W.

25b, 26a. He that believeth in me, though he were dead, yet shall he live: and whosoever liveth and believeth in me shall never die.

Jesus presses harder. In the statement *He that believeth in me, though he were dead, yet shall he live,* Jesus uses the word *dead* in a literal, physical sense

HOW TO SAY IT

Bethabara	*Beth-**ab**-uh-ruh.*
Bethany	*Beth-uh-nee.*
Judea	Joo-*dee*-uh.
Nicodemus	*Nick-uh-**dee**-mus.*
Perea	Peh-*ree*-uh.
Quran	Kuh-*ran*.

and the word *live* in a spiritual sense: even if a person physically dies (as has happened to Lazarus), he or she will live forever spiritually based on belief in Christ. Verse 26a states the same thing in reverse: anyone who believes in Jesus while physically alive, as Lazarus had believed in Him, will never die spiritually. In other words, the person of faith has an eternal hope that goes beyond the grave.

All this makes sense to us in hindsight. But for Martha, full of grief over her loss, the entire matter may seem hopelessly confusing. Perhaps she wonders why Jesus is waxing philosophical when what she really needs is sympathy, a shoulder to cry on. Little does she realize that Jesus will soon provide a source of comfort beyond her wildest dreams.

26b. Believest thou this?

This is not a question about Martha's belief in resurrection. Martha has already affirmed her belief in that. This is, rather, a question about her personal trust in Jesus. Her answer follows.

D. Belief (v. 27)

27. She saith unto him, Yea, Lord: I believe that thou art the Christ, the Son of God, which should come into the world.

The Gospel of John is filled with situations where people respond in varying ways to something that Jesus has done or said. Sometimes the response is in faith, but sometimes the response is one of confusion or downright disbelief. These give us a chance to think about our own response to Jesus.

In this particular case, Martha serves as a model of faith in the face of loss. Despite her grief and confusion, she comes closer to a genuine understanding of Christ's identity than any other character in John's story at any point before the resurrection. John 20:30, 31 indicates that the Gospel of John is written to lead the reader to believe that "Jesus is the Christ, the Son of God"; Martha's words here closely echo John's stated objective, although it seems doubtful that she fully understands the implications of her own words.

As a faithful Jew of her day, Martha probably believes that the Christ will come to deliver Israel from political bondage. She may also understand that the Christ will be *the Son of God* in the same sense that the great Jewish kings were sometimes called sons of God in the Old Testament (example: 2 Samuel 7:14). Beyond this, the Jewish people are certainly not expecting a human Messiah who actually will be God in the flesh (John 1:11, 14).

Some may find fault with Martha for not sorting through Jesus' intentionally ambiguous words to attempt a deeper answer. But sometimes a simple affirmation of trust that Jesus is the promised Messiah is the best position to adopt in the face of grief and confusion. Whether or not we understand why a tragedy has happened, we can still turn to God with faith and trust, believing that He has everything under control.

What Do You Think?
  What differences have you noticed in the ways believers and unbelievers respond to death? Should there be a noticeable difference? Explain.
Talking Points for Your Discussion
  ▪ Expressions of anger
  ▪ Expressions of hope
  ▪ Questions of *Why?*
  ▪ Expressions of grief

II. Freed from the Grave
(John 11:41-44)

John 11:28-40 (not in today's text) deals primarily with Jesus' interaction with Mary, sister of Martha. This interaction and certain comments by others who are present (vv. 36, 37) set the stage for the resurrection of Lazarus.

A. Source of Jesus' Power (vv. 41, 42)

41, 42. Then they took away the stone from the place where the dead was laid. And Jesus lifted up his eyes, and said, Father, I thank thee that thou hast heard me. And I knew that thou hearest me always: but because of the people which stand by I said it, that they may believe that thou hast sent me.

Jesus utters a prayer that reveals the ultimate purpose of the miracle to follow: *that they may believe that thou hast sent me.* While many of Jesus' miracles demonstrate God's compassion for the sick and needy, all are intended to point people to

The Resurrection and the Life

God through Christ. There can be no doubt about the source of Jesus' power, as He directs all credit for what is about to happen to the Father. Jesus designs this prayer with the listeners in mind.

❧ *Getting Indirectly to the Point* ❧

The old expression *going around the barn at high noon* means to do something in an unnecessarily indirect way. This expression came to mind recently when my wife told me a very detailed story about why she decided to clean out our daughter's closet and how many boxes were filled. The real point was to convince me to take the boxes to the garage. That was something I would have done gladly even without the long explanation!

Even so, an indirect approach may be appropriate when it comes to sharing our faith. Pointing out someone else's need for forgiveness can be off-putting; pointing out our own need and how Christ met it can be winsome. Telling someone what to think feels controlling; asking what she thinks raises curiosity. Talking about the Christian life can seem hypocritical; living it can silence criticism.

Notice that Jesus did not simply march up to Lazarus's tomb and say, "Hey, everybody—watch this resurrection!" Instead, Jesus used an indirect approach that included prayer. Our own indirect approaches also should do so as well. Without God's help, we would all miss the point. —A. W.

B. Lazarus Loosed (vv. 43, 44)

43. And when he thus had spoken, he cried with a loud voice, Lazarus, come forth.

This verse is a graphic illustration of what John envisions happening at the end of time, when Christ will call all the faithful to Him when He returns. At John 5:25-28, Jesus promises that a time is coming when the dead will hear the voice of the Son of God and be raised to eternal life. Lazarus's resurrection is thus a foreshadowing of what will happen to all those who believe.

44. And he that was dead came forth, bound hand and foot with graveclothes: and his face was bound about with a napkin. Jesus saith unto them, Loose him, and let him go.

In ancient times, dead bodies are wrapped in strips of cloth with spices before burial to control the odor of decay. Many comparisons have been drawn between the grave clothes and napkin (or "sweat cloth") of Lazarus and Jesus (John 20:6, 7; see Lesson 6). We can only wonder how the crowd reacts while watching Lazarus emerge from the tomb wrapped in these items! The fact that he is *bound hand and foot with graveclothes* bring a comical image to mind: Lazarus, unable to remove the wrappings, perhaps is able only to hop as he emerges. Clearly, when Jesus calls, you come!

What Do You Think?
How does your confidence in Jesus' (and your) resurrection make a practical difference in how you live?
Talking Points for Your Discussion
- In terms of your priorities
- In your response to illness
- In the way you grieve

Conclusion

A. Pleasant Surprises

While it's always nice to get what you've worked for, sometimes a pleasant surprise goes a long way. Things we don't expect—like a bonus at work or a letter from an old friend or a word of thanks from a surprising source—make us feel appreciated because they show that someone cares for us. In our story today, Martha got the ultimate pleasant surprise as she saw something unfold before her eyes that was humanly impossible. Since Jesus really does have power over death, power to call His people back from the grave, why should we fear anything? Since He secures our eternal destiny, can He not also provide everything else we need in this world now?

B. Prayer

Father, death is a fearful thing. We're afraid of the thought of leaving people behind, of leaving things undone, and we miss loved ones who have died. Please help us trust You more in the face of death. In Jesus' name, amen.

C. Thought to Remember

The grave is not the end.

INVOLVEMENT LEARNING

Some of the activities below are also found in the helpful student book, Adult Bible Class.
Don't forget to download the free reproducible page from www.standardlesson.com to enhance your lesson!

Into the Lesson

Place in chairs copies of the Key Words from a Miracle activity from the reproducible page, which you have downloaded. Learners can begin working on this as they arrive.

Alternative: Distribute handouts of a tombstone graphic (photo or clipart). Across the top, have the heading "Fears or Anxieties About Death." In large letters, have the word *GRAVE* displayed vertically down the center of the page. Ask learners to use the acrostic to jot words or phrases (horizontally, to intersect with the word *grave*) that express people's anxieties about death. Wrap up this activity by displaying a poster board with the same acrostic. As people share some of their word choices, write those words on the poster board.

Under either approach, make the transition to Bible study by saying, "Jesus is the one who can calm our fears about death. He did it in the first century, and He still does it today."

Into the Word

Divide the class into four study teams. Distribute handouts with the following assignments; provide teams with the resources noted. If your class is too small for four teams, delete Team 1 and/or Team 3, as those assignments deal with material outside the range of the printed text for today (but give priority to keeping Team 1 of the two).

Team 1: Dramatize the events of John 11:1-16, which lead up to today's encounter with Jesus. String and paper are provided for you to create identification signs for actors/actresses to wear around their necks. *Team 2:* List for sharing some of the emotions and feelings that Martha probably experienced in John 11:20-28, 39. *Team 3:* List for sharing some of the frustrations, emotions, and feelings that Mary expressed in John 11:29-37. *Team 4:* Be ready to explain the wonderful significance and applications of Jesus' saying in John 11:25, 26.

After Team 1 makes its presentation, introduce Teams 2 and 3 by saying, "We all know that the death of a loved one is accompanied by a flood of emotions for those who feel the loss. Teams 2 and 3 will explore some of the emotions present in Lazarus's family."

Before calling for the presentation of the conclusions of Team 4, say, "Team 1, you discovered in your preparations that Jesus delayed going to see Lazarus. Why do you think He waited two days before going?" Discuss observations.

Next say, "Team 2, after Jesus claimed to be the resurrection and the life, He asked Martha if she believed this. Why do you think Jesus asked that question? What is the significance of Martha's answer in verse 27?" Discuss observations.

Next say, "Team 3, as Jesus prayed in verses 41, 42, He said that the first part of the prayer was for the benefit of people standing near. Why did He want them to hear that statement? What does this tell us about prayer?" Discuss observations.

Finally, address Team 4 as you say, "Jesus claims to be the resurrection and the life. Naturally, we apply this to eternity. But what does this fact signify in the here and now for the Christian?" Use Team 4's observations to lead smoothly into the Into the Life segment, which will expand this discussion.

Into Life

Write *Unbelievers* on the board as the head of a column on the left. Similarly, write *Believers* on the board as the head of a column on the right. Say, "Jesus' claim to be the resurrection and the life should—indeed, *must*—affect one's life-attitude, values, worldview, and behavior. How are believers different from unbelievers in this regard?" Jot responses on the board. After discussion, close with prayer that asks that the fact of John 11:25, 26 will be evident in your learners' lives in the week ahead.

The Way, the Truth, and the Life

DEVOTIONAL READING: Matthew 7:13-20
BACKGROUND SCRIPTURE: John 14

JOHN 14:1-14

1 Let not your heart be troubled: ye believe in God, believe also in me.

2 In my Father's house are many mansions: if it were not so, I would have told you. I go to prepare a place for you.

3 And if I go and prepare a place for you, I will come again, and receive you unto myself; that where I am, there ye may be also.

4 And whither I go ye know, and the way ye know.

5 Thomas saith unto him, Lord, we know not whither thou goest; and how can we know the way?

6 Jesus saith unto him, I am the way, the truth, and the life: no man cometh unto the Father, but by me.

7 If ye had known me, ye should have known my Father also: and from henceforth ye know him, and have seen him.

8 Philip saith unto him, Lord, show us the Father, and it sufficeth us.

9 Jesus saith unto him, Have I been so long time with you, and yet hast thou not known me, Philip? he that hath seen me hath seen the Father; and how sayest thou then, Show us the Father?

10 Believest thou not that I am in the Father, and the Father in me? the words that I speak unto you I speak not of myself: but the Father that dwelleth in me, he doeth the works.

11 Believe me that I am in the Father, and the Father in me: or else believe me for the very works' sake.

12 Verily, verily, I say unto you, He that believeth on me, the works that I do shall he do also; and greater works than these shall he do; because I go unto my Father.

13 And whatsoever ye shall ask in my name, that will I do, that the Father may be glorified in the Son.

14 If ye shall ask any thing in my name, I will do it.

KEY VERSE

Jesus saith unto him, I am the way, the truth, and the life: no man cometh unto the Father, but by me.

—John 14:6

Photo: Comstock / Comstock / Thinkstock

GOD'S CREATIVE WORD

Unit 3: I Am . . .

LESSONS 10–13

LESSON AIMS

After participating in this lesson, each student will be able to:

1. Paraphrase Jesus' reaction to the disciples' concern.

2. Discuss the significance of Jesus' claim to be "the way, the truth, and the life" in light of a postmodern worldview.

3. Write a note to someone who needs the comfort provided in Jesus' words from John 14.

LESSON OUTLINE

Introduction

A. "Can You Tell Me How to Get to . . . ?"

Do you ever stop and ask for directions? Many of us won't do this because it hurts our pride. Sometimes we may be hesitant because we don't trust the source of help. More than once I've followed directions only to end up more lost than before. Once while traveling in a major city in Europe, I asked a taxi driver (who didn't speak English) to take me somewhere, and I ended up miles away from my desired destination.

In some cultures, people believe they should always be helpful to strangers, and so they will offer directions even when they have no idea where you're going. Accepting directions obviously requires a high level of trust that your helper knows what he or she is talking about. Modern GPS systems are reliable, but not foolproof.

If good directions to a store or restaurant are important, then knowing the right way to God is critical! Many different faith systems and philosophies claim to set us on the correct path. But how do we know which one is right when they contradict each other?

B. Lesson Background

Our previous three lessons each focused on one of the seven famous "I am the [something]" sayings that appear in the Gospel of John. The context of those three statements was that of Jesus' public ministry. Our "I am the [something]" study for today, however, involves the private context of Jesus' farewell discourse.

The Gospel of John naturally divides into three major sections. After a brief introduction (1:1-18), chapters 1–12 relate the events of Jesus' public ministry; chapters 13–17 recount His private teachings in the upper room on the last night of His life; and chapters 18–21 finish the story with Christ's death and resurrection. Almost all the material in the second section of the book, chapters 13–17, is unique to the Gospel of John. This section is typically called "the farewell address" because it relates Jesus' final words to His disciples. Here He discloses His true identity and the purposes of His mission.

The Way, the Truth, and the Life

I. Promised Place

(JOHN 14:1-4)

A. Comfort in Belief (v. 1)

1. Let not your heart be troubled: ye believe in God, believe also in me.

As Jesus speaks these words, the disciples likely are pondering Jesus' prediction that one of them will betray Him (John 13:21-26) and/or His insistence that Peter will deny Him three times (13:37, 38). These comments certainly are troubling enough, but they are nothing compared with what Jesus is about to tell them: He himself will be leaving soon (14:19, 28-30), and the disciples will be hated and persecuted (15:18–16:4). But in the face of difficulty, the disciples may find supernatural peace through their faith in God and Jesus (14:27).

The Greek verbs in the second half of this verse can be translated in various ways. In Greek, as in English, the statement "ye believe" can express the simple fact of belief (as in "ye are believing"). If this is the intent here, then Jesus is stating a fact something like this: "Ye [disciples] already believe in God, and ye also believe in me." However, the statement "ye believe" also can function as a command (as in "ye need to believe"). If this is the intent here, then Jesus is stating a command something like this: "Ye [disciples] need to trust in both God and in me."

A third possibility is that Jesus is combining the simple fact of belief with the command to believe: "Ye already believe in God; ye need to believe in me as well." This is the thrust of the translation of the *King James Version*. In any case, the Gospel writer is drawing our attention to the close relationship between the Father and Jesus. Together they provide comfort for believers.

What Do You Think?

What things tend to trouble you the most? How does belief in God and Jesus help you in these areas?

Talking Points for Your Discussion

- Spiritual issues
- Nonspiritual issues

B. Facts of Heaven (vv. 2-4)

2. In my Father's house are many mansions: if it were not so, I would have told you. I go to prepare a place for you.

The term *mansions* has generated confusion about the nature of Heaven. In modern English, the word *mansion* refers to a large and elegant home. If this is what Jesus has in mind, one wonders why there would be *many mansions* inside the *Father's house,* since houses normally are not built inside of other houses.

The translators of the *King James Version* did not have a problem with this, however, because the word *mansion* simply meant "dwelling place" in their day. We may compare the translation *mansions* here with John 14:23, where the same Greek word is translated "abode." These are the only two places in the New Testament where this particular Greek word occurs.

Obviously, the Father's house is Heaven, and Jesus is promising the disciples that He will make a place for them there. While the disciples will suffer for their faith and will not find a place in this world, they can rest assured that Christ will provide an eternal dwelling where they will truly be at home.

3. And if I go and prepare a place for you, I will come again, and receive you unto myself; that where I am, there ye may be also.

While popular images of Heaven focus on pearly gates and streets of gold, the Bible consistently emphasizes that Heaven is a place where God and His people can be together forever. The Gospel of John rarely refers to the second coming of Christ directly, but this verse is a notable exception: Jesus will die, go to Heaven, then return later to take the disciples back with Him. Knowing this fact provides them (and us) with hope in the face of pain and persecution.

The word *if* here should not be taken as an indication of doubt. In Greek, this sentence structure means that the second clause will always follow from the first: if Jesus goes, then He will certainly come back—He will not abandon His people. In this particular case, there is no real doubt about the "if" part either, since Jesus is well aware of His pending death, resurrection, and ascension.

4. And whither I go ye know, and the way ye know.

As verse 5 will indicate, the disciples find this comment confusing. Perhaps Jesus knows this and is hoping they will ask Him to take the discussion to a deeper level. At the same time, however, Jesus' statement here is literally true: inasmuch as the disciples know Jesus—having seen His miraculous works and having heard His words of truth—they do indeed know the way to the Father's house.

> *What Do You Think?*
> What impact does Jesus' promise have on you?
> *Talking Points for Your Discussion*
> - In terms of your Christian witness
> - In terms of the smaller things of daily living
> - In terms of the larger things of life choices

II. Promised Way
(John 14:5-11)
A. Thomas's Question (vv. 5-7)

5. Thomas saith unto him, Lord, we know not whither thou goest; and how can we know the way?

This question reveals that Thomas (and probably the other disciples too) has not come to grips fully either with Jesus' true nature or His destination. Ancient Jews have no real expectation that the Messiah would be what Christ actually is: God in the flesh (John 1:11, 14). At least some of Jesus' followers have confessed Him to be "the Christ" (Matthew 16:16; John 11:27), but we wonder how complete their understanding really is.

The disciples do not seem yet to understand that Jesus is the preexistent Son of God. If they can understand Jesus' true nature, then they will know where He is going and how they can get there. Thus Thomas's question shows incomplete understanding of Jesus' nature.

As a side note, this blunt question is typical of Thomas's personality. As on the occasions in John 11:16 and 20:24-29, Thomas does not hesitate to speak his mind.

6. Jesus saith unto him, I am the way, the truth, and the life: no man cometh unto the Father, but by me.

This is one of the most famous verses in the New Testament. Many Christians can quote it by heart. But we must remember it in its original context: Jesus is answering Thomas's question in verse 5.

The emphasis in Jesus' answer falls on the word *I*: He himself, and He alone, is *the way* to the Father. His insistence that no one can come to the Father except through Him has two implications: (1) faith in Christ is required for admission to Heaven and (2) Christ's teachings and actions perfectly illustrate the type of life that pleases God.

The three terms *way, truth, life* are closely related and can be understood in two broad senses. Traditionally, these words have been taken primarily in a doctrinal sense, meaning that true or accurate belief in Christ is the only way to gain access to eternal life with God. Put another way, this means we can't get to Heaven if we don't believe the right things about Jesus.

Another approach, however, views these terms as more dynamic descriptions of Jesus' example, which He expects all disciples to imitate. Viewed from this angle, Jesus demonstrates what it means to be "true/faithful" to God by showing His followers the way to behave; He thus models a lifestyle of faith.

Both approaches are consistent with the thinking of the writer. John everywhere insists that people must think about Christ correctly and must also live as Jesus lived (see 1 John 3:23, 24). We walk the path that leads to our eternal home as we believe in Christ and imitate His example.

> *What Do You Think?*
> In the current culture, which of the three affirmations about Jesus gives unbelievers the most difficulty? Why?
> *Talking Points for Your Discussion*
> - Jesus as *the way*
> - Jesus as *the truth*
> - Jesus as *the life*

7. If ye had known me, ye should have known my Father also: and from henceforth ye know him, and have seen him.

Because Jesus and the Father are one (John 10:30; 17:11, 21-23), then anyone who sees Jesus sees God. Knowing Jesus is the key to knowing the Father. The phrase *from henceforth* probably means that Jesus expects His disciples to understand this in the future because of what He now says explicitly. In effect, Jesus is saying, "You've seen how I live and teach. When you saw all that, you were seeing God in action. Now that I've clarified all this, there can be no further doubt, right?"

B. Philip's Request (vv. 8-11)

8. Philip saith unto him, Lord, shew us the Father, and it sufficeth us.

While Thomas focuses on Jesus' statements about "the way," Philip's inquiry raises a question about *the Father*. Philip seems to be repeating the request of Moses to God in Exodus 33:18: "I beseech thee, shew me thy glory." Philip doesn't seem to realize that God's glory is visible in the Son.

This is one of four scenes in John's Gospel where Philip appears. Each scene leads to a deeper revelation of Christ's divine identity. At John 1:43-46, Philip tells Nathanael that Jesus is the one promised by Moses and the prophets; at 6:5-7, Philip unwittingly highlights the miraculous power displayed in the feeding of the 5,000 by telling Jesus of the impossibility of buying enough bread for the crowd; at 12:20-33, after the triumphal entry, Jesus explains the significance of His impending death after Philip brings some Greeks to meet Him.

As on these other occasions, Philip's question gives Jesus an opportunity to explain His relationship with God and why faith in His teachings is critical.

9. Jesus saith unto him, Have I been so long time with you, and yet hast thou not known me, Philip? he that hath seen me hath seen the Father; and how sayest thou then, Shew us the Father?

Jesus' frustration is understandable. Philip was one of Jesus' very first disciples (John 1:43). In view of this fact, Philip's lack of understanding is incredible. Thus Jesus simply repeats what He earlier said to Thomas: anyone who has seen Him in action has seen God (compare John 12:45; Colossians 1:15; Hebrews 1:3). It's bad enough that Jesus' enemies do not recognize who He really is.

How much worse that His closest followers display such ignorance!

❧ *UNDERESTIMATED* ❧

Few people in Vancouver, British Columbia, gave Laurence Gilbert a second thought. The unassuming letter carrier never married and lived his whole life in the house in which he grew up. People recalled him as "a nice man, a quiet man" and "a very gentle soul." After his death at age 71, though, many people certainly wished they had taken the time to get to know him! For you see, Laurence was a millionaire. At his death, numerous charities received very large financial gifts.

Looks can be deceiving. Many people underestimated Jesus in His time on earth (compare Isaiah 53:2b). How could a simple carpenter's son also be the Son of God? How could a rural peasant with a funny Galilean accent be a prophet? Even those who experienced His power firsthand seemed to "not quite get it." Just think—the crowd in John 6:15 expected someone who was entitled to sit on the very throne of God in Heaven to diminish himself to being the king of a minor earthly nation!

What about us? Do we come to Christ with a laundry list of petty complaints and requests that are all about making ourselves comfortable in our temporary circumstances? Or do we come to Him

HOW TO SAY IT

Galilean	Gal-uh-*lee*-un.
Messiah	Meh-*sigh*-uh.
Nathanael	Nuh-*than*-yull (*th* as in *thin*).

in faith that He can change us and our circumstances beyond our wildest dreams? —A. W.

10. Believest thou not that I am in the Father, and the Father in me? the words that I speak unto you I speak not of myself: but the Father that dwelleth in me, he doeth the works.

Three themes in the Gospel of John intersect in this verse. First, the phrase *in the Father* touches on Christ's unity with God, a theme that will be highlighted in Jesus' final prayer in John 17 (also John 10:38; 14:20). Second, Jesus never says anything on His own without God's directive because Christ and the Father are one; thus when Christ speaks, we hear the voice of God (see 7:16; 8:28; 12:49). Third, and closely related, *the works* that Jesus does—which include both His sayings and His miracles—are expressions of God's power (see 5:19, 36; 8:29; 9:4; 10:25). Because Jesus is one with the Father, He says what the Father wants Him to say and does what the Father wants Him to do.

Taken together, the three principles expressed in this verse explain Jesus' claim to be "the way, the truth, and the life." Throughout John's Gospel, Jesus frequently refers to himself as the one whom God has sent into the world (see John 3:17; 5:24, 36-38; 6:29, 38, 39; 7:28; 12:45). While God previously had sent Moses and other prophets to speak His words, none of these people could lay claim to the authority that Christ bears as God's Son. This being the case, Jesus' teachings are the certain way to truth and salvation.

11. Believe me that I am in the Father, and the Father in me: or else believe me for the very works' sake.

In the synoptic Gospels (that is, Matthew, Mark, and Luke), miraculous healings often follow the faith of those who come to Christ for aid (examples: Matthew 9:22, 29; 15:28; Mark 10:52; Luke 17:19). In John's Gospel, Jesus' miracles generally are not preceded by faith; rather, Christ first does something to reveal His divine power, and this may or may not lead someone to believe in Him (compare John 2:1-11 and 4:43-54 with 5:1-18 and 9:18). For John, the things that Jesus does point to the true source of His power and His oneness with God. These things should result in belief.

III. Promised Work
(John 14:12-14)
A. Believe and Do (v. 12)

12. Verily, verily, I say unto you, He that believeth on me, the works that I do shall he do also; and greater works than these shall he do; because I go unto my Father.

When we read this verse, we wonder how it will be possible for the disciples ever to do anything "greater" or more impressive than, say, Jesus' raising of Lazarus or the feeding of the 5,000. The key is the phrase *because I go unto my Father.* That will happen only after Jesus' death and resurrection. Those events introduce what one commentator calls "an age of clarity and power." Many more people will come to believe in Jesus after His death, burial, resurrection, and ascension than before. We continue Christ's ministry today when we share His message and demonstrate His love.

> *What Do You Think?*
> How will you go about doing the "greater works" that Jesus predicted and promised?
> *Talking Points for Your Discussion*
> ▪ While participating in the local ministries of your church
> ▪ While supporting the ministry of a missionary
> ▪ While performing a ministry of your own

B. Ask and Receive (vv. 13, 14)

13, 14. And whatsoever ye shall ask in my name, that will I do, that the Father may be glorified in the Son. If ye shall ask any thing in my name, I will do it.

The phrase *in my name* ties these verses to the theme of our lesson: because Christ is the way to the Father, we can appeal to God through faith in Jesus. Further, Christ is not only the way that we gain access to God, but also the channel through which God's blessings and power flow to us. Hence, anything we accomplish through Christ brings glory to God, as everything Jesus did brought glory to God. In a very real sense, we, as disciples, are continuing Jesus' work of revealing God to the world.

Viewed in this light, it becomes obvious what these verses do *not* mean: they do not mean that we can have anything we want merely by asking. Aside from the fact that experience teaches that we don't always get what we pray for, the context of Jesus' remarks make the meaning of *whatsoever* and *any thing* clear. Jesus clearly is not referring to prayers for wealth, health, or prosperity; in fact, in the very next chapter He will promise the disciples that faith leads to hardship (John 15:18–16:4).

Jesus is promising that God will empower the disciples to continue the work of witnessing after He (Jesus) is gone. God equips Jesus with everything He needs to complete His mission, and God, through Christ, will equip the disciples to fulfill their missions. The goal of all this is indicated clearly in verse 13: bringing glory to God.

❧ *In Jesus' Name* ❧

As a child, I ended each of my prayers with "in Jesus' name I pray, amen." To me it was a bit like putting a postage stamp on a letter: if I were to drift off to sleep before finishing this formula, I thought the prayer didn't really count. So strong was this habit that one night, in a sleepy mental fog, I actually said "in Jesus' name" to my mother instead of saying "Goodnight"!

Having my own children has given me a bit more insight into what it means to be "in" someone's name. Because my children are related to me, they share my family name, but they don't have to remind me of this fact in order to persuade me to do things for them. Because I love them dearly, I will gladly do what they ask me if I am able and if it is good for them. There is no "magic formula" to get my response—our relationship is secure enough that they can come to me freely, without formalities.

A vital part of praying specifically "in Jesus' name" is that this phrase reminds us of whose we are. Problems arise, however, when we merely tack on this phrase at the end of a prayer as if it were a way to "push the God button" and be heard. We do need to show God the ultimate respect He deserves, but treating Him like a cold computer that does not respond unless the proper buttons are pushed is not the way. Romans 8:15 and

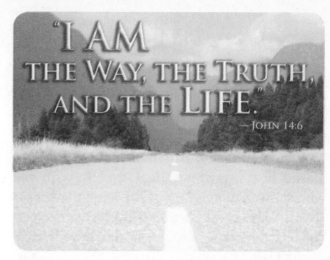

Visual for Lesson 13. *Use this visual to introduce the discussion question that is associated with John 14:6.*

Hebrews 2:11 further show how we are "in" His family name.
—A. W.

Conclusion
A. Only One Way

When I was growing up, I often heard my grandfather use the expression, "There's more than one way to get there." As a carpenter and later as a construction manager, he had learned to look for ways around obstacles to completing a task. His wise saying was based on the fact that there are very few places that can be reached by only one path—there's normally more than one road.

According to the Gospel of John, however, this principle doesn't apply to God: there is only one way to get to Him, and that way is Jesus. While many religions claim to lead us to God, Christ says that He himself is "the way, the truth, and the life"—the *only* way, truth, and life. Jesus is the way to God. Jesus is the way that God empowers us to witness to the world. There is only one way.

B. Prayer

O God, we never could have found You without Jesus. Please send us Your power through Him so that we can glorify Your name as He did. In Jesus' name, amen.

C. Thought to Remember

Jesus is our source of truth and life.

INVOLVEMENT LEARNING

Some of the activities below are also found in the helpful student book, Adult Bible Class.
Don't forget to download the free reproducible page from www.standardlesson.com to enhance your lesson!

Into the Lesson

Before class begins, mount several pieces of poster board on the walls. On each, write the phrase *Phobias and Fears.* Distribute markers as learners arrive; ask them each to sketch one personal fear or phobia (snakes, heights, crowds, etc.). Begin class by thanking class members for sharing their vulnerable points. Say, "Some fears are very serious and debilitating; other fears may be fleeting. Today's lesson addresses what should be everyone's greatest fear: eternity without God."

Alternative: Ask learners to share true stories of times when they got lost. After a few of these, share a personal experience of your own that resulted in great uncertainty on your part. After noting your uncertainty, make the transition to Bible study by saying, "Uncertainty can be an awful feeling. Uncertainty can lead to fear, which in turn can generate even more uncertainty in a vicious cycle. Even those closest to Jesus experienced uncertainty. Let's look to see how they and Jesus handled the situation."

Into the Word

Divide the class into small groups or study pairs. Give each learner a handout with the following questions:

1. What was troubling the disciples in the setting of today's text (John 14:1)? 2. Why were Jesus' statements to His disciples comforting—or why *should* they have been comforting (vv. 1-4)? 3. What is the nature of the "disconnect" when we compare Jesus' statement "the way ye know" (v. 4) with Thomas' immediate response, "We know not whither thou goest; and how can we know the way?" (v. 5)? 4. What do verses 10, 11 reveal about Jesus' nature? 5. Does Jesus' threefold claim to be *the way, the truth,* and *the life* teach us three distinct things about Jesus (v. 6)? Explain. 6. In what ways is the comfort of today's passage the same to us as it was to the first-century disciples? 7. In what ways is the comfort of today's passage different for us and the first-century disciples?

Follow questions 6 and 7 by distributing copies of the Encouraging Words and Phrases activity from the reproducible page, which you have downloaded. Have learners discuss and complete these within their small groups or study pairs. Allow time for a whole-class discussion.

Into Life

Give to small groups a handout that offers two activity choices. Groups will share their work with the class as a whole. *Choice 1:* Write a Communion meditation based on Jesus' claim in John 14:6. What should be the main point(s) of the meditation? What prayer thought will come at the conclusion? *Choice 2:* Create an artistic expression of the truths in John 14:6. You may do a sketch, poem, origami, etc.

After groups share their work, ask the class, "What life circumstances call for the comfort offered in today's Scripture?" List answers on the board. You may expect the resulting list to describe life-threatening health concerns, tragedies that result from holding a non-Christian worldview, the distress of children who have just lost a grandparent, and the various crises that unbelievers suffer through.

Next, distribute sheets of nice stationery and ask learners to write a comforting or encouraging note to an acquaintance who would appreciate it. Allow time for writing. Suggest that learners include at least one phrase from today's text. Learners are to take their notes home to mail them. Encourage learners not to use e-mail, which is less personal in nature.

As learners depart, distribute copies of the Facebook Caption activity from the reproducible page, which you have downloaded. Ask learners to complete this at home and be prepared to discuss the results next week.

GOD CALLS FOR JUSTICE

Special Features

Lessons

Unit 1: Justice Defined

Unit 2: Justice Enacted

Unit 3: Justice Promised

QUARTERLY QUIZ

Use these questions as a pretest or as a review. The answers are on page iv of This Quarter in the Word.

Lesson 1

1. The Israelites were not to help the wicked by serving as an unrighteous _____. *Exodus 23:1*

2. Moses taught that the opinion of the crowd is a reliable guide. T/F. *Exodus 23:2*

Lesson 2

1. The wages of a day laborer were to be paid the same day the work was done. T/F. *Leviticus 19:13*

2. The opposite of loving one's neighbor as oneself is to bear a _____. *Leviticus 19:18*

Lesson 3

1. Leviticus taught that every 50th year was to be a year of _____ in Israel. *Leviticus 25:10*

2. The Lord repeatedly reminded the people that He had brought them forth from where? (Egypt, Canaan, Sheba?) *Leviticus 25:38, 55*

Lesson 4

1. Which groups deserve special consideration for help? (pick three: widows, widowers, eunuchs, kings, fatherless, strangers?) *Deuteronomy 10:18*

2. The ancestors of the Israelites numbered ____ when they entered Egypt. *Deuteronomy 10:22*

Lesson 5

1. *Ebenezer* was the name of a tree blessed by Samuel. T/F. *1 Samuel 7:12*

2. The prophet Samuel was also a what? (king, army general, judge?) *1 Samuel 7:15*

Lesson 6

1. King David was also known as the sweet _____ of Israel. *2 Samuel 23:1*

2. David claimed that God had made a temporary covenant with him. T/F. *2 Samuel 23:5*

Lesson 7

1. Two women who brought a case to Solomon were what? (slaves, harlots, old?) *1 Kings 3:16*

2. Solomon committed a murder to resolve the case of the two women. T/F. *1 Kings 3:25-27*

Lesson 8

1. Elisha advised a Shunammite woman to flee from Israel because of a coming what? (invasion, plague, famine?) *2 Kings 8:1*

2. Elisha's assistant was named *Gehazi*. T/F. *2 Kings 8:4*

Lesson 9

1. King Jehoshaphat failed to appoint judges as he was supposed to. T/F. *2 Chronicles 19:5*

2. Jehoshaphat warned that the Lord was not a respecter of _____. *2 Chronicles 19:7*

Lesson 10

1. The psalmist says "Praise the Lord, O my _____." *Psalm 146:1*

2. The Lord turns _____ _____ the way of the wicked. *Psalm 146:9*

Lesson 11

1. Which territories did Isaiah associate with the coming Messiah? (pick two: Dan, Naphtali, Zebulun, Gad, Reuben?) *Isaiah 9:1*

2. The Messiah will establish peace in the land. T/F. *Isaiah 9:7*

Lesson 12

1. God promised to set up _____ to feed His flock. *Jeremiah 23:4*

2. God promised to "raise unto David a _____ Branch." *Jeremiah 23:5*

Lesson 13

1. How many shepherds did Ezekiel prophesy that God would establish over His people? (one, twelve, "a multitude"?) *Ezekiel 34:23*

2. Ezekiel prophesied that there would be "showers of _____." *Ezekiel 34:26*

QUARTER AT A GLANCE

by Douglas Redford

THE NUMBER of Old Testament books used to address the topic of justice this quarter (12 books in all!) indicates that this theme was very important for God's covenant people, Israel. But what exactly is justice as God sees it? Many people think of justice in terms of making sure that appropriate punishment is administered for crimes. We say that "justice is served" when that happens.

At the risk of sounding a bit trite, consider justice as treating people *just as* you would want to be treated if you were in their position. Yes, biblical justice does include punishing wrongdoing. But it is also expressed in promoting the opposite of wrongdoing, that is, in doing good to others. This is seen quite clearly in the lessons covered under the theme of *Unit 1: Justice Defined*.

The passages to be studied in Unit 1 deal very little with punishing wrongdoing. Instead, they cover such areas as returning a lost animal when it is found, refusing to accept bribes, and providing opportunities for the poor to glean during harvest time. Justice is proactive: it is exercised in doing good, not simply in punishing wrongdoers. Biblical justice is "served" in serving others.

These standards of justice are applied often throughout the Old Testament in evaluating the leaders of God's people. Near the completion of his term of leadership, Samuel put his reputation on the line by challenging his fellow Israelites to cite any instance of abuse that had occurred on his watch. The people responded, "Thou hast not defrauded us, nor oppressed us, neither hast thou taken ought of any man's hand" (1 Samuel 12:4).

Obviously, such a leadership style does not happen automatically; it is the product of a life that is lived by a principle later stated by David: "He that ruleth over men must be just, ruling in the fear of God" (2 Samuel 23:3; Lesson 6). Those who know justice best and rule justly are those who allow God to define what justice is. Some examples of just leaders at work are provided in the lessons of *Unit 2: Justice Enacted*.

Eventually God's people in the Old Testament, especially their leaders, are called to account for their failure to administer justice as defined by God. But the prophets (some of whose ministries are the focus of *Unit 3: Justice Promised*) do more than simply highlight failures and shortcomings. They also foretell the coming of a king who will be the ideal of what "ruling in the fear of God" means. That king is, of course, Jesus.

Christians are to learn justice primarily from the example of Jesus. But we can also learn much from considering the ideals set forth for God's people in the Old Testament. Many secular groups today promote causes that reflect those ideals (taking care of the poor, for example). However, the acts of justice or kindness of those groups are carried out by people who have a variety of motivations. What must distinguish our actions from theirs is our desire to do what we do in the name of Jesus.

As followers of Jesus, our witness should make clear that the justice we promote is not of this world because the kingdom to which we belong is not of this world (John 18:36). Our actions are

> **Biblical justice is "served" in serving others.**

done, not simply to make this present world a better place to live (although that should result from our being salt and light), but to prepare people for the "new heavens and a new earth, wherein dwelleth righteousness" (2 Peter 3:13).

In his prediction of the messianic kingdom, the prophet Isaiah declared, "The zeal of the Lord of hosts will perform this" (Isaiah 9:7; Lesson 11). May our zeal be directed toward the advancement of that same cause.

by Lloyd M. Pelfrey

B E FAIR! Small children learn early what those words mean. Indeed, fairness is desirable at every level of society. A report from studies at UCLA in 2008 concludes that fairness is a part of the makeup of humanity. This concept therefore dates back to creation.

God's People Receive the Law!

Our studies this quarter reveal how God demanded justice from the nation of Israel after it left Egypt. The Israelites were free, but this freedom was not a license for selfishness. There was to be fairness in interpersonal relationships.

The law code for Israel began with the Ten Commandments as given in Exodus 20. This is followed by three chapters of approximately 70 ordinances that give details for the  types of infractions that could create chaos for an encamped group of people. In the centuries that followed, God sent prophets to remind the people that ignoring their covenantal responsibilities would have dire consequences.

The Laws of Other Nations

In the centuries after the flood of Noah's day, the developing nations discovered that it was in their best interests to have codes of conduct. A dozen or more ancient kingdoms had such codes. At least seven of these predate by several centuries the establishment of the nation of Israel in the fifteenth century BC.

For example, consider the Code of Hammurabi, dated at about 1790 BC. It lists nearly 300 laws along with punishments for infractions. Property rights are emphasized; the rights of individuals receive little attention. Archaeologists working at Hazor in the summer of 2010 found cuneiform tablets of a similar code. These are being dated to the eighteenth and seventeenth centuries BC.

Compassion in Israel's Code

God's expectations for Israel were different. His law expressed concerns for those we would call the disadvantaged or disenfranchised. An authentic follower of the Lord does not take advantage of such people. Those who were relatively better off were to provide conditions that would allow the poor to work to provide for themselves. Land that had been sold was to return to the original family every 50 years (the Year of Jubilee). Such a practice provided the means for one generation to escape from a state of poverty that circumstances of the past had produced. This was not to be an unfair, forced redistribution of wealth in a socialistic sense. Since Leviticus 25:16 made clear what the rules were, it was fair to everyone. It was simply treating others as one would want to be treated.

The Law of Moses was distinctive also in that much information was given about what the Lord expected in acceptable worship. There were to be dramatic differences between Israel's worship and those of her neighbors. Other nations used sacrifices for clairvoyance, trying to tell the future by examining parts of the sacrificial animal; Israel did not. The God of Israel declared himself holy; holiness was absent from the lives of others gods. Israel had a sacred, covenantal relationship with God; the concept of covenant was not a part of the worship by others. The laws of Israel never required the sacrifice of infants or virgins; this was often done by others. Israel's sacrificial system even gave special consideration to the poor.

Justice for All

Some people will take advantage of the goodness of others, but a society that values justice and fairness will work to ensure justice for all. The best place to begin is to determine the expectations of the Creator.

THIS QUARTER IN THE WORD

Answers to the Quarterly Quiz on page 338

Lesson 1—1. witness. 2. false. **Lesson 2**—1. true. 2. grudge. **Lesson 3**—1. jubile (jubilee). 2. Egypt. **Lesson 4**—1. widows, fatherless, strangers. 2. 70 ("threescore and ten"). **Lesson 5**—1. false. 2. judge. **Lesson 6**—1. psalmist. 2. false. **Lesson 7**—1. harlots. 2. false. **Lesson 8**—1. famine. 2. true. **Lesson 9**—1. false. 2. persons. **Lesson 10**—1. soul. 2. upside down. **Lesson 11**—1. Naphtali, Zebulun. 2. true. **Lesson 12**—1. shepherds. 2. righteous. **Lesson 13**—1. one. 2. blessing.

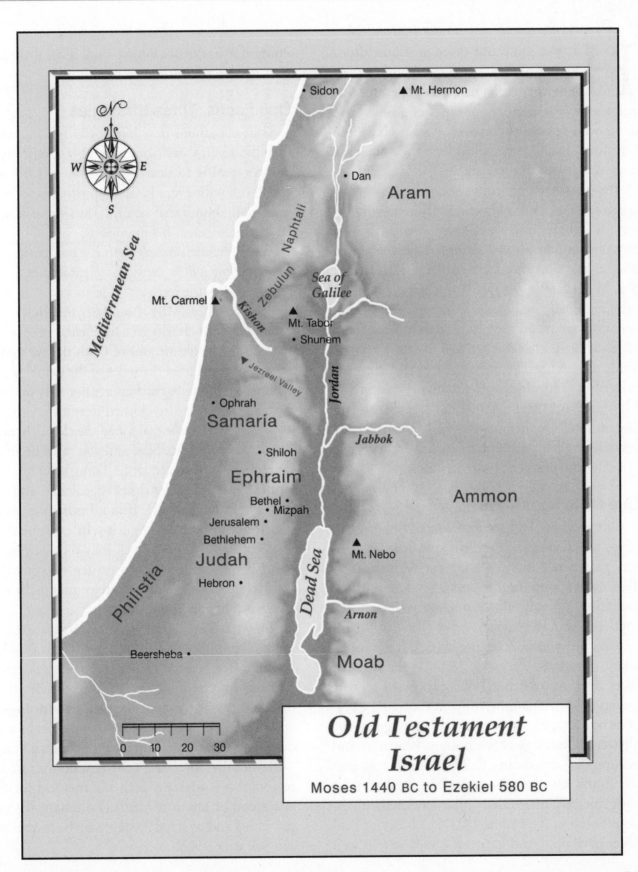

Old Testament Israel

Moses 1440 BC to Ezekiel 580 BC

TEACHING THE BOMBER

Teacher Tips by Brent L. Amato

HAVING READ our three previous install-ments of Teacher Tips, you know by now that *the bored, the barrier, the boss,* and *the bomber* are the four types of problem students who present themselves in your classroom. Our final installment will address the fourth and most dangerous of these.

The bomber enters your classroom looking for targets. He or she may take verbal aim at your lesson, the other learners, and/or you personally! For some reason, *the bomber* seems to have the proverbial "chip on his shoulder" that results in lashing out. Whether *the bomber* is sincerely misguided or intentionally malicious, failure to deal with the situation can mean the destruction of your class.

Jesus, the master teacher, had to deal with both kinds of bombers. Peter was one of the "sincerely misguided" kind on at least one occasion (see Matthew 16:21-23). Many Pharisees were of the "intentionally malicious" ilk (see Mark 12:13-17). Jesus didn't let the bombers' agendas succeed in His day, and neither can we in ours.

One More Imperative

Our previous Teacher Tips offered three imperatives for all types of problem students: intercessory prayer, relating in accordance with the New Testament's "one another" passages, and spiritual parenting. One additional imperative specifically applies to you, the teacher: *never give up.*

After an especially vexing class, haven't we all asked ourselves, "Why do I continue to teach? Why do I even bother?" We easily can picture the apostle Paul asking himself the same questions many times, especially after undergoing the physical bombings of whippings, beatings, and stoning (2 Corinthians 11:23-29). Paul continually found his teaching under bombardment by both sincerely misguided and intentionally malicious bombers (Galatians 2:11-14; 3:1-5). But Paul never gave up. "And let us not be weary in well doing: for in due season we shall reap, if we faint not" (Galatians 6:9).

One Focus, Three Strategies

Your classroom may have nice lighting, comfortable chairs, etc., but it is also a battlefield. Satan's goal is to destroy, and he will fill your classroom with every kind of spiritual land mine, bullet, and bomb that he can. Thus we need some strategies to defeat his intentions.

First, prepare yourself with the realization that your teaching will be subject to spiritual attack. This just goes with the territory. If Jesus and Paul experienced bombers, why shouldn't you? Before you walk onto your classroom battlefield, make sure to "put on the whole armour of God, that ye may be able to stand against the wiles of the devil" (Ephesians 6:11). Effective teachers are not only prepared with a lesson, but also clothed in spiritual armor.

Second, guard the truth and the class. There are doctrinal nonnegotiables, and you must be able to defend them from attack (2 Timothy 2:15). Seek to defuse *the bomber* quickly, calmly, and graciously (Proverbs 15:1). If at all possible, defer a confrontation until after class. In extreme cases, the protection of your flock may require that *the bomber* not be allowed to return to your class (Titus 3:10). Our third strategy may help keep that from happening.

Third, minister to the bomber outside the classroom. The root of the problem may be unresolved conflict, deep-seated emotional pain, a doctrinal agenda, unrepentant sin, or a personality issue directed toward you in particular. Finding out what's going on inside *the bomber* should be a priority, and this may require lots of time and tact.

Remember that the goal is redemption and restoration (Galatians 6:1); the method for that is a blend of love and truth (Ephesians 4:15). A redeemed and restored *bomber* may be the best lesson you ever teach!

PRACTICE
JUSTICE

DEVOTIONAL READING: Deuteronomy 32:1-7
BACKGROUND SCRIPTURE: Exodus 22:1–23:9

EXODUS 23:1-9

1 Thou shalt not raise a false report: put not thine hand with the wicked to be an unrighteous witness.

2 Thou shalt not follow a multitude to do evil; neither shalt thou speak in a cause to decline after many to wrest judgment:

3 Neither shalt thou countenance a poor man in his cause.

4 If thou meet thine enemy's ox or his ass going astray, thou shalt surely bring it back to him again.

5 If thou see the ass of him that hateth thee lying under his burden, and wouldest forbear to help him, thou shalt surely help with him.

6 Thou shalt not wrest the judgment of thy poor in his cause.

7 Keep thee far from a false matter; and the innocent and righteous slay thou not: for I will not justify the wicked.

8 And thou shalt take no gift: for the gift blindeth the wise, and perverteth the words of the righteous.

9 Also thou shalt not oppress a stranger: for ye know the heart of a stranger, seeing ye were strangers in the land of Egypt.

KEY VERSE

Thou shalt not follow a multitude to do evil; neither shalt thou speak in a cause to decline after many to wrest judgment. —**Exodus 23:2**

GOD CALLS FOR JUSTICE

Unit 1: Justice Defined

LESSONS 1–4

LESSON AIMS

After participating in this lesson, each student will be able to:

1. List several "do nots" that characterize godly interpersonal behavior.

2. Predict some results of keeping God's commands.

3. Identify the command that he or she has the hardest time keeping and make a plan for change.

LESSON OUTLINE

Introduction
  A. God's Justice for God's People
  B. Lesson Background
 I. Alliances (EXODUS 23:1, 2)
  A. Wrong Partnership (v. 1)
    Honest Testimony
  B. Wrong Following (v. 2)
 II. Compassion (EXODUS 23:3-5)
  A. No Favoritism (v. 3)
  B. No Neglect (vv. 4, 5)
 III. Justice (EXODUS 23:6-9)
  A. Respect Innocence (vv. 6, 7)
  B. Reject Bribes (v. 8)
    Blinded by Bribes
  C. Protect Strangers (v. 9)
Conclusion
  A. Justice in the Church
  B. Prayer
  C. Thought to Remember

Introduction

A. God's Justice for God's People

Though traditional junk mail has always been a nuisance, junk e-mail takes the annoyance to a whole new level. Junk e-mail, also known as *spam,* costs senders almost nothing for promoting the product or idea of their choosing. Christian spam is no different. Some well-intended Christians use spam to encourage other believers with inspirational messages, to enlist them in various causes, etc. One of the most common causes is that of supporting or trying to elect public officials who vow to administer godly justice in the land.

Such spam may promote divisive debates among Christians. Some of the debates center on which official's policies are most just. Other debates revolve around whether Christians have any business at all trying to engineer justice through the world's political machinery. These debates have driven many Christians to a false choice between advocating justice on the world's terms or ignoring justice altogether. They think they must choose between fighting worldly politics the world's way or neglecting political concerns altogether.

Scripture's approach to justice moves beyond false choices. God's people make their most fundamental contribution to justice by ordering their personal lives before the watching world according to God's ideals. Beginning with Abraham, God began forming a people whose common life was intended to reflect God's justice in every way, regardless of what the nations around them believed or practiced. Though some of the world's elected officials will waffle with the changing polls, God's people are called to remain steadfast in their witness to divine justice. This witness began with ancient Israel and continues with the church. In today's passage we catch a glimpse of the justice to which God called the Israelites shortly after He delivered them from Egypt.

B. Lesson Background

After the flood, God covenanted with all creation never to destroy the earth again by water (Genesis 9:9-17). Sin would come back, but repeating a cycle of destructive floods to bring renewal could not be the permanent answer. Thus God committed himself to bring permanent peace and order to a world made violent and chaotic by sin.

God's solution began with making Abraham and his descendents into a special people through whom all nations would be blessed (Genesis 12:1-3). Before He could do this, however, this people would be enslaved in Egypt for 400 years. During that time, God increased their number and prepared the then-current occupants of the promised land for judgment (Genesis 15:13-16).

After delivering His people from Egypt with a show of great power, God declared them to be His "peculiar treasure" and "a kingdom of priests, and an holy nation" (Exodus 19:5, 6). If the Israelites were to be a kingdom of priests, they first had to order their lives according to God's principles.

This "holy cultivation" would provide the proper soil through which the Messiah could come. In this light, it is a mistake to view God's laws for Israel as a legalistic formula to achieve a form of righteousness by means of good works. Rather, these laws were God's means of forming a special people who would get the world's attention by their faithfulness to God's will. God's laws cover a wide range of topics. Today's passage focuses on the everyday practice of justice.

I. Alliances
(EXODUS 23:1, 2)

A. Wrong Partnership (v. 1)

1. Thou shalt not raise a false report: put not thine hand with the wicked to be an unrighteous witness.

This verse echoes the ninth of the Ten Commandments: "Thou shalt not bear false witness against thy neighbour" (Exodus 20:16). This command is critical to Israelite justice. Since this era lacks video surveillance, fingerprinting, and the

HOW TO SAY IT

Amos	*Ay*-mus.
Deuteronomy	Due-ter-*ahn*-uh-me.
Israelites	*Iz*-ray-el-ites.
Leviticus	Leh-*vit*-ih-kus.

ability to perform DNA testing, the legal system relies most heavily on eyewitness testimony.

As a result, the most significant threat to the legal system of the day is witness tampering. The best way to engineer a false verdict is to convince a witness that it is in his or her best interest to mislead the judge into believing that the innocent party is guilty and/or the guilty party is innocent (compare 1 Kings 21:1-14). Therefore, this verse warns the Israelites not to partner with wicked people who would subvert justice by means of engineering false eyewitness evidence. Verse 8 (below) discusses bribery as a primary problem in witness tampering.

What Do You Think?
  How should you respond if a fellow employee asks you to say you saw him at his workstation at a time when you did not?
Talking Points for Your Discussion
  - Dealing with peer pressure
  - Dealing with guilt trips
  - Avoiding rationalization
  - Romans 12:2

❧ HONEST TESTIMONY ❧

In the helter-skelter days of the 2007–2009 financial crisis, media attention was focused on the multibillion-dollar Ponzi scheme of Bernard Madoff. A similar scheme in Utah didn't get much notice. Jeffrey Mowen's $18 million Ponzi scam wasn't even in the same league with that of Madoff. However, Mowen's case had a twist to it that the Madoff case didn't.

When Mowen's scheme was uncovered, he fled to Panama, where he was arrested. After being extradited, Mowen was charged with witness tampering, including attempting to have four witnesses killed so they could not testify against him. Mowen allegedly dictated a "hit list" in Morse code to another jail inmate. But that prisoner was working with law enforcement and wearing a recording device. Mowen's trial on the charges of fraud and witness tampering was to begin in late 2010.

In an evil sort of way, Mowen knew the value of honest testimony: such testimony could put him away for a long time, so he tried to stop it. The average law-abiding citizen is properly outraged at Mowen's attempts to do so. Do we ever wonder about God's outrage when our own lives fail to testify to Christian truth?   —C. R. B.

B. Wrong Following (v. 2)

2. Thou shalt not follow a multitude to do evil; neither shalt thou speak in a cause to decline after many to wrest judgment.

Sometimes an outside party will bribe witnesses to falsify evidence. But at other times a witness will feel the pressure of a crowd that is somehow subverting justice. To *speak in a cause to decline after many* is a way of describing that problem.

To be truthful when the multitudes are lying is to invite the scorn of many and to risk being ostracized by one's community. Nevertheless, God demands that His people rise above the fray of peer pressure. Pagans may try to cheat the system either individually or collectively. But this must not happen among God's people. The Israelites must set themselves apart as different—holy.

What Do You Think?

How do we teach our children and grandchildren to avoid following a crowd in doing wrong?

Talking Points for Your Discussion

- Peer pressure issues
- Media influence issues
- Deuteronomy 6:7
- Proverbs 22:6

II. Compassion
(Exodus 23:3-5)

A. No Favoritism (v. 3)

3. Neither shalt thou countenance a poor man in his cause.

God shows a special concern for the poor throughout Scripture (examples: Leviticus 19:9, 10; James 2:1-4). When justice is subverted, frequently it is the poor who are cheated (examples: Amos 5:12; Luke 20:47). The poor are prime targets for legal abuse because they lack the funding and connections to influence judges and witnesses. Even when modern society provides legal representation through public defenders, the quality of such representation can pale in comparison with the best lawyers money can buy.

Yet as sympathetic as God is to the plight of the poor, He insists that true justice does not show favoritism to them (Leviticus 19:15, next week's lesson). The divine answer to a system that is ripe for favoring the rich is not one that favors the poor, but one that favors none. All the guilty are equally guilty before their Creator. None may hide behind economic status. None are immune to divine scrutiny and justice. Discrimination in any form is wrong.

B. No Neglect (vv. 4, 5)

4, 5. If thou meet thine enemy's ox or his ass going astray, thou shalt surely bring it back to him again. If thou see the ass of him that hateth thee lying under his burden, and wouldest forbear to help him, thou shalt surely help with him.

The practice of godly justice extends beyond the formal procedures of the ancient legal system. Godly justice also is to affect one's everyday treatment of neighbors. Though many will speak truthfully in court and under oath, these same truth-tellers may be inclined to look the other way when no one else is around. This is especially so when they have the opportunity to see a personal foe suffer economic loss.

This foe may be a neighbor who has cheated or slandered a person. When such a foe appears to suffer loss, it is tempting to think that he or she is receiving "just deserts." It is tempting to smile on the inside as such a neighbor gets what seems to be deserved. Yet this too fails to reflect God's nature.

The God who teaches Christians (through Jesus) to pray for their persecutors teaches the Israelites to care for the property of their enemies. This involves going out of one's way to restore stray animals or otherwise protecting enemies from suffering loss. As Jesus notes, this kind of love reflects the Father's own love and moves beyond the self-interested love of pagans (Matthew 5:43-48). God's people are called not just to avoid practicing evil, but to overcome evil with good (Romans 12:17-21; quoting Proverbs 25:21, 22). God's justice moves beyond human conceptions of justice. It is too small a task that God's people merely avoid contributing to injustice; God expects His people to join Him in acting out godly concern for the good of all.

What Do You Think?
What are some ways to apply this verse in a nonagricultural context of the twenty-first century?
Talking Points for Your Discussion
- Next-door neighbors
- Coworkers
- Fellow church members

III. Justice
(Exodus 23:6-9)

A. Respect Innocence (vv. 6, 7)

6. Thou shalt not wrest the judgment of thy poor in his cause.

Though God warns the Israelites not to show partiality toward the poor when it comes to justice (v. 3, above), He also stresses that injustice is unacceptable for the poor as well. Thus God keeps steady pressure on His people to understand the pure, unbiased nature of justice.

This pressure is just as necessary today. The economic, cultural, and political forces of sinful society may place certain parties at a disadvantage. To do nothing to correct this is to displease God. A system that reflects God's justice will be sensitive to abuses of the legal system so that injustices that are normal in the world will not be seen as normal among God's people.

This concern is equally important within the church. Paul notes that some church members are more prominent and thus tend to receive more honor (1 Corinthians 12:12-31). By contrast, other members seem naturally to be less noteworthy; without deliberate attention these will receive less honor. So Paul suggests that the seemingly less important members be given great attention and that the seemingly more important members be given less attention. His goal is not a body in which a certain set of members dominates, but that no set of members dominates (v. 25). Each part is to experience equal honor as befitting God's people.

Modern society tries to root out discrimination by legal means. Within the church, however, it is grace that makes us sensitive to those who are being alienated, oppressed, or ignored. God's people can remain sensitive because we are committed to honoring one another (Romans 12:10). We can remain sensitive because we are not competing for positions of power and influence. We have rejected the world's power-mongering ways (Mark 10:42-44). Those who have received positional power from God are instructed to use it to serve those in their care the way Jesus loved and served us. Noble intentions within a broken system can produce devastating effects. So God has formed a people whose life together should reflect His justice from the inside out.

7. Keep thee far from a false matter; and the innocent and righteous slay thou not: for I will not justify the wicked.

The text moves to outline the most common forms of injustice that God's people must avoid. He begins by warning us to keep far from a falsehood. To *keep thee far from* prohibits a person of God from having anything to do with false accusations. There is to be no waffling or rationalizing in this regard. To partner with injustice and deny a true verdict to the innocent is to participate firsthand in the evil that wrongfully befalls the righteous. God will not turn a blind eye to such actions, particularly since justice is a foundation of His throne (Psalm 89:14). Thus God presents the Israelites with a choice: they can show the world what true justice looks like by their common life, or they can suffer at God's hand the punishment that awaits those who ignore His justice, for He *will not justify the wicked*.

B. Reject Bribes (v. 8)

8. And thou shalt take no gift: for the gift blindeth the wise, and perverteth the words of the righteous.

At the root of injustice is often the desire for money or status. The wicked can thus use the practice of gift-giving as a means of injustice. Indeed, humans seem to be able to find ways to turn all good things into instruments of wickedness. So bribery is entirely out of the question for

Visual for Lesson 1. *Point to this visual as you ask, "How can we stand up for justice in ways that don't involve being active in politics?"*

God's people. To receive bribes is just as sinful as to give them because to do either is to participate in and endorse the same web of deception (Deuteronomy 16:19; 27:25).

The righteous are not immune to the power of a bribe. The righteous can be tempted to rationalize how God's work might be able to use for good the "gift" that they are receiving. Perhaps the money can free the recipient from debt so he or she can be more generous in giving. "Maybe I can give a portion of the money to a worthy cause." Even the godliest people can deceive themselves into embracing evil as a supposed means for good.

❧ BLINDED BY BRIBES ❧

Randy "Duke" Cunningham was decorated highly for his valor as a Navy fighter pilot during the Vietnam War. He emerged from that conflict as an *ace*—having shot down five enemy aircraft. He later was an instructor in the Navy's famous TOPGUN fighter tactics training program. His military record became a springboard to being elected to Congress in 1990.

Cunningham's military experience landed him membership on the Appropriations Subcommittee on Defense, U.S. House of Representatives. This subcommittee determines spending on defense programs. While serving on that subcommittee, Cunningham succumbed to temptation. He resigned from Congress under pressure in 2005, admitting to bribery, mail and wire fraud,

and tax evasion. Over a period of several years, he had accepted more than $2 million in bribes from at least three defense contractors. U.S. Attorney Carol Lam said, "The citizens who elected Cunningham assumed that he would do his best for them. Instead, he did the worst thing an elected official can do—he enriched himself through his position and violated the trust of those who put him there." Cunningham went to prison.

The fact that America traditionally has held its elected officials to a higher standard than Cunningham practiced obviously does not always prevent bribery from taking place. The issue is not only the dishonesty involved, but also the fact that the "little guy"—the small businessperson who cannot afford to buy his way to power—is prevented from having a fair chance. In effect, elected officials become blind to their existence. God expects better of His people. Will He get it?
—C. R. B.

C. Protect Strangers (v. 9)

9. Also thou shalt not oppress a stranger: for ye know the heart of a stranger, seeing ye were strangers in the land of Egypt.

One temptation that the Israelites might face is to think that justice is only for the pureblood Israelite. After all, God's laws clearly distinguish between Israelites and non-Israelites, right?

God will not allow the oppression of injustice on non-Israelites who live among His people. The world was created for everyone. God's gift of life is for all humanity. The order God intended for His creation applies to everyone.

God did not free the Israelites from slavery so they could become a new Egypt that enslaves others. This precept is so important that God mentions it more than once (Exodus 22:21; Leviticus 19:33, 34—next week's lesson). The "congregation of Israel" consists of those who are born into the tribes of Israel and those who are not (Exodus 12:19). There are not separate laws for each (Exodus 12:49; Leviticus 17:8-16; 20:2).

The Israelites were once strangers in the land of Egypt. That fact means that the Israelites know how it feels to be in that position. Their memory in that regard should cause them to treat kindly

Practice Justice

the stranger in their midst, now that the shoe is on the other foot.

After Christ's ascension, God will send His people—the Christians—out into the world to win the lost. Yet God's people of the New Testament era are strangers in a world that does not accept Christian values (1 Peter 1:1; 2:11). Thus we know what it feels like to be strangers in the world. Let us make sure that unbelievers or new Christians who come into our church are not made to feel like "foreigners." Lead them gently!

What Do You Think?

How should the fact that we were once strangers in the land of sin affect how we treat others?

Talking Points for Your Discussion

- Treatment of fellow Christians
- Treatment of nonbelievers, those still held captive by sin

Conclusion

A. Justice in the Church

Hindsight makes it easy to see how Israel should have witnessed God's justice to the world. Israel was a God-chosen people that had to enforce a God-given legal code throughout her God-chosen territory. It is a bit more difficult to discern how the church should best represent God's justice in concrete ways today.

As God sends us throughout the world to make disciples, we realize that our primary identity is not tied to a particular nation inhabiting a specific location. Even so, the church can and must reflect God's justice. The apostle Peter quoted Exodus 19:6 to support his claim that the church, like Old Testament Israel, possesses a distinct identity: "But ye are a chosen generation, a royal priesthood, an holy nation, a peculiar people; that ye should shew forth the praises of him who hath called you out of darkness into his marvellous light" (1 Peter 2:9).

The church is not a "normal" sort of nation, but it is still a nation. Its people live throughout the earth but are citizens of Heaven (Philippians 3:20). It has a king who makes demands of His

subjects and calls them to live just lives that point the watching world to the splendor of His kingdom. So we should not be surprised that Jesus and the New Testament writers frequently instruct Christians to live out many of the same principles of justice that we see in Exodus 23. We are instructed to be hospitable to strangers (Hebrews 13:2), love our enemies (Matthew 5:44; Romans 12:19, 20), see to the needs of the poor (Galatians 2:10; James 1:27), avoid wrong partnerships (2 Corinthians 6:14; James 4:4), and resist showing partiality to those who are financially well off (1 Timothy 5:21, 22; James 2:1-9).

In this way the church continues Israel's witness to God's justice. When we order our lives accordingly, we serve as God's sign to the world that its twisted versions of justice stand under His supreme judgment.

What Do You Think?

How can our church do better at extending hospitality to the "strangers" who show up?

Talking Points for Your Discussion

- Spiritual hospitality
- Physical hospitality
- Matthew 10:16

B. Prayer

Lord God, we thank You for so loving this world that You refuse to abandon us to our own faulty visions of justice. We thank You for entrusting Your people with Your laws and Your teachings regarding the shape of true justice. Help us to discern how we ought to live this out in our daily lives. In Jesus' name we pray, amen.

C. Thought to Remember

Order your life according to God's justice.

VISUALS FOR THESE LESSONS

The visual pictured in each lesson (example: page 350) is a small reproduction of a large, full-color poster included in the *Adult Resources* packet for the Summer Quarter. That packet also contains the very useful *Presentation Helps* on a CD for teacher use. Order No. 020049212 from your supplier.

INVOLVEMENT LEARNING

Some of the activities below are also found in the helpful student book, Adult Bible Class.
Don't forget to download the free reproducible page from www.standardlesson.com to enhance your lesson!

Into the Lesson

Form learners into groups of two to four. Give each group at least one copy of a newspaper and/or news magazine. Ask groups to search for illustrations of unjust or unfair practices, actions, or perspectives. Say, "Be ready to explain why you chose the illustration or example that you did."

After the reports, make the transition to Bible study by saying, "Often our perspectives on justice and injustice are influenced (even tainted) by our personal circumstances. That's why we must discover how God defines or interprets social injustice. We'll find several illustrations and principles in today's Old Testament Scripture."

Into the Word

Read the lesson text (Exodus 23:1-9) with the class. Say, "This passages raises many issues and questions about social justice. We'll tackle these issues in study teams." Form five teams or pairs; give the teams the following written assignments:

"Don't" Team: Make three columns on a poster board. In the first column, make a list of "things not to do." In the second column, answer the question "What are the consequences of disobeying?" In the third column, make a list of "opposites or behaviors desired." (Supplies needed: large poster board and marker.)

"Do" Team: Paraphrase verses 4 and 5, which are the only two verses that list something we must "do." In your paraphrase, substitute an illustration from modern life. Write that newly illustrated paraphrase on a poster board. Be ready to explain the overall principle God is giving to His people in this illustration. (Supplies needed: large poster board and marker.)

"Just" Team: Discuss why it is sometimes difficult to know what is "just." Think about two groups arguing for different positions or outcomes, yet each group claiming that its position is "just." Why does that happen? Be ready to share an illus-

tration of this issue. Suggest ways to achieve a "meeting of the minds" when two groups or individuals have differing ideas of fairness or justice.

"Rights" Team: After reading today's text, read also Matthew 5:38-42 and 1 Corinthians 6:7. What do these imply about a believer insisting on his or her "rights"? Be ready to propose to the class circumstances in which one should demand justice and when one should surrender that claim.

"Principles" Team: Suggest how to apply the principles of justice in Exodus 23:1-9 to the church in today's culture. Read the following passages to discover general principles of justice God asks of Christians: Matthew 5:44; Acts 6:1-6; Romans 12:14, 19, 20; 1 Timothy 5:21; James 1:27; 5:1-6. (Supplies needed: poster board and marker.)

Into Life

Say, "Christians, both individually and collectively as the church, are to demonstrate God's idea of social justice. Let's look at the last verse of our text and try to identify a way that we can put that into practice in today's world." Write *Strangers/Aliens/Foreigners* at the top of the board.

Step 1. Reread verse 9. Brainstorm: "Who are strangers or aliens in our culture?" **Step 2.** Brainstorm: "How should Christians—both individually and collectively—interact with these groups? (*Caution:* Do not let this turn into a political discussion regarding how the secular authorities should handle immigration policy.) **Step 3.** Select one of the ideas suggested that the class will develop. Appoint a leadership team for the project.

Alternative: Distribute copies of the Observations activity from the reproducible page, which you can download. Use as a whole-class brainstorming activity.

As learners depart, distribute copies of the A Change of Heart activity from the reproducible page.

• Practice Justice

LIVE AS GOD'S JUST PEOPLE

DEVOTIONAL READING: Luke 10:25-37
BACKGROUND SCRIPTURE: Leviticus 19

LEVITICUS 19:9-18, 33-37

9 And when ye reap the harvest of your land, thou shalt not wholly reap the corners of thy field, neither shalt thou gather the gleanings of thy harvest.

10 And thou shalt not glean thy vineyard, neither shalt thou gather every grape of thy vineyard; thou shalt leave them for the poor and stranger: I am the LORD your God.

11 Ye shall not steal, neither deal falsely, neither lie one to another.

12 And ye shall not swear by my name falsely, neither shalt thou profane the name of thy God: I am the LORD.

13 Thou shalt not defraud thy neighbour, neither rob him: the wages of him that is hired shall not abide with thee all night until the morning.

14 Thou shalt not curse the deaf, nor put a stumblingblock before the blind, but shalt fear thy God: I am the LORD.

15 Ye shall do no unrighteousness in judgment: thou shalt not respect the person of the poor, nor honor the person of the mighty: but in righteousness shalt thou judge thy neighbour.

16 Thou shalt not go up and down as a talebearer among thy people: neither shalt thou stand against the blood of thy neighbour; I am the LORD.

17 Thou shalt not hate thy brother in thine heart: thou shalt in any wise rebuke thy neighbour, and not suffer sin upon him.

18 Thou shalt not avenge, nor bear any grudge against the children of thy people, but thou shalt love thy neighbour as thyself: I am the LORD.

. . . .

33 And if a stranger sojourn with thee in your land, ye shall not vex him.

34 But the stranger that dwelleth with you shall be unto you as one born among you, and thou shalt love him as thyself; for ye were strangers in the land of Egypt: I am the LORD your God.

35 Ye shall do no unrighteousness in judgment, in meteyard, in weight, or in measure.

36 Just balances, just weights, a just ephah, and a just hin, shall ye have: I am the LORD your God, which brought you out of the land of Egypt.

37 Therefore shall ye observe all my statutes, and all my judgments, and do them: I am the LORD.

KEY VERSE

The stranger that dwelleth with you shall be unto you as one born among you, and thou shalt love him as thyself; for ye were strangers in the land of Egypt: I am the LORD your God. —**Leviticus 19:34**

GOD CALLS FOR JUSTICE

Unit 1: Justice Defined

LESSONS 1–4

LESSON AIMS

After participating in this lesson, each student will be able to:

1. Identify the issue at hand each time God reminds His people, "I am the Lord."

2. Explain how obedience to God's laws helps one to be more like the Lord.

3. Identify one way he or she can act as God's agent to bring justice to a contemporary situation.

LESSON OUTLINE

Introduction

A. What We Owe

Sitcoms seem to revolve around a handful of recurring plotlines. One involves extreme gratefulness to a lifesaver. It begins when Person A finds himself in a life-threatening situation until Person B selflessly intervenes to save him. Motivated by extreme gratitude, Person A decides that the only proper response is to offer his own life in servitude to Person B. Eventually, the service becomes a burden. Then Person B falls into peril and Person A is there to repay by saving Person B. Having balanced the scales, life returns to normal. This comical plotline reveals an earnest desire each party has to repay what is received from the other.

In real life, it is inappropriate to attempt payment for a gift given generously with no thought of reciprocity. But an attempt may be made anyway if the original recipient doesn't want to feel "indebted" (compare Luke 14:12). For Christians, the sin-debt we owed has been paid by Christ, and it is wrong for us to try to figure out what God wants from us in return payment for the salvation He has granted us. To the psalmist's question, "What shall I render unto the Lord for all his benefits toward me?" (Psalm 116:12) we must answer, "Nothing!" God is not like us. He neither wants nor expects repayment. Even so, we are called to do good works (Ephesians 2:10); we render those good works to Him in gratitude *because* we have been saved, not as repayment for having been saved. In this way, we become people who show and teach the world what God has done for us.

But this imperative is not unique to the New Testament era. God has always expected the behavior of His people to reflect His nature. That's what today's lesson is about. Our service to God cannot be reduced to a spiritual ceremony. It must take the form of a life ordered in every way according to His justice.

B. Lesson Background

The background to last week's lesson is no different from this one. Thus that information need not be repeated here. However, we can point out a noteworthy difference between last week's

Scripture of Exodus 23 and this week's passage from Leviticus 19. The latter makes use of a literary device that helps us both outline the passage and learn why Old Testament Israel was called to God's particular way. This device is the repetition of the phrases "I am the Lord" and "I am the Lord your God." Together, these two phrases occur 15 times over a space of 37 verses in Leviticus 19.

Although these same lines are used elsewhere in Leviticus, they stand out in Leviticus 19 by how often they are used. The significance of these phrases is stated at the beginning of Leviticus 19, where the Lord instructs Moses by saying, "Speak unto all the congregation of the children of Israel, and say unto them, Ye shall be holy: for I the Lord your God am holy" (Leviticus 19:2; quoted in 1 Peter 1:16). God called Israel to live a particular way of life *because that life reflects His holiness.*

We should not think of the imitation to which God calls His people as some kind of divine ego management. Though imitation may be the highest form of flattery among humans, God is not like us in this regard. He wants us to imitate His holiness because we are in His image and because this imitation is what is best for us. To live in accord with God's nature is to live with the grain of the universe rather than constantly fighting against it.

I. How to Treat One Another
(LEVITICUS 19:9-18)
A. Benevolence (vv. 9, 10)

9, 10. And when ye reap the harvest of your land, thou shalt not wholly reap the corners of thy field, neither shalt thou gather the gleanings of thy harvest. And thou shalt not glean thy vineyard, neither shalt thou gather every grape of thy vineyard; thou shalt leave them for the poor and stranger: I am the LORD your God.

Our obligation to God cannot be separated from our obligation to one another. Thus the Israelites are called to the rather mundane practice of sharing food. In ancient Israel as today, people fall on hard times for various reasons. Some make poor choices that cost them their possessions. Others are stricken with a natural disaster that leaves them with little more than the shirts on their backs. Still others suffer the loss of the family breadwinner (compare Ruth 1:3-5). So God states how the Israelites are to help out.

The verse before us does not call for straight handouts. Neither does it call people to give a portion of their produce to public officials who will decide how to distribute it to the poor. Instead, God calls His people to leave some food behind during harvest. Farmers are to leave some food on the stalks and vines so the impoverished will have a means of getting food. To the Israelites, their land isn't private property, but God's property (Leviticus 25:23). The first-century Christians seem to operate with similar convictions (Acts 4:32).

> *What Do You Think?*
> Under what circumstances, if any, should churches require those in need to do some work in order to receive assistance from the church? Why?
> *Talking Points for Your Discussion*
> - Luke 10:25-37
> - Acts 4:32-35
> - 2 Thessalonians 3:6-12

❧ SHARING THE HARVEST ❧

The Old Testament's instructions for helping the poor can be difficult to apply literally in modern culture. Something like 98 percent of people lived on farms in ancient times, but only about 2 percent do so in modern America. Thus a literal application of not reaping the corners of a field probably would result in wasted food because most of the urban poor would not have access to it—and

HOW TO SAY IT

elohim *(Hebrew)*	el-o-*heem.*
ephah	*ee*-fah.
Leviticus	Leh-*vit*-ih-kus.
meteyard	*meet*-yard.
Moses	*Mo*-zes or *Mo*-zez.
Yahweh *(Hebrew)*	*Yah*-weh.

few food crops are grown in modern metropolitan areas! Some creative thinking is thus required.

Members of one California church saw their location adjacent to a military base as a ministry opportunity. With permission from the manager of a large grocery store, church members stood outside the store at Christmastime. As customers entered the store, volunteers distributed lists of nonperishable items needed by the community food pantry. Shoppers were asked to add some items to their shopping list and then leave them at the door as they left the store. As a result, several pickup truckloads of food, diapers, laundry soap, etc., were taken to the food pantry for distribution to needy military families and others. A little effort made a big difference.

We might be surprised to discover how much need there is for the necessities of life in our communities. What effort will you make to discover and meet these needs? What effort should be required of the recipients to receive help?

—C. R. B.

B. Honesty (vv. 11, 12)

11. Ye shall not steal, neither deal falsely, neither lie one to another.

God also calls the people to honest dealings. The prohibitions we see here apply to a wide variety of exchanges: selling and bartering goods, negotiating property lines, settling conflict at the town gate, etc.

Lying and stealing are usually very straightforward issues, easy to define (compare Exodus 20:15, 16). But to *deal falsely* can be a little slippery, and it's easy to rationalize in this area. Think about how we communicate "how busy we are" to avoid commitments to serve. Think about how we deal with (or avoid dealing with) issues that divide us. We could say that putting on a front that pretends such conflict doesn't exist is to "deal falsely."

Christ did not say that God's people will never have conflict and will never struggle to agree (Matthew 18:15-17; Acts 15:36-41). Christ has shown us better ways of dealing with conflicts and disagreements. If God's people cannot be forthright with one another, why should the world think Christ's truth is uniquely mediated through us?

What Do You Think?
Does the requirement not to lie or deal falsely mean that brutal honesty is the only alternative? Why, or why not?
Talking Points for Your Discussion
- The issue of tact (Daniel 2:14)
- The issue of Rahab's deceit (Joshua 2)

12. And ye shall not swear by my name falsely, neither shalt thou profane the name of thy God: I am the LORD.

The term LORD (with small capital letters) is God's personal name. It is sometimes rendered in English letters as *Yahweh*. This term is distinct from the word *Lord* (with only the first letter capitalized), which in the Old Testament is a translation of the word *elohim,* the general word for deity. For example, *elohim* is the word behind the translation "all gods" in Exodus 18:11 and "their gods" in Exodus 23:24. The name LORD, then, is a specific name for Israel's God and Him alone.

God's personal name means "I am." Israel's God is not a god of philosophical abstraction but of actual being. All people can know something about Him through creation (Romans 1:20). We know even more about Him through the special revelation of the Bible. The verse before us, which is part of that special revelation, tells us something about God: His name is important.

From the beginning of Israel's existence as a nation, God has called His people to respect His name (Exodus 20:7; Deuteronomy 5:11). To not *profane the name of thy God* means more than not using it as a swear word. It also means not using God's name to endorse human agendas. The world will continue to toss God's name around carelessly for rhetorical effect. But God's people must stand out as those who so honor God that we invoke His name only when we sincerely mean it (Romans 2:24; 2 Corinthians 1:23; 1 Timothy 6:1).

C. Dignity (vv. 13, 14)

13. Thou shalt not defraud thy neighbour, neither rob him: the wages of him that is hired shall not abide with thee all night until the morning.

Live as God's Just People

Workers in the ancient world typically are paid on a daily basis. Thus to withhold a worker's pay *all night until the morning* is mistreatment. In ancient times, it was easier for employers to mistreat employees since government oversight was not what it is today. Mistreatment happens when employers underpay (or simply don't pay) workers, when employers lie about the agreed upon compensation, etc. Genesis 29–31 tells us how Laban deceived and mistreated Jacob, his own relative, when Jacob was in Laban's employ. In a world full of Labans, Jacob's descendants are called to be a witness to God's justice when it comes to labor (compare Jeremiah 22:13).

The fact that fraud against workers still exists in New Testament times (James 5:4) indicates a continuing problem. Jesus repeats the imperative "defraud not" in Mark 10:19.

14. Thou shalt not curse the deaf, nor put a stumblingblock before the blind, but shalt fear thy God: I am the LORD.

Israel is called to respect the dignity of those with disabilities. Think of what an act of cowardice it is to curse to their face those who cannot hear the curse or to place obstacles before those who cannot see! Yet some find perverse pleasure in doing so. This happens not only to those who are physically impaired, but also to those who may be thought of as figuratively blind or deaf—naïve people who end up being easy targets of those with more education or more experience.

This passage implies that taking advantage of people reveals no fear of God on the part of the perpetrator. Those who truly fear the Lord know that He sees everything and that He calls every deed into account. They know that He calls His people to honor Him by treating "the least of these" (Matthew 25:40, 45) with the dignity they possess in God's sight. If they cannot treat with respect those whom they can see, how can they respect God, whom they cannot see (1 John 4:20)?

❧ GRAPPLING WITH "THOU SHALT NOT" ❧

At one time the question, "What does the Bible say about such-and-such?" would be answered with an authoritative—and occasionally legalistically expressed—statement. The answer might

Visual for Lesson 2. *Point to this visual as you ask, "What was a time when you had a difficult time balancing justice with compassion?"*

include the quotation of a Bible verse. Better yet, the answer might be several verses quoted from different places in the Bible to demonstrate that the answer is really what the Bible teaches and not just one or two proof texts pulled out of context.

Then some Christians began to think that certain instructions to people in an ancient culture might not apply literally to modern life. We began to hear, "Well, I think what the Bible means by that is . . ." followed by a sometimes well-reasoned attempt to apply scriptural principles to modern circumstances. Thinking about the instructions on treating the deaf and blind (v. 14), how should Christians deal with this command when the categories of disabilities that society recognizes have increased vastly in number? Should we share society's changing sensitivity to such handicaps?

Then comes the more recent shift to "Well, I feel . . ." That is often followed by an explanation that has more to do with one's knee-jerk emotions than with what God has spoken. As we wrestle with this issue in good conscience, we keep in mind that what God thinks about something trumps any way we may "feel" about it. Our goal is to think God's thought after Him. —C. R. B.

D. Justice (vv. 15, 16)

15. Ye shall do no unrighteousness in judgment: thou shalt not respect the person of the poor, nor honor the person of the mighty: but in righteousness shalt thou judge thy neighbour.

This verse reminds us that true justice is impartial. Though worldly justice is tilted toward the mighty, God's standards are binding on all people, regardless of social or economic status. God's ideal is a system of justice that reflects His own unbiased righteousness. Neither *the poor* nor *the mighty* are to receive preferential treatment because of their status (see last week's lesson).

16. Thou shalt not go up and down as a talebearer among thy people: neither shalt thou stand against the blood of thy neighbour; I am the LORD.

The first half of this verse instructs God's people not to spread lies, and the second half indicates the reason: that by misrepresenting the truth, one can endanger another's life. For an example of this happening, see 1 Kings 21.

James 3 reminds us that the human tongue is dangerous. God will hold us accountable not only for intentionally malicious words, but also for careless, idle words (Matthew 12:36). If the Israelites are to demonstrate God's will in this world, they must expunge wrong speech. The life of the innocent neighbor is more important than the fleeting satisfaction of gossip or slander.

E. Love (vv. 17, 18)

17, 18. Thou shalt not hate thy brother in thine heart: thou shalt in any wise rebuke thy neighbour, and not suffer sin upon him. Thou shalt not avenge, nor bear any grudge against the children of thy people, but thou shalt love thy neighbour as thyself: I am the LORD.

A society that shares food generously, speaks truth plainly, honors dignity routinely, and practices justice daily will be a remarkable society! Yet such a society could still fall short of God's design if His people fail to love one another. This idea is central to the Old Testament law and is still binding on Christians today (Matthew 19:19; James 2:8). It moves beyond merely not hating one another. It moves from correcting one another's sins (Matthew 18:15) to dropping any ill will against another, to loving the neighbor as oneself. The Israelites are called, as Christians after them, to look after the needs of their neighbors. "Neighbor love" summarizes God's law (Romans 12:9).

II. How to Treat Strangers
(LEVITICUS 19:33-36)
A. Love (vv. 33, 34)

33, 34. And if a stranger sojourn with thee in your land, ye shall not vex him. But the stranger that dwelleth with you shall be unto you as one born among you, and thou shalt love him as thyself; for ye were strangers in the land of Egypt: I am the LORD your God.

The bulk of Israel's laws focuses on how the people should order their lives together and with God. The ultimate purpose is to be God's vehicle of blessing to all nations. But looking forward to this ideal first requires looking back. The Israelites had been foreigners in Egypt. They know first-hand what it is like to be "strangers."

So as God brings the Israelites into the promised land, He calls them to be hospitable to the non-Israelites who choose to be part of "the congregation of Israel" (see again the discussion of Exodus 23:9 in last week's lesson). More than that, He calls them to love those strangers in the same way they love one another.

B. Justice (vv. 35, 36)

35, 36. Ye shall do no unrighteousness in judgment, in meteyard, in weight, or in measure. Just balances, just weights, a just ephah, and a just hin, shall ye have: I am the LORD your God, which brought you out of the land of Egypt.

An *ephah* is a dry measure, equal to about six-tenths of a bushel; a *hin* is a liquid measure, equal to about a gallon. A *meteyard* is a measuring rod. Proverbs 11:1 and 20:23 speak of God's abhorrence of dishonest balance scales and weights. The love that God calls the Israelites to show strangers must manifest itself in concrete acts of justice. Strangers are vulnerable to being cheated since they have no family connections. Crooked merchants are less likely to cheat family members than to cheat strangers, so God calls for righteous measurements in economic transactions. This is love in action.

The Israelites are instructed not to intermarry with foreigners of the land (Deuteronomy 7:3; Joshua 23:12). Nor are foreigners to take part in governance (Deuteronomy 17:15). But a common point of contact is the marketplace. Economic transactions with non-Israelites are allowed (Deuteronomy 14:21; 15:3; 23:20). Both Israelites and non-Israelites may ply their trades, buying and selling to their neighbors.

The dishonest merchant has two sets of weights —one set that is honest and one set that is dishonest—for weighing out transactions. Sensing the stranger's vulnerability, the crooked merchant will use the dishonest set of weights so the vulnerable person will either pay more for purchases or take less for goods sold. The Israelites may have been treated this way in Egypt. God calls the Israelites to extend the same justice to all (see Deuteronomy 25:13, 14; Proverbs 20:10, 23).

> **What Do You Think?**
> How are dishonest business transactions today similar to and different from those of the ancient world? How do we stay on guard against either perpetrating or falling victim to clever new schemes?
> *Talking Points for Your Discussion*
> - Predatory lending practices
> - Insider trading
> - The problem of rationalization

III. What Perspective to Have
(Leviticus 19:37)

37. Therefore shall ye observe all my statutes, and all my judgments, and do them: I am the Lord.

What the Israelites owe God is simple: they owe Him obedience. This obedience is not about earn-

ing God's favor. It is about mission. If God's people observe all of His laws and live out His justice, then God can use them to accomplish His mission of being a blessing to all nations.

All is the key word in this verse. God's set of laws is not a smorgasbord of optional, pick-and-choose life principles. It is a complete way of life. It all hangs together because no part of human existence is outside of God's jurisdiction.

> **What Do You Think?**
> How can we obey God's laws fully without becoming legalistic in the process?
> *Talking Points for Your Discussion*
> - Issues of motive (Matthew 6:5)
> - Issues of the spirit of God's law (Luke 11:42)
> - The problem of equating human tradition with God's law (Mark 7:5-13)

Conclusion
A. Legitimate Spirituality

There are many forms of spirituality. Some focus on self as the source and destination of spiritual development. Others acknowledge a "higher power" beyond oneself, making submission to that power central to the spiritual walk. But legitimate spirituality is represented in today's passage.

This passage acknowledges that the Lord is the one who knows best. But personal submission to God is not just about loving Him. Right relationship with God includes right relationship with others. Serving Him requires loving one another. We do for one another what God would do if He were here personally.

B. Prayer

Lord, You have called us to a life of justice that demands more than we may prefer to give. Please soften our hearts and open our eyes. Help us see the life that You have set before us as the wonderful gift it is. Please triumph over our fears and replace them with humble obedience, which is what You require of us. In Jesus' name, amen.

C. Thought to Remember
Serve God on His terms.

INVOLVEMENT LEARNING

Some of the activities below are also found in the helpful student book, Adult Bible Class.
Don't forget to download the free reproducible page from www.standardlesson.com to enhance your lesson!

Into the Lesson

Place in chairs copies of the Searching for Life-Changing Words activity from the reproducible page, which you can download. Learners can work on this as they arrive.

Write these nine words on nine slips of paper, one each: *Love thy neighbour as thyself. I am the Lord.* Use capital letters and punctuation as given. Put the nine slips into an envelope. Make enough envelopes so that each group of three to four learners will have one set of the nine puzzle pieces. Distribute envelopes and say, "These envelopes contain one of the most familiar commands in the Bible. Who can be the first to unscramble the message?"

After the correct answer is given, ask, "Where does this command occur originally?" *(answer: Leviticus 19:18)* "Where do we find this statement in the New Testament?" *(answers: Matthew 19:19; 22:39; Mark 12:31; Luke 10:27; Romans 13:9; Galatians 5:14; and James 2:8)* Say, "The importance of this command should be quite apparent. Today's text provides examples of how to live it."

Into the Word

Prepare in advance three posters with the following headings, one each: *What God's People Owe One Another (Leviticus 19:9-18) / What God's People Owe All People (Leviticus 19:33-36) / What God's People Owe God (Leviticus 19:37).* Divide the first two posters into two columns each. Head each of the first columns "Israelites Owed . . ." and both second columns "Modern Applications."

Read the Scripture for the first poster, then ask the class to help you fill in the first column, based on what they see in the text. (Answers may include the ideas of honesty, dignity, justice, and love.) Then ask your class to help you fill in the second column. Read James 2:1-8. Note that God still calls His people to practice fairness and justice.

Complete the second poster as you did the first. Answers for the first column may include love, jus-

tice, fairness, and honesty. As you work on completing the second column, ask, "Why would God want us to treat nonbelievers this way? What are possible outcomes of this kind of behavior?"

Read aloud the single verse for the third poster. Then ask the following questions: 1. What is different about what the Israelites owed God from what they owed others? Why is this significant? 2. What is the danger of not practicing *all*? Jot answers on the poster board.

Into Life

Pose the following discussion questions. Jot responses on the board.

1. Why does God emphasize compassion, justice, dignity, and love? *(Answers can revolve around issues of a strong social structure, prevention of uncontrolled greed, and embracing proper values.)*

2. What are the major messages coming from this text to (a) our church's finance ministry? (b) our church's ministerial staff and church elders? (c) our church's benevolence ministry? and (d) you? (List these four categories on the board and jot answers underneath them). When mentioning the benevolence ministry, ask about how to treat a stranger who walks into the church office asking for cash to buy a tank of gas. Push deeper by asking how the response to the stranger would be the same as or different from a response to a church member who asks for help with utility bills.

Give each person an inexpensive, pocket-sized notebook. Say, "Use this to keep a log for the week ahead of every act of compassion (1) directed toward you, (2) you see directed toward others, and (3) you perform. At the conclusion of the week, mentally 'give back' the log to God, thanking Him for His wisdom in teaching you this important discipline."

Distribute copies of the Acting with Compassion activity from the reproducible page, which you can download, as learners depart.

CELEBRATE JUBILEE

DEVOTIONAL READING: **Nehemiah 1:5-11**
BACKGROUND SCRIPTURE: **Leviticus 25**

LEVITICUS 25:8-12, 25, 35-40, 47, 48, 55

8 And thou shalt number seven sabbaths of years unto thee, seven times seven years; and the space of the seven sabbaths of years shall be unto thee forty and nine years.

9 Then shalt thou cause the trumpet of the jubile to sound on the tenth day of the seventh month, in the day of atonement shall ye make the trumpet sound throughout all your land.

10 And ye shall hallow the fiftieth year, and proclaim liberty throughout all the land unto all the inhabitants thereof: it shall be a jubile unto you; and ye shall return every man unto his possession, and ye shall return every man unto his family.

11 A jubile shall that fiftieth year be unto you: ye shall not sow, neither reap that which groweth of itself in it, nor gather the grapes in it of thy vine undressed.

12 For it is the jubile; it shall be holy unto you: ye shall eat the increase thereof out of the field.

. . . .

25 If thy brother be waxen poor, and hath sold away some of his possession, and if any of his kin come to redeem it, then shall he redeem that which his brother sold.

. . . .

35 And if thy brother be waxen poor, and fallen in decay with thee; then thou shalt relieve him: yea, though he be a stranger, or a sojourner; that he may live with thee.

36 Take thou no usury of him, or increase: but fear thy God; that thy brother may live with thee.

37 Thou shalt not give him thy money upon usury, nor lend him thy victuals for increase.

38 I am the LORD your God, which brought you forth out of the land of Egypt, to give you the land of Canaan, and to be your God.

39 And if thy brother that dwelleth by thee be waxen poor, and be sold unto thee; thou shalt not compel him to serve as a bondservant:

40 But as an hired servant, and as a sojourner, he shall be with thee, and shall serve thee unto the year of jubile.

. . . .

47 And if a sojourner or stranger wax rich by thee, and thy brother that dwelleth by him wax poor, and sell himself unto the stranger or sojourner by thee, or to the stock of the stranger's family:

48 After that he is sold he may be redeemed again; one of his brethren may redeem him:

. . . .

55 For unto me the children of Israel are servants; they are my servants whom I brought forth out of the land of Egypt: I am the LORD your God.

KEY VERSE

Ye shall hallow the fiftieth year, and proclaim liberty throughout all the land unto all the inhabitants thereof: it shall be a jubile unto you. —**Leviticus 25:10**

GOD CALLS FOR JUSTICE

Unit 1: Justice Defined

LESSONS 1–4

LESSON AIMS

After participating in this lesson, each student will be able to:

1. Summarize the ideal practice of the Year of Jubilee.

2. Compare and contrast the ideal of the Year of Jubilee with modern proposals of economic justice.

3. Suggest some contemporary methods of helping the poor and disadvantaged that the church can practice and that reflect the principles of Jubilee.

LESSON OUTLINE

Introduction

A. Emancipation Proclamation

America's Emancipation Proclamation is often remembered as the official declaration of Abraham Lincoln to end slavery in America. But things were much more complicated than that. The proclamation was issued not once, but twice (in 1862 and 1863), and only certain states actually were affected by these executive orders. Nonetheless, the Emancipation Proclamation served as a clarion call in its day for the liberation of persons who were deemed to be the property of others.

In Christian memory, human liberation goes back much further. In Exodus 8:1, the Lord issued His famous charge to Moses, "Go unto Pharaoh, and say unto him, Thus saith the Lord, Let my people go, that they may serve me." Indeed, this prior act of deliverance loomed large in the imaginations of American slaves who sought to be released. Though the similarities between these events should not be overstated, what is important for our purposes is that God did not liberate His people from slavery so they would turn around and enslave one another. To counteract any tendency to do so, God designed an economic framework that corrected the economic practices that could drive people into economic slavery.

Last week we saw this in laws that required Israelites to care for their poor neighbors and leave food in the fields for them to harvest. Yet some people would still find themselves in hard times, needing to take refuge under the care of fellow Israelites. So God erected a giant guardrail within the social and economic vision He had for His people. That guardrail was *the Year of Jubilee.*

B. Lesson Background

The Year of Jubilee is best understood in light of the broader Sabbath laws, which are rooted in God's creation of the world (Genesis 1, 2). God created the world in six days, and He rested on the seventh. When God rescued the Israelites from slavery in Egypt, He gave them a calendar that reflected that rest in concrete ways. The Israelites were to complete all their work in six days so that they could rest on the seventh as God did (Exodus 20:8-11; Leviticus 23:3). The original Sabbath (which means "ceasing") was thus God's gift to His people so they could enjoy His gift of life. It was a gift for all Israelites as well as for the animals.

As Leviticus 25:1-7 makes clear, the Sabbath principle was not limited to the seventh day. It also extended to a seventh-year rest. God instructed the Israelites to sow their fields for only six years. He vowed to so bless them on year six that they would have enough to carry them through the seventh year. Under this legislation, all who lived in the land, the land itself, and even the animals rested an entire year. For a full year, the people could enjoy the goodness of life in God's creation. But God's Sabbath laws did not end here. We see the Sabbath principle extended to an even greater degree in today's passage.

I. Concept of Jubilee
(LEVITICUS 25:8-12)

A. Calculation and Proclamation (vv. 8, 9)

8. And thou shalt number seven sabbaths of years unto thee, seven times seven years; and the space of the seven sabbaths of years shall be unto thee forty and nine years.

As noted in the Lesson Background, every seven years the Israelites are to rest for a full year. This is ecologically sensitive insofar as it allows the soil to replenish its natural resources. It is socially sensitive insofar as the poor will not be denied the rest and relaxation that wealth affords the few who possess it. It is spiritually sensitive insofar as God's people are given more time to worship God, enjoy His gifts, and reflect on His will.

Yet God doesn't stop here. He further requires counting off every seven cycles of Sabbath years and sets apart the fiftieth year to be especially significant. The fiftieth year is known as *the Year of Jubilee,* as we shall see below.

HOW TO SAY IT

jubile	*ju*-buh-lee.
Leviticus	Leh-*vit*-ih-kus.
victuals	*vih*-tulz.
Yom Kippur	Yom Kih-*purr.*

9. Then shalt thou cause the trumpet of the jubile to sound on the tenth day of the seventh month, in the day of atonement shall ye make the trumpet sound throughout all your land.

Given the importance of the seventh day and year, it is fitting that *the seventh month* (late September and early October to us) is also special. The first day of this month is commemorated as a day of rest and offerings (Leviticus 23:24, 25). The people cease working on the tenth day and celebrate the Day of Atonement (23:27-31); this particular day is also described as "a sabbath of rest" (23:32). On the fifteenth day, the people cease work at the start of the seven-day Festival of Booths or Tabernacles (23:34).

The tenth day of the seventh month of the forty-ninth year is set apart by a trumpet blast. The trumpet signals God's special presence (Exodus 19:19; 20:18; Numbers 10:9). Perhaps we would expect the trumpet to sound for the Year of Jubilee on the first day of the first month. But the fact that it sounds on the Day of Atonement (Hebrew *Yom Kippur*) indicates that God has something very special in store. The Day of Atonement is explained fully in Leviticus 16:29-34.

B. Consecration and Restriction (vv. 10-12)

10. And ye shall hallow the fiftieth year, and proclaim liberty throughout all the land unto all the inhabitants thereof: it shall be a jubile unto you; and ye shall return every man unto his possession, and ye shall return every man unto his family.

As the Day of Atonement means a clean slate with regard to sin, the Year of Jubilee means a new start in an economic sense. God's desire is that Israelite clans and tribes are to maintain possession of the property that God assigns them (Leviticus 25:23; compare Numbers 26:1-27; Joshua 13–21; Judges 21:24; 1 Kings 21:1-3). Even so, some Israelites will fall into hardship and have to sell land to pay off debt or provide for their families. As hardship befalls more families, it inevitably happens that those in a position to buy property end up with more and more land. Many people will find themselves under the thumb of the rich. The debt-slavery this causes will be "Egypt all over again."

God has a corrective plan. The Year of Jubilee is God's deliberate strategy for breaking the destructive economic cycle. The trumpet blast signals that whoever has had to surrender land can return *unto his possession* and *unto his family*. Those who have acquired additional land have to let it return to the original owner. But is it really fair to force the new "owner" of the land to give it back without compensation? The details of how this works fairly are given in Leviticus 25:14, 15 (not in today's text).

❧ IS IT REALLY THAT CURIOUS? ❧

Perhaps we find ancient Israel's ideal practice of property ownership to be curious and unthinkable today. But modern society has its own curiosities in this regard! Take the case from 2009 of a Pennsylvania couple who for 30 years owned a piece of property a few miles from their home only to find out that they didn't really "own" it!

When the couple tried to sell the land, they discovered that some friends who lived adjacent to the property had been using it for more than 20 years. Because the owners had done nothing to stop the use, the neighbors claimed *squatter's rights* —the popular term for what the law calls *adverse possession*.

Several legal standards determine what adverse possession is. Acts such as mowing the grass, planting shrubbery, or installing a fence across the property line can trigger the principle of adverse possession. The rightful owners must take action to prevent it, something that the Pennsylvania couple didn't do. The end result was that the "squatters" ended up with 55 percent, the owners' attorney 25 percent, and the owners 20 percent.

We may have trouble deciding which is more startling: the jubilee concept or the case of the Pennsylvania couple! But in reflecting on this, we keep in mind that the underlying principle in the case of ancient Israel was that only God owned the land. Were we to adopt that mind-set today (even without the particulars of the jubilee requirement), how would our lives be different?   —C. R. B.

11, 12. A jubile shall that fiftieth year be unto you: ye shall not sow, neither reap that which groweth of itself in it, nor gather the grapes in it of thy vine undressed. For it is the jubile; it shall be holy unto you: ye shall eat the increase thereof out of the field.

The Year of Jubilee is also an additional year of rest. It is a second consecutive Sabbath year since the previous year—the forty-ninth year—is one of the seventh years. The poor who return are able to enjoy their first year back. But this seems to present a logistical problem. If land is not worked for two consecutive years, then a full harvest will not be available until the following year. How can one year's harvest (in the forty-eighth year) provide enough food for more than two years following? Leviticus 25:20-22 (not in today's text) provides God's answer: God himself will provide enough produce in the forty-eighth year to sustain the people for three years.

> **What Do You Think?**
> In what ways do God's values regarding work and rest agree and conflict with modern cultural values? How can you bring your own values on work and rest into line with God's?
> *Talking Points for Your Discussion*
> - Forty-hour work week
> - Vacations
> - Sabbatical
> - "All work and no play make Jack a dull boy"

II. Redemption of Land
(LEVITICUS 25:25)

25. If thy brother be waxen poor, and hath sold away some of his possession, and if any of his kin come to redeem it, then shall he redeem that which his brother sold.

The Israelites have not yet entered the promised land to take possession of it at this time. After that happens, the leaders are to parcel out the land proportionally by lot (Numbers 26:52-56). By the end of this process, each family will have its own land. The goal (actually, requirement) is to keep it in the tribe (36:1-9). The Year of Jubilee ensures that this goal is met at least once every 50 years.

But what about the time between the jubilees? God's answer is the redemption system. When a particular family loses the ability to manage its property, the nearest kin has first rights to purchase it. This serves at least two purposes. First, it keeps property among relatives. Second, a blood relative may be willing to restore land to a poverty-stricken Israelite even before the Year of Jubilee rolls around. This practice is most popularly illustrated in Ruth 4.

What Do You Think?

What can we do to assist family members or fellow Christians who have lost jobs or are otherwise experiencing financial setbacks?

Talking Points for Your Discussion

- Identifying obstacles to assisting
- Grappling with the issue of accountability
- Giving assistance with and without strings attached
- Applying 2 Thessalonians 3:6-14

III. Rescue of People
(Leviticus 25:35-40, 47, 48, 55)
A. Providing Support (vv. 35-38)

35. And if thy brother be waxen poor, and fallen in decay with thee; then thou shalt relieve him: yea, though he be a stranger, or a sojourner; that he may live with thee.

When poverty-stricken Israelites are forced to sell their land, they will need a new place to stay. So God calls the other Israelites to open their hearts to those who are *waxen poor, and fallen in decay with thee*. Those with land must create space in the property of their inheritance.

The phrase *though he be* means "as if he were." To be treated as *a stranger, or a sojourner* means the poverty-stricken Israelite will have to rent land. For some, this will mean relocating to the land of someone who is hospitable. For others, it will mean continuing to work on their former property while watching much of the land's produce go to the purchaser. What is most important is that the poverty-stricken family remains on Israelite turf, which is the idea of *that he may live with thee.*

36, 37. Take thou no usury of him, or increase: but fear thy God; that thy brother may live with thee. Thou shalt not give him thy money upon usury, nor lend him thy victuals for increase.

Some Israelites may be tempted to take advantage of their disenfranchised relatives. So God requires that those who provide relief must not jack up the prices or exact interest *(usury)*. The purpose of loans of money or food *(victuals)* is to help neighbors get through tough times, not to profit from someone else's misery.

What Do You Think?

What was the most helpful assistance you ever received? What made that assistance more helpful than other instances?

Talking Points for Your Discussion

- Assistance from a Christian source that met an immediate need or provided a long-term solution
- Assistance from a secular source that met an immediate need or provided a long-term solution

---

38. I am the Lord your God, which brought you forth out of the land of Egypt, to give you the land of Canaan, and to be your God.

God now provides some perspective. Any Israelite who starts to get miserly and cold-hearted toward someone in need should pause and think of what God himself has done. It is He who has *brought you forth out of the land of Egypt, to give you the land of Canaan.* The Israelites must not forget that their hard work does not make the land theirs. It remains God's property (Leviticus 25:23).

God does not free the Israelites and grant them land so that they can build miniature kingdoms for themselves. Rather, He does it in order to create a people whose life together will reflect His justice and compassion. This is their heritage as God's "peculiar people" (Deuteronomy 14:2; 26:18).

B. Providing Employment (vv. 39, 40)

39, 40. And if thy brother that dwelleth by thee be waxen poor, and be sold unto thee; thou shalt not compel him to serve as a bondservant: but as an hired servant, and as a sojourner, he shall be with thee, and shall serve thee unto the year of jubile.

To avoid falling into the pattern of the nations around them, the Israelites need to give careful consideration regarding how they treat the poor. It is OK for Israelites to employ one another as hired hands. It is not OK to make them slaves. Employers are to regard their hired hands as temporary travelers who eventually will return to their own land. Each poor person has the same future in God's economic plan for Israel: restoration to his or her original land, which is God's land.

> **What Do You Think?**
> What are some implications of hiring a family member or a fellow Christian?
> *Talking Points for Your Discussion*
> - Unique risks or challenges
> - Unique benefits

C. Providing Redemption (vv. 47, 48, 55)

47, 48. And if a sojourner or stranger wax rich by thee, and thy brother that dwelleth by him wax poor, and sell himself unto the stranger or sojourner by thee, or to the stock of the stranger's family: after that he is sold he may be redeemed again; one of his brethren may redeem him.

The *sojourner or stranger* is a non-Israelite. The continuing presence of such foreigners among the covenant people was presumed when God gave instructions for celebrating Passover (Exodus 12:19, 48, 49). Such people are not to be mistreated (Exodus 22:21; 23:9; Deuteronomy 24:17; etc.).

Scripture is clear that the Israelites are supposed to expel all foreigners from the promised land so God's people will not be corrupted by pagan practices (Deuteronomy 7:16). However, the reference to *sojourner or stranger* here probably is to those foreigners who choose to identify themselves with God's covenant people by accepting and obeying God's laws (Numbers 9:14; 15:13-16). Ruth is an example of someone like this (Ruth 1:4, 16). There are many passages that require such foreigners to live by the same standards as the Israelites (Leviticus 16:29; 17:8-16; 20:2; etc.).

The case of a foreigner having to provide a financial bailout of an Israelite makes us wonder why the kin of the impoverished Israelite did not do so! But financial assistance from foreigners is presumed to happen in the future by the two verses before us. Yet God places limits on this. There is to be no debt-slavery either for a fellow Israelite or a foreigner. Should Israelites sell themselves into the hands of wealthy foreigners, God's people are to redeem them.

55. For unto me the children of Israel are servants; they are my servants whom I brought forth out of the land of Egypt: I am the LORD your God.

The Israelites must not be enslaved by foreigners because the Israelites already have a master. The Lord who delivered them from Egypt possesses sole rights to them. God later sells them temporarily into the hands of the Babylonians, but that is His right.

> **What Do You Think?**
> What attitudes keep you from assisting those in need? How will you correct this problem?
> *Talking Points for Your Discussion*
> - Psalm 24:1
> - Mark 7:9-13
> - Luke 6:38

❧ SERVANTS TO WHOM? ❧

Much of what Americans buy—from clothing to technology to automobiles to food—is produced elsewhere in the world. The value of products and services consumed in 2007 in excess of what America produced that year was greater than the gross domestic product of Brazil!

Without getting into the complexities of economic theory, the result is that America is becoming more and more "in debt" to other countries. Economists debate how long the situation can continue before such indebtedness to foreign countries begins to control America's foreign and domestic policy (if it isn't doing so already).

In ancient Israel, God's concern regarding "debt slavery" extended down to its effects on individual Israelites. God wanted the Israelites to be *His* servants, not owing their allegiance to others. That fact should cause us to question whose servants *we* really are. Do we serve God or an addiction to material things that results in ever-increasing credit card debt? Remember: "the borrower is servant to the lender" (Proverbs 22:7).   —C. R. B.

Conclusion

A. Jubilee Ideal and Practice

Jubilee was to be the year in which (1) liberty was proclaimed for all Israelites who were enslaved for debt; (2) the remission of debt occurred; (3) land was restored to families who had sold it in the previous 49 years; and (4) the land had to lie fallow. This is described in today's text and referred to in Leviticus 27:16-25 and Numbers 36:4.

We may wonder if Israel ever practiced jubilee as a nation. We don't really have any firm evidence that they did (Isaiah 37:30 is a possible reference to jubilee ideas). We know that the generation that followed Moses rebelled against God (Judges 2:10-13). The lack of reference to jubilee in the historical narratives of the Old Testament does not mean that jubilee was not practiced. That would be an argument from silence. We simply do not know.

After Solomon's reign, the kingdoms of Israel and Judah were ruled by many kings who would not have welcomed the practice of jubilee. Other ancient Near Eastern kingdoms did practice the remission of debts at the accession of a new king, but nothing exactly like jubilee. Despite its possible disuse, the prophets appealed to the jubilee ideal metaphorically as part of the coming kingdom of God (example: Isaiah 61:1-3).

B. New Testament Jubilee

Jesus launched His public ministry with His own emancipation proclamation: "The Spirit of the Lord is on me, because he has anointed me to preach good news to the poor. He has sent me to proclaim freedom for the prisoners and recovery of sight for the blind, to release the oppressed, to proclaim the year of the Lord's favor" (Luke 4:18, 19; quoting Isaiah 61:1, 2). This *year of the Lord's favor* is nothing less than jubilee. Christ frees those held captive to sin. He calls His followers to announce this freedom.

God's freedom call in Christ must never be ignored. It is central to the identity of Christians.

Visual for Lesson 3. *Point to this visual as you ask, "In what way does this visual remind us of the new beginning we have in Christ?"*

As the church proclaims the eternal jubilee available in Christ, she needs to discern whether she is practicing an earthly jubilee ideal as Jesus would have us do. Yet as we engage in prayer and soul-searching in this regard, we will be careful not to "read into" the New Testament an Old Testament law that was operative only for ancient Israel.

The jubilee principle as stated by Paul to the Corinthians is this: "At the present time your plenty will supply what they need, so that in turn their plenty will supply what you need. Then there will be equality, as it is written: 'He who gathered much did not have too much, and he who gathered little did not have too little'" (2 Corinthians 8:14, 15; quoting Exodus 16:18). Practicing this ideal will be easier when we come to grips with the fact that we are "aliens and strangers" (1 Peter 2:11).

C. Prayer

Lord God, we thank You for redeeming us through Christ. We sometimes forget what is good for us as we enslave ourselves to "things" and to our own selfish desires. Please give us the boldness to name slavery when we see it, to assist one another when we need it, and to proclaim Your freedom at all times to all people. In Jesus' name, amen.

D. Thought to Remember

Live freely and free those in bondage.

INVOLVEMENT LEARNING

Some of the activities below are also found in the helpful student book, Adult Bible Class.
Don't forget to download the free reproducible page from www.standardlesson.com to enhance your lesson!

Into the Lesson

Form groups of three to five learners to share circumstances in which they would have liked to have had the opportunity to start over. Some may also share times when they *did* receive such an opportunity. After a few minutes, transition to Bible study by saying, "There may be many circumstances in which we may wish for a fresh start: rearing children, dealing with finances, etc. Today's study will reveal God's plan for a fresh start for the people and land of ancient Israel."

Into the Word

Alternative 1: Early in the week, recruit two individuals to prepare brief presentations. The first mini-lecture will describe the principles of Sabbath laws that are the background for the Year of Jubilee. Give a copy of the Lesson Background to the person preparing this. This presentation is to occur before the reading of today's text. After the reading of the lesson text (Leviticus 25:8-12, 25, 35-40, 47, 48, 55), introduce your second presenter to describe the Year of Jubilee. Give the second presenter a Bible dictionary that describes this event and a copy of the lesson commentary.

After the second presentation, ask the following questions: 1. What problems needed to be resolved in making the Year of Jubilee work for the Israelites? 2. Was the Year of Jubilee fair to everyone? Why, or why not? 3. Who, if anyone, would "take a loss" when the Year of Jubilee rolled around? (Hint: See Leviticus 25:15, 16, not in today's text.)

Alternative 2: Ask research groups of three to five learners to do one of the following two assignments. If your class is large enough, form more than two teams and give duplicate assignments. Try to have even numbers of groups. Give the groups these written task descriptions plus the resources implied: *Team A:* Read the Lesson Background and today's text. Discuss the Sabbath laws that are the background for the Year of Jubilee described in today's study. Select a team spokesperson to summarize your findings. *Team B:* Read today's text and an article from a Bible dictionary describing the Year of Jubilee. Be prepared to share the principles and activities of the Year of Jubilee.

After teams have researched their tasks, ask each team to join another team that studied a different assignment and exchange information discovered. Follow this activity by asking the questions in *Alternative 1,* above.

Option: If your class needs more of a discussion regarding the facts of the Year of Jubilee (and less discussion of background, implications, etc.), distribute copies of the Discovering the Facts activity from the reproducible page, which you can download. You may wish to use this in place of discussing the principles of Sabbath laws.

Into Life

Ask learners to discuss the similarities and the differences between the principles of the Year of Jubilee and today's economic and business structures and practices. These questions may be helpful in stimulating discussion: 1. Is the jubilee principle of giving the land a rest important today, and do we have any modern provisions for that principle? 2. What obstacles are built into our structures that make it difficult for people to start over economically? 3. What vehicles exist for giving people a fresh start today? How do they work? 4. What general principles of the Year of Jubilee may be helpful in today's world, if any?

Ask a church leader to share (1) a success story in helping someone make a fresh start and/or (2) a description of your church's benevolence program. Be sure the speaker understands that the presentation is to be brief—limit of 10 minutes.

As learners depart, distribute copies of the My Journal Notes activity from the reproducible page, which you can download, as take-home work.

LOVE GOD;
LOVE PEOPLE

DEVOTIONAL READING: Micah 6:1-8
BACKGROUND SCRIPTURE: Deuteronomy 10:1-22; 16:18-20

DEUTERONOMY 10:12-22

12 And now, Israel, what doth the LORD thy God require of thee, but to fear the LORD thy God, to walk in all his ways, and to love him, and to serve the LORD thy God with all thy heart and with all thy soul,

13 To keep the commandments of the LORD, and his statutes, which I command thee this day for thy good?

14 Behold, the heaven and the heaven of heavens is the LORD's thy God, the earth also, with all that therein is.

15 Only the LORD had a delight in thy fathers to love them, and he chose their seed after them, even you above all people, as it is this day.

16 Circumcise therefore the foreskin of your heart, and be no more stiffnecked.

17 For the LORD your God is God of gods, and Lord of lords, a great God, a mighty, and a terrible, which regardeth not persons, nor taketh reward:

18 He doth execute the judgment of the fatherless and widow, and loveth the stranger, in giving him food and raiment.

19 Love ye therefore the stranger: for ye were strangers in the land of Egypt.

20 Thou shalt fear the LORD thy God; him shalt thou serve, and to him shalt thou cleave, and swear by his name.

21 He is thy praise, and he is thy God, that hath done for thee these great and terrible things, which thine eyes have seen.

22 Thy fathers went down into Egypt with threescore and ten persons; and now the LORD thy God hath made thee as the stars of heaven for multitude.

DEUTERONOMY 16:18-20

18 Judges and officers shalt thou make thee in all thy gates, which the LORD thy God giveth thee, throughout thy tribes: and they shall judge the people with just judgment.

19 Thou shalt not wrest judgment; thou shalt not respect persons, neither take a gift: for a gift doth blind the eyes of the wise, and pervert the words of the righteous.

20 That which is altogether just shalt thou follow, that thou mayest live, and inherit the land which the LORD thy God giveth thee.

KEY VERSES

And now, Israel, what doth the LORD thy God require of thee, but to fear the LORD thy God, to walk in all his ways, and to love him, and to serve the LORD thy God with all thy heart and with all thy soul, to keep the commandments of the LORD, and his statutes, which I command thee this day for thy good? —**Deuteronomy 10:12, 13**

GOD CALLS FOR JUSTICE

Unit 1: Justice Defined

LESSONS 1–4

LESSON AIMS

After participating in this lesson, each student will be able to:

1. Define "fear of the Lord."

2. Explain how fear of the Lord relates to justice.

3. Participate in a role-play that dramatizes acting in the fear of the Lord to address an unjust situation in a modern office.

LESSON OUTLINE

Introduction

A. Different Love

Those who do not know the God of Scripture may be confused about the nature of godly love. In a people-to-people sense, *love* often refers to a deep appreciation for another that encourages one to give sacrificially of self. The term *love* is also routinely applied to inanimate objects such as ice cream, television shows, etc. In such cases, *love* means something like "preference for."

In light of this wide range of applications, some people may not be sure what to make of the biblical invitation to love God. Loving the unseen God is necessarily different from loving people, whom we can see and touch. We can express love for people by meeting their needs. God, by contrast, lacks nothing (Psalm 50:9-12); He has no needs that we can meet. Thus it is important for those who strive to love God to pay careful attention to Scriptures such as today's passage, which teach us how to love God.

B. Lesson Background

The word *Deuteronomy* literally means "second law." This points to the fact that this book recounts how Moses gave God's laws to the Israelites a second time. He had to do so because the first generation, which had been taught the law at Mount Sinai, had been forbidden to enter the promised land. That generation lacked the faith to follow God's lead into Canaanite territory. They wished instead to return to Egypt (Numbers 14:1-4). God therefore decided that it would be the following generation to enter the land instead.

Deuteronomy, as the second presentation of the law, brings together much of the legal material in Exodus, Leviticus, and Numbers, but presents it more like a sermon and less like legal code. We see in Deuteronomy that God's just requirements have not changed. But since the people and times have changed, the requirements have been repackaged in such a way as to address the unique needs of the next generation.

Beginning in Deuteronomy 9:4 and continuing though 10:11, Moses stressed to these younger Israelites that there was nothing special about their nation that God should have set it apart for its unique mission. He chose the Israelites by grace. Moses then recounted how God nearly destroyed their parents' generation altogether. Yet because of Moses' plea to spare them, God relented.

After this reality check, Moses set forth God's requirements in concise form. Our passage for today is an overview of the life to which God had called His people.

I. Lord's Requirements
(DEUTERONOMY 10:12-16)
A. Imperatives (vv. 12, 13)

12. And now, Israel, what doth the LORD thy God require of thee, but to fear the LORD thy God, to walk in all his ways, and to love him, and to serve the LORD thy God with all thy heart and with all thy soul.

God's requirements for Israel are summarized in terms of four things the people must do: *fear, walk, love,* and *serve.* What this verse does not clarify is the precise relationship between these terms as Moses uses them. It is tempting to think of these four imperatives as distinct actions and then to interpret each one in light of the aspects of its meaning that do not overlap with the meanings of the others. For example, to *walk* in His ways would focus on living a moral and holy life; to *love* Him would emphasize emotional attachment to God.

But another way of interpreting this verse takes almost an exact opposite approach. This method holds that the intended meaning of each action is what all of them have in common. If we were to sketch their meanings in terms of four overlapping circles, the core meaning in this passage would be where they all overlap. Each imperative may bring unique elements, but these are not the cur-

rent focus. The next verse shows us that this "overlap meaning" approach is probably intended.

13. To keep the commandments of the LORD, and his statutes, which I command thee this day for thy good?

The fifth imperative, *keep,* completes the thought of verse 12. This imperative stands out from the previous four imperatives as the organizing principle of those four: the Israelites cannot claim to *fear* the Lord, *walk* in His ways, *love* Him, or *serve* Him if they refuse to *keep* His commandments.

A careful reading of the rest of Deuteronomy confirms this interpretation. One way to see this is to note every occurrence of the idea of doing something "with all of one's heart and soul." In Deuteronomy 6:5, 6, loving God with one's heart, soul, and might is linked with keeping God's commands. In 11:13, heeding God's commands is linked with loving God and serving Him with all of one's heart and soul. See also Deuteronomy 13:3, 4; 26:16, 17; and 30:2-6, 10.

The unifying principle in all these passages is obedience to God's commands. This principle is the core message of Deuteronomy as a whole. Moses is calling the Israelites of the second generation to align their lives with the commands set forth in this book. God has entrusted to them the keys to the blessed life. He is giving them "inside information" about the way this world is designed to operate. Their mission involves living this out so convincingly that God can use them as a witness to all nations (Deuteronomy 4:5-8).

> **What Do You Think?**
> How have you observed that following God's commands is beneficial for you personally?
> *Talking Points for Your Discussion*
> - In terms of physical health
> - In terms of spiritual health
> - In terms of relationships

HOW TO SAY IT

Canaanites	*Kay*-nun-ites.
Deuteronomy	Due-ter-*ahn*-uh-me.
differentiation	dif-uh-*ren(t)*-she-*a*-shun.
Justitia	*Yus*-tih-tee-uh.
Leviticus	Leh-*vit*-ih-kus.
Moses	*Mo*-zes or *Mo*-zez.

❧ DIFFERENTIATION, GOOD AND BAD ❧

As children mature, they have the need to separate themselves from their parents and become individuals in their own right. This process, which psychologists call *differentiation,* may create parent-child struggles of epic proportions. Sometimes grandparents can be the bridge between the children and their parents, easing the separation process. A comic once noted that, "Grandparents get along so well with their grandchildren because they have a common enemy!"

The humor in that punch line is of the uneasy kind. But if we dig below the humor, we discover a helpful nugget: a grandparent may be able to recognize the differentiation that is taking place because he or she has been through it twice already—once as a child and once as a parent. In a sense, Moses was like this grandparent. First he went through his own traumatic separation process (Exodus 2:11-15). Then he guided the exodus generation in their separation from Egypt—but the differentiation that resulted was the bad kind (Exodus 32; Numbers 14; etc.).

The time came for Moses to teach those of the next generation how to avoid the errors of their parents. Would the resulting differentiation be the good kind or the bad? The passage of time reveals the answer! And so it is with us.   —C. R. B.

B. Facts (vv. 14, 15)

14, 15. Behold, the heaven and the heaven of heavens is the LORD's thy God, the earth also, with all that therein is. Only the LORD had a delight in thy fathers to love them, and he chose their seed after them, even you above all people, as it is this day.

Visual for Lessons 4 & 10. *Have this visual on display as you work your way through the various categories of people mentioned in today's text.*

Before beginning his summary of God's commandments, Moses reminds the Israelites of their special place in God's heart. The God of the entire universe chose the Israelite forefathers and their descendants to be uniquely His. He could have chosen a nation that was already fully established in its land. He could have chosen a nation with a powerful army to subdue His enemies. He could have chosen a nation with a massive trade network to disseminate His decrees. But He didn't. He chose the Israelites instead.

God delights in the Israelites despite the fact that there is nothing inherently good or beautiful in them that is not also in other peoples of the earth. Moses reminds this second generation that they should not take God's favor for granted.

What Do You Think?
  How does being identified as a "chosen one," a
    child of the Almighty, affect your decisions and
    actions?
Talking Points for Your Discussion
  ▪ In exercising your priestly duties (1 Peter 2:9)
  ▪ In how you worship (Ephesians 1:11, 12)
  ▪ In personal holiness (Colossians 3:12)

C. More Imperatives (v. 16)

16. Circumcise therefore the foreskin of your heart, and be no more stiffnecked.

Moses drives his point home with a circumcision analogy. The practice of physical circumcision started over 600 years previously with Abraham (Genesis 17:10-14). It is a covenant sign between God and His people. But a mark of the flesh is not enough. Witness the fact that their circumcised fathers could not enter the promised land due to disobedience. If this generation is to do better, it must go beyond a mark of the flesh to allow God's mark on their inmost being. This is the second time that circumcision of the heart is mentioned in the Bible (the first time is Leviticus 26:41), and it will not be the last (see Deuteronomy 30:6; Jeremiah 4:4; and Romans 2:29).

As Moses speaks, physical circumcision has not been practiced for quite some time (see Joshua 5:2-7). Thus there is no sense of "Now that you have been circumcised physically, take the next step and be circumcised spiritually." For this generation, spiritual (heart) circumcision is first; physical circumcision comes later (again, Joshua 5:2-7). In the Christian era, physical circumcision is irrelevant in a religious sense (1 Corinthians 7:19; Galatians 5:6; 6:15) while spiritual (heart) circumcision remains vital (Romans 2:28, 29; Colossians 2:11).

Does Moses sense resistance among the people of this generation—the same kind of resistance that led to God's displeasure with their parents? Moses cautions the people not to be stiff-necked. They must be pliable and bendable to God's will.

II. Lord's Nature
(Deuteronomy 10:17, 18)
A. Preeminent (v. 17a)

17a. For the LORD your God is God of gods, and Lord of lords, a great God, a mighty, and a terrible.

Moses begins to encapsulate God's unique requirements. The first step is to reaffirm the utter superiority and majesty of Israel's God above all pretender gods and lords. God is the ultimate God and the ultimate Lord. There is none like Him. The word *terrible* has the sense of "inspiring terror."

B. Impartial (v. 17b)

17b. Which regardeth not persons, nor taketh reward.

God is not like us. He does not regard one person as better than another (Acts 10:34), nor can He be influenced by a bribe (*reward;* 2 Chronicles 19:7). Moses is thus teaching the people that God's own character, which is unlike the character of any ruler or god they have previously known, is the foundation to the commands by which He calls them to live.

C. Loving (v. 18)

18. He doth execute the judgment of the fatherless and widow, and loveth the stranger, in giving him food and raiment.

The phrase *He doth execute the judgment* means something like "He stands up for" or "He intercedes for" *the fatherless and widow*. God's own track record is one of love. Foreigners as a group *(the stranger)* are closely linked in God's estimation with the fatherless and the widow. Together they represent those who are most vulnerable. To lose a father or a husband to death may leave a surviving child or widow without support. Such disenfranchised people are therefore God's special concern. They have a special place in His heart; by contrast, the lords of this world routinely push such people to the margins (Mark 12:40).

> **What Do You Think?**
> Who are the disenfranchised today? How can we express love to them?
> *Talking Points for Your Discussion*
> - In our local community
> - In our wider culture
> - In the world

III. Israel's Duty
(Deuteronomy 10:19-21; 16:18-20)
A. To the Stranger (v. 19)

19. Love ye therefore the stranger: for ye were strangers in the land of Egypt.

It says something about Israel's God that the first command Moses lists, which is rooted in God's own character, is that of love. God exhibited His love for strangers by choosing a bunch of *strangers in the land of Egypt* to be His people. If the Israelites are to bear witness to God's love in this world, they must love such persons in turn.

B. To the Lord (vv. 20, 21)

20. Thou shalt fear the LORD thy God; him shalt thou serve, and to him shalt thou cleave, and swear by his name.

In the next few verses, Moses echoes much of what he has said above, with an emphasis on exclusivity. Though the Israelites must be hospitable to strangers, they are to remain firm in their rejection of rival gods and rival masters.

The normal sentence order in Hebrew is verb-subject-object, which contrasts with the English preference for subject-verb-object. In every clause of this verse, however, the object comes first in Hebrew: *the Lord* they shalt fear; *him* they shalt serve; *to him* they shalt cleave; *by his name* they must swear. This change in word order reflects the author's deliberate emphasis. The Lord, and the Lord only, is to be at the center of Israel's world.

What Do You Think?

How can you ensure that God has first priority in your life? Be specific.

Talking Points for Your Discussion

- In honor
- In trust
- In time commitments

21. He is thy praise, and he is thy God, that hath done for thee these great and terrible things, which thine eyes have seen.

This verse provides the reason for the absolute requirements of verse 20, above. It has now been 40 years since the exodus from Egyptian slavery (Deuteronomy 1:3). Some who are listening to Moses are eyewitnesses to the miracles of that deliverance, since the penalty of death against the first generation applied only to those age 20 and older (Numbers 14:29-32; Joshua 5:6). The survivors are not to forget that God alone is the one who has done marvelous things before their very eyes! (On the word *terrible,* see v. 17a.)

C. To Memory (v. 22)

22. Thy fathers went down into Egypt with threescore and ten persons; and now the LORD thy God hath made thee as the stars of heaven for multitude.

God is the one who has multiplied the Israelites from 70 persons (Genesis 46:27; Exodus 1:5) to a number akin to *the stars of heaven* (see Genesis 15:5; 22:17; 26:4). God promised to multiply Abraham's seed, bless his offspring, bring them to the promised land, and use them to bless all nations. God is keeping this promise. The people are numerous (compare Numbers 26), they are blessed, and they now stand directly before the promised land. But their cohesion as God's people will not be permanent unless they accept God's plan.

D. To Justice (16:18-20)

16:18. Judges and officers shalt thou make thee in all thy gates, which the LORD thy God giveth thee, throughout thy tribes: and they shall judge the people with just judgment.

God does not plan to judge cases supernaturally from Heaven; nor does He trust that His people will be so righteous that they will not need an organized system of justice. So His plan is for the Israelites to appoint those who will enforce the laws that God has given them. He confers power on people, and He expects them to use that power to serve those who are under their jurisdiction.

When the people end up in a dispute, they can bring their cases and any witnesses to the gates of the towns that God is giving His people. The judges preside over cases at these gates. They are expected to give the rulings that God himself would give if God were presiding personally over the case. Only in this way can justice prevail.

16:19. Thou shalt not wrest judgment; thou shalt not respect persons, neither take a gift: for a gift doth blind the eyes of the wise, and pervert the words of the righteous.

This verse identifies certain obstacles to justice. Judges may be tempted to render verdicts according to personal preference; this can come about by showing partiality. Judges also will be tempted to accept bribes; sadly, some will succumb to the temptation (1 Samuel 8:3; Isaiah 1:23; etc.).

The standards to which God holds judges are God's personal standards. As we have seen above in Deuteronomy 10:17, God does not show partiality and cannot be manipulated by gifts. God cannot be influenced by the amount of money placed in the offering plate. No number of sacrifices can coax Him into turning a blind eye to justice. Since judges are presiding on God's behalf, they must preside according to His just standards.

❧ *THE GOOD KIND OF BLINDNESS* ❧

Justitia was the Roman goddess of justice. She is often depicted today as a woman holding a balance scale and a sword (see photograph on page 409 of this quarter's studies). The sword represents the power of reason and justice that the government should wield appropriately in every case. The scale symbolizes the weighing that should be given to the evidence involving a case being considered.

To further the symbolism of impartiality, Justitia (or "Lady Justice") is often portrayed wearing a blindfold. Her first known depiction in this fashion is a statue placed in Berne, Switzerland, in 1543. The idea is that justice should be "blind" to any factor other than the weight of truth itself. God's concern for blind justice predates by many centuries all these representations, seen in the fact that He ordered judges to judge the disputes as if God himself were ruling in the case.

Although very few of us serve as judges in courtrooms, we realize that we make judgments all the time in other ways. For example, parents routinely judge and resolve disputes between their children, and this responsibility must not be shirked. Comedian Bill Cosby observed many years ago that children quickly discover that parents are not interested in *justice*, parents are interested in *quiet!* That's humorous, but sadly so. Do you administer proper justice in areas you are called to do so, or do you "wrest justice" in various ways?   —C. R. B.

What Do You Think?

What manipulations of justice do you see today? What actions that do not involve partisan politics can Christians take to prevent such distortions?

Talking Points for Your Discussion

▪ In government
▪ In the business world

16:20. That which is altogether just shalt thou follow, that thou mayest live, and inherit the land which the Lord thy God giveth thee.

Moses wraps up this summary of God's law with a rhetorical flourish that doesn't always translate well into English. The first part of this verse literally reads, "Justice, justice, you shall pursue." It is a passionate plea that reflects a sense of urgency. The reason is clear in the second half of the verse: the people's very lives and presence in the promised land are riding on it.

Put simply, if God's people do not live according to God's commandments, He will drive them out of the land just as He will do to the unjust Canaanites who currently inhabit the area. God does not give His people the land as an end unto itself, as if He arbitrarily wants them to have it and not the Canaanites. He gives the Israelites the land because He intends to form them into a just people who will showcase His justice to the nations. To forsake justice is therefore to forsake God's calling and mission. This is their reason for being.

The phrase *that thou mayest live* can have an additional meaning in referring to quality of life. To live according to God's justice is to "really live." There is no point to living in the promised land if the quality of life there is no different from life in Egypt. Living a life of justice is to live a life worthy of God's mission in God's land.

Conclusion
A. Loving a God of Justice

Loving the God of justice is different from loving food, from loving forms of entertainment, and from loving people. To love God is to embrace His character, to seek His will, and to obey His commands. This core teaching of Deuteronomy is central to New Testament faith. Jesus makes this clear several times (see John 14:15, 21; 15:10, 12). Loving God cannot be separated from loving Jesus, which cannot be separated from keeping God's commands, which cannot be separated from loving one another (1 John 3:16, 17). How unique is our God! How unique and wonderful are His love and His justice! Let us love God by demonstrating His justice for the sake of His mission in this world.

B. Prayer

Lord God, teach us to love You in ways that are appropriate to Your holiness and Your majesty. Teach us Your justice and empower us to be faithful to Your requirements. We are humbled to be Your people. Thank You for entrusting us with a task as important as Your mission in this world. In Jesus' name, amen.

C. Thought to Remember

True justice cannot be separated from loving God and loving people.

INVOLVEMENT LEARNING

Some of the activities below are also found in the helpful student book, Adult Bible Class.
Don't forget to download the free reproducible page from www.standardlesson.com to enhance your lesson!

Into the Lesson

Ask learners to create a list of definitions or uses of the word *love.* If your class needs an example, say, "Love can be used to express favorites, as in 'I love this TV program.'" This activity may be done as a whole class, in small groups, or in pairs. If using groups or pairs, add a touch of competition by seeing who can make the longest or most detailed list.

Make the transition to Bible study by asking, "How would you define *love for God*?" Also discuss what threads of emotions and thoughts may be included in the phrase *I love God.* Say, "The word *love* is used in so many different ways that we may have difficulty defining love for God. Today we'll try to clear up this murkiness as we take a look at a Scripture that teaches us how to love Him."

Into the Word

Early in the week, give a class member a photocopy of the Lesson Background. Ask this learner to prepare a brief introduction to Deuteronomy. The presentation should address why the book was written and its target audience. The mini-lecture should conclude with the last sentence of the Lesson Background. *Alternative:* Deliver this mini-lecture yourself.

Give study teams or pairs the following written assignments and photocopies of the appropriate page(s) of the lesson commentary. *Team 1:* Define the four key words *fear, walk, love,* and *serve* of Deuteronomy 10:12, 13. What do these words teach us about loving God? *Team 2:* Read Deuteronomy 10:13-16. What is the unifying principle in verse 13, and why was this for the good of the Israelites? Why was the reminder to the Israelites in verses 14, 15 important in this teaching about loving God? What is the significance of the symbolism of circumcision and stiff necks in verse 16? *Team 3:* What are the ways we can demonstrate love for God according to Deuteronomy 10:17-

22? Be sure to include in your report the reason God reaffirmed His superiority in verse 17. *Team 4:* Why did God ask for the appointment of judges and officers in Deuteronomy 16:18-20? What were God's expectations, and why were these expectations important?

Ask the class to brainstorm answers to these questions: "What have you learned about loving God from this passage? What elements would you include in a definition of *love for God* in particular or in *expressing love* in general?" Write responses on the board. At the conclusion of this activity, write the title of today's lesson on the board: *Love God; Love People!*

Alternative: Use the Love God—How? activity from the reproducible page, which you can download, instead of the above. This can be better for smaller classes.

Into Life

Give each learner an unlined index card. Say, "Let's move this study into everyday life. We need to talk about how we express love for God and love for others in our culture and world. Write *Love God* on the top of one side of your card. Below it write three ways we can express our love for God. Those ideas may or may not come from today's text." Allow learners to share some of the ideas that have not already been mentioned in the brainstorming activity above.

Then say, "Now write *Love People* on the other side. Below it write three ways that we can express God's love for others. Again, the ideas may or may not come from today's text." Allow learners to share ideas not already mentioned in the brainstorming activity. Then ask learners to circle or rewrite one idea on each side of the card that they intend to do.

Distribute copies of the Love People activity from the reproducible page, which you can downloaded, as learners depart.

Love God; Love People

SAMUEL ADMINISTERS JUSTICE

DEVOTIONAL READING: **Ezekiel 18:25-32**
BACKGROUND SCRIPTURE: **1 Samuel 4–7**

1 SAMUEL 7:3-17

3 And Samuel spake unto all the house of Israel, saying, If ye do return unto the LORD with all your hearts, then put away the strange gods and Ashtaroth from among you, and prepare your hearts unto the LORD, and serve him only: and he will deliver you out of the hand of the Philistines.

4 Then the children of Israel did put away Baalim and Ashtaroth, and served the LORD only.

5 And Samuel said, Gather all Israel to Mizpeh, and I will pray for you unto the LORD.

6 And they gathered together to Mizpeh, and drew water, and poured it out before the LORD, and fasted on that day, and said there, We have sinned against the LORD. And Samuel judged the children of Israel in Mizpeh.

7 And when the Philistines heard that the children of Israel were gathered together to Mizpeh, the lords of the Philistines went up against Israel. And when the children of Israel heard it, they were afraid of the Philistines.

8 And the children of Israel said to Samuel, Cease not to cry unto the LORD our God for us, that he will save us out of the hand of the Philistines.

9 And Samuel took a sucking lamb, and offered it for a burnt offering wholly unto the LORD: and Samuel cried unto the LORD for Israel; and the LORD heard him.

10 And as Samuel was offering up the burnt offering, the Philistines drew near to battle against Israel: but the LORD thundered with a great thunder on that day upon the Philistines, and discomfited them; and they were smitten before Israel.

11 And the men of Israel went out of Mizpeh, and pursued the Philistines, and smote them, until they came under Bethcar.

12 Then Samuel took a stone, and set it between Mizpeh and Shen, and called the name of it Ebenezer, saying, Hitherto hath the LORD helped us.

13 So the Philistines were subdued, and they came no more into the coast of Israel: and the hand of the LORD was against the Philistines all the days of Samuel.

14 And the cities which the Philistines had taken from Israel were restored to Israel, from Ekron even unto Gath; and the coasts thereof did Israel deliver out of the hands of the Philistines. And there was peace between Israel and the Amorites.

15 And Samuel judged Israel all the days of his life.

16 And he went from year to year in circuit to Bethel, and Gilgal, and Mizpeh, and judged Israel in all those places.

17 And his return was to Ramah; for there was his house; and there he judged Israel; and there he built an altar unto the LORD.

KEY VERSE

If ye do return unto the LORD with all your hearts, then put away the strange gods and Ashtaroth from among you, and prepare your hearts unto the LORD, and serve him only: and he will deliver you out of the hand of the Philistines. —**1 Samuel 7:3**

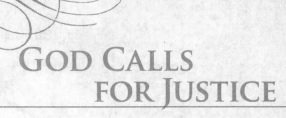

GOD CALLS FOR JUSTICE

Unit 2: Justice Enacted

LESSONS 5–9

LESSON AIMS

After participating in this lesson, each student will be able to:

1. Tell how repentance and renewed devotion to the Lord brought security to the Israelites.

2. Tell why personal spiritual renewal is necessary before the church can be effective in addressing the needs in its surroundings.

3. Organize or participate in a special time of rededication to the Lord individually, in his or her family, in class, or as a church.

LESSON OUTLINE

Introduction

A. "Out of Order"

The three words found in the heading above can be some of the most annoying there are, whether posted on a vending machine, an ATM, or a gasoline pump. In those cases, the hungry person, the individual needing cash quickly, and the driver running on empty all feel *out of order* themselves because they can't get what they need.

Out of order describes the entire world under the impact of sin. What God had declared "very good" (Genesis 1:31) became a place of disruption and disorder when those made in the Creator's image turned from Him and listened to the appeal of the master of disorder, Satan. A sense of order can come only when we return to the God who is "not the author of confusion, but of peace" (1 Corinthians 14:33).

B. Lesson Background

Out of order is also a fitting label to describe Israel during the period of the judges (roughly 1380–1050 BC). The previous four lessons in our survey of the Old Testament this quarter called attention to the order that God provided for His chosen people, Israel, as He gave them His laws. God made it abundantly clear that disobedience would produce devastating consequences. The people's lives would become *out of order*. If they persisted in their rebellion, they eventually would find themselves *out of Israel*—exiled to foreign soil.

The Israelites entered the promised land in triumph under the leadership of Joshua. But the nation entered the chaotic period of the judges after the deaths of Joshua and the elders who had served with him (Judges 2:8-23). The disarray of this time is captured best in the closing statement of the book of Judges: "every man did that which was right in his own eyes" (Judges 21:25).

God's answer to this moral and spiritual cesspool was to raise up a series of judges as deliverers. It can be argued that the most important of these was Samuel—the last of the 15 judges—who judged approximately 1067–1043 BC. As a result of Samuel's ministry, the Word of the Lord flourished throughout the land (1 Samuel 3:19–4:1a).

A good example of how spiritually inept the nation had become is the treatment of the ark of the covenant in 1 Samuel 4. That passage describes how the people viewed it as a "good luck charm," carrying it into battle with the hopes that its presence (and thus God's presence) would ensure victory over the Philistines.

Instead, the people suffered a humiliating defeat. The ark remained in Philistine territory seven months, during which time it made the Philistines' lives very much *out of order* (1 Samuel 5:1–6:1)! The Philistines returned the ark to Israel; eventually it was brought to a place called Kirjathjearim, located about eight miles west of Jerusalem. The ark has been there for 20 years (1 Samuel 7:1, 2) by the time of the incident described in today's printed text.

I. Problems from Within
(1 Samuel 7:3-6)
A. Solemn Act (vv. 3, 4)

3. And Samuel spake unto all the house of Israel, saying, If ye do return unto the LORD with all your hearts, then put away the strange gods and Ashtaroth from among you, and prepare your hearts unto the LORD, and serve him only: and he will deliver you out of the hand of the Philistines.

The verse just before this one, 1 Samuel 7:2, tells us that "all the house of Israel lamented after the Lord." This statement immediately follows a reference to the ark remaining in Kirjathjearim for 20 years (it stays there about 70 years in total, until the reign of David; 1 Chronicles 13:5, 6; 2 Chronicles 1:4). God's people eventually come to realize that they have abused the privilege of having God's presence with them (which is what the ark represented).

At the point represented by the verse before us, the people seem to realize that their real enemy since arriving in the promised land has not been the Philistines or other foreign threats. Rather, the Israelites have been their own worst enemy because they have forsaken God. As a result, Samuel encourages the people to take specific steps to show that they are serious about their mourning. He speaks

unto all the house of Israel, probably meaning that he addresses the tribal leaders or elders. They relay his instructions to the rest of the people.

The command to *put away the strange gods and Ashtaroth from among you* is uncompromising. The word *Ashtaroth* is a plural term in Hebrew. Ashtoreth (the singular form) is the name of a goddess of sex and war known in Canaan as Ashtar or Astarte, the consort or lover of Baal. The use of the plural form may suggest that different forms of the deity are worshipped in different towns. Any and all forms of this deity must be destroyed. The allegiance of the people's hearts must be redirected to the Lord to the point that they *serve him only.*

> *What Do You Think?*
> At what point does something or someone we value become an idol or object of worship? How do we keep this from happening?
> *Talking Points for Your Discussion*
> - Celebrities
> - Possessions
> - Vocations
> - Relationships

4. Then the children of Israel did put away Baalim and Ashtaroth, and served the LORD only.

The people obey. Although Samuel's counsel in the previous verse did not mention the Baalim (which is the plural form of Baal), these generally are worshipped alongside the Ashtaroth.

B. Sacred Assembly (vv. 5, 6)

5. And Samuel said, Gather all Israel to Mizpeh, and I will pray for you unto the LORD.

In addition to commanding the people to rid themselves of idols, Samuel determines to take a further role in spurring the people to remain true to their commitment. Thus we see his instructions for the people to gather at Mizpeh so he can pray for them. As in verse 3, *all Israel* likely describes the elders or tribal leaders of Israel. Mizpeh is a town in the territory of the tribe of Benjamin (Joshua 18:26), about eight miles north of Jerusalem.

To *pray for* (intercede for) others is one of the most important functions of Old Testament prophets (1 Kings 13:1-6; Amos 7:1-6). Samuel is recognized later, along with Moses, as one of Israel's greatest intercessors (Psalm 99:6; Jeremiah 15:1).

6a. And they gathered together to Mizpeh, and drew water, and poured it out before the Lord, and fasted on that day, and said there, We have sinned against the Lord.

The people gather as directed. The actions of drawing water and pouring *it out before the Lord* are not directly commanded in the Law of Moses. This appears to have its roots in the drink offering that is to accompany the burnt offering made twice daily (Numbers 28:1-7). The pouring out of such an offering represents pouring out one's self as an offering to the Lord (compare 2 Timothy 4:6). Here the people are pouring out their hearts before the Lord in repentance.

The Israelites also fast. Fasting involves abstaining from food (and sometimes water) to focus on spiritual matters. The time normally given to preparing and consuming physical sustenance is devoted to prayer and/or worship.

Along with these acts of contrition come appropriate words of confession: *We have sinned against the Lord.* The people have already "put away" their false gods (v. 4, above), but a nationwide confession such as we see here is an instrumental step on the road to nationwide renewal and revival.

> *What Do You Think?*
> How do our actions verify genuine repentance? Can repentance be real without a change in behavior? Explain.
> *Talking Points for Your Discussion*
> - Matthew 3:8
> - Acts 19:18, 19
> - Acts 26:20
> - James 4:17

6b. And Samuel judged the children of Israel in Mizpeh.

While at Mizpeh, Samuel apparently hears certain cases that are brought before him so that he may render verdicts. Perhaps this is a consequence of the period of fasting and confession: some in the crowd may realize that they have violated God's law and need to make amends.

II. Problems from Without
(1 Samuel 7:7-12)
A. Israelites Fear (vv. 7, 8)

7. And when the Philistines heard that the children of Israel were gathered together to Mizpeh, the lords of the Philistines went up against Israel. And when the children of Israel heard it, they were afraid of the Philistines.

At some point, news of the gathering at Mizpeh reaches the Philistines. The *lords of the Philistines* are five in number (Judges 3:3) and include the chief officials of the five key Philistine cities listed in Joshua 13:3. The closest of these cities to Mizpeh is approximately 25 miles to the southwest. The Philistines are a primary enemy of Israel at this time; perhaps they see a convenient target. When the Israelites hear of the approaching Philistine army, their initial reaction is fear.

8. And the children of Israel said to Samuel, Cease not to cry unto the Lord our God for us, that he will save us out of the hand of the Philistines.

The Israelites plead with Samuel to *cry unto the Lord* on their behalf. Samuel told the people earlier that he would pray for them (v. 5). But the Israelites likely have not foreseen that the need for Samuel's prayer would suddenly become so urgent!

B. Samuel Prays (v. 9)

9. And Samuel took a sucking lamb, and offered it for a burnt offering wholly unto the Lord: and Samuel cried unto the Lord for Israel; and the Lord heard him.

HOW TO SAY IT

Ashtaroth	*Ash*-tuh-rawth.
Ashtoreth	*Ash*-toe-reth.
Astarte	A-*star*-te (first *a* as in *had*).
Baal	*Bay*-ul.
Baalim	Bay-uh-*leem*.
Kirjathjearim	*Kir*-jath-***jee***-uh-rim or jee-***a***-rim.
patriarchs	*pay*-tree-arks.
Philistine	Fuh-*liss*-teen or *Fill*-us-teen.
Ramah	*Ray*-muh.

Samuel's intercessory prayer is preceded by *a burnt offering*. A *sucking lamb* is still young enough to be nursing milk from its mother. A lamb offered as a burnt offering has to be at least seven days old (Leviticus 22:26, 27).

Perhaps Samuel offers the lamb at this point to remind the people that the Lord's battle strategy is quite different from man's. Although the people have had no time to organize themselves for battle, it does not matter. The Lord hears Samuel's cry on behalf of his people; that is all that matters.

C. Philistines Panic (vv. 10, 11)

10. And as Samuel was offering up the burnt offering, the Philistines drew near to battle against Israel: but the LORD thundered with a great thunder on that day upon the Philistines, and discomfited them; and they were smitten before Israel.

The Lord responds to Samuel in an unforgettable display of power. Thunder is sometimes associated in poetic passages of the Bible with the voice of God (Psalm 18:13; 29:3). On this occasion, the thundering that the Philistines hear throws them into a panic (the meaning of the word *discomfited*). Their defeat is devastating.

11. And the men of Israel went out of Mizpeh, and pursued the Philistines, and smote them, until they came under Bethcar.

After the victory comes the mopping up action. Although the Lord has won the victory, *the men of Israel* have an important role to play. Bethcar may be the location of a Philistine fortress where the tattered remnants of the Philistine army flees for refuge. The name *Bethcar* means "house of the lamb," an ironic name since the Lord has come to the aid of His people in the process of Samuel's sacrificing a lamb. *Under* indicates a lower elevation.

What Do You Think?

What was a time you saw God act in an unexpected way? How did this surprise change the way you pray?

Talking Points for Your Discussion
- Issues of God's timing
- Issues regarding the nature of your requests

D. Samuel Celebrates (v. 12)

12. Then Samuel took a stone, and set it between Mizpeh and Shen, and called the name of it Ebenezer, saying, Hitherto hath the LORD helped us.

Stones are used to commemorate significant events (Joshua 4:19-24; 24:26, 27). A stone symbolizes reliability and permanence, thus serving as a lasting witness to the event being celebrated.

Here Samuel takes a stone and sets it up *between Mizpeh and Shen*. The word *Shen* means "tooth" and likely refers to a sharp, pointed rock that may have such an appearance. The exact locations of Shen and Bethcar (v. 11) are unknown.

The word *Ebenezer* means "stone of help." The name is certainly fitting for what has just happened on behalf of God's people. But it also reflects an awareness that God's help has guided the entire history of the people to this point *(hitherto)* and implies that His help will be needed in any future endeavors. Perhaps you remember singing the line "Here I raise mine Ebenezer" in the old hymn "Come, Thou Fount of Every Blessing." That line and others were modified in the 1970s to create a different emphasis; but the original wording can be found on the Internet.

❧ LIVING UP TO THE NAME ❧

For many, the word *Ebenezer* brings to mind the image of Ebenezer Scrooge, a famous character in the Charles Dickens novel *A Christmas Carol*. Ebenezer, a greedy old skinflint, is about the furthest thing from a "stone of help" that one can imagine! Thus there is sharp irony in his name. But Ebenezer eventually becomes a source of great assistance to many, becoming like the Ebenezer of Scripture: a symbol of God's help.

Literary critics have speculated about the person who might have been the model for the Scrooge character. They needn't bother: the world is filled with people whom sin has marred to the point where they have become rocks of oppression. But God can change people. Our challenge is to allow God to work through us so we live up to the meaning of the name *Christian*. We can each become *an Ebenezer*—a symbol of the love of God that gladly gives help in the name of Christ. —C. R. B.

III. Peace Prevails
(1 Samuel 7:13-17)

A. Subduing the Philistines (vv. 13, 14)

13. So the Philistines were subdued, and they came no more into the coast of Israel: and the hand of the LORD was against the Philistines all the days of Samuel.

The Philistines remain at bay for the remainder of Samuel's period of leadership. That enemy no longer menaces *the coast* (the borders) of Israel, meaning they are no further threat. The Philistines experience a resurgence during the reign of Saul (1 Samuel 13:5-7; 31:1-7), but David brings them under control (2 Samuel 5:17-25).

14. And the cities which the Philistines had taken from Israel were restored to Israel, from Ekron even unto Gath; and the coasts thereof did Israel deliver out of the hands of the Philistines. And there was peace between Israel and the Amorites.

Israelite territory that has been under Philistine control is now reclaimed. Most likely the Philistine cities of Ekron and Gath are not taken by Israel, only the towns between them *(the coasts)*.

The term *Amorites* means "mountain dwellers." They, along with the Canaanites, were the primary inhabitants of the promised land prior to the conquest by Israel. According to Deuteronomy 7:1, 2, the Israelites were supposed to "utterly destroy" the Amorites when entering the promised land. The Amorites' continued presence apparently has sparked some degree of conflict with Israel, which now comes to an end under Samuel's influence.

B. Serving the Israelites (vv. 15-17)

15. And Samuel judged Israel all the days of his life.

We have reached the summary of the remainder of Samuel's ministry to God's people. He judges not so much in the sense of providing military leadership (as the leaders in the book of Judges do), but in seeing that justice is administered in cases brought before him.

16. And he went from year to year in circuit to Bethel, and Gilgal, and Mizpeh, and judged Israel in all those places.

In judging Israel, it appears that Samuel's itinerary is fairly localized as he rides a regular *circuit to Bethel, and Gilgal, and Mizpeh.* If Samuel starts from his home in Ramah (v. 17, below) and makes the circuit of the other three cities and back home, the result is a trip of perhaps 25 miles.

We may wonder why Samuel's travels are so limited. Why doesn't he extend his influence into other areas of Israel? The answer may lie in recognizing that this is still the time when judges are ruling in Israel. From what the book of Judges tells us, the work of each judge is fairly localized. Such limitations may provide one reason behind the request for a king that is found in 1 Samuel 8:1-5.

17. And his return was to Ramah; for there was his house; and there he judged Israel; and there he built an altar unto the LORD.

Ramah is Samuel's hometown (compare 1 Samuel 1:19). There he returns at the completion of his circuit. There he continues his judging of Israel, presumably handling whatever cases are brought before him.

Samuel's building of an *altar unto the Lord* reminds us of what the patriarchs did (Abraham in Genesis 12:8; Isaac in 26:23-25; Jacob in 35:6, 7). It appears that the purpose of such an altar is similar to the purpose of the altars of those patriarchs: to mark a spiritual milestone. For Samuel, it perhaps marks the Lord's calling him to return home after being away for so long while he was serving in the tabernacle as a result of his mother's vow (1 Samuel 1:9-11).

❧ *CIRCUIT RIDERS* ❧

Circuit-riding preachers were common in the early days of America. They typically ministered to several churches as they rode from place to place on horseback. Francis Asbury (1745–1816), founder of American Methodism, was perhaps the most famous circuit rider in America. He is said to have traveled 270,000 miles and preached 16,000 sermons along the way.

As a judge of Israel, Samuel also was a circuit rider—although he may have walked rather than ridden. His circuit of four venues (including his home in Ramah) was much shorter than Asbury's, but may have been about as large as that of the average circuit-riding preacher on the American frontier. In all of these cases, the underlying principle was the same: people needed God's message, so God's spokesman took that message to them.

Some today still are called to such "nomadic" ministries. They must rise to the challenge, however difficult it may be. What service is God calling you to perform for Him? Will you accept the challenge of that ministry?   —C. R. B.

Visual for Lesson 5

Keep this map displayed throughout the quarter for a geographical perspective on the lessons.

> ### What Do You Think?
> What are some creative ways you can serve God beyond where you live?
> ### Talking Points for Your Discussion
> - While on vacation
> - While traveling on business
> - While on a short-term mission trip

Conclusion

A. Winning the War Within

Like God's people of old, we who are God's people today must acknowledge our own idolatry and do away with anything that has come between us and God. We must repent of sins that are keeping us from effective service in God's kingdom and that interfere with His Spirit's work in us. We cannot look at the world the way God wants us to until we see ourselves the way He sees us. We cannot confront a sin-stained world until we have properly addressed the sin in our own lives.

We have observed how the Israelites poured out water before the Lord and fasted (1 Samuel 7:6). The lesson comments suggest that the pouring out of water represented the people's pouring themselves out to God as they pledged themselves to be loyal to Him alone. Are there similar actions that can serve a purpose like that for us today?

Some time ago, my church held a service in which a nail was distributed to each person in attendance. A wooden cross had been placed at the front of the sanctuary, near the pulpit. At the conclusion of the sermon, each person was invited to bring his or her nail to the front and hammer it into the cross. The action represented an individual's dealing with whatever sin, idol, or other obstacle to spiritual growth that had become an issue in his or her life. By this gesture the person was declaring, "I want to rid myself of this problem because it is keeping me from being what God wants me to be."

Once the Israelites under Samuel's direction dealt with their sin, the Lord provided an amazing act of deliverance. Who knows what great things we will witness when we present ourselves to God—with no strings attached!

B. Prayer

Father, help us to take a good, honest look at ourselves in light of Your Word and Your holiness. Forgive us when we fail to take seriously the power and influence of sin. Remind us that we cannot influence the world around us until we ourselves have been surrendered to You—and that must happen each day. In Jesus' name, amen.

C. Thought to Remember

We must order our own lives before we can bring God's order to a chaotic world.

INVOLVEMENT LEARNING

Some of the activities below are also found in the helpful student book, Adult Bible Class.
Don't forget to download the free reproducible page from www.standardlesson.com to enhance your lesson!

Into the Lesson

Prepare 11 large index cards that feature the following 11 words, one to a card: *THE / LORD / LET / NONE / OF / SAMUEL'S / WORDS / FALL / TO / THE / GROUND.* Put *1 Samuel 3:19* on a twelfth card. Ask a learner to stand next to you with a hand extended toward you, with thumb and index finger spread widely. Hold the cards (in sequence) above your assistant's hand. Say, "I am going to drop these cards one at a time. Let's see how many you can catch." At the end, note how successful the assistant was and what the words indicate about Samuel's ministry: *the Lord let none of Samuel's words fall to the ground.*

Into the Word

Recover the two cards containing *SAMUEL'S* and *WORDS*. Use that phrase to "label" today's text. Affirm that "Samuel's words were God's words, and when Israel heard and heeded them, they were blessed, as we see in today's text."

Ask learners to circle the words of Samuel in today's text (you can announce that these are in vv. 3, 5, 12, or you can let learners discover them on their own). Now ask your learners to underline the results of Samuel's words in the lives of the Israelites. After allowing opportunity to do so, ask the group to identify those results as you make a list. The following may be noted: idols put away (v. 4); assembly to hear (v. 6); drink offering to God (v. 6); fasting (v. 6); sins confessed (v. 6). Ask, "In what sense are these acts the kinds of things the messenger of God always wants?"

Note that further words of Samuel in verse 12 ("hitherto hath the Lord helped us") do not have an obvious and immediate consequence stated. Ask, "What do you see as the results of the truth *the Lord has helped us to this point in time?*" Let learners respond, but at some point note that the other results seen in the closing verses are certainly true: enemies subdued (v. 13); restoration (v. 14);

God's people empowered for good (v. 14); peace (v. 14); leadership succeeds (vv. 15-17). All was possible because of the Lord's presence and help.

Reinforce the idea that *Samuel's words were God's words.* Have learners read the following verses about the effect of God's Word: 2 Samuel 22:31; Psalm 119:105; Isaiah 55:11; Jeremiah 23:29; Hebrews 4:12; Luke 6:46-49. The last entry will draw an appropriate conclusion, as Christ affirms the power of abiding by His words.

Into Life

Say, "A classic rock song carried the title 'This Is Dedicated to the One I Love.' For the one who would be godly, his or her song might be, 'This life is dedicated to the God I love.'" Have a musically talented class member find (or compose) a melody for the following verse. Distribute copies, and ask the class to join you in a rededication by singing these words:

> *This life of mine is His;*
> *His will I make my own;*
> *His Word will all my standard be;*
> *His purpose, mine alone.*
>
> *This life of mine is God's;*
> *I live it unto Him;*
> *I dedicate all that I am;*
> *I want no life of whim.*
>
> *This life of mine is gift;*
> *A gift from Him I love;*
> *A gift to Him I give today,*
> *From me to God above.*

Suggest that learners post the poem for a time as a regular reminder of our need to rededicate ourselves to God's will.

Alternative: Use the Out of Order activity from the reproducible page, which you can download, instead of the above.

The activity A Promise and a Response on the reproducible page can be either a concluding devotional exercise or a take-home exercise.

DAVID EMBODIES GOD'S JUSTICE

DEVOTIONAL READING: Isaiah 32:1-8
BACKGROUND SCRIPTURE: 2 Samuel 22:1–23:7; 1 Chronicles 18:14

2 SAMUEL 23:1-7

1 Now these be the last words of David. David the son of Jesse said, and the man who was raised up on high, the anointed of the God of Jacob, and the sweet psalmist of Israel, said,

2 The Spirit of the LORD spake by me, and his word was in my tongue.

3 The God of Israel said, the Rock of Israel spake to me, He that ruleth over men must be just, ruling in the fear of God.

4 And he shall be as the light of the morning, when the sun riseth, even a morning without clouds; as the tender grass springing out of the earth by clear shining after rain.

5 Although my house be not so with God; yet he hath made with me an everlasting covenant, ordered in all things, and sure: for this is all my salvation, and all my desire, although he make it not to grow.

6 But the sons of Belial shall be all of them as thorns thrust away, because they cannot be taken with hands:

7 But the man that shall touch them must be fenced with iron and the staff of a spear; and they shall be utterly burned with fire in the same place.

1 CHRONICLES 18:14

14 So David reigned over all Israel, and executed judgment and justice among all his people.

KEY VERSE

David reigned over all Israel, and executed judgment and justice among all his people.

—1 Chronicles 18:14

GOD CALLS FOR JUSTICE

Unit 2: Justice Enacted

LESSONS 5–9

LESSON AIMS

After participating in this lesson, each student will be able to:

1. Describe the ideal ruler according to David's "last words."

2. Compare and contrast David's ideal ruler with the ideal role of a political leader in a modern democracy.

3. Tell how someone today who is not in politics can follow David's example in his or her own sphere of influence.

LESSON OUTLINE

Introduction

A. Famous Last Words

Today's printed text records "the last words of David" (2 Samuel 23:1)—at least the last of his songs or psalms. The last words of someone often reveal much about what that person saw as the true passion or purpose of his or her life. Jesus' last words on the cross—"Father, into thy hands I commend my spirit" (Luke 23:46) and "It is finished" (John 19:30)—reveal His focus on His mission. The heavenly Father had sent Him on the mission to die for sin, He had completed that mission, and He was returning to the one who had sent Him on that mission.

Paul's last words (as far as his writings in Scripture are concerned) are found in 2 Timothy. There one can read of the apostle's unshaken confidence and joy even in the face of death. It is clear that he had no regrets whatsoever about his choice to follow Jesus.

We will see in today's text how David's last words express an attitude of thanksgiving to God for His blessings through the years and also a firm conviction that the future is under God's control. Such perspectives do not happen by accident. If we want to conclude our earthly lives on a triumphant note with no regrets, then we must cultivate the proper attitudes *today* and each day that we live. Our last words will not become a part of sacred Scripture, but they can "last" beyond ourselves and leave a legacy to others, testifying to our faith and our devotion to the Lord.

B. Lesson Background

Samuel, whose leadership of God's people was the focus of last week's study, anointed the first two kings of Israel—Saul and David. David rose from humble beginnings as a shepherd in the household of his father, Jesse of Bethlehem, to become Israel's greatest king. The key to David's greatness lay in the fact that he was "a man after [God's] own heart" (1 Samuel 13:14). David's passion for the Lord is quite evident when one reads the many psalms that he wrote. He became known, as today's text indicates, as "the sweet psalmist of Israel" (2 Samuel 23:1).

David's stellar, consistent walk of faith and obedience was tragically marred by his adulterous affair with Bathsheba and his arrangement of the murder of her husband. Turmoil was the trademark of David's household from that point on (2 Samuel 12:10; 12:15-19; 13:1-19; etc.). But David was repentant.

The conclusion of 2 Samuel includes two songs of David that provide summaries of his life. The one found in 2 Samuel 22 (also found in Psalm 18) is much longer than the one recorded in our printed text from 2 Samuel 23. Both songs acknowledge God's guidance and faithfulness through the years.

I. God's Presence
(2 Samuel 23:1-4)
A. David's Words (v. 1a)
1a. Now these be the last words of David.

The fact that what follows is called *the last words of David* does not mean that these are David's *very* last words. First Kings records other words that David speaks just before dying, to make certain that Solomon succeeds him as king. First Kings 2:1-9 includes what would be David's literal "last words," when he gave counsel to Solomon and assured him of the steadfastness of God's promises. What we have in the passage before us may be considered David's last inspired song or psalm.

What Do You Think?
What would you want your last words to say about what was important to you?

Talking Points for Your Discussion
- Life priorities
- Personal holiness
- Exercise of spiritual gifts

B. David's Titles (v. 1b)

1b. David the son of Jesse said, and the man who was raised up on high, the anointed of the God of Jacob, and the sweet psalmist of Israel, said.

Some may question whether David could have written the kind of introduction found in this verse since it is in the third person, whereas the contents of the psalm to follow are written in first person. Perhaps the inspired author of 2 Samuel (no author of the books is actually given) included this introduction. At the same time, biblical poetry is sometimes characterized by a frequent "shift in persons" (see, for example, Psalm 32), so perhaps David himself did include these introductory words.

David is referred to by four titles or descriptions in this verse. Each calls attention to a special way in which God directed David's life. The first of these, *son of Jesse,* highlights David's humble background. There was nothing especially outstanding about David's family line. David was watching his father's sheep when the prophet Samuel came to Jesse's house in Bethlehem, at God's command, to anoint a king to replace Saul. Apparently David, being the youngest of eight sons, was thought to be an unlikely candidate. Thus he was relegated to his shepherding duties until Samuel asked that he be brought in from the field (1 Samuel 16:1-13).

The phrase *the man who was raised up on high* also reflects an awareness of David's modest beginnings. David did not seek the kingship over Israel. He knows that God raised him up to this position. When the Lord announced to David the special covenant that He was making with him, David's response expressed a keen understanding of his unworthiness to receive such favored treatment (2 Samuel 7:18-29).

Next, David is described as *the anointed of the God of Jacob.* David understands that although it was Samuel who had anointed him to be Israel's king, Samuel was guided by God in his selection. Had it not been for God's intervention, Samuel would have anointed someone else (1 Samuel 16:6, 7). The Hebrew word translated *anointed* is where the term *Messiah* comes from.

HOW TO SAY IT

Bathsheba	Bath-*she*-buh.
Belial	*Bee*-li-ul.
Bethlehem	*Beth*-lih-hem.
Solomon	*Sol*-o-mun.

Finally, David is referred to as *the sweet psalmist of Israel*. Of the 150 psalms in the book of Psalms, 73 are attributed by title to David. Two that have no author given (namely, Psalms 2 and 95) are credited to David in the New Testament (Acts 4:25, 26; Hebrews 4:6, 7).

The Psalms reflect various circumstances in David's life. Perhaps the most familiar one is Psalm 23, in which David uses the imagery of the shepherd to describe God's degree of care for him. Psalm 18 (found also in 2 Samuel 22) includes several references to how the Lord has guided David to victory on the battlefield. David's legacy of praise in the Psalms continues to exert a profound effect on readers today.

The change from *of Jacob* in one title to *of Israel* in the next title may simply be the kind of variation one encounters in poetry. Or perhaps it is a way for David to acknowledge how the Lord has guided his life. Just as the Lord directed Jacob's steps and eventually changed his name to Israel (Genesis 32:27, 28), so the Lord has directed David's life and made him the man described by the series of titles in this verse.

We should also note that the thoughts of being *raised up* and *anointed* are themes mentioned at the beginning of the books of Samuel, in Hannah's song of praise found in 1 Samuel 2:7, 8, 10. These themes become exemplified especially in the experience of David, whose life and reign form the primary focus of the books of 1 and 2 Samuel.

Visual for Lesson 6. *As you study 2 Samuel 23:3, point to this statement as you ask, "How can Christian politicians do this in the year 2012?"*

C. David's Testimony (vv. 2-4)

2. The Spirit of the LORD spake by me, and his word was in my tongue.

When Samuel anointed David to be king, "the Spirit of the Lord came upon David from that day forward" (1 Samuel 16:13). *The Spirit of the Lord*, who has empowered David ever since that point, now provides guidance as David conveys his "last words." David's statement tells us that his words are not really his at all; they are the Lord's. The words are important enough that they are not just in David's mind, but on his tongue also. Further, he does not just speak them, he also commits them to writing.

3. The God of Israel said, the Rock of Israel spake to me, He that ruleth over men must be just, ruling in the fear of God.

Again, David emphasizes the source of what he is conveying: *the God of Israel said, the Rock of Israel spake to me*. Likening God to a rock or stone occurs elsewhere in the Old Testament (Genesis 49:24; Deuteronomy 32:4; Psalm 92:15); the same imagery is used of Jesus in the New Testament (1 Corinthians 10:4; Ephesians 2:19, 20; 1 Peter 2:4-8). It is a fitting comparison, for a rock is associated with firmness and dependability, especially in the face of adverse conditions.

The declaration of God that *He that ruleth over men must be just, ruling in the fear of God* is vitally important. "The fear of the Lord is the beginning of wisdom" (Proverbs 9:10), but according to David it is also the vital aspect of justice. Justice implies a sense of order within a society that results in encouraging and promoting what is good and punishing what is wrong. This is how order in a society is maintained.

The more a society drifts from God and His righteous standards, the less likely it is that true justice will be upheld. Ironically, faith in God and an acknowledgement of His standards are viewed in many circles today as liabilities for exercising justice, not as assets. More and more we see that adherence to God's standards is touted as an obstacle to getting elected or to doing one's job in the public arena.

4. And he shall be as the light of the morning, when the sun riseth, even a morning with-

David Embodies God's Justice

out clouds; as the tender grass springing out of the earth by clear shining after rain.

The images here are those of refreshment and renewal. The book of Proverbs often points out the positive effects of rulers who discharge their duties faithfully (Proverbs 16:10, 12, 13; 20:28; 28:2; 29:4, 14). Also noted are the negative characteristics and consequences of a ruler who executes his responsibilities with no sense of accountability of God or any respect for His ultimate authority (Proverbs 17:7; 28:15, 16; 29:4, 12).

II. God's Power
(2 Samuel 23:5-7)
A. His Covenant Promises (v. 5)

5. Although my house be not so with God; yet he hath made with me an everlasting covenant, ordered in all things, and sure: for this is all my salvation, and all my desire, although he make it not to grow.

The negative statement at the beginning of this verse *(although my house be not so with God)* and the one at the conclusion *(although he make it not to grow)* sound discordant notes given the positive tone of David's words to this point. Consequently, various interpretations are proposed.

One suggestion is that the negative statements are David's reflections on his own failures as a godly leader. David's house therefore does not receive all the blessings that it could. But despite these failures, God still has chosen to make *an everlasting covenant* with David.

On the other hand, some students suggest that it is preferable to translate the two negative statements as rhetorical questions. The Hebrew text allows for this possibility. Under this idea, the first phrase of the verse would read something like, "Is not my house so with God?" This would refer back to the promises of refreshment in the previous verse. David would be declaring how the Lord has favored not only him, but also his entire house by virtue of the covenant blessings recorded in 2 Samuel 7:4-16.

As a rhetorical question, the last phrase of this verse would read, "Will he not make it to grow?" If this is valid, it means David is recognizing that

human effort cannot bring about something that is everlasting—in this case, an everlasting covenant. Such a covenant and its blessings must come from the Lord.

The text between the opening and concluding phrases adds depth of insight. The fact that God *hath made with me [David] an everlasting covenant, ordered in all things, and sure* acknowledges God's commitment to carry out everything He has promised to do. There are no loopholes, no escape clauses, no fine print, or anything else to give David reason to question the Lord's word to him. The fact that God has indeed made such a covenant with David also reflects 2 Samuel 7:16. This covenant includes foreshadowings of Jesus, the Son of David. The New Testament describes Jesus as being on the throne of David and possessing an eternal kingdom (Luke 1:30-33). How assuring when one's "last words" can express the utmost confidence in the Lord's promises!

David acknowledges the blessing of protection from the Lord in the statement *for this is all my salvation, and all my desire.* For David personally, this salvation undoubtedly includes deliverance from earthly enemies (see 2 Samuel 22:1). But it also may reflect David's insight into the impact of the coming Messiah as the source of salvation in a spiritual sense—from sin. Peter describes David as "a prophet" in Acts 2:29-31, where David is said to have spoken of the resurrection of Jesus (in Psalm 16, which is quoted in Acts 13:35).

Whenever we read David's many psalms, we come away with an appreciation of this man's heart of praise and worship of the Lord. It is humbling to consider that David lived prior to the cross of Jesus and His empty tomb. Just think of what David's praise would have been in response to those!

What Do You Think?
 What shapes your expectations of God? How do
  you test the validity of those expectations?
Talking Points for Your Discussion
 ▪ In your relationships
 ▪ In your work or ministry
 ▪ In what brings you happiness
 ▪ In what brings you a sense of blessing

B. His Coming Judgment (vv. 6, 7)

6. But the sons of Belial shall be all of them as thorns thrust away, because they cannot be taken with hands.

The word *Belial* literally means "no value." *The sons of Belial* therefore are people who have chosen to live lives that are worthless before God. David appropriately compares such individuals to worthless thorns. The fact that thorns *cannot be taken with hands* means that one does not use bare hands when clearing a field of thorns, as the next verse shows us.

7. But the man that shall touch them must be fenced with iron and the staff of a spear; and they shall be utterly burned with fire in the same place.

Most of us know the pain of trying to handle thorns without first having donned protective gloves. In the Old Testament world as today, one may also use certain tools to clear away a thicket of thorns. A person *must be fenced,* or protected, by means of an implement in this situation. This may involve the use of *iron and the staff of a spear* (functioning as a pitchfork) to pick up the thorns and place them in a pile. There they can be burned, never to be a problem again.

A similar word picture is used in Scripture to depict the wicked as chaff—the husk or shell of grain. Chaff, like thorns, is good for nothing except to be consumed in the fire (Psalm 1:4; Matthew 3:11, 12). Those who reject the Lord's covenant, established through Jesus the Son of David, face everlasting punishment, as Jesus himself taught (Matthew 13:36-43; 25:41-46).

What Do You Think?

What was a situation in which you suffered harm because you didn't "handle" a malevolent person properly? What can you do to protect yourself against such people?

Talking Points for Your Discussion

- Romans 16:17
- 1 Corinthians 5:11; 15:33
- Ephesians 6:10-18
- 2 Thessalonians 3:6
- Titus 3:10

Residents of the American Southwest flock to the desert in spring to see the beautiful cactus blossoms that transform an otherwise forbidding landscape. The blossoms can range from ¼" to 10" in size. They cover the spectrum from pale greenish-yellow to vivid magenta hues. Such beauty!

However, almost everyone knows of the pain a cactus can cause. Indeed, the word *cactus* seems almost synonymous with the word *prickly.* No one intentionally grabs a cactus with bare hands!

David was aware that many people willingly choose lifestyles that are morally prickly or thorny. He warns us of the dangers of being around such people. Their lives appear very attractive at times, but their "thorns" may wound us severely.

—C. R. B.

III. David's Reign
(1 CHRONICLES 18:14)

14. So David reigned over all Israel, and executed judgment and justice among all his people.

The text of today's lesson includes one verse from 1 Chronicles. This verse summarizes David's reign *over all Israel.* David's reign was characterized by justice. That was a result of David's closeness to the heart of God, for whom justice is always a passion (Deuteronomy 32:4; Psalm 89:14; Isaiah 9:6, 7; Jeremiah 23:5; 33:15).

David therefore exemplifies the principle stated in 2 Samuel 23:3, part of today's text. With rare exceptions, there was no contradiction between David's words and his actions. David on his best days is a fitting model for leaders in any setting to follow.

What Do You Think?

What are some things you can do to leave a positive, godly legacy? Be specific!

Talking Points for Your Discussion

- Example (John 13:15; 1 Corinthians 11:1)
- Persistence (Romans 2:7)
- Holiness (Hebrews 12:14)

In America's advocacy of democratic ideals around the world, one of the most intractable obstacles is that of political corruption. It has been true in both Afghanistan and Iraq, places where attempts to implement democracy have run up against the problem of corruption.

Yet before we look condescendingly at political corruption in other countries, we should examine the corruption and lack of justice in our own backyard. For example, NBC Chicago reported in February 2010 on a study by the University of Illinois at Chicago that concluded that Cook County had been a "dark pool of political corruption" for over a century. Since the mid-1970s, 31 "sitting or former Chicago aldermen have been convicted of corruption or other crimes." It happens in other American cities as well.

The word *executed* has an interesting range of possible meanings. It can mean "carried out," but it can also mean "killed." The verdict of Scripture is that during David's reign justice was executed in the positive sense of the term. Which of those two senses of *executed* describes justice in your town?

—C. R. B.

Conclusion

A. Leaders Are "Needers"

Ruling in the fear of God (2 Samuel 23:3) is certainly a noble ideal. Godly individuals add a moral dimension to leadership that, sadly, is all too often lacking in the current climate. But how can this principle realistically be applied in the modern political scene, where money and power seem to determine whose agenda prevails? Those who try to bring a Christian perspective to a particular issue are often ridiculed in the media, lampooned as narrow-minded and intolerant. Is there even a place for the godly leader?

Jesus desires that His followers be salt and light, adding godly seasoning and illumination to every sphere of life (Matthew 5:13-16). The political realm is not excluded. However, anyone who senses a call by the Lord to represent Him in that arena must recognize that he or she is in for a fight! Jesus warned His disciples as He sent them

out that they needed to be "wise as serpents, and harmless as doves" (Matthew 10:16). That combination will certainly be required of anyone venturing into politics.

When considering David's example of leadership, it is instructive to study the verses immediately following the ones that are part of today's printed text. Second Samuel 23:8-39 records actions of the various "mighty men" who supported David and in some cases saved his life. And 1 Chronicles 18:15-17 lists some of the important officials in David's administration. These lists indicate that David had help in carrying out a wise and just rule.

Anyone who desires to serve God in the political sphere today dare not face such a task alone. Such a person must acknowledge (and this is true of a leader in any setting) that he or she is a "needer"—one who needs a group of people to offer prayer support and encouragement. This group will hold the leader accountable, warning and rebuking when necessary. This will help keep the leader fit for running the larger race (1 Corinthians 9:24-27), fit for gaining the larger prize (Philippians 3:12-14).

> *What Do You Think?*
> What one cultural norm do you most need to set aside so you can become a "needer"? How will you do that?
>
> *Talking Points for Your Discussion*
> - Cultural norm of nuclear (vs. extended) family
> - Cultural norm that stresses task over relationship
> - Cultural norm of pride in "rugged individualism"

B. Prayer

Father, the more our world drifts from You the more it drifts from an understanding of what is truly right and just. We pray that You will raise up leaders who acknowledge their dependence on You. In Jesus' name, amen.

C. Thought to Remember

Fear of God makes good people great
and intelligent people wise.

INVOLVEMENT LEARNING

Some of the activities below are also found in the helpful student book, Adult Bible Class.
Don't forget to download the free reproducible page from www.standardlesson.com to enhance your lesson!

Into the Lesson

Display (or create a handout of) the following list of names: Thomas Edison, Julius Caesar, Winston Churchill, Joan Crawford, Bing Crosby, Leonardo da Vinci. Say to your class, "Last words are often difficult to verify, but I have a series of attributed dying words. I am going to read them to you, and I want you to identify the probable speaker from this list of names. One name will not be used." Read the following five quotes, allowing time for response before you reveal the answer:

"Et tu, Brute?" *(Julius Caesar).* "That was a great game of golf, fellers" *(Bing Crosby).* "I have offended God and man because my work did not reach the quality it should have" *(Leonardo da Vinci).* "Don't you dare ask God to help me!" *(Joan Crawford).* "I'm bored with it all" *(Winston Churchill).*

At the end say, "Today we study what are labeled as the last words of another famous person, King David." (You may wish to use the lesson commentary to explain why these aren't the *very* last words of David.)

Into the Word

Display on a large sheet of butcher paper a life-size outline of a human figure. Label it *The Embodiment of Justice.* Distribute to each learner a half-sheet of paper featuring an outline of a human figure. Point out the title of today's study: "David Embodies God's Justice."

Read the last verse of today's text (1 Chronicles 18:14) and note the way that verse summarizes David's reign of justice. Say, "Let's think about what it was that personified divine justice and rightness in the reign of David as we look at 2 Samuel 23:1-7. On your outline figure, write in one element of David's character and behavior that exemplified his life of divine justice." (If your learners need a starter, give this example from verse 1: *David sensed that his exalted position was entirely God's doing;* this statement can be tagged

to a body part that "senses"—the eyes, for example.) Ask several to share orally; write their statement onto the large figure on the butcher paper.

Alternative: To emphasize the positive nature of David's last words, read the following fictional, "opposite" version. Pause as you read each line. Ask learners to state why the line is wrong based on what they see in 1 Samuel 23. Use the commentary to resolve issues of interpretation.

> "The Last Words of King Undavid"
> *The lament of Undavid, son of the Evil One [v. 1]*
> *The poem of a man humbled and humiliated by the
>   Most High [v. 1]*
> *A man made king by his own hand of violence [v. 1]*
> *Israel's curser of curses! [v. 1]*
> *The spirit of evil spoke through me [v. 2]*
> *Empty words filled my mouth [v. 2]*
> *When one rules over men in unrighteousness [v. 3]*
> *When he rules with no fear of God [v. 3]*
> *He is like the darkness of midnight on a cloudy
>   night [v. 4]*
> *He is like the threatening clouds before a storm [v. 4]*
> *A storm that uproots trees and destroys homes [v. 4]*
> *He has refused to covenant with me [v. 5]*
> *I have no desire [v. 5]*
> *I gather evil men around me [v. 6]*
> *It is a good thing to shake hands with evil men [v. 6]*

Into Life

Distribute copies of the Feeling Like David? activity from the reproducible page, which you can download. *Option 1:* If time allows, have learners fill this out and discuss their reactions in study pairs. *Option 2:* If time is short, have learners take this home for completing during a devotional time. Suggest that they post it on a "morning mirror" for a reminder as they begin each day in the week ahead.

If you use *Option 1* above, distribute copies of the Confident Last Words segment of the reproducible page for learners to take home and post on a "morning mirror."

SOLOMON JUDGES WITH WISDOM AND JUSTICE

DEVOTIONAL READING: Psalm 37:27-34
BACKGROUND SCRIPTURE: 1 Kings 3; 2 Chronicles 9:8

1 KINGS 3:16-28

16 Then came there two women, that were harlots, unto the king, and stood before him.

17 And the one woman said, O my lord, I and this woman dwell in one house; and I was delivered of a child with her in the house.

18 And it came to pass the third day after that I was delivered, that this woman was delivered also: and we were together; there was no stranger with us in the house, save we two in the house.

19 And this woman's child died in the night; because she overlaid it.

20 And she arose at midnight, and took my son from beside me, while thine handmaid slept, and laid it in her bosom, and laid her dead child in my bosom.

21 And when I rose in the morning to give my child suck, behold, it was dead: but when I had considered it in the morning, behold, it was not my son, which I did bear.

22 And the other woman said, Nay; but the living is my son, and the dead is thy son. And this said, No; but the dead is thy son, and the living is my son. Thus they spake before the king.

23 Then said the king, The one saith, This is my son that liveth, and thy son is the dead: and

the other saith, Nay; but thy son is the dead, and my son is the living.

24 And the king said, Bring me a sword. And they brought a sword before the king.

25 And the king said, Divide the living child in two, and give half to the one, and half to the other.

26 Then spake the woman whose the living child was unto the king, for her bowels yearned upon her son, and she said, O my lord, give her the living child, and in no wise slay it. But the other said, Let it be neither mine nor thine, but divide it.

27 Then the king answered and said, Give her the living child, and in no wise slay it: she is the mother thereof.

28 And all Israel heard of the judgment which the king had judged; and they feared the king: for they saw that the wisdom of God was in him, to do judgment.

2 CHRONICLES 9:8

8 Blessed be the LORD thy God, which delighted in thee to set thee on his throne, to be king for the LORD thy God: because thy God loved Israel, to establish them for ever, therefore made he thee king over them, to do judgment and justice.

KEY VERSE

All Israel heard of the judgment which the king had judged; and they feared the king: for they saw that the wisdom of God was in him, to do judgment. —**1 Kings 3:28**

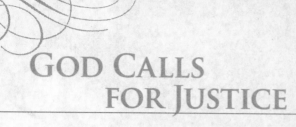

GOD CALLS FOR JUSTICE

Unit 2: Justice Enacted

LESSONS 5–9

LESSON AIMS

After participating in this lesson, each student will be able to:

1. Retell the story of Solomon's ruling concerning two women who both claimed the same baby.

2. Explain how Solomon's ruling showed divine insight.

3. Join with others to pray for divine insight for church and/or political leaders.

LESSON OUTLINE

Introduction

A. "Judge Solomon"

When a court case gets extensive coverage in the media, a high-profile individual is usually involved. Think of the criminal trial of O. J. Simpson in 1995. People may remember the name of the judge in such cases, but more often than not that person stays in the background.

Of course, this is not the case with the TV programs that feature judges rendering decisions daily. The focus there is on the judges, not on the litigants. The fact that many people are fascinated by such programs is reflected in the salaries commanded by these judges. According to a 2008 article on www.forbes.com, "Judge Judy" (Judith Sheindlin) was earning $45 million a year!

Certain elements of the case brought before Solomon in today's lesson text may seem quite familiar to those who watch the TV judges regularly. Two people stood before Solomon, each claiming that the other was not telling the truth, and it was one person's word against another's. But before we get lost in the details of the case, we should remind ourselves that the primary focus that day was on the judge—a man who had succeeded his noteworthy father as king of Israel. Obviously the new king had enormous shoes (or sandals) to fill. How would he handle this responsibility? The case confronting him in today's text provided a clue.

B. Lesson Background

Solomon recognized the vast scope of the task that lay before him as the new king of Israel. King David, his deceased father, had set the bar high by virtue of his exemplary life (other than the incident involving Bathsheba and Uriah, which the Bible does not try to downplay). In addition, David had made extensive preparations to transfer the kingdom to Solomon, recording plans for building the temple and arranging various groups of officials who would serve in the kingdom. These included priests, gatekeepers, and musicians. (The lists of these individuals and the account of David's other preparations are recorded in 1 Chronicles 23–29.) Much had been given to Solomon; no doubt much was expected from him.

Solomon Judges with Wisdom and Justice

In spite of the generous assistance provided by his father, Solomon still recognized his deep need for help from the Lord. So when the Lord spoke to him one night in a dream and told him to ask for whatever he wanted, Solomon prayed, "Give therefore thy servant an understanding heart to judge thy people, that I may discern between good and bad: for who is able to judge this thy so great a people?" (1 Kings 3:9).

Solomon's understanding heart, especially the ability to "discern between good and bad," was put to the test in the incident described in today's text. It is recorded in the Scriptures immediately following Solomon's dream, so it appears to have occurred fairly early in his 40-year reign as king of Israel, which began around 970 BC.

I. Explaining a Dilemma
(1 KINGS 3:16-22)
A. Story Conveyed (vv. 16-21)

16. Then came there two women, that were harlots, unto the king, and stood before him.

We do not know if the *two women, that were harlots* who approach King Solomon reside in Jerusalem or if they have come some distance to see the king. There are references to harlots (prostitutes) throughout the Bible (Leviticus 21:14; Joshua 2:1; Proverbs 6:26; 23:27; Hosea 4:13, 14; Matthew 21:31, 32). It appears that prostitution was tolerated in Israel, although prohibited by the Law of Moses (Leviticus 19:29).

We may wonder how these two women have such direct access to the king of Israel, although elsewhere we are told of other situations where individuals approach a king for a judgment (2 Samuel 14:1-4; 2 Kings 8:1-6). Perhaps those who do so have already brought their case before

HOW TO SAY IT

Aqaba	*Ock*-uh-buh.
Bathsheba	Bath-*she*-buh.
Eziongeber	*Ee*-zih-on-*ge*-ber (g as in get).
Mesopotamia	*Mes*-uh-puh-*tay*-me-uh.
Solomon	*Sol*-o-mun.
Uriah	Yu-*rye*-uh.

a "lower court" (a gathering of the elders or judges in the town in which they live; compare Deuteronomy 1:15-17). Because of the sensitive nature of the matter that the two women bring to Solomon, possibly no verdict has yet been reached; or if it has, it is now being appealed before the king.

> *What Do You Think?*
> Under what circumstances, if any, should the fact that people are engaged in immoral behavior affect how justice is administered?
> *Talking Points for Your Discussion*
> ▪ In the church
> ▪ In civil lawsuits
> ▪ In criminal cases

17. And the one woman said, O my lord, I and this woman dwell in one house; and I was delivered of a child with her in the house.

One of the women proceeds to explain the situation that brings them both before Solomon.

18. And it came to pass the third day after that I was delivered, that this woman was delivered also: and we were together; there was no stranger with us in the house, save we two in the house.

A vitally important fact is that the two women were alone at the time each gave birth, just three days apart. The fact that no one else was present means that there are no other witnesses available to shed light on what really happened.

19. And this woman's child died in the night; because she overlaid it.

Most likely these two women are rather poor. They live alone, having no husbands or servants. The only "company" they tend to keep is temporary. The contempt in which they are probably held because of their occupation means that hardly anyone takes pity on them or offers assistance. Also, any income from their prostitution probably has been minimal during much of the time of their pregnancies.

Under such circumstances, furniture in the women's house probably is rather limited. If they have no other beds in which to place their infants, then each woman's child has been sleeping in the bed with her.

One night tragedy strikes. The second woman who gave birth turned on top of her son during the night, smothering him.

It is in this verse and the next that the gender of the children becomes clear: they are both male. The Hebrew word for *child* in this verse is the standard word for "son." Had one child been a boy and the other a girl, then the controversy that follows still could have occurred, since there was no third party present to witness which woman gave birth to a boy and which gave birth to a girl.

20. And she arose at midnight, and took my son from beside me, while thine handmaid slept, and laid it in her bosom, and laid her dead child in my bosom.

One may question how the first woman (the one who is speaking) knows all these details regarding how and when the tragedy took place since she was asleep at the time. To have such detailed knowledge could cast suspicion on her as the mother of the dead infant since this is the kind of knowledge the perpetrator would have! Perhaps we can presume that this time line of events is merely logical reasoning that is based on the end result.

We also wonder about what is unsaid. Did the woman who accidentally smothered her son express any grief or alarm *at midnight,* when she discovered the tragedy? Did she try to revive him? Did she ponder her options before taking the action claimed for her? We do not know. We are simply told of her efforts to cover up this tragedy by switching the dead infant for the live one. Certainly the callous heart of this woman is clear in such a "solution."

The first woman had been keeping her child at *her bosom,* reflecting her own tender care for him. She uses the word *handmaid* to describe herself, perhaps as a way of acknowledging her dependence on the king for help.

21. And when I rose in the morning to give my child suck, behold, it was dead: but when I had considered it in the morning, behold, it was not my son, which I did bear.

Imagine the first woman's horror when she rises *in the morning* to nurse her child, only to discover that the child she thinks to be her son is dead! But then, on looking at the infant closely in the morning, she sees that this child is not hers. After giving the matter some thought—and perhaps after a conversation with the other woman and/or taking a close look at the living infant—she realizes to her additional horror what has happened.

We do not know how much time has elapsed between the death of one of the infants and the appearance of these two women before Solomon. If this case has already been brought before other authorities or officials, then several days may have passed. It is hard to imagine the sense of frustration that must have been building within the mother of the living child or the level of tension that has escalated between the two women.

B. Story Challenged (v. 22)

22. And the other woman said, Nay; but the living is my son, and the dead is thy son. And this said, No; but the dead is thy son, and the living is my son. Thus they spake before the king.

At this point, we can picture *the other woman* suddenly interrupting the first woman's account to state her own position. She flatly contradicts the first woman's testimony. Most likely the anger of both women intensifies rapidly as each accuses the other of lying. How can this situation possibly be resolved when there is no third party to consult and when the issue is essentially a matter of "she said/she said"?

❧ CHANGING CHALLENGE ❧

The case before Solomon would be easy today. Just identify the mother with a DNA test!

But modern science makes things not only easier at times, but also more difficult. For example, science has given us various medical procedures to enable surrogate parentage in ways that were undreamed of a hundred years ago. Such capability has raised various moral and legal questions.

Focusing strictly on the legal issue of "whose child is it?" in our limited space here, we occasionally read of a case where a person, by contract, is supposed to give up the newborn, but refuses to do so. Then come the legal battles. Often presenting themselves are questions about what is legally "conscionable" in such cases, regardless of the wording of the contract.

Solomon Judges with Wisdom and Justice

We see the issue of surrogate parentage in Genesis 16, but modern technology has taken the moral and legal issues to a whole new level! One thing is certain: if we do not ask God for wisdom in these matters, disaster will loom. —C. R. B.

II. Exercising Wisdom
(1 KINGS 3:23-28)
A. Solomon's Proposal (vv. 23-25)

23. Then said the king, The one saith, This is my son that liveth, and thy son is the dead: and the other saith, Nay; but thy son is the dead, and my son is the living.

Solomon doesn't dive right in and give a decision. Instead, he begins his response to the two women by summarizing the heart of the dilemma before him. People want to know that they've been heard. Thus Solomon is showing some wisdom in this regard by summarizing or reflecting back.

24. And the king said, Bring me a sword. And they brought a sword before the king.

Solomon's next words surely leave the women (and everyone else present) startled. What can the king possibly want with a sword?

25. And the king said, Divide the living child in two, and give half to the one, and half to the other.

Even more bizarre is the king's command! Since (1) each woman claims that the child in question is hers, and (2) there is no evidence to support either claim over the other, then (3) each woman is to receive a "fair share" of the child. The technical "fairness" of such a verdict is, of course, completely outweighed by its gruesomeness.

B. Mother's Protest (v. 26)

26. Then spake the woman whose the living child was unto the king, for her bowels yearned upon her son, and she said, O my lord, give her the living child, and in no wise slay it. But the other said, Let it be neither mine nor thine, but divide it.

Immediately, the real mother of *the living child* passionately protests this "solution." The Hebrew expression is literally, "Her bowels ached for her son." In biblical times, the bowels are believed to

Visual for
Lesson 7

Challenge your learners to compare and contrast the imperative on this visual with Proverbs 3:5.

be the center of one's emotions. (That belief is still reflected today in expressions like "gut feeling" or "gut reaction.") The mother pleads with the king to let the other woman have *the living child*. Even though the real mother will not be able to carry out her role as the child's mother, she will not allow any bitterness toward the other woman (or toward Solomon for his decision) to result in the death of her child. Although this woman makes her living through prostitution, she still possesses motherly instincts to want to preserve the life of her child.

The other woman, however, sees the king's ruling very differently. She is perfectly satisfied with Solomon's reasoning. In her mind, she and the other woman will now be on equal footing: each woman's son will be dead.

> *What Do You Think?*
> What was a circumstance where you thought it wise not to insist absolutely on "justice"? How did things turn out?
> *Talking Points for Your Discussion*
> ▪ In a family situation
> ▪ In the church
> ▪ In the workplace

C. Solomon's Ruling (v. 27)

27. Then the king answered and said, Give her the living child, and in no wise slay it: she is the mother thereof.

The reaction of each woman has revealed who the real mother is. Clearly the woman who pleads for the life of the child is his mother. Solomon thus rules in her favor. We do not know if any additional rulings are issued by Solomon regarding this matter. Is the other woman punished for perjury? Is she punished in some way for causing the death of her own child, even though unintentional? The Bible does not say. We may also wonder if the two women continue to share a house after this incident! Of primary significance is the impact Solomon's handling of this case has on the entire nation of Israel, as the next verse reveals.

What Do You Think?
When did you experience a situation of someone using knowledge of human nature to get at the truth?
Talking Points for Your Discussion
- Situation involving parent and child
- Situation involving teacher and student
- Situation involving boss and employee

D. Nation's Respect (v. 28)

28. And all Israel heard of the judgment which the king had judged; and they feared the king: for they saw that the wisdom of God was in him, to do judgment.

The word about Solomon's decision spreads quickly throughout *all Israel*. It is clear that no ordinary intelligence is at work here. Solomon possesses *the wisdom of God . . . to do judgment.* He has used an adroit procedure to reach a verdict that is completely just. The mother of the child in question has been given back her child; the other woman has been exposed for the liar that she is.

What Do You Think?
What was a situation where divine wisdom from Scripture helped you make a difficult decision?
Talking Points for Your Discussion
- A situation involving simple misunderstanding
- A situation involving someone's hidden sin
- A situation involving the secular authorities
- A situation involving children

III. Exalting Wisdom's Source
(2 Chronicles 9:8)

8. Blessed be the Lord thy God, which delighted in thee to set thee on his throne, to be king for the Lord thy God: because thy God loved Israel, to establish them for ever, therefore made he thee king over them, to do judgment and justice.

Second Chronicles 9 records the visit of the queen of Sheba to see King Solomon, and she is the one speaking here. Sheba is located in the southwestern corner of the Arabian Peninsula, perhaps in the territory occupied by modern Yemen. This location places it close to the trade routes linking Mesopotamia, Africa, India, and Israel.

Most likely there is more than just curiosity concerning Solomon that sparks this visit by the queen. Solomon's efforts to establish a headquarters for his trading ventures at Eziongeber (2 Chronicles 8:17, 18, mentioned just before the record of the queen's visit) probably interferes with Sheba's commercial interests. (Eziongeber is located at the northwestern end of the Arabian Peninsula, at the northern tip of what is today the Gulf of Aqaba.)

The queen does not travel alone; accompanying her is a large entourage bearing "spices, and gold in abundance, and precious stones" (2 Chronicles 9:1). First Kings 10:1 also notes that she comes "to prove [Solomon] with hard questions." The queen is overwhelmed with amazement on experiencing the scope of Solomon's wisdom. She has heard rumors of his wisdom, but now she witnesses it firsthand. Among her words of tribute to Solomon is the verse before us.

The queen of Sheba appears to express faith in the Lord, acknowledging Him to be the one responsible for placing Solomon on the throne of Israel. She also observes the Lord's special favor toward Israel. Solomon's reign over Israel reflects that favor, for through him the Lord provides *judgment and justice* for the people.

However, the queen's acknowledgment of the Lord most likely is not a personal confession of faith in Him as the only God. She may be expressing her recognition of the Lord only as sovereign

Solomon Judges with Wisdom and Justice

God over Israel. Clearly the queen is aware of Solomon's reputation for exercising justice. In her mind, that testifies not only to Solomon's greatness but also to the greatness of his God.

❧ WHAT'S A REPUTATION WORTH? ❧

There once was a time when people seemed more concerned with their reputation than they do these days. Witness the fact that so few celebrities sue the gossip tabloids for damage to reputation. Perhaps most celebrities subscribe to Oscar Wilde's famous statement, "The only thing worse than being talked about is not being talked about." This is in line with the familiar saying, "There's no such thing as bad publicity."

But perhaps there is. Toyota suffered a big drop in sales in late 2009 and early 2010 as a result of bad publicity concerning that company's vehicles. Millions of cars were recalled at huge cost. In 2010, BP suffered massive damage to its reputation as a result of the *Deepwater Horizon* oil spill in the Gulf of Mexico.

In terms of articulated wisdom, Solomon's reputation stood far above his peers. The queen of Sheba's statement is testimony to that fact. Unfortunately, Solomon did not always apply that wisdom to his own life as he should (1 Kings 11:1-13), and his reputation is sullied to this day as a result. Godly people seek to excel not only in wise words but in wise actions. More than our own reputation is at stake. What the world thinks of Christ and His church is also affected. —C. R. B.

What Do You Think?
How does your relationship with Jesus make a difference when you face a difficult decision?
Talking Points for Your Discussion
- In your motives
- In your credibility
- In your interpersonal skills

Conclusion

A. Compassion vs. Justice

Solomon's verdict in today's lesson demonstrated a healthy combination of compassion and justice. Solomon figured that his proposal to cut the child in two would reveal the love of the mother and the bitterness of the pretender. He was right. Compassion saw that the child was returned to his rightful mother; justice saw that the liar was exposed for what she was.

Today we may not face circumstances exactly like those confronting King Solomon. But we are sometimes faced with difficult circumstances involving having to determine whether or not someone is telling the truth. Numerous scams and con artists take advantage of unsuspecting victims, especially the elderly. Churches have been abused by such professionals, who make preying (rather than praying) a way of life.

How can the church exercise both compassion and justice in such situations? If we are going to err (and we most certainly will), is it better to err on the side of compassion or on the side of justice? Each congregation must look carefully at its surroundings and determine how best to address the needs for help that exist. In some cases, churches in a community can share information and pool resources in order to make sure that dishonest people who move from church to church do not take advantage of others' generosity.

Sometimes a fear of "being used" can keep Christians or churches from acting. This is unfortunate. Jesus has called His followers to be salt and light (Matthew 5:13, 14). This should become a matter of prayer as we determine what needs to be done. If we are not certain what to do in a particular area, perhaps we can investigate what other churches have done and network with them. Will we make mistakes in the process? No doubt. But isn't this better than to make the larger mistake of doing nothing at all?

B. Prayer

Father, we live in a time that requires us to be wise as serpents and harmless as doves. Help us to maintain that balance as we minister to a broken world. Help us to represent a Christlike perspective to Your glory. In Jesus' name, amen.

C. Thought to Remember

True wisdom includes viewing others
as God sees them.

INVOLVEMENT LEARNING

Some of the activities below are also found in the helpful student book, Adult Bible Class.
Don't forget to download the free reproducible page from www.standardlesson.com to enhance your lesson!

Into the Lesson

Place in chairs copies of the Who's on the Bench? activity from the reproducible page, which you can download. Your learners can begin working on this as they arrive.

Have one of your good oral readers read aloud 2 Chronicles 9:1-9 to begin class. As the reading is concluded, say, "Wow! The queen was impressed! Imagine what it would take to impress a queen of a rich and successful nation. Today's text is just one small picture of Solomon's demonstrating God's wisdom in human affairs."

Into the Word

Give each learner a simple sketch of a courtroom setting, including judge's bench, witness stand, jury box, prosecutor's table, defendant's table, and bailiff/guard position. Ask learners to fill in the courtroom setting, as best they can, from the case introduced in today's text. Expect learners to identify that Solomon sits on the judge's bench; the two women are litigants; the king's attendants may be in the bailiff/guard position; etc.

Point out the case before Solomon ended up being in modern parlance a "bench trial," not a "jury trial." Ask, "But what if it had been a jury trial, and you received a notice for jury duty?" Draw attention to the jury box as you say, "I am going to ply you with questions to see if you are qualified to sit on this jury." Use the following questions, as well as others of your own devising.

1. "Both the plaintiff and defendant are prostitutes. Knowing that, can you judge fairly in this case?" [v. 16] 2. "The babies in this case are both illegitimate children. How do you see that affecting your thinking?" [vv. 17, 18] 3. "On what basis do you normally distinguish between liars and truth-tellers?" [v. 22] 4. "Emotions will run high in this case. Will you be able to judge the case strictly on facts, not emotions?" [vv. 17-22] 5. "The judge has the ultimate authority in this case. Do you have confidence in this judge? Why, or why not?" 6. "Since this case will involve conflicting testimony, should prosecution of perjury be made after this case is decided? Why, or why not?" [v. 27]

Let learners respond freely, but make sure to use the questions as a means to work through the text, as indicated by the bracketed verse numbers.

Into Life

Say, "Everyone who heard of Solomon's decision in the matter of the disputed baby was impressed that he demonstrated the wisdom of God (1 Kings 3:28). What judicial decisions have you heard that impressed you with the rightness and justice of the outcome in a criminal case? What characterizes such decisions?" (To keep the discussion from becoming political, such as with Supreme Court decisions regarding interpretations of the constitution, keep the stress on criminal cases.)

The thought in 2 Chronicles 9:8 lends itself to the following questions you may wish to pose to your class: 1. Do you ever praise God when you see justice done? If not, why not? 2. Do you sense the presence and wisdom of God when leaders do the right thing? 3. Do you see the hand of God at work when righteous men and women are put into places of authority?

Lead the class in a time of directed prayer for divine insight for leaders, both in the church and in the government. Pray for the following; add others as you see fit: *our church leaders*—for insight into how to make better disciples of the Christians in our church; *our community's chief elected leader(s)*—for wisdom to promote development that will be godly, wholesome, and family enriching; *our country's chief leader*: for insight that humility is better than pride, righteousness is better than success.

Distribute copies of the So You Want Wisdom? activity from the reproducible page, which you can download, as a take-home exercise.

Solomon Judges with Wisdom and Justice

A King Acts on a Widow's Behalf

DEVOTIONAL READING: Luke 15:11-24
BACKGROUND SCRIPTURE: 2 Kings 4:1-37; 8:1-6

2 KINGS 8:1-6

1 Then spake Elisha unto the woman, whose son he had restored to life, saying, Arise, and go thou and thine household, and sojourn wheresoever thou canst sojourn: for the LORD hath called for a famine; and it shall also come upon the land seven years.

2 And the woman arose, and did after the saying of the man of God: and she went with her household, and sojourned in the land of the Philistines seven years.

3 And it came to pass at the seven years' end, that the woman returned out of the land of the Philistines: and she went forth to cry unto the king for her house and for her land.

4 And the king talked with Gehazi the servant of the man of God, saying, Tell me, I pray thee, all the great things that Elisha hath done.

5 And it came to pass, as he was telling the king how he had restored a dead body to life, that, behold, the woman, whose son he had restored to life, cried to the king for her house and for her land. And Gehazi said, My lord, O king, this is the woman, and this is her son, whom Elisha restored to life.

6 And when the king asked the woman, she told him. So the king appointed unto her a certain officer, saying, Restore all that was hers, and all the fruits of the field since the day that she left the land, even until now.

KEY VERSE

So the king appointed unto her a certain officer, saying, Restore all that was hers, and all the fruits of the field since the day that she left the land, even until now. —**2 Kings 8:6**

Photo: Stockbyte / Thinkstock

GOD CALLS
FOR JUSTICE

Unit 2: Justice Enacted

LESSONS 5–9

LESSON AIMS

After participating in this lesson, each student will be able to:

1. Tell how God's providence led to the Shunammite's having her land restored after her return from a lengthy absence.

2. Suggest ways God's providence may be at work today in the restoration of assets to those who have been displaced.

3. Identify some situations in which he or she may be God's instrument for justice for someone in need.

LESSON OUTLINE

Introduction

A. A Place for the Displaced

The term *displaced* came into prominence during World War II. It described people who were uprooted from their homes as a result of the war. *Displaced* has since come to be used for people who are forced to vacate their homes because of disasters. One often heard it used in the aftermath of Hurricane Katrina in 2005.

Of course, people have been displaced from the very beginning of humanity's existence. Adam and Eve were displaced from the Garden of Eden as a consequence of their sin against God, not because of circumstances beyond their control. By contrast, Abraham was displaced from his homeland in obedience to God's command to go to a destination unknown at the time of the call.

Today's text tells of a woman who was displaced as a result of a famine. It also records how God provided for this woman—through His prophet and through a king of Israel—so she could survive and recover from the devastation of the famine.

B. Lesson Background

Today's lesson describes an incident that occurred during the ministry of the prophet Elisha, although in this case he is not the main character. The ministry of Elisha is difficult to date with precision. Apparently, it began sometime around 850 BC and extended through most, if not all, of the second half of that century.

Elisha's call to become a prophet came while he was plowing a field. The prophet Elijah approached him and "cast his mantle upon him" (1 Kings 19:19). This act amounted to an anointing of Elisha to succeed Elijah (vv. 15, 16). After bidding farewell to his family and his life as a farmer, Elisha "went after Elijah, and ministered unto him" (v. 21), serving in a kind of apprentice relationship (see also 2 Kings 3:11). Elisha continued Elijah's prophetic ministry after Elijah was taken to Heaven in a chariot of fire (2 Kings 2:11).

These two served as the Lord's prophets during a pivotal time in the history of the northern kingdom of Israel (in contrast with the southern kingdom of Judah, during the divided monarchy).

A King Acts on a Widow's Behalf

Elijah's ministry had begun during the reign of King Ahab, who was "stirred up" in doing evil by Jezebel, his wife (1 Kings 21:25). God used Elijah and Elisha to counter the paganism promoted by Ahab (16:30-33; 21:26). After Ahab's death, he was succeeded by two of his sons—first Ahaziah, who reigned for only two years (1 Kings 22:51), and then by Jehoram (also spelled Joram), who reigned for 12 years (2 Kings 3:1). Both sons followed the wicked path set by their father.

Although not mentioned by name, it appears that Jehoram (Joram) is the king of Israel at the time of various incidents during the ministry of Elisha. These include the healing of Naaman (2 Kings 5) and a period when the Syrians posed a serious threat to the northern kingdom (6:8–7:2). Jehoram is also most likely the king mentioned in today's study from 2 Kings 8:1-6. Although an evil king, he wasn't as evil as his father, Ahab (3:1-3).

At one point in his travels, Elisha had passed through Shunem, a village in Galilee located at the eastern end of the Valley of Jezreel. A prominent woman in the village invited him to share a meal with her and her husband. Elisha began stopping there whenever he passed that way (2 Kings 4:8). The woman, who had recognized Elisha to be a "holy man of God," suggested to her husband that they provide a room for Elisha so he could stay with them whenever he passed by (vv. 9, 10).

On one occasion when Elisha was staying in Shunem, he asked the woman if there was anything he could do for her to repay her kindness to him. Upon hearing from his assistant, Gehazi, that the couple was childless (2 Kings 4:14), Elisha told the woman that she would give birth to a son. At first the woman was quite taken aback by such an announcement (4:16), but Elisha's word came true at the promised time (4:11-17).

One day tragedy struck, and the child died (2 Kings 4:19-21). The woman quickly mounted a donkey and rode to see Elisha to tell him what had happened. The prophet came to the house and brought the child back to life (vv. 32-37).

We do not know how much time elapsed between that miracle and the incident described in today's text. We suspect that the woman's husband has died in the interim because (1) he is not men-

tioned in today's text and (2) he was described as "old" back in 2 Kings 4:14. One may assume that Elisha continued to keep in touch with the family and stopped whenever he was in the vicinity.

I. Woman's Departure
(2 KINGS 8:1, 2)
A. Command (v. 1)

1. Then spake Elisha unto the woman, whose son he had restored to life, saying, Arise, and go thou and thine household, and sojourn wheresoever thou canst sojourn: for the LORD hath called for a famine; and it shall also come upon the land seven years.

The account of Elisha's raising this woman's son from the dead is recorded in 2 Kings 4:18-37 (see the Lesson Background). In the verse before us, Elisha instructs the woman to travel with her household (which includes her family and perhaps any servants) to another location. The Lesson Background discusses the likelihood that her husband is dead by this time.

The prophet does not specify a particular destination. What matters is that the woman leave her homeland, for the Lord has decreed a seven-year famine in that area. We note that Jacob and his family also had to relocate because of a famine (Genesis 45).

> *What Do You Think?*
> What was a situation in which a "big event" that affected many people tested your trust in God? How did you grow spiritually as a result?
> *Talking Points for Your Discussion*
> ▪ Natural disaster
> ▪ Economic hardship
> ▪ Military conflict

B. Compliance (v. 2)

2. And the woman arose, and did after the saying of the man of God: and she went with her household, and sojourned in the land of the Philistines seven years.

The woman is acquainted enough with Elisha to know that he is indeed a *man of God*. His word can be trusted. Thus she takes her household and lives *in the land of the Philistines seven years.*

What Do You Think?
Whose advice do you trust so much that you do not question it, even if it leads to hardship initially? What caused you to develop that level of trust?

Talking Points for Your Discussion
- In spiritual matters
- In family matters
- In financial matters

The Philistines are a thorn in Israel's side on various occasions, most notably during the time of Samson (1075–1055 BC; see Judges 13–16) and the reign of Saul (1050–1010 BC; 1 Samuel 13:19-23; 14:47; 23:27; 31:1-7). David will bring the Philistines into submission (2 Samuel 5:17-25; 8:1), and it does not appear that they ever become a formidable threat to Israel again. By the time of Elisha, the Philistines seem to be exerting little influence. The Shunammite woman apparently has little to fear in traveling to their territory with her household.

❧ CAN YOU TRUST A PROPHET? ❧

One of the strangest experiences I ever had on the mission field was an encounter with a woman who claimed to be a reincarnation of Jesus. At the request of some members of our church, I took some other church leaders along to see her and find out what she was teaching. With a sudden thunderstorm adding drama to her words, the woman pointed at me, prophesying that I would be the first of 12 disciples who would help her start a new world religion. Truthfully, I felt disconcerted by this odd prediction. But with God's help, I found the words in her language to reject this prophecy and invite her to accept Jesus Christ.

The Shunammite woman, by contrast, had no hesitation about Elisha's prediction. She believed him so completely that she abandoned her property and went to live in a foreign nation.

What's the difference between these two examples? The woman I encountered bore several signs of a false prophet, including making false predictions (Deuteronomy 18:21, 22), diverting worship away from God (Deuteronomy 13:1-3), and bearing bad spiritual fruit (Matthew 7:15-17). Unlike the Shunammite's ongoing friendship with Elisha, I did not personally know or trust this "prophet." Most significantly, Elisha had raised the woman's son from the dead, proving his commission by God. In the end, this is the basis for putting faith in Jesus Christ. His self-resurrection is the proof of His divinity. Our ongoing relationship with Him helps us grow in our trust in Him day by day.

—A. W.

HOW TO SAY IT

Ahaziah	Ay-huh-*zye*-uh.
Elijah	Ee-*lye*-juh.
Elisha	Ee-*lye*-shuh.
Gehazi	Geh-*hay*-zye (G as in *get*).
Jehoram	Jeh-*ho*-rum.
Jezebel	*Jez*-uh-bel.
Jezreel	*Jez*-ree-el or *Jez*-reel.
Joram	*Jo*-ram.
Mordecai	*Mor*-dih-kye.
Naaman	*Nay*-uh-mun.
Naboth	*Nay*-bawth.
Shunammite	*Shoo*-nam-ite.
Shunem	*Shoo*-nem.
tsunami	sue-*nah*-me.

II. Woman's Return
(2 KINGS 8:3-6)
A. Appeal to the King (vv. 3-5)

3. And it came to pass at the seven years' end, that the woman returned out of the land of the Philistines: and she went forth to cry unto the king for her house and for her land.

The woman returns to her homeland when the famine is over. But to her great dismay she discovers that someone else apparently has taken over her homestead. Thus the need to go *forth to cry unto the king for her house and for her land.*

We do not know whether the woman consults any other authority before taking her plight to the king himself (most likely King Jehoram, as noted in the Lesson Background). When Elisha had offered to do some favor for the woman previously, he had suggested that he could intervene on her behalf to the king (2 Kings 4:12, 13). Her reply at the time had been, "I dwell among mine own people" (v. 13). She seemed to be content with nothing more than that. Now, after being away from her people for several years, she returns to dwell among them once again, but is unable to do so.

Other questions that are not addressed directly in Scripture may be raised about the woman's situation. For example, does she not have access to a "kinsman" as did Naomi in the person of Boaz (Ruth 2:1, 20)? As mentioned earlier, the woman's husband likely is dead by this time. If so, did his family take possession of her land when she left? Do they now refuse to grant her access to a kinsman, thus forcing her to go to a "higher court" (the king)? Has the king himself seized the property? The text highlights only the woman's desperate circumstances; she has returned home, yet "home" is in the hands of someone else.

4. And the king talked with Gehazi the servant of the man of God, saying, Tell me, I pray thee, all the great things that Elisha hath done.

As the woman makes her way to the king, he is having a conversation with *Gehazi the servant of the man of God* (Elisha). Gehazi is acquainted with the Shunammite woman, and he knows of the miracles provided for her through the birth of her son and then his resurrection from the dead (2 Kings 4:11-37). Gehazi is also mentioned in the account of how Naaman was healed of his leprosy. There, however, Gehazi acts in a deceptive, self-centered manner, taking items from Naaman under false pretenses. As a result, Gehazi is stricken with the leprosy that had afflicted Naaman (2 Kings 5:20-27).

Since Gehazi is speaking in the presence of the king in the passage before us, some suggest that the account here in 2 Kings 8 occurs chronologically before the incident involving Naaman in 2 Kings 5 since the king is unlikely to admit a leper into his presence. The fact that 2 Kings 5:27 says that the leprosy will cling to Gehazi "for ever" speaks against the possibility that Gehazi has been healed of this affliction.

On this occasion, King Jehoram is asking Gehazi about *all the great things that Elisha* has done. As noted previously, this king is not quite as evil as his parents (2 Kings 3:1, 2). He seems to have some measure of interest in the things of the Lord, especially the acts of the prophet Elisha. Several of Elisha's miracles have already occurred by this point (2 Kings 4:1–7:20).

What Do You Think?

How can we create an eagerness in others to hear about what God or godly people are doing?

Talking Points for Your Discussion

- Through obvious results
- Through being alert for receptiveness (proper timing)
- Through intercessory prayer

5. And it came to pass, as he was telling the king how he had restored a dead body to life, that, behold, the woman, whose son he had restored to life, cried to the king for her house and for her land. And Gehazi said, My lord, O king, this is the woman, and this is her son, whom Elisha restored to life.

Perhaps Gehazi's account of Elisha's "great things" begins with telling of Elisha's restoring a *dead body to life*. After all, this is a miracle that Gehazi himself has witnessed (2 Kings 4:27-37). One can only imagine Gehazi's utter disbelief when, after seven years, in walks the very woman of whom he is speaking! She has come to plead with *the king for her house and for her land*. She is accompanied by her son, perhaps in an effort to stir the king's sympathy for her predicament.

What Do You Think?

When was a time you obtained help or justice in an unexpected way? How might God have had a hand in it?

Talking Points for Your Discussion

- In a personal matter
- In the workplace
- In a legal matter
- Involving a church issue

B. Answer from the King (v. 6)

6. And when the king asked the woman, she told him. So the king appointed unto her a certain officer, saying, Restore all that was hers, and all the fruits of the field since the day that she left the land, even until now.

As we read that *the king asked the woman,* we do not know if he is asking her about Elisha's miracle or about why she has come to see him. This verse reads as if the latter situation is the case, since the words *so the king appointed* indicate his response to what the woman tells him. Perhaps the king is interested initially in hearing the woman's personal testimony about what Elisha has done for her and her son. But then he desires to know the reason for her coming to see him, so she proceeds to explain her dilemma.

The king, to his credit, appoints *a certain officer* to handle the woman's problem and restore her house and land. If, as suggested earlier, the king himself is the one who seized the woman's property after she left it behind, then perhaps hearing the account of the miracles that Elisha has done for the woman moves him to return what he has taken.

However, the king does not stop there. He also commands that *all the fruits of the field since the day that she left the land, even until now* be restored. This refers to whatever profits have been received from the land during the seven years of her absence (although those profits certainly are minimal because of the famine). Thus the Shunammite woman, who may wonder if she will even be allowed to see the king, discovers that she will receive more than she dreams possible.

Although the Lord is not specifically mentioned in the account of the woman's return to her homeland or that of the king's decision concerning her property, one can be sure that His hand is present in this turn of events. It is not just by luck that Gehazi is describing what Elisha has done for the woman just as she shows up to speak to the king!

The influence of divine providence in this case is reminiscent of what happens on several occasions within the book of Esther, which demonstrates God's special care to preserve His people from destruction. (See, for example, Esther 6:1-11, where Haman's plot to kill Mordecai results in Haman's praise of Mordecai!) Although the name of the Lord is not found anywhere in the book of Esther, His care is nevertheless evident in numerous "behind the scenes" ways.

> *What Do You Think?*
> Is it a mistake to see divine providence in all outcomes? Why, or why not?
> *Talking Points for Your Discussion*
> - What God "causes" vs. what God "permits"
> - The extreme view that "God causes everything"
> - The extreme view that God lets the world function solely through the laws of nature

It is noteworthy that King Jehoram's attitude toward another's property is quite the opposite of his parents' (Ahab and Jezebel). They had falsely accused righteous Naboth so that he could be stoned to death and Ahab could take possession of his vineyard (1 Kings 21:1-16). The prophet Elijah (Elisha's mentor) had been quick to confront Ahab with the evil of his actions (vv. 17-24).

❧ *ASKING PERMISSION* ❧

Christians in China have used various strategies to survive under a communist regime. Many tens of millions worship in secret house churches, while others participate in officially registered "Three-Self" churches. Although the official churches have been criticized for being too heavily influenced by the government, they do teach essential Christian doctrines and are growing rapidly.

One of these churches was having problems managing the large number of children attending its services. Rather than improvising a solution, they followed protocol and took the question to the local department of religious affairs. Surprisingly, the Communist authorities advised that they organize a separate children's worship meeting and even gave permission for a foreign missionary couple to be invited in to help them figure out how to do it!

Clearly, this is not the typical situation in China, no more so than it was typical for Israelite widows to have their land and seven years of produce returned to them. Sometimes, though, it is

God's plan to use the civil authorities as a channel of blessing.

Christians who obey the scriptural teaching to submit to the governing authorities (Romans 13:1-7) can experience these blessings as well as being a positive witness. Obviously, we must resist when we are commanded to violate God's law, and this too is a witness to those in power (Acts 4:18-20; 5:27-29). But before we look for subversive ways to carry out the work of God's kingdom, maybe a first step is just to ask permission. We might be surprised at the results. —A. W.

Conclusion

A. God's Care—Through Us?

We have noted in this study how God providentially cared for the Shunammite woman. It was no accident that she arrived to see the king at the very moment Gehazi was describing how Elisha had miraculously helped her. Many can testify how God used a confluence of events to bless them in a way that caught them completely by surprise.

In thinking about meeting the needs around us today, the importance of placing one's ultimate faith in God's care must not be overlooked. David once made this observation: "I have been young, and now am old; yet have I not seen the righteous forsaken, nor his seed begging bread" (Psalm 37:25). Many in our churches have gone through or are now going through difficult economic circumstances. Certainly we should never preach "have faith in God" as a way to avoid our responsibility to help others (James 2:14-17). But the Bible often highlights our heavenly Father's care for His children of faith and His promise not to abandon them. Difficult circumstances should not be made light of, but they can be prime opportunities for one's faith to prevail under pressure and, in turn, to provide a testimony to others of the Lord's faithfulness.

In truth, we live in a society where many people feel displaced—alone, unwanted, and unloved. In a word, they are *forgotten,* sadly in some instances by the church. Often a response to these situations does not require a significant amount (or any

Visual for Lesson 8. *Use this visual to start a discussion regarding how James 1:27 relates to today's lesson text.*

amount) of money—just some time. In nursing homes, for example, are many residents who seldom if ever hear from a family member or friend. For these individuals, one day runs into another with little variety. What a blessing it is to such a person when a caring Christian develops a friendship and visits on a regular basis! Such a ministry can include special days such as the person's birthday. Taking the person out for an occasional meal (if he or she is able) or inviting the person to one's home (again, if able) can provide a pleasant break from the daily routine. And older folks usually enjoy being around children; time spent with them can be delightful as well.

This is just one example of forgotten people who may be in your neighborhood. Can you think of others? Make a list. Start a ministry to them in your church, or involve your family in such a ministry. Such service to forgotten people will not be forgotten—by them or by you.

B. Prayer

Father, how grateful we are for Your care for us and for the way You use people and circumstances around us to provide in times of need. As we have freely received from You, may we be generous and gracious to others. In Jesus' name, amen.

C. Thought to Remember

Make every effort to see that the "displaced"
do not become the "misplaced."

INVOLVEMENT LEARNING

Some of the activities below are also found in the helpful student book, Adult Bible Class.
Don't forget to download the free reproducible page from www.standardlesson.com to enhance your lesson!

Into the Lesson

Have the phrase *Coincidence or Providence?* in view as learners assemble. Ask, "How can we discern between mere coincidence and God's interventional providence?" As the discussion runs its course, make sure to point out that God's providential actions involve God's working out His will in a nonmiraculous way. Note that in today's text the fact that Gehazi is recounting the raising of the widow's son with the king just as the widow and her son walk in shows God's providence.

Option: Before learners arrive, place in chairs copies of the All the Great Things Elisha Has Done exercise from the reproducible page, which you can download. This will allow your early arrivers a chance to review Elisha's ministry as a prelude to today's study.

Into the Word

Divide your class into groups to receive these assignments, for which you have created handouts: *Woes of Widows Group*—Today's text of 2 Kings 8:1-6 relates how a widow was displaced by famine and dispossessed of property. Compare and contrast this with the relief for widows you see in Acts 6:1-6. *Providential Provision Group*—Today's text of 2 Kings 8:1-6 reveals a time when God made sure the right people came together at the right time for a blessing. Compare and contrast this with how you see God working out His will in Acts 23:12-18. *Evil People Doing Good Group*—In today's text of 2 Kings 8:1-6, an evil king of Israel does the right thing. Compare and contrast this with what is described in Luke 18:1-5.

Allow groups to present their conclusions. *Option:* Following these, you can distribute copies of the Evil People and Right Behaviors exercise from the reproducible page, which you can download, for further small-group discussions.

Alternative: Write on the board the sentence *How is the widow of 2 Kings 8:1-6 like _____?* Then read the following list of names and situations for the blank, pausing between each for learners to give their reactions. Expected responses (although not the only possible responses) are in italics; don't read those unless everyone is stumped:

1. Abraham *(left home by faith in God's Word; Genesis 12:4);* 2. Jacob *(left home to escape a famine; Genesis 45:6; 46:1-6);* 3. The widow of Nain *(had a resurrected son; Luke 7:11-15);* 4. Samson *(spent time in Philistine territory; Judges 16);* 5. Esther *(she interrupted a king at the opportune time; Esther 5:1-8);* 6. Naomi *(went to a pagan place with her family to escape famine; Ruth 1:1);* 7. The prostitutes who argued over a baby before Solomon *(asked a king for justice; 1 Kings 3:16-28).*

Ask, "Are there other Bible people you can relate to the incident in today's text?" The compare-and-contrast discussion that follows will encourage a close reading of today's text.

Into Life

Display a world map. Have cut-out arrows and reusable adhesive available. Ask several people to come to the map and use the arrows to identify places where people have been displaced recently from their homes for any reason; allow only brief explanations of their choices.

Then ask, "What do you see that we as a class or as individuals can do to encourage justice and restoration in one of these places?" Allow free response. Consider a group commitment to a single project, whether through a church-related or social nonprofit organization. Perhaps provide contact information for those church benevolent agencies you know to be doing worthy and efficient projects.

Alternative: Distribute copies of the Widows Indeed in Need activity from the reproducible page, which you can download. Have learners wrestle with this either in small groups or as a whole class.

A King Acts on a Widow's Behalf

Jehoshaphat Makes Judicial Reforms

DEVOTIONAL READING: James 2:1-5
BACKGROUND SCRIPTURE: 2 Chronicles 18, 19

2 Chronicles 19:4-11

4 And Jehoshaphat dwelt at Jerusalem: and he went out again through the people from Beersheba to mount Ephraim, and brought them back unto the LORD God of their fathers.

5 And he set judges in the land throughout all the fenced cities of Judah, city by city,

6 And said to the judges, Take heed what ye do: for ye judge not for man, but for the LORD, who is with you in the judgment.

7 Wherefore now let the fear of the LORD be upon you; take heed and do it: for there is no

iniquity with the LORD our God, nor respect of persons, nor taking of gifts.

8 Moreover in Jerusalem did Jehoshaphat set of the Levites, and of the priests, and of the chief of the fathers of Israel, for the judgment of the LORD, and for controversies, when they returned to Jerusalem.

9 And he charged them, saying, Thus shall ye do in the fear of the LORD, faithfully, and with a perfect heart.

10 And what cause soever shall come to you of your brethren that dwell in their cities, between blood and blood, between law and commandment, statutes and judgments, ye shall even warn them that they trespass not against the LORD, and so wrath come upon you, and upon your brethren: this do, and ye shall not trespass.

11 And, behold, Amariah the chief priest is over you in all matters of the LORD; and Zebadiah the son of Ishmael, the ruler of the house of Judah, for all the king's matters: also the Levites shall be officers before you. Deal courageously, and the LORD shall be with the good.

KEY VERSE

[Jehoshaphat] said to the judges, Take heed what ye do: for ye judge not for man, but for the LORD, who is with you in the judgment. —**2 Chronicles 19:6**

GOD CALLS FOR JUSTICE

Unit 2: Justice Enacted
LESSONS 5–9

LESSON AIMS

After participating in this lesson, each student will be able to:

1. List the steps Jehoshaphat took as king of Judah to ensure that justice was administered in the land.

2. Compare and contrast the instructions that Jehoshaphat gave his judges with what is expected of judges today.

3. Suggest how the principles Jehoshaphat stressed can be used as criteria when deciding how to cast votes for judges in a democracy.

LESSON OUTLINE

Introduction

A. "For the Lord"

Brother Lawrence (born Herman Nicholas) was a monk who lived in the seventeenth century. He is known for his devotional classic *The Practice of the Presence of God*. Brother Lawrence's desire was to glorify God even in what seemed to be the least significant of activities. For him the "common business" of attending to his kitchen duties in the monastery was an act of worship.

One insight that is attributed to Brother Lawrence should cause us all to think: "Nor is it needful that we should have great things to do. . . . We can do little things for God; I turn the cake that is frying on the pan for love of him, and that done, if there is nothing else to call me, I prostrate myself in worship before him, who has given me grace to work; afterwards I rise happier than a king. It is enough for me to pick up but a straw from the ground for the love of God."

If it's important to cook and clean for God's glory, how much more important is it to render just legal verdicts in His sight! That's the topic of today's lesson. No matter what we do, it is always of more lasting import if we do it *for the Lord*.

B. Lesson Background

Today's lesson involves an action of King Jehoshaphat. He was one of the more godly kings of Judah during the period of the divided monarchy in Old Testament history. He ruled from about 873 to 848 BC. Second Chronicles 17:3, 4 says this of him: "And the Lord was with Jehoshaphat, because he walked in the first ways of his father David, and sought not unto Baalim; but sought to the Lord God of his father, and walked in his commandments."

Jehoshaphat's reign overlapped the ministry of the prophet Elijah, with the king's reign reaching its conclusion just as Elisha's prophetic ministry was beginning. We must keep in mind that the efforts of these two prophets were concentrated primarily in the northern kingdom (Israel), where (as we noted last week) they were used by the Lord to counter the influence of Kings Ahab (and his wife Jezebel), Ahaziah, and Jehoram (Joram).

The Bible does not mention any contact between Elijah and Jehoshaphat, but it does tell of one occasion when Elisha and King Jehoshaphat (of Judah) and King Jehoram (of Israel) were together. On that occasion, Elisha told Jehoram that he was granting the king's request for help only because of the presence of Jehoshaphat: "As the Lord of hosts liveth, before whom I stand, surely, were it not that I regard the presence of Jehoshaphat the king of Judah, I would not look toward thee, nor see thee" (2 Kings 3:14).

When Jehoshaphat's reign is first mentioned in 2 Chronicles, he is cited for his efforts to rid Judah of idol worship and to promote the teaching of God's law throughout Judah (2 Chronicles 17:1-9). Also noted is the respect in which he was held by surrounding peoples and the attention he gave to various projects and reforms (vv. 10-19).

On the downside, however, Jehoshaphat entered into an ill-advised alliance with King Ahab of Israel, who desired Jehoshaphat's aid in retaking some territory from the Syrians. At Ahab's behest, Jehoshaphat wore his royal robes into battle while Ahab disguised himself in an effort to keep a prophet's prediction of his death from being fulfilled (2 Chronicles 18:1-31). This episode nearly cost Jehoshaphat his life, but "the Lord helped him" (v. 31) and he was spared.

Jehoshaphat then "returned to his house in peace to Jerusalem" (2 Chronicles 19:1), but that peace was short-lived. After he returned, he was met by Jehu, the son of a "seer" (not to be confused with another Jehu who was a king of Israel). Jehu soundly rebuked Jehoshaphat for his attempt to "help the ungodly" and told him that "therefore is wrath upon thee from before the Lord" (2 Chronicles 19:2). But Jehu also commended Jehoshaphat for the "good things" he had done, including setting his heart on seeking the Lord (v. 3).

It seems that Jehoshaphat took the Jehu's chastening words seriously, for there follows the account of additional reforms, initiated by Jehoshaphat, that is found in today's printed text.

I. Reforms Beyond Jerusalem
(2 Chronicles 19:4-7)
A. Seizing the Initiative (v. 4)

4. And Jehoshaphat dwelt at Jerusalem: and he went out again through the people from Beersheba to mount Ephraim, and brought them back unto the LORD God of their fathers.

After being criticized by Jehu (see the Lesson Background), perhaps King Jehoshaphat of Judah spends some time reflecting on what he has heard. Maybe Jehoshaphat realizes that the time he spent trying to assist King Ahab of Israel in a questionable venture could have been invested in a far wiser and more God-honoring way.

Determined to alter his priorities and move both himself and his kingdom in the proper direction, Jehoshaphat goes *out again through the people from Beersheba to mount Ephraim*. Beersheba is located in the southernmost part of the territory belonging to the tribe of Judah. *Mount Ephraim* describes the hill country of central Palestine that belongs to the tribe of Ephraim, which is part of the northern kingdom of Israel. However, Ephraim's territory is at the southern end of the north's territory and is only 12 miles or so from Jerusalem. The distance *from Beersheba to mount Ephraim* is thus about 60 miles.

Why the territory of Ephraim is included in the scope of Jehoshaphat's interest is explained in 2 Chronicles 17:2. Not long after Jehoshaphat began his reign, "he placed forces in all the fenced cities of Judah, and set garrisons in the land of Judah, and in the cities of Ephraim, which Asa his father had taken." That is why the verse before

HOW TO SAY IT

Ahaziah	Ay-huh-*zye*-uh.
Amariah	*Am*-uh-**rye**-uh.
Baalim	Bay-uh-*leem*.
Elijah	Ee-*lye*-juh.
Ephraim	*Ee*-fray-im.
Ishmael	*Ish*-may-el.
Jehoram	Jeh-*ho*-rum.
Jehoshaphat	Jeh-*hosh*-uh-fat.
Jehu	*Jay*-hew.
Joram	*Jo*-ram.
Levites	*Lee*-vites.
Zebadiah	Zeb-uh-**dye**-uh.

us says that Jehoshaphat is going through this territory *again*. Jehoshaphat has already provided for the defense of this area against possible military attack. But now he is more concerned with the people's spiritual welfare—that they return *unto the Lord God of their fathers*.

❧ FAITH OF OUR FATHERS ❧

I have a Hindu friend who has visited my church, but he has made it clear that he is not interested in becoming a Christian. Even though he does not accept some of the core beliefs of Hinduism, he still identifies as a Hindu because it is his parents' faith. In his words, "I don't know what happens after we die, but I want to follow my family's religion so I can be with them wherever they end up."

In the same way, many who identify themselves as "Christians" today follow their family's faith without having truly made it their own. They may go for years appearing to be solid believers. They may even rise to positions of leadership in the church. But the reality is that their Christianity might be more an expression of culture and family ties than of genuine faith. A crisis or moment of temptation can expose the weakness of this spiritual foundation, to the great surprise of onlookers.

We, like Jehoshaphat, need to call people to return to the "God of their fathers." We are referring, of course, to the God of our *spiritual* fathers, which is not necessarily that of our *physical* fathers (see Luke 14:26). Our fathers in the faith—men like Moses, Paul, and Stephen—had relationships with God that motivated them to lives of sacrificial service. This is the kind of faith that saves and is worth passing on.   —A. W.

B. Selecting Judges (vv. 5-7)

5. And he set judges in the land throughout all the fenced cities of Judah, city by city.

Jehoshaphat's project of bringing the people "back unto the Lord God" (v. 4, above) includes appointing *judges in the land throughout all the fenced cities of Judah*. This is in accordance with Deuteronomy 16:18. In all the places where he has been intent on defending the residents from military attack, Jehoshaphat now seeks to defend from injustice. Perhaps an "every man for himself" or "might makes right" philosophy has been determining how disputes are handled if there have been no judges for some time in these cities.

> **What Do You Think?**
> Which criteria are most important when Christians cast their votes to elect judges? Which criteria are of lesser importance? Why?
> *Talking Points for Your Discussion*
> ▪ Church membership
> ▪ Community involvement
> ▪ Legal experience as a prosecutor
> ▪ Legal experience as a defense attorney
> ▪ Character
> ▪ Endorsements

6. And said to the judges, Take heed what ye do: for ye judge not for man, but for the LORD, who is with you in the judgment.

Jehoshaphat's counsel to the judges he appoints is wise indeed! To see one's judgment as being done *for the Lord* will mean bringing it into submission to His laws—God's standards of right and wrong. Judging that is done for the Lord will not allow factors such as social standing, gender, or race to determine how a given case should be decided.

> **What Do You Think?**
> What challenges do you think a Christian might face in seeking or rendering verdicts according to Jehoshaphat's *for the Lord* standard?
> *Talking Points for Your Discussion*
> ▪ As a judge
> ▪ As a juror
> ▪ As an attorney

The statement that the Lord is *with you in the judgment* provides encouragement to the appointed judges. The Lord will bless their efforts if they seek to honor Him. The phrase may also imply that the Lord will be watching whenever they issue judgments. If they fail to respect God's authority or if they do anything that prejudices their judgment, then the Lord will not ignore what they have done. As "the Judge of all the earth" (Genesis 18:25), God will hold them accountable. There has always been a court that is more supreme than humanity's highest courts.

7. Wherefore now let the fear of the LORD be upon you; take heed and do it: for there is no iniquity with the LORD our God, nor respect of persons, nor taking of gifts.

Judging in *the fear of the Lord* will keep one from harboring attitudes and participating in actions that will pervert the cause of justice. The Lord provides the ultimate example for judges: *there is no iniquity with the Lord our God, nor respect of persons, nor taking of gifts.*

The principles of impartiality and refusing bribes are based on instructions found in the Law of Moses. *Respect of persons* (showing partiality) is prohibited in Exodus 23:6, 7; Leviticus 19:15; Deuteronomy 1:17; 16:19a (see also Proverbs 24:23). Bribes are forbidden in Exodus 23:8; Deuteronomy 16:19b; 27:25 (see also Proverbs 17:23; Micah 3:11). We serve a God who does not show favoritism (Acts 10:34; Romans 2:11; 1 Peter 1:17).

II. Reforms Within Jerusalem
(2 CHRONICLES 19:8-11)
A. Appointing Officials (v. 8)

8. Moreover in Jerusalem did Jehoshaphat set of the Levites, and of the priests, and of the chief of the fathers of Israel, for the judgment of the LORD, and for controversies, when they returned to Jerusalem.

After covering the territory "from Beersheba to mount Ephraim" (v. 4), Jehoshaphat returns to Jerusalem and addresses the need for administering justice there as well. Here his appointments are somewhat more extensive than they were in the territory he previously covered.

The Levites and priests are involved primarily in the religious life of Israel, being engaged in activities such as offering sacrifices, leading worship, and teaching God's law to the people. Thus any judgments they render may deal primarily with questions pertaining to religious practices. Those numbered among *the chief of the fathers of Israel* are likely some of the elders or heads of families and clans. Their primary responsibility may

Visual for Lesson 9. *Point to this visual as you pose to your learners the various discussion questions in today's lesson.*

be to address controversies that are not as religious in nature.

Jehoshaphat's use of the Levites and priests may be an effort to bring the judicial system in Jerusalem under the close scrutiny of the religious leaders. While such a practice would likely meet with significant resistance today because of the often cited idea of "separation of church and state," it is very appropriate for Old Testament Israel due to its status as the chosen people of God.

Because Jerusalem is the city of God's special presence (1 Kings 9:3; 11:36) on account of the temple built by Solomon, it should be an exemplary place in the matter of following God's law faithfully. Thus extra measures are taken by Jehoshaphat as he continues to bring the people back to the God of their fathers.

What Do You Think?
  Which parts of the Bible can and should a judge use to inform his or her thinking while hearing cases in a modern courtroom?
Talking Points for Your Discussion
  ▪ Criminal cases
  ▪ Civil cases

B. Assigning Duties (vv. 9-11)

9. And he charged them, saying, Thus shall ye do in the fear of the LORD, faithfully, and with a perfect heart.

As with the judges of verse 7 above, Jehoshaphat emphasizes to the officials in Jerusalem that they must fulfill their duties *in the fear of the Lord.* He also encourages them to do their work *faithfully, and with a perfect heart.* The Hebrew word translated "perfect" is a form of the word *shalom,* often translated "peace." In this context, the word conveys the idea of wholeness or completeness. Today we might think of the concept of *integrity,* which also carries with it the idea of completeness. (An *integer* in mathematics is a "whole number," and to be *integrated* is to be united.)

What Do You Think?

How should you apply the judging principles in today's text to your own life personally?

Talking Points for Your Discussion

- In a role as a parent
- In a role as a church leader
- In a role as a teacher
- In a role as a boss

---

10. And what cause soever shall come to you of your brethren that dwell in their cities, between blood and blood, between law and commandment, statutes and judgments, ye shall even warn them that they trespass not against the LORD, and so wrath come upon you, and upon your brethren: this do, and ye shall not trespass.

Jehoshaphat also instructs the appointed judges concerning the kinds of cases they will decide. The meaning of the phrase *between blood and blood* is difficult to determine with certainty. It may refer to cases involving closely related family members (blood relatives), which may develop into full-scale feuds. The idea of "bloodshed" (loss of life) may be in view as well. Special wisdom will be necessary in handling such cases and making certain that justice is fairly and correctly administered.

The terms *law and commandment, statutes and judgments* are all words used in the Old Testament to describe the requirements that God gave His people to live by. It may be best not to try to distinguish shades of meaning between these terms; the point of Jehoshaphat's instruction is that *any* matter involving something covered within God's

law must be handled in a manner that is consistent with the holy, righteous character of the giver of that law. Thus these individuals appointed by Jehoshaphat are warned not to *trespass . . . against the Lord.*

11. And, behold, Amariah the chief priest is over you in all matters of the LORD; and Zebadiah the son of Ishmael, the ruler of the house of Judah, for all the king's matters: also the Levites shall be officers before you. Deal courageously, and the LORD shall be with the good.

Now Jehoshaphat names those whom he has designated to administer justice in specific areas. First, *Amariah the chief priest is over you in all matters of the Lord.* With any disputes of a more religious nature, this man will see that proper decisions are rendered. For example, a case involving the presence of an alleged false prophet among the people (see the warnings in Deuteronomy 13:1-5; 18:20-22) might be a matter for Amariah and those under him to evaluate.

A certain Zebadiah, described as *the ruler of the house of Judah,* is to be in charge of *all the king's matters.* Such matters may concern issues of a more secular nature (perhaps a question involving restoration of stolen property).

The Levites are then given the responsibility to be *officers before you.* Their specific duties are not highlighted—possibly they simply are to serve as assistants wherever needed, whether the issue in question is one of the *matters of the Lord* or one of *the king's matters.* If there is uncertainty concerning which category a given case falls (religious "matters of the Lord" or secular "matters of the king"), perhaps the Levites will be responsible for making that decision.

The final portion of Jehoshaphat's challenge notes one ingredient that has not been mentioned previously: courage. It takes courage for a judge to stand for what is right, especially when an evil king comes to power. It takes courage to defy those who would use power or wealth to influence a judge to decide a case a certain way.

For now, a righteous king—Jehoshaphat—is in power in Judah. True justice will be promoted during his reign, for he is a king whose heart is "lifted up in the ways of the Lord" (2 Chronicles 17:6). In fact, the name *Jehoshaphat* means "the Lord judges." But what will happen when Jehoshaphat dies? For justice to continue to prevail throughout Judah, those in power (including judges) must remember that the Lord is Judah's true king. He *shall be with the good*—with those who see themselves as the Lord's ambassadors for justice and righteousness in this world.

❧ *A Courageous Judge* ❧

In 1955, President Eisenhower appointed Frank M. Johnson, Jr. (1918–1999) to the U.S. District Court in Montgomery, Alabama. At a time when most courts in the South were working to suppress civil rights for African-Americans, Johnson took a courageous stand to guarantee the constitutional rights of all Americans.

Among other things, Judge Johnson ruled against segregated city buses, struck down unfair voter registration practices, and curtailed the abuses against civil rights protesters. His principled actions put him and his family in grave danger: his mother's home was bombed, and a cross was burned in his yard. Refusing to be intimidated, he persisted for many years on the bench.

Generations of judges before Johnson had issued rulings that stayed in line with popular opinion more than the principles of the law. But Judge Johnson and others who shared his courage made profound changes. You and I may not have the authority of a federal judge, but we do influence those around and after us. Will you take a courageous stand for what is right? Will you leave a legacy of godliness for future generations?   —A. W.

> *What Do You Think?*
> What does Jesus' command to "judge not" (Matthew 7:1) imply for Christians? How has this passage been misunderstood?
>
> *Talking Points for Your Discussion*
> - Matthew 7:15-20
> - John 7:24
> - Romans 14:4, 10, 13
> - 1 Corinthians 5:12, 13
> - Titus 3:10
> - James 2:13; 4:12

Conclusion
A. Giving Justice

In the process of appointing judges, King Jehoshaphat issued a very bold command for them to fear the Lord and respect His law. Such a request was quite appropriate for God's chosen, covenant people. They were expected to apply His law to every part of life.

But what about Christians today who live in highly secular settings? Justice often is seen as an inalienable right today. People who believe they have been wronged will "demand justice." They insist on getting their "rights" or "entitlements." Justice is viewed primarily as something to be extracted from the judicial system—the courts. Seldom is justice seen as something that we have the privilege of *giving* to others. In striving to promote justice, sometimes we will have to initiate it instead of depending on the judicial system.

Part of promoting justice and righteousness involves living as salt and light (Matthew 5:13-16). In Paul's letter to Titus, the repeated emphasis on goodness (whether it is good people or good works) cannot be missed (Titus 1:8; 2:3, 7, 14; 3:1, 8, 14). Peter, in addressing Christians who have been victims of unjust persecution, encourages his readers to be faithful in "well doing" (1 Peter 2:15; 4:19); though they may not receive justice from the authorities, they can still treat others in a just and right manner (2:21-23).

Today we may wish for the kind of judges whom Jehoshaphat appointed in his time—those who would carry out their duties in the fear of God. But even if such judges are not in power or are in a distinct minority, that does not lessen our duty as Christians to live in the fear of God.

B. Prayer

Father, we live in a world that has turned away from Your standards. Help us to initiate your justice at the most basic level: in transforming hearts and lives through the gospel of Your Son. In Jesus' name, amen.

C. Thought to Remember
Live by Heaven's just standards.

INVOLVEMENT LEARNING

Some of the activities below are also found in the helpful student book, Adult Bible Class.
Don't forget to download the free reproducible page from www.standardlesson.com to enhance your lesson!

Into the Lesson

Prepare in advance 11 slips of paper with the following Scripture segments printed on them, one segment per slip: 17:3, 4 / 17:6 / 17:7-9 / 18:3, 4 / 18:6 / 20:2, 3 / 20:5, 6 / 20:18 / 20:20, 21 / 20:27, 28 / 20:32. Distribute the slips of paper as learners arrive. Write *2 Chronicles* on the board. Say loudly and emphatically, "Great Jumpin' Jehoshaphat!" Ask if anyone has heard that expression. Then say, "Let's listen to what some passages from 2 Chronicles reveal about King Jehoshaphat's attitudes and decisions." Call for the texts to be read in sequence, without commentary.

At the end say, "We don't really see any reference to Jehoshaphat's doing any jumping, but the label *great* is not out of line, is it? Today's study text reveals one aspect of his greatness." (*Alternative:* Put all the passages on a single sheet of paper for one of your good oral readers to read.)

Note that in 2 Chronicles 19:3, which immediately precedes today's text, a man named Jehu said to the king, "There are good things found in thee, in that thou . . . hast prepared thine heart to seek God." Comment: "Jehoshaphat had just returned from the military humiliation that he and Ahab, king of Israel, suffered at the hands of God's enemies (see 2 Chronicles 18:1–19:2). Jehoshaphat needed God's word of encouragement, for he had been foolish. Today's text seems to indicate he had learned his lesson, even if by the hard way!"

Into the Word

Create a handout of the following questions, headed *You Be the Judge.* The verse references given in brackets indicate where the answers are found, but don't include those on the handout.

1. How did Jehoshaphat ensure that the people were aware of where their allegiance should lie? *[v. 4]* 2. Why is the fact that judges were appointed by the king significant? *[v. 5]* 3. What difference did it make that judges resided in "fenced" cit-

ies? *[v. 5]* 4. What difference should it have made to a judge to remember that he answered first of all to God? *[v. 6]* 5. In what ways was a judge to resemble God himself? *[v. 7]* 6. What sorts of cases could the judges in Jerusalem be called on to settle? *[vv. 8-10]* 7. In what sense should living "in the fear of the Lord" control the judicial decisions made? *[vv. 9, 10]* 8. Why were the separate appointments of chief justices for "all matters of the Lord" and "all the king's matters" important? *[v. 11a]* 9. What did courage have to do with wise judgment? *[v. 11b]* 10. How did Jehoshaphat's final blessing "the Lord shall be with the good" encourage justice? *[v. 11b]*

After your class discusses each question, ask, "What implications does this have for today?" (Try to keep the resulting discussions from turning political.) Since this exercise may be very time-consuming for a whole-class discussion, you may wish to use small groups and assign only half or a third of the questions to each group; groups should be prepared to summarize their answers for the class as a whole.

Into Life

Say, "How does today's study provide clues for casting votes for judges during elections?" Let the class offer suggestions. *Option:* Distribute copies of the Judge's Checklist activity from the reproducible page, which you can download, to enhance this discussion. Consider having a Christian judge or lawyer briefly address your class on the issue of what makes a good judge.

Close by noting that although few are set apart formally as judges, all Christians are commissioned as priests (1 Peter 2:5). In this light, lead the class in singing the hymn "A Charge to Keep I Have." For convenience, the stanzas are included in the Commissioned and Charged section of the reproducible page. Allow learners to note parallels between the hymn and today's text.

Jehoshaphat Makes Judicial Reforms

PRAISE FOR GOD'S JUSTICE

DEVOTIONAL READING: Luke 4:16-21

BACKGROUND SCRIPTURE: Psalm 146; Exodus 21–23; Isaiah 58

PSALM 146

1 Praise ye the LORD. Praise the LORD, O my soul.

2 While I live will I praise the LORD: I will sing praises unto my God while I have any being.

3 Put not your trust in princes, nor in the son of man, in whom there is no help.

4 His breath goeth forth, he returneth to his earth; in that very day his thoughts perish.

5 Happy is he that hath the God of Jacob for his help, whose hope is in the LORD his God:

6 Which made heaven, and earth, the sea, and all that therein is: which keepeth truth for ever:

7 Which executeth judgment for the oppressed: which giveth food to the hungry. The LORD looseth the prisoners:

8 The LORD openeth the eyes of the blind: the LORD raiseth them that are bowed down: the LORD loveth the righteous:

9 The LORD preserveth the strangers; he relieveth the fatherless and widow: but the way of the wicked he turneth upside down.

10 The LORD shall reign for ever, even thy God, O Zion, unto all generations. Praise ye the LORD.

KEY VERSES

Happy is he that hath the God of Jacob for his help, whose hope is in the LORD his God. . . . Which executeth judgment for the oppressed: which giveth food to the hungry. —**Psalm 146:5, 7**

Photo: Domus / Digital Vision / Thinkstock

GOD CALLS FOR JUSTICE

Unit 3: Justice Promised

LESSONS 10–13

LESSON AIMS

After participating in this lesson, each student will be able to:

1. List the attributes of God that relate to justice.

2. Relate the attributes of God and His justice to situations both in ancient Israel and in situations of his or her experience where those attributes address a need for justice.

3. Write a poem or song that praises God's justice.

LESSON OUTLINE

Introduction

A. Everyone Wants Justice

In September of 2009, the small community of Beason, Illinois (a few miles from where I live), experienced a horrific mass murder when five members of a family were bludgeoned to death. Only a 3-year-old survived. Everyone who has heard of this case wants justice done for this family.

Hundreds of other examples of criminal acts could be offered. They all have a common thread: every decent and honorable person wants justice. The problem is that not everyone gets justice in this world. For perfect justice we must turn to the only one who can give it, and that is the God of the universe.

B. Lesson Background

Traditionally, the book of Psalms, also known as *the Psalter,* has been divided into five sections; you can see their divisions in all major English translations of the Bible. The overall structure of the collection of these books points to the desire of God's people for justice. Books I and II suggest the establishment and climax of the Davidic dynasty (example: Psalms 2 and 72, respectively). The Babylonian captivity of 586 BC points to the failure of this dynasty in Judah, an emphasis in Book III (example: Psalm 89).

The answer to the failure of David's earthly kingdom is found in Book IV, where Yahweh God is king (examples: Psalms 96–99) during "wilderness wanderings" (examples: Psalm 90–94, 105, 106). Book V, for its part, looks forward to the reestablishment of the Davidic dynasty in a coming king-priest (Psalm 110). Thus, the Psalter ends with an exiled remnant praying for justice from the only one who can give it: the true king of Israel, the Creator of the universe.

Today's text is an individual hymn of praise for God's justice. It is a continuation of the psalm before it, which ends with this statement: "My mouth shall speak the praise of the Lord: and let all flesh bless his holy name for ever and ever" (Psalm 145:21). Psalm 146 is the beginning of a series of psalms of praise (namely, 146–150) within Book V that wraps up the entirety of the Psalter.

All are praise hymns, with the phrase *Praise ye the Lord* occurring at the beginning and end of each.

Why such praise? Because the Creator God is a God of justice, and one day He will allow His people to prevail over the injustices of the world. Psalm 146 is primarily about justice for the downtrodden. The rest of the Psalms in this subgrouping hint at this theme (see Psalm 147:6, 11; 148:11; 149:6-9) as these Psalms progress to total praise in Psalm 150.

I. Call to Praise
(PSALM 146:1, 2)
A. Present Exhortation (v. 1)

1. Praise ye the LORD. Praise the LORD, O my soul.

The phrase *praise ye the Lord* is a translation of a Hebrew word most Christians know very well: *Hallelujah.* This word functions as bookends for each of the concluding psalms in Psalm 146–150. After challenging the reader to *praise ye the Lord,* the psalmist repeats the exhortation to himself—*praise the Lord, O my soul.* People are more likely to follow you when you give them an example. If you praise the Lord, perhaps others will too.

The fact that the word *LORD* occurs with small capital letters indicates that *Yahweh* is the word being translated. This is God's personal name. It is *Yahweh,* the God who revealed His name to Moses (Exodus 3), whom we praise. God's personal name is used 11 times in this psalm if we count the short form of *Yah* in *Hallelujah* at the beginning and the end.

HOW TO SAY IT

Babylonian	Bab-ih-*low*-nee-un.
Davidic	Duh-*vid*-ick.
Josiah	Jo-*sigh*-uh.
Judah	*Joo*-duh.
Megiddo	Muh-*gid*-doe.
Pharaohnecho	*Fay*-ro-*nee*-ko.
Psalter	*Sal*-ter.
Thessalonians	*Thess*-uh-**lo**-nee-unz (*th* as in *thin*).
Yahweh (Hebrew)	*Yah*-weh.

B. Future Intent (v. 2)

2. While I live will I praise the LORD: I will sing praises unto my God while I have any being.

This verse is a good example of Hebrew parallelism. This is where ideas are repeated using slightly different words. We easily see that *while I live* is parallel to *while I have any being.* The phrase *will I praise* is parallel to *I will sing praises.* Finally, *the Lord* is parallel to *my God.* More than likely, the psalmist is referring to the very psalm we are studying in expressing his intent to praise. In singing a psalm, one makes music to the eternal God, something we should do as long as we live. This is a commitment to praise for a lifetime. Such a commitment, like that of a marriage, cannot be sporadic or intermittent.

What Do You Think?

How do your experiences praising the Lord compare with the psalmist's?

Talking Points for Your Discussion
- In difficult circumstances
- In good circumstances
- In combining continual praise with sincerity

II. Trust in Whom?
(PSALM 146:3-5)
A. Capabilities of Mortals (v. 3)

3. Put not your trust in princes, nor in the son of man, in whom there is no help.

The word for *princes* is a general word for "nobility" (see Proverbs 8:16; 25:6, 7). In Psalm 149:8 we see a word translated *nobles* standing parallel to the word *kings.* In Numbers 21:18, *princes* is parallel to *nobles.* Judah's experiences with kings after David and Solomon were generally negative. Those kings were responsible for Judah's being in exile and for the suffering of an entire nation.

The phrase *son of man* is a description of these leaders as merely frail humans (mortals). To be "son of [something]" in this context means to have the characteristics of that something—hence *son of man* emphasizes the mortality of a leader. To put too much trust in earthly leaders is dangerous! They are, after all, only human.

III. Attributes of God

(PSALM 146:6-10)

A. Creator (v. 6a)

6a. Which made heaven, and earth, the sea, and all that therein is.

Many teachings about God flow from the fact that He is the Creator of the universe (Acts 4:24; 14:15; 17:24; Revelation 10:6; 14:7). Can one's help come from any other source? Compare Psalm 121:1, 2. The Creator naturally cares for and protects that which He has created.

❧ REFLECTIONS OVER ICE CREAM ❧

One afternoon when nothing seemed to go right, I left work early and treated myself to a bowl of ice cream. A few minutes into my sundae, a family walked into the restaurant. The family included a girl of about 9 years old; she was bald and wearing a face mask to protect herself from infection. Tears sprang to my eyes as I thought about my own daughter. Suddenly my issues didn't seem important anymore, but now my mind began to turn over a much bigger problem. God has the power to spare this child from sickness and suffering. Why doesn't He?

The above reflections may seem a little off topic in our consideration of God's actions as Creator in Psalm 146:6. But what we see here is very similar to God's response to Job's questions about unjust suffering: God simply points out the marvels of creation and Job's own limitations (Job 38–41).

Looking out the restaurant window at the trees blowing in the wind, I thought about the complexity of nature. Surely a God who creates and sustains this fragile, interconnected world must know what He is doing in the life of a sick little girl. Somehow this wise Creator, whose ways are mysterious like the wind (John 3:8), will work out even the worst situations for the good of His children (Romans 8:28).

—A. W.

B. Frailty of Plans (v. 4)

4. His breath goeth forth, he returneth to his earth; in that very day his thoughts perish.

Humans are destined to die (Genesis 3:19), with some notable exceptions (see Genesis 5:24; 2 Kings 2:11; 1 Thessalonians 4:17). The intentions of a ruler, whether good or bad, cease at that ruler's last breath of life.

Perhaps the psalmist is thinking of King Josiah (ruled 640–609 BC), who truly wanted to help Judah during her dark days (2 Kings 22:1–23:30). But all the good help that Josiah did was cut short when he died at the Battle of Megiddo, at the hands of Pharaohnechoh (23:29). Josiah's four successors undid all of Josiah's godly reforms (23:32, 37; 24:9, 19). Josiah's intentions died with him.

C. Blessed in God (v. 5)

5. Happy is he that hath the God of Jacob for his help, whose hope is in the LORD his God.

The Hebrew behind the word *happy* is also translated *blessed* in various places. It is the first word of Psalm 1:1, where the blessed person takes delight in the instruction of Yahweh. In the verse before us, the blessing is that of having the *God of Jacob* as one's help in life. This is a distinct commitment to a worldview in which one's hope is in the one who has worked in history to bring about the redemption of not only God's people but of the entire universe. The God of Jacob is none other than Yahweh, as again we see the word *LORD* in small capital letters. From this point, the psalmist gives us numerous attributes of Yahweh God to demonstrate that He is a God of justice.

B. Reliable (v. 6b)

6b. Which keepeth truth for ever.

Someone has said that "truth is the first casualty of war." We are in a spiritual war! Keeping evil from overwhelming our lives requires constant

Praise for God's Justice

vigilance for the truth. But we have the best ally one can have: God. One of the great attributes of the Creator is that He is the keeper of truth. Without truth there can be no justice. In this sense God keeps faith forever with His creation.

C. Advocate (vv. 7-9)

7a. Which executeth judgment for the oppressed.

The oppressed, by definition, have trouble getting justice. Often the oppressed are those who are in economic distress. God has special concern for such folks. The God who is able to create Heaven and earth is quite willing and able to see that the oppressed get justice (see Psalm 76:8, 9; 103:6). We will discuss some specific categories of oppressed people as we consider verse 9, below.

7b. Which giveth food to the hungry.

While it is true "man doth not live by bread only" (Deuteronomy 8:3), we must still have food. God may use supernatural means to feed His people (Exodus 16; Matthew 14:16-21). More often, God works through His people to provide food for others (Leviticus 19:9, 10; Matthew 25:34-40). To give food to the hungry is thus to act on behalf of God (compare Isaiah 58:7). Jesus shows us that we should ask for our "daily bread" (Matthew 6:11). Regardless of how God does it, we should trust that He will feed the hungry.

7c. The Lord looseth the prisoners.

It is a self-evident truth that God sets prisoners free! He gave birth to Israel by delivering the Israelite slaves from Egyptian bondage. Hundreds of years later, He releases His people again, from Babylonian captivity. In ancient Israel, people could sell themselves into indentured servitude in order to pay off debt, but Yahweh God placed limitations by law upon this kind of slavery (see Exodus 21:2).

Setting prisoners free is a jubilee act (Leviticus 25:39-55; see Lesson 3). When Isaiah presents the coming Messiah, he does it in the context of a jubilee in which he will "proclaim liberty to the captives, and the opening of the prison to them that are bound" (Isaiah 61:1; quoted by Jesus in Luke 4:18). The most important prison to be released from is that of sin (Acts 8:23; 2 Timothy 2:26).

What Do You Think?
How has God worked in your life when you have faced the things described in verse 7?
Talking Points for Your Discussion
- When you felt oppressed
- When you didn't have enough food
- When you were in bondage of some kind

8a. The Lord openeth the eyes of the blind.

Some students think this phrase belongs with the one before it—setting prisoners free. Prisoners in ancient times often are held in complete darkness. Being set free means being able to see again after adjusting to the light. Figuratively, *the blind* refers to people who are groping around in the darkness of their minds or hearts, what we may call *spiritual darkness* (Romans 1:18-32).

Jesus' healings included giving sight to the blind (see Mark 8:22-26; 10:46-52; etc.). But the worst kind of blindness is spiritual blindness, and that is the most important thing to fix. Jesus criticized those who could see but refused to perceive (Matthew 13:14, quoting Isaiah 6:9; also compare Acts 28:26, 27).

8b. The Lord raiseth them that are bowed down.

This phrase connects this psalm with the previous psalm: "The Lord . . . raiseth up all those that be bowed down" (Psalm 145:14). Certainly, we

Visual for Lessons 4 & 10. *Have this visual on display as you work your way through the various categories of people mentioned in today's text.*

can take *bowed down* in a physical sense. However, the figurative sense is more powerful, with reference to those bowed down in mind, spirit, and heart. These are people who cannot get up spiritually on their own. Jesus addresses this problem as He ministers to "sheep having no shepherd" (Matthew 9:36).

> **What Do You Think?**
> How do we continue to praise God when He doesn't seem to answer our prayers for relief?
> *Talking Points for Your Discussion*
> ▪ When promoting the gospel brings hardship (2 Corinthians 11:16-31)
> ▪ When holy living brings hardship (Daniel 6)
> ▪ The injustice of the cross (Mark 14:36; 15:34)

8c. The LORD loveth the righteous.

Psalms 33:5 and 45:7 speak of the Lord's love of righteousness. The text before us pushes the idea further in proclaiming the Lord's love for *the righteous,* meaning "righteous people." Each item in Proverbs 6:16-19 reflects the opposite of righteousness—things the Lord hates. Part of knowing what it means to be righteous (and thus to be loved by God) is to know what it means to be unrighteous. The best way to avoid unrighteousness is to pursue righteousness. God especially loves those who pursue righteousness (Proverbs 15:9).

The concepts of *righteousness* and *judgment* (meaning "justice") are virtual synonyms in many passages (examples Psalms 9:8; 37:6; 72:2). Indeed, righteousness and judgment (justice) underpin God's very throne (Psalm 89:14; 97:2).

9a. The LORD preserveth the strangers.

The phrase *the strangers* reveals a specific category of "the oppressed" in verse 7a, above. Other words for *strangers* are *alien* (Psalm 69:8; Ephesians 2:12) and *sojourner* (Genesis 23:4; Psalm 39:12). Such people have no inherited rights or land, yet God takes care of them; examples include Abraham (Genesis 23:4) and Moses (Exodus 2:22; 18:3). Israel is not allowed to oppress a stranger (Exodus 22:21; 23:9; Leviticus 19:33) because the Israelites themselves had been strangers in Egypt. Strangers are to be treated in a way similar to the poor (Leviticus 19:10). This is at least one way *the*

Lord preserveth the strangers: through the kindness of His own people.

Jesus is presented in John's Gospel as a stranger who is rejected (John 1:11). The apostle Peter considers Christians to be strangers in this world, with no true inheritance on this earth (1 Peter 1:1, 4). He appeals to Christians to live righteous lives because we are "strangers and pilgrims" here (1 Peter 2:11). We are not home yet! In the meantime, God takes care of us.

9b. He relieveth the fatherless and widow.

Here we see two more specific categories of "the oppressed" from verse 7a, above. *The fatherless and widow* typically are mentioned together in Scripture (examples: Job 24:3; Isaiah 10:1, 2). Combined references to strangers, the fatherless, and widows are also quite common (examples: Deuteronomy 10:18; 24:17-21; Zechariah 7:10).

The word *relieveth* can mean "restores." This concept is used in the psalm that follows this one to bind it to this subgrouping on God's justice: "The Lord lifteth up the meek: he casteth the wicked down to the ground" (Psalm 147:6).

God has given strict laws and dire warnings about the abuse of orphans and widows (Exodus 22:22-24; Deuteronomy 27:19). The prophets seek justice for these two groups (see Isaiah 1:17, 23; Jeremiah 22:3; etc.). Jesus refers to widows to make a strong statement about injustice (see Luke 20:47). The first-century church paid close attention to the need to assist widows (Acts 6:1-5; 1 Timothy 5:3-16) and orphans (James 1:27). God always is concerned with the helpless of society, and often He works through His people to assist them.

9c. But the way of the wicked he turneth upside down.

The Hebrew text literally reads, "And way of wicked ones he bends [makes crooked]." Understanding *way* as figurative, the translation *turneth upside down* seems very appropriate. No one can stop God from carrying out His plans against the wicked. "Consider the work of God: for who can make that straight, which he hath made crooked?" (Ecclesiastes 7:13). God will not fail to frustrate the plans and designs of wicked people who plot against His righteous and helpless ones (see Psalm 1:6; Micah 2:1-3).

❧ LESSONS FROM A HAPLESS HIJACKER ❧

Reginald Chua boarded Philippine Airlines Flight 812 in May 2000. He subsequently brandished a gun and a grenade as he robbed passengers. On his orders, the flight crew reduced altitude to 6,000 feet, depressurized the plane, and opened the door so that he could jump out with a homemade parachute. The wind was so strong he had to get a "helpful" push from a flight attendant. Witnesses saw him separate from the parachute in midair and plunge to his death; his body was recovered the next day.

We may wish that all criminals received immediate justice for their evil deeds! But that just doesn't happen. Neither do righteous people always enjoy immediate benefits of their righteousness. This may seem unfair until we remember that none of us is innocent (Romans 3:10). What if God instantly gave us what we deserved whenever we sinned against Him?

Peter reminds us that God is "not slack concerning his promise," but rather "is longsuffering to usward"; God wants everyone to come to repentance (2 Peter 3:9). This too is a way of turning the way of the wicked upside down. It's the way we should hope, pray, and work for. —A. W.

D. Eternality (v. 10a)

10a. The LORD shall reign for ever, even thy God, O Zion, unto all generations.

The kings of Israel and Judah do not reign forever (see discussion on vv. 3, 4, above). The great injustices they bring upon God's people come to an end eventually. But Yahweh God reigns forever, and His reign is one of righteousness and justice. This is the heartbeat of the "Yahweh reigns" psalms (see Psalms 96:10; 97:1, 2; 99:1, 4).

Taken literally, *Zion* refers to a mountain adjacent to Jerusalem (2 Kings 19:31). Figuratively, however, Zion refers to the people of God. He forever lives so that our descendants *(unto all generations)* will be able to praise this same king until Jesus returns. When everything around us seems to be failing and wickedness seems to be winning, God still reigns as eternal king. His reign is one of justice and equity. Amen.

IV. Reminder to Praise
(PSALM 146:10b)

10b. Praise ye the LORD.

This short command—literally, *Hallelujah*—repeats the opening of this psalm. There is no better way to end a psalm such as this!

Conclusion
A. The Justice of God

Often there seems to be no justice to be found with human leaders, even in the twenty-first century. Human leaders and institutions cannot save us. In fact, in their clumsy attempts to "save" us, they actually may harm us. Our help, and thus our hope, must be in Yahweh God alone. To Him belong attributes that indicate His perfection and worthiness of praise that we have seen in this lesson. Therefore, all generations of God's people should praise Yahweh God. One day all the injustices of the world will be judged, and justice will prevail in the new heavens and the new earth (see Revelation 21, 22; compare Isaiah 60).

B. Prayer

O Lord our God, we put our trust in You and not in man. We pray for justice for the oppressed, and we pray for the strength to be Your agents who provide that justice. Overturn the plans of the wicked. In Jesus' name, amen.

C. Thought to Remember

Praise Yahweh God—again!

INVOLVEMENT LEARNING

Some of the activities below are also found in the helpful student book, Adult Bible Class.
Don't forget to download the free reproducible page from www.standardlesson.com to enhance your lesson!

Into the Lesson

Create a handout entitled "Book Titles" with the following 10 entries:

> *A Symphony of Praise: Psalm ___*
> *Astronomical Praise: Psalm ___*
> *Bandages: Psalm ___*
> *Dancing and Music in Praise: Psalm ___*
> *God the Creator: Psalm ___*
> *Have Breath, Will Praise: Psalm ___*
> *New Song of Praise: Psalm ___*
> *Praise from Highest High and Lowest Low: Psalm ___*
> *Princes—Who Needs 'Em? Psalm ___*
> *Weather Wonders: Psalm ___*

Put these instructions on the handout: "Each of Psalms 146–150 begins and ends with a call to *Praise the Lord!* like bookends of emphasis. Look at these 10 book titles (which are in alphabetical order) and find which of Psalms 146–150 best identifies each. Each of these five psalms will be used twice." Place copies of the handout in chairs so learners can begin working on this activity as they arrive.

The answers (not to be put on the handout) are *Symphony,* Psalm 150 (based on vv. 3-5); *Astronomical,* Psalm 148 (based on v. 3); *Bandages,* Psalm 147 (based on v. 3); *Dancing,* Psalm 149 (based on v. 3); *God,* Psalm 146 (based on v. 6); *Breath,* Psalm 150 (based on v. 6); *New Song,* Psalm 149 (based on v. 1); *Praise from Highest,* Psalm 148 (based on vv. 4, 7); *Princes,* Psalm 146 (based on v. 3); *Weather,* Psalm 147 (based on vv. 16-18).

Option: Have an artistic member create the handout with the book titles depicted vertically along the spines of books, one each. Include two bookends with the word *hallelujah* displayed prominently on each.

After discussing the results, have your class sing the first stanzas of a series of hymns and/or choruses that call for praise to God. Titles such as "Praise God from Whom All Blessings Flow," "Praise to the Lord, the Almighty," and "Praise Him! Praise Him! Jesus, Our Blessed Redeemer" are appropriate. At the end, call out *Hallelujah!* and ask for a translation of that Hebrew imperative, which is *Praise the Lord!*

As an alternative to singing a series of hymns and/or choruses, conclude this segment with the antiphonal (back and forth) reading Hallelujah! from the reproducible page, which you can download.

Into the Word

Say, "The author of Psalm 146 lists many reasons for praising God. As I read through this psalm, jot down at least 10 reasons as you hear them; pay special attention to verses 6-9 for these readings." Read Psalm 146 aloud and discuss learners' discoveries.

Option: Do the above in conjunction with a two-column handout entitled "Reasons to Praise Him." The heading of the first column on the handout will be *The Psalmist's Reasons.* The heading of the second column will be *My Reasons.* Put the numerals 1 through 10 down the left side of the handout. Learners can complete the first column as they hear you read Psalm 146. Learners can complete the second column during a time of sharing in small groups. Encourage learners to connect the psalmist's reasons for praise to specific times or incidents in their own lives.

Into Life

Have the class sing the children's antiphonal song "Praise Ye the Lord, Hallelujah." This song involves rapid standing and sitting as the halves of the class take turns singing. If rapid standing and sitting is not appropriate for your class, you can use raising and lowering of arms.

Ask learners how they will take that praise with them into the week ahead. Launch this discussion by stating how you will do so. This can be discussed in small groups if time allows.

Praise for God's Justice

GOD PROMISED A RIGHTEOUS LORD

DEVOTIONAL READING: John 8:12-19
BACKGROUND SCRIPTURE: Isaiah 9:1-7

ISAIAH 9:1-7

1 Nevertheless the dimness shall not be such as was in her vexation, when at the first he lightly afflicted the land of Zebulun and the land of Naphtali, and afterward did more grievously afflict her by the way of the sea, beyond Jordan, in Galilee of the nations.

2 The people that walked in darkness have seen a great light: they that dwell in the land of the shadow of death, upon them hath the light shined.

3 Thou hast multiplied the nation, and not increased the joy: they joy before thee according to the joy in harvest, and as men rejoice when they divide the spoil.

4 For thou hast broken the yoke of his burden, and the staff of his shoulder, the rod of his oppressor, as in the day of Midian.

5 For every battle of the warrior is with confused noise, and garments rolled in blood; but this shall be with burning and fuel of fire.

6 For unto us a child is born, unto us a son is given: and the government shall be upon his shoulder: and his name shall be called Wonderful, Counsellor, The mighty God, The everlasting Father, The Prince of Peace.

7 Of the increase of his government and peace there shall be no end, upon the throne of David, and upon his kingdom, to order it, and to establish it with judgment and with justice from henceforth even for ever. The zeal of the LORD of hosts will perform this.

KEY VERSE

For unto us a child is born, unto us a son is given. —**Isaiah 9:6**

God Calls for Justice

Unit 3: Justice Promised

LESSONS 10–13

LESSON AIMS

After participating in this lesson, each student will be able to:

1. List the images of hope found in Isaiah 9:1-7.

2. Explain how Jesus fulfills the prophecy of Isaiah 9:1-7.

3. Suggest a way to bring the hope promised in Isaiah 9:1-7 to a contemporary situation of oppression or prejudice.

LESSON OUTLINE

Introduction
  A. The Birth of a Boy
  B. Lesson Background
I. Future of Galilee (ISAIAH 9:1-5)
  A. Changing Status (v. 1)
  B. Great Light (v. 2)
    Shedding Light . . . and Heat
  C. Multiplied Nation (v. 3)
  D. Shattered Yoke (v. 4)
  E. New Peace (v. 5)
II. King from Galilee (ISAIAH 9:6, 7)
  A. Son Given (v. 6a)
  B. Son Named (v. 6b)
  C. Son Reigns (v. 7)
    Government Increase, Good and Bad
Conclusion
  A. The Kingdom of God at Work
  B. Prayer
  C. Thought to Remember

Introduction

A. The Birth of a Boy

I was never more excited than the day my son was born. My wife and I already had a daughter, so we were hoping for a boy. Our only son came into the world on August 28, 1971. I was scheduled to preach the next day on Moses and the burning bush, but I do not remember anything I said. The congregation simply laughed at my exuberance and the fact that my feet did not touch the floor. I was flying high! God had answered our prayers by giving us a healthy beautiful boy.

No one in the congregation claimed that this child was "their" child. My wife and I had to pay the bills, bring the infant boy to our home, and take care of his needs from that day until he was on his own. No one rejoiced as much as my wife and I did that we had a baby boy. We had high hopes for him, but we could not predict what he would grow up to become. The doctors of that time could not tell us the sex of the child in advance of the birth.

Not so the boy in today's text! This child was predicted hundreds of years earlier. He was predicted to be a king reigning on David's throne, bringing justice and righteousness to the earth. He was to be a child who, in a sense, belonged to all of us: "For unto *us* a child is born, unto *us* a son is given" (Isaiah 9:6). He has made a difference in the world ever since His birth. Our study today will reveal how and why He is "our" child.

B. Lesson Background

Isaiah 9:1-7 must be understood in the larger context of Isaiah 7–12. That section of Isaiah is concerned with the Syro-Ephraimite War against Judah as well as Assyria's threat of overwhelming the entire region. Both Syria and Ephraim (another name for the northern kingdom of Israel; see Isaiah 7:1-17) had plans to besiege Jerusalem, capture her, and put a puppet king on the throne. Then they would be able to use Judah's army with theirs in defense against the mighty Assyrians (Isaiah 7:6).

The young and inexperienced King Ahaz (2 Kings 16:2) was frightened, along with all of Judah, by these political winds (Isaiah 7:2). The

God Promised a Righteous Lord

prophet encouraged Ahaz to trust the Lord in this matter rather than seek any kind of alliance with the Assyrians to help him out of this mess. Isaiah even offered Ahaz a sign from the Lord (7:11).

For some reason, Ahaz refused to ask for a sign (Isaiah 7:12). Perhaps he already had in mind an alliance with the Assyrians (2 Kings 16:7). But the Lord gave Ahaz ("the house of David") a sign anyway: *Immanuel*, meaning "God with us" (Isaiah 7:14; Matthew 1:23). Before this child could reach an age of accountability (Isaiah 7:15), the Assyrians would have destroyed the two threats in the north. But Ahaz refused this sign. It therefore remained a "distant" prophecy for a remnant of God's people, not to be fulfilled until Immanuel truly would come in ultimate victory.

Instead, Ahaz received another sign: the birth of Isaiah's son Maher-shalal-hash-baz (meaning "spoil speeds, prey hastens"), who would incarnate victory over Syria and Ephraim/Israel by the Assyrians (compare Isaiah 7:14-17 with 8:1-4). This is the "near" prophecy that ended up being relevant to Ahaz's day. The northern part of Galilee was overrun with Assyrians when Syria was attacked. Our lesson text is involved in the context of these prophecies (about 734 BC).

I. Future of Galilee
(ISAIAH 9:1-5)
A. Changing Status (v. 1)

1. Nevertheless the dimness shall not be such as was in her vexation, when at the first he lightly afflicted the land of Zebulun and the land of Naphtali, and afterward did more grievously afflict her by the way of the sea, beyond Jordan, in Galilee of the nations.

The threat to Syria by the Assyrians began to be felt soon after 734 BC. By 733 BC the northern portion of Ephraim (Israel), described here as *the land of Zebulun and the land of Naphtali*, also was feeling the heavy hand of Assyria. Naphtali lies along the western shore of the Sea of Galilee and extends northward, while Zebulun is west and southwest of Naphtali, midway between the Sea of Galilee and the Mediterranean (see Joshua 19:10-16, 32-39). These areas plus Gilead (east of

the Jordan River) are taken by Tiglathpileser III of Assyria when he overwhelms Syria (2 Kings 15:29). Damascus is destroyed in 732 BC.

The dimness mentioned here is related to the verse just before this one (Isaiah 8:22), where "dimness of anguish" predicts what is to happen in Galilee. God's people have a choice to make. They can either live in this dark and anxious world where they have abandoned God, or they can return "to the law and to the testimony" (Isaiah 8:20).

The translation *did more grievously afflict* is tricky because the Hebrew can have two meanings. The Hebrew verb can mean "cause to be heavy," that is, "to increase the affliction"; this is the choice the translators of the *King James Version* have made. On the other hand, the Hebrew verb also can mean "cause to honor," as it does in Exodus 20:12. Thus, the Bible student is faced with two possible interpretations: (1) *at the first he [God] lightly afflicted the land*, but afterward the people there are afflicted more heavily—referring to the total destruction in 722 BC; or (2) God has afflicted His people in the past *(at the first)*, but in the future *(afterward)* He will honor this area. Neither interpretation diminishes the understanding of the verses that follow.

The verse before us is unique in describing Galilee as being *of the nations* (Matthew 4:15, quoting this verse, has "Galilee of the Gentiles," which is the same thing). It seems that the prophet Isaiah is emphasizing the melting-pot nature of this area, where people from many nations end up living alongside one another after forced resettlement by the Assyrians (see 2 Kings 17:24).

B. Great Light (v. 2)

2. The people that walked in darkness have seen a great light: they that dwell in the land of the shadow of death, upon them hath the light shined.

The prophetic word is so certain that the author speaks of the prophecy as having already been fulfilled. The people have continued to walk (that is, "live") as if in the darkest part of the night (compare Isaiah 5:30; 8:22). They apparently have no desire to walk in the light (compare John 3:19, 20). They prefer the *land of the shadow of death*, a

Visual for Lesson 11. *Point to this visual as you introduce the discussion question that is associated with Isaiah 9:2.*

deep darkness of mind and spirit in a land bereft of God's presence.

Yet it is on people who seem to prefer darkness that a great light comes. They *have seen* (personal experience) this light and *upon them hath the light shined* (objective fact). Light is a figure of speech for God himself or for His divine presence (see Isaiah 60:1-3; 2 Corinthians 4:6; 1 John 1:5; Revelation 21:23; 22:5).

Matthew quotes this verse to refer to Jesus (Matthew 4:16). Jesus' ministry, centered in Capernaum (see 4:13), is like a great light bursting on an unworthy people. Yet in spite of Jesus' great miracles and authoritative teachings, most choose not to walk in the light. As a result, Jesus condemns them (see Matthew 11:21, 23).

What Do You Think?

How do your experiences with darkness help you appreciate the great light of Christ?

Talking Points for Your Discussion
- Experiences of spiritual darkness
- Experiences of physical darkness

❧ SHEDDING LIGHT . . . AND HEAT ❧

When I was in graduate school, my wife and I served as apartment building managers for a small complex of 11 units. My duties were varied: I had to collect the rent, mow the grass, trim the shrubs, replace burned out lightbulbs in the hallways, etc.

Changing lightbulbs taught me a certain lesson. On the bases of the lightbulb fixtures were stamped the words "Do not use higher than 60-watt bulbs." I was never sure why. Then one day I had to replace some bulbs, but I didn't have any 60-watt bulbs on hand. I had some 100-watt bulbs, so I used them instead. New bulbs usually lasted several months. However, the 100-watt bulbs I used lasted only about two weeks. In the enclosed area of the glass diffuser, the 100-watt bulbs simply created so much heat that they burned themselves out quickly.

Jesus came to bring light. However, the light He brought was so intense that it created unbearable heat for His enemies. Their response was to attempt to extinguish His light—they wanted Him "burned out" permanently. For three days they appeared to have succeeded. But all Jesus' enemies, from any era, eventually find out that the light of God cannot be extinguished. A day is coming when the light and heat of God's wrath will doom them (2 Peter 3:10-12). Make sure you're not one of God's enemies!　—J. B. N.

C. Multiplied Nation (v. 3)

3a. Thou hast multiplied the nation.

The nation of Israel will be multiplied many times over (see Isaiah 26:15; 54:1-3). This is caused by the great influx of Gentiles in fulfillment of the first promise of God to Abraham (Genesis 12:3). It will not happen overnight. However, what better place to begin that process than Galilee, where people from many nations rub shoulders daily?

3b. And not increased the joy: they joy before thee according to the joy in harvest, and as men rejoice when they divide the spoil.

The rapid shift from the positive "thou hast multiplied the nation" of verse 3a to the negative *and not increased the joy* here is startling. This has led to different interpretations. One interpretation proposes that the prophet is foreseeing different times in history. First, the people dwell in darkness; then the light dawns (v. 2), and the nation is multiplied (v. 3a). But that is followed by a time of difficulty and corruption (lack of joy).

A different interpretation proposes that although the *King James Version* is precisely accurate in its translation here, there is an uncertainty in what

God Promised a Righteous Lord

the Hebrew word behind the translation really is. The word for *not* in Hebrew sounds exactly like the word for *to it* (a homonym). Thus it would be easy for a copyist of Hebrew to write *not* when another person actually is saying *to it* (or vice versa) during verbal dictation. If *to it* was the original intent, then the idea is something like, "To it [the nation] you have increased the joy!" This uncertainty between *not* and *to it* (or *to him*) occurs over a dozen times in the Old Testament Hebrew text. Context usually makes clear which is intended, but the case before us is a difficult one.

Regarding *the joy in harvest,* we recall that bountiful crops are a cause for celebration (Exodus 23:16). Dividing *the spoil* after a battle is an extremely happy occasion for men who have risked their lives fighting an enemy (Numbers 31:25-47; Psalm 119:162). Both events are considered gifts from God (see Deuteronomy 28:2-8).

> **What Do You Think?**
> How will God use your church to increase joy this week?
> *Talking Points for Your Discussion*
> - In meeting spiritual needs
> - In meeting physical needs
> - In meeting relational needs

D. Shattered Yoke (v. 4)

4. For thou hast broken the yoke of his burden, and the staff of his shoulder, the rod of his oppressor, as in the day of Midian.

HOW TO SAY IT

Assyria	Uh-*sear*-ee-uh.
Ephraim	*Ee*-fray-im.
Gilead	*Gil*-ee-ud (G as in *get*).
Maher-shalal-hash-baz	*May*-her-*shal*-al-**hash**-bas.
Midian	*Mid*-ee-un.
Naphtali	*Naf*-tuh-lye.
Syria	*Sear*-ee-uh.
Syro-Ephraimite	*Sigh*-roe-*Ee*-fray-im-ite.
Tiglathpileser	*Tig*-lath-pih-*lee*-zer.
Zebulun	*Zeb*-you-lun.

The blessing in view here is freedom from foreign domination. The historical note of *the day of Midian* refers to Gideon's defeat of the Midianites, over 400 years in the past at this point. Gideon's actions (Judges 6–8) triggered knowledge that his victory could only have been an act of God (7:2-14). The fact that Gideon's actions included men of Asher, Zebulun, and Naphtali (6:35) enhances the imagery for what God will do in this territory around the Sea of Galilee. No one expected it in Gideon's day, and no one will expect it in Jesus' day. Skeptics will say things like "Shall Christ come out of Galilee?" (John 7:41) and "Search, and look: for out of Galilee ariseth no prophet" (John 7:52).

The suffering of the people is described by three phrases: *the yoke of his burden, the staff of his shoulder, the rod of his oppressor.* The imagery is of a disenfranchised, subjugated people. This will be the status of the Jews under Roman rule in the time of Jesus. But Jesus comes to grant deliverance from bondage to a different master: sin.

Some students see echoes of the events surrounding the exodus from Egypt in the use of such words as *yoke* (Leviticus 26:13), *burden* (Exodus 1:11), *shoulder* (Psalm 81:6), and *oppressor* ("taskmasters" in Exodus 5:6, 10, 14). The exodus events were of divine origin, as will be the future birth of a special child (Isaiah 9:6, below).

> **What Do You Think?**
> When was a time you were surprised by the way God worked to lighten or remove a burden from your life?
> *Talking Points for Your Discussion*
> - Through a person
> - Through His word
> - Through a change of circumstance

E. New Peace (v. 5)

5. For every battle of the warrior is with confused noise, and garments rolled in blood; but this shall be with burning and fuel of fire.

Another reason for great rejoicing is the end of warfare. Once the people are liberated (v. 4, above), a spreading peace will allow the burning of the warrior's blood-stained garments. There will be no more need for these. This outcome matches what the prophet foresees in Isaiah 2:4 (compare Psalm 46:9; Zechariah 9:10).

II. King from Galilee
(ISAIAH 9:6, 7)
A. Son Given (v. 6a)

6a. For unto us a child is born, unto us a son is given: and the government shall be upon his shoulder.

The final reason for joy is the birth of a child. He is to be extraordinary! He is *given* to us. This is not said of other births, although this child was to have been a sign to Ahaz—a sign refused!

Isaiah 7:14; 8:1, 8, 10 require us to conclude that this child is to be the coming *Immanuel* ("God with us"). The government—that is, rule and dominion—will be His (see Matthew 28:18). When His shoulder bears the rule of government, it releases the beating from the shoulder of the people (Isaiah 9:4, above).

B. Son Named (v. 6b)

6b. And his name shall be called Wonderful, Counsellor, The mighty God, The everlasting Father, The Prince of Peace.

Names are significant throughout Isaiah's ministry and in his confrontation with kings, especially Ahaz (Isaiah 7:3; 8:1-3; etc.). The set of names we see now reminds us of "throne names" used for newly crowned kings. Egyptian coronation liturgies exhibited such names to encourage qualities desired of the newly crowned monarch. These names give the character of this child and His perfect rule.

Wonderful is a word that can stand by itself. It simply means "wonder," as close to the idea of supernatural as we have in Hebrew (see Psalm 78:12, where the same Hebrew word is translated "marvellous things"). It refers to something out of the ordinary (see Isaiah 29:14). Since this child is "God-with-us," then He is a wonder!

Counsellor describes the true wisdom of this child. Solomon, David's son, also was given great wisdom that could be explained only supernaturally (see 1 Kings 3). This child perhaps is

presented as the "new Solomon," who gives supernatural counsel to His subjects (see Isaiah 11:2). Even so, the child will be greater than Solomon (Luke 11:31). The child's wise, supernatural counsel is the exact opposite of that of the supposedly "wise" counselors of Isaiah 19:11.

The mighty God describes the child's divinity (see John 1:1). The exact title *the everlasting Father* is found only here in the Old Testament. The child will bring about conditions in the new government that will fulfill the role of the divine fatherhood of God (see Psalm 103:13; Isaiah 63:16). His rule will be for all eternity (see Isaiah 57:15).

The Prince of Peace is the chief characteristic of this child's rule. War is the character of earthly kings. The only son of David we know of who did not go to war was Solomon, yet Solomon established his kingdom with bloodshed (1 Kings 2:25, 46). Solomon's name means "peace," but the promised child will be the ultimate *Prince of Peace*. He brings peace between God and humanity by way of reconciliation and redemption (see John 14:27; Romans 5:1-11).

What Do You Think?
Which description of Christ is most meaningful to you personally? Why?
Talking Points for Your Discussion
- Wonderful
- Counselor
- Mighty God
- Everlasting Father
- Prince of Peace

C. Son Reigns (v. 7)

7. Of the increase of his government and peace there shall be no end, upon the throne of David, and upon his kingdom, to order it, and to establish it with judgment and with justice from henceforth even for ever. The zeal of the LORD of hosts will perform this.

The promise to Abraham in Genesis 12:3 became, at Sinai, the purpose of Israel's existence (Exodus 19:5, 6). The broader redemptive work through David is found in a promise that his dynasty will never end (compare 2 Samuel 7:16).

God Promised a Righteous Lord

The eternal kingdom derives its authority and power from God's plan for the throne of David (see Luke 1:32). It is established on *judgment and with justice*. As with the exodus events, only God's zeal can do this. Through Jesus' death, burial, resurrection, and ascension to the right hand of God, the kingdom continues on earth through the church (see Ephesians 1:20-23; Colossians 1:13).

What Do You Think?

How would you respond to someone who says real life doesn't match the description of Christ's rule in verse 7?

Talking Points for Your Discussion

- Regarding continuing wars in the world
- Regarding the influence of unrighteousness in the world
- Regarding the shocking injustice in the world

❧ *GOVERNMENT INCREASE, GOOD AND BAD* ❧

Historians often see the American Civil War as the great dividing line in U.S. history. Part of the reason for this viewpoint is that the federal government took on a greater responsibility for things during the war, and this trend continued after the war's end. For example, the government gave railroad companies millions of acres of land to facilitate the building of transcontinental railroads.

Most Americans agree that certain instances of increased governmental authority are beneficial. After the Civil War, housing laws regulated the safety of urban construction of apartment buildings. The Pure Food and Drug Act of 1906 regulated products for consumer safety and health. New laws prohibited various forms of child labor. The list goes on.

Some instances of governmental increase, however, are not always regarded as positive. I don't want to get into a political discussion, but the nightly news reminds us of the continuing protests of those opposed to what they see as governmental intrusions into their lives. But imagine a perfect government whose increase is also identified with peace. We should all long for such a government, and indeed it is coming. It is the government of God's eternal kingdom.   —J. B. N.

Conclusion

A. The Kingdom of God at Work

Pilate asked Jesus, "Art thou the king of the Jews?" Jesus replied, "Thou sayest" (Matthew 27:11). The high priest asked, "Art thou the Christ?" Jesus' direct response was, "I am" (Mark 14:61, 62). With these answers the preliminary words of Jesus were reaching their climax: "The time is fulfilled, and the kingdom of God is at hand: repent ye, and believe the gospel" (Mark 1:15). What remained were the essential historical facts of the gospel—the death, burial, resurrection, and ascension of Jesus to God's right hand.

When the Holy Spirit came upon the disciples on the Day of Pentecost (Acts 2), the kingdom of God on earth entered a new phase. The ancient hope for a prince from the lineage of David who would reign in peace, bringing justice and righteousness to the earth, began to be preached in earnest. On that day 3,000 believers were baptized, receiving forgiveness of sins and the gift of the Holy Spirit. The Lord has continued to lead His church to bring righteousness and justice to the earth from that day until now.

Can the church today duplicate the growth of the first-century church? It can happen only if we depend on our righteous Lord and submit fully to His rule. "Until men can find some redemptive community which is capable of bridging the schism of society and uniting . . . all races and classes . . . under its righteous rule, a world of peace and justice must remain forever a dream. The church affirms that there is but one redemptive community . . . the all-embracing commonwealth of the Kingdom of God" (John Bright).

B. Prayer

Father, teach us to depend on Your righteous rule through our Lord Jesus Christ. In these dangerous and difficult times, help us not to fear the power and evil of human governments. Rather, help us to embrace Your kingdom and work for peace and righteousness. In Jesus' name, amen.

C. Thought to Remember

He is wonderful!

INVOLVEMENT LEARNING

Some of the activities below are also found in the helpful student book, Adult Bible Class.
Don't forget to download the free reproducible page from www.standardlesson.com to enhance your lesson!

Into the Lesson

Purchase (or prepare on a computer) inexpensive copies of an *It's a Boy!* birth announcement, one copy for each class member. Distribute these as class members arrive. Leave them blank for a later activity. This will result in questions and speculation, but don't respond or comment on the announcements yet. Have visible a map of ancient Palestine. You will use this in an activity below.

Into the Word

Say, "Isaiah's message, like that of most of God's prophets, was largely negative. It announced punishment for Israel's sinfulness. Yet there are glimmers of positive hope and blessing." Give each learner a half-sheet of paper that features the image of a flashlight battery. Have one end of the battery clearly marked as positive (+) and the other end marked negative (–). Lightly screen the word *EVERLASTING* lengthwise along the battery. You can ask a class member who enjoys computer graphics to prepare this.

Say, "Let's look at today's text, Isaiah 9:1-7, and note the negative and positive words and phrases. As you discover each, write it next to the appropriate end of the battery. Take about five minutes."

When time is up, ask one learner to read his or her negative list and another learner to read his or her positive list. The lists may vary from learner to learner, but expect to see entries such as the following: **negative**—*dimness, vexation, afflicted, darkness, shadow, death, yoke, rod, oppressor, battle, noise, blood, fire;* **positive**—*light, shined, rejoice, harvest, spoil, Wonderful, Counsellor, mighty, everlasting, peace, increase, judgment, justice, forever, zeal.* (*Option:* At this point, you can use the two Darkness and Light activities from the reproducible page, which you can download, to extend these areas of discussion.)

After the two lists are read, note how the historical context fits the negative list (use the Lesson Background). Note also how the Messiah's kingdom removes all that and replaces it with the delights of God's presence and reign.

Have someone read Matthew 4:12-17. As the class hears Matthew's affirmation, ask, "How is the fulfillment of Isaiah's prophecy fully seen in Jesus' coming?" Let the class respond freely. Indicate on your map how Jesus' work in Galilee ties in with the geographical boundaries of Isaiah's day.

Return to the *It's a Boy!* announcements with which you began class. Say, "How would you fill in this announcement for the birth of Jesus?" Since birth announcements usually include the length and weight of the baby, challenge your class to be creative here. For example, *weight* might be "will weigh heavily on the conscience of all people." Encourage learners to let the full scope of Isaiah 9:1-7 inform their creativity in this regard.

Into Life

Share with your class information regarding "places of spiritual darkness" that you have researched in advance. Reference to nations where a false religion dominates life and behavior would be a good choice. A visual presentation of some kind will help drive home the reality of the spiritual darkness.

Establish a fund using a traditional piggy bank that you have labeled "A Bit of Light for the Darkness" and on which you have drawn (or pasted an image of) a lightbulb. Collect money for a short time period, a month or so, and then send the collected amount—large or small—to a ministry of the class's choice. Make clear that you're not soliciting for an indefinite commitment, only "a bit of light for the darkness" for a bit of time.

If your budget allows, give each learner a flashlight battery with this note attached as a reminder: "There's a positive and negative end on this battery. Which will you choose to emphasize this week in your life for Christ?"

God Promised a Righteous Lord

GOD PROMISED A RIGHTEOUS BRANCH

DEVOTIONAL READING: Psalm 33:1-5
BACKGROUND SCRIPTURE: Jeremiah 23:1-8; 33

JEREMIAH 23:1-6

1 Woe be unto the pastors that destroy and scatter the sheep of my pasture! saith the LORD.

2 Therefore thus saith the LORD God of Israel against the pastors that feed my people; Ye have scattered my flock, and driven them away, and have not visited them: behold, I will visit upon you the evil of your doings, saith the LORD.

3 And I will gather the remnant of my flock out of all countries whither I have driven them, and will bring them again to their folds; and they shall be fruitful and increase.

4 And I will set up shepherds over them which shall feed them: and they shall fear no more, nor be dismayed, neither shall they be lacking, saith the LORD.

5 Behold, the days come, saith the LORD, that I will raise unto David a righteous Branch, and a King shall reign and prosper, and shall execute judgment and justice in the earth.

6 In his days Judah shall be saved, and Israel shall dwell safely: and this is his name whereby he shall be called, THE LORD OUR RIGHTEOUSNESS.

JEREMIAH 33:14-18

14 Behold, the days come, saith the LORD, that I will perform that good thing which I have promised unto the house of Israel and to the house of Judah.

15 In those days, and at that time, will I cause the Branch of righteousness to grow up unto David; and he shall execute judgment and righteousness in the land.

16 In those days shall Judah be saved, and Jerusalem shall dwell safely: and this is the name wherewith she shall be called, The LORD our righteousness.

17 For thus saith the LORD; David shall never want a man to sit upon the throne of the house of Israel;

18 Neither shall the priests the Levites want a man before me to offer burnt offerings, and to kindle meat offerings, and to do sacrifice continually.

KEY VERSE

Behold, the days come, saith the LORD, that I will raise unto David a righteous Branch, and a King shall reign and prosper, and shall execute judgment and justice in the earth. —**Jeremiah 23:5**

GOD CALLS FOR JUSTICE

Unit 3: Justice Promised

LESSONS 10–13

LESSON AIMS

After participating in this lesson, each student will be able to:

1. Recount the leadership characteristics of the righteous shepherd.

2. Compare and contrast the ways Jesus fulfills the image of the righteous shepherd with the ways human leaders do.

3. Write a note of appreciation to an elder or other leader in his or her church.

LESSON OUTLINE

Introduction

A. Bad Leadership

I have been doing interim ministries for over 35 years, ever since I started teaching full-time at a Bible college. It is a peculiar type of ministry but necessary. Many churches need some "in between time" of an interim ministry in order to be able to move successfully from one preaching minister to the next. Often a preacher leaves because there is a problem in the church, and leaving is the proverbial "lesser of two evils." If the next preacher is to be successful, the interim minister must deal with the problem in such cases. I have observed both good and bad leadership while doing so.

Bad leadership often seems to be no leadership at all. It has lost its focus on the future in terms of a vision for the people and knowledge of how to get there. Bad leadership has a tendency to perpetuate itself by not preparing future leaders. The younger person who is a potential, future leader remains apathetic and unchallenged.

Bad leadership in a church has recognizable traits. One such trait can be called *the ruling elder syndrome* or *the ruling preacher syndrome*. This is a top-down attitude: "I am the boss!" Churches *do* need strong leadership, but that is not the same as being a dictator.

Lack of communication and lack of delegation are also traits of bad leadership. Also, immoral people sometimes are in leadership positions. I remember three churches I have served as an interim minister where I thought a key leader was living an immoral life and was attempting to hide it. Three is bad enough, but I am thankful it wasn't more! Our lesson today addresses the issue of bad leadership and God's solution.

B. Lesson Background

Leaders in ancient Israel were often referred to as *shepherds,* a common image in that day. The prophet Ezekiel described bad leadership in great detail in terms of shepherd imagery (compare Ezekiel 34). The prophet Jeremiah also called the irresponsible civil and religious leaders *shepherds;* they misled the people and brought destruction to the kingdom.

God Promised a Righteous Branch

Jeremiah ministered in the southern kingdom of Judah from about 626 BC to a little beyond the fall of Jerusalem in 586 BC. His ministry saw the deterioration and destruction of Judah due to bad, unholy leadership. Jeremiah may have encouraged King Josiah's reforms of about 622 BC, but those reforms ended when Josiah lost his life in battle in about 609 BC (2 Kings 23:29). It was all downhill from there (23:31–25:21).

Jeremiah 22, just prior to today's text, discusses three evil kings who succeeded Josiah. These three were responsible as bad shepherds for the destruction of Judah, although the death knell had already been sounded (see 2 Kings 23:26, 27). The Lord's charges against these men included the shedding of innocent blood, failing to pay workers, and ignoring the just cause of the powerless.

Last week's lesson promised a coming Davidic king against the historical background of the Assyrian threat (about 734 BC). This week's lesson concerns the same promise, except the threat is now the Babylonian hordes (597–586 BC).

I. Shepherds' Failure
(JEREMIAH 23:1, 2)
A. Their Sin (v. 1)

1. Woe be unto the pastors that destroy and scatter the sheep of my pasture! saith the LORD.

The source of Judah's woes is the worthless pastors (shepherds) who have ruled Judah unwisely. The terms *pastors* and *shepherds* refer primarily to kings in this context (see Jeremiah 21, 22), but also can refer to those who give them counsel. These include priests and false prophets (Jeremiah 23:16, 25-40; 32:32; 2 Chronicles 36:14).

Chief among the evil kings was Manasseh. He ruled for 55 years, from about 698 to 644 BC (2 Kings 21:1). His evil was shocking (21:2-11, 16). Josiah's law reform after Manasseh was a case of too little, too late (22:1–23:27).

The Lesson Background mentions three evil kings of Jeremiah 22, which is immediately prior to today's lesson text. The "woe oracle" of judgment we see in the verse before us is probably uttered in the early part of the reign of Zedekiah, who fol-

lows those other three. He ends up being the last king of Judah (see Jeremiah 21:1-10). These four do not champion justice in the land (see 21:11–22:9). Instead, they *destroy and scatter* God's people by failing to keep the covenant with Yahweh, primarily by worshipping other gods. This one-verse description of the shepherds' sin is paralleled in the prophet Ezekiel's oracle of Ezekiel 34:1-6.

B. Their Judgment (v. 2)

2. Therefore thus saith the LORD God of Israel against the pastors that feed my people; Ye have scattered my flock, and driven them away, and have not visited them: behold, I will visit upon you the evil of your doings, saith the LORD.

The leaders of God's people—the succession of kings and their advisors—are judged accordingly. They are supposed to feed the people, but they feed only themselves (compare Jude 12). The prophet Ezekiel's parallel oracle of judgment proclaims that the shepherds have not searched "for my flock, but the shepherds fed themselves, and fed not my flock" (Ezekiel 34:8). Simple neglect would be bad enough, but these evil shepherds take an active role in scattering the flock.

There is a play on words in the Hebrew that is apparent also in the English. The Hebrew for *visited* applies not only to what the bad shepherds have *not* done for the flock, but also to what God *will* do in response: He will visit them in judgment.

> *What Do You Think?*
> What advance plans does your church have in place to deal with leadership failure? What improvements need to be made?
>
> *Talking Points for Your Discussion*
> - For a matter of doctrinal defection
> - For a matter of moral failure
> - For causing divisiveness
> - For personal or family issues

❧ *Bad Shepherds Through the Centuries* ❧

In the Middle Ages, one of the duties of every bishop was to visit each parish in his diocese at least once a year. The purpose of this policy was to see to it that the people were being cared for properly by their priest—taught properly, instructed in correct moral living, and encouraged as active members of the church. Unfortunately, many bishops did not perform their annual visitations. Some did, however, and the results were often sadly humorous.

For example, one bishop asked a local priest if he knew the Lord's Prayer. "No," said the priest, "but whatever the king wants, I'll do it." In another parish, the bishop asked if the priest could name any of the 12 apostles. "Yes," said the priest, "David and Moses." When Boniface, the archbishop of Germany, was given jurisdiction over Bavaria in the eighth century, he visited some of the priests and discovered they did not understand Latin, the official language for all ceremonies of the church. Because some of the priests did not understand gender differences in Latin case endings, they were baptizing "in the name of the Father, the Daughter, and the Holy Spirit"!

Bad shepherding can take many forms. General ignorance and shabby biblical understanding are just two. But the result is the same: a flock that is inexcusably scattered—spiritually if not physically. What evidence do you see of inadequate shepherding today, and how can you help correct this problem? —J. B. N.

II. Lord's Actions
(JEREMIAH 23:3-6)

A. Gathers Remnant (v. 3)

3. And I will gather the remnant of my flock out of all countries whither I have driven them, and will bring them again to their folds; and they shall be fruitful and increase.

In contrast with verse 1, this verse indicates that God is the one who drives the Israelites from their homeland. There is no contradiction here, for the bad shepherds of God's people lead them along the path of idolatrous worship and rebelliousness. Jeremiah 44:17 notes the guilt of "our fathers, our kings, and our princes" in this regard (compare 44:21). But the people are also to blame for following the evil leadership willingly, especially given Jeremiah's warnings (44:23). So God allows mighty nations to conquer them: Israel in 722 BC by the Assyrians, and Judah in 586 BC by the Babylonians.

The concept of a remnant returning is found throughout the prophets (see Jeremiah 24, 40–44; Isaiah 1:9; 10:20-22; 11:11; 37:4; Micah 4:7; 7:18). Ezekiel 34:11-22, a parallel oracle, is lengthy in this regard. Not only will God gather the remnant, the people of that remnant also *shall be fruitful and increase* (see Amos 9:11-15; Hosea 2:21-23; Zechariah 8:9-13).

B. Replaces Shepherds (v. 4)

4. And I will set up shepherds over them which shall feed them: and they shall fear no more, nor be dismayed, neither shall they be lacking, saith the LORD.

The remnant that returns will not experience the same kind of leadership that existed before the exile. Instead, God will provide new shepherds who will do what shepherds are supposed to do: feed the sheep and provide for their needs. Fear and dismay will vanish with these new leaders.

Since it is evident we are talking about a supernatural act by God, it is reasonable to look to the messianic age for its fulfillment. Jesus is "the good shepherd" (John 10:11, 14; compare Hebrews 13:20). He serves as the model shepherd in that capacity. His disciples are under-shepherds. After

God Promised a Righteous Branch

the resurrection, Jesus says to Peter three times "Feed my lambs/sheep" (John 21:15-17).

After the church is founded on the Day of Pentecost, the apostles establish leadership that understands the pastoral role (see 1 Timothy 3; Titus 1:5-9; 1 Peter 5:1-4). These new shepherds would not exist were it not for the successful rule and authority of the good shepherd, the chief shepherd (1 Peter 5:4).

Neither shall they be lacking is a continuation of the play on Hebrew words that we saw in Jeremiah 23:2. The word that means "visited" there is now used with a negative word to mean *neither shall they be lacking*. The picture is one of absolute safety and provision.

> ### What Do You Think?
> What are some ways to make sure your church "will set up shepherds" for her future?
> ### Talking Points for Your Discussion
> - Awareness of consequences of not doing so
> - Methods of identifying future leaders
> - Methods of leadership training
> - Having younger leaders "at the table" vs. having them merely "in the loop"

C. Raises Branch (vv. 5, 6)

5. Behold, the days come, saith the LORD, that I will raise unto David a righteous Branch, and a King shall reign and prosper, and shall execute judgment and justice in the earth.

The word *Behold,* which translates a word that exists in the Hebrew, is missing from some modern English translations. That is unfortunate, because it is an important word. It is saying "Look! I am about to say something very important! Pay attention!"

The statement *the days come* is very general and does not give us any sense of a time frame. It is simply a fact, a promise from God that something will happen. That "something" is that God is going to reestablish the Davidic dynasty through *a righteous Branch.* The word *Branch* is an important way of describing the coming Messiah, who is to sit on David's throne (see Isaiah 4:2; 11:1; Jeremiah 33:15; Zechariah 3:8; 6:12). The same idea

(but not the word itself) is found in Isaiah 6:13; 53:2. This Branch is a king, and He shall be successful because He rules wisely. This Branch produces *judgment and justice in the earth.* This is in contrast with the evil kings who come before.

6. In his days Judah shall be saved, and Israel shall dwell safely: and this is his name whereby he shall be called, THE LORD OUR RIGHTEOUSNESS.

The first half of this verse shifts perspective slightly, from the Messiah himself to the messianic age. In that age, both Judah and Israel *shall be saved.* Whether God's people are saved from external foes or internal troubles, they shall live safely.

This means that all the genuine people of God in the last days will experience the rule of the coming Messiah (see Jeremiah 30, 31). His name *THE LORD OUR RIGHTEOUSNESS* describes the chief characteristic of the age to come. This is probably an ironic wordplay on the name of the last king of Judah, Zedekiah, which means "My righteousness is Yahweh." Zedekiah was anything but righteous or just (see 2 Kings 24:19)!

III. Promise Fulfilled
(JEREMIAH 33:14-18)

A. Righteousness Instituted (vv. 14-16)

14. Behold, the days come, saith the LORD, that I will perform that good thing which I have promised unto the house of Israel and to the house of Judah.

Chapters 30–33 in Jeremiah are known as The Book of Consolation. These four chapters are a collection of messianic prophecies and hope for the exiled remnant. The next few verses in today's text form part of the conclusion to this section of Jeremiah.

What is *that good thing* that God *promised unto the house of Israel and to the house of Judah?* It is the fulfillment of His promise to David through the prophet Nathan: "And thine house and thy kingdom shall be established for ever before thee: thy throne shall be established for ever" (2 Samuel 7:16). Our next verse expands on this a bit.

15. In those days, and at that time, will I cause the Branch of righteousness to grow up

unto David; and he shall execute judgment and righteousness in the land.

This verse is parallel to Jeremiah 23:5, which we considered above. The time designator *in those days, and at that time* is referring to the messianic age—the era when the Messiah himself will come. It also is parallel to "Behold, the days come" from 33:14, above. The Branch is called "a righteous Branch" in 23:5, whereas here He is called *the Branch of righteousness*. There is no difference, since the last four words in both verses are identical in Hebrew.

Hence, the Messiah will do that which is just and that which is right in the land/earth. That very last word—*land* here in 33:15, but *earth* in 23:5—could go either way in translation. Our Christian perspective tells us that the Messiah's rule includes the entire earth. The ancient Israelites, for their part, have a tendency to think only in terms of their own land—the promised land.

16. In those days shall Judah be saved, and Jerusalem shall dwell safely: and this is the name wherewith she shall be called, The LORD our righteousness.

This verse is parallel to Jeremiah 23:6, considered above, with some variation and a slight twist at the end. *In those days* is parallel to "in his days" of 23:6. "Shall Judah be saved" is similar in both. However, *Jerusalem shall dwell safely* here is expressed as "Israel shall dwell safely" in 23:6. The change from *Israel* in 23:6 to *Jerusalem* here in

Visual for Lesson 12. *Have this visual on display as you explore the "branch language" of Isaiah 4:2; 11:1; Jeremiah 23:5; 33:15; Zechariah 3:8; 6:12.*

33:16 allows for Jerusalem to receive a new name. It is the same name that the Messiah is given: *The Lord our righteousness.*

A verb can be supplied to cause this name to be a full sentence: "The Lord [is] our righteousness." If this is the idea, then the emphasis falls back on the Messiah, who has been sent by God to bring about the peace and security that God's people (a remnant in Jerusalem) will one day experience. We take special note of Isaiah's renaming of Jerusalem after she has been purified from her sins: "The city of righteousness, the faithful city" (Isaiah 1:26).

> **What Do You Think?**
> How do the qualities of church leaders in 1 Timothy 3 connect with or reflect the idea of "the Lord our righteousness"?
> *Talking Points for Your Discussion*
> ▪ In terms of reputation
> ▪ In terms of temperament
> ▪ In terms of ability or aptitude

❧ PREDICTIONS ❧

I remember my dad telling me one day in the mid-1950s that I would live to see a man on the moon. "I won't be alive to see it, but you will" were his two predictions. I didn't believe him.

Children's television programs at the time included Buck Rogers and Captain Video, and I watched these regularly. These series featured spaceships going to and fro, plus similar science-fiction stuff. But I knew it was all fiction. To really put a man on the moon? Dad was just being silly and unrealistic. I dismissed his comments for about a decade. My prediction was that his two predictions would not come to pass.

My prediction turned out to be wrong. One of dad's predictions was wrong too because he did live to see a man on the moon. Human predictions are notoriously unreliable. But it is a different story with regard to predictions made by the Lord. He has a perfect track record of accurate predictions. What the Lord promises He is certain to accomplish, and that includes safety as well as justice. Will we trust Him in this?   —J. B. N.

B. Failure Impossible (vv. 17, 18)

17. For thus saith the LORD; David shall never want a man to sit upon the throne of the house of Israel.

God had promised to David that his dynasty would be forever (2 Samuel 7:12-16; compare Psalm 89:4, 29, 35-37). But what if David does indeed fail to have a son sit on his throne? Does that mean that God's promise has failed?

From Jeremiah's viewpoint, the sin of Judah is so serious that nothing can prevent her destruction and exile. The kingship will be suspended for many years; the punishment is severe, with only a remnant surviving (Jeremiah 30–33). But survive she will! Yet even before this, there's a sense that *the throne of the house of Israel* is no longer the throne it was meant to be following the death of Solomon. Only when the Messiah, David's true "son," comes on the scene can the throne be occupied legitimately. Only the "righteous Branch" can sit on this throne.

18. Neither shall the priests the Levites want a man before me to offer burnt offerings, and to kindle meat offerings, and to do sacrifice continually.

We recall that all priests are Levites, but not all Levites are priests. Thus there is an overlapping reference here. The priests are not exempt from the prophet's criticism (see Jeremiah 6:13; 8:10, 11). As Jeremiah looks forward to a legitimate king to sit on the throne of Israel (a true son of David), he also looks forward to a legitimate priesthood to offer continual sacrifices (compare 1 Peter 2:5).

The priesthood and kingship of ancient Israel are never combined into one office. Perhaps Jeremiah cannot yet see how the two will be combined in terms of the coming Messiah (Psalm 110:4; see Genesis 14:18-20). Hebrews 4:14–10:18

HOW TO SAY IT

Assyrians	Uh-*sear*-e-unz.
Babylonians	Bab-ih-*low*-nee-unz.
Josiah	Jo-*sigh*-uh.
Manasseh	Muh-*nass*-uh.
messianic	mess-ee-*an*-ick.
Zedekiah	Zed-uh-*kye*-uh.

gives details regarding the Messiah's priesthood and how it is an eternal priesthood with a sacrifice that is effective forever. We have a high priest we can turn to and "obtain mercy, and find grace to help in time of need"—Jesus (Hebrews 4:14-16).

Conclusion
A. Good Leadership

There is a reason God chose David to be king: David was a man "after [God's] own heart" (1 Samuel 13:14). In spite of David's sins (2 Samuel 11, 12), he was a good leader. Toward the end of his life, he uttered great words that apply to every good leader: "The God of Israel said, . . . He that ruleth over men must be just, ruling in the fear of God. And he shall be as the light of the morning, when the sun riseth, even a morning without clouds; as the tender grass springing out of the earth by clear shining after rain" (2 Samuel 23:3, 4). The greatest son of David, Jesus Christ, is the ultimate leader in this regard.

Jesus turns leadership on its head for the church. Whereas secular leaders exercise authority and power, leaders in God's church are to be servants (Mark 10:42-45). Jesus washes His disciples' feet (John 13:14-17). He is the good shepherd who lays down His life for the sheep (John 10:11-15).

Peter never forgot that model. In his twilight years, Peter could write to the church elders, "Feed the flock of God which is among you, taking the oversight thereof, not by constraint, but willingly; not for filthy lucre, but of a ready mind; neither as being lords over God's heritage, but being examples to the flock. And when the chief Shepherd shall appear, ye shall receive a crown of glory that fadeth not away" (1 Peter 5:2-4). Amen!

B. Prayer

O Lord God, we pray for good leadership in the church. May Your Spirit move those of humble spirits to rise in our moment of greatest need to care for Your flock. In the name of the good and righteous shepherd, Jesus our Lord, amen.

C. Thought to Remember

Good leaders lead justly in the fear of God.

INVOLVEMENT LEARNING

Some of the activities below are also found in the helpful student book, Adult Bible Class.
Don't forget to download the free reproducible page from www.standardlesson.com to enhance your lesson!

Into the Lesson

Recruit an artistic class member to prepare an image of an ancient shepherd leaning on his staff with his eyes closed, appearing to be asleep. Hand a copy to each arriving learner.

As class begins, ask, "What's wrong with this image of a shepherd?" The obvious answer: a shepherd with eyes closed cannot watch out for the sheep's safety and well-being! Note that today's text starts with Jeremiah's indictment of bad shepherds and ends with a prediction of God's ultimate justice as seen in His coming king. Be sure to connect the promises of this week's study with that of next week when the time arrives.

Alternative: Place in chairs copies of the From Woe to Joy activity from the reproducible page, which you can download. Learners can begin working on this as they arrive. After you go over your learners' solutions, say, *"Woe to Joy* summarizes today's study."

Into the Word

Put the following 20 words or phrases on 20 pieces of paper, one each: *David / David / Righteous Branch / Righteous Branch / Judah / Judah / safely / safely / days / days / judgment / judgment / saved / saved / the Lord Our Righteousness / the Lord Our Righteousness / name / name / king / throne.* Make sure the words are large enough to be readable throughout your learning space. Randomize the word cards and affix them to the board underneath 20 flaps of paper, one each, in rows of 4 or 5. Number the flaps conspicuously from 1 through 20. Do all this before class begins.

Have two learners read aloud today's two texts of Jeremiah 23:1-6 and 33:14-18, one each. After your readers finish, point out that the texts are closely parallel (which should be fairly obvious). Then gesture toward the board and indicate that you want learners, one at a time, to select two flaps to discover matching words/phrases from the two texts (in the manner of the old television game show *Concentration®*). Flaps are closed back down when selections don't match. Correct matches are left uncovered (remove flaps).

When the class eventually realizes that the words *king* and *throne* are unmatchable, ask, "How do those two words encapsulate the key idea of today's study texts?" Expected response: Jeremiah's prophecy is that God's people will one day have a righteous king on an eternal throne. He will be completely unlike the bad kings they had experienced.

Option 1: Distribute handouts that have the text of Jeremiah 23:1-6 printed in a column on the left and Jeremiah 33:14-18 printed in a column on the right. Also distribute highlighters or colored pencils. Have learners work in small groups to trace parallel words and ideas across the two columns. After they finish, use the commentary to explain the uniqueness of the words and thoughts in each column (that is, words and thoughts in a column for which no parallel exists in the other column).

Option 2: If time allows, have learners complete the Gracious Promises exercise from the reproducible page, which you can download. This activity is ideal for discussion in small groups or pairs.

Into Life

Purchase and distribute *Thank You* note cards. Such cards are available for as little as 10 cents each at dollar stores. Assign the names of spiritual leaders of your congregation to your learners. Ask them to jot brief notes of thanks for the work their leaders do for Christ. Suggest that this can be done anonymously ("from a fellow Christian you have blessed"). Encourage learners to complete and mail these within the next two days.

Distribute copies of the Beautiful Names activity from the reproducible page, which you can download, as learners depart. This will be a take-home exercise.

GOD PROMISED TO BE WITH US

DEVOTIONAL READING: **Psalm 23**
BACKGROUND SCRIPTURE: **Ezekiel 34**

EZEKIEL 34:23-31

23 And I will set up one shepherd over them, and he shall feed them, even my servant David; he shall feed them, and he shall be their shepherd.

24 And I the LORD will be their God, and my servant David a prince among them; I the LORD have spoken it.

25 And I will make with them a covenant of peace, and will cause the evil beasts to cease out of the land: and they shall dwell safely in the wilderness, and sleep in the woods.

26 And I will make them and the places round about my hill a blessing; and I will cause the shower to come down in his season; there shall be showers of blessing.

27 And the tree of the field shall yield her fruit, and the earth shall yield her increase, and they shall be safe in their land, and shall know that I am the LORD, when I have broken the bands of their yoke, and delivered them out of the hand of those that served themselves of them.

28 And they shall no more be a prey to the heathen, neither shall the beast of the land devour them; but they shall dwell safely, and none shall make them afraid.

29 And I will raise up for them a plant of renown, and they shall be no more consumed with hunger in the land, neither bear the shame of the heathen any more.

30 Thus shall they know that I the LORD their God am with them, and that they, even the house of Israel, are my people, saith the Lord GOD.

31 And ye my flock, the flock of my pasture, are men, and I am your God, saith the Lord GOD.

KEY VERSE

I will set up one shepherd over them, and he shall feed them, even my servant David; he shall feed them, and he shall be their shepherd. —**Ezekiel 34:23**

GOD CALLS FOR JUSTICE

Unit 3: Justice Promised

LESSONS 10–13

LESSON AIMS

After participating in this lesson each student will be able to:

1. List three blessings of being in covenant relationship with God.

2. Identify the "one shepherd" of Ezekiel 34:23.

3. Keep a journal for seven days regarding how he or she finds peace and blessing in Christ.

LESSON OUTLINE

Introduction

A. Experiencing God's Presence

There have been three times in my life when I have experienced God's presence in what can only be called a "supernatural" manner. One was in the summer of 1965, when a friend and I were doing youth evangelism. I had just graduated from Bible college, and my friend was entering his senior year. He led the singing, and I did the preaching. As we were walking across a field from the parsonage to the church building for one service, a strange sensation came over me—a sensation that led me to go back and change my sermon for the evening.

I had only 14 sermons developed at that point in my young career. I told my friend to go ahead and start the service, and I would come as soon as possible. I made it to the service just in time to witness a young man interrupt the singing by standing up with great difficulty from a wheelchair. He gave a testimony to the young people about his addiction to alcohol and wild living.

A year earlier he had had a car accident that resulted in his lying on the highway with legs crushed, the smell of gasoline and alcohol all around. He said, "I met Jesus on the highway that day, and He saved not only my physical life but my life for all eternity. I want you to meet Jesus tonight, not on the highway like I did, but here tonight before it is too late." He sat down, my friend finished leading the singing, and I stood to preach. The sermon I went back and selected was entitled "When You Meet Jesus."

Before I could finish my sermon, young people were running to the front to give their lives to Jesus. It was a supernatural moment when we knew God was present and working through us and in us.

The other two experiences? They will have to wait for another time. But we hasten to remind ourselves that we do not really need to experience God's presence in a supernatural way to know that He is with us. All we really need to do is remind ourselves of His promise always to be with us (Matthew 28:20). His presence meets our deepest needs and gives us peace and wholeness. It did for ancient Israel as well.

God Promised to Be with Us

B. Lesson Background

Ezekiel began to prophesy in Babylon in 593 BC. We calculate this date by combining 2 Kings 24:8-14 with Ezekiel 1:2, 3. Thus Ezekiel was already in Babylon for several years when Jerusalem fell in 586 BC (see Ezekiel 24:1, 2; 33:21). The first 7 years of Ezekiel's ministry concerned the judgment against Jerusalem and its pending destruction (Ezekiel 1–24). A series of judgments against the nations followed (Ezekiel 25–32). The remaining 15 years of Ezekiel's ministry concerned his message of hope (Ezekiel 33–48). Ezekiel's last dated oracle was given in 571 BC (29:17). If we subtract "the fifth year" of Ezekiel 1:2 from "the seven and twentieth year" of 29:17, we calculate that his prophetic ministry lasted at least 22 years.

Ezekiel ministered during a very turbulent time in Judah's history. The Assyrians had threatened Jerusalem in 701 BC. Judah survived to see the destruction of Nineveh (the capital of Assyria) in 612 BC. At the famous Battle of Carchemish, a clash between Babylon and Egypt in 605 BC, the Babylonians emerged as the new superpower of the day (Jeremiah 46:2).

A few years later, in 598/7 BC, King Nebuchadnezzar of Babylon sent a force against Jerusalem to put down a rebellion (2 Kings 24:1b). The result was exile for King Jehoiachin, Ezekiel, and thousands of their fellow Judeans (24:14-16). The Babylonians eventually came back, laid siege to Jerusalem, and destroyed the city in the summer of 586 BC. The result: yet another deportation.

Ezekiel's message of hope was a vision of restoration and revitalization. The name of the restored city would be "The Lord is there" (Ezekiel 48:35). The promise of God's presence in this renewed kingdom of God is the essence of our lesson today.

I. Promise of a Shepherd
(Ezekiel 34:23, 24)
A. Actions (v. 23)

23. And I will set up one shepherd over them, and he shall feed them, even my servant David; he shall feed them, and he shall be their shepherd.

Ezekiel is God's "watchman" (Ezekiel 33) who offers the exiles hope for a future unlike anything they have ever known. God is going to restore and revitalize all that the exiles have lost. The visionary hope includes restoring of the Davidic kingship (chapter 34), restoration of land (chapters 35, 36), restoration of the nation (chapter 37), respite from enemies (chapters 38, 39), and the return of God's glory (chapters 40–48). Ezekiel, having foretold and experienced the demise of the Davidic dynasty (chapter 17), now announces its restoration.

The *servant David* will be a shepherd who will feed the flock. His care will contrast starkly with the evil of the bad shepherds (Ezekiel 34:1-22). The great golden age of David's reign (1010–970 BC) is a focal point for prophetic hope of a new kind of king for God's people (see Isaiah 9:5, 6; 11:1; Jeremiah 23:5; Ezekiel 37:24; Amos 9:11).

The *one shepherd* image implies the reuniting of Israel and Judah, never again to be divided (1 Kings 12:1-24 Ezekiel 37:15-19; John 10:16). It may also imply the eternal reign of this king, who lives forever (see Ezekiel 37:25). How else could this one shepherd reign (Revelation 7:17)?

What Do You Think?
  In what ways can church leaders, being accountable to the chief shepherd Jesus, tend the flock (1 Peter 5:2-4)?
Talking Points for Your Discussion
- In whole-church gatherings
- In smaller group settings
- In church discipline
- One-on-one

B. Results (v. 24)

24. And I the LORD will be their God, and my servant David a prince among them; I the LORD have spoken it.

Yahweh himself is the God of this kingdom revitalized. *My servant David* is the one Yahweh has chosen. The prophet Hosea yearns for the day when all Israel will "seek the Lord their God, and David their king; and shall fear the Lord and his goodness in the latter days" (Hosea 3:5; see the same idea in Jeremiah 30:9).

This David is not the historical David come to life again, nor is he to be merely a representative of a series of kings as before. This David is a singular person who will occupy David's heavenly throne forever (see Luke 1:32). Under Babylonian domination, the exiles have witnessed David's throne being cast to the ground (Psalm 89:44). God will one day restore it (see Psalm 110:1).

When that happens, this "David" will be *a prince among* his people. Perhaps the designation *prince* instead of *king* is to downplay the recent bad kings of Judah. The Davidic prince-king is first and foremost a servant of God. He will be humble and gentle, God's representative on earth. God has spoken—it is a fact!

❧ *THE VOICE OF AUTHORITY* ❧

We instinctively recognize "the voice of authority" in an earthly sense. We need only visit a busy supermarket to prove this: all around us we will hear parental voices of authority correcting children's behavior. (Whether or not such authoritative voices are actually obeyed is another matter!)

Hollywood has learned to use the voice of authority for dramatic effect. In the 1956 movie *The Ten Commandments,* Pharaoh often delivers pronouncements with the finality expected of his position: "So let it be written; so let it be done." His words are final. Even when some murmur their disappointment, Pharaoh is relentless. "So let it be written; so let it be done." He's the boss.

Old Testament prophets reflected the same kind of finality when they spoke for God or passed along God's direct words. Isaiah did so concerning

HOW TO SAY IT

Assyrians	Uh-*sear*-e-unz.
Babylonians	Bab-ih-*low*-nee-unz.
Carchemish	*Kar*-key-mish.
Hosea	Ho-*zay*-uh.
Jehoiachin	Jeh-*hoy*-uh-kin.
messianic	mess-ee-*an*-ick.
Nebuchadnezzar	*Neb*-yuh-kud-**nez**-er.
Nineveh	*Nin*-uh-vuh.
Yahweh *(Hebrew)*	*Yah*-weh.
Zedekiah	Zed-uh-*kye*-uh.

the Babylonians ("I, even I, have spoken"; Isaiah 48:15). Jeremiah spoke of the land being desolate and the heavens being blackened ("because I have spoken it"; Jeremiah 4:28). Ezekiel thus stands in good company in pronouncing God's truth. Whether the Israelites would heed and obey that authoritative voice was another matter. The same is true for us today.
—J. B. N.

II. Promise of Blessings
(EZEKIEL 34:25-29)
A. Peace (v. 25)

25a. And I will make with them a covenant of peace.

The phrase *covenant of peace* also occurs in Numbers 25:12; Isaiah 54:10; and Ezekiel 37:26. The covenant being discussed here is what will characterize the messianic age. The covenant Jesus institutes on the night He is betrayed (see Mark 14:22-25) fulfills the prediction of Jeremiah for such a covenant. Peace is to prevail in the relationship between God and His people. The curses of Genesis 3 are to be reversed.

The blessings of the covenant of peace are set forth in verses 25b-30, below. We can see a double structure for all the blessings noted in these verses, except for the last blessing in verse 30. This structure looks like this:

> *peace,* verses 25b and 28b
> *fruitfulness,* verses 26, 27a and 29a
> *deliverance,* verses 27b, 28a and 29b

25b. And will cause the evil beasts to cease out of the land: and they shall dwell safely in the wilderness, and sleep in the woods.

We should read carefully Leviticus 26:4-13, which seems to be the source of many of the phrases and ideas in Ezekiel 34:25b-30. Leviticus 26 functions as a ratification of the original covenant from Sinai in terms of promised curses and blessings. For the half-verse before us, compare Leviticus 26:5 ("and dwell in your land safely") and 26:6 ("and I will give peace in the land, and ye shall lie down, and none shall make you afraid: and I will rid evil beasts out of the land").

Ezekiel sees this peace in terms of the absence of fearful wild beasts, the presence of security in the wilderness, and the ability to *sleep in the woods* without fear (see Ezekiel 5:17; 14:15, 21; 33:27). The *evil beasts* could be figurative for the oppressive empires of Assyria and Babylon. But these oppressors are mentioned plainly in Ezekiel 34:27 alongside "the beast of the land" in 34:28; thus *beasts* here in 34:25b is probably literal. Also, "sword" and "beast" are separate instruments of punishment in 14:21.

The woods is not a place where an Israelite normally would sleep without fear of ferocious beasts that attack at night! But there shall be genuine peace in the heart of the one in covenant relationship with God. We must keep in mind the idea that we are sheep in a wilderness and woods of sin, and God's servant Jesus is the shepherd that protects us. This goes above and beyond a mere literal application of protection from bears in the woods!

Visual for Lesson 13

Point to this visual as you ask, "How has the Lord been your shepherd in the past week?"

What Do You Think?

If Ezekiel were writing today, what imagery might he use for readers living in a modern, industrialized society?

Talking Points for Your Discussion

- Instead of "evil beasts," he might use . . .
- Instead of "dwell safely in the wilderness," he might use . . .
- Instead of "sleep in the woods," he might use . . .

B. Abundance (vv. 26, 27a)

26, 27a. And I will make them and the places round about my hill a blessing; and I will cause the shower to come down in his season; there shall be showers of blessing. And the tree of the field shall yield her fruit, and the earth shall yield her increase, and they shall be safe in their land, and shall know that I am the LORD.

Many verses in Ezekiel promise famine as punishment for disobedience (see Ezekiel 5:12, 16, 17; 6:11, 12; 7:15; 14:13, 21). Famine often is a result of drought (see 22:24). But here we see a promise that the land will be productive because of the timely rains that come—the early rains in late October and November, and the later rains that come between December and March. Rarely

does the land receive too much rain (but see Ezekiel 13:10-16; 38:22).

Comparison of Ezekiel 34:26, 27a here can be made with Leviticus 26:4 ("and the land shall yield her increase, and the trees of the field shall yield their fruit"); 26:5 ("and dwell in your land safely"); and 26:13 ("I am the Lord your God . . . and I have broken the bands of your yoke, and made you go upright"). The fruitfulness of the land is a characteristic sign of the age to come (see Hosea 2:21-23; Isaiah 29:17; Jeremiah 31:4-14; 32:40-44). The remnant of God's people in exile will know that Yahweh is God when they experience deliverance from Babylonian bondage. The people will return to a land of their hearts' desire, a land God blesses with rain.

As with the beasts just discussed, so with the *showers of blessing*—the ultimate application is more than literal. God gives to His people spiritual blessings that are as essential to peaceful existence as the rain is to the land's productivity (see Malachi 3:10). The passage before us is the origin of the grand old hymn "There Shall Be Showers of Blessing," seldom heard today in contemporary worship. The chorus expresses the need for spiritual blessings that satisfy the soul: "Showers of blessing, Showers of blessing we need: Mercy drops round us are falling, But for the showers we plead."

My hill probably refers to all the land God promised to Israel, rather than being a limited reference to Mount Zion, God's "holy hill" (Psalm 2:6).

The rains in Palestine could be irregular, and the land was often plagued by drought. Sometimes too much rain was the problem since torrential rain can erode the land and wash out the crops. Modern irrigation techniques allow us to avoid much of the drought problems of the ancient world. But the problem of too much rain still seems unmanageable.

For a while I had a ministry in southern Indiana, a rural church in a farming community. One August we had a three-day rain. It was never heavy, but it was virtually constant for three days, yielding about five inches of rainfall. One member of the congregation joyfully told me that this was a "good" rain. It had not been heavy enough to wash out the crops, but it had come slowly enough to soak the ground down to the roots of the plants. "This rain set the crops," he said. The corn would be finished growing in five weeks, and this rain was the last the corn needed.

God's showers of blessings are like that. He knows what we need. He knows not to give us all we ask for, lest we be overwhelmed. Instead, He sends the right amount of blessings, which settle deeply enough to be all that we need for the time we need them. Thank Him for that!   —J. B. N.

C. Freedom (vv. 27b, 28)

27b, 28a. When I have broken the bands of their yoke, and delivered them out of the hand of those that served themselves of them. And they shall no more be a prey to the heathen, neither shall the beast of the land devour them.

Phrases such as *broken the bands of their yoke* and *delivered them out of the hand of those that served themselves of them* allude to a second exodus, when the people return from Babylonian captivity. The first exodus, from Egypt, also is described by such statements (see Leviticus 26:13). Ezekiel uses the language of covenant law to express the new state of the age to come.

As a result of the covenant of peace and the Davidic servant's leadership, the flock of God will experience a peaceful life. This will be life free from fear of the pagans (*the heathen*) or beasts. Notice the similar language in Leviticus 26:6.

> **What Do You Think?**
> How can God's presence free us from modern yokes?
> *Talking Points for Your Discussion*
> - The yoke of worry
> - The yoke of debt
> - The yoke of health problems
> - The yoke of addictions

28b. But they shall dwell safely, and none shall make them afraid.

The presence of God and His servant-shepherd David is the reason that *none shall make them afraid.* Their presence will bring a peaceful life.

E. Land (v. 29)

29a. And I will raise up for them a plant of renown, and they shall be no more consumed with hunger in the land.

These blessings of the covenant of peace are real, and they are described in superlative imagery. A good example is the prediction that God *will raise up for them a plant of renown.* The picture is that of paradise regained. Famine will no longer be found in the land in contrast with the experiences of the patriarchs (see Genesis 12:10; 26:1).

29b. Neither bear the shame of the heathen any more.

The pagans will no longer shame the people through exile and slavery. The same is true in the covenant blessings of Leviticus 26:7, 8: "And ye shall chase your enemies, and they shall fall before you by the sword. And five of you shall chase an hundred, and an hundred of you shall put ten thousand to flight: and your enemies shall fall before you by the sword." Because of such victory, God makes His people "go upright" (26:13).

III. Knowledge of God
(EZEKIEL 34:30, 31)
A. In His Presence (v. 30)

30. Thus shall they know that I the LORD their God am with them, and that they, even the house of Israel, are my people, saith the Lord GOD.

This verse lies outside the double structure of verses 25b-29 (see comments above on v. 25). It is the climax of the list of blessings belonging to God's people as a result of the covenant of peace. There should be no greater comfort than the assurance of God's divine presence. This is a vision of all God's people gathered together (Israel and Judah) as *the house of Israel*. Whenever we see the two ideas "their [or your] God" and "my people" together, the image is that of a covenant relationship. It is within this covenant relationship that God promises His divine presence for His people (see Leviticus 26:12; Jeremiah 7:23; 11:4; 30:22; Ezekiel 36:28; a negative example is Hosea 1:9).

The phrase *the Lord GOD* is characteristic of how Ezekiel writes God's name—Ezekiel uses *Lord GOD* more than all the other prophets combined. The rendering of *GOD* with small capital letters indicates that the word Yahweh is being translated. The word *saith* carries the authority of the very words from God's mouth. The greatest blessing anyone can claim is the divine presence of God in his or her life (see Ephesians 2:22).

What Do You Think?
What do you find most helpful in heightening your awareness of God's presence? Why?
Talking Points for Your Discussion
- Corporate worship
- Observing the Lord's Supper
- Personal prayer or devotional time
- Other

B. In His Flock (v. 31)

31. And ye my flock, the flock of my pasture, are men, and I am your God, saith the Lord GOD.

Our text ends as it began: with the shepherd and sheep figure. The imagery of the messianic age suspended this briefly in verses 25-30, but now the metaphor is warmly applied to the people of verse 30. The people of God have always been God's pasture. The bad shepherds (leaders) of Israel and Judah have allowed and caused His people to be scattered (Jeremiah 23:2; Ezekiel 34:7-10). So God himself will gather His far-flung flock from the nations of the world and deliver them from their exile (Jeremiah 23:3; Ezekiel 34:11-22). At just the right moment (see Galatians 4:4), God sends His servant "David," the one shepherd, to feed the sheep and care for them (Jeremiah 23:4-6; Ezekiel 37:23, 24). That one shepherd is Jesus. The divine presence of God is assured by the new covenant relationship between God and His people.

What Do You Think?
What are some crises that people go through that cause them to realize that their primary allegiance has been misplaced?
Talking Points for Your Discussion
- In allegiance to country ahead of God
- In allegiance to career ahead of God
- In allegiance to family ahead of God

Conclusion

A. God's Presence in Christ

Jesus identified himself with the shepherd imagery of the Old Testament when He said He was sent "unto the lost sheep of the house of Israel" (Matthew 15:24). The extended imagery of the good shepherd in John 10:1-30 reflects the imagery of Jeremiah 23 and Ezekiel 34, 37. Jesus was "moved with compassion" because the people "fainted, and were scattered abroad, as sheep having no shepherd" (Matthew 9:36). Jesus' teaching featured imagery of lost sheep (see Matthew 18:12-14; Luke 15:3-7).

Leaders in the church are to feed the flock without thought of reward (see 1 Peter 5:2, 3). They do so with the realization that they and their flock have the divine presence of God at all times in Christ. No one needs a special supernatural sign or feeling to be assured of His presence. God's promise is enough.

B. Prayer

Father, we thank You for the blessings of Your covenant of peace that delivers us from wrath. May Your peace and presence be reflected in our lives to an unbelieving world. In Jesus' name, amen.

C. Thought to Remember

"The Lord is my shepherd; I shall not want."

INVOLVEMENT LEARNING

Some of the activities below are also found in the helpful student book, Adult Bible Class.
Don't forget to download the free reproducible page from www.standardlesson.com to enhance your lesson!

Into the Lesson

Say, "Restoring things to original condition is a satisfaction known to some of us. Who here has restored a car, house, a piece of furniture, or some other valuable object to its original status?" Let learners respond. If you know of a class member who has done so, ask him or her to bring "before and after" pictures to share.

Point out that Ezekiel's concluding chapters are about God's restorative power and intent. Display on the board these incomplete phrases and chapter numbers:

Restoration of _____, chapter 34
Restoration of _____, chapters 35, 36
Restoration of _____, chapter 37
Restoration of _____, chapters 38, 39
Restoration of _____, chapters 40–48.

You can let class members examine the chapters from the book of Ezekiel and suggest completions. But for the sake of time, you may wish to fill in the blanks yourself: *God's shepherd/leader; the land; the nation; security; God's glorious presence/temple.* Note the key verses of Ezekiel 34:23 (found in today's text); 36:33-35; 37:22; 38:14; 43:1, 2.

Into the Word

Give each learner a cutout image of a sheep that is about 4" in length, head to tail. Sketch a large image of a shepherd (at least 2' tall) on the board. Indicate that you want learners to play a non-blindfolded game of "Pin the Sheep on the Shepherd." Explain: "Looking at today's text in Ezekiel 34:23-31, write on your sheep one attribute of the shepherd or his sheep based on the text. Then come forward, reveal what you've written, and stick it on the shepherd." Have reusable adhesive or tape available.

Do the first one yourself as an example: on your sheep write (and read aloud) "God will put one chief shepherd over His flock" (Ezekiel 34:23a).

Continue until a variety of truths are affirmed and posted.

Alternative: If you wish for your learners to see a contrast between bad shepherds and the promised good shepherd, form small groups or study pairs to complete the What a Contrast! activity from the reproducible page, which you can download. This exercise adds a consideration of Ezekiel 34:1-10, which is not part of today's printed text.

Option: If your class needs help with the concept of *covenant* in verse 35, ask, "In what senses is a *covenant* the same as an *agreement*?" Expect responses such as (1) both involve promises to be fulfilled, (2) both are binding, (3) both involve two or more parties, (4) both involve peaceful relationships, (5) both generally are entered voluntarily, (6) both offer something to all parties involved, and/or (7) both have an anticipated consummation.

Into Life

Give each learner a handout entitled "My Peace and Blessings Journal." Have the following seven entries down the left-hand side:
Peace and Blessings of Sunday:
Peace and Blessings of Monday:
Peace and Blessings of Tuesday:
Peace and Blessings of Wednesday:
Peace and Blessings of Thursday:
Peace and Blessings of Friday:
Peace and Blessings of Saturday:
Say, "We take God's blessings for granted most of the time. To reverse this problem, sit down each evening this week and write something you received from God that day. This exercise can encourage you to make a regular practice of meditative thanksgiving." Allow a time of free expression of blessings received during the week just completed.

As learners depart, distribute copies of the If the Lord Is My Shepherd, Then . . . activity from the reproducible page, which you can download.

God Promised to Be with Us